Mastering
Autodesk VIZ 2005

Mastering™
Autodesk® VIZ 2005

George Omura with Scott Onstott

San Francisco   London

Associate Publisher: Dan Brodnitz

Acquisitions Editor: Willem Knibbe

Developmental Editor: Jim Compton

Production Editor: Susan Berge

Technical Editor: Ryan Spruston

Copyeditor: Rebecca C. Rider

Compositor: Maureen Forys, Happenstance Type-O-Rama

CD Coordinator: Dan Mummert

CD Technician: Kevin Ly

Proofreaders: Laurie O'Connell, Nancy Riddiough

Indexer: Nancy Guenther

Book Designer: Maureen Forys, Happenstance Type-O-Rama

Cover Designer: Design Site

Cover Illustrator: Tania Kac, Design Site

Library of Congress Card Number: 2004104230

ISBN: 0-7821-4343-1

SYBEX and the SYBEX logo are either registered trademarks or trademarks of SYBEX Inc. in the United States and/or other countries.

Mastering is a trademark of SYBEX Inc.

Screen reproductions produced with FullShot 99. FullShot 99 © 1991-1999 Inbit Incorporated. All rights reserved.
FullShot is a trademark of Inbit Incorporated.

The CD interface was created using Macromedia Director, COPYRIGHT 1994, 1997-1999 Macromedia Inc. For more information on Macromedia and Macromedia Director, visit http://www.macromedia.com.

Autodesk VIZ is a 3D solution for modeling, rendering, animating, and creating photorealistic design visualizations. It can be used to explore design concepts, communicate design intent, and share work with clients, colleagues, and consultants. Straightforward modeling features and unique interoperability with other Autodesk design applications add flexibility and efficiency to the creation process. It allows clear and accurate sharing of design ideas with advanced global illumination processes (including the mental ray renderer) to capture even subtle effects for realistic 3D visualizations.

Autodesk, AutoCAD, Design Web Format, and DWF are either registered trademarks or trademarks of Autodesk, Inc., in the U.S.A. and/or certain other countries. mental ray is a registered trademark of mental images GmbH & Co. KG, licensed for use by Autodesk, Inc. Certain content, including trial software, provided courtesy Autodesk, Inc., © 2004. All rights reserved.

TRADEMARKS: SYBEX has attempted throughout this book to distinguish proprietary trademarks from descriptive terms by following the capitalization style used by the manufacturer.

The author and publisher have made their best efforts to prepare this book, and the content is based upon final release software whenever possible. Portions of the manuscript may be based upon pre-release versions supplied by software manufacturer(s). The author and the publisher make no representation or warranties of any kind with regard to the completeness or accuracy of the contents herein and accept no liability of any kind including but not limited to performance, merchantability, fitness for any particular purpose, or any losses or damages of any kind caused or alleged to be caused directly or indirectly from this book.

To my children
— George Omura

To my loving partner, Jenn
— Scott Onstott

Acknowledgments

THIS BOOK COVERS A topic that has always been one of my favorites, so I am glad to have the opportunity to be involved as the author. But so many other people have helped bring this book to you, and they certainly deserve recognition. I'd first like to thank Willem Knibbe for his early efforts in making this book a reality and helping to keep it alive and Jim Compton for developing the book. On the production side, I want to thank Susan Berge, production editor, for her masterful coordination of the project, and Rebecca Rider for her fine editorial work. A big thanks also goes to Ryan Spruston, technical editor, who gave many excellent comments and suggestions. I also want to acknowledge the people "in the trenches" who are responsible for the production side of things: Maureen Forys of Happenstance Type-O-Rama, Dan Mummert, and Kevin Ly.

I'd like to thank the many members of ELS Architecture and Planning with whom I've had the great pleasure to work: Clarence Mamuyac, Ed Noland, Jamie Rusin, Bruce Bullman, and David Petta all contributed samples from their projects for reproduction in this book. The 3D modeling work of Jeff Zieba, Chris Jung, and William Gordon appear in a number of the ELS renderings as well. I would also like to give a special thanks to David Fawcett for including me in so many great 3D projects.

At Autodesk, a special thanks to Jim Quanci for his help and positive encouragement in the early stages of this book, and to Denis Cadu for his help in obtaining software. Thanks also goes to Shaan Hurley for keeping me up to date on the beta software.

And finally, I've worked with Scott Onstott many times in the past. He always gives his best effort and has been a great guy to work with, so I was quite pleased to hear that he was going to update this latest revision. Thanks, Scott, for doing a great job.

—*George Omura*

I'D FIRST LIKE TO thank George Omura for the opportunity to update his successful book. I share his enthusiasm for all things VIZ and appreciate the opportunity to take on greater responsibility as an author. I'd like to thank Willem Knibbe for his insight and support. Thanks to Susan Berge and Rachel Gunn for keeping me on schedule. Thanks to Jim Compton for his exacting editorial work and many helpful suggestions. Ryan Spruston has my appreciation for acting as technical editor; he did a great job correcting my mistakes and offering creative suggestions. Rebecca Rider also deserves thanks for her beneficial work as copy editor.

Thanks to Denis Cadu, program manager of the Autodesk Developer Network for access to the latest builds and his personal support. I'd also like to thank the beta program participants for their expertise and active involvement with the development and testing of Autodesk VIZ 2005.

Finally, thanks to my wife Jenn for her understanding and support throughout this project.

—*Scott Onstott*

Contents at a Glance

Contents

Introduction

Much of your work as a designer involves sketches and drawings throughout the design process. Such graphic representations of designs not only help convey your ideas to others, they also help you see problems with a design and help you refine your ideas. 3D computer modeling and animation take design visualization way beyond hand drawn sketches by allowing you to create a complete replica of your design and look at it from virtually any point of view.

With Autodesk VIZ 2005, you can apply color, texture, and lighting to see how variations of these elements affect your design. You get a realistic view of your design so that you can make better decisions as you progress through the design process.

Mastering Autodesk VIZ 2005 is intended to help architects and designers visualize and present their designs through images, 3D models, and animations. This book focuses on the use of Autodesk VIZ 2005 as a modeling and presentation tool. Because *Mastering Autodesk VIZ 2005* is focused on design issues, you won't find an in-depth study of character animation or animated special effects; nor will you find a book that describes every single tool and function that's available.

You *will* find step-by-step tutorials covering the major functions that you'll need as a designer. These tutorials are based on years of experience using earlier versions of VIZ and its precursor, 3D Studio MAX (now known as 3ds max), on real projects with real deadlines and requirements. You'll learn how to construct complex geometric forms and how to apply lighting and materials to study a design. You'll also learn how to create effects to emphasize parts of your design for presentations.

How to Use This Book

The goal of this book is to give you the appropriate skills to produce professional-level presentations of your ideas, from conceptual designs to finished renderings and animated walkthroughs. Once you've mastered those skills, you'll be equipped to confidently explore Autodesk VIZ 2005 and its rich set of tools and options on your own.

To get the most from this book, you'll want to read the chapters sequentially from front to back, doing the tutorial exercises as you go along. Each chapter builds on the skills you learned from the previous chapters, so you can think of this book as your personal, self-paced course on Autodesk VIZ 2005.

The first three chapters help you to become familiar with the way Autodesk VIZ 2005 works and how it is organized. If you are already familiar with VIZ, you may want to skim through these chapters to become familiar with some of the new features. Chapters 4 and 5 show you how to build a fairly complex building, using a variety of tools. These chapters introduce you to some of the more common methods of construction in VIZ. Chapters 6 through 9 show you how to use lighting and materials. Chapters 10 and 11 show you advanced rendering techniques using radiosity and mental ray. Chapters 12 and 13 cover animation, and Chapters 14 through 16 delve into some of the finer points of modeling and rendering. Chapter 17 shows you techniques for generating interactive content for the World Wide Web.

At the back of the book, you'll find a set of appendixes that offer general reference information on some of the more commonly used tools in VIZ. Once you've worked through the first half of the book, you can use the appendixes as an aid in your own exploration of VIZ. In fact, you may find it useful to skim over the appendixes once you've completed the first three or four chapters so that you'll have some understanding of their content. You can then refer to the appendixes as you work through the rest of the book.

Finally, before you get started with the tutorials, make sure you've installed the sample files from the companion CD. You'll need those files to complete many of the exercises. See Appendix A for details on installing the sample files.

NOTE *It is important that you set up VIZ to recognize the location of the sample files from the companion CD. Make sure you perform the instructions given in the section entitled "Adding a Map Path to Help VIZ Find Bitmaps" in Chapter 7. If you like, you can set up VIZ as described in that section right after you've installed the samples.*

What You'll Find

To give you a better idea of what you'll find in this book, here is a summary of the chapters and their contents.

In Chapter 1, you'll get an introduction to the VIZ interface, and you'll get your first look at VIZ objects and how they are created. You'll also learn how to perform some basic editing operations, such as moving, scaling, and copying objects. Toward the end of Chapter 1, you'll be introduced to the different ways you can view your designs in VIZ.

Chapter 2 delves deeper into the workings of VIZ objects. You'll learn about the different types of objects available in VIZ and how you can use them to create the shapes you want. You'll learn how to manipulate VIZ's core set of shapes, called primitives, into more complex shapes. You'll also learn about the different ways you can duplicate shapes, and why these different duplication methods can help you quickly build your design.

Chapter 3 looks at how you can create complex forms from simple lines. Here you'll learn how to manipulate a basic type of object called a spline shape and to turn it into a wineglass. You'll look at creating walls and doors as well.

Chapter 4 introduces you to object and editing methods that are common to architectural projects. You'll begin to model a well-known building, using a hand-drawn sketch as a background. You'll also focus on drawing objects that have unusual shapes.

In Chapter 5, you'll continue working on the building you started in Chapter 4 by exploring ways to organize parts of the design. You'll learn how to use object names and layers to help identify parts of the design. You'll also continue your exploration of modeling complex forms by building a complex roof form.

Chapter 6 uses another well-known building as a vehicle for introducing you to digital light and rendering. You'll also learn about the different types of lighting and shadow and how to use them together. In addition, you'll learn how you can create a more realistic effect in your renderings by placing lights in strategic locations.

In Chapter 7, you'll build on the work you will have done in Chapter 6 while exploring materials. You'll read about the many different properties of materials, such as color and bump map textures. You'll also learn how to align a texture to a surface. You'll also be introduced to methods for adding entourage, such as trees and foliage, to a design.

Chapter 8 continues with placing cameras in the model and setting the model in an environment. You'll learn how to control the background to affect the mood of your renderings. You'll also see how to selectively render parts of your model to save time.

Chapter 9 shows you different ways of using VIZ files. You'll learn how to combine files efficiently to allow distribution of work among other members of a design team. You'll also discover ways to share data between files. The latter part of the chapter shows how you can share models on the Internet.

Chapter 10 gives you an introduction to the ins and outs of radiosity rendering. Radiosity is a rendering method that accurately simulates the way light bounces off materials and surfaces, and it produces some of the most lifelike views available in a computer simulation.

Chapter 11 shows you how to get started rendering with mental ray. This renderer offers the highest level of realism and you will learn how to simulate global illumination and caustic optical phenomena in a step-by-step tutorial. The latter part of the chapter shows you how to light a scene using the soft light of a skylight in conjunction with image-based lighting and high dynamic range images (HDRI).

Chapter 12 introduces you to animation. You'll learn how to create and control the animation of a camera to produce an animated flyby of the building you worked on in earlier chapters. You'll also see how to edit an animated object's motion, preview your animation, and control lights over time.

Chapter 13 continues your look at animation by exploring the options for file animation output, backgrounds and props, and other walkthrough animation tools.

Chapter 14 explains how you can utilize Photoshop and other image-editing programs to enhance your use of VIZ. You'll learn how to quickly convert your own scanned images into custom-made props for your VIZ design, such as trees or foliage. You'll also learn how to use bitmap images to create geometric forms in VIZ.

Chapter 15 continues your look at Photoshop and VIZ by showing how you can convert a scanned image of a car into a 3D model of a car. Here you'll learn methods for editing meshes to shape them into smooth forms. In the second half of the chapter, you'll learn how to match a design to a background image to create a montage.

Chapter 16 shows you how you can use AutoCAD-based files with VIZ. You'll learn the different ways that you can combine both 2D and 3D AutoCAD data with VIZ design files. You'll learn the best ways to prepare an AutoCAD drawing for import into VIZ, and you'll learn how you can use a single AutoCAD file as a shared data source for both AutoCAD and VIZ designs. Toward the end of this chapter, you'll be shown how to create stairs and to import truss models from AutoCAD.

Finally, Chapter 17 shows you how to export interactive content to the Internet including panoramas, virtual reality worlds, and Shockwave 3D. You will also learn how to bake scene lighting into textures for use in real-time simulation engines.

In addition to the chapters, this book contains four appendices. Appendix A has important installation notes, Appendix B is a reference for all the modifiers and materials used in VIZ 2005, and Appendix C has information about patches and NURBS surfaces, which are optional modeling tools. Finally, Appendix D contains reference material on helper objects and rendering effects.

You'll also find a bonus chapter on the companion CD that covers some of the more technical issues you'll face when you're ready to distribute your animations. You'll learn about the different video storage options that are available and how they work. You'll also learn methods for getting the best quality from your animations.

System Requirements

This book assumes that you already have Autodesk VIZ 2005 and a PC on which to run the software. In addition, you should perform a full installation of Autodesk VIZ 2005, including the optional tutorials and plug-ins. (See Appendix A for more on the installation of VIZ for this book.) The following list shows you the minimum system requirements for VIZ:

Intel- or AMD-based Processor at 300MHz

512MB RAM

3GB free disk space before VIZ software installation

Graphics card supporting 1024×768 16-bit color display with 64MB RAM

CD-ROM drive

Microsoft Windows 2000 or XP (Professional or Home Edition)

Autodesk does not support VIZ on Windows Me, NT, 98, 95, or 3.1.

TIP   You can obtain a trial version of VIZ from an Autodesk VIZ 2005 reseller. Check `www.autodesk.com` *for details.*

The 3GB of free disk space includes space for sample files and general work space for your projects. For later chapters, you may want to have a copy of AutoCAD version 2005 or 2004 and Photoshop CS or 7. You can obtain a trial version of Photoshop from the Adobe website. As of this writing, you can order a trial version of AutoCAD 2005 from Autodesk's website. It's not essential to have these other programs, but you may find them useful companions to VIZ.

What's on the Companion CD

As mentioned earlier, you'll want to make sure that you've installed the sample files from the companion CD that's included with this book. They are needed for many of the exercises that you'll encounter. You'll find installation instructions for the sample files in Appendix A. The companion CD also contains a VIZ trial version and a bonus chapter on distributing VIZ animations on videotape.

Chapter 1

Getting to Know VIZ

WELCOME TO *Mastering Autodesk VIZ 2005*. Once again, Autodesk VIZ 2005 benefits from the development of its sister product, 3ds max, to give architects and other design professionals an indispensable design tool. VIZ 2005 gives designers cutting edge rendering technology, easier-to-use architectural materials, improved communication with other software, enhancements to modeling and animation tools, and improvements in the user interface.

This chapter introduces some of VIZ 2005's special features and then gets you started working with the VIZ 2005 interface.

◆ Introducing VIZ 2005 Features

◆ Getting Started

◆ Touring the Interface

◆ Working with Objects

◆ Getting the View You Want

◆ Working with the Custom UI and Defaults Switcher

Introducing VIZ 2005 Features

With the new Architectural material (Figure 1.1), it has become far easier to render realistic real-world materials in VIZ 2005. Featuring a preset list of commonly used building surfaces, this new material type will certainly save you time texturing your models.

NOTE *Architectural is now the default material in VIZ 2005.*

If you're an AutoCAD or Architectural Desktop user, you'll find that importing and linking your building data into VIZ has been completely overhauled and greatly improved. A new Layer manager has been designed to work seamlessly with your existing AutoCAD and/or Architectural Desktop models and helps you to maintain the same project organization, materials, and layer standards.

FIGURE 1.1

The new Architectural material

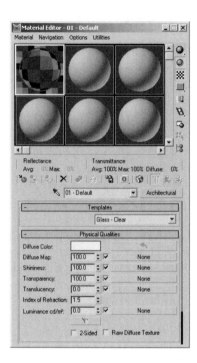

VIZ 2005 now includes *mental ray*, which was formerly sold as a separate high-end rendering plug-in. mental ray is a film-quality rendering solution, fully integrated with VIZ 2005, that allows the most realistic rendering possible today, including global illumination, caustics, soft shadows, area and volume lights, ray tracing, reflections and refractions, motion blur, and depth-of-field effects. Mental ray includes a robust shader language for those with a programming bent, and a highly efficient rendering pipeline, where incremental changes in an animation are the only portions of the frames that get rendered. In addition, VIZ 2005 now supports High Dynamic Range Image (HDRI) files, keeping up with the cutting edge in computer graphics.

The *radiosity rendering* system that was introduced in VIZ 4 is still available, and it remains a time-tested way to create accurate study models of a design by inserting light-fixture specifications. By simulating the way light works in the real world, radiosity rendering takes much of the guesswork out of lighting design. With VIZ 2005, you won't need to wait until a project is built to see if your lighting design works the way you intended. Natural outdoor lighting has also been improved to give you a realistic representation of your design.

If your computer is connected to a computer network, you can harness processor time from the other computers to reduce the time it takes to render a single image or even an entire animation. A new stand-alone command-line rendering tool with access to rendering presets (also available in VIZ itself) allows for more efficient unattended processing of your rendered artwork. As with earlier versions of VIZ, you can also take advantage of multiprocessor systems to improve speed.

Autodesk VIZ 2005 is also designed to take advantage of the Internet both as a reader and publisher. With its Asset Browser and an Internet connection, you can quickly acquire 3D models and props that are available on the Web. You can also publish your own interactive content to the Web in the form of wraparound panoramas, virtual reality worlds, and Shockwave 3D models. Render to Texture, also known as Texture Baking, is a new feature that allows you to "bake" your beautifully lit rendered views into surfaces for use in real-time interactive models.

Finally, VIZ 2005 offers a set of improvements based on user feedback. The interface has been updated to match the improvements recently made to VIZ's sophisticated sibling, 3ds max 6. The animation Track view has been better organized by being split into two specialized editors, the Dope Sheet and the Curve Editor. There are numerous improvements to modeling tools including enhancements to Editable Splines, patches, and polys. In addition, the new Shell modifier offers you a new way of modeling by giving thickness to surfaces.

Getting Started

Although many of VIZ's components are typical for a Windows program, quite a few are unique. To begin exploring the VIZ 2005 interface, start the program by doing one of the following:

◆ Double-click the Autodesk VIZ 2005 icon on the Desktop.

◆ Choose Start ➢ Programs ➢ Autodesk VIZ 2005 ➢ Autodesk VIZ 2005.

You'll see a variety of components in the VIZ window (see Figure 1.2)—some that are familiar and others that are not.

FIGURE 1.2

The standard Autodesk VIZ 2005 window

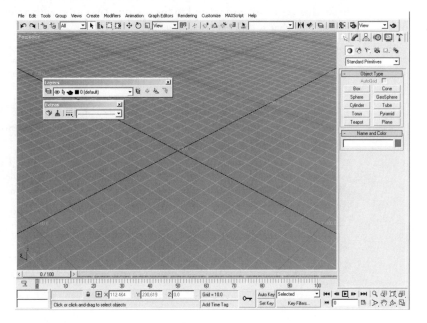

At the top, you see a typical menu bar and toolbar. There are two new floating toolbars called Layers and Extras. The Tab panel from VIZ 4 is gone, thus simplifying the interface. In the center, you see the viewport area, which currently shows a perspective view. At the lower right corner of the screen, you see the viewport navigation tools for adjusting your views in the main viewport. You also see the time controls for creating animations, the prompt line and status bar, and something called the MAXScript Mini Listener (for creating macros). On the right side, you see the Command Panel, which contains nearly all the tools you'll use to create and edit objects in VIZ. Let's take a closer look at each of these components.

Touring the Interface

VIZ offers a wealth of tools, and their sheer number can be overwhelming. To get a basic understanding of the VIZ window, let's look at each of the window components individually, starting with the menu bar.

The Main Menu Bar

At the top of the screen is the main menu bar. Here, you find the typical Windows commands for file maintenance, as well as commands specifically for Autodesk VIZ 2005.

The options in the menu bar are organized in the same way as they are in most other Windows applications. Clicking an option issues a command, and you're expected to take some action. An option that's followed by three periods, called an ellipsis, opens a dialog box, usually to allow you to make changes to settings related to the option. An option with a right-pointing arrow displays more options in what is called a *cascading menu*.

Try out the menu bar by taking a look at the Units Setup dialog box.

1. Choose Customize ➢ Units Setup. The Units Setup dialog box displays.

2. Select the US Standard radio button, and make sure that Feet w/Decimal Inches is selected below it, and that the Feet radio button is selected for Default Units.

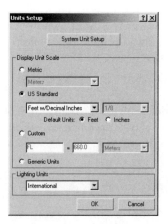

3. Click the System Unit Setup button and you will see another small dialog box. Make sure 1 system unit is set equal to 1 inch. Do not change anything else in the System Unit Setup dialog box and click OK twice to close both dialog boxes.

By checking the Units Setup dialog box, you ensure that in future exercises, you'll be working with the same units that are discussed in this book.

NOTE *Autodesk VIZ 2005 is something of a chameleon. It can change its appearance, depending on the focus of your modeling needs. If your VIZ 2005 window doesn't look the way it does in the figures in this book, choose Customize ➤ Revert to Startup Layout. You'll see a warning message telling you that any user interface (UI) changes you have made will be lost. Click OK to set up your VIZ windows to match the interface you see in this book.*

The Main Toolbar

Just below the menu bar is the main toolbar. The tools on this toolbar offer tool tips to help you remember their purpose.

To the far left of the toolbar are the Undo and Redo options.

Next is a set of tools for selecting objects. These selection tools let you select objects by clicking them or by selecting them by name. You can also set the method for selecting objects by using a selection window, which provides a way of indicating a selection by placing a rectangle, circle, or other border around the objects.

To the right of the selection tools are the transform tools. This set of tools lets you move, rotate, and scale objects. You can also choose the reference coordinate system, set the center of the transform using the pivot options, use different snap options, work with named selection sets, and use tools to mirror and align objects.

The next group of tools to the right of the layer tools are the materials and rendering tools. The materials tools give you control over the appearance of objects. With these tools, you can create color, texture, opacity, and other material characteristics, and then apply these characteristics to objects in your model. You can also open the new render dialog, select the render type, and perform a quick render with these buttons.

The rendering tools give you control over the output of your Autodesk VIZ 2005 model. Unlike output from most applications, output from VIZ 2005 is most likely to be image, animation, or web3d files. The rendering tools let you set the type and size of output, from single, large format stills to video-ready animations.

TIP *If you're working with a screen resolution of 1024×768 or less, you won't see all the tools on the main toolbar. Some of the tools are off the screen to the far right. To access these tools, place the cursor on the toolbar so that a hand icon appears, and then click and drag the toolbar to the right. The hidden tools will emerge. You can also click the Rendering tab to expose all the rendering tools. The smallest supported resolution in VIZ 2005 is 1024×768, but the recommended resolution is 1280×960 or higher.*

Docked and Floating Toolbars

In addition to the main toolbar, you see two "floating" toolbars sitting on top of the perspective view (see Figure 1.2) and one that is hidden. You can open hidden toolbars by right-clicking on a blank part of the main toolbar. A context menu will appear listing the available toolbars. Let's take a quick look at the visible floating toolbars.

Two toolbars float over the Perspective viewport, the Layers toolbar and the Extras toolbar. As with most toolbars, you can move these floating toolbars to the side or hide them altogether to gain better access to objects in the main viewport.

Layers are like overlays that help you organize the objects in your model. If you are an AutoCAD or Photoshop user, you should have an idea of how layers work. You'll learn more about layers in Chapter 5.

You can dock the floating toolbars, or float the docked toolbars. You can try the following exercise to see how to change the location of toolbars:

1. Click and drag the title bar of the Layers toolbar so that the toolbar is below the main toolbar (see Figure 1.3). The Layers toolbar appears ghosted as a horizontal outline just before you release the mouse button.

FIGURE 1.3

Docking the Layers toolbar under the main toolbar

2. When the outline is in the position shown in Figure 1.3, release the mouse button. The Layers toolbar is now in a docked position.

3. Dock the Extras toolbar just to the right of the Layers toolbar (also just under the main toolbar).

4. Right-click the two vertical lines (called the toolbar handle) on the left side of the Extras toolbar to open the shortcut menu.

TIP You can also open the toolbar shortcut menu by right-clicking a blank part of the interface. For example, try right-clicking next to the Extras toolbar and you'll see the shortcut menu that allows you to open or close any of the toolbars by name.

5. Select Float from the shortcut menu. The Extras toolbar returns to its floating position. Another way to do this is to drag the toolbar by its handle down into the viewport.

6. Right-click the title bar of the Extras toolbar and notice that the Axis Constraints toolbar is unchecked in the shortcut menu.

7. Select the Axis Constraints toolbar from the shortcut menu to open it, and then dock both the Extras and Axis Constraints toolbars to the right of the already docked Layers toolbar as shown in Figure 1.4.

FIGURE 1.4
All three optional toolbars docked under the main toolbar

In this brief exercise, you learned how to dock and float toolbars, and how to access the shortcut menu where you can toggle the toolbars on and off.

Toolbar Flyouts

You may have noticed that some of the tools in the main toolbar show a small arrow in the lower right corner of the tool icon.

That arrow indicates that the tool is one of several offered in a *flyout*. A flyout is like a graphical version of options in a menu bar. If you click and hold a tool that's part of a flyout, you see a set of other tools appear. For example, if you click and hold the Select and Uniform Scale tool, two additional tools appear.

Once you select an option from a flyout, it becomes the default button that you see in the toolbar.

The Viewport

At the center of the window is the *viewport* (see Figure 1.5). This is where you'll be doing most of your modeling work. In a blank file, the viewport shows a grid that you can use as a reference for orientation and size. The grid is labeled with distances in the current, default unit setting. The labels also indicate the X and Y axes.

FIGURE 1.5

A typical Perspective viewport in the opening screen

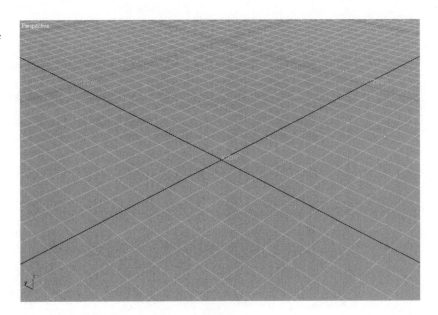

If you look in the lower left corner of the viewport, you see the world axis that indicates the orientation of the X, Y, and Z axes. The world axis helps you get your bearings when looking at other types of views.

Currently, the viewport shows the perspective view, as indicated by the label in the upper left corner. You can also tell that it's a perspective view by the way the grid squares get smaller and converge in the distance. As you'll see toward the end of this chapter, you can configure and view your model in a variety of ways, depending on your needs.

Tools for Working with the Viewport

At the bottom of the window, there are several other options that are grouped into four sections: the status bar, the prompt line, the time controls, and the viewport navigation tools (see Figure 1.6). Most of these tools affect the viewport, either by modifying the display of the viewport directly or by affecting the way you interact with objects within the viewport.

FIGURE 1.6
The bottom sections of the Autodesk VIZ 2005 window

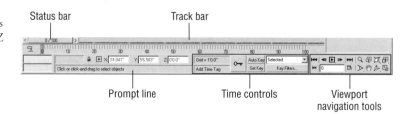

The viewport navigation tools give you control over the main graphic display in the center of the window. With these tools, you can zoom and pan over the display, as well as alter the viewpoint of your model. You can also switch between multiple views and a single view. Try the following:

1. Click the Min/Max Toggle button in the far lower right corner of the window. This is a tool you'll be using often. You can also press Alt+W on the keyboard.

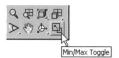

The graphic display changes to display four separate viewports. Each viewport shows a different type of view, as shown in Figure 1.7. Notice that the viewports are labeled in their upper left corners.

FIGURE 1.7
Four viewports, showing the top, left, front, and perspective views

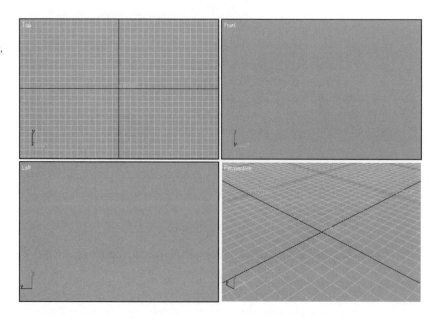

2. Right-click the upper left viewport, labeled Top. Notice that the border of the Top viewport becomes highlighted in yellow.

3. Click the Min/Max Toggle tool again. Now the Top viewport fills the graphic area. Notice how you can quickly expand the view of a viewport to see more detail.

4. Click the Min/Max Toggle tool again. Then right click anywhere within the Perspective viewport.

5. Click the Min/Max Toggle tool to restore your original window setup.

You've just seen how you can expand the graphic area into multiple viewports showing the top, front, left, and perspective views. Several other views and viewport arrangements are available, as you'll see later in this chapter.

TIP   You can set the current, active viewport to display a top, front, or left side view by pressing the T, F, or L key. You can also press B for the bottom view. Pressing P will display the perspective view, and pressing U will display an isometric user-defined view. If you have added a camera, you can press C to select from a list of camera views. The hotkeys of R for right view and K for back have been removed from the defaults in VIZ 2005. You can easily assign your own hotkeys to commands; this procedure is covered later in the chapter.

To the left of the viewport navigation tools are time control tools. These tools give you control over the animation functions of VIZ. Here, you can set your creations in motion by selecting the length of time for your animation, as well as setting the precise location of objects within that time frame.

Near the bottom center of the interface there is a large button with the symbol of a key on it and two smaller buttons to the right that are used to create animation keyframes, called *keys*.

The long horizontal elements across the bottom of the viewport are the time slider and track bar, used for animation. You can hide the track bar to save space on the screen. Choose Customize ➢ Show UI ➢ Show Track Bar to toggle this part of the interface off until you're ready for making animations.

Just to the left of the animation controls are the transform type-in text boxes. This area displays the location of your cursor in X, Y, and Z coordinates. It also displays other types of data, depending on your current activity. For example, if you're rotating an object, the coordinate readout displays the rotation angle of the object being rotated. If you're scaling the data, these text boxes will show percentages.

In addition to the transform type-ins, there is a Grid panel, which may lie hidden to the right if your display is set to low resolution. To find it, place the cursor on the vertical bar just to the left of the prompt line until you see a double-pointed arrow.

When you see the arrow, click and drag to the left. The Grid panel will be revealed to the right of the transform type-ins.

You can display a grid in the current, active viewport by clicking this panel. Right-click the panel to open a dialog box that lets you set the grid spacing and other grid parameters.

Finally, to the far left at the bottom of the VIZ window is the MAXScript Mini Listener. MAXScript is a language that allows you to create custom *macros* in Autodesk VIZ 2005. A macro is like a prerecorded series of instructions. The MAXScript Mini Listener serves two functions: the pink area displays your activity when the MAXScript MacroRecord function is turned on, and the white area provides a space where you can enter commands through the keyboard.

Getting to Know the Command Panel

You'll be using the Command Panel for most of your work in VIZ. If you're an experienced AutoCAD user, you might think of the Command Panel as the equivalent of the AutoCAD command line; it's a single entry point for nearly all of the program's functions. The Command Panel offers nearly all the tools for creating and editing in VIZ.

Across the top of the Command Panel, you see a set of six tabs, each displaying an icon.

From left to right, the tabs are Create, Modify, Hierarchy, Motion, Display, and Utilities. If you place the cursor on a tab, you'll see a tool tip displaying the name of the tab. When you click a tab, the functions relating to the tab appear in the rest of the Command Panel. Here's a brief rundown of what each tab offers:

Create Allows you to create two-dimensional and three-dimensional objects. You can also create light sources, cameras, and helper objects that are used to determine distance and relationships between objects. Light sources, cameras, and helpers are objects that don't appear when your view is rendered.

Modify Gives you control over the dimension and shape of your objects. You find tools to extrude, twist, and bend your objects. You can also control methods for applying material definitions to objects (called *mapping coordinates*) in this tab.

Hierarchy Offers a set of tools aimed primarily at animation. The options in this tab let you build relationships between objects to simulate joint movement or to constrain motion of one object in relation to another. It also offers a way to control the location of an object's pivot point.

Motion Another tab that gives you control over animation. Here, you can control the actual motion of objects over time and view the trajectories of objects.

Display   Lets you turn objects on or off in your model. There may be times when you don't want a particular object visible while you render your model or while you're editing a complex model full of objects. Display lets you temporarily hide objects from view and lock them out from being selected.

Utilities   A kind of catchall tab that provides access to special features and plug-ins. This is where you find the Camera Match utility that lets you match your model view to a photograph. You can also get access to the MAXScript customization features in this tab.

TIP   You can move the Command Panel just like any toolbar or close the panel entirely by clicking the Close button (the one with the X, in the upper right corner of the window). To bring the Command Panel back, right-click the blank area of any toolbar and then select Command Panel from the shortcut menu. (You can also right-click the Command Panel's title bar to dock the panel on the left side of the screen.)

Understanding VIZ's Tools

There are a few ways of working in VIZ that are a bit unusual for a Windows program. In this section, you'll explore the Create tab of the Command Panel as a way to understand some of VIZ's quirks. There aren't many, but understanding them now will make it easier for you to learn how to use the program.

GETTING TO KNOW SCROLLING PANELS AND ROLLOUTS

Autodesk VIZ 2005 has a rich set of creation and editing tools—so many, in fact, that VIZ's programmers had to come up with a way to get to them easily without making the program too arcane. Two of these tools help you navigate its interface: the *scrolling panel* and the *rollout*. A scrolling panel is an area that can be scrolled up or down using a hand cursor. A rollout is a set of tools that can be opened or closed, much like a drawer in a dresser. Let's start by looking at how a scrolling panel works:

1. Click the Create tab of the Command Panel. Notice the row of icons just below the title of the tab. These icons are buttons, or tools, that offer different categories of objects.

2. Place the cursor over the tool that looks like a movie camera. Notice that a tool tip displays, offering the name of the tool.

3. Click the Camera tool. You see the options change below the tools.

4. Click the Target button. A set of additional options appears. Although it may not be obvious, these options extend beyond the bottom of the Command Panel.

5. Move your cursor down to a blank spot in the Command Panel. The cursor changes to a hand.

6. Click and drag upward with your mouse. Notice that the options in the Command Panel scroll upward, following the motion of your mouse. This is an example of a scrolling panel. This scrolling action exposes the rest of the options in the lower portion of the Command Panel. Release the mouse button at any time once you've seen how this scrolling action works.

7. Place the cursor on a blank area again so that the hand cursor displays. Then click and drag downward to view the Target and Free buttons under the Object Type bar.

8. You can also scroll the Command Panel by rolling the wheel on your mouse or by dragging the dark gray slender vertical scroll bar on the right side of the command panel. Try both of these methods.

9. Another way to see more of the Command Panel is to increase its width by dragging the vertical border between the Command Panel and the viewport. Position your mouse along this edge and drag to the left and expand the Command Panel to two and then three columns.

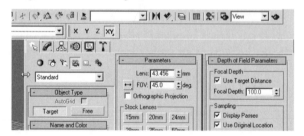

10. The advantage to having a three-column Command Panel is obvious—you can see all the controls within the Command Panel at once. The disadvantage is equally apparent—the viewport becomes much smaller. Drag the Command Panel back to one vertical column to give yourself the maximum amount of screen space. It's better to learn how to scroll within the Command Panel than to sacrifice valuable viewport space.

In this exercise, you see that the entire set of options can be changed by clicking a single tool. You can also see that the set of tools can extend beyond the bottom of the Command Panel. You can scroll the options upward or downward within the Command Panel in several ways. This allows VIZ to offer a wide variety of options within the limited space of your display.

The main toolbar also acts like a scrolling panel whenever a portion of the toolbar extends beyond the screen area. For example, if your screen resolution is 1024×768, a portion of the Rendering toolbar isn't visible to the right of the screen. If you place the cursor on a blank area of the Rendering toolbar, it turns into a hand cursor. You can then click and drag to the left to display the additional tools.

When you clicked the Target button in step 4 of the preceding exercise, a set of options appeared under a button labeled Parameters. There are three other buttons, labeled Depth of Field Parameters, Object Type, and Name and Color. Notice the minus (–) sign to the far left of these buttons. These buttons are called *rollouts.* They let you open and close a set of options to get them out of the way, or to roll them out for use. Try the following:

1. Click the rollout labeled Parameters. The options below the Parameters rollout disappear. Also notice that the minus (–) sign to the left of the rollout changes to a plus (+) sign. This indicates that the rollout is in its closed state. The plus tells you that there is more information inside, waiting to be rolled out.

2. Click the rollout labeled Name and Color. It also closes and displays a plus (+) sign to the left. Right-click a black part of the interface within any one of the rollouts and you'll see a context menu. Select Close All.

3. Notice that the Parameters and Depth of Field Parameters rollouts closed but Object Type and Name and Color remained open. This is because all objects on the Create Panel have Object Type and Name and Color rollouts, and these always remain open. Any additional rollouts belong to the object you have chosen to create and can be controlled with this context menu. Try dragging the Depth of Field Parameters rollout above the Parameters rollout.

4. You will see a horizontal blue bar appear with an image of the rollout you are dragging ghosted. When you release the mouse, the rollout you are dragging gets docked where the blue bar was. Now the Depth of Field Parameters rollout should appear above the Parameters rollout.

5. Click the Parameters and Depth of Field Parameters rollouts again to display the options.

Now you can see how easy it is to control and customize the Command Panel interface. In this and later chapters, you'll explore the rollouts that appear in the Command Panel and throughout the program.

CREATING OBJECTS AND SETTING THEIR PARAMETERS

By now, you've seen most of VIZ's interface and how it functions. However, you will want to know about a few more tools and methods before you really delve into using VIZ. In the following exercises, you'll get a chance to create a simple object, and in the process, you'll be introduced to a few new tools.

1. In the Create tab of the Command Panel, click the Geometry tool at the top of the panel.

You see the Object Type rollout with a set of object types.

2. Click the Box button. Additional rollouts appear in the Command Panel. These include Creation Method, Keyboard Entry, and Parameters. Notice that a message displays in the prompt line at the bottom of the screen that says, "Click and drag to begin creation process." Also, the cursor in the graphic area displays as a cross, telling you that you're in object creation mode.

3. Place the cursor at the center of the graphic area at coordinates 0,0 and click and drag diagonally to the upper right corner of the screen—don't release the mouse button just yet. As you move the mouse, a rectangle follows your cursor. Notice that the values in the Length and Width input boxes in the Parameters rollout change as you move the mouse.

4. Place the cursor so that the rectangle looks similar to the one shown in Figure 1.8, and then release the mouse button. (You don't need to match the rectangle in the figure exactly.) Now, as you move the cursor, the rectangle changes in height. Notice that the Height parameter in the Parameters rollout also follows the change in height.

FIGURE 1.8
The rectangle so far

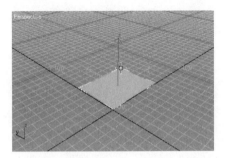

5. Adjust the height so that the Height parameter shows about 20 and click your mouse. The box is now fixed at the height you selected. It should look similar to Figure 1.9.

FIGURE 1.9
The finished box

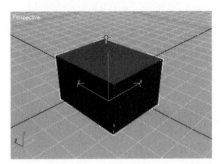

You've just created your first object in VIZ, and in the process, you've seen how the dimensions of an object are reflected in the Parameters rollout. Once you've created an object, you can continue to modify its parameters, as the following exercise demonstrates.

1. In the Parameters rollout, locate the Width input box and click the upward-pointing arrow to the right of the box several times. Arrows like this one are called *spinners,* and they allow you to graphically adjust the value of the input box they are associated with. Notice that the box in the perspective view begins to widen as the value in Width input box increases.

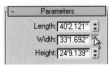

2. Click and hold down the left mouse button while pointing to the upward arrow of the Width spinner. Notice that the box continues to grow in width as you hold down the mouse button.

3. Right-click the spinner arrow. The box shrinks in width to 0. Right-clicking the spinner changes the spinner value to its default, which is 0 in this case.

4. Click and drag the mouse upward from the Width spinner. The box gradually grows in width. Click and drag downward, and the width shrinks back down.

5. Click and drag the Width spinner upward until the cursor reaches the top of the screen. Then continue moving the mouse upward. Notice that the cursor reappears at the bottom of the screen. This *circular* action of the spinner lets you scroll continuously without being limited by the screen area.

TIP   *While adjusting a spinner, you can immediately undo any changes you make by right-clicking the mouse while still holding the left mouse button. This allows you to quickly experiment with spinner settings while you work.*

You've just seen how you can change the parameters of an object by using the spinner. Now let's take a look at the old-fashioned way of entering values into input boxes.

1. Click the Length input box in the Parameters rollout and type **20↵**. Notice how the box's length changes.

2. Press the Tab key. Notice that the Width value is now highlighted.

3. Type **20↵** for the width and press Tab again. The Height value is highlighted.

4. Enter **20↵** again. The box is now a cube 20 units square.

NOTE   *You can also create a cube directly by selecting the Cube check box in the Creation Method rollout.*

If there is a series of related input boxes—such as the Length, Width, and Height boxes in the previous exercise—the Tab key lets you advance from one value to the next. You'll find that numeric input boxes and spinners are quite common throughout Autodesk VIZ 2005.

TIP   *If you hold down the Ctrl key while you move a spinner, the rate of change in the spinner value increases. The Alt key has the opposite effect, decreasing the rate of change. The higher the numeric value in the spinner, the faster the rate of change, and vice versa. Also, if you right-click a spinner, it sets the value to zero.*

Working with Objects

Now that you've seen the main elements of the VIZ interface, let's take a look at how you interact with objects in the viewport. You'll start by looking at a way to move the box you've just created. Then you'll learn how you can view your box from different angles.

Selecting and Moving Objects

VIZ's basic editing tools are simple and straightforward, although it may take a little explaining for you to grasp the finer points. As with most graphics programs, you use a selection tool to select objects. This tool is typically shown on the toolbar as an upward-pointing arrow that looks like the standard Windows cursor.

1. Click the Select Object tool in the main toolbar.

2. Click in a blank area of the viewport. This clears any selections that may currently be active.

3. Move the cursor over the box. Notice that the cursor turns into a plus (+) sign. This tells you that the cursor has found a selectable object.

4. Click the box. A graphic displays, showing the X, Y, and Z orientation of the box in relation to the viewport. Also notice that marks like 3D *corner marks* appear at the corners of the box. These are called *selection brackets,* and they indicate graphically the objects that are selected.

    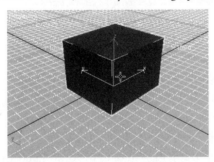

    With the box selected, you can go to the Modify tab of the Command Panel and edit its properties, or you can use any number of other editing tools to affect the box.

Let's continue by looking at one of the more basic editing tools you'll use—the Select and Move tool.

1. Click the Select and Move tool. Notice that the graphics indicating the box selection change and new ones appear.

2. Place the cursor on the box. It changes into the Select and Move icon.

3. Click the box. A graphic known as the Move gizmo displays, showing the X, Y, and Z orientation of the box in relation to the viewport. Selection brackets also appear at the corners of the box.

4. Place the cursor on the Z axis handle of the Move gizmo; the blue arrow represents the Z axis. Notice that the Z axis label is highlighted in yellow and the X axis label turns back to red. When you move the cursor away from the Z axis, the X axis is highlighted again and the Z axis returns to blue.

   The yellow highlighting shows you which axis is currently active. The Y axis is the default constraint direction. If you look at the Constraints toolbar to the left of the VIZ window, you'll see that the Y axis button is selected. As you've seen in this step, you can select an axis to constrain just by placing your cursor on the axis coordinate arrow.

TIP *The axis that is highlighted in yellow is the last axis constraint that was used. For example, if you transform an object in the Y direction, the next time you go to transform an object, the Y axis will be highlighted.*

5. Place the cursor on the XY plane handle of the Move gizmo. Notice that the XY plane handle is highlighted in yellow. Click and drag the box on the grid. The box now moves in the XY plane. When you click and drag the X arrow, movement is constrained along the X axis only.

6. Click and drag the blue Z coordinate arrow upward. Now, movement is constrained in the Z axis, away from and toward the grid. As you may guess, clicking and dragging the green Y coordinate arrow constrains movement in the Y axis.

7. Click the Restrict to XY Plane tool in the Constraints toolbar.

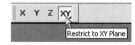

8. Click and drag the box slowly in a circular motion, taking care not to click a coordinate arrow. (You still must have the cursor over the box.) If you click an object in a location other than the coordinate arrows, but still on the object, you can freely move the object in the XY plane. Notice that the coordinate location of the object is displayed in the status line just below the drafting tools.

CONSTRAINING MOTION

The tools in the Constraints toolbar constrain the motion of an object in the X, Y, or Z axis. For example, to constrain motion in the X axis, click the Select and Move tool, and then click the X tool in the Constraints toolbar. The selected object's motion is constrained to the X axis. In 3D Studio VIZ 3 and before, this was the only method available to constrain motion.

Another important function that the Constraints toolbar offers is the selection of the default *free motion* plane. In step 8 of the preceding exercise, you were able to move the box freely in the XY plane, but you were constrained to that plane. The Constraints toolbar lets you select the default plane to which you are constrained. The Restrict to XY Plane tool is a flyout offering three options: XY, YZ, and ZX. You can select the plane in which you want to constrain motion by selecting one of these three options. The XY option is fine for nearly all of your work; every now and then, though, you'll want to use one of the other options, so it's good to be aware of this tool. You can also access these constraint planes simply by dragging the appropriate parts of the Transform gizmo—it's very intuitive.

Finally, a tool that is related to the transform tools is the Selection Lock Toggle tool.

This tool helps prevent the accidental loss of a selection due to a mouse click. It also allows you to use the transform tools without actually placing the cursor on the selected objects. You can toggle this tool on and off by clicking it or by pressing the spacebar while in a selection mode.

As you see, moving an object in VIZ is fairly straightforward. But what if you want to move an object a specific distance or to a known position? The following exercise demonstrates how this is done.

1. With the box still selected and the Select and Move tool still active, click the Absolute/Offset Mode Transform Type-In button at the bottom of the VIZ window.

The tool changes to show that the Offset mode is active.

When the Absolute/Offset Mode Transform Type-In button is in the "up," or Absolute, mode, you can enter the specific coordinates of the point where you want to move your object. When it's in the "down," or Offset, mode, you can enter a relative distance from the object's current location.

2. Click in the X input box in the coordinate readout and type **10**↵. The box moves 10 units to the right.

3. Click and drag the Z axis coordinate readout spinner upward. The box moves vertically.

4. Click the Absolute/Offset Mode Type-In button to switch to Absolute mode. Then click in the Z coordinate readout input box and enter 1↵. The box moves so that its base is exactly at 1 for the Z coordinate.

5. Right-click the X coordinate readout spinner. Remember that right-clicking a spinner converts the value associated with the spinner to its default, which is 0 in this case. Notice that the box moves to 0 for the X coordinate.

6. Right-click the spinners for the Y and Z coordinates in the coordinate readout. The box moves to the center of the screen at the origin (coordinates 0,0,0).

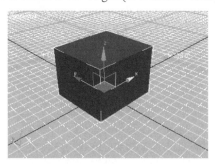

Just as with the spinners in the Command Panel, the transform type-in spinners let you set values by clicking and dragging. You can also return to the default values of zero by right-clicking the spinners. The spinners in the coordinate readout appear when you turn on the Select and Move, Select and Rotate, or Select and Scale tools from the main toolbar.

TIP If you are used to earlier versions of VIZ, you can still use the floating Transform Type-In dialog box that appears when you right-click the Select and Move, Rotate, and Scale tools.

Rotating and Scaling Objects

New!

Besides the Move tool, the transform tools also include the Rotate and Scale tools. The look and functionality of these Transform gizmos has been improved in VIZ 2005. Try the following set of exercises to see how these tools work.

TIP You can also activate the Move, Rotate, and Scale tools by right-clicking an object and selecting Move, Rotate, or Uniform Scale from the shortcut menu.

1. With the box selected, click the Select and Rotate tool in the main toolbar. A graphic known as the Rotate gizmo, a kind of virtual trackball, displays showing rings for rotation about the X, Y, and Z axes.

2. Place the cursor on the ring that circumscribes the X axis. Notice that the ring is highlighted in yellow. Click and drag the X axis ring upward. The box rotates about the X axis. A tangent indicator arrow will appear indicating the direction of rotation and a transparent red slice along with a text tool tip will appear displaying the amount of rotation.

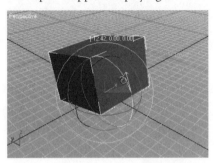

Make sure the Absolute/Offset Mode Transform Type-In button is in the Absolute mode and look at the coordinate readout. Notice that the X value is not zero, because you rotated it in step 2. It now shows a number of degrees.

3. Right-click the X spinner in the coordinate readout to set the X value rotation back to zero. Notice that the box snaps back to its original orientation.

The Select and Rotate tool's methods are the same as those for the Select and Move tool. You can rotate an object graphically by clicking and dragging the object, or, with an object selected, you can enter an exact rotation value in the coordinate readout. When the Absolute/Offset Transform Type-In button is in the Absolute mode, you can control the orientation in relation to the object's original orientation when it was created. In the Offset mode, you can control the orientation relative to the object's current orientation.

Now try out the Scale tool:

1. With the box selected, click the Select and Uniform Scale tool in the main toolbar. A graphic known as the Scale gizmo displays, showing the X, Y, and Z orientation of the box in relation to the viewport.

2. Click anywhere on the Scale gizmo or the box and drag the box upward. The box grows uniformly in size.

3. Click and hold the Select and Uniform Scale tool. Then select the middle tool, which is the Select and Non-uniform Scale tool.

4. Drag the XY plane handle of the Scale gizmo (highlighted in yellow) to nonuniformly scale the box in the XY plane in this case. Similarly, the axis handles can be dragged to constrain the scaling of an object to one axis.

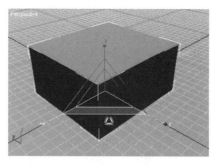

Now, take a look at the coordinate readout. The values you see are percentages of scale. When the Absolute/Offset Transform Type-In button is in the Absolute (up) position, the values are percentages of the original size of the object. When it's in the Offset position, the values are the scale in relation to the current size, and are immediately reset to 100% when you release the mouse button.

1. With the Absolute/Offset Transform Type-In tool in the Absolute position, click and drag the Z spinner upward. Notice that the box grows in the Z axis.

2. Right-click the Y axis spinner. The box distorts to a 0 value in the Y axis.

3. Click in the X value input box and enter **100.↵**. The box's X value is restored to its original size.

4. Press the Tab key to move to the Y value input box and enter **100.↵**.

5. Press Tab again to move to the Z input box and enter **100.↵**. The box is now restored to its original size.

The Select and Scale tool works in a slightly different way from the other two transform tools. For one thing, a zero value in the coordinate readout doesn't return the selected object to its original shape. This is because the values in the coordinate readout represent percentages, where 100% is the original size.

The new Scale gizmo allows you to both uniformly and nonuniformly scale an object by automatically switching between scale modes. Which operation you perform depends on which part of the Scale gizmo you drag.

1. Try dragging the center of the Scale gizmo. You will see the object get uniformly bigger or smaller, when you drag up or down.

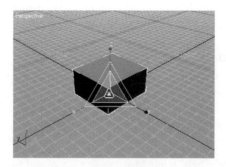

2. This time, put your mouse over one of the edges of the Scale gizmo. When you drag over one of the plane handles, you are performing a nonuniform scale in two directions at once. Look closely at the gizmo and you can see the axes labeled. Try nonuniformly scaling the box in the YZ plane.

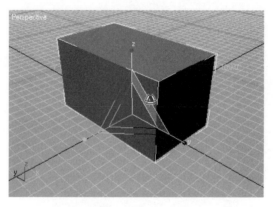

3. The last operation you can perform using the Scale transform gizmo is a nonuniform scale in one direction. To accomplish this, put your mouse directly over the axis handle at the tip of an axis. For example, put your mouse over the green dot at the end of the Y axis and drag to scale in that direction only.

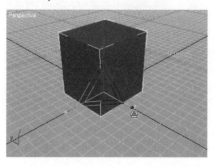

Once you master the mechanics of the new transform gizmos, you will find that you have much finer and more intuitive control over your objects as compared to previous versions of VIZ.

Copying an Object

You've covered just about all the ways of moving, rotating, and scaling an object in the Perspective viewport. If you want to copy an object, you use the same methods you would use to move, rotate, or scale objects—with the addition of holding down the Shift key. Try the following steps to see how copying, or cloning as it's called in VIZ, works. (Copying is one of the forms of a more general function called *cloning*.)

1. Make sure that the Select and Move tool is active and that the box is selected.

2. While holding down the Shift key, drag the box to the right. A second box appears.

3. Release the mouse button. The Clone Options dialog box displays. This dialog box lets you control the type of copy you're making, as well as the name of the new object.

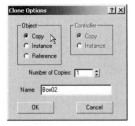

4. In the Object group of the Clone Options dialog box, make sure Copy is selected.

5. Click OK. The new box is now added to your model.

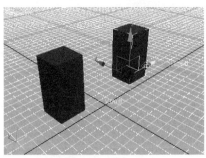

TIP   You may experience times when you want to make a copy of an object in exactly the same location as the original object. To accomplish this, first select the object you wish to copy, and then select Edit ➤ Clone from the menu bar or Ctrl+V on the keyboard. You see the Clone Options dialog box that you saw in the preceding exercise. Set your options and click OK. Note that the new copy doesn't appear at first, because it occupies the same space as the original. (You can accomplish the same thing by Shift+clicking an object with the Select and Move tool or by selecting Clone from the transform quad menu, which can be accessed by right-clicking the object.)

In step 4, you selected the Copy option in the Clone Options dialog box. This option creates a distinct copy of the original object. The other two options, Instance and Reference, create clones that are linked to the original, so that changes in one object affect the other. You'll learn more about these options in Chapter 2.

Selecting Multiple Objects

You've now learned how to select, move, and copy a single object, but what do you do if you want to move or copy several objects at once? You can select multiple objects, or *selection sets* as they are called in VIZ, using two methods. The first is one that is also employed in other graphics programs.

1. Click the Select Object tool on the main toolbar.

2. Click a blank area of the viewport to clear any selections you may already have.

3. Click and hold your mouse at a point below and to the left of the original box. Then drag to the right and upward. Notice that a dotted rectangle follows your cursor, as shown in Figure 1.10.

4. Continue to drag the cursor up and to the right until it encloses both boxes. Then release the mouse button. Both boxes are selected.

FIGURE 1.10

Placing the selection rectangle around the boxes

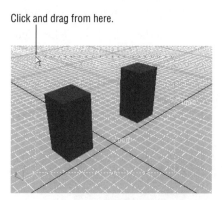

Click and drag from here.

Notice that selection brackets (or bounding boxes) appear at the corners of both boxes, and a Transform gizmo appears between the two boxes, showing you that the two objects are selected. You can select objects in a couple of other ways, which you'll learn about in a moment, but first, let's use the current selection to make a few more copies of the box.

1. Click the Select and Move tool in the main toolbar.

2. Shift and drag the Y axis arrow downward so that copies of the two boxes appear in the location shown in Figure 1.11. (You don't need to be exact about the placement of the copies.)

FIGURE 1.11
Place the copies just
beyond your first
two boxes.

3. When you have the copies in place, release the mouse button.

4. In the Clone Options dialog box, make sure Copy is selected in the Object group and click OK.

The four boxes help to demonstrate some of the other selection methods available to you. First, let's look at another property of the selection window.

1. Click the Select Object tool.

2. Click a blank spot in the viewport to clear your selection set.

3. Click and drag the cursor from the point indicated in Figure 1.12.

FIGURE 1.12
Selecting points for a
crossing window

Click and drag from here.

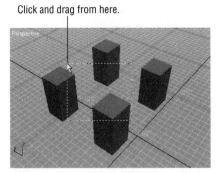

4. Drag the rectangle up and to the right so that it encompasses just a portion of all the boxes, as shown in Figure 1.12. Then release the mouse button. Three of the four boxes are selected.

Notice that you didn't need to enclose the boxes completely to select them. In the current selection mode, you only need to have the selection window cross over the desired objects. This is known as a *crossing window*. If you're an AutoCAD user, this type of window should be familiar to you.

You can change the way the selection window works by using the Window/Crossing Selection tool. The following exercise demonstrates this.

1. Click a blank area in the drawing in order to clear your selection set.

2. Click the Window/Crossing Selection tool in the Main toolbar.

Notice that the icon changes to one showing a sphere that's completely within a dotted rectangle. This tells you that you are now in Window Selection mode.

3. Click a point below and to the left of the box in the center foreground, as shown in Figure 1.13.

FIGURE 1.13

Placing a selection window

Click here to start the selection window.

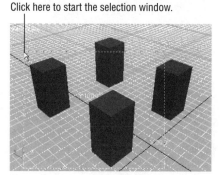

4. Drag the rectangle up and to the right until it includes part of the boxes on the right, as shown in Figure 1.13. Then release the mouse button. Notice that the only objects selected are the two boxes on the left.

When you use Window Selection mode, only objects that are completely within the selected window are selected. Unlike with the crossing window, objects that are partially inside the selected window are left out of the selection.

You can use the Ctrl key in conjunction with a window or crossing selection to continue to add more objects to your selection set. You can also remove objects from your selection set by using the Ctrl key with a window or crossing selection. Let's see how adding and subtracting from selections works:

1. Ctrl+click and hold a point above and to the left of the box in the upper right of the viewport, as shown in Figure 1.14.

2. Drag the window down and to the right so that it completely encloses the two boxes to the right. Then release the mouse button. Now all four boxes are selected.

3. Hold down the Ctrl key and then click the box in the upper right of the screen, as shown in Figure 1.15. Now all boxes except the upper right one are selected.

FIGURE 1.14
Adding objects to your selection set using the Ctrl key and a window

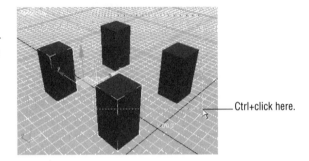

— Ctrl+click here.

FIGURE 1.15
Removing an object using the Ctrl key and a click

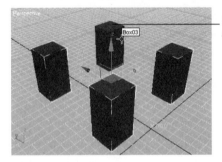

— Place a window around this box.

New!

You can change the shape of your selection window to help select objects. As in VIZ 4, there are rectangular, circular, and polygonal selection window options. New to VIZ 2005 is the Lasso selection region that allows freeform sketching for a selection.

1. Drag open the selection window flyout and choose the Lasso button.

2. Sketch a Lasso selection region by dragging the mouse in a freeform manner around two of the boxes to select them.

Right now, you have only a few objects in your model, but as your model develops, you'll find that selecting objects in a crowded model becomes more of a challenge. Knowing about the different selection modes you've just used will go a long way toward making your work easier.

One more selection method will be an invaluable tool as your model becomes more complex. You can select objects by their names, using the Select Objects dialog box. The following is a quick exercise that will introduce you to this important tool.

1. Click the Select by Name tool in the main toolbar or press H on the keyboard.

The Select Objects dialog box displays. Notice that it contains a list showing the names of the objects in your drawing. Right now, the list shows the default names given to the objects by VIZ. You can always change the name of an object in the Command Panel. (You can rename an object on every tab except Utilities.)

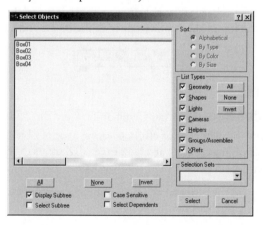

2. Click the None button near the bottom left of the dialog box. This clears the selection set.

3. Click Box02 and then Ctrl+click Box04 in the list of object names. This list lets you select multiple names as you would in a typical Windows list box. You can Shift+click to select a group of adjacent names or Ctrl+click to select a group of individual names.

4. Click the Select button. The two boxes are selected.

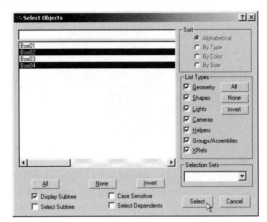

The preceding exercise showed you how to select objects based on their names, but it also indirectly showed you the importance of the names of objects. Giving objects meaningful names helps you locate and select them more easily, especially in a crowded model.

NOTE *VIZ is a parametric, object-oriented program (unlike AutoCAD), and every object has its own name. Each object has its own parameters that can be accessed from the Modify tab.*

Whenever you create an object in Autodesk VIZ 2005, you have the opportunity to give the new object a name. If you don't indicate a new name, VIZ provides a name for you. If the new object is a copy of an existing one, the new name that VIZ provides is the name of the original object, with a number appended to its name. If you don't give an object a meaningful name when you create the object, it's easy enough to change it later. Just select the object, and then enter a new name in the object name input box at the top of the Modify tab or in the Name and Color rollout of the Create tab.

Naming Selection Sets

Suppose you've gone through a lot of effort selecting a set of objects, and you know you will want to select the same set of objects again at a later time. VIZ offers the Selection toolbar, which lets you name a selection set for later recall. Here's how it works:

1. Make sure two of the boxes are selected. It doesn't really matter which two, because you're just practicing using the Selection toolbar.

2. Click inside the Selection input box that's just to the left of the Mirror tool in the main toolbar.

3. Type the name **Sample.**↵. You've just given the current selection set a name. (You can enter a selection set name up to 15 characters long.)

4. Click in a blank area of the viewport to clear the current selection set.

5. In the main toolbar, click the downward-pointing arrow to the right of the Selection input box. Select Sample. The two boxes you selected earlier are now the current selection set.

In these early stages of learning VIZ, the concept of named selection sets may seem simple, but it's one tool you'll likely use quite a bit as you expand your skills.

TIP *The Edit option in the menu bar offers some additional selection commands, such as Select All, Select None, and Select Invert. You can also use the Edit ➤ Select By cascading menu to select objects by color or name.*

Editing Named Selection Sets

Named selection sets are not fixed in stone. You can add to or subtract from them, or you can delete them entirely through the Named Selection Sets dialog box.

1. Open the Named Selection Sets dialog box by choosing Edit ➤ Edit Named Selection Sets, or by clicking the Named Selection Sets button just to the left of the Selection input box you used before. The Named Selection Sets dialog box appears with a list of all of the selection sets that have been created.

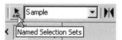

2. Click the plus (+) symbol next to your Sample named selection to see which objects are contained within this set.

3. Click Sample in the list. Then click the Select Objects by Name button in the Named Selection Sets toolbar. The Select Objects dialog box displays. Select one of the names in the list that doesn't already appear in the Named Selection Sets dialog box, and then click the Select button.

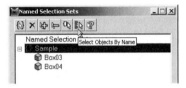

4. Click the Add Selected Objects button within the Named Selection Sets dialog box.

The name of the object you selected now appears in the list of objects contained in the selection set.

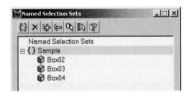

5. Close the dialog box and deselect all by clicking off to the side in the viewport.

6. Select Sample from the Selection toolbar's drop-down list to refresh the selection. Now you see that three of the boxes are selected.

There are several other tools in the Named Selection Sets dialog box. These tools let you select objects from a set, highlight selected objects, delete objects from a set, or remove a set altogether. You can also create new named selection sets using the Create New Set tool at the far left of the Named Selection Sets toolbar.

You've now seen most of the selection tools you'll need to get started with VIZ. You'll learn about a few other selection tools as you work with VIZ, and you'll also get a chance to apply the tools you've already learned as you start to build and edit 3D models in later chapters.

In the next section, you'll learn about the tools that enable you to view your model from different angles, and how these different views can aid you in creating and editing your model.

Getting the View You Want

So far in this chapter, you've done all of your work without making any modifications to the *point of view* of your model. Now let's take a look at ways you can control your view. Understanding the viewport controls is essential for manipulating objects in your model, so take some time to become familiar with all the tools discussed in this section.

Understanding the Perspective Viewing Tools

If you look at the viewport tools in the lower right corner of the VIZ window, you'll see some tools that are common among most graphics programs. These include the magnifying glass and the hand. Other tools in this area may be a bit more mysterious. In this section, you'll learn how these tools let you get around in your model.

PANNING AND ZOOMING YOUR VIEW

Let's start by looking at the tool with the hand icon, known as the Pan tool. Like similar tools in other programs, the Pan tool displaces your view up or down, or to the left or right. But in VIZ's Perspective viewport, you're also changing your point of view. Do the following to see what this means.

1. Click the Pan tool.

2. Click and drag the viewport to the left and upward until the boxes are roughly centered in the viewport.

3. Click and drag the viewport in a circular fashion. Notice that your view of the model appears to change as if you were moving sideways while looking at the boxes.

Next, try the Zoom tool.

1. Click the Zoom tool.

2. Click and drag the Zoom tool upward from the center of the viewport. Notice how you appear to get closer to the boxes.

3. Click and drag the cursor downward in the viewport. Now you appear to be moving away from the boxes.

4. Continue to click and drag downward until your view looks similar to the one shown in Figure 1.16.

You may have also noticed that, as you moved farther away, the grid became denser. Then, at a certain point, the grid changed to a wider interval. VIZ does this so that the grid doesn't overwhelm the view when it becomes too dense.

Again, as with other graphics programs, the Zoom tool enlarges or reduces your view. In addition to the Zoom tool, the wheel of the mouse can also be used to zoom in and out within a viewport. In VIZ's Perspective viewport, zooming has the effect of moving you closer to or farther away from the objects in your model.

FIGURE 1.16
Zooming out to view
a larger area

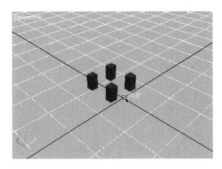

Now, suppose you don't like the last view change you made and you want to go back to the previous view. Try the following steps to return to the previous view.

1. Choose Views ➤ Undo View Change. You return to the previous view. (Alternatively, press Shift+Z.)

2. Choose Views ➤ Undo View Change or press Shift+Z again. Your view returns to the view prior to the last view.

3. Choose Views ➤ Undo View Change a third time. You return to the view you had before you panned your view.

The Views ➤ Undo View Change command lets you step back to a previous view in case the last view change you made is one you don't like. Views ➤ Undo View Change undoes any view change, regardless of which viewport tool you used last.

WARNING   *Don't confuse Views ➤ Undo View Change with the Edit ➤ Undo command. Edit ➤ Undo undoes creation and editing operations but not view changes.*

SAVING A VIEW YOU LIKE

If you happen to get a view that you know you want to go back to later, you can save the view with the Views ➤ Save Active command from the menu bar. Use it in the next exercise to save a view that you'll return to later in this chapter. And, as you'll see in Chapter 8, you can also create a camera object and align it to a view.

1. Click the Zoom Extents tool to set up your view for the next exercise. Zoom Extents causes the viewport to display the entire model.

2. Save this view by choosing Views ➤ Save Active Perspective View.

The Zoom Extents tool repositions your view so that the entire model just fits within the viewport, filling the viewport as much as possible. If you're an AutoCAD user, you're familiar with this tool, because its counterpart in AutoCAD performs the same function.

TIP   You can restore the default perspective view (the one you see when you open a new file) in a blank file by clicking the Zoom Extents tool or by choosing File ➤ Reset to reset the design.

CHANGING YOUR VIEWING ANGLE

Two other tools are specifically designed for viewing 3D objects: Field-of-View and Arc Rotate Selected. The Field-of-View tool changes your field of view. The Arc Rotate Selected tool lets you rotate your view around a selected object.

The Field-of-View tool appears to do the same thing as the Zoom tool, but as you'll see in the following exercise, there is a significant difference between the Zoom and Field-of-View tools.

1. Save the current view by choosing Views ➤ Save Active Perspective View. This lets you return to the current view later.

2. Click the Field-of-View tool.

3. Place the cursor in the viewport and click and drag downward until your view looks similar to Figure 1.17.

FIGURE 1.17
View of perspective after increasing the field of view

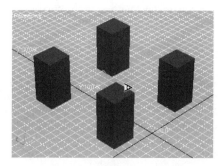

In one sense, it appears as though you've zoomed out from the boxes, but if you compare this view to the zoomed-out view in the previous exercise, you'll notice a difference. When you use the Zoom tool in the Perspective viewport, your view changes as though you were physically moving closer to or farther away from the boxes. As the name implies, the Field-of-View tool widens or narrows your field of view, much as a zoom lens on a camera does. You're not actually changing the distance from the object; instead, you're changing the area that your viewport displays. The Field-of-View tool has the potential to distort your view, just as a super-wide-angle fish-eye lens or a super-telephoto lens tends to distort a photograph. Until you find yourself in a situation where you really need to change the field of view, you may want to refrain from using the Field-of-View tool.

Now let's take a look at the Arc Rotate Selected tool.

1. Return to the view you had before you used the Field-of-View tool by selecting Views ➤ Undo View Change.

2. Click the Select Object tool. Click in a blank space in the viewport to clear any selections that may be active. In the next exercise, you'll see why this is significant.

3. Click the Arc Rotate Selected tool.

You see a yellow circle with squares at each of the four cardinal points on the circle. If you place the cursor inside the circle, the cursor looks like two overlapping ellipses.

4. Place the cursor on the square at the far left of the circle. Notice that the cursor changes shape to what looks like a horizontal ellipse.

5. With the cursor on the square, slowly click and drag the cursor to the right. Notice how the view rotates.

6. Place the cursor on the square at the top of the circle. Now the cursor changes to a vertically oriented ellipse.

7. With the cursor on the square, click and drag the cursor downward. The view now rotates in that direction.

The squares on the yellow circle are like handles that you can grab and turn to change your view orientation. The left and right squares constrain the rotation to the horizontal plane, and the top and bottom squares constrain the rotation to the vertical plane. If you prefer, you can adjust the view freely without constraint in the vertical or horizontal direction by clicking and dragging the cursor anywhere within the circle. You can also rotate the view by clicking and dragging anywhere outside the circle. The following exercise demonstrates these features. Pay attention to the shape of the cursor in each step.

1. Place the cursor anywhere within the circle. Then slowly click and drag in a small, circular motion. Notice how the view changes as if your point of view was rotating around the group of boxes.

2. Place the cursor anywhere outside the circle. Then slowly click and drag in an up-and-down motion. Now the view rotates around the circle as if you were tilting your head from side to side.

You may have noticed that the cursor changes, depending on whether you're inside or outside the circle. This gives you further cues regarding the way the Arc Rotate tool affects your view.

You've been introduced to nearly all of the viewport tools. However, there's one more feature of the Arc Rotate Selected tool that you'll want to know about before you move on. The Arc Rotate

Selected tool uses the center of the viewport as the center about which it rotates when no object is selected. But the Arc Rotate Selected tool works in a slightly different way when objects are selected. Try the following exercise to see how this variation works.

1. Choose Views ➤ Restore Active Perspective View to restore the view you saved earlier.

2. Click the Select Object tool from the main toolbar.

3. Click the box in the left side in the back row.

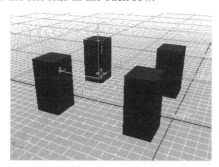

4. Click the Arc Rotate Selected tool again.

5. Slowly click and drag the cursor within the circle. Notice how the view appears to be fixed at the center of the selected box.

6. Slowly click and drag the cursor in a vertical motion outside the circle. The view appears to rotate around the selected box.

7. Return to the saved view by choosing Views ➤ Restore Active Perspective View.

If you click and hold the Arc Rotate Selected tool, you'll see two other Arc Rotate tools in the Arc Rotate flyout. The tool at the top, called simply the Arc Rotate tool, rotates the view about the view center, regardless of whether an object is selected. You've already seen how the second tool, the Arc Rotate Selected tool, works. The tool at the bottom of the Arc Rotate flyout is the Arc Rotate Sub-Object tool. This tool rotates a view about a sub-object-level selection. You'll learn about sub-object-level editing in Chapter 4.

TIP *You can Arc Rotate by holding down the Alt key on the keyboard and dragging the wheel button of your mouse in a viewport. Don't turn the wheel, but drag it as if the wheel was a middle mouse button. This is a huge timesaver because you'll find that you don't have to spend time clicking the Arc Rotate button when you want to rotate your viewing angle.*

By being able to select an object or set of objects as the center of rotation for your view, you are better able to set up your views for rendering or editing. The combination of the Zoom, Pan, and Arc Rotate tools allows you to obtain just about any view you may need as you work within VIZ's Perspective viewport. But you aren't limited to a perspective view of your model. In fact, there are many situations where the perspective view is not ideal, especially when editing your model. In the next section, you'll look at other viewport types that give you greater flexibility in creating and editing objects in your model.

Using Multiple Viewports

So far, you've done all your work in the Perspective viewport, but this isn't the only view you have available. You saw earlier how you can divide the VIZ window so that it displays four equal viewports, each representing a different view. Let's go back to that viewport arrangement to explore the uses of some of VIZ's display tools. The first item you'll look at is the way that the Field-of-View tool changes when your active viewport changes.

1. Click the Min/Max Toggle tool in the set of viewport navigation controls.

VIZ's window changes to display four viewports.

2. Right-click anywhere in the viewport labeled Top in the upper left corner of the display. Notice that the Field-of-View tool changes to a magnifying glass with a rectangle. This is the Region Zoom tool.

Also notice that the Top viewport now shows a thick border around it, indicating that it is the current, active viewport.

3. Click the Region Zoom tool.

4. Click and drag the cursor on a point below and to the left of the boxes, as shown in Figure 1.18. As you drag the cursor, you see a rectangle appear. Don't release the cursor just yet.

5. Position the rectangle above and to the right of the bottom row of boxes, as shown in Figure 1.18, and then release the mouse button. The view enlarges to the region you just indicated with the Region Zoom tool.

FIGURE 1.18

Selecting a view to enlarge with the Region Zoom tool

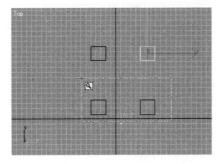

The Region Zoom tool acts like the magnifying tools in many other graphics programs. Also, the Zoom and Pan tools perform the same functions in orthogonal views in VIZ as they do in other programs, allowing you to zoom in and pan over the view.

You may have noticed two other tools in the viewport navigation controls that haven't been discussed yet: the Zoom All and Zoom Extents All tools. Now that you have multiple viewports displayed, you can try out these two tools.

1. Click the Zoom All tool.

2. In any viewport, click and drag the cursor upward. Notice that the view in all of the viewports is enlarged to take in as much of the four boxes as can be displayed.

3. Click and drag the cursor downward, and the views expand to show more of the model area.

4. Click the Zoom Extents All tool.

All of the viewports change to show enlarged views of the boxes.

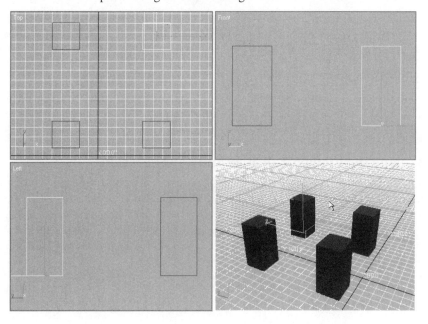

Although not as frequently used as the other viewport navigation tools, the Zoom All tool and the Zoom Extents All tool can be helpful when you need to adjust the overall view of your model in multiple viewports.

You should be aware that the Arc Rotate Selected tool you used in the Perspective viewport also works in the other viewports. Try it out on the Top viewport in the next exercise.

1. Click the Arc Rotate Selected tool.

2. Click and drag the cursor from the center of the Top viewport upward and to the right, so it shows a view similar to Figure 1.19.

FIGURE 1.19

Top view after using Arc Rotate Selected

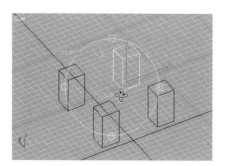

The view changes to a type of 3D view known as an *isometric projection.* Also notice that the label in the upper left corner of the viewport now reads User. This indicates that the view is a custom view based on your changes.

3. Click the Zoom Extents tool to center the view in the viewport.

The 3D view in the upper left corner of the display differs in many ways from the perspective view. But, as you'll see in the next section, it's different only because a few of the settings for that viewport are different from those of the Perspective viewport.

Changing the Viewport Display and Configuration

If you compare the User viewport with the Perspective viewport, you notice two things that are different. First, as mentioned in the previous exercise, the User viewport shows a 3D orthographic projection. The second difference is that the User viewport isn't shaded; the boxes are displayed as simple line outlines called a *wireframe view.* These display characteristics can be modified for each viewport.

In the following exercise, you'll see how you can alter viewport settings to obtain specific view characteristics such as shading and perspective.

1. Right-click the User label in the upper right corner of the User viewport. A pop-up menu displays.

2. Select Smooth + Highlights from the menu. The boxes now appear shaded, just as they do in the Perspective viewport.

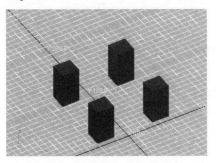

3. Right-click the Perspective viewport label. Then select Wireframe from the pop-up menu. The perspective view changes to a wireframe representation.

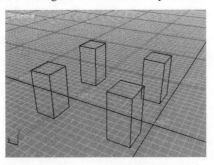

Notice that the pop-up menu is the same for both the User and Perspective viewports. This menu gives you control over the display characteristics of the viewport. Try out a few other options in the Viewport pop-up menu.

1. Right-click the User label, and then select Views ➢ Perspective. The user view changes to a perspective view. Notice that the label changes to read Perspective, so that you now have two Perspective viewports.

2. Right-click the Perspective label of the upper left viewport, and then select Views ➤ Top. The view now changes back to the original top view. Notice that the boxes are still shaded.

3. Right-click the Top label and select Wireframe. The view returns to its original state.

Now all the viewports show wireframe views of the boxes. Wireframe views are often better for many types of editing operations. Wireframes also redraw faster when your model is very large and full of complex geometry. Another type of view, called *bounding box*, is even faster than a wireframe view, but bounding box views reduce the representation of objects to rectangular boxes.

Besides changing the way the viewport displays your model, wireframe view also gives you control over the layout of the viewports themselves. The following exercise shows you the variety of layouts you can create in VIZ.

1. Choose Customize ➤ Viewport Configuration. The Viewport Configuration dialog box displays.

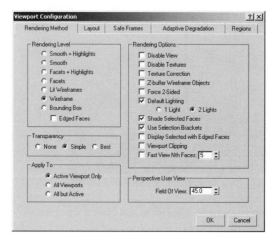

2. Click the Layout tab. You see the current viewport layout. Above it is a set of predefined layouts.

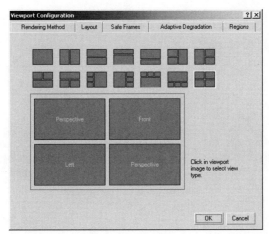

3. Click the layout that looks like three small rectangles stacked on the left side with one large rectangle on the right.

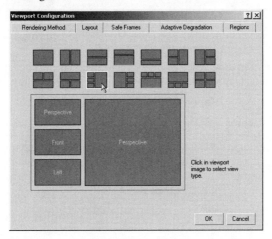

4. Click OK. The viewports change to the selected layout.

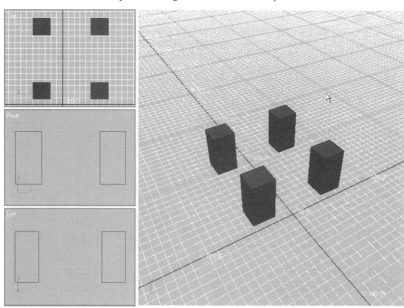

Users of previous versions of VIZ may find this layout comfortable. It has been the default layout for a few of the early 3ds max and 3D Studio VIZ versions.

You aren't limited to the canned layouts either. You may decide that you want the layout to reflect a more traditional mechanical drawing layout, with a top, front, and right side view. Here's how you can set up such a viewport arrangement:

1. Choose Customize ➤ Viewport Configuration.

2. With the Layout tab selected, click the layout showing four equal viewports, which is the right-most layout in the bottom row of layout options.

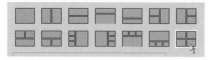

3. Click the sample viewport labeled Front in the upper right corner of the large sample layout and select Perspective in the pop-up menu.

4. Click the sample Perspective viewport in the lower right corner and select Right from the pop-up menu.

5. Click the sample left viewport in the lower left corner and select Front from the pop-up menu. The sample layout should now look like Figure 1.20.

FIGURE 1.20

The four-viewport layout with modifications

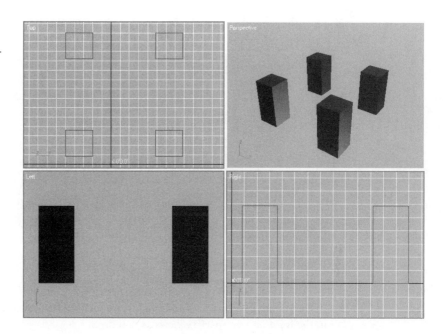

6. Click OK. Now you have a layout that shows the top, front, and right views, plus a perspective view, arranged in a more traditional manner.

TIP   *When VIZ displays multiple viewports, you can resize those viewports on the fly by clicking and dragging the viewport borders. Place the cursor on the border and, when you see a double-headed arrow, click and drag to change the viewport size.*

As you can see from what you've learned so far, Autodesk VIZ 2005 provides a wide array of display options, but most of the time, you'll stick with one viewport layout that you are comfortable with. For the purposes of this book, you'll use the default layout that shows the four equal-size viewports.

Before you conclude your tour of the VIZ interface, let's see how the Move tool acts in the non-Perspective viewports. The following exercise will give you a feel for the ways that you can use multiple viewports.

1. Click the Select and Move tool.

2. In the Top viewport, click and drag the cursor from a point below and to the left of the bottom row of boxes.

3. Drag the selection rectangle above and to the right of the two boxes in the lower row, so that they are enclosed in the rectangle. The two boxes are selected.

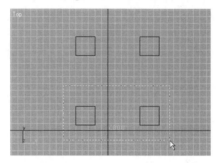

4. Right-click in the Right viewport.

TIP   By right-clicking in a viewport, you can make it active without disrupting any selections you may have active at the time.

5. In the Right viewport, click and drag the green Y arrow upward. Notice how the boxes move in the front and perspective views as you do this.

6. Position the boxes so they are higher by about one-half the height of a box.

7. Click and drag the red X axis of the boxes to the right of the screen, so they merge with the box to the right, as shown here.

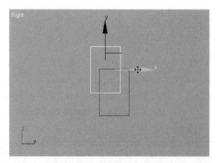

8. You can discard this file. You won't need it anymore.

In this exercise, you've seen a number of methods in action. First, the Select and Move tool can be used to select objects as well as move them. This can help you move objects quickly by reducing the number of clicks. But be careful, or you might select and move the wrong object when you're in a hurry.

You also saw how you can right-click in a viewport to make it active. Had you simply clicked in the Right viewport in step 4, you would have lost the selection set you created in step 3.

Finally, you saw how objects in VIZ don't conform to one of the basic rules of physics. In VIZ, more than one object *can* occupy the same space at the same time. This characteristic can be useful in a number of ways as you build models in Autodesk VIZ 2005.

Working with the Custom UI and Defaults Switcher

New!

The new Custom UI and Defaults Switcher provides an easy and unified method for managing all the myriad preference settings within VIZ 2005. Let's explore what the Custom UI and Defaults Switcher has to offer.

1. Choose Customize ➢ Custom UI and Defaults Switcher.

2. Click on the DesignVIZ initial settings for tool options in the upper left of the dialog to see the settings listed in Figure 1.21.

FIGURE 1.21
Custom UI and Defaults Switcher settings

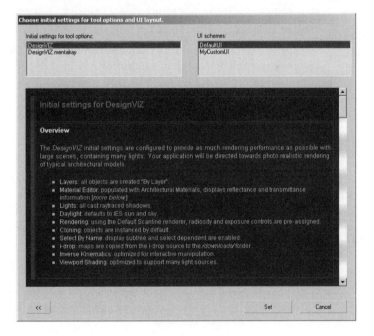

3. Scroll down in the dialog box and read through the changes that the DesignVIZ settings represent in the HTML file that is part of the Custom UI and Defaults Switcher dialog box. There are two initial settings for tool options: DesignVIZ and DesignVIZ.mentalray.

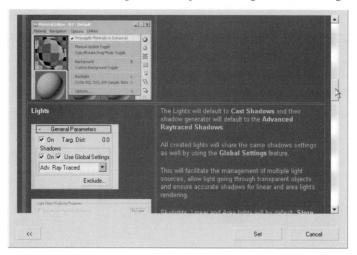

The DesignVIZ settings are configured to provide you with good rendering performance in large scenes with many lights; this assumes you'll be using the radiosity renderer and photometric lights.

The DesignVIZ.mentalray initial settings are meant to be used in conjunction with the mental ray renderer. Each of these settings automatically configures multiple preferences in layers, the Material Editor, Lights, Daylight System, Rendering, Cloning, Select by Name, i-drop, Inverse Kinematics, and Viewport Shading.

NOTE *See Chapter 10 to learn more about the radiosity renderer and Chapter 11 to learn how to use the new mental ray renderer.*

On the right side of the Custom UI and Defaults Switcher dialog box, you'll see a list of UI schemes you have already saved. Here, you can conveniently select which UI scheme you'd like to use. UI schemes hold in one place all the customization you can make to the keyboard hotkeys, toolbar, quad menus, standards menus, and color schemes. To make changes to an existing UI scheme, you'll use the Customize User Interface dialog box.

1. Choose Customize ➢ Customize User Interface to display this window.

2. Click each of the tabs at the top of this dialog to become familiar with all the ways you can customize your user interface (changes can be made to the keyboard, toolbars, quads, menus,

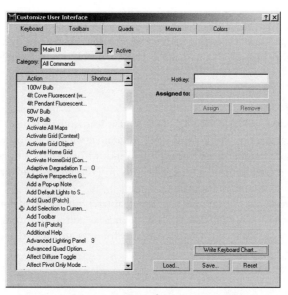

and colors). If you do decide to make any changes, simply click the Save button on the tab within this dialog box to record your specific changes to disk.

3. Choose Customize ➤ Save Custom UI Scheme. Open the Save As Type popup. You will notice five different file formats that can be saved (and loaded) through Save (and Load) Custom UI Scheme from the Customize menu. Each one of the lower four formats —UI File (*.cui), Menu File (*.mnu), Color File (*.clr), and Shortcut File (*.kbd)—correspond to each of the tabs in the Customize User Interface dialog—Toolbars and Quads, Menus, Colors, and Keyboard, respectively.

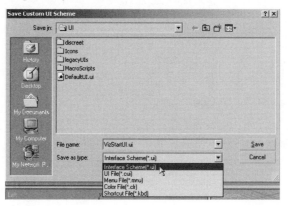

When you choose to save the first format in the Save Custom UI Scheme dialog (Interface Scheme format), you are saving a composite file that contains all the customization present in all the other formats combined. It is this Interface Scheme format (*.ui) that is displayed in the UI Schemes portion of the new Custom UI and Defaults Switcher.

Summary

In this introduction to Autodesk VIZ 2005, you've learned how to use the many different tools available in VIZ. You saw how some tools work in familiar ways, while others, like the spinners and rollouts, are a slight departure from other typical Windows programs. You were also introduced to some of the basic object-creation and editing methods in VIZ. These basic methods are the foundation on which you will build your skills in this program.

You've covered a lot of ground in this first chapter. Don't worry if you can't remember everything. You'll be exposed to many of these tools frequently as you work through the following chapters. In the next chapter, you'll take a closer look at how objects are created and edited.

Chapter 2

Introducing VIZ Objects

IF YOU'VE NEVER USED a 3D modeling program, you may find the behavior of objects in VIZ to be rather unusual. Objects in VIZ are very dynamic and malleable, and they can be fairly complex. In this chapter, you'll get introduced to the ways you can create and form objects, and, in the process, you'll see that you can create just about any shape from just a handful of basic object types.

Most 3D modeling programs typically offer basic building blocks called *primitives*. Primitives are basic shapes on which you can build to form your model. VIZ offers three types of primitives that you can use to build forms: standard primitives, extended primitives, and splines. Let's start by looking at standard primitives. We'll get to splines in Chapter 3.

- ◆ Understanding Standard Primitives
- ◆ Molding Standard Primitives with Modifiers
- ◆ How VIZ Sees Objects
- ◆ Making Clones That Share Properties
- ◆ Introducing Extended Primitives
- ◆ Working with Groups

Understanding Standard Primitives

In Chapter 1, you used the Create tab of the Command Panel to create a box. Let's take another look at the Command Panel to see what else it has to offer.

1. Start VIZ 2005.

2. Click the Create tab in the Command Panel.

3. Click the Geometry button just below the Create tab label.

NOTE   *Notice that the list box just below the Create tools displays the Standard Primitives option. You can use other types of objects by selecting them from this list box. For now, you'll concentrate on the Standard Primitives.*

You see the Object Type rollout that contains the standard primitives. You've already used the Box type in Chapter 1.

There are nine other object types, as shown in Figure 2.1. To create any of these primitives, you use a method that's similar to the one you used to create the box in Chapter 1.

FIGURE 2.1
A view showing all the standard primitives

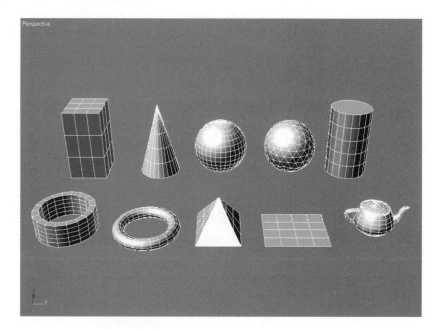

To create a box, first click and hold inside the viewport to establish one corner of the base of the box, and then drag and release the mouse button to select the other corner of the base. You can then adjust the height of the box by moving the mouse. When you've found the height you want, click the mouse again. In short, you click and drag to determine the base dimension, and then click to establish the height. To create a sphere, click and hold to set the center point of the sphere, and then drag and release to set the radius. Try it out in the following exercise.

1. In the Object Type rollout, click the Sphere button.

2. Click and hold in the viewport near the origin.

3. Drag the mouse slowly forward. The sphere grows as you do this. Also notice that the Radius input box in the Parameters rollout displays the radius of the sphere as you move your mouse.

NOTE   *If the Parameters rollout doesn't display dimensions in feet and inches, choose Customize ➤ Units Setup to open the Units Setup dialog box. Select the US Standard radio button, and Feet w/Decimal Inches.*

4. Release the mouse to complete the sphere.

   You may recall that you were able to adjust the parameters of the box after you created it. You can do the same with the sphere.

5. Click the Radius input box in the Parameters rollout.

6. Type 6↵. The cube now has a 6-foot radius.

7. Click and drag the Radius spinner upward. The sphere grows in size.

Notice that, by default, VIZ places the sphere's center on the plane defined by the grid. The grid shows the World Coordinate System, which is the main coordinate system for your model. As you'll see later, you can use other coordinate systems.

Adjusting an Object's Parameters

You can see from the sphere (and from the box example in Chapter 1) that the form of a standard primitive is not fixed. You can change its size and other properties by using the tools in the Command Panel. This ability to adjust the parameters of an object is referred to as *parametric modeling*. This means that you don't need to be precise in your initial placement and creation of a primitive object, because you can refine its form later by entering values in the Parameters rollout.

COORDINATES IN VIZ

One feature that stands out in VIZ's Perspective viewport is the grid. The grid offers some orientation in an otherwise empty space, and it also shows the coordinates of the space. You may remember from high school geometry that the X and Y axes form the basis of a standard two-dimensional grid, with the X axis defining the horizontal (or width) dimension and the Y axis forming the vertical (or length) dimension. Here, you also have the additional Z axis, which forms the height dimension.

The grid you see in a new file shows the World Coordinate System, which is the basis of your model's coordinates. In a new file, you can see the *origin* of the World Coordinate System at the center of the grid. The World Coordinate System is also called the Home Grid in VIZ. The origin is where the X, Y, and Z zero coordinates intersect. The origin is frequently used as a reference point for your model. It is also used as a common reference point among separate model files that need to be combined later. If you're an AutoCAD user, you'll know how the World Coordinate System's origin can be used to keep external reference drawings aligned. In VIZ, you can use the origin to align different models in a similar way.

The World Coordinate System is fixed and cannot be moved. You can, however, adjust the spacing of the grid and the type of units you wish to use. Later, you'll learn about user grids, which allow you to create local coordinates that can be placed anywhere.

VIZ also uses another coordinate system based on what is called *object space*. Object space is the coordinate system of individual objects. You see evidence of this object space in the form of a graphic showing the X, Y, and Z orientation of an object when it's first created or when it's selected. This graphic, along with the transform gizmos (the Move gizmo, the Scale gizmo, and the Rotate gizmo), represents both the position of the object in world space, and the origin point of the object in its own space—the object space. There are two classifications of modifiers in VIZ, the World-Space modifiers (WSMs) and the Object-Space modifiers (OSMs).

Try modifying the sphere's other parameters to see the variety of forms you can generate from just one type of object.

1. In the Parameters rollout, click the Radius input box and enter **2↵**. This changes the radius of the sphere to 2 feet.

2. Scroll down the rollout until you see the Hemisphere input box.

3. Click and drag the Hemisphere spinner upward and watch the sphere. It starts to collapse into a dome from the bottom up.

4. Highlight the entire value in the Hemisphere input box, and then enter **0.5↵**. This gives you an exact hemisphere.

NOTE *For the sake of clarity on the printed page, you will see a leading zero before a decimal measurement. You don't need to type this zero.*

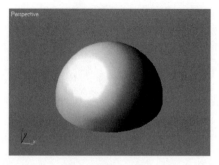

You can further adjust the shape of the sphere by removing a section. The Slice From and Slice To input boxes allow you to do this.

5. Locate the Slice From input box below the Hemisphere input box. Click the Slice On check box, and then click and drag its spinner upward until it reads 135. This value is the angle in degrees from the Y axis to the beginning of the slice.

6. Click and drag the Slice To spinner downward until it reads –135 (minus 135). Your hemisphere now looks like a segment was removed.

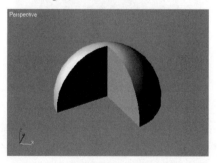

As you can see, you can use a variety of parameters to modify the shape of an object, and each object has a different set of parameters that's appropriate to that object. For example, the Cylinder type offers parameters for radius and height, as well as Slice From and Slice To. The Slice From and

Slice To parameters for the Cylinder type let you create a segment of a cylinder in a manner similar to the sphere example.

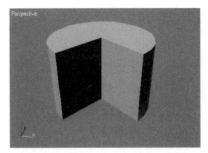

In the Parameters rollout for the Sphere type, there are a couple of other parameters. The Smooth parameter is a check box that turns smoothing on and off. *Smoothing* is a feature of VIZ that's found in most 3D modeling programs. It removes the hard edges between the facets that make up the object. Let's see how smoothing works with the hemisphere you've created.

1. Click the Slice On check box to remove the check mark from this setting. The hemisphere returns to its full shape.

2. Make sure the sphere is selected.

3. Click the Smooth check box to remove the check mark. (The Smooth check box is just below the Segments input box in the Parameters rollout.) Notice that the sphere now looks faceted. You're seeing the facets that make up the sphere.

4. To see the construction of the sphere more clearly, right-click the Perspective viewport label in the upper left corner of the viewport and select Wireframe.

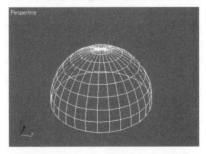

With smoothing turned off, the sphere looks as if it had a rough surface. In fact, all objects are faceted, even if they appear to be smooth. The Smooth parameter is present for all of the curved primitives—the Cone, Sphere, GeoSphere, Cylinder, Tube, Teapot, and Torus (donut shape) types.

Now let's look at another parameter that is somewhat related to the Smooth parameter. The Segments parameter gives you control over the number of facets that make up an object. Try the following to see how the Segments parameter affects the sphere.

1. Click and drag the Segments spinner downward until the Segments value is 12.

Notice that the sphere appears to have fewer surface segments.

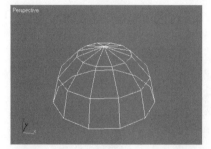

2. Right-click the Perspective label in the upper left corner of the viewport and select Smooth + Highlight from the shortcut menu. This view clearly shows the faceting.

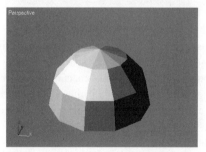

3. Click the Smooth check box to turn on smoothing. You see that the sphere's surface appears smoother, although you can detect the faceting.

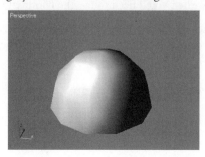

4. Click and drag the Segments spinner downward so that the Segments value reads 4. The sphere becomes a pyramid shape with the edges smoothed.

5. Click the Smooth check box again to turn off smoothing. The sphere now looks like a pyramid with flat surfaces.

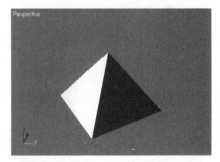

Smoothing provides the illusion of a gradual curve, hiding the facets that are required to construct objects. In the extreme case where a sphere is reduced to four sides, smoothing still provides the illusion of a smooth edge, but it does not hide the sharp corners along the profile of the sphere.

In situations where you need to show a smooth, curved surface, the Smooth parameter is essential. You can apply smoothing to all objects, even if they do not have a Smooth parameter by default. You'll learn more about applying smoothing to objects in later chapters.

Accessing Parameters

You can set an object's parameters in the Create tab of the Command Panel immediately after you create the object. But if you create several objects, and then decide you want to modify the parameters of an object you created earlier, you'll need to use the Modify tab of the Command Panel.

1. Click in a blank area of the viewport to clear your selection set. (When you create an object, it's automatically the current selection, so you need to click to clear the previous selection of the sphere.)

2. Click the Select Object tool, and then click the sphere, which at this point looks like a pyramid with flat surfaces. Notice that the sphere's parameters do not appear in the Create tab of the Command Panel.

3. Click the Modify tab of the Command Panel. You see the parameters for the sphere. You can now make adjustments to the sphere from the Parameters rollout.

The Modify tab displays the parameters of any object you select. Your selection must, however, be a single object. The Modify tab is the doorway to editing all objects in your model, as you'll see a little later in this chapter.

Introducing the Standard Primitive Tools

As you've seen, there are 10 standard primitive object types. So far, you've used the Box and Sphere tools to create objects. Now let's take a quick look at how each of the standard primitives works. Although you won't be trying out every standard primitive in this chapter, the method of creation for all of these objects is quite similar to the procedure for creating Box and Sphere objects, so you shouldn't have any trouble if you want to experiment with them.

The Plane primitive is perhaps the simplest of all. Click and hold to establish one corner of the plane, and then drag to locate the other corner. Once you are satisfied with the size of the plane, release the mouse. Figure 2.2 illustrates the procedure for creating a plane.

The Box, Cylinder, and Pyramid tools all work in a similar way. First, click and hold to set one corner of the box or pyramid, or for a cylinder, the center point. Drag to locate the other corner of the box or pyramid, or the radius of the cylinder. Release the mouse when you are satisfied with the size of the base. Next, move the mouse forward or backward to establish a height. Click when you want to fix the height. Figure 2.3 shows how to create these objects.

FIGURE 2.2
Drawing a plane

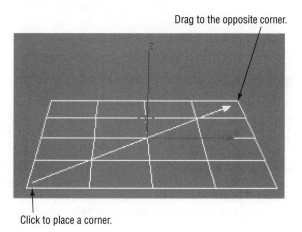

Drag to the opposite corner.

Click to place a corner.

FIGURE 2.3
Drawing a box, cyl-
inder, and pyramid

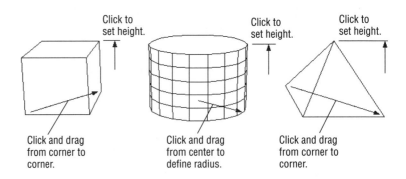

The Sphere and GeoSphere primitives are created in the same way. Click and hold to establish the center point, and then drag to locate the radius. When you're satisfied with the radius, release the mouse button. Figure 2.4 illustrates the process.

FIGURE 2.4
Drawing a sphere
and geosphere

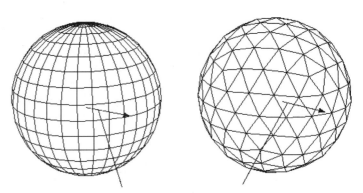

Click and drag from center to radius.

WHAT'S THE DIFFERENCE BETWEEN SPHERE AND GEOSPHERE?

You may notice that, on a superficial level, both the Sphere and GeoSphere tools create the same thing—a sphere. But if you look at the wireframe view of each of these objects, you'll see that there's a structural difference. The sphere is created with horizontal and vertical segments, much like the longitude and latitude lines on a globe. The geosphere is constructed like a geodesic dome, with triangles.

The sphere's construction lets you convert it into a dome of varying configurations, but the geosphere can be only an exact hemisphere. The advantage of the geosphere is its modeling *plasticity*. Because its shape is derived from a less regular construction, it can be molded more easily into other shapes. Also, it requires fewer facets to simulate a smooth surface, which is important when you're creating a very complex model that contains a lot of objects.

The Cone, Torus, and Tube primitives are a bit more complicated to construct, requiring a few more steps than the other types.

The cone starts with a click and drag to establish its center and base, just like the cylinder. And as with the cylinder, the next step is to establish the height by positioning the mouse, and then clicking to set the height. But unlike the cylinder, the cone requires an additional step to establish the radius of the top of the cone, as shown in Figure 2.5.

The Torus object is the most unusual of the standard primitives in its construction method. First, click and hold to establish the center point of the torus, and then drag to locate the overall radius. Release the mouse button when you're satisfied with the radius. Next, move the mouse forward or backward to establish the diameter of the torus body. Click the mouse when you're satisfied with the diameter. Figure 2.6 shows how to draw a torus.

FIGURE 2.5

Drawing a cone

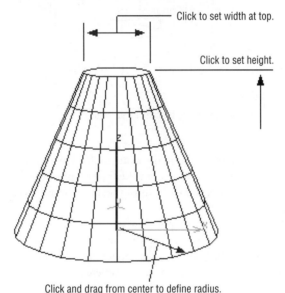

Click to set width at top.

Click to set height.

Click and drag from center to define radius.

FIGURE 2.6

Drawing a torus

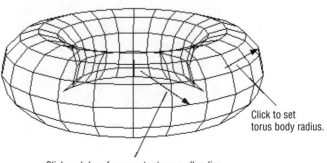

Click to set torus body radius.

Click and drag from center to overall radius.

The method for creating a Tube primitive is similar to the method for creating a Cylinder primitive, but with a slight twist. Click and hold to select the center of the tube, and then drag to establish the inside radius. Release the mouse to fix the inside radius. Move and click the mouse to establish the outside radius. (The order can also be reversed so that the outside radius is set first, followed by the inside radius.) Finally, move and click the mouse to establish the height. Figure 2.7 illustrates this process.

FIGURE 2.7
Drawing a tube

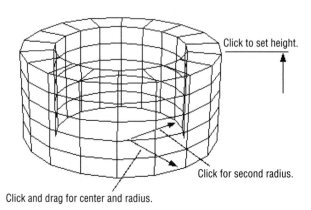

Click to set height.

Click for second radius.

Click and drag for center and radius.

Remember that you can make adjustments to the dimensions of the primitives after their creation. In fact, you may find it easier to just quickly place a primitive in your model, without giving much care to determining its size, and then adjust the dimensions of the primitive in the Parameters rollout to fine-tune its shape.

New!

The method for drawing a teapot (Figure 2.8) is similar to creating a sphere. Click and hold to select the center of the teapot, and then drag to establish the overall teapot size. There are options to toggle the visibility of the body, handle, spout, and lid. As with many of the other primitives, there is a smoothing checkbox and a segments parameter.

FIGURE 2.8
Drawing a teapot

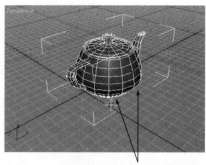

Click and drag for center and radius.

NOTE   *The teapot primitive is new to VIZ 2005, but has been in 3ds max since the beginning. The teapot is a sort of mascot of computer graphics. People have been using teapots, with their intersecting and curved surfaces, as test objects in renderings ever since Martin Newell modeled this teapot form at the University of Utah in 1975 to test shading algorithms.*

Molding Standard Primitives with Modifiers

You've seen how standard primitives have basic parameters that can be modified any time after the creation of the primitive. Also, tools called *modifiers* can further act on a primitive to change its form. You might think of modifiers as invisible attachments that add functions to a primitive, in much the same way that a software plug-in adds functions to your Internet browser or other program.

Adding a Modifier

In this section, you'll explore a few of the more commonly used modifiers offered in the Modify tab of the Command Panel. Think of this section as a general introduction to modifiers. You'll explore the use of other modifiers in later chapters.

You'll start your exploration of modifiers by creating a box. You'll use the box to try out the modifiers.

1. Choose File ➤ New to start a new file. You'll see a message asking you whether you want to save changes to the current design. Click No. Next, you'll see another dialog box with three options.

2. Click the New All radio button, and then click OK.

3. Click the Zoom Extents tool to display the default view for a new file.

4. Click the Create tab in the Command Panel, and then click the Box button.

5. In the Creation Method rollout, click the Cube radio button.

6. Click a point near the origin, and then drag the base of the box so that the Length and Width parameters show a value of approximately 4 feet. Then drag upward and click when the Height parameter shows a value of four feet.

7. If the box you created is shaded, right-click the Perspective label in the upper left corner of the viewport and select Wireframe. You'll use a wireframe view so that you can better see the effects of changes that you make to the box's parameters. You should have a view that looks similar to Figure 2.9.

FIGURE 2.9
The box in the viewport

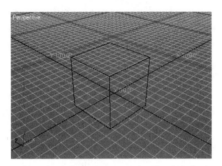

Now let's add a modifier to change the shape of the box to a curved box.

1. Make sure the box is selected. Click the Modify tab in the Command Panel.

Notice the list box with only Box listed. This is the *modifier stack list*. You'll use it in the following exercises. Also notice the options in the Parameters rollout. You'll see the standard Length, Width, and Height options, as well as the Length Segs, Width Segs, and Height Segs options shown here.

In the next section, you'll see what these Segs options do.

2. Click the Modifier List drop-down list arrow near the top of the Command Panel. This expands to show a scrollable list of modifiers. Notice that the list is divided into several categories.

3. Click the Bend modifier, which is under Object-Space Modifiers in the list. Notice that Bend now appears in the modifier stack list just below the Modifier List drop-down list. You'll also see an orange outline appear, superimposed on the box. This orange box is another gizmo, like the Move, Rotate, and Scale gizmos introduced in Chapter 1, and it shows the general effect of the modifier. Also notice that the Parameters rollout changes to show a set of Bend options.

4. In the Bend group of the Parameters rollout, click and drag the Angle spinner upward, and watch what happens to the box: it bends to the right. Right-click the Perspective label in the upper left corner of the viewport and select smooth and highlights.

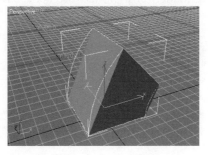

5. Adjust the Angle spinner so that its value reads 60. Alternatively, you can highlight the Angle value, and then enter **60**↵.

The Bend modifier has its own set of parameters that can alter the shape of an object. This is typical for any modifier you might use on an object. But adding a modifier doesn't mean that you cannot return to the original parameters of the object to make changes there.

Accessing Modifier Parameters

You've just applied the Bend modifier to the box, but the result may not be exactly what you expected. The box now looks like a trapezoid. To get the box to appear curved, you need to use the Segs parameters you saw earlier as part of the box's original set of parameters.

Currently, the object's modifier stack list contains Bend, the modifier you just added, and Box, which is the current object type. You also see the modifier you just added.

1. Click Box in the modifier stack list (beneath the Modifier List drop-down list). Notice that the original box parameters appear in the Parameters rollout.

2. Click and drag the Height Segs spinner slowly upward. Notice what happens to the box. Right-click the Perspective label in the upper left corner of the viewport and select edged faces.

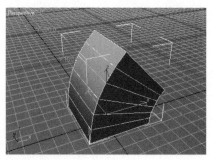

You see horizontal lines appear, dividing the box horizontally. The value in the Height Segs input box shows the number of segments. Also notice that the box now appears to be curved.

3. Set the Height Segs value to 8.

In this exercise, you saw how you can increase the number of segments in the box, which allows the Bend modifier to give the box a curved appearance. You also saw how the modifier stack offers access to the box's original parameters. The modifier stack plays a key role in your ability to edit objects in VIZ, as you'll see as you work through the examples in this book.

Now let's try making another adjustment to the Bend parameters.

1. Click Bend in the modifier stack list (beneath the Modifier List drop-down list).

2. Click the Direction spinner in the Parameters rollout and drag it upward. Notice how the box rolls around as you change the Bend direction.

3. Adjust the Direction value to 180. This causes the Bend modifier to point in a direction that is at an angle of 180 degrees from its original direction.

Once again, you moved from one set of parameters to another. This time, you switched from the box's basic parameters to the Bend modifier's parameters. When you adjusted the Direction spinner in step 3, you saw how the box appeared to roll around as it changed the direction of the bend.

You may have noticed the plus (+) sign to the left of the Bend item in the modifier list. If you click the plus (+) sign, the list expands to show additional parameters available for the modifier. For the Bend modifier, Gizmo and Center are two additional options.

As noted earlier, the Gizmo option refers to the orange shape superimposed over the box. It lets you see how the modifier is being applied to the object. The Center option refers to the origin of the modifier object, which is usually the first point you pick when you create the object. Both the Gizmo and Center options can be edited as you learn in later chapters.

Now let's try another modifier. The Taper modifier does just what you might guess: it tapers an object.

1. Start by changing the view to one that will show more of the box. Arc Rotate your view to get a better look at the box.

2. Click the Zoom Extents tool in the viewport navigation controls.

3. Click the Modifier List drop-down arrow and select Taper from the list. (It's in alphabetic order under Object-Space Modifiers in the list.) Now the Parameters rollout shows a different set of options.

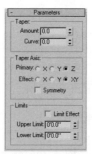

4. In the Parameters rollout, click and drag the Amount spinner downward. The box tapers vertically. You also see the orange gizmo change shape as you adjust the Amount spinner.

5. Click and drag the Curve spinner upward, and watch how the box bulges.

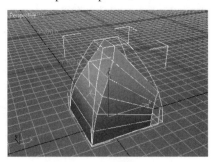

6. Set the Curve spinner back to zero for now.

Although this is an interesting form, you may have expected the box to taper along its curved length instead of straight up. You can change the effect of the Taper modifier by changing its position in the modifier stack list, as explained in the next section.

Inserting Modifiers Where You Want Them

The modifier stack is like a collection of modifiers, each one stacked on another one, just as they appear in the modifier stack list. Currently, Taper is at the top of the modifier stack list, because it is the last modifier you added to the box. Below Taper is Bend, and below Bend is the Box object itself. You can change the order of the modifiers in the stack to obtain a slightly different effect on the box. Try the following to see how this works.

1. Click the Taper label in the modifier stack list to select it.

Take care not to click the plus (+) sign or the lightbulb icon in the list. (Clicking the plus (+) sign shows additional levels of the modifier, as you saw earlier, and clicking the lightbulb toggles the modifier off and on, as you'll learn in the next section.)

2. Right-click and select Cut from the shortcut menu to cut the Taper label.

3. Click the Box label in the list to select it.

4. Right-click and select Paste from the shortcut menu. The Taper modifier is pasted just above Box in the list, changing the order of the modifiers. Notice the change in the shape of the box. It now tapers along the length of the bend.

TIP   *Instead of cutting and pasting to move a modifier in the modifier stack, you can simply click and drag a modifier into a different location in the list. The blue bar previews where you will paste the modifier in the stack before you release the mouse button.*

WHAT CAN YOU DO WITH PRIMITIVES AND MODIFIERS?

Some examples of objects that are built with the help of modifiers are the binoculars and drawer pulls shown here.

Several objects were used for the binoculars, including cylinders and a few splines. A Taper modifier was used to taper the large end of the binoculars, and a combination of Taper and Skew modifiers was used in the main body. The drawer pulls are just cylinders with a Squeeze modifier applied. The Squeeze modifier gives the cylinder a slight bulge at the top, while tapering the sides down.

This exercise demonstrated a couple of things. First, you saw how to change the order of modifiers in the modifier stack. You also saw how a change in the order affects the way multiple modifiers work on the box. When the Taper modifier is below the Bend modifier, the box is tapered *before* it is bent, giving the modified box a completely different shape. Therefore, you can see how VIZ evaluates the stack from the bottom up in sequential order. Remember that the order of the modifiers in the stack affects the way that the modifiers work.

You also saw how the shortcut menu lets you manipulate the modifiers. You can cut, paste, and even delete modifiers using the shortcut menu that appears when you right-click a modifier label.

Using the Modifier Stack Tools

You've seen how you can make changes to the modifier stack to fine-tune the shape of an object. Some additional tools offer ways to manage the modifier stack. The following set of exercises will let you see what these tools do.

1. Choose Edit ➢ Hold from the menu bar. This command acts like a place marker to which you can return if you want to experiment.

TIP The Edit ➢ Hold command performs the same function as AutoCAD's Mark option under the Undo command. You can save your drawing in its current condition in case you want to return to this condition later. It lets you try out various what-if scenarios without the risk of losing your work up to a certain point.

2. Click the lightbulb icon to the left of the Bend option in the modifier stack list.

Clicking the lightbulb icon turns off the modifier. Notice that the box reverts to the shape it had without the Bend modifier.

3. Click the Bend lightbulb again to turn Bend back on.

4. Click the lightbulb next to the Taper modifier. Notice how the box reverts to the shape it had before Taper was added.

5. Choose Edit ≻ Fetch. You see a message box asking if it's okay to restore. Click OK. Your box returns to its original state (as it was before step 1).

The lightbulb icon lets you turn on or off a modifier, so you can quickly view the effects of removing a modifier from the stack without actually needing to delete it. A somewhat similar tool is the Show End Result tool. The Show End Result tool simply shows you the shape of the object at the currently selected modifier stack level. The following example demonstrates this.

1. Select Taper in the modifier stack list.

2. Click the Show End Result tool in the toolbar just below the modifier stack list.

The viewport shows the box in its form before the Bend modifier is applied. Also notice that the Show End Result icon changed. This helps you remember whether the Show End Result tool is on or off.

3. Click the Select Object tool, and then click a blank area of the model to clear the selection. The box returns to its original form, with all of the modifiers active.

4. Click the box to select it again, and then choose Taper from the Modifier Stack drop-down list. The box again returns to the form it had before the Bend modifier was applied. This shows that the Show End Result On/Off tool doesn't actually affect the end result of the box.

5. Click the Show End Result On/Off tool again. The viewport again displays the box in its final form.

Now suppose you want to simply delete a modifier from the stack. This is easy to do with the shortcut menu.

1. Select the Taper in the modifier stack list.

2. Right-click and select Delete from the shortcut menu. Now the Taper modifier is removed from the modifier stack. The box reverts to the form it had before you added the Taper modifier.

3. Choose Edit ≻ Fetch to restore the Taper modifier.

TIP   Another way to remove a modifier from the modifier stack list is to select it and then click the garbage can icon in the toolbar below the modifier stack list. This is the Remove Modifier from Stack tool.

The Delete shortcut menu option is a quick way to remove a modifier. You can accomplish the same thing by selecting the Cut option from the shortcut menu. Another modifier stack tool (available on the toolbar beneath the modifier stack list) is Make Unique. This tool works with special types of clones, which you'll learn about in the "Making Clones That Share Properties" section, coming up shortly.

How VIZ Sees Objects

Let's take a break from the tutorial for a moment to understand how VIZ 2005 sees objects. When you create and edit an object in VIZ, you are creating data that VIZ evaluates to display your model. The order in which that data is evaluated is known as the *object data flow*. VIZ sees objects as a stream, or flow, of data in a particular order. The order in which this data is evaluated affects the outcome of the data; in other words, the order affects the behavior and appearance of the object in your model.

You already saw an example of object data flow when you rearranged the modifiers in the modifier stack list. You saw that the order in which modifiers appear in the stack affects the shape of a box. VIZ also applies this data flow to the overall object by evaluating all modifications made to an object in a specific order.

The first piece of data VIZ looks at is the *master object*. This is the object as you first create it, including a set of parameters, its position, and its orientation.

The next item is the modifier or set of modifiers you apply to an object. Modifiers are evaluated in their order in the modifier stack, as you've already seen. Of course, if there are no modifiers, VIZ skips to the next piece of data.

The third item in the data flow is the transformations applied to the object. Transformations refer to the movement, cloning, scaling, or rotation of an object. For example, even though you may have moved the object *before* you applied modifiers, VIZ will evaluate the object's move transformation after it evaluates its modifiers. The one exception to this occurs when you use the Xform (transform) modifier, which places transform operations within the bounds of the modifier stack.

VIZ evaluates the properties of an object last. Properties include the object's name, color, layer assignment, display, rendering, shadow casting and receiving, motion blur, and so on. For example, even though an object acquires a default color and name as soon as it's created, VIZ evaluates the name and color last.

So to summarize object data flow, VIZ looks at object data in the following order:

1. Master object

2. Modifiers

3. Transforms

4. Properties

The ramifications of object data flow are not obvious at first, but keep the concept in the back of your mind as you work with VIZ. It will help you understand the behavior of the program and ultimately give you better control over your models.

Making Clones That Share Properties

The modifier stack plays a major role in allowing you to mold objects to a desired form, but you can go a step further and have modifiers act across several objects instead of on just one. In Chapter 1, when you learned about copying objects, you may have noticed two clone options in the Clone Options dialog box: Instance and Reference.

Instances and references are more than just clones of objects; they share modifiers, so the changes you make to one clone affect all the other clones. This can be a great editing aid when you have multiple copies of the same object, such as columns in a building or lighting fixtures. By making instance clones, for example, you can place the objects in your model before you've actually finalized the particular parameters of the objects.

Creating an Instance Clone

The instance and reference clones are quite similar, but with a subtle but powerful difference. You'll start by examining the simpler of the two types of clones—the instance clone.

1. Make sure the modified box you created is selected, and then click the Select and Move tool.

2. Shift+click and drag the red X coordinate arrow to the right. Then move the copy of the box along the X axis toward the upper right corner of the viewport, so that its bottom corner is at about the 110-inch X axis mark. You can use the grid to see the distance of your copy.

3. Release the mouse button. The Clone Options dialog box displays.

4. If it is not already selected, click the Instance radio button in the Object group, and then click OK. You now have an instance clone of the original box.

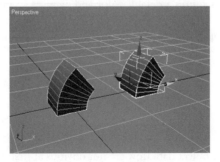

You now have two identical boxes. The similarities of the two boxes go beyond appearances, as the following steps demonstrate.

5. With the box to the right selected, make sure the Modify tab in the Command Panel is selected.

6. Make sure the Bend modifier is selected in the modifier stack list.

7. In the Parameters rollout, click and drag the Angle spinner downward until its value reads –60. Notice that both boxes change shape simultaneously.

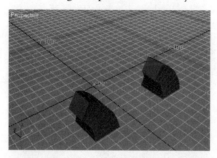

Any parameter change you make to either of the boxes will be reflected in its instance clone. Furthermore, if you add other modifiers to either of the clones, each will have the modifier applied to its modifier stack. This is true because instance clones share modifiers in their respective modifier stacks. This sharing of the modifiers is what distinguishes an instance clone from an ordinary copy.

Creating a Reference Clone

Like an instance clone, a reference clone also shares modifiers in its modifier stack, but in addition, it allows you to include modifiers that are not shared. The following example shows how this works.

1. Select the box in the foreground.

2. With the Select and Move tool, Shift+click and drag its green Y axis arrow to the left to a location similar to the one shown in Figure 2.10.

FIGURE 2.10
The location of the reference clone

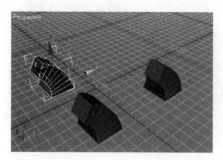

3. In the Clone Options dialog box, click the Reference radio button, and then click OK.

4. Click the clone farthest to the right to select it.

5. Change the Bend modifier's Angle parameter back to 60. Now all three of the clones change shape.

6. Click the newest clone to the far left to select it. Look carefully at the modifier stack, and you'll see a gray bar at the very top of the stack list. This line divides the shared modifiers from potential unshared modifiers.

The shared modifiers of all the clones are still accessible through the reference clone.

1. With the reference clone selected, select Taper from the modifier stack list.

2. In the Parameters rollout, adjust the Amount spinner downward to read –0.85. All of the clones change shape.

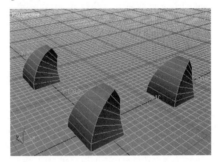

3. With the reference clone to the left selected, click the blank, gray line at the top of the modifier stack list.

4. Open the Modifier List drop-down list and select Twist. (It's in alphabetic order under Object-Space Modifiers in the list.) The Twist modifier is now added to the top of the modifier stack of the selected box.

5. In the Parameters rollout, click and drag the Angle spinner upward so that its value reads 70. Notice that the box changes shape independently of the other boxes.

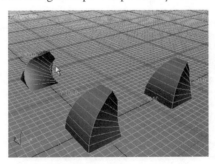

Here, you see that the blank line in the modifier stack allows you to apply a modifier independent of the other shared modifiers. Try testing this by moving the Twist modifier below the line.

1. In the modifier stack list, select Twist, then select Cut from the shortcut menu. Twist is removed from the list.

2. Click the Bend modifier to select it, right-click, and then select Paste to paste the Twist modifier above Bend. You'll see Twist appear above Bend but below the blank line.

Now all three boxes share the twist modifier.

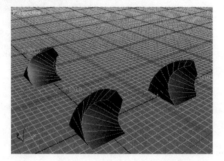

3. Select the Twist modifier, right-click, and select Cut to remove it.

As you see, you can manipulate the reference clone's modifier stack in quite a number of ways to achieve an effect across multiple objects. Next, you'll see another way that the stack can be used in conjunction with a modifier to apply the transform tools to multiple objects.

TIP If you're an AutoCAD user, you might think of instance and reference clones as being similar to blocks in AutoCAD. But as you can see from these exercises, they are far more flexible in VIZ. Reference clones can share some parameters and also include parameters that are independent of other instances.

Scaling and Rotating Objects with Transform Tools

Now that you have a set of objects in your model, let's take a break from our look at modifiers to examine the transform tools. In Chapter 1, you learned how you can scale and rotate a single object using the transform tools in the main toolbar. You can also scale and rotate a collection of objects by selecting the set of objects and applying the Scale or Rotate tools. When you do this, by default, VIZ affects all of the selected objects uniformly. For example, if you rotate a collection of objects, they all rotate about a common axis, as illustrated in Figure 2.11. If you scale a collection of objects, they all change their scale, including the distance between objects in the collection, as illustrated in Figure 2.11.

VIZ offers a few options that alter the way objects are affected by the transform tools. In this section, you'll learn how the Transform Center options give you a higher degree of control over the transform tools.

FIGURE 2.11
Scaling and
rotating objects
in a selection set

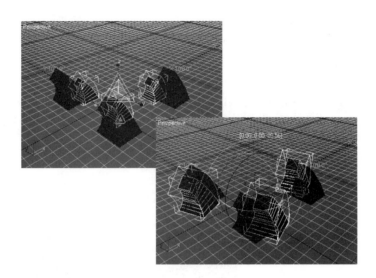

NOTE *Although the exercise involves a set of cloned objects, the transform tools in the main toolbar don't care whether the selected objects are clones of each other or a set of dissimilar objects.*

First, try rotating one of the clones by itself.

1. Click the Select and Rotate tool in the main toolbar.

2. Click the box in the middle of the viewport in the foreground.

3. Click and drag the red X coordinate axis upward. The box rotates independently of the others.

4. Click the Undo button to return the box to its original orientation.

Here, you see that the Rotate tool affects only the currently selected clone. You also see that you can use the new rotate gizmo's rings to control the orientation of the rotation.

Now, let's take a look at how the Rotate tool affects a group of objects.

1. Click the Select Object tool, and then select all three objects. You can either click and drag a region enclosing all of the objects or Ctrl+click each object.

2. Click the Select and Rotate tool in the main toolbar.

3. Click the Use Pivot Point Center tool in the main toolbar. If you don't see it, click and hold the tool just to the right of the View drop-down list in the main toolbar, and then select the Use Pivot Point Center tool from the flyout.

4. Click and drag the red X axis ring. Now all of the cloned boxes rotate in unison with the original box, each on its own axis.

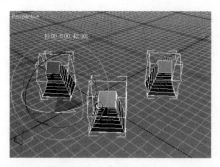

Next, try the Select and Uniform Scale tool.

1. Click the Undo button to return the boxes to their original orientation.

2. Click the Select and Uniform Scale tool in the main toolbar.

3. Click the Use Pivot Point Center tool in the main toolbar, and then click and drag the Scale gizmo or any of the boxes. Each of the three boxes now scales in unison with the others, each about its own center.

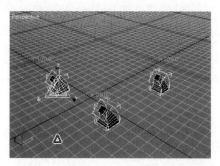

4. Click the Undo tool to return the boxes to their original size.

You've seen how the Use Pivot Point Center tool affects the Rotate and Scale transform tools. Next, try the Use Transform Coordinate Center tool to see its effect on the Scale tool.

1. Click and hold the Use Pivot Point Center tool, and then select the Use Transform Coordinate Center tool from the flyout.

Notice that the transform gizmo now appears at the origin of the World Coordinate System on the home grid.

2. Click and drag the Scale gizmo or any of the boxes. Notice that they all change in scale about the origin of the model.

3. Click the Undo button twice to return all of the clones to their original orientation.

TIP   You can use the Undo tool to undo as many as 20 steps back. You can also set the number of steps VIZ will allow for Undo. To set the number of steps, choose Customize ➤ Preferences. Choose the General tab of the Preferences dialog box, and then set the Scene Undo Levels option to the value you want. Holding more undo steps consumes more memory.

As you can see from the previous exercise, the Transform Center options allow you to select the center location of the currently active transform tool. They are a simple set of options that enhance your ability to control the transform tools. You haven't had a chance to try all of the options with all of the transform tools, so here's a summary of the Transform Center tool functions:

Use Pivot Point Center   Places the center of the transformation at the center of the selected object. If multiple objects are selected, each object is transformed about its own object space.

Use Selection Center   Places the center of the transformation at the center of the set of selected objects. This differs from Use Pivot Point Center in that all objects move, scale, or rotate about a common, single point, rather than about their individual object space center points.

Use Transform Coordinate Center   Places the center of transformation at the origin of the World Coordinate System. Or, if you're using a user grid, the center of transformation will be at the origin of the user grid. This option, in conjunction with a user grid, is useful for moving, scaling, or rotating an object or set of objects in relation to a specific point in a model.

TIP   The Xform modifier lets you scale and rotate objects from the modifier stack. This has the advantage of allowing you to apply transform tools to cloned objects without needing to individually select the objects. It also has the effect of applying the transform tools to a specific position in the object data flow. Normally, transforms are evaluated after the modifiers, but you can insert transforms within the modifier stack using the Xform modifier.

Making a Clone Unique

At some point, you may decide that you want to turn a clone into a unique object, so that it no longer reacts in unison with other clones. You can do this easily with the Make Unique tool.

1. Click the Select Object tool, and then select the clone to the far left.

2. Make sure the Modify tab is selected in the Command Panel, and then select the Bend modifier, the modifier just below the blank line, in the modifier stack list.

3. Click the Make Unique button in the toolbar below the modifier stack list. The selected box is now an independent object that is no longer connected to the other two clones.

The blank line in the modifier stack separates the basic object type from the modifiers listed above it. If you add more modifiers to a reference clone above the blank line, those additional modifiers will only affect that clone and not the others. You can think of the line as a "uniqueness" modifier.

Cloning a Modifier

You've learned the many ways that you can clone an object and edit those clones together. You've also seen most of the major methods used to create objects from primitives. But there is one more feature related to clones and modifiers that you'll want to know about. At times, you may want to clone just one modifier instead of an entire object. This allows you to have an object maintain a degree of uniqueness and still have at least one modifier cloned so that it acts on a set of objects. The following exercise will demonstrate the principle.

First, make a copy of one of the clones.

1. Click the Select and Move tool, and then Shift+click and drag the red Y coordinate arrow of the box to the far right.

2. Drag the copy to a location behind the box in the foreground, so the set of boxes forms a square.

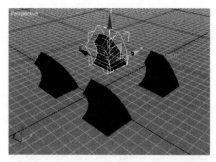

3. In the Clone Options dialog box, click the Copy radio button, and then click OK.

Now let's add a cloned Bend modifier to the new copy. You can do this by copying the modifier to the clipboard, and then pasting it back into the modifier stack list.

1. With the box in the foreground selected, click the Bend modifier in the modifier stack list, right-click, and select Copy.

2. Click the new box you created.

3. In the modifier stack list, click Bend, right-click, and then select Paste Instanced from the context menu to place the new Bend modifier above the old one. Notice that the new instanced Bend modifier is italicized to show that it is an instanced modifier.

4. Delete the old Bend modifier.

You've just created an instance clone of the Bend modifier. Now let's see the results.

1. Click the box in the foreground.

2. Click Taper in the modifier stack list. Notice that the Taper gizmo appears for two of the boxes. The gizmo does *not* appear for the copy you just created, nor does it appear for the box that you made unique.

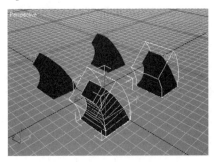

3. Try adjusting the Amount spinner in the Parameters rollout. The instance and reference clones move in unison with the original box, but the newest copy does not.

4. Click Bend in the modifier stack list. Notice how three of the boxes show the Bend gizmo.

5. Change the Angle value to 90. Three of the objects change their shape.

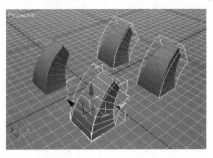

By placing an instance copy of a modifier in an object's modifier stack, you can apply a cloned modifier to an object, so a unique object can share a few characteristics with other similar objects. An example of this might be a set of windows across the facade of a building, as shown in Figure 2.12.

FIGURE 2.12
A facade of a building using cloned references for windows

Most of the windows are identical, with the exception of one or two. The window design can be modified for one window, and all the windows are affected. Some of the windows may need to share only a few (but not all) of the parameters of the rest of the windows. It saves memory to make instances of objects that are identical.

Introducing Extended Primitives

Before moving on to the next chapter, you may want to be aware of the *extended primitives*. These are a set of primitives that offer a few more parameters than the standard primitives. In most cases, the extended primitives offer shapes with smoothing applied to their corners. Some of the other extended primitives are complex shapes, such as the Hedra and Gengon objects. Figure 2.13 shows the extended primitives and some of the parameters that control their shape.

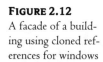

You can get to the extended primitives by clicking the Geometry tool in the Create tab of the Command Panel, and then selecting Extended Primitives from the drop-down list that appears just below the Create tools.

NOTE *Five new extended primitives have made it into VIZ 2005: Torus Knot, L-Extrusion (L-Ext), C-Extrusion (C-Ext), Hose, and RingWave. These five extended primitives have been in 3ds max for a while, but have finally been added to VIZ 2005 for increased compatibility with its sister product.*

For several of the extended primitives, you'll see a Fillet parameter. This controls the radius of the corners. For example, the Chamfer Cylinder (ChamferCyl) primitive has a Fillet parameter that works in conjunction with a Fillet Segment parameter to control the rounding of its top and bottom edges. The Oil Tank and Spindle primitives use a Blend parameter to round their corners.

FIGURE 2.13

Examples of extended primitives

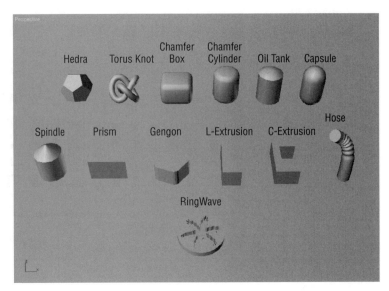

Modeling a Couch

Up until now, you've just been creating random forms using the primitives. In this chapter's last set of exercises, you'll get a chance to create a small couch to try out some of the tools you've learned about so far.

Start by setting up a new file.

1. Save your sample drawing as **MySample.max**, and then choose File ➤ New.

2. In the New Design dialog box, choose New All, and then click OK.

3. Click the Min/Max Toggle tool in the viewport navigation controls to view all four viewports.

4. Click the Zoom Extents All tool in the viewport navigation controls to set all of the viewports to their default views.

You'll start your model by creating the base frame. For this, you'll use one of the extended primitives.

1. Click the Create tab of the Command Panel.

2. Click the Geometry tool and select Extended Primitives from the drop-down list.

3. Click the ChamferBox tool, and then click the Keyboard Entry rollout.

4. Click the Length input box in the Keyboard Entry rollout and enter **20″**↵.Press Tab to advance to the Width input box and enter **44″**↵.

5. Press Tab again to advance to the Height input box and enter **9″**↵.

6. Press Tab and enter **1″**↵ for the Fillet value.

7. Click Create. The base is created.

8. Click Zoom Extents All to get an enlarged view of the base.

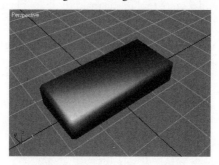

In this exercise, you created the base strictly by using the Keyboard Entry rollout. Now create the back of the couch.

1. Click the Length input box of the Keyboard Entry rollout to select the entire value, and then enter **8″**↵.

2. Press Tab twice to go to the Height input box, leaving the Width input box unchanged. Then enter **26″**↵.

3. Press Tab again, and then enter **2″**↵.

4. Click the Create button. The couch back is created in the middle of the base.

5. Click the Select Move tool in the main toolbar, and then right-click in the Top viewport to make it active.

6. Click and drag the green Y axis arrow of the seat back upward, to move the seat back to the back side of the base, as shown in Figure 2.14. Click the Zoom Extents All tool to get a better view.

FIGURE 2.14

Moving the seat back into position

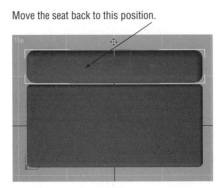

Move the seat back to this position.

Let's also rotate the seat back so it is angled slightly backward.

1. Click the Select and Rotate tool in the main toolbar. Then right-click in the perspective viewport to make it active.

2. Click and drag the red X axis ring upward, and watch the coordinate readout on the transform gizmo. When the readout shows –8 (minus eight) degrees, release the mouse button.

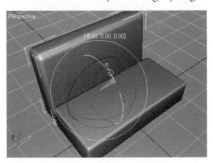

Now apply a Squeeze modifier to the back to add an arch to its shape.

1. Click the Modify tab in the Command Panel. Then open the Modifier List drop-down list and select Squeeze. (It's in alphabetic order under Object-Space Modifiers in the list.)

2. Go to the Axial Bulge group in the Parameters rollout, and click and drag the Amount spinner upward until its value reads 0.14.

3. Press Tab and set the Curve value to 3. Notice that the seat back shows a gizmo bending upward, but the back itself does not bend. This is because the back is made up of only a single segment in the horizontal direction.

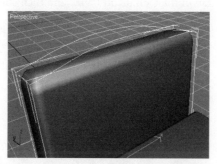

To allow the Squeeze option to take effect, you need to increase the number of horizontal segments in the seat back.

4. Select ChamferBox in the modifier stack list.

5. Scroll the Command Panel up until you see the Width Segs input box in the Parameters rollout.

6. Click the Width Segs input box and enter **20**↵. The back divides into 20 segments, and a curve appears at the top of the back.

7. Click the Zoom Extents All tool to get a better look at your work so far.

Now let's add the arms. Once again, you'll use the ChamferBox extended primitive, but this time you'll use a different modifier to adjust its shape.

1. Click the Create tab in the Command Panel, and then click ChamferBox again.

2. Click the Keyboard Entry rollout to open it. Enter **28″** for the Length, **7″** for the width, **22″** for the height, and **2″** for the Fillet value.

3. Click the Create button. The arm appears in the center of the base.

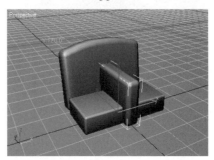

4. Click the Select and Move tool. Right click in the top viewport to make it active. Click and drag the arm into the position shown in Figure 2.15.

TIP *If you place the Select and Move cursor on the plane handle at the corner of the transform gizmo, you can move the arm freely in the XY plane.*

5. Shift+click and drag the red X axis arrow of the arm to the right until you see a copy of the arm in the position shown in Figure 2.16.

6. In the Clone Options dialog box, click the Instance radio button, and then click OK. (You made an instance copy because you want to taper both arms simultaneously.)

7. Click the Modify tab of the Command Panel.

FIGURE 2.15
Moving the arm
into position

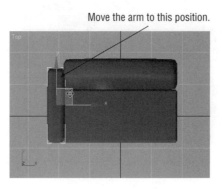

Move the arm to this position.

FIGURE 2.16
Creating a copy
of the arm

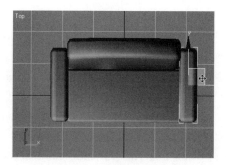

FIGURE 2.16
Creating a copy
of the arm

8. Open the Modifier List drop-down list and select Taper (under the Object-Space Modifiers heading toward the bottom of the list).

9. In the Parameters rollout, click and drag the Amount spinner until its value reads 0.17. Both arms taper, narrowing at their bases.

You're nearly finished with the couch. The final part is the seat cushions. For that, you'll use a copy of the base.

1. Click the Select and Move tool in the main toolbar.

2. Right-click in the Left viewport to make it active. This viewport offers the clearest view of the seat base.

3. Click the seat base to select it, and then Shift+click and drag the green Y axis arrow upward until you have a copy of the seat base, as shown in Figure 2.17.

4. In the Clone Options dialog box, click the Copy radio button, and then click OK. You don't want this copy to be linked to the base.

You need to change a few parameters for the cushion. It's a bit too thick, and you want two cushions to fit in the seat, so you need to reduce the width of the cushion.

FIGURE 2.17
The copy of the
seat base

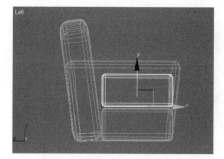

5. Click the Modify tab of the Command Panel.

6. In the Parameters rollout, change the Length and Width values in the Parameters rollout to **22"**, and change the Height value to **7"**.

7. With the Select and Move tool selected, right-click the Top viewport. Then click and drag the red X axis arrow of the cushion to the left to place the cushion as shown in Figure 2.18.

8. Shift+click and drag the red X axis arrow to the right to make a copy of the cushion on the right side of the couch.

9. In the Clone Options dialog box, click Instance, and then click OK.

The couch is complete. Let's get a better view of it.

1. Right-click the Perspective view to make it active.

2. Arc Rotate for a better view.

3. Click the Zoom Extents All tool.

4. Click the Min/Max Toggle tool. Your view should look like Figure 2.19.

5. Save the file as **MyCouch.max**.

FIGURE 2.18
The new position of the cushion

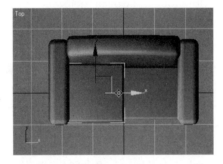

FIGURE 2.19
The completed couch

Working with Groups

Now that you've modeled the couch, it is important to organize the many primitive objects that compose this piece of furniture into a group. As a group, you'll be able to easily select and transform this piece of furniture within your architectural space as a single object.

Grouping the Components of the Couch

The couch is made up of several ChamferBox extended primitive objects. For convenience, you'll want this set of objects to act like one object when it is selected. To do this, you can use the VIZ Group feature. You'll create a group containing a single object; then you'll add other objects to that group.

1. Select the seat cushions and base of the couch.

2. Choose Group ➤ Group. The Group dialog box displays.

3. Replace the default Group01 name with **Couch01**; then click OK.

TIP   *It is always a good idea to name the first object in a series with an 01 suffix. For example Couch01 is a good name. If you ever instance this group, the clones will be automatically numbered in sequence by VIZ.*

4. Now, select the couch back and both arms; then choose Group ➤ Attach.

5. Place the cursor on the couch back and notice that a selection cursor displays, as shown in Figure 2.20. This selection cursor will display whenever the cursor passes over a group. Click the seat cushion, which is now part of the Couch01 group. Now all the components of this piece of furniture are contained in the Couch01 group.

6. Click the Select by Name tool on the main toolbar. You'll see the name *Couch01* in square brackets, indicting that Couch01 is a group. Click Cancel when you're done looking at the list.

FIGURE 2.20
The selection cursor appears as you pass the cursor over the couch back.

Even though you could have created the Couch01 group all at once by selecting all the components of the couch in step 1, this exercise gave you the opportunity to see how you can add objects to a group that has already been created.

The couch will now act as a single object for selection and transform operations. It will now be much easier to locate this piece of furniture in a complex scene because it shows up in the Select by Name dialog box as Couch01, rather than six rather anonymous sounding ChamferBoxes.

Working within Groups

After you've contained objects within a group, you can always open it up to work on the objects inside. When you're done making changes, remember to close the group to stay organized.

1. Select the Couch01 group you made previously.

2. Choose Group ➤ Open. All open groups display pink selection brackets as seen in Figure 2.21.

FIGURE 2.21
Open groups display pink selection brackets.

Pink bounding box shown for open group

3. In the left viewport, select the couch back and rotate it back a bit more to have a more relaxed seating position.

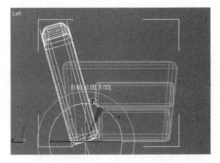

4. Move the couch back forward to eliminate any gap that may have opened up between the back and seat.

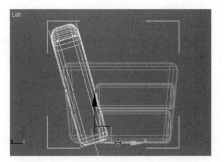

5. Open the Select Objects dialog box by typing H on the keyboard and observe how the objects within the group are displayed while the group is open. Observe how the objects belonging to the group are indented to let you know they belong to the Couch01 group.

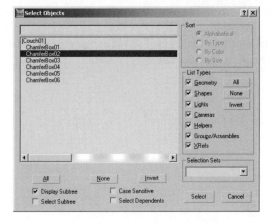

6. Now that you have finished editing the objects contained within the group, it is time to close the group. Choose Group ➢ Close.

7. Click Select by Name again and observe how the edited and then closed group looks identical to the group just after we created it.

You have seen how easy it is to work with groups. If you're familiar with blocks in AutoCAD, you will recognize the similarity to groups in VIZ. They are both structures that contain objects and yield higher levels of organization for your data. They differ in the way that VIZ does not automatically instance the objects contained within groups, whereas in AutoCAD, blocks are always made as instances. Grouping in VIZ is independent of cloning; the choice of whether to instance, reference, or copy is yours to make separately from any organizational structures of convenience you choose to make with groups.

Summary

In this chapter, you learned how to create and manipulate primitive objects. Primitives offer a quick way to generate the most common forms you'll be working with in your modeling. You saw how the Command Panel plays a key role in object creation and editing. In particular, you examined the role of the modifier stack in modeling objects. You'll come back to the modifier stack frequently throughout this book, but this introduction will serve as the foundation on which you'll build other skills.

While there is still a lot to cover, you've now learned about the basic tools you'll need to explore VIZ 2005 with confidence. In the next chapter, you'll learn more about the spline primitive. The spline offers a way to quickly create complex shapes without surfaces. You can manipulate splines using the same modifier tools you learned about in this chapter, plus you have the added advantage of being able to control the basic outline of the form.

Chapter 3

Creating Shapes with Splines

IN THE PREVIOUS CHAPTER, you learned about VIZ's geometry primitives and how they can be shaped by parameters and modifiers into an infinite variety of forms. In this chapter, you'll continue your introduction to primitives with an exploration of *splines*. Splines are a type of primitive and they are classified as shapes in VIZ. In a way, shapes are even more primitive than the geometry primitives you looked at in Chapter 2. You can create more varied forms with splines than you can with the geometry primitives, but they require a bit more work to use.

In general, you can think of splines as objects composed of straight-line or curved-line segments. Splines can be two- or three-dimensional, but unlike geometry, splines do not define surface areas or volumes. Splines are defined only along their edge segments. Strictly speaking, a spline is a line or curve whose shape is controlled by its *vertices*, which are the points along the spline. *Bézier* splines are a type of spline that includes features for controlling its curvature. Splines are initially created as two-dimensional objects (with the exception of the Helix spline, which is a line that curves in 3D space like DNA). Like the standard primitives in VIZ, most splines are parametric; that is, they can be modified using parameters like the Width and Length parameters of the Box standard primitive. All the splines can be made three-dimensional by editing their vertices and handles.

One beauty of splines is that you can use them to create an outline of virtually any two-dimensional shape, and then *extrude* (displacement that defines a volume) the outline into the third dimension. You can use splines as paths for a variety of purposes, such as camera motion for animated sequences or the path for a *loft*, which is a type of extruded form along a path. Splines can be *lathed* (revolved around an axis) making a surface or volume. You can also create a complex 3D armature with splines that a surface can be draped over.

New!   Now in VIZ 2005, a *shell* that defines a volume can be extruded out of a three-dimensional surface, which itself may be made from splines. Suffice it to say that splines are used almost everywhere in VIZ and are definitely worth learning to use well.

NOTE   *You will use splines to model surfaces and shells in Chapter 5.*

In this chapter, you'll learn how to use splines to create complex extruded and lathed forms. You'll see how you can apply modifiers to enhance splines, just as you did with geometry primitives. You'll also begin to explore methods for editing objects on what are called the *sub-object* levels. These are levels of editing at which you can manipulate the components that make up an object.

◆ Drawing with Splines

◆ Modifying a Shape Using Sub-object Levels

◆ Outlining and Extruding Splines

◆ Combining and Extruding Primitive Splines

◆ Joining Closed Splines with Boolean Tools

◆ Creating a Solid Form with Splines

◆ Introducing the Spline Types

◆ Editing Splines

◆ Creating Tubular Splines

◆ Using the AEC Walls and Doors

Drawing with Splines

As you'll see in this and later chapters, the ability to edit the location and characteristics of an object's vertices is an essential part of creating and editing forms in VIZ. In this chapter, you'll begin work with splines and their associated vertices to gain a better understanding of how you can manipulate objects in general. You'll start with the most primitive of the shape objects: the Line spline. With the Line tool, you can draw line segments, curves, squares, circles, or just about any shape you want. Such shapes can then be extruded in a manner similar to the standard primitives you saw in the last chapter.

NOTE   *I mentioned that most VIZ shapes are parametric, which means that they offer a set of parameters that let you modify the shape at will. The Line spline is an exception. The Line spline does not offer parametric editing. Once you've created a Line spline, you cannot use parameters to modify its shape. Lines behave more like the common splines used in other computer design and drafting programs.*

Let's get started by drawing a simple rectangle using a Line spline.

1. Start VIZ 2005, then type **T** to change the viewport to a top view.

2. If it isn't selected already, click the Create tab in the Command Panel.

3. Click the Shapes tool. Notice that the drop-down list shows Splines.

NOTE *Like Splines, NURBS Curves are also classified as shapes. NURBS (non-uniform rational basis splines) are more complex mathematically than splines—as such, they are harder to use but offer more accuracy. You can read more about NURBS in Appendix C.*

4. Click the Line button in the Object Type rollout (or select Line from the Shapes tab of the Tab panel).

Notice that a set of new rollouts appears in the bottom half of the Command Panel. The Line options that appear in the Command Panel offer a variety of ways to construct a spline from line segments.

Drawing Straight-Line Segments

Now you're ready to draw a spline made of line segments. Use Figure 3.1 to help you select points as you draw the spline in the next exercise. You don't need to be too exact because you're just practicing.

1. Click a point near coordinate 0.0″,10′0.0″,0.0″ just above the 0,0 origin in the viewport. You can use the coordinate readout at the bottom of the VIZ window to locate the point. Now, as you move the cursor, a rubber-banding line follows from the point you just clicked.

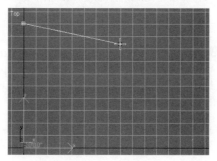

2. Place the cursor near the 15-foot X coordinate, directly to the right of the first point, and click. You can use the coordinate readout again to locate a relative coordinate near 15′0.0″,0.0″,0.0″. A line segment is fixed between the two points you selected. (Don't worry if your line segment is not exactly straight.)

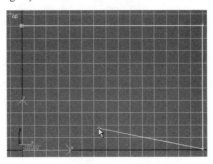

3. Click a point near the origin point of the grid, and then click again (see Figure 3.1).

4. Click the beginning of the line segment near where you started drawing the line. You'll see a dialog box asking you whether you want to close the spline.

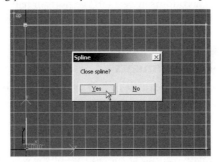

5. Click Yes. The rectangle is complete, and VIZ awaits your next point selection to draw another spline.

You've just drawn a rectangle. It's not necessarily straight, but now you know that you can draw a rectangle by clicking points in the drawing area. You also saw that you can close the set of line segments by clicking the beginning point. The Spline dialog box appears, offering you the option of either closing the set of line segments or leaving it open. When you select Yes, the beginning and ending points of the spline are connected exactly end to end.

TIP *Right-click to stop drawing an open spline whose ending vertex isn't connected to its starting vertex.*

Figure 3.1

Drawing a rectangle with the Line tool

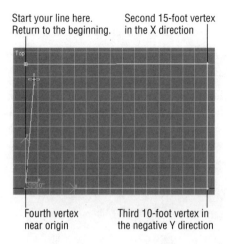

Constraining Lines Vertically and Horizontally

Some of the lines you drew in the previous exercise may not be perfectly horizontal or vertical. VIZ offers some tools that constrain your lines to perfectly horizontal and vertical lines, much like a T-square and triangle constrain your lines when you draft on a drafting board.

One way to constrain lines vertically or horizontally is to use the Shift key. Let's try drawing another rectangle using this technique.

1. Make sure the Line button in the Object Type rollout is still active; it should be orange and appear to be in a down position.

2. Click a point about 10 inches directly below the 0,0 coordinate. Once again, you see a rubber-banding line as you move your cursor around the screen.

3. Hold down the Shift key as you move the cursor. The rubber-banding line is restrained in a vertical or horizontal direction.

4. Point the cursor downward and click a point 5 feet below the last point. A vertical line is drawn.

5. Right-click to exit the Line tool, and then press the Delete key to delete the line you just drew.

WARNING *The former Ortho and Polar tools have been eliminated from VIZ 2005. Most of their functionality is retained by using the Shift key, plus the object and grid snap used in conjunction with user grids. You'll usually find many ways to get the same job done in VIZ.*

Drawing Curves

The Spline tool also allows you to draw curves, as the following exercise demonstrates.

1. With the Line button selected, click and drag from a point near the origin to the right, as shown in Figure 3.2.

2. Continue to drag the mouse approximately 5 feet to the right, and then release the mouse button. You can use the coordinate readout to estimate your distance. Now, as you move the mouse, the line becomes a curve emerging from the starting point in the general direction indicated by the first two points you selected.

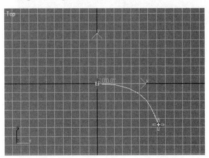

3. Click a point about 6 feet to the right and 6 feet downward, as shown in Figure 3.3. The spline's curved shape is now fixed, and a straight rubber-banding line appears from the last point you picked.

4. Click another point near the origin of the drawing at coordinate 0,–6″. A straight-line segment is added.

5. Right-click to end your line input.

6. Click each spline you just drew and press the Delete key to erase each one. You won't need them anymore.

FIGURE 3.2
Placing the first point of a curved-line segment

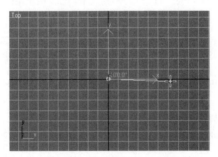

FIGURE 3.3

Drawing a curved spline

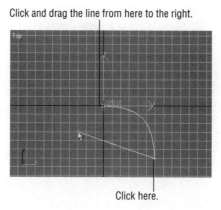

Click and drag the line from here to the right.

Click here.

WARNING *It is fairly easy, especially when you're in a hurry, to accidentally click and drag a point, in which case, you'll get a curve in your line segment. If you just want a straight-line segment, take care not to accidentally drag your mouse while clicking. You can also set the Drag Type to Corner in the Creation Method rollout of the Line object to ensure that you'll get a straight line, even if you drag.*

Here, you see that by clicking and dragging a point, you can add a curve to the spline. A single click gives you a straight *corner* point. Once you've drawn a spline, you can later edit a curve in the spline, add more vertices, remove existing ones, or even convert a corner vertex into a curved one for rounded corners.

Lathing a Spline

Next, you'll create a wineglass using a spline. This will give you a chance to see how you can edit a spline to achieve a desired affect.

1. Click the Min/Max Toggle tool in the viewport navigation controls to view all of the viewports. Then click the Front viewport to activate it.

2. If it isn't active already, click the Line button in the Object Type rollout of the Create tab of the Command Panel.

3. Draw the profile of the wineglass. You can use the grid and Figure 3.4 to locate the points indicated in the figure. If the grid doesn't already appear, click the Grid panel at the bottom of the screen. Don't click and drag any of the points and don't worry if your placement isn't exact. You just need to create the general outline. Later, you'll learn how to apply a curve to a spline. It is easier to start with straight-line segments and later curve them to your liking than to start directly with imperfect curved segments.

TIP *If you click a point accidentally, you can go back to the previous vertex by pressing the Backspace key.*

FIGURE 3.4
Drawing the wine-
glass profile

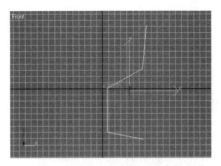

TIP *The dimensions of the glass are exaggerated to fit the Front viewport. To save some effort, you're just drawing the profile in the space provided, without rescaling the view. You can always scale the glass down to a normal size later. The next step is to turn the profile into a 3D wineglass.*

4. With the spline profile selected, click the Modify tab in the Command Panel.

5. Open the Modifier List drop-down list. Then click the Lathe modifier.

The cylinder is revolved with the profile of the spline.

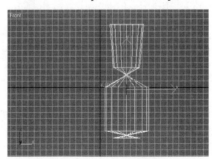

The shape isn't quite what you would expect. The Lathe tool extruded the spline profile about the profile's center, which is not necessarily where you want the extrusion to occur. You can make some simple adjustments to a spline on a sub-object level to get the exact shape you want, as described in the next section.

NOTE *You could also click the Min button in the Lathe modifier without resorting to entering a sub-object level, but you would still need to make some fine adjustments to make sure the stem had some volume.*

Modifying a Shape Using Sub-object Levels

Objects in VIZ are fairly complex entities that offer built-in parameters for controlling their shape. As you saw in Chapter 2, you can add even more control by using modifiers. But parameters and modifiers are limiting when it comes to some of the more minute and detailed changes you might want to make to objects. For example, parameters allow you to adjust the overall height and width of a box, and modifiers allow you to taper the overall shape, but what do you do when you want to add a bulge to one surface or remove one side of a box? To make these types of changes, you need to gain access to objects on a more fundamental level than parameters and modifiers provide. VIZ offers that access through sub-object modeling.

There are three basic methods for gaining access to an object's sub-object levels. One method is to use the red buttons in the Selection rollout in the Modify tab of the Command Panel. Another method is to click the plus sign next to the name of an object in the modifier stack list, and then select the sub-object level from the expanded list.

Still another way to access an object's sublevels is to use the quad menus that appear when you right-click in a viewport. The tools 1 quad contains a listing of each of the available sub-object levels as well as the top (or object) level.

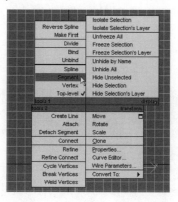

Sub-objects in a spline are the lines or curve segments of the spline and the vertices at each line-segment intersection. When you enter the sub-object level of an object, you gain access to these sub-objects. You can alter the characteristics of each sub-object to fine-tune the overall object's shape.

You can also edit modifiers on a sub-object level, although you are usually more limited in the number of levels to choose from within modifiers. Still, using these levels, you can make adjustments to the way modifiers affect the object. You'll start your exploration of sub-object editing by adjusting the Lathe modifier's axis level.

Adjusting the Lathe Axis

The wineglass profile you created in the previous exercise isn't quite where it should be in relation to the center of the Lathe axis. You can move the center axis of the Lathe modifier to the location you want by moving the modifier's axis of rotation. Let's try that now.

1. Click the plus sign to the left of the Lathe listing in the modifier stack list. Axis appears as an option under the Lathe modifier.

2. Click the Axis option, and it will be highlighted in yellow to indicate that you can now edit on this level. Also notice that the Select and Move tool in the main toolbar is automatically selected.

3. In the Front viewport, click and drag in the red arrow at the end of the X axis handle of the transform gizmo to the left until it looks like Figure 3.5. Now the extruded spline looks more like a wineglass.

4. Click the Zoom Extents All tool to get a better view. Your perspective view should look similar to Figure 3.6.

TIP   *As a shortcut to steps 1 and 2 of this exercise, you can click the plus symbol next to Lathe in the modifier stack list so that it is expanded. You can first use the Min button in the Align group of the Parameters rollout to get a shape closer to the one you want, and then fine-tune the shape by entering the Axis level and transforming the gizmo.*

FIGURE 3.5
Moving the
Lathe axis

Click and drag the red arrow at the
end of the X axis handle to the left.

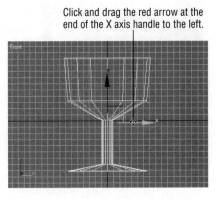

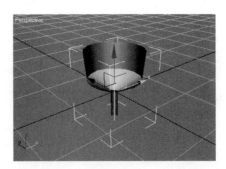

Here, you see how the transform gizmo can be moved to alter the way the Lathe axis affects the resulting three dimensional object. The Lathe axis offers control over the way modifiers act on an object.

Flipping Surface Normals

At this point, you might notice that your perspective view of the wineglass looks a bit odd. Some of the parts seem to be missing. As you model other objects in VIZ 2005, you will find that sometimes surfaces seem to disappear. You know the surfaces are there, because you can see them in wireframe view. Where do these surfaces go?

To understand why surfaces disappear, you need to know one basic fact about 3D computer models: a surface has only one visible side. The other side of a surface is invisible. Like a one-way mirror, an object appears solid from one direction and transparent from the other.

Surfaces are visible or invisible, depending on the direction of their normals. A *normal* is a mathematical concept indicating a vector pointing perpendicularly away from a plane (as defined by at least three points); the direction of the normal is determined by the order and direction in which these points are created. Here is an example of a typical object face and its normal.

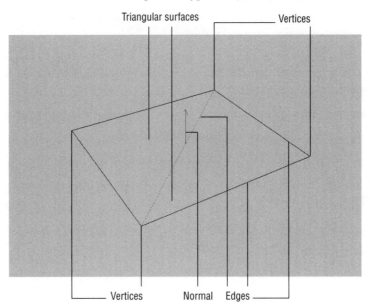

You will now flip the normals of the wineglass so that the surface faces the opposite direction.

1. Select the top level of the Lathe modifier by clicking Lathe in the stack.

2. Click the Flip Normals button in the Parameters rollout.

Observe how the surface appeared to flip to the other side in Figure 3.7. Now you can see the exterior of the wineglass while the interior remains hidden. Computer graphics surfaces usually are visible from one side only.

In most situations, you'll be creating *volumes* in VIZ. When you create a volume such as a box or the lathed outline of a wineglass, VIZ will automatically align the normals of the surfaces so that they all point outward, away from the interior of the volume. You'll see this happen later, when you use the Outline option on the spline for the wineglass, effectively creating a double walled surface to represent the glass. Instead of creating a surface using a single layer of surfaces, the Outline option creates a closed volume with a distinct interior and exterior. If you look between the lathed outline splines, you will see that from the inside out, the wineglass is invisible!

In most situations, VIZ takes care of the normals in objects, but if you import objects from AutoCAD, sometimes surfaces disappear. You can use a number of methods to fix these disappearing surfaces from AutoCAD. You'll learn about those methods as you begin to work with materials later in this book.

Smoothing Spline Corners

You now have a wineglass that looks a bit crude. Next, you'll smooth some of the rough spots by returning to the Spline primitive and editing it.

1. Select Line from the modifier stack list. Your view of the wineglass returns to the flat spline you drew earlier. Notice that the options below the modifier stack list change to a set of options related to the spline.

2. Click the Vertex option in the Selection rollout so that it is highlighted.

3. Click the second vertex of the spline to select it.

FIGURE 3.7
Flipping normals
on the wineglass

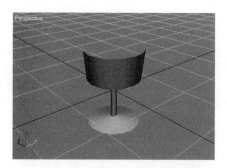

4. Right-click in the viewport to open the quad menus.

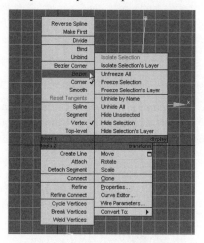

5. Click the Bézier option. The line curves and two handles appear, emerging from the vertex.

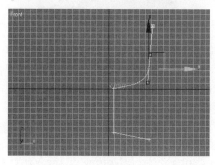

The Bézier option turns a vertex into a control point for a Bézier curve passing through that vertex. You can then manipulate the curve by adjusting the tangent handles that appear.

1. First hover your mouse over the XZ plane handle of the transform gizmo to make sure it is active. Then With the Select and Move tool active, click and drag one of the Bézier tangent handles to deform the spline to the shape shown in Figure 3.8. Notice that as you move the handle, the opposite handle moves in the opposite direction in a parallel fashion. You may also want to drag the vertex itself to a new position by clicking and dragging the axis and plane handles of the transform gizmo.

TIP   If you find that you can move the Bézier handles in only one direction, try hovering your mouse over the proper plane on the Move transform gizmo and then drag to move in your chosen plane. Another problem you may encounter is that often the Bézier handles are on top of the X and Y axes, so when you try to click and drag the handle, you simultaneously click the X or Y axis arrow, restraining your motion to that axis. To get around this problem, click the Bézier handle a little off to the side. You may also drag the handle away from the arrow first, then select the Restrict to XY Plane tool, and then move the handle freely. Another option is to type **X** *to temporarily toggle off the transform gizmo.*

2. Click the next vertex toward the stem of the wineglass, as shown in Figure 3.9.

3. Right-click in the viewport after you select the vertex, and then select Bézier Corner from the quad menu. Now you see two handles from this vertex, but this time, the handles are not opposite each other. Instead, they point in different directions.

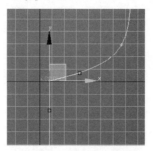

4. Click and drag each of the Bézier handles into position, as shown in Figure 3.10. Notice that the Bézier Corner option lets you control the curve from the vertex in both directions.

5. Click Lathe in the modifier stack list. You now see how your changes to the spline translate to the form of the wineglass, as shown in Figure 3.11.

In this exercise, you have begun to see that splines are really made up of components, or sub-objects. You used the transform gizmo to reposition the axis used by the Lathe modifier. You also changed the characteristics of a vertex by editing on the Vertex level. For example, the quad menu options allow you to change the shape of a spline just by changing the type of vertex being used. Four of the options on the vertex shortcut menu relate to the way the vertex affects corners:

Smooth   Turns a sharp corner into a rounded one. This has an effect similar to that of the Bézier option without offering the Bézier handles.

Corner   Turns a Bézier or smooth corner into a sharp corner with no curve.

Bézier   Converts a corner into a Bézier curve with symmetric handles that allow you to adjust the *pull* and direction of the curve.

Bézier Corner   Converts a corner to a Bézier curve with handles that allow you to adjust the pull and direction of the curve. Unlike the regular Bézier option, Bézier Corner allows you to control the handles independently in both directions from the vertex.

Remember that to use these corner options, you need to be editing on the Vertex sub-object level.

FIGURE 3.8

Click and drag the vertex and its tangent handle.

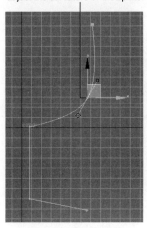

Use the Move tool to drag the selected vertices to a new position. Also drag the green handles to adjust the curvature of the spline.

FIGURE 3.9

Click the next vertex to select it.

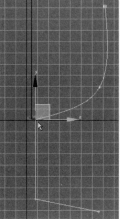

Select this vertex.

FIGURE 3.10

The new location for the Bézier corner handles

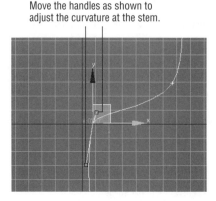

Move the handles as shown to adjust the curvature at the stem.

FIGURE 3.11

The view of the wineglass so far

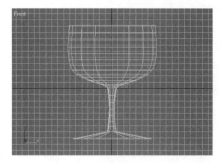

USING QUAD SHORTCUT MENUS

In the wineglass exercise, you used a shortcut menu that appeared when you right-clicked the vertex of a selected spline. You may have been a bit surprised by the appearance of this particular shortcut menu—it's really several menus arranged in a quad fashion. In fact, VIZ calls this a *quad menu*. The options on the quads vary depending on the context.

Many of the options in the quad menu are actually duplicates of options in the Modifier tab of the Command Panel and on the main toolbar. These options provide a quick way to get to options that relate specifically to the object you're editing. By using the quad menu, you don't need to sort through a set of buttons in the Command Panel, many of which may be grayed out.

Be aware that the options in the quad menu are often abbreviated versions of those found in the Command Panel, and they frequently don't offer keyboard input. If you want to edit an object visually, the shortcut menu options work just fine. However, if you need to enter exact dimensions, you'll want to go to the Modify tab of the Command Panel and use the tools and options there.

Enhancements to Tangent Handles

In VIZ 2005 a few improvements have been made to the way you can work with spline vertices and their tangent handles. Let's explore these new features.

1. Off to the side of your wineglass, draw a spline in the Top viewport alternating straight and curved segments. Do this by alternately clicking and dragging the mouse while using the Line tool. Right-click to finish drawing the spline.

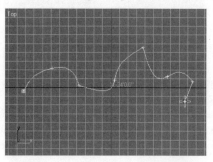

2. Switch to the Modify panel and right-click in the viewport to bring up the quad menu. Select Vertex from the tools 1 quad to enter the vertex sub-object level for editing.

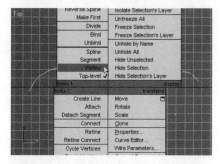

3. Select a few vertices of your choosing either by dragging a selection window or by Ctrl-clicking individual vertices.

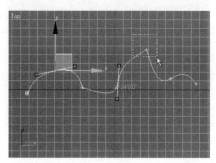

New!

4. Right-click and change the tangent handle type for the entire selection to Bézier Corner from the tools 1 quad.

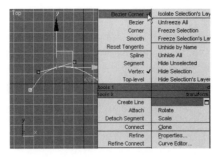

Being able to change the tangent type of multiple vertices in a selection set is new to VIZ 2005. This is much better than it was in VIZ 4, where you had to change each vertex one at a time by right-clicking directly on top of the vertex you wanted to work on. Another new feature is the way you can now copy and paste tangent handle orientations between handles.

1. While you are still in the vertex sub-object level for editing, scroll way down in the Geometry rollout and locate the Tangent group. Click the Copy button.

2. When the Copy button is active, you are in a mode where you can select a tangent handle to copy its orientation to the clipboard. Click one of the handles of either a Bézier or Bézier Corner vertex. You will automatically exit Copy mode when you click.

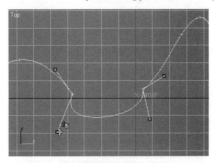

3. Click the Paste button in the Tangent group.

New!

4. Click the handle of another vertex. This matches the tangent handle orientation stored on the clipboard to the vertex where you choose to paste it. Notice that your cursor changes to a clipboard paste icon while over a green tangent handle.

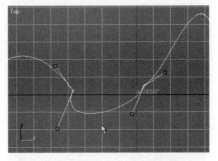

As you copy and paste handle orientations between vertices, you are essentially making these handles parallel to each other. This can be convenient when shaping splines and is new in VIZ 2005.

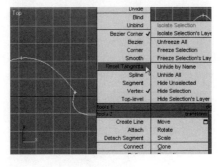

Another minor enhancement made to splines is the Reset Tangents option in the tools 1 quad menu. Use this option when you want the orientations of the tangent handles you already copied and pasted to revert back to their original orientations. You can think of it as a specialized undo tool for tangent handles.

Creating Thickness with a Spline

The wineglass is currently an object with no thickness. To make this glass appear more realistic, you can give it some thickness. Here's how it's done.

1. Select the wineglass and click Line in the modifier stack list.

2. Select the Spline level in the Selection rollout.

3. Click the spline. Notice that now the entire spline turns white, indicating that it's selected.

4. Scroll down the Modify tab until you see the Outline button in the Geometry rollout.

5. Click the input box to the right of the Outline button, change its text value from 0'0.0" to 2", and press Enter. The spline is outlined and now is represented by a double wall.

6. Go back up to the modifier stack list and select Lathe. You now see the entire glass, including those portions of the glass that did not appear because of the arrangement of the normals.

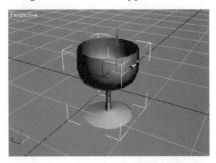

7. Zoom into closely to the rim of the wineglass. Toggle the Flip Normals check box and see if you can tell which direction the surfaces ought to point. When Flip Normals is unchecked, you should be able to see the tiny top surface of the rim.

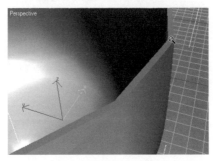

8. When you zoom in close, you will see that the wineglass appears chunky or faceted. Try increasing the number of Segments in the Lathe modifier to make it appear more rounded.

9. Choose File ➢ Save and save your wineglass model.

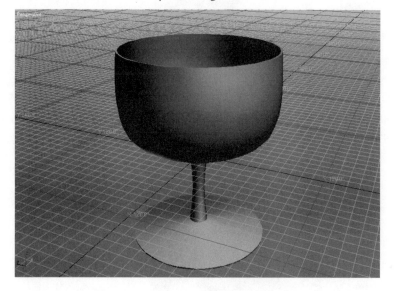

In step 5, when you entered a value for the Outline, VIZ changed the single-line spline into an outline using the spline, thereby creating a double-lined spline. In this context, entering an Outline value has the effect of creating a cross section with thickness.

The Outline option generates an outline using the existing spline as one side of the outline. To determine the side on which the outline appears, check the direction in which the original spline was created. For example, if a spline is drawn from left to right, the outline will appear on the top side, as shown in Figure 3.12.

FIGURE 3.12

How to determine the side of the outline

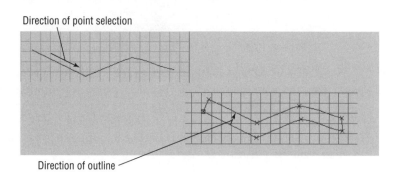

TIP *The Center check box just below the Outline input box causes the outline to be centered on the original spline instead of creating the outline on either side of the spline.*

If you're not sure of the order in which a spline was drawn, expand the Line item in the modifier stack list, select Vertex, and then click the Show Vertex Numbers check box in the Selection rollout of the Modify tab.

With the Show Vertex Numbers check box selected, you'll see each vertex labeled with a small, black number, indicating the order in which the vertices were created.

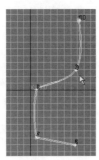

If you want the outline to appear on the opposite side, either you can enter a negative value for the offset distance or you can reverse the order of the vertices using the Reverse button in the Geometry rollout of the Modify tab. The Reverse button is active only when you select Spline from the Selection rollout or the modifier stack list. You must also have a Spline sub-object selected.

So far, you've used the sub-object options and parameters to adjust the spline curve to a shape that really gives the impression of a wineglass. The steps you took while editing the spline are similar to what you would do for other types of objects. As you've seen in some of the rollouts, there is a bewildering array of options you can apply to a sub-object, but you've covered the main points regarding sub-object editing. Throughout this book, you'll continue to work on a sub-object level to edit items such as segments and vertices.

Outlining and Extruding Splines

You've just seen how you can create a wineglass using a spline and the Lathe modifier. Now, let's look at drawing a type of object that is simpler in many ways but that requires quite a different approach to using splines. Walls are usually drawn with straight-line segments, and they require a fairly high degree of accuracy. In the following exercise, you'll learn how to draw a spline using exact coordinates.

NOTE *This example is intended primarily to demonstrate a technique of working with splines, not necessarily a method you'll use in the real world to draw walls. (I do make my walls this way in fact.) VIZ provides a set of architecture, engineering, and construction (AEC) tools, which includes a Wall tool. The AEC tools offer specialized functions geared toward the creation of building components such as walls and stairs. VIZ's AEC Wall tool works in a way that is slightly different from the splines described here, and it offers some timesaving features for inserting doors and windows. You'll learn about the AEC tools at the end of this chapter.*

Drawing Accurate Line Splines

You'll start by setting up a top view in a new file that will include the area in which you'll draw the walls. The walls will cover a 20-foot square area, so you'll want to include an area that covers about 20 feet square.

1. Choose File ➢ New, choose New All in the New Design dialog box, and click OK.

2. Choose Customize ➢ Units Setup. In the Units Setup dialog box, make sure that US Standard and Feet w/Decimal Inches are selected, and click the Inches radio button for the Default Units setting. Then click OK.

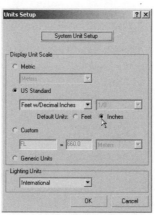

3. Click the Zoom Extents All tool to restore the views to their default orientation.

4. Click the Top viewport, and then click the Min/Max Toggle tool to enlarge it.

5. Click the Zoom tool and zoom out until you see the 10′0.0″ grid appear in the viewport.

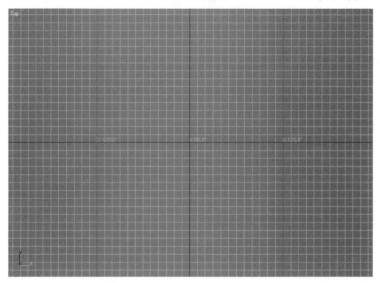

6. Click the Pan tool and pan the view downward and to the left so that the 0,0 coordinate is in the lower left corner of the viewport.

Now you're ready to start drawing. You'll draw an L-shaped room that is 20 feet by 20 feet, with each leg 10 feet long.

1. If it isn't already selected, click the Create tab of the Command Panel.

2. Make sure the Shapes tool and Splines are selected. Then click the Line button.

3. Use the hand cursor to scroll the Create tab upward until you see the Keyboard Entry rollout at the bottom of the panel, and then click it.

You see three coordinate input boxes and three buttons labeled Add Point, Close, and Finish. These are the tools you'll use to accurately place the wall.

1. Click the Add Point button. This starts the wall by inserting the start point at the coordinates shown in the coordinate input boxes. Because the input boxes show the coordinates 0,0,0 for the X, Y, and Z coordinates, the line starts at 0,0,0.

2. Click the X coordinate input box and enter **20′**↵.

3. Click the Add Point button again. It isn't obvious, but you've just added a line segment from coordinate 0,0,0 to 20′,0,0.

4. Click the Y coordinate input box, enter **10′**↵, and click the Add Point button. Another line segment is added. This time, you can see the line segment.

5. Click the X coordinate input box, enter **10′**↵, and click the Add Point button.

6. Click the Y coordinate input box, enter **20′**↵, and click Add Point.

7. Click the X coordinate input box, enter **0**↵, and click Add Point.

8. Click the Close button.

   You've just drawn the basis for the walls.

9. Click the Zoom Extents tool to get an overall view of your walls.

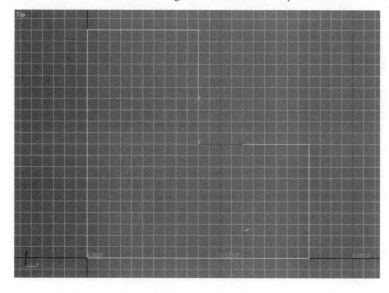

As you can see from this exercise, you can enter coordinate values to place the corners of the walls accurately. Because you started at the World Coordinate System origin 0,0,0, it's fairly easy to determine the coordinate location of your walls.

Giving Walls Thickness

Right now, you have only a single-line representation. To give the walls thickness, you can use the Outline tool, which you used earlier in the wineglass exercise.

1. Click the Modify tab of the Command Panel. Because you just created the wall outline, the outline is still selected, and you can see the options for the spline in the Modify tab.

2. Click the Spline button in the Selection rollout.

3. Scroll down the Modify panel to the Geometry rollout so you can see the Outline button.

4. Double-click the input box next to the Outline button and enter **5"**↵. Notice that a new spline outline appears inside the original outline. This is the inside face of the wall.

5. Exit the spline sub-object level by clicking Line in the stack.

When you used the Outline option in the wineglass example, VIZ turned the single line into a single, continuous outline of the wineglass section. In this wall example, you actually have two splines, with one inside the other. Even though there are two splines, VIZ considers this to be one object. This is so because the new spline was created while you were in the sub-object spline level of the line. As you'll see in the next exercise, concentric closed splines behave in an unusual manner.

1. Click the Min/Max Toggle tool to view the other viewports.

2. Click the Zoom Extents All tool to see the entire outline in all the viewports.

3. Click the Modifier List drop-down list arrow near the top of the Command Panel and click Extrude, which is in the Object-Space Modifier category.

4. In the Parameters rollout, click the Amount input box and enter **8′**↵.

5. Make sure the Segments input box shows a value of 1. Walls are usually vertical planes, so you don't need the extra segments in the wall's vertical plane. You now have a wall that is 8 feet tall.

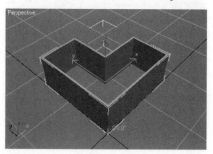

TIP *AutoCAD users will find it easier to import 2D floor plans into VIZ and then extrude the walls of the floor plan in VIZ. You'll learn how to import 2D plans in Chapter 16.*

If you're an AutoCAD user, you may find drawing walls with accurate dimensions a bit more difficult in VIZ. It can be done, but as you've just seen, you need to translate the wall dimensions into coordinates. You can use a tool called the user grid as an aid to drawing accurately.

Using Grids and Snaps to Align Objects Accurately

You've seen how you can enter coordinate data for splines using the Keyboard Entry rollout in a simple example. As you can imagine, entering coordinates can become quite cumbersome and tedious for any wall configuration that is even slightly more complex. There are several tools that can help make drawing walls easier: user grids and snaps.

User grids are nonprintable grids that you can align to any orientation or object geometry you want. You can use them to set up a *local* coordinate system in which to add other objects.

Snaps are a set of options that let you accurately select specific geometry on existing objects such as endpoints of line segments, midpoints of lines, and intersections. Snaps also let you select grid points.

In the next exercise, you'll use grid objects and snaps to add some walls to the existing set of walls. Start by setting up a view that will allow you to see your work.

1. Right-click the Top viewport, and then click the Min/Max Toggle tool.

2. Arc Rotate the model around to the other side.

3. Click the Zoom Extents tool to fit the model in the view. If it is not already selected, choose the Smooth & Highlights viewport display by right-clicking the viewport label and selecting it from the pop-up menu. From the same pop-up menu, select Perspective from the Views flyout.

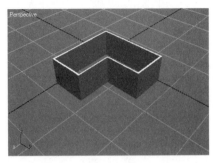

Now you're ready to add a user grid. First, you'll place it randomly in the drawing, then you'll move it into a position that makes it easier to add a new wall.

1. If it isn't selected already, click the Create tab of the Command Panel.

2. Click the Helpers tool.

3. Click the Grid button in the Object Type rollout.

4. Click and drag downward from a point in the upper right corner of the view, as shown in Figure 3.13. Just approximate the location—it doesn't need to be exact.

You don't need to be too accurate about the shape and size of the grid. As with all other VIZ objects, you can fine-tune its parameters in the Command Panel after it is created. You can set the width and length, as well as the grid spacing. In this set of exercises, you're just using the grid to create a local coordinate system, from which you can draw additional walls.

FIGURE 3.13
Adding a user grid

First click here to start the grid placement.

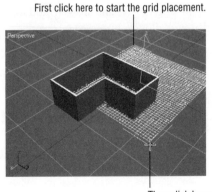

Then click here.

Next, you'll move your user grid into a position that will allow you to enter coordinates relative to an existing feature of the walls you've drawn so far. To accurately place the grid, you'll use snaps. First, set up the snaps to connect to the geometry you plan to work with. In this case, you'll want to snap to grid points and endpoints of objects.

1. Right-click the Snap Toggle button in the main toolbar at the top of the VIZ window.

The Grid and Snap Settings window displays.

2. If it isn't already selected, click the Snap button, and then click the Grid Points check box. If the Endpoint check box is not already checked, click it as well. Then close the Grid and Snap Settings window.

3. Click the Snap Toggle button to make it active or type S on the keyboard. (You'll know it's active if the button looks like it is down.)

Now you're ready to move the grid using the snap settings to guide your movements.

1. Click the Select and Move tool in the main toolbar. Now, as you move the cursor over the viewport, you'll see a cyan snap marker appear on the grid.

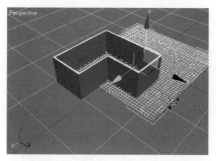

The cursor jumps to grid points on the user grid. You may also notice that it also jumps to the endpoints of the walls you've drawn so far.

2. Place the cursor so that it is on the 0,0 origin of the user grid. You can spot the origin by locating the transform gizmo. You may need to Arc Rotate at any time to get a better view.

3. Click and hold the origin, and then drag the grid to the corner of the wall, as shown in Figure 3.14.

4. Make sure that the cursor shows the endpoint graphic before you release the mouse button.

Now you're ready to start drawing the wall addition.

1. Click the Shapes tool in the Create tab of the Command Panel.

2. Click the Line button in the Object Type rollout.

FIGURE 3.14
Dragging the grid to
the corner of the wall

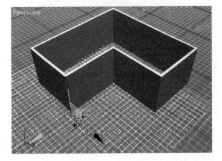

3. Scroll up the Command Panel until you see the Keyboard Entry rollout, and then click it to open it.

4. With the X, Y, and Z values set to 0 in the Keyboard Entry rollout, click the Add Point button. This starts the new line at the 0,0 coordinate of the user grid (on the corner of the existing wall).

5. Click the X value, enter **12′**↵, and click the Add Point button.

6. Click the Y value, enter **10′**↵, and click the Add Point button.

7. Click the X value again, enter **−10′**↵, and click the Add Point button.

8. Click the Finish button to exit the Line tool.

By using the user grid, you were able to draw the additional wall line using coordinates relative to the corner of the existing wall. This is far easier than trying to translate world coordinates into the coordinates relative to the existing walls. You can place as many user grids as you need in a model, and they can be oriented in any direction you choose. You can also align them to the surfaces of objects if you so choose. You'll learn how to do this in later chapters.

TIP   If you're an AutoCAD user, you can think of the user grid as a kind of User Coordinate System (UCS) as it is known in AutoCAD. The methods for using the user grid may differ from the UCS, but its purpose is the same. In addition, VIZ offers an autogrid, which is like a quick, temporary grid that works on the fly.

Now let's finish the additional wall by giving it some thickness and height.

1. With the new wall selected, click the Modify tab. (Since the wall has just been created, it's already selected.)

2. Click the Spline level in the stack.

3. Select the spline. Scroll down the Command Panel until you see the Outline button and enter **5″**↵ in the input box next to the Outline button. Once you press ↵, the wall will be given a thickness of 5 inches. Exit the spline level.

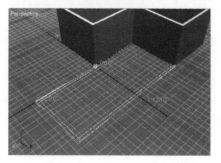

4. Scroll up to the top of the Command Panel so you can see the modifier stack list and apply the Extrude modifier. Make sure that the Amount value in the Parameters rollout is set to 8′. Your additional wall now appears in place.

5. Click the Zoom Extents tool to get an overall view of your model so far.

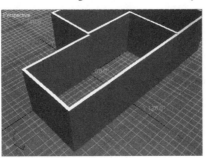

Once again, you used the Outline option to convert a single-line spline into an outline, giving the wall a thickness. Unlike other parameters, an outline cannot be changed by simply changing a parameter once it's in place. This is true for most sub-object functions. You can make changes at sub-object levels, such as changes to the vertices or line segments.

TIP *Another way to draw line segments is to set the snap setting to Grid Points (on the Snaps tab of the Grid and Snap Settings window), and then set the grid spacing to the smallest value you need to work with (on the Home grid tab). Then, as you select points for the line, you can read the coordinates readout at the bottom of the VIZ window. You'll see that the coordinates show your current position relative to the last point you selected in the X, Y, and Z coordinate format.*

While you were working to add the new wall, you got a glimpse of the Grid and Snap Settings window. That window contains quite a few snap options (on the Snaps tab), of which you only used two. Table 3.1 describes the snap options. (You won't be using all of these options in this book.)

TABLE 3.1: GRID AND SNAP SETTINGS OPTIONS

SETTING	DESCRIPTION
Standard/NURBS	Drop-down list reveals a different set of snaps for NURBS objects
Grid Points	Snap to intersection of grid lines
Pivot	Snap to an object's pivot point as represented by transform gizmo
Perpendicular	Snap to perpendicular to line segments and edges
Vertex	Snap to vertices
Edge	Snap to edges
Face	Snap to faces
Grid Lines	Snap to the intersection of grid lines
Bounding Box	Snap to bounding box corner

TABLE 3.1: GRID AND SNAP SETTINGS OPTIONS *(continued)*

SETTING	DESCRIPTION
Tangent	Snap to tangent of curves and circles
Endpoint	Snap to endpoints
Midpoint	Snap to midpoints of line segments and edges
Center Face	Snap to the center of face
Clear All	Clear all snap settings

You may have noticed a graphic next to each of the options on the Snaps tab of the Grid and Snap Settings window. When a snap setting is selected, the cursor will display the graphic associated with the snap setting whenever the cursor approaches a geometry that matches the snap setting. For example, if you select the Endpoint snap setting, when snap is turned on and the cursor approaches and touches an endpoint, the cursor will display the graphic associated with the endpoint snap.

Adjusting a Wall Location

The wall you just added isn't quite aligned properly with the first set of walls. If you look at a top view of the walls, you'll see that the new wall is offset by the width of the wall where the new wall meets one of the corners of the old wall.

To move the new wall section into place, you need to work with the vertices of the wall. Once again, this means working with the wall on a sub-object level. The following exercise will give you some hands-on experience with some simple vertex transformations. Start by returning to the top view of the walls.

1. Type **T** to switch to a Top viewport. If it is not already selected, choose Wireframe viewport display from the viewport label pop-up menu.

2. Click the Select Object tool, click the user grid, and then press the Delete key. You don't need the user grid anymore.

3. Click the Zoom Extents tool to get an overall view of the model. Your view will look similar to Figure 3.15.

FIGURE 3.15

Top view showing the new wall offset

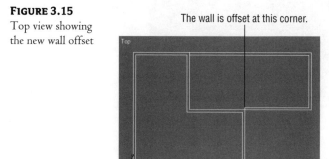

The wall is offset at this corner.

Now you can see the offset more clearly. Let's go on to the work of moving the wall into alignment with the existing wall. First, set up the snap for endpoints. You don't want to accidentally snap to a grid point.

1. Right-click the Snap Toggle button at the bottom of the VIZ window.

2. In the Grid and Snap Settings window, make sure that Grid Points is not checked and that Endpoint is checked, and then close the window.

   Next, you'll move the wall section.

3. Click the Select Object tool, and then click the new wall.

4. Click the Modify tab of the Command Panel and select Line from the modifier stack list.

5. Expand Line in the stack and click the Vertex level.

6. With the Select Object tool active, place a window around the vertices you want to move. Do this by clicking and dragging a window, as shown in Figure 3.16. You'll see the selected vertices turn red, with arrows showing the coordinate directions.

7. Click the Select and Move tool on the main toolbar.

8. Place the cursor on the wall vertex, as shown in Figure 3.17.

9. Arc Rotate into User view so that you can see the object in three dimensions.

10. When you see the Endpoint Snap marker, click and drag the vertex downward to the location of the vertex just below it, as shown in Figure 3.18.

FIGURE 3.16

Placing a selection window around the vertices

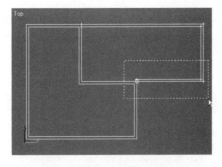

FIGURE 3.17
Selecting the
vertex to move

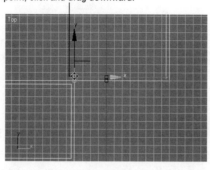

With the endpoint marker on this
point, click and drag downward.

FIGURE 3.18
Selecting the new
location of the
vertex

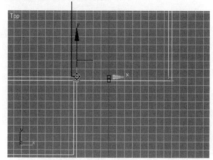

When the cursor snaps to the endpoint,
release the mouse button.

You've moved the selected vertices into place. Now let's take a look at the results.

1. Click the Min/Max Toggle tool to view all of the viewports.

2. Click the Zoom Extents All tool to show all of the model in all viewports. Notice that the new walls no longer appear as walls. Because you are editing the lines in the modifier stack, VIZ displays the wall as a spline.

3. In the modifier stack list, select Extrude. The wall reappears at its full height.

You've just moved a set of vertices, thereby stretching a wall into a new location. As you can see, you need to enter the sub-object level of editing before you can make changes to vertices, but once you do, you have a good deal of freedom to edit parts of an object. As you've seen through these exercises, you can easily get to the sub-object level by selecting the level, such as Vertex, from the Selection rollout or from the modifier stack list.

If you're working with architectural models, you'll use this operation frequently to fine-tune parts of a model. You'll get a chance to edit the vertices of objects in a number of ways as you work through the exercises in this book.

TIP If you find that you cannot select another object while editing your model, it may be because you currently are editing an object on a sub-object level. Check to see if a sub-object level is selected in the Modify tab. If it is, select the object level in the modifier stack list, and then select the next object to be edited. For example, if you are in the Vertex sub-object level of a line, select Line from the modifier stack list. This places you in the object level of the line.

Combining and Extruding Primitive Splines

You've learned how you can create walls with simple lines. Lines are perhaps the most basic type of object you can draw with, and you'll use them often when creating your models. But for walls of a floor plan, you can use another object type that can simplify your work.

VIZ offers a number of 2D shapes that can help make quick work of your modeling efforts, as long as you know how to apply them. In this section, you'll use the Rectangle spline to add a room to your current plan.

1. Click the Top viewport, and then click the Min/Max Toggle tool to enlarge it.

2. Click the Zoom tool, and then click and drag downward on the Top viewport so that you get a view of a larger area.

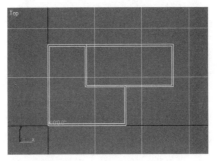

3. Click the Create tab of the Command Panel and click the Rectangle button in the Object Type rollout.

4. Right-click the Snap Toggle button to open the Grid and Snap Settings window, click the Grid Points option, and close the window. You'll use the Grid Points snap to help you create the next set of walls.

5. Make sure the Snap Toggle tool is turned on. Then click and drag from coordinate 26',14',0 to draw a rectangle that is 14 feet wide by 15 feet deep. You can use the coordinate readout at the bottom of the screen to read the dimensions of your rectangle as you move the mouse.

Just as in the exercise in the previous section, you started out with a single-line representation of the wall. In this case, it's a rectangle that is 14 feet by 15 feet. You were able to use the grid and snap together in this exercise to place the rectangle and determine its size.

The next step in adding the wall is to combine it with the existing walls. The rectangle needs to have a portion of its upper left corner removed. To make the plan a little more interesting, you'll also add a curve to the lower right corner.

Combining Splines

You've learned that Spline objects can be composed of multiple splines, accessible on the spline sub-object level. In this section, you'll see how to combine two Spline objects into one and edit the new object to form new shapes.

1. Click the Select Object tool in the main toolbar and click the wall that intersects the rectangle you just drew, as shown in Figure 3.19.

2. Click the Modify tab in the Command Panel and select Line in the modifier stack list.

3. Scroll down the Command Panel to the Geometry rollout and click the Attach button.

4. Move the cursor on top of the rectangle you added in the previous exercise. You'll see the Attach cursor appear when the cursor finds an available object to attach.

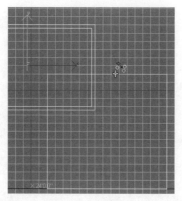

5. Click the rectangle. Notice that it turns white as it becomes part of the selected object.

6. Click the Attach button again to deactivate it.

You've just attached the rectangle to the wall you selected at the beginning of this exercise. Earlier, you saw how the Outline option created two concentric rectangles to form a rectangular wall. That was a clue that objects can contain multiple splines. The outer and inner walls of that rectangular wall are separate splines contained within the same object. In this exercise, you added the rectangle you just created to the wall of the previous exercise.

Next, you'll see how you can trim the parts of the rectangle that you don't need.

1. Click the Region Zoom tool.

2. Place a zoom window around the area shown in Figure 3.20 to enlarge that area.

FIGURE 3.19
Click the wall you created in the previous exercise, and then select Line from the modifier stack list.

Use the Select Object tool to select the wall.

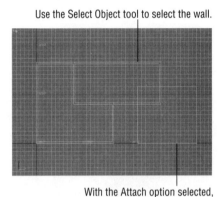

With the Attach option selected, click the rectangle.

FIGURE 3.20
Placing a Region Zoom window around the rectangle corner

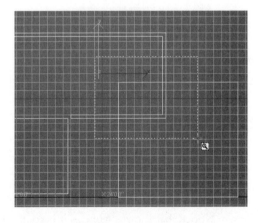

3. With the wall selected, click the Spline button in the Selection rollout.

4. Locate the Trim button in the Geometry rollout (you may need to scroll down the rollout) and click it.

5. After you click the Trim button, place the cursor on the upper left corner of the rectangle. Notice how the cursor changes to a graphic that indicates the Trim operation.

6. Click the rectangle in the location shown in Figure 3.21. The corner of the rectangle is trimmed back to the wall.

7. Click the Trim button to deactivate it.

8. Click the Zoom Extents tool to get an overall view of the walls.

The Trim tool will trim a spline to the nearest spline that is a part of the same object. Trim ignores any splines that are not included in the current object. This is why you needed to attach the rectangle before you used the Trim tool.

You can continue to trim a spline by clicking the side you wish to trim. The spline will then trim back to the nearest spline that is part of the currently selected object. Figure 3.22 shows an example of what the rectangle would look like if you continued to click the remaining endpoints of the rectangle with Trim activated.

You won't be trimming the rectangle any farther than you have in step 6. Instead, in a later exercise in this chapter, you'll use the rectangle in its current configuration to learn how you can merge two sets of lines using the Boolean option.

NOTE *AutoCAD users will find that the Fillet tool is similar in effect to the AutoCAD Fillet tool, although it works in a very different way.*

FIGURE 3.21
Selecting the portion of the rectangle to be trimmed

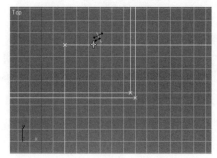

FIGURE 3.22

Click the endpoints of the rectangle to trim it back to the outside of the wall.

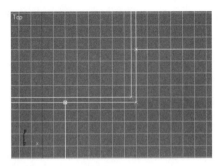

Now let's see how you go about adding a rounded corner to a spline using the Fillet tool.

1. Scroll to the Selection rollout and click the Vertex tool.

2. Click the Select Object tool and click the lower right corner of the rectangle. Then click the Select and Move tool. You'll see the transform gizmo appear at the corner, along with the Bézier handles.

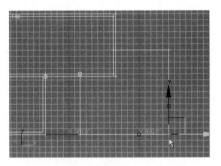

3. Scroll down the Command Panel until you see the Fillet button in the Geometry rollout.

4. Click and drag the Fillet input box spinner upward. Notice what happens to the corner: as you move the spinner, the corner turns into a radius. Don't release the mouse button just yet.

5. Adjust the spinner until the Fillet value reads 5′ and then release the mouse button. (If you release the mouse button before you get to 5′, click the Undo button and try again.) You could also just type in 5′↵ in the Fillet text box.

The Fillet tool is an option of the Vertex sub-object level, so you need to be in the Vertex sub-object editing mode before you can use it.

Now, to finish off the new wall, use the Outline tool once again.

1. Scroll up to the Selection rollout and click the Spline tool.

2. If it isn't already selected, click the Select Object tool, and then click the filleted rectangle. It turns red when it's selected.

3. Scroll down the Command Panel to get to the Outline tool on the Geometry rollout.

4. Enter 5"↵ in the Outline tool's input box. The rectangle is outlined.

5. Click the Min/Max Toggle tool to view all of the viewports.

6. Scroll up the Command Panel, and then click Extrude in the modifier stack list.

Because the rectangle is attached to the wall spline you created earlier, it's also affected by the Extrude modifier. Figure 3.23 shows your model up to this point, from an angle that shows all of the components.

As you work with splines, you'll see that the type of tool options you can use to edit a spline depend on the sub-object type you select in the Selection rollout or the modifier stack list. Fillets and Bézier curves can be edited when the Vertex sub-object level is selected. Trim is available when you select the Spline sub-object level. The Attach option is available in object mode as well as in all sub-object levels.

Joining Closed Splines with Boolean Tools

In the previous exercise, you combined the rectangle with a wall to form a wall object that is made up of two splines. The added rectangle protrudes into the wall that it is joined with, as shown in an enlarged view of the walls in Figure 3.24.

FIGURE 3.23
The perspective view of the walls

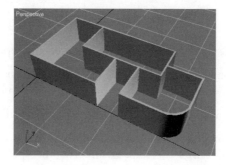

FIGURE 3.24

The walls joined
at a corner

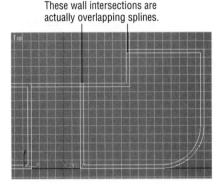

Although these wall intersections do not adversely affect your ability to work with the model, you may eventually want to merge the wall intersections into a clean joint. You can do this by using the Boolean option.

1. Make sure the Top viewport is active, and then click the Min/Max Toggle tool to enlarge the Top viewport.

2. Select Line from the modifier stack list. The newest addition to your drawing appears in red because it's selected.

3. Make sure that Spline is selected in the Selection rollout, and then scroll down the Command Panel to the Geometry rollout until you see the Boolean tool.

4. Click the Boolean button. Then, in the Top viewport, move your cursor to the other wall that is connected with the currently selected wall, as shown in Figure 3.25.

5. Notice that the cursor shows a graphic indicating that it has found a candidate for the Boolean operation.

6. Click the wall. The wall intersections form a neat connection.

7. Scroll up the Command Panel and click Line in the modifier stack list to exit the sub-object level. You can now see the corners more clearly, as shown in Figure 3.26.

8. Select Extrude from the modifier stack list to restore the wall height.

You can use the Boolean tool to join any closed splines, such as those that form the two walls from the previous exercise. Figure 3.27 shows some examples of other splines that are joined using this tool. Besides joining spline outlines, you can subtract outlines or obtain the intersection of two outlines.

FIGURE 3.25
Selecting the wall for the Boolean operation

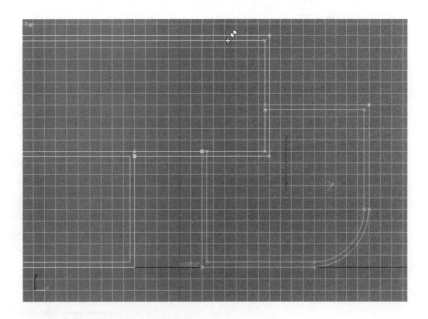

FIGURE 3.26
The wall intersections after using the Boolean tool

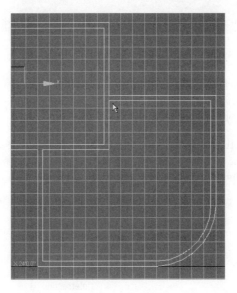

FIGURE 3.27
Examples of Boolean
operations on closed
splines

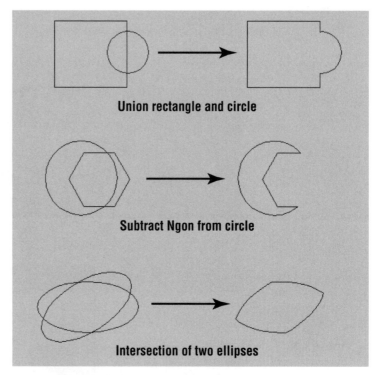

Union rectangle and circle

Subtract Ngon from circle

Intersection of two ellipses

NOTE *In Chapter 4, you'll learn about the Boolean tool for the Compound Objects type, which creates new objects by combining existing ones through Boolean operations. Boolean operations with compound objects are different from those created through the Boolean options in the Spline object's sub-object level.*

To perform these other types of Boolean operations, follow the same steps you used to join the wall intersections in the previous exercise, but before you select the object to be joined, click the appropriate Boolean option (the buttons to the left of the Boolean tool button).

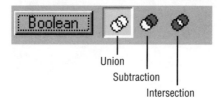

Union
Subtraction
Intersection

TIP *Remember that to perform Boolean operations on splines, the splines need to be attached and they need to be closed. You also need to be at the Spline sub-object level to use the spline Boolean operations.*

WARNING   Don't confuse the Boolean operations that are part of sub-object spline modeling with the Boolean compound object that you will learn about in Chapter 4. They are both the same kind of math used in different parts of the program for different purposes.

Creating a Solid Form with Splines

You've been using splines to create outline shapes such as the profile of the wineglass and the walls of a floor plan. You can also create solid forms like those of the primitive objects you saw in the previous chapter. Splines let you go beyond the primitive forms of circles, rectangles, and squares to make just about any shape you need.

In the following exercise, you'll use a spline to create a ceiling for the walls that you've created so far. This involves creating an outline of the walls, and then using the Extrude modifier to give the outline some thickness.

Start by setting up a view that will make it easier to add the ceiling.

1. Arc Rotate in the Perspective viewport so that you can see the entire top edge of the walls.

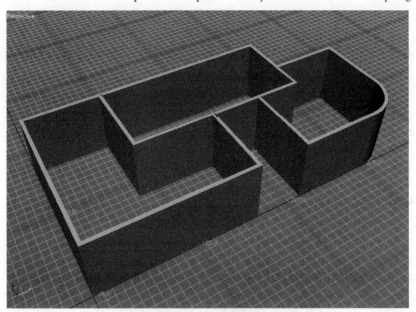

2. Next, set up the snaps to accurately place the spline at the perimeter of the walls. Right-click the Snap Toggle tool.

3. In the Grid and Snap Settings window, click Clear All, and then click the Endpoint check box.

4. Close the Grid and Snap Settings window.

5. Make sure the Snap Toggle is on.

Now you're ready to add the spline that will become the ceiling.

1. Click the Create tab of the Command Panel, and then click the Shapes tool if it isn't already selected.

2. Click the Line tool.

3. Click the outside corners of the walls, as shown in Figure 3.28. When you get to the rounded corner, click the point indicated in the figure. You'll move and reshape that corner later.

4. When you return to the starting corner, click it. In the Spline dialog box, click Yes to close the spline.

Now you have the roof plane outlined with a spline. Next, you need to make an adjustment to the corner where the walls are rounded.

1. With the ceiling spline selected, click the Modify tab in the Command Panel.

2. Click the Vertex tool in the Selection rollout, and then click the Select and Move tool in the main toolbar.

3. Click the vertex at the corner where the wall is rounded, as shown in Figure 3.29.

4. Click and drag the green arrow at the end of the Y axis handle of the transform gizmo toward the right and align the wall, as shown in Figure 3.30.

5. Scroll down to the Geometry rollout in the Modify tab of the Command Panel until you see the Fillet tool.

6. Click the Fillet tool input box so that the entire value is highlighted, then enter 5'↵. The corner is filleted to match the wall, as shown in Figure 3.31.

7. Exit the Vertex sub-object level by clicking on the Line object in the Selection rollout.

FIGURE 3.28
Selecting the vertex

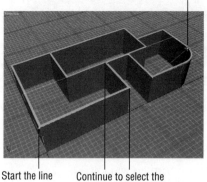

Select the new endpoint at the top of the wall on the outside for the rounded corner.

Start the line at this corner.

Continue to select the top outside endpoints.

FIGURE 3.29
Moving the vertex

FIGURE 3.30
Aligning the wall

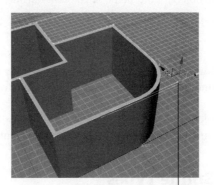

Move this vertex to align
with the outer wall edge.

FIGURE 3.31
The spline after
filleting

For the final operation, you need to give the new spline an area with thickness. Typically, you would make a ceiling around 10 to 12 inches thick between floors of a building. Use the Extrude modifier to extrude the spline to a thickness of 12 inches.

1. Scroll up to the top of the Command Panel and click the Modifier List drop-down arrow.

2. Click the Extrude modifier (in the Object-Space Modifier category).

3. Go to the Parameters rollout, click the Amount input box, and enter **12″**↵. The spline extrudes into a thick, slab-like object in the shape of the wall outline, as shown in Figure 3.32.

4. Click the Min/Max Toggle tool to see all the viewports of the walls.

5. Save the walls you've drawn as a file named **Mywalls.max**.

You extruded the wall outline only 12 inches, but it could easily have been extruded several feet. You could also copy the spline vertically and use the outline tool to form the exterior walls of a second floor.

You've seen a few examples of using splines to create walls and a ceiling. There are many ways to create walls, as you'll learn in later chapters. For now, let's move onto a look at other spline types.

Introducing the Spline Types

You've already used the Line spline and the Rectangle spline, and you've gotten some practice in editing them. Before you continue, you'll want to know a little about the other spline types. Table 3.2 shows the different spline options, how they are created, and some of the editing characteristics of each object.

You may want to experiment by creating some different splines in a separate file. Remember that you can extrude most of them into the third dimension using the Extrude modifier and the Loft creation tool, which extrudes a shape along a spline path (you'll learn about lofting in Chapter 5). The Helix spline cannot be extruded straight, but it can be used as a path for animated motion or as a path for extrusions (as in *lofts*).

FIGURE 3.32
The finished ceiling on top of the walls

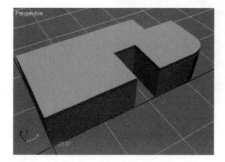

TABLE 3.2: CREATION METHODS FOR SPLINES

SPLINE NAME AND FUNCTION	CREATION METHOD	CREATION OPTIONS*	PARAMETERS*
Line—Draws splines	Click points to place line segments. Click and drag adds smoothing when Smooth is selected for Initial or Drag type group.	*Initial Type:* Corner/ Smooth *Drag Type:* Corner/ Smooth/Bézier	*Interpolation:* Steps, Optimize, Adaptive *Rendering:* Renderable (as tube), Thickness, General Mapping Coords.
Circle—Draws circles	Click center and drag radius [Center]. Or click two points to locate points on circumference edge [Edge].	Edge/Center	Radius
Arc—Draws arcs	Click start point and drag to place endpoint, then adjust and click for radius [End-End-Middle]. Or click center, drag to radius and first end, click second end [Center-End-End].	End-End-Middle/Center-End-End	Radius, From, To, Pie Slice (creates pie-slice shape), Reverse
Ngon—Draws regular polygons	Click center, then drag to place radius [Center]. Or click to place one edge, then drag for other edge [Edge].	Edge/Center	Radius, Radius, Inscribe/ Circumscribe, [number of] Sides, Corner Radius, Circular
Text—Draws text	Click to place text.	Input box for entering text	Font, Size, Kerning, Leading, Text, Manual Update
Section—Draws a section plane and creates a 2D outline of intersecting objects	Click to place section center point, drag to place corner. Create Shape button creates spline outline of object intersecting Section shape.	*Update:* When section moves/When section selected/ Manually *Selection Extent:* Infinite/ Section Boundary/Off	Length, Width
Rectangle—Draws rectangles	Click first corner and drag for other corner [Edge]. Or click center and drag for corner [Center].	Edge/Center	Length, Width, Corner Radius
Ellipse—Draws ellipses	Click first tangent edge and drag for other edge [Edge]. Or click center and drag for edge [Center].	Edge/Center	Length, Width

TABLE 3.2: Creation Methods for Splines *(continued)*

SPLINE NAME AND FUNCTION	CREATION METHOD	CREATION OPTIONS*	PARAMETERS*
Donut—Draws Donut—Draws two concentric circles	Click first point on circumference and drag for second point on circumference, click for second radius [Edge]. Or click center and drag for first radius, click for second radius [Center].	Edge/Center	Radius 1, Radius 2
Star—Draws star shapes	Click center and drag for first radius, click again for second radius.		Radius 1, Radius 2, [number of] Points [of star], Distortion [twist], Fillet Radius 1, Fillet Radius 2
Helix—Draws a 3D helix (spiral)	Click first circumference point, drag second circumference point, click height, click second radius [Edge]. Or click center, drag first radius, click height, click second radius [Center].	Edge/Center	Radius 1, Radius 2, Height, Turns, Bias CW [clockwise]/ CCW [counter-clockwise]

Items separated by / denote radio button options. Italics denote button group names.

Editing Splines

You've seen how you can edit the rectangle and line through the Modify tab of the Command Panel. In most cases, you need to select the Edit Spline modifier from the Modifier List drop-down list to gain access to the sub-object levels of a spline as parametric controls are usually shown.

The exception to this is the Line spline, which will display its sub-object level options as soon as you select the Modify tab.

Once you've selected Edit Spline, you can make changes to the vertices, line segments, or whole spline by entering the corresponding sub-object level of the Edit Spline modifier. You can even attach or detach components of a spline to create new forms, as you'll see in the next chapter.

Another way to gain access to a spline's sub-object level is to right-click the object name in the modifier stack list and select Convert To: Editable Spline from the shortcut menu.

This exposes the sub-object level of the selected spline in a way similar to the Edit Spline modifier, but it does so by permanently converting the spline to an Editable Spline. The spline then loses its parametric functions. If you know you won't need to parametrically modify a spline, however, this can be a good way to simplify your model.

TIP   Reducing a spline to an Editable Spline also helps reduce the memory requirements of your model. VIZ must reserve additional memory from your system in order to maintain the parameters of objects. By converting a spline into an Editable Spline, VIZ no longer needs to reserve that additional memory for the spline. And as your model becomes larger, these memory issues become more important. On the other hand, using the Edit Spline modifier consumes more memory than converting a primitive spline shape to an Editable Spline, but you have the best of both worlds—parametric and explicit control.

Using AEC Walls and Doors

You've seen how to create walls using the Spline tool. By doing this, you were able to learn about many of the spline's characteristics, and you were introduced to the concept of editing in sub-object levels. VIZ also offers another tool that is tailored to drawing walls: the AEC Wall tool. This tool works in a way similar to the Spline tool, but you don't need to extrude or offset the wall to get a thickness and height—it's handled parametrically instead.

Try drawing some walls and adding some doors in the following exercise.

1. Choose File ➢ New and create an all new file.

2. Click the Min/Max Toggle tool, and then click the Zoom Extents All tool to set up the default views.

3. If the upper left viewport's label shows User, right-click the label and select Views ➢ Top from the shortcut menu, or type **T** on the keyboard.

4. Click the Create tab of the Command Panel.

5. Select AEC Extended from the Geometry type drop down list and then select Wall from the Object Type rollout.

Notice that the Parameters rollout includes Width and Height parameters. You also see a set of Justification options, which allow you to determine how the walls are drawn in relation to the points you select.

6. In the Top viewport, click near the origin to start your wall. As you move the cursor, you see a rubber-banding wall display in the viewports.

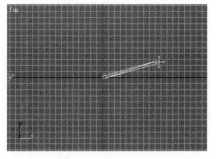

7. Click a point to the right, as shown in Figure 3.33, and then click another point above that first point so that you create an L-shaped wall configuration.

8. Right-click to finish drawing wall segments.

9. Click the Zoom Extents All tool to get a better view of your wall.

FIGURE 3.33
Drawing the
AEC wall

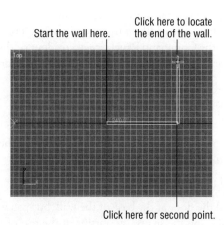

Placing the points for a wall works the same way as placing points for straight-line segments. You can use the Keyboard Entry rollout to input coordinates, just as you did earlier with the spline walls. The AEC Wall tool offers a quick way to lay out a basic floor plan.

In addition to a simplified wall-creation method, the AEC tools also allow you to add doors and windows that automatically create openings. Try adding a door to your walls in the next exercise to see how this works.

TIP *First, set up snap settings for snapping to the edge of objects. This is important, because the AEC Door and Window tools require the use of the edge snap to work properly with AEC Walls.*

1. Right-click the Snap Toggle button. In the Grid and Snap Settings window, click Clear All and click the Edge check box. Then close the window.

2. Make sure the snap toggle is on. If it is off, type **S** on the keyboard.

3. Make the Perspective viewport active, and then Arc Rotate so that you can see the top edge of the wall.

4. Click the Zoom Extents tool, click the Min/Max Toggle tool, and then click the Zoom Extents tool to center the view of the wall.

Now you're ready to place a door.

1. Click the Pivot Door tool after selecting Doors from the Geometry drop down list on the Create panel.

2. Place the cursor on the top edge of the wall, as shown in Figure 3.34. Then click and drag along the top edge to establish the width of the door opening. You can watch the Width parameter in the Create tab of the Command Panel to get a readout of the door width. Release the mouse button when you are ready to set the width value of the door. You can also edit the Width parameter later.

3. Move the cursor to the opposite side of the wall so you see the Edge Snap marker, and then click that location. This sets the depth of the door.

4. Move the cursor down the wall to its base, and then click the bottom edge of the wall. This sets the height of the door.

5. Right-click to end the door placement.

You could have started the door at the base of the wall, but you would not have been able to indicate the width of the wall using the snaps. By starting at the top of the wall, you were able to select the width graphically by using the Edge Snap cursor.

To finish off this exercise, make some final adjustments to the door you just created.

1. Click the Modify tab in the Command Panel.

2. In the Parameters rollout, change the door height to 6′7″ and the width to 3′.

3. Click and drag the Open spinner to set the value to 45. This sets the door swing to 45 degrees. The door opens and reveals an opening in the wall.

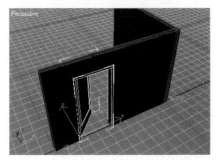

Here, you see a unique feature of the AEC Pivot Door tool: it automatically places an opening in the AEC wall. AEC doors will not do this for walls you create using splines; it works only with AEC walls. Another feature of AEC doors is that you can move the door, and the opening will move with it.

If you look at the parameters for the door you created in this exercise, you'll see that you can adjust quite a few parameters. You can set the door frame size and the dimensions of the door leaf. You can even get down to details like adding glass or beveled panels.

FIGURE 3.34
Starting the door
placement

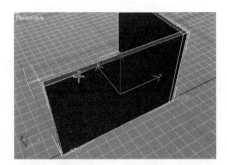

Summary

In this chapter, you've seen how splines can be created and edited, and you've also had a brief introduction to the concept of sub-objects. You've really just scratched the surface of what splines can do.

In the next chapter, you'll use an architectural project as a basis for exploring a number of VIZ's features. You'll get a chance to see how you can trace over a scanned image, and you'll continue to look at splines with a focus on sub-object editing. You'll also learn how you can sculpt objects by subtracting one shape from another or by adding shapes together.

Chapter 4

Editing Meshes for Complex Objects

In the previous three chapters, you spent time getting familiar with VIZ. In this chapter, you'll continue your exploration of VIZ's features, while exercising your newfound skills. You'll start by learning how to add openings to the walls you created in Chapter 3. Then you'll learn how you can import scanned images that you can use to trace over. In the process of tracing over a floor plan, you'll further explore methods for creating and editing forms using splines. You'll also be introduced to ways you can edit extruded shapes.

- ◆ Creating an Opening in a Wall with Boolean Operations
- ◆ Tracing over a Sketch
- ◆ Editing Meshes
- ◆ Using Instance Clones to Create Symmetric Forms
- ◆ Attaching Objects to a Mesh
- ◆ Smoothing Meshes

Creating an Opening in a Wall with Boolean Operations

In the Chapter 3, you created a set of walls that completely enclosed a space. You'll need to add wall openings between the enclosed spaces of your model. To do this, you'll use *Boolean* operations to remove portions of a wall.

NOTE *Boolean operations are named after George Boole, who developed a mathematical branch of symbolic logic. Boolean logic includes AND, OR, and NOT operators, which correspond to geometric union, intersection, and subtraction.*

Boolean operations are methods you can use to join two objects together, subtract the shape of one object from another, or obtain a shape that is the intersection of two objects. Figure 4.1 illustrates the effect of Boolean operations on some sample shapes.

VIZ allows you to use two objects to form new shapes using Boolean operations. Those shapes are referred to as the *operands* of the Boolean operations. In the following exercise, you'll use a simple box to form the opening in your walls. The existing wall is one operand, and the box that forms the opening is the other operand.

Hiding Shapes That Get in the Way

Start by setting up your wall model and creating an object you'll use to subtract from the walls.

1. Open the Mywalls.max model you created in the last chapter. (This file is also included on the companion CD as Mywalls04.max.)

2. If your VIZ window shows only a single viewport, click Min/Max Toggle to view the four viewports.

    You'll need to hide the ceiling of your model in order to more easily work on the model. Here's a quick way to temporarily hide objects if they're in your way.

3. Use the Select Object tool to select the ceiling.

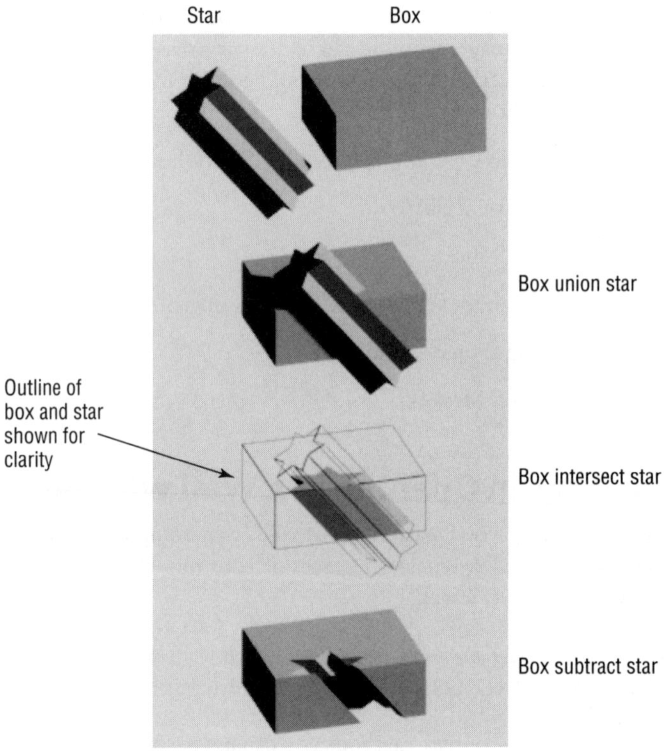

FIGURE 4.1

Examples of Boolean operations

Star   Box

Box union star

Outline of box and star shown for clarity

Box intersect star

Box subtract star

4. Click the Display tab of the Command Panel, then, in the name input box just below the Display label, change the name to **Ceiling**. This will help you find the ceiling later.

5. Look for the Hide rollout in the Command Panel and click the Hide Selected button. The ceiling disappears.

6. The ceiling hasn't really gone anywhere. You've just hidden it. Just so you know where to look when you do need to turn it back on, click the Unhide by Name button in the Hide rollout.

The Unhide Objects dialog box displays.

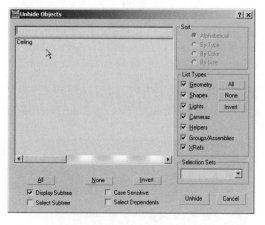

7. You can see that the Ceiling is listed in the dialog box. To turn it back on, you would click the name in the list, and then click Unhide. You want to keep it off for now, so click Cancel.

Creating the Shape of the Opening

Now you're ready to get to work on the walls. Your first step is to create the shape of the opening. You can think of this shape as the negative space of the opening, or as the shape that is to be removed from the wall.

1. Click the Top viewport to make it active.

2. Click the Zoom Extents tool so that you can see the entire plan in the viewport.

3. Click the Geometry tool in the Create tab of the Command Panel and make sure Standard Primitives is selected in the drop-down list.

4. Click the Box button in the Object Type rollout. Then, in the Top viewport, click and drag a rectangle that is roughly 3 feet by 3 feet square, to the location shown in Figure 4.2. You don't need to draw the box precisely, since you'll enter the exact dimensions in the Parameters rollout.

5. Make the height of the box roughly 7 feet.

6. Go to the Parameters rollout of the Create tab and set the Length and Width input boxes to 3 ′ and the Height to 6 ′8″.

   You now have a box that will be used to create an opening. The next steps are to place the box in the location for the opening.

7. Click the Select and Move tool in the main toolbar and move the box to the location shown in Figure 4.3. Remember that you need to place the cursor on the selected object. Then, when you see the Move cursor, click and drag the object into position.

8. Shift+click and drag the box to make a copy of the box in the location shown in Figure 4.3.

9. In the Clone Options dialog box, click Copy, and then click OK.

FIGURE 4.2
Placing the box in the plan

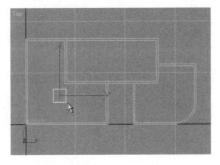

FIGURE 4.3
Positioning the box in the doorway locations

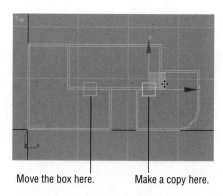

Move the box here.   Make a copy here.

Subtracting the Opening from the Wall

Now that you have the shape ready, you can use the Boolean tool to subtract it from the wall. First, select the object from which you want to subtract the opening.

1. Click the Select Object tool and click the first wall you created, as shown in Figure 4.4.

2. Click the Geometry tool in the Create tab and select Compound Objects from the drop-down list just below the row of tools.

3. Click the Boolean button in the Object Type rollout.

The Boolean options appear in the Command Panel.

4. Click the Pick Operand B button in the Pick Boolean rollout.

5. Click the box that intersects the wall, as shown in Figure 4.4.

6. Scroll down the Command Panel to the Parameters rollout and make sure that the Subtraction (A-B) radio button is selected.

If you look in the Perspective viewport, you'll see that an opening appears in the wall where you located the box, as shown in Figure 4.5.

Now repeat the operation for the other wall.

1. Click the Select Object tool and click the second wall, as shown in Figure 4.6.

2. Click the Boolean button in the Object Type rollout of the Command Panel.

3. Click the Pick Operand B button, and then select the box, as shown in Figure 4.6. The second opening appears, as shown in Figure 4.7.

FIGURE 4.4
Selecting the wall and the box for the Boolean operation

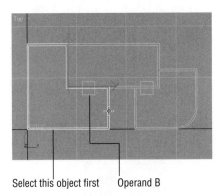

Select this object first   Operand B

FIGURE 4.5
The opening in the wall

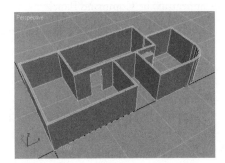

FIGURE 4.6
Selecting the wall and box for the second opening

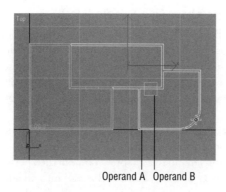

Operand A   Operand B

FIGURE 4.7
The Perspective view showing the second opening

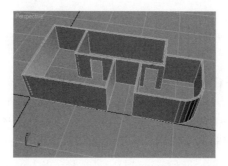

In this example, you created a simple rectangular opening in the wall. The shape of the opening can be anything you want it to be. You just need to create the geometry, using primitives or extruded splines. In addition, the object that you're subtracting from doesn't need to be a thin plane such as the wall in this example. It can be any geometry you want, and the subtracted shape will leave its impression. Figure 4.8 shows some examples of other Boolean subtractions to give you an idea of other possibilities.

FIGURE 4.8
Some samples of Boolean subtractions

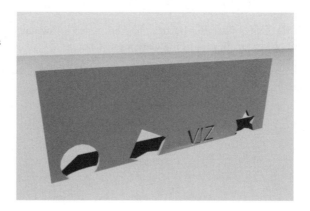

Creating Multiple Openings in a Single Wall

You can perform only one Boolean operation on an object at a time. But what if you need to do multiple Boolean operations, such as create several openings in one wall? To do this, you can create the opening shapes, convert them to editable meshes, and then use the editable mesh Attach option in the Modify tab to join several meshes together into one object. You can then subtract that single object from the wall. You can also attach several boxes together to form a single object, and then subtract it from the wall at once.

Another method is to perform the Boolean operation to create one opening as described in the previous exercise, and then convert the resulting wall and opening into an editable mesh, as described in the "Editing Meshes" section later in this chapter. You can then perform another Boolean subtraction on the same wall. For the next opening, convert the wall into an editable mesh again, then perform the next Boolean subtraction. The drawback to this method is that you cannot edit the openings by going back and changing the size of the boxes. You can, however, edit openings in the mesh at sub-object levels.

TIP   You can also perform multiple nested Boolean operations. Just click the Boolean button again while the previous Boolean is selected to initiate the next operation. This method preserves access to all the operands.

Making Changes to the Opening

Now suppose that you decide to increase the size of one of the openings. You can go back and modify the box so that it's wider. This, in turn, will increase the opening size.

1. Click the Select Object tool in the main toolbar and click the first wall, as shown in Figure 4.9.

2. Click the Modify tab in the Command Panel and scroll down the panel to the Display/Update rollout. Click the Display/Update rollout label to open the rollout.

3. Click the Operands radio button. The box (also known as Operand B of the Boolean compound object) reappears in the viewports.

4. Scroll up to the top of the Modify tab. In the Parameters rollout, click the B: Box01 option in the Operands group.

FIGURE 4.9

Moving the operand
to change the loca-
tion of the wall
opening

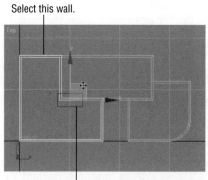

Select this wall.

Resize operand and move to this location.

5. Notice that Box is now listed in the modifier stack list. Click the Box item.

The Command Panel options change to show the parameters for the box.

6. In the Parameters rollout, change the Width input box value to **6 '**. Notice how the box changes in the viewports as you edit the Width parameter.

7. Go back to the top of the modifier stack list and select Boolean.

8. Scroll down to the Display/Update rollout and click the Result radio button.

Now you can see the result of your edit in the Perspective viewport. The opening is now 6 feet wide instead of 3 feet wide.

Besides altering the shape of the box, you can also reposition it to change the location of the wall. Here's how it's done.

1. Click the Operands radio button in the Display/Update rollout again to view the box.

2. Scroll up the Command Panel to the modifier stack list and click Boolean. It should turn yellow. (If it isn't yellow, click it again until it turns yellow.) You can also click the plus (+) sign next to the Boolean modifier to expand the list, and then click Operands.

3. Click the Select and Move tool in the main toolbar. Then click and drag the box to the left so that it passes through the corner of the wall, as shown in Figure 4.9.

4. Click Operands again in the modifier stack list to exit the sub-object level (the yellow color disappears).

5. Scroll down the Command Panel to the Display/Update rollout and click the Result radio button. The new wall opening configuration appears in the Perspective viewport, as shown in Figure 4.10.

6. Save the Mywalls02.max file.

The tricky part of moving Operand B in this exercise is making sure that the sub-object level is active and that Operand B is selected in the Operands list in the Parameters rollout.

These exercises demonstrate that you can alter the shape of the opening by modifying the parameters of the object you used to create the opening. The trick here is to know how to get to the box operand in order to edit its parameters. It's a good idea to first make the subtracted operand visible. It's not absolutely necessary, but it helps to see the operand as you make changes. Use the modifier stack list to gain access to the operand. Once there, you can access the operand's parameters and make changes to its geometry or change its location. To change the location of either of the operands within a compound object, you go to the Operands sub-object level and select the operand. The operands are considered sub-objects of the Boolean compound object construction.

FIGURE 4.10
The result of moving
the box operand

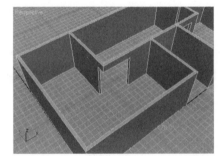

Tracing over a Sketch

You cannot always predict when or where you'll have a brilliant design idea. Frequently, ideas arise when you're sitting at a table sketching out ideas in a brainstorming session or perhaps even during lunch. The basic tools of pencil and paper offer the spontaneity needed to express ideas freely.

Once you've created an inspired sketch, VIZ offers a way to quickly transfer your inspiration into a 3D model. Among its view options, VIZ supplies a tool that displays a bitmap image in a viewport for a variety of purposes, including the tracing of scanned design sketches.

In this section, you'll continue your exploration of splines by importing a sketch and tracing over it. You'll use a sketch that is a rough approximation of the building known as the Chapel at Ronchamp, designed by Le Corbusier. Figure 4.11 shows a 3D-massing model based on this sketch.

This building model offers the opportunity to examine how you might use splines to create shapes other than simple straight walls such as those you created in the previous chapter. You'll also be introduced to other methods for modeling forms by combining splines and primitives. (My apologies to Le Corbusier for creating a less-than-perfect representation of one of his most admired buildings!)

Importing a Bitmap Image

Importing a bitmap image is fairly simple, but you need to watch out for a few settings. In the following exercise, you'll import an image that is a sketch of the Ronchamp floor plan. The sketch shows a grid that is spaced at approximately 4.5 meters, as shown in Figure 4.12. The bitmap image is on the book's companion CD.

You'll import this image into the Top viewport, so first set up VIZ so that you can see only the enlarged Top viewport.

NOTE   *You'll need a file from the companion CD, so make sure you've installed the sample files before you start.*

1. Choose File ➤ Reset and click Yes at the Reset warning message.

NOTE   *The difference between using File ➤ Reset and File ➤ New is subtle but there is an important distinction. When you reset the scene, you are starting completely over and everything defaults to the way it was when you first launched VIZ. When you create a new scene, it merely erases all the objects, leaving your scene seemingly empty—but the new scene still has all the materials, units, and other settings as they were set before.*

FIGURE 4.11
A 3D model of the
Chapel at Ronchamp

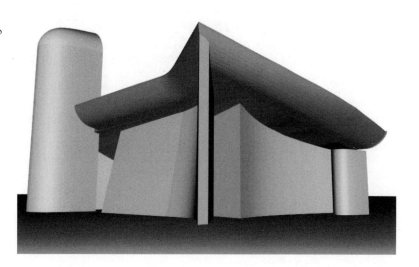

FIGURE 4.12
The bitmap image
of the Chapel at
Ronchamp
floor plan

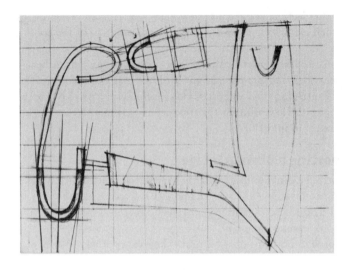

2. Type **T** to go to the Top viewport.

   Now you're ready to import and set up your scanned floor plan.

3. Click Views ➤ Viewport Background. The Viewport Image dialog box displays.

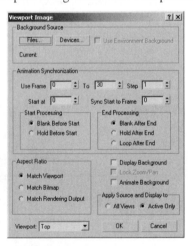

4. Click the Files button at the top of the dialog box in the Background Source group. The Select Background Image dialog box displays.

5. Make sure that All Formats is selected in the Files of Type drop-down list, and then locate the `Ronchampscan.gif` file. Click the file, and then click Open.

6. In the Viewpoint Image dialog box, click the Match Bitmap radio button in the Aspect Ratio group, toward the lower left corner of the dialog box.

7. To the right of the Aspect Ratio group, click the Lock Zoom/Pan check box. This is important, because it locks the image to the viewport. Any pans or zooms you perform will act on the imported bitmap image as well as the viewport.

8. Click OK. The image appears in the Top viewport.

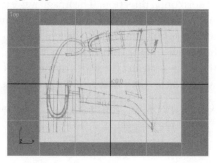

Scaling the Image to the Model's Space

The image's size appears in a somewhat arbitrary fashion. It would be most desirable to size the image so that it's to scale—that is, so that the distances represented by the image are the same as those in the VIZ model. You can approximate the correct scale, although you won't be able to get it exactly the same. Here's how it's done.

Start by setting up the units you'll be working with.

1. Choose Customize ➢ Units Setup. The Units Setup dialog box displays.

2. Click the Metric radio button and make sure Meters is displayed in the Metric drop-down list. Then click OK.

You'll use meters in this example, because this is a European building project. Now let's proceed to scaling the image to the proper size.

If you look at the scanned image carefully, you'll see a grid whose spacing is about 4.5 meters. You see 10 grid spaces in the horizontal direction. The image was carefully cropped to be as close as possible to a width of 10 grid units. VIZ imports an image so that its width will just fit in the viewport, so if you set the width of the viewport to match the width of the image, you have a fairly close scale relationship between the sketch and the dimensions in VIZ.

To begin adjusting the image scale, set the width of the viewport to match the width of the bitmap image. The simplest way to do this is to first set up a grid that matches the grid in the sketch.

1. Right-click the Grid Panel at the bottom of the VIZ window.

The Grid and Snap Settings window displays, with the Home Grid tab selected.

2. In the Grid and Snap Settings window, set the Grid Spacing to **4.5m** and make sure the Major Lines Every Nth Grid Line input box shows 10.

3. Close the Grid and Snap Settings window. Then click the Zoom tool.

4. Click and drag the Zoom cursor from the center portion of the viewport downward until you see 10-grid spacing just fit horizontally in the viewport, as shown in Figure 4.13. When you click and drag from the center, the view will stay centered as you zoom out. If you need to, use the Pan tool to adjust the horizontal position so that the Y axis is at the center of the viewport.

5. Choose Views ➢ Reset Background Transform. The image will fill the entire viewport. Note that the vertical grid lines of the image are fairly close to the vertical grid lines of the viewport, as shown in Figure 4.14.

FIGURE 4.13
Adjust the grid spacing so that 10 horizontal grid spaces just fit in the viewport.

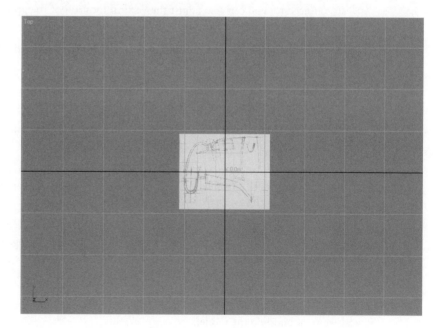

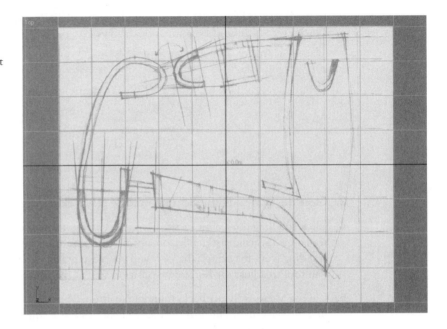

If you need to, you can also adjust the vertical location of the grid. This will require the use of a low-tech device: a sticky-back note.

1. Take a sticky-back note and place it so its top edge is aligned with one of the horizontal grid lines of the scanned image.

2. Click the Pan tool and carefully pan the view downward until one of the horizontal viewport grid lines is aligned with the top edge of the sticky-back note.

3. Choose Views ➤ Reset Background Transform. The grid will align vertically with the grid in the image.

4. Once you have the viewport grid as closely aligned to the image's grid as possible, choose Views ➤ Save Active Top View. By saving this view, you can quickly reset the image to the viewport in the event that you inadvertently lose the image.

The grids may not align perfectly, but for this sketch, you should have the alignment close enough. You now have a fairly close match to the scale of the actual building. As this exercise shows, there is some preparation of the image involved. First, you should place a grid on the sketch so that you have some scale reference. Second, the width of the image needs to be cropped to a whole grid unit so that you can use the image width to match the viewport.

Now that you have the image to a size that makes some sense scale-wise, you can get on with the real work of building the model.

Tracing Over the Image

To trace over the bitmap, you'll use the Line spline that you were introduced to in the previous chapter. You won't trace all of the walls at first.

Start by tracing the small, U-shaped wall on the exterior of the chapel.

1. In the Top viewport, use the Region Zoom tool to zoom into the U-shaped wall area so that your view looks similar to Figure 4.15.

   You may get a message warning you of memory use. Click Yes in the warning dialog box.

TIP   *If you accidentally select No in the warning dialog box in step 1, the background image may disappear. If this happens, you can choose Views ➤ Viewport Background, and then make sure the* Ronchampscan.gif *file has Display Background checked in the Viewport Background dialog box in the Top viewport.*

2. Click the Create tab of the Command Panel, and then click Shapes.

3. Click the Line button in the Object Type rollout of the Command Panel.

4. Trace over the outside of the wall, using single clicks to select the points shown in Figure 4.15.

5. For the last point, click the beginning of the spline. In the Spline dialog box, click Yes to close the spline.

The line needs to be curved, so use the Bèzier Vertex option to form the curve of the wall.

1. Click the Modify tab of the Command Panel, click the plus (+) sign next to Line in the modifier stack list, and then click Vertex in the expanded list. (You can also click the Vertex button in the Selection rollout of the Modify tab.)

FIGURE 4.15
Tracing the wall

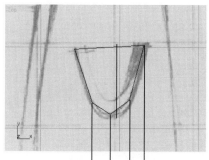

Continue selecting points in
a counter-clockwise fashion.

2. With the Select Object tool, click the middle vertex of the wall, as shown in Figure 4.16.

3. Right-click to open the quad menu and select Bèzier from the list of vertex type options.

4. Click the Select and Move tool in the main toolbar, and then click and drag the tangent handles to a position similar to the one shown in Figure 4.16. You'll want to smooth the bottom curve to match the bitmap image.

5. Right-click the second vertex to the left of the one you just edited and select Bèzier from the shortcut menu.

6. Right-click the other vertex to the right, select Bèzier from the shortcut menu, and adjust the Bèzier handle so that the wall looks symmetrical, as shown in Figure 4.18.

7. Adjust the tangent handles to smooth the curve at this vertex, as shown in Figure 4.17.

Now you have the general outline of the wall. You could extrude the spline now to get the general shape of the wall, but the design calls for a bit more elaboration.

Building Objects from Traced Lines

The shape of the wall starts at its base as a solid form, and as you move up the height of the wall, it becomes partially open. In the transition area, you have a sloped roof that covers the enclosed portion of this piece of the chapel, as you can see in Figure 4.19.

FIGURE 4.16
Editing the
middle vertex

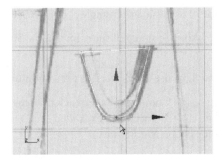

FIGURE 4.17
Editing the second
vertex to the left of
the middle vertex

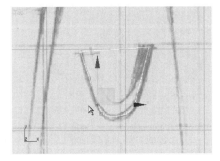

FIGURE 4.18
Editing the fourth
vertex to the right of
the middle vertex

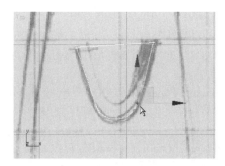

FIGURE 4.19
Looking at the form
of the U-shaped wall

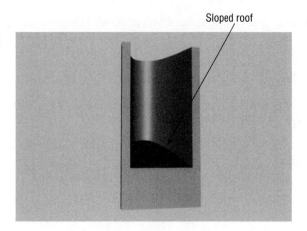

Sloped roof

To obtain this shape, you'll make a copy of the wall outline you've just drawn and then form it to create an object matching the void of the upper part of the piece. Once you have the void object, you can subtract it from the main outer part of the wall using the Boolean operation you learned about earlier in this chapter.

CREATING THE VOID OUTLINE

While you're creating the void object, you'll get a chance to explore some spline-editing tools. First, you'll make a copy of the existing wall outline, and then you'll edit the copy to get the outline of the void object.

1. Click Line in the modifier stack list to deactivate the Vertex sub-object level.

2. With the Select and Move tool selected, Shift+click and drag the wall you just created to the right so that you have a copy, as shown in Figure 4.20.

3. In the Clone Options dialog box, click Copy, and then click OK. You don't need an instance or reference copy for this part because the new object is destined to be different from the original.

Next, you'll work on the copy to form the void outline.

1. With the copy of the wall selected, expand the Line modifier in the modifier stack list, and then select Spline. (You can also click the Spline tool in the Selection rollout of the Command Panel.)

2. Scroll down the Command Panel to the Outline input box in the Geometry rollout, click the input box, and enter **0.4**↵. This creates an outline that is 0.4 meter thick.

3. Scroll up to the top of the Command Panel and click the Segment tool in the Selection rollout. (You can also select Segment from the modifier stack list.)

4. Click the straight-line segment at the top of the interior wall outline, as shown in Figure 4.21, and then press the Delete key to delete the line.

With the straight segment deleted, you can extend the remaining portion of the line to the outside edge of the wall.

1. Click the Spline tool in the Selection rollout again, and then click the remaining portion of the interior wall outline so that it turns red.

2. Scroll down the Command Panel and click the Extend button. (You can also right-click and select Extend from the shortcut menu.)

FIGURE 4.20
Copy the wall as shown here.

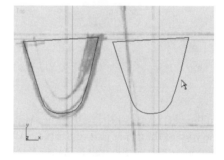

FIGURE 4.21
Delete the straight-line segment.

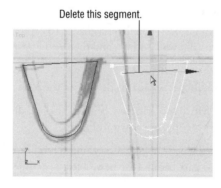

3. Place the cursor on the left endpoint of the inside wall so that the Extend cursor displays, as shown in Figure 4.22, and click the line. It extends to the outside line.

4. Click the other end of the inside wall so that it too extends to the straight-line segment of the outside line.

5. Click the Extend button in the Command Panel to deactivate it, and then click the Close button in the Command Panel. This generates a new straight-line segment across the top.

6. Click the Select Object tool, and then click the outside wall outline, as shown in Figure 4.23. Then press the Delete key to delete it.

7. Scroll up to the top of the Command Panel and click the Spline button to deactivate it.

You have the outline of the shape you want to subtract from the wall. Now move it into position.

1. Right-click the Snap Toggle tool in the main toolbar.

2. In the Grid and Snap Settings window, click the Clear All button, and then click Midpoint. Close the Grid and Snap Settings window.

FIGURE 4.22
Extending the inside wall to the straight-line segment of the outside wall outline

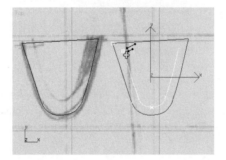

FIGURE 4.23
Select the outside wall, and then press the Delete key.

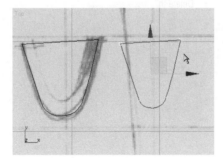

3. If it isn't already active, click the Snap Toggle tool to make it active.

4. With the Select and Move tool selected, place the cursor on the midpoint of the straight-line segment of the wall copy.

5. When you see the Midpoint cursor appear on the line, click and drag the wall outline to the straight segment of the original wall, as shown in Figure 4.24.

FORMING THE WALL VOID

Now you're ready to extrude both the wall and the wall void. First, move the void object to the elevation where the void begins.

1. Click the Min/Max Toggle tool to see all four viewports.

2. Right-click the Perspective viewport and then click the Zoom Extents tool.

3. Click the Select and Move Tool. With the inside wall outline selected, right-click to open the quad menu and click the small square symbol next to Move to open the transform type-in dialog box.

Segment	Hide Unselected
Vertex	Hide Selection
Top-level	Hide Selection's Layer
tools 1	display
tools 2	transform
Create Line	Move
Attach	Rotate
Detach Segment	Scale
Connect	Clone
Refine	Properties...
Refine Connect	Curve Editor...
Cycle Vertices	Wire Parameters...
Break Vertices	Convert To:
Weld Vertices	

NOTE *You can also use the transform type-ins that are integrated into the bottom of the user interface. Opening the Transform Type-In dialog box from the quad menu is just a way of focusing your attention on entering coordinate values. The dialog box has the advantage that you can see both absolute and offset (relative) values simultaneously.*

FIGURE 4.24
Selecting and moving the wall copy using the Midpoint snap

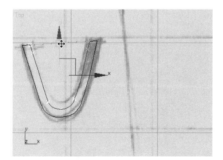

4. Click the Z input box of the Absolute: World group, then enter **2.5**↵, for 2.5 meters. Then close the Move and Transform Type-In dialog box.

5. Click Zoom Extents again to see both wall outlines. The inside wall outline now appears to be somewhat above the outside wall outline.

Now it's time to extrude the two outlines. This piece of the chapel is about 7.5 meters high, so you can extrude both pieces to this height. The height of the void is somewhat arbitrary, because it's to be subtracted from the main, outside form of the wall.

1. Click the Snap Toggle tool or type S on the keyboard to turn it off. It may be a distraction during the next few operations.

2. Click the original, outside wall outline to select it.

3. In the Modify tab, select Extrude from the Modifier List drop-down list.

4. In the Parameters rollout, click the Amount input box and enter **7.5**↵, for 7.5 meters. The outside wall appears at its full height.

Now extrude the interior void shape.

5. In the Top viewport, click the wall outline copy that forms the interior outline of the wall, as shown in Figure 4.25.

6. Select Extrude from the Modifier List drop-down list again. The object extrudes to the same height as the other wall. VIZ applies to the current extrusion the last value you entered for the first extrusion.

7. Click the Perspective viewport, and then click the Zoom Extents tool to get a better look at the two extrusions. Because one extrusion is inside the other, you won't really see both extrusions.

FIGURE 4.25
Select the form of the interior outline.

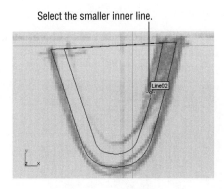

Select the smaller inner line.

ADDING A TAPER TO THE VOID

You're almost ready to subtract the interior void object from the outer wall object. You need to apply the taper modifier to the void object to get the sloping roof (shown earlier in Figure 4.19).

1. With the Perspective viewport selected, click the Min/Max Toggle tool to enlarge the view.

2. Click the Arc Rotate Selected tool in the viewport navigation controls. The yellow Arc Rotate circle appears in the viewport.

3. Click and drag the left square on the circle to the right so that you get a view similar to Figure 4.26.

4. Click the Select Object tool, and then click the interior void object.

5. Right-click and select Isolate Selection from the display quad menu. The viewport changes to show only the interior wall object and the Isolated Selection dialog box displays.

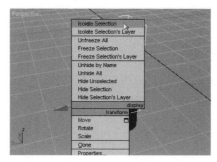

By using the Isolate tool, you can more easily view and edit an object that may be partially hidden by other objects in your model. Now you can apply the Taper tool to the selected object and see its effects more clearly.

1. Select Taper from the Modifier List drop-down list.

2. In the Parameters rollout, click the Primary Y radio button in the Taper Axis group. This causes the taper to occur in the Y axis.

FIGURE 4.26
Match this view using the Arc Rotate Selected tool.

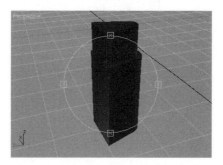

3. Click the Effect Z radio button in the Taper Axis group. This constrains the taper effect to the Z axis.

4. In the Parameters rollout, set the Amount input box to **−0.38** to specify the amount of the taper. The top of the extrusion now slopes down toward outside of the curve.

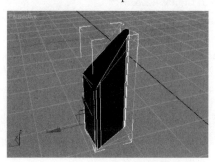

5. Click the Exit Isolation button in the Isolated Selection dialog box to restore the view of the other wall object.

6. Type **T** to go to the Top viewport. When you see a display warning message, click Yes. If you click No, you'll lose the orientation of the bitmap image to the Top viewport.

You're just about ready to subtract the inside wall shape from the outside shape, but there are a couple little details you'll want to take care of. You need to change the Taper modifier so that it affects the bottom of the extrusion instead of the top. You also need to align the taper to the extrusion.

ALIGNING THE TAPER MODIFIER TO THE OBJECT

The Taper modifier acts on the shape in a direction that is aligned with the World Coordinate System. You really want the Taper modifier to be aligned with the void object, which is slightly skewed in relation to the World Coordinate System. You may recall from earlier chapters that you can adjust the orientation of a modifier by adjusting its gizmo. In the next exercise, you'll rotate the taper gizmo to align it with the inside wall shape.

1. With the Taper modifier still active, click the plus (+) sign next to Taper in the modifier stack list. You should see Gizmo in the expanded list.

2. Click Gizmo, and then click the Select and Rotate tool in the main toolbar.

3. Carefully click and drag the blue, Z axis ring of the Transform gizmo downward, until the rectangular Taper gizmo is aligned with the top edge of the wall, as shown in Figure 4.27.

4. Adjust the gizmo so that its top edge is aligned with the straight segment of the void object, and release the mouse button.

5. Click the Taper gimzo level in the stack again to return to object-level editing.

The taper is now aligned with the extrusion.

You're now ready to subtract the void object from the outer wall object.

1. Click the Select Object tool in the main toolbar. In the Top viewport, select the outer wall object, as shown in Figure 4.28.

TIP   *The rule of thumb with Boolean subtractions is to always select the object that is to remain first. This makes your first object Operand A of the Boolean. The second object you select becomes Operand B and is subtracted by the default setting of (A–B). Note that if you do get it backward you can always reverse the operand order (B–A), but that can lead to some confusion.*

2. Click the Create tab in the Command Panel, and then click the Geometry tool.

3. Click the drop-down list just below the Create buttons and select Compound Objects.

FIGURE 4.27
Click and drag the Z axis to rotate the Taper gizmo.

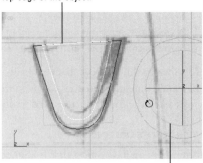

Align Taper gizmo's edge with top edge of the object.

Drag the blue Rotate gizmo down to align the Taper gizmo with the object.

FIGURE 4.28
Selecting the outside wall shape

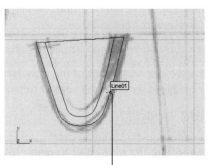

Select the larger outer object.

4. Click the Boolean button, and then click the Pick Operand B button in the Pick Boolean rollout. Make sure Subtraction (A-B) is still selected in the Operation group in the Parameters rollout.

5. Click the void shape. It is subtracted from the outer wall object to form the final shape of the wall. You can see the result in the Perspective viewport.

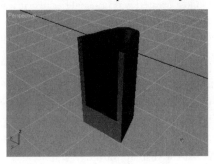

WARNING *If for some reason you don't get the results shown here, it may be because the Subtraction option is not selected under the Operation group in the Parameters rollout. Scroll down the Command Panel and check to make sure that Subtraction (A-B) is selected.*

You've just created part of the Chapel at Ronchamp building. The method shown here is just one of a number of ways you could have used to create the wall. By using this method, you were able to try out some spline-editing tools, and you also got a chance to practice using some other methods you learned in previous chapters.

Now let's move onto another part of the building to examine another way of editing objects.

Editing Meshes

You've been introduced to VIZ objects in the form of the standard primitives, splines, and AEC tools. It also helps to think about VIZ objects in terms of parametric and nonparametric objects. This can be a bit confusing, because virtually all objects in VIZ start out as parametric objects. But, as you'll see, a lot of your work with objects will depart from the parametric level of editing as soon as you begin editing objects in earnest. In fact, you've already seen this with the spline examples in this and the previous chapter.

In your introduction to VIZ objects, you created simple forms and adjusted them through the use of the object's parameters. Parameters are great for establishing the initial dimensions and characteristics of an object. They can also serve as a convenient way to make adjustments to objects as you progress through the design process. But eventually, you'll begin to make changes on a deeper level, bypassing the parameters altogether. At this point, you'll be editing 3D objects as *editable meshes*. Editing 3D objects as editable meshes is similar to the sub-object level editing you've already performed on splines. The main difference is that you have some additional sub-object levels to work with, in the form of faces and edges.

In this section, you'll begin to explore editable meshes by creating the south wall of the chapel. You'll learn how you can convert an extruded spline into an editable mesh, and then you'll proceed to modify the mesh on a sub-object level.

Creating a Tapered Wall

The part of the chapel you just created was unusual because it was a curved wall. Ronchamp contains many curved walls, but they shouldn't pose a problem to you now, because you've had some experience drawing such shapes and extruding them. One wall of the chapel is quite unusual, however. The south wall tapers in two directions, plus it has a curve in it. In the following set of exercises, you'll look at a way to create such a wall in VIZ, and in the process, you'll be introduced to some additional methods for editing sub-objects.

You'll start, as usual, by outlining the plan of the wall. Once again, you'll trace over the imported bitmap sketch using a line. First, set up your view to prepare for tracing.

1. Click the Top viewport to make it active, and then click the Min/Max Toggle tool to enlarge the view. Click Yes at the display warning.

2. Choose Views ➤ Restore Active Top View. Click the Pan tool and pan the view so the south wall is centered in the view. Then use the Zoom Region tool to enlarge the south wall to fill as much of the viewport as possible.

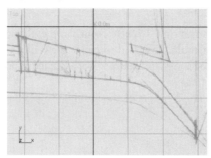

Now you're ready to trace the wall.

1. If it isn't already selected, click the Create tab of the Command Panel and click the Shapes tool.

2. Click Line and draw the line, as shown in Figure 4.29. Pay special attention to the vertices at the curved portion of the wall. You'll want to place three vertices around the curve so that you can later change them into Bèzier vertices.

3. At the last point, click the beginning of the line and close the shape.

4. Click the Modify tab of the Command Panel, expand the Line item in the modifier stack list, and then click Vertex in the expanded list.

FIGURE 4.29

Trace the south wall as shown here. The vertices are shown here for clarity.

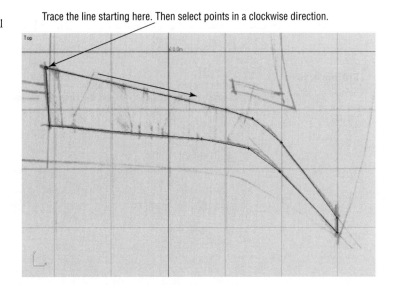

Trace the line starting here. Then select points in a clockwise direction.

5. Click the Select and Move tool in the main toolbar, right-click the vertex shown in Figure 4.30, and select Bèzier from the shortcut menu.

6. Using the tangent handles, adjust the curve of the wall so that it looks similar to Figure 4.30. You'll want the curve of the wall to join the straight portions of the wall in a tangent.

7. Right-click the vertex across the wall from the one you just edited and select Bèzier.

8. Adjust the curve of this vertex so it looks similar to Figure 4.31. Click Vertex in the modifier stack list to exit the vertex sub-object mode when you're finished.

Now it's time to extrude the wall. The wall forms a peak at its eastern-most end, and that peak is approximately 14 meters high. You'll want the wall to be at least 14 meters high so that you have enough material to work with.

1. You're already in the Modify tab of the Command Panel, so open the Modifier List drop-down list and select Extrude. If you're continuing from the last section, the wall will extrude to the last height you entered.

2. In the Parameter rollout, change the Amount input box value to **14**, for 14 meters. Also, make sure that the Segments value is set to 1.

3. Click the Min/Max Toggle tool, right-click the Perspective viewport, and then click the Zoom Extents tool to get a better look at the south wall so far.

4. Click the Arc Rotate Selected tool, and then click and drag the right-most square of the Arc Rotate circle to the left until your view looks similar to Figure 4.32.

5. Click the Min/Max Toggle tool to enlarge the Perspective view.

FIGURE 4.30
Selecting and editing the vertex

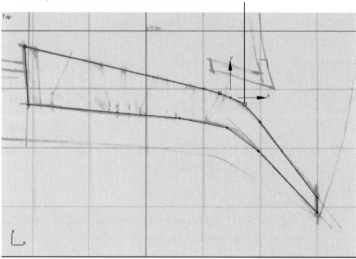

Right-click this vertex and select Bézier.
Then adjust the handles to achieve the curve shown here.

FIGURE 4.31
Editing the second vertex

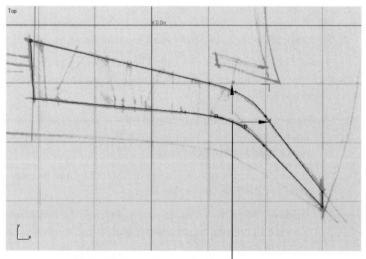

Right-click this vertex and select Bézier.
Then adjust the curve to match the one shown here.

FIGURE 4.32
The Perspective view after rotating with the Arc Rotate Selected tool

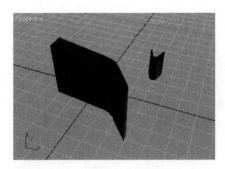

You now have the basic form of the wall, but it tapers vertically. Not only that, but the taper is not uniform across the entire wall. It tapers more at its west end, and it doesn't taper at all at its east end. You won't be able to use the Taper modifier to accomplish this non-uniform taper. Instead, you'll edit the mesh directly by rotating some of the edges.

Converting the Spline to a Mesh

To edit the south wall, you need to convert the extruded spline to an editable mesh to take advantage of the special features of mesh objects. You can then make the appropriate changes at the sub-object level of the mesh to get the volume you want. Start by setting up the view to aid in your editing.

1. Right-click the Perspective label in the upper left corner of the Perspective viewport and select Wireframe.

2. Click the Arc Rotate Selected tool, and then click and drag the square at the top of the Arc Rotate circle downward so your view looks similar to Figure 4.33. You want to get a good view of the top of the wall.

3. Click the Zoom tool, and then click and drag upward in the viewport to enlarge the view of the wall. It should look similar to Figure 4.34.

EDITING THE EDGE OF A MESH

Now you're ready to start editing the wall. You'll convert the object to an editable mesh to gain access to the sub-object tools, and then you'll learn how to use a new selection tool, the Lasso Selection Region tool, to select an edge of the wall for editing.

1. Make sure that the south wall is selected.

2. In the modifier stack list, right-click Extrude, and select Collapse All from the pop-up menu. You'll see a warning message telling you that "This will remove everything in the stack of all selected objects."

3. Click Yes at the warning message. You've just converted your extruded spline into an editable mesh.

FIGURE 4.33
Rotating the view
to see the top of
the wall

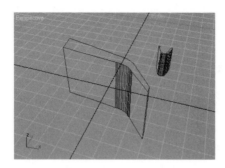

FIGURE 4.34
Enlarging the view
of the top of the
south wall

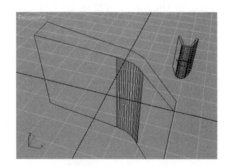

TIP *You can right-click anywhere in the modifier stack list to open a shortcut menu that offers a limited set of conversion options.*

The shortcut menu options you see when you right-click an item in the modifier stack list depend on the item that is currently selected. Usually, this menu will include the Editable Mesh item. Now let's proceed with editing the wall.

1. Expand the Editable Mesh item in the modifier stack list and click Edge. (You can also click the Edge tool in the Selection rollout.)

New!

2. In the main toolbar, click and hold the Rectangular Selection Region tool until its flyout displays and then drag the mouse down to the bottom option, the Lasso Selection Region tool.

You're going to select the top edge of the wall that is closest to you, so you'll need a selection tool that lets you select a free-form area.

3. Click the Crossing Selection tool in the main toolbar so that it changes to the Window Selection tool (the icon changes to a dotted square enclosing a sphere). This causes VIZ to select only objects that fall completely within the selection window.

4. Click the Select Object tool, and then start dragging a selection lasso around the wall, as shown in Figure 4.35.

5. Continue to drag the lasso so that the front, top edge of the wall is completely enclosed by the selection. Release the mouse button and your selection should appear as shown in Figure 4.36.

FIGURE 4.35
Drawing the lasso selection

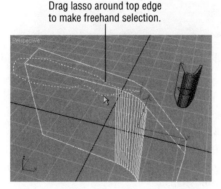

FIGURE 4.36
Top edge selected

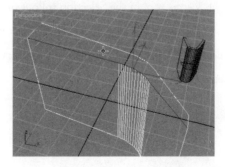

Now that you have the edge selected, you want to rotate it. The best view for this operation is the top view, so the first thing to do is to go to the top view.

1. Click the Min/Max Toggle tool to view all of the viewports, right-click the Top viewport, and then click Min/Max Toggle again to enlarge it.

2. Click the Select and Rotate tool in the main toolbar.

3. Place the cursor on the Z ring of the Rotate gizmo, and then click and drag clockwise until the edge is rotated in such a way that it appears to be parallel to the other edge of the wall. You can look at the coordinate readout and set the angle to –7 (minus seven) degrees.

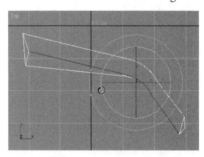

4. Click the Select and Move tool, and then click and drag the edge upward so that the top edges are closer together, as shown in Figure 4.37.

5. Exit the Edge sub-object level and return to the top level.

Moving a Single Mesh Vertex

You've managed to taper the south wall. The right end of the wall is a vertical surface that does not taper, so you need to realign the upper corner to its original location. You can do this by moving the vertex and using the endpoint snaps.

1. Switch back to the Top view and select the curved wall again. Select Vertex from the modifier stack list (or click the Vertex tool in the Selection rollout of the Command Panel).

2. Click the vertex at the corner of the top of the wall to select it, as shown in Figure 4.38.

   Before you move the vertex, set endpoint snaps, so you can get a perfect alignment.

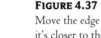

3. Right-click the Snap Toggle button in the main toolbar.

FIGURE 4.37

Move the edge so it's closer to the top edge of the wall and parallel to it.

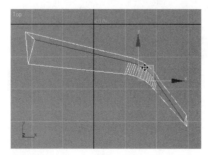

FIGURE 4.38
Select the corner of
the top of the wall.

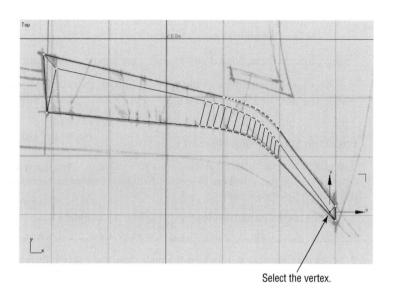

Select the vertex.

4. In the Grid and Snap Settings window, click the Clear All button, and then click Endpoint. Close the Grid and Snap Settings window.

5. Click and hold the Snap Toggle tool to expose its flyout. Select the 2.5D Snap Toggle tool. (The 2.5 Snap Toggle tool allows you to select any vertex in 3D space while restricting the motion to a 2D plane.)

6. Click the Select and Move tool. Then place the cursor on the selected vertex so that the Endpoint Snap cursor displays.

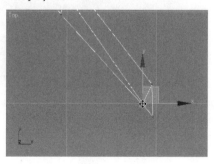

7. Click and drag the cursor to the vertex shown in Figure 4.39. When the Endpoint Snap cursor displays, release the mouse button.

8. Click the Min/Max Toggle tool to get a look at the results in the Perspective viewport.

Now that you have the east end of the wall back to its original configuration, you can move onto editing the interior side of the wall.

CREATING SPLINES FROM MESHES

It is possible to create a flat 2D spline from a 3D mesh object. You can create a spline where a section plane intersects the 3D form. This can be useful when you are trying to create section drawings of complex forms like in the following example.

1. Switch to the Perspective view by typing **P** on the keyboard.

2. Isolate the curved wall you have been working on by selecting Isolate selection from the quad menu.

3. Click the Create tab and click the Shapes button. Make sure Splines in shown in the drop-down list and then click the Section tool.

4. Drag out a section plane on the home grid at the base of the curved wall. It doesn't matter how large you make this plane because it is only a placeholder representing the section cut you are making through the curved wall.

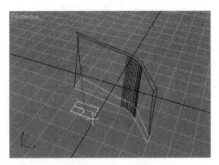

Continued on next page

CREATING SPLINES FROM MESHES *(continued)*

5. Move the section plane upward in the Z direction.

As you move the section plane, notice there is a yellow highlight that shows where the section plane cuts through the mesh. Observe how the yellow highlighting changes shape as the section plane moves because the curved wall's cross section changes with height.

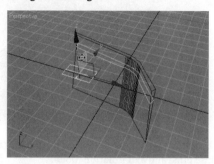

1. Try rotating the section plane. See how the highlighting always represents the intersection of the section plane with the mesh object.

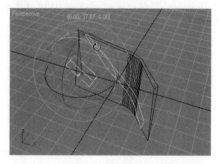

2. Still with the section plane selected, switch to the Modify tab of the Command Panel. Click the Create Shape button.

3. Give a name to the new spline you are creating in the Name Section Shape dialog box.

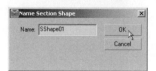

Continued on next page

CREATING SPLINES FROM MESHES *(continued)*

4. Delete the section object. Notice that there is still something intersecting the mesh—this is the new spline you created from the mesh.

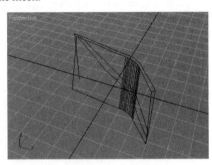

5. Select the object that is intersecting the mesh. It is an Editable Spline as seen in the Modify panel. Finally, delete this spline and exit isolation mode.

You have seen how you can use the Section tool to highlight the relationship between your 3D mesh object and a plane. After positioning and orienting the section plane, you created a spline crystallizing this intersecting relationship. This procedure can be useful when you go to generate any number of splines from a mesh.

FIGURE 4.39

Moving the vertex

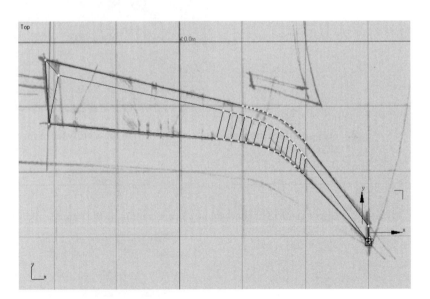

USING THE SNAP TOGGLE OPTIONS

In the previous exercise, you were able to move a vertex to a point exactly above another vertex by using endpoint snaps in conjunction with the 2.5D Snap Toggle tool. You might have thought the two vertices would merge into one point, and in fact, that is what would have happened if you used the 3D Snap Toggle tool. Instead, the vertex you moved was constrained to its Z axis location, and it remained above the vertex you snapped to.

The 2.5D Snap Toggle tool automatically constrains the movement of objects to the plane of the current view, plus it allows you to select any vertex on the screen when snaps are turned on. It's called 2.5D Snap because you can select any vertex in 3D space, while restricting the motion to a 2D plane. In the previous exercise, you were moving the vertex in the Top viewport, so the vertex's movement was restrained to the plane of the top view. Had you been in the left or front view, the movement of the vertex would have been restrained in the plane defined by those views.

You also saw the 2D Snap Toggle option in the Snap Toggle flyout. This option not only restrains motion to the view plane, but it also restricts your selection of vertexes to those on the currently active working grid, which is usually the world grid, unless you have created a user grid.

FLATTENING A SURFACE

The interior side of the wall also tapers inward toward the top, but that taper occurs only along the straight portion of the wall, starting from the curve and progressing to the left. In this situation, you need to move only the vertex at the end of the wall corner.

1. Click in the Left viewport, and then click the Zoom Extents tool. You'll use this view to help adjust the taper of the wall.

2. Right-click in the Perspective view, and then use the Select Object tool to select the two vertices on the top left corner of the wall. You can use the Rectangular Selection Region setting from the main toolbar to select the vertices with a rectangular window, as shown in Figure 4.40.

FIGURE 4.40

Selecting the corner vertex

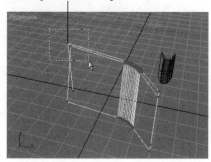

Select these two vertices with a rectangular selection region.

3. Right-click the Left viewport and turn off Snap.

4. With the Select and Move tool selected, click and drag the green X axis to the right. Adjust the wall so that is looks similar to Figure 4.41.

Now you have both sides of the wall tapering inward. But there's one problem with the wall: the west end to the left of the wall is twisted and not flat because of all of the changes you've made to the vertices. You can quickly flatten that end of the wall using the View Align tool.

1. Click the Select Object tool. In the Top viewport, click and drag a selection region so that all of the vertices of the left end of the wall are selected, as shown in Figure 4.42.

2. Right-click in the Left viewport to make it active.

FIGURE 4.41
In the Left viewport, move the vertices so the wall looks like this.

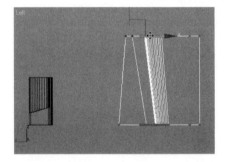

FIGURE 4.42
Selecting the vertices of the left side of the wall

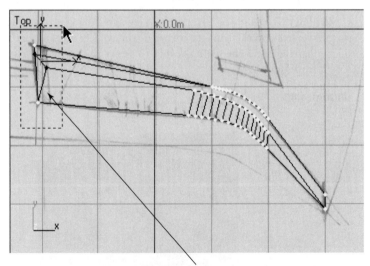

Select all of the vertices at this end of the wall.

3. Scroll down the Command Panel until you see the View Align button toward the bottom of the Edit Geometry rollout, and then click it.

Alternatively, you can right-click in the Left viewport and select View Align from the tools 1 quad of the shortcut quad menu.

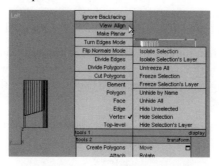

The selected vertices are aligned to the left viewport, forming a flat plane.

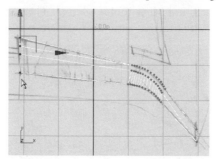

The View Align tool flattened the left side of the wall so that it became a plane parallel to the active viewport (the Left viewport in this case).

TIP   You might have noticed a few other buttons in the group with the View Align button. Grid Align aligns the points to the current active user grid or to the nearest grid line in the world grid. Make Planar causes all of the selected points to be coplanar, taking the average location of all of the points to determine the plane. Collapse causes all of the selected points to converge into a single point.

Tapering the Top of the Wall

To finish off the wall, you need to slope the top of the wall downward from right to left. This will be a uniform slope, so you can use the Taper modifier for the operation.

1. Right-click the Front viewport, and then click the Zoom Extents tool to get a better view of the wall.

2. Click the Vertex button in the Selection rollout to deactivate it (or click Vertex in the modifier stack list).

3. Open the Modifier List drop-down list and select Taper. (You may need to scroll toward the bottom of the list to find it.)

4. In the Parameters rollout, set the Amount input box value to **0.09**. This is roughly equivalent to 8 degrees.

5. In the Taper Axis group of the Parameters rollout, click the X Primary radio button and the Z Effect radio button. This causes the taper to occur only in the X axis.

The Taper occurs from roughly the midpoint of the wall, which causes the left side to drop and the right side to rise, as with a balance scale. But you want to maintain the height of the wall at its highest point instead of having it rise. You can adjust the center of the taper by moving the Transform gizmo.

1. Expand Taper in the modifier stack list and select Center.

2. Make sure the Select and Move tool is selected. Then, in the Front viewport, click and drag the red X axis arrow to the right until the Y axis arrow is aligned with the right edge of the wall.

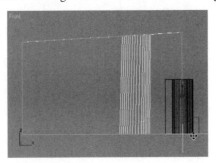

3. Exit the Center sub-modifier level.

Notice that the wall drops down in height. If you play with the Amount parameter spinner, you'll see that the top of the wall now changes its taper angle in relation to the right end of the wall. Make sure that you set the Amount value back to 0.09 when you're finished experimenting.

The wall is also tapered to the north, so you want to apply the Taper modifier again.

1. Select Taper from the Modifier List drop-down list.

2. In the Parameters rollout, set the Taper Amount input box value to **–0.1** (minus zero point one). This is equivalent to roughly 10 degrees.

3. In the Taper Axis group of the Parameters rollout, click the Y Primary radio button and the Z Effect radio button. This causes the taper to occur only in the Y axis.

USING THE EDIT MESH MODIFIER

In the beginning of this section, you converted an extruded spline into an editable mesh. You could have used the Edit Mesh modifier to gain access to the same mesh sub-object level you used to edit the south wall. The advantage to using the modifier is that you can return to the Spline level in the modifier stack to make changes at that level. The disadvantage is that your model uses more memory to store the Edit Mesh modifier. The Edit Mesh modifier also inserts more complexity into the object data flow, which can cause unpredictable results as your model becomes more complicated.

The Edit Mesh modifier is a great option while you're in the process of creating an object and you aren't quite sure you want to commit to a particular set of changes. It allows you to return to other levels of the modifier stack and experiment. It also helps to maintain the parametric characteristics of objects so that you have more flexibility in shaping an object. But once you've created an object you're satisfied with, it's a good idea to convert objects to editable meshes for the sake of data flow simplicity and efficient memory use.

You now have an editable mesh to which you've applied two Taper modifiers. You could convert the wall to an editable mesh again, thereby combining the effects of the Taper modifiers into a single editable mesh. But later, you'll need to make further adjustments to the taper of the wall to fit the roof, so for now, keep the modifiers in place.

Now you've completed the main shape of the south wall. Next to the roof, the south wall is the most complex part of the building, so it took quite a bit of effort to construct. In the next set of exercises, you'll create the towers of the chapel. These towers are a bit easier to build, but they're also a bit tricky.

Using Instance Clones to Create Symmetric Forms

The towers of Ronchamp actually enclose smaller mini altars apart from the main altar at the east end of the building. The towers' forms reflect the shape of a nun's hat. To create the towers, you'll create half of the tower plan, then mirror that half to complete the rest of the plan. This will ensure that the walls are symmetrical, and it will also give you the parts you need to construct the top of the tower.

Adding a User Grid to Aid Tracing

First, set up the top view to trace the plan of the tower. The tower is slightly skewed from the axis of the main floor, so adding a user grid will help you create it.

1. Click the Top viewport to make it active, and then click the Min/Max Toggle tool to enlarge it.

2. Click the Pan tool and pan the view so that the large tower plan is centered in the viewport, as shown in Figure 4.43.

3. Click the Zoom Region tool and place the zoom region around the tower plan, as shown in Figure 4.43.

4. Click the Create tab in the Command Panel, and then click the Helpers button.

5. Click Grid, and then click and drag a grid across the viewport, starting in the lower left corner of the viewport, as shown in Figure 4.44. As you're aligning the grid, place its vertical center-line at the center of the plan, as indicated in Figure 4.44.

6. The grid is a bit too dense. To adjust its spacing, go to the Spacing group in the Parameters rollout and change the Grid value to **2**, for 2 meters.

7. To align the grid with the tower, click the Select and Rotate tool in the main toolbar, and then carefully click and drag the blue Z axis ring clockwise so that it is aligned with the lines indicating the top edge of the tower, as shown in Figure 4.45. The angle is very slight, so you just need to rotate the grid slightly.

Building the Tower Walls

Now you're ready to lay out the tower. Start by tracing the left side of the tower plan.

1. Click the Shapes button in the Create tab of the Command Panel, and then click the Line tool in the Object Type rollout.

2. Draw the lines shown in Figure 4.46, starting from the upper left corner of the plan. Finish the line at the centerline of the grid. Right-click when you're finished drawing the lines.

FIGURE 4.43

Centering the tower plan and selecting the zoom region

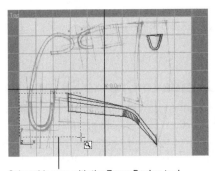

Select this area with the Zoom Region tool.

FIGURE 4.44

Adding a grid to the viewport

Place the grid so it is centered on this point.

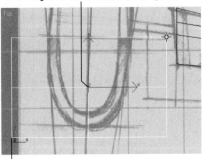

Drag the grid helper starting from here.

3. Click the Modify tab in the Command Panel and click the Vertex tool in the Selection rollout (or expand the Line item in the modifier stack list and select Vertex).

4. Right-click the last vertex in the lower half of the viewport and select Bèzier from the shortcut quad menu.

5. Click the Select and Move tool and adjust the Bèzier handle of the selected vertex to the location shown in Figure 4.47.

NOTE   *If you find that you cannot move the Bèzier handle, make sure the Constraints toolbar shows the Restrict to XY Plane tool selected. Avoid clicking the Transform gizmo.*

6. Right-click the middle vertex, choose Bèzier from the shortcut menu, and adjust the handles so that the line looks similar to Figure 4.48.

7. To add thickness to the wall, click the Spline tool in the Selection rollout and scroll down the Command Panel to find the Outline option.

FIGURE 4.45
Aligning the grid with the tower plan

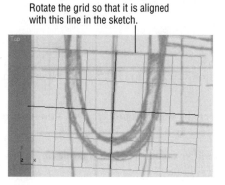

FIGURE 4.46
Drawing the left half of the tower plan

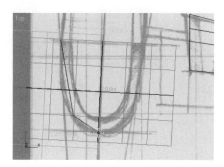

FIGURE 4.47
Moving the vertex handle of the end of the line

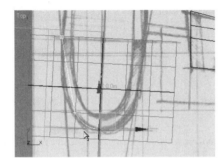

FIGURE 4.48
Adjusting the middle vertex

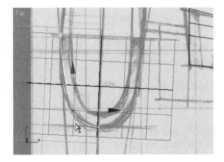

8. Click the Outline input box and enter **0.5↵**. The line becomes a wall with a thickness of 0.5 meter.

The next step is to mirror the wall you just created. You want to use the Y axis of the user grid you set up earlier as the mirror axis.

1. Click Line in the modifier stack list to exit the sub-object level. (Alternatively, click the Spline tool in the Selection rollout.)

2. In the main toolbar, click the Reference Coordinate System drop-down list to view its options.

3. Select Grid from the list. Notice that the Transform gizmo rotates slightly to match the user grid orientation.

4. Click the Mirror Selected Objects tool in the main toolbar.

5. In the Mirror: Grid Coordinates dialog box, make sure that the X radio button in the Mirror Axis group is selected.

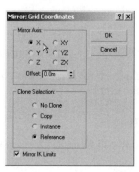

6. Click the Reference radio button in the Clone Selection group. Then click OK. You see a mirrored copy of the wall you just drew.

7. Click the Select and Move tool and click the Snap Toggle button. In the main toolbar, Endpoint snaps are still set from the last time you set the snap settings.

8. Using the endpoint snaps, click and drag the bottom endpoint of the wall half you just created to the bottom endpoint of the original wall, so that they meet end to end, as shown in Figure 4.49.

FIGURE 4.49
Moving the second half of the wall into place

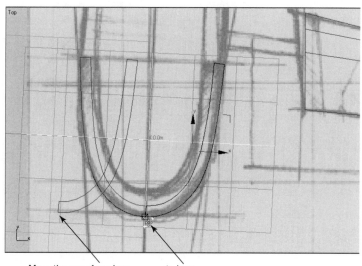

Move the copy from here ...   to here.

The plan of the tower is a bit too wide at the opening. You can adjust one side of the plan, and because the two halves are references, adjustments you make to one side will affect the other side.

1. Turn off the Snap Toggle tool. Then select the left half of the tower plan.

2. Click Vertex in the Selection rollout of the Command Panel. Then use the Rectangular Selection Region setting to select the two wall corner vertices at the top of wall, as shown in Figure 4.50.

3. Make sure Grid is selected from the Reference Coordinate System drop-down list.

4. Click the Select and Move tool. Click and drag the red arrow at the end of the X axis handle of the Transform gizmo to the left a slight amount so that the walls look similar to Figure 4.51.

Because they are reference clones, both ends of the wall move in unison toward the centerline of the tower plan.

Adding the Vaulted Ceiling

You need another copy of the wall half to use later to cap the tower. This copy will be extruded using the Lathe modifier to form the vaulted ceiling of the tower.

1. Click the Vertex button in the Selection rollout to deactivate it. Then, using the Select and Move tool, Shift+click and drag the right half of the tower plan to the right.

FIGURE 4.50
Select these two vertices.

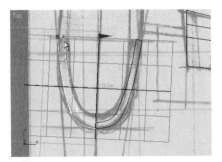

FIGURE 4.51
Moving the ends of the tower wall inward

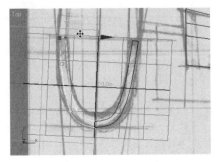

2. In the Clone Options dialog box, click Copy. Then enter the name **Vault** into the Name input box and click OK.

Now you're ready to extrude the plan into a tower. The overall height of the tower is 22 meters. Subtract 2 meters for the vaulted ceiling, for a height of 20 meters for the straight portion of the tower.

1. Click the Min/Max Toggle tool.

2. Click the Select Object tool and click the left half of the tower plan.

3. In the Command Panel, select Extrude from the Modifier List drop-down list.

4. In the Parameters rollout, change the Amount input box value to **20m**.

5. Right-click the Perspective viewport and click the Zoom Extents tool to get a better view of your model.

To finish off the basic shape of the tower, you need the vaulted ceiling.

1. In the Top viewport, select the right-most copy of the tower plan outline.

2. In the Command Panel, select Lathe from the Modifier List drop-down list.

3. In the Parameters rollout, change the Degrees value to **180**. The ceiling won't look quite right, but in the next step, you'll fix things.

4. Click the plus (+) sign next to Lathe in the modifier stack list and select Axis.

5. Use the Select and Move tool to click and drag the red X axis arrow to the left until the shape of the vault appears to be about the same width as the extruded tower plan, as shown in Figure 4.52.

FIGURE 4.52
Using the Lathe modifier to form the ceiling

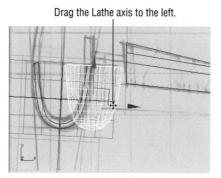

Drag the Lathe axis to the left.

Next, you'll move the vaulted ceiling into position and adjust its width to fit exactly over the vertical walls of the tower. You don't want the next operation to operate on a sub-object level, so begin by turning off this option.

1. Click Lathe in the modifier stack list to exit the sub-object level.

2. Right-click the Select and Move tool to open the Move Transform Type-In dialog box.

3. In the Absolute: World group, change the Z input box to **20** to raise the vault to 20 meters. Then close the dialog box.

The vaulted ceiling is in its proper Z axis location. Now you need to place the ceiling exactly over the vertical wall.

1. Right-click the Top viewport and click the Min/Max Toggle tool to enlarge it. This will help you move the ceiling more accurately.

2. Click the Snap Toggle tool to activate it, and then place the cursor on the upper left corner of the vaulted ceiling, as shown in Figure 4.53.

3. When you see the Endpoint Snap cursor, click and drag the mouse to the upper left corner of the wall, as shown in Figure 4.53.

   Next, adjust the ceiling width so that it fits precisely over the vertical wall.

4. Turn off the Snap Toggle tool.

5. Click the Axis level in the modifier stack list. Then click and drag the red X axis arrow to adjust the width of the vault so that it fits exactly over the wall on the left side of the vault, as shown in Figure 4.54.

6. Click the Min/Max Toggle tool to view the other viewports.

7. Delete the user grid you created earlier. You won't need it anymore.

FIGURE 4.53

Moving the vaulted ceiling into place above the vertical wall

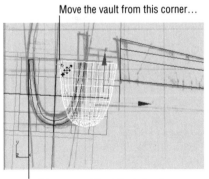

Move the vault from this corner…

…to this corner of the extruded walls.

Creating the Smaller Towers

You have completed one tower. There are two smaller towers of a similar configuration. You can make a copy of the large tower you just created, and then edit the copy to create the smaller tower. First, copy the tower and move the copy into its new location at the north side of the building.

1. Click the Top viewport and click the Min/Max Toggle tool to enlarge it.

2. Click the Zoom Extents tool to get an overall view of the plan so far.

3. Click the Select Object tool and make sure the Rectangular Selection Region tool is selected on the main toolbar.

4. Click and drag a rectangular window around the tower you just created, as shown in Figure 4.55. This will select all three components of the tower: the two wall halves and the ceiling.

5. Click the Select and Move tool, then Shift+click and drag the tower to the location of the smaller tower, as shown in Figure 4.56.

6. In the Clone Options dialog box, click Copy and click OK.

FIGURE 4.54

Adjusting the width of the vaulted ceiling to fit the wall

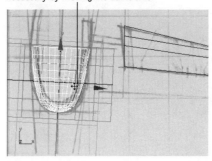

Adjust the width of the vault if necessary by moving the Lathe axis.

FIGURE 4.55

A rectangular window around tower

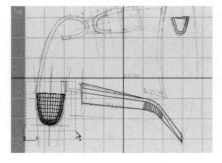

The copy is a bit too large, and it's oriented in the wrong direction. You need to rotate the tower copy, and then scale it down.

1. Pan the view so that the tower copy is centered in the viewport, and use the Region Zoom tool to enlarge the view of the tower, as shown in Figure 4.57.

2. Click the Rotate tool, and then click and drag the blue Z axis ring clockwise until the tower is aligned with the image of the smaller tower in the imported bitmap sketch. You can use the centerline in the sketch to help you align the tower.

3. Use the Select and Move tool to center the tower over the sketch.

4. Click the Scale tool and click and drag the tower downward until it is about the same width as the sketch of the smaller tower, as shown in Figure 4.58.

5. Recenter the tower using the Select and Move tool. Use the Select and Scale tool to refine the size of the tower until it fits over the sketch, similar to Figure 4.58.

You may also need to play with the rotation of the tower to get the tower in the correct orientation. You don't need to be too fussy about the tower, however. Just use this as an opportunity to get used to VIZ's Move, Scale, and Rotate tools.

FIGURE 4.56
Moving the tower copy to a new location

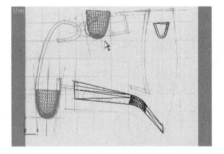

FIGURE 4.57
Centering the tower copy in the viewport and selecting a region to enlarge

Use the Region Zoom tool to enlarge this area.

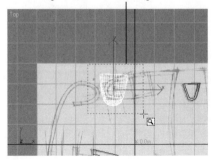

When you scaled the copy of the tower, VIZ scaled it down in all directions. This causes the tower copy to appear to be floating in space. It needs to be brought back down to the ground level.

1. Click the Min/Max Toggle tool, and then right-click in the Front viewport.

2. Make sure the entire tower copy is selected, and then use the Select and Move tool to move the tower downward so that its base rests on the plane of the World Coordinate System, as shown in Figure 4.59.

Editing the Tower Walls

You have the tower in the location and orientation you like. Now you need to adjust the wall thickness. Because you scaled the tower down in size, the thickness of the walls was also scaled down. You need to set them to the same thickness as the other walls. Here's where VIZ's ability to edit at sub-object levels really helps.

1. Right-click the Top viewport and click the Min/Max Toggle tool to enlarge the viewport.

2. Click the Select Object tool, and then click the tower ceiling. You'll be able to tell if you've selected the ceiling by the name Vault01 just below the Modify tab label.

FIGURE 4.58
Fine-tune the size and location of the tower over the sketch so that it looks similar to this figure.

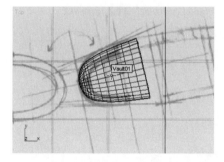

FIGURE 4.59
Move the tower down to ground level.

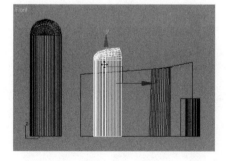

3. Click the Display tab of the Command Panel. Then click Hide Selected. You want to temporarily turn off the ceiling vault so you can see the walls more clearly.

4. Click the tower wall half, as shown in Figure 4.60.

5. In the Modify tab of the Command Panel, select Line in the modifier stack list, and then select Segment in the expanded list.

6. Click the line segment of the wall shown in Figure 4.61, and then press the Delete key to delete the inner side of the wall.

7. Continue to delete the other three segments, as shown in Figure 4.61. Do not delete any of the segments that represent the outside edge of the wall.

You may notice that, as you delete the line segments, they are also deleted in the cloned half of the wall.

FIGURE 4.60
Select the tower wall.

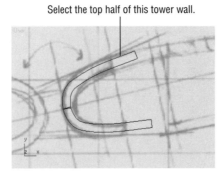

Select the top half of this tower wall.

FIGURE 4.61
Deleting the line
segments of the
tower wall

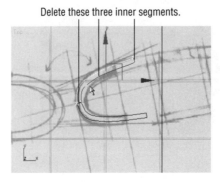

Delete these three inner segments.

Now you need to reconstruct the inside of the tower wall.

1. Select Spline from the modifier stack list.

2. Click the remaining outline of the wall, as shown in Figure 4.62.

3. Scroll down the Command Panel to the Outline button, then enter **0.66**↵ in the Outline input box. The outline of the wall appears in both halves of the tower wall.

Although you edited only one half of the tower wall, the changes are reflected in the other half and in the vaulted ceiling. This shows one of the big advantages of careful use of instance and reference clones. The cloning occurred at the spline level, so changes to the spline affect the reference clone.

You also saw that you can edit the spline without affecting the Extrude modifier that you applied to the spline higher up in the stack. Here is an example that shows when it's appropriate not to immediately convert an object into an editable mesh as you did with the south wall. You were able to make changes to the tower wall thickness, while still maintaining the overall shape of the tower. Later, when you're satisfied with the tower's general shape, you can convert it to an editable mesh.

The walls are now at the appropriate thickness. You need to change the ceiling in the same way.

1. Select Extrude from the Modifier List stack list.

2. Click the Display tab at the top of the Command Panel, and then click Unhide All to turn on the ceiling vault.

3. Use the Select Object tool to select the ceiling. The Vault01 name should appear under the Display label of the Command Panel, letting you know that the ceiling is indeed selected.

4. Click the Modify tab in the Command Panel, and if it isn't already expanded, expand the Line item in the modifier stack list. Then select Segment.

5. Delete the line segments on the inside of the ceiling outline, as shown in Figure 4.63.

FIGURE 4.62
Selecting the remaining outline of the wall

Select the remaining wall spline.

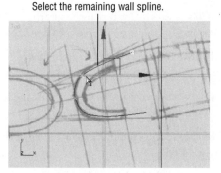

FIGURE 4.63
Deleting the inside
lines of the ceiling

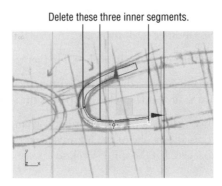

Delete these three inner segments.

6. Click the Spline tool in the Selection rollout.

7. Scroll down the Command Panel to the Outline button and set the Outline value to **0.66** to match the walls. (Although the original tower walls were 0.5 meter thick, you need to set the scaled-down cloned walls to 0.66 meter because of the way VIZ works with parametric objects.)

8. Select Lathe from the modifier stack list. The lathe portion of the ceiling is restored. Now the second tower is complete.

Once again, you were able to edit a spline without affecting the modifier that is applied to the spline higher in the stack.

You have one more tower to create. This one will be easy, because it's a mirror of the smaller tower you just created.

1. Use the Select Object tool and the Rectangular Selection Region tool to select all of the tower you just created.

2. Click the Mirror Selected Objects tool in the main toolbar.

3. In the Mirror: Screen Coordinates dialog box, make sure the X radio button is selected in the Mirror Axis group and the Instance option is selected in the Clone Selection group. Then click OK.

4. Click the Select and Move tool, and then move the tower copy to the left to the location of the second smaller tower, as shown in Figure 4.64.

5. Click the Pan tool and pan your view to the right so that the second tower appears in the center of the screen, as shown in Figure 4.65.

6. Use the Select and Rotate tool to rotate the new tower so that it is oriented in a way similar to that shown in Figure 4.65.

7. To see your results so far, click the Min/Max Toggle tool.

The smaller towers could use a little more work to refine their forms, but for now, you have the general form of the towers in place.

FIGURE 4.64
Moving the second smaller tower into place

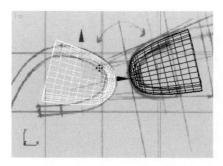

FIGURE 4.65
The final location of the second smaller tower

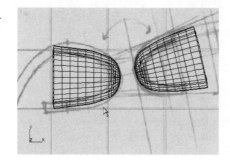

Drawing the Remaining Walls

There are still a few other walls that need to be added to the model, as well as the roof. As a review of some of the earlier skills you've learned, go ahead and add the other walls, starting with the west wall on the left side of the floor plan.

1. Click the Min/Max Toggle tool to enlarge the top view again. Then click the Zoom Extents tool to view the entire top view.

2. Use the Region Zoom tool to zoom into the area shown in Figure 4.66.

3. In the Create tab of the Command Panel, click the Shapes button if it isn't already selected, and then draw the line shown in Figure 4.66.

4. Click the Modify tab of the Command Panel, and then click the Vertex button in the Selection rollout.

5. Select all the vertices and then right-click to open the quad menu. Convert all of the points on the line to Bèzier curves. Adjust the tangent handles to match as closely as possible the curve shown in Figure 4.67.

FIGURE 4.66
Draw the west wall as shown here. The vertices are marked for clarity.

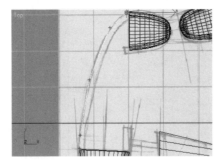

FIGURE 4.67
Match the curve shown here.

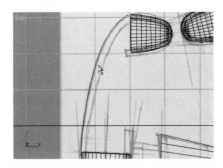

6. In the Modify tab, click the Spline tool in the Selection rollout. Then scroll down the panel to the Outline input box and enter **0.5**↵. The west wall will convert to a thick wall.

7. Scroll up to the top of the Command Panel and select Extrude from the Modifier List drop-down list.

8. In the Amount input box of the Parameters rollout, enter **9.5**↵.

The west wall will need some editing later. For now, continue with the addition of the north wall.

1. Choose Views ➢ Undo View Change, then zoom into the area shown in Figure 4.68.

2. Draw the line shown in Figure 4.68 and convert the vertex indicated in figure to a Bèzier curve. Adjust the Bèzier handles so the line follows the curve of the sketch. By now, this should be a familiar process.

3. Click the Spline tool in the Selection rollout and scroll down to the Outline button to set the wall outline to **0.5** meter. If your wall outline appears on the wrong side of the line, click the Undo tool and reenter the Outline value as **−0.5** (minus zero point five). (Or you can click the Reverse button and reenter the **0.5** Outline value.)

4. Scroll up to the top of the Command Panel and select Extrude from the modifier stack list. VIZ uses the last value you entered for the Extrude amount, so the wall automatically extrudes to 9.5 meters.

OBJECT DATA FLOW, SCALED PARAMETRIC OBJECTS, AND EDITABLE MESHES

You may have noticed that when you edited the wall thickness for the cloned tower, you needed to use an outline value that was greater than the actual thickness of the typical walls of the chapel. The original tower wall had a thickness of 0.5 meter, yet, on a sub-object level, you needed to make the new tower walls 0.66 meter to make them the same width as the other walls. This is because when you scale an object, the dimensional parameters of the original spline from which the walls were extruded are not affected.

When you cloned the tower, then scaled down the clone, the width of the cloned walls remained at their original 0.5 meter at a sub-object level, even though the walls are thinner than before relative to the rest of the model. To see this more clearly, try creating a 24-inch cube. Scale the cube down to about half its size, then check its parameters in the Modify tab. You'll see that the parameters still show that it is a 24-inch cube, even though you know it is half its original size. This can cause a good deal of confusion.

The reason for this seemingly odd behavior becomes clearer when you consider the object data flow in VIZ. You may recall that VIZ evaluates the data associated with an object in a particular order before the object is displayed. The order of that data evaluation is master object, modifiers, transforms, and properties. The object's parameters fall under master object, which is the first item in the object data flow. Transforms are third in the evaluation order. Transforms affect the way the master object is displayed, but they have no effect on the master object's internal parameters or other data at its sub-object level. The net result of this is that when parametric objects are scaled up or down in size, their parameters remain at their original values before being scaled, even though the object itself appears larger or smaller than its original size.

Another way of saying all this is that the object really exists in its own space, called object space (*space* means a 3D Cartesian coordinate system with an origin and a grid). Objects are defined, sculpted, and modified in object space. Objects can be transformed in object space using the XForm modifier. Moving, rotating, and scaling (in other words, transforming) an object actually occurs in world space and is applied later in the object data flow. (Objects can be transformed in world space to align with object space by using the Local Reference Coordinate System.)

Another way to look at it is to consider the master object as having internal data that include their own unit of measure and coordinate system, called object space. These internal data are unaffected by modifiers, transforms, and properties. The modifiers, transforms, and properties you apply to an object really only affect the object's appearance in the VIZ viewport.

This all changes when you convert an object to an editable mesh. In terms of VIZ data, an editable mesh is a more fundamental way of representing the object on a mathematical level, even though its appearance is identical to that of the original object from which it was derived. Once you convert an object to an editable mesh, the editable mesh becomes the master object in the data flow. This new master object then inherits the properties and structure of the original object, while the modifiers are collapsed into the original master object. You can then apply more modifiers and transforms to this new master object, and the process goes on.

Finally, add the east wall to the model.

1. Choose View ➤ Undo View Change or type Shift+Z on the keyboard to return to the overall view of the plan, and then zoom into the area shown in Figure 4.69.

2. Draw the line shown in Figure 4.69.

3. Convert the vertices shown in Figure 4.70 into Bèzier curves and adjust the tangent handles to match the curve of the sketch.

4. Use the Outline option to create an outline that is 0.5 meter wide.

5. Extrude the east wall to a height of 11 meters.

6. Click the Min/Max Toggle tool to view all of the viewports.

7. Save your work as `Ronchamp01.max`.

You've created most of the major structure of the chapel. If you're familiar with the Chapel at Ronchamp, you'll see that there are a few areas where the model doesn't quite match the real building, but in general, you do get the overall flavor of the design. Refining the details will come later. There's also the roof to be created, which you'll work on in the next chapter. For a view of the chapel so far, see Figure 4.71.

FIGURE 4.68

Drawing the north wall

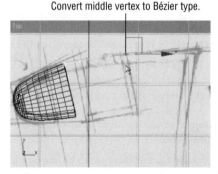

FIGURE 4.69

Drawing the east wall

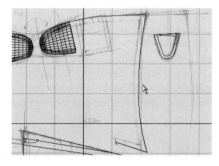

FIGURE 4.70
Convert these
vertices into curves.

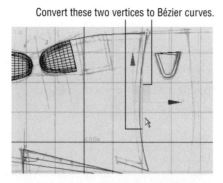

Convert these two vertices to Bézier curves.

FIGURE 4.71
A view of the
chapel so far

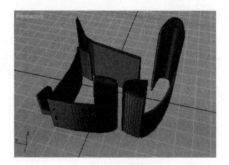

Attaching Objects to a Mesh

As you have been modeling the Chapel at Ronchamp, you have been creating a series of objects. Sometimes, and particularly in more complicated projects where you anticipate creating hundreds of objects, it can be helpful to attach multiple objects to a mesh. By aggregating objects together by attachment, you reduce the total number of objects in the scene. It often makes sense to attach the objects that logically belong together to a mesh object for simplified organization of your scene, but it is not strictly necessary. You will learn how to attach objects to a mesh next.

1. Select the east wall, which is the last object you made.

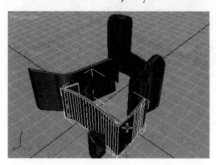

2. In order to attach other objects to this one, you'll have to first either convert this object to an editable mesh, or use the Edit Mesh modifier. Apply the Edit Mesh modifier to this wall.

3. Click the Attach button in the Edit Geometry rollout.

4. Click each one of the three adjacent tower objects to attach them to the east wall, as seen in Figure 4.72. These objects should be named Line05, Line06, and Vault01.

5. Click the Attach button again to turn it off.

6. Type **H** on the keyboard to open the Select Objects dialog box. Notice that the objects you attached no longer appear in the list. Instead the attached no longer appear as objects because they have become part of the east wall (currently named Line11).

7. Now that you have seen how attachment works, try the opposite—detaching. Enter the Element sub-object level of the east wall Edit Mesh modifier.

8. Select the element that was formerly known as Vault01 within the east wall object as seen in Figure 4.73.

FIGURE 4.72
Attaching the adjacent tower to the east wall

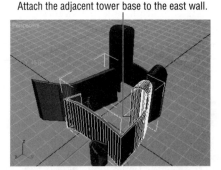

Attach the adjacent tower base to the east wall.

9. Click the Detach button in the Edit Geometry rollout. The Detach dialog box appears to prompt you for the name of this new object. Type in **Vault01** and click OK.

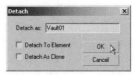

WARNING   *Once you detach an object from a mesh, it too becomes an editable mesh. The modifiers you may have used before the attachment occurred are lost. Because of this, it is important not to attach objects to a mesh until you are done editing their stacks.*

10. Exit the Element sub-object level. Observe how the Vault is no longer part of the bounding box of the east wall object as seen in Figure 4.74. It has become its own "object" once again.

You have seen how you can organize a complex scene by attaching multiple objects to a single mesh object. You have also learned how to detach elements from a mesh, returning them to their former object-status. The two opposites of attaching and detaching to and from meshes are a powerful optional way to organize your scenes.

FIGURE 4.73
Selecting elements within a mesh

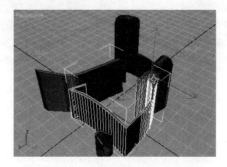

FIGURE 4.74
After detaching an element from the mesh

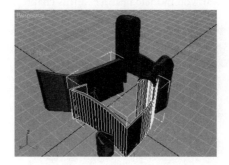

TIP *You may choose to organize your scene using mesh attachment as an alternative to using groups. Objects that are attached to a mesh lose the modifiers in their stacks and require the use of more complicated Multi/Sub-Object materials, which you will learn about in Chapter 7. However, mesh elements require much less memory compared to grouped objects.*

Smoothing Meshes

You learned in Chapter 2 that many of the primitive objects have a Smooth parameter. *Smoothing* is an inherent quality of mesh objects.

All meshes are composed of vertices that are themselves connected by straight lines called edges. Sets of edges define surfaces called faces or polygons (depending on whether they are three-sided or multisided). Constellations of polygons form elements as you learned before.

The relatively simple surfaces set up by the sub-objects literally define a faceted overall surface. Smoothing is an illusion that gives the appearance of a continuously curved surface over a discrete set of vertices, edges, faces, and so on.

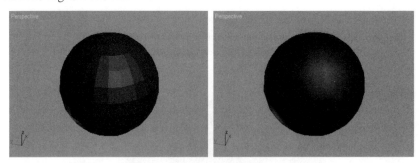

Each mesh object stores smoothing information that can be edited. You will learn two different ways to adjust smoothing—both within a mesh and by using the Smooth modifier.

Smoothing within a Mesh

You can adjust smoothing in a sub-object level within a mesh object. The smoothing data is part of the mesh itself. You will learn how to convert an object to an editable mesh and adjust its smoothing next.

1. Select the Tapered wall you modeled earlier in this chapter.

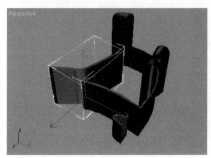

2. Right-click in the stack and the context menu appears. Choose Collapse All and the object becomes an editable mesh. A warning message will appear asking you if you are sure you want to continue. Click yes.

3. Zoom into the area indicated in Figure 4.75.

TIP   The Field of View navigation tool in a Perspective viewport is actually a flyout. Use the flyout and discover the Region Zoom tool underneath.

4. Observe that there is a smoothing discontinuity, or *seam* that shows up along the backside of the tapered wall as seen in Figure 4.76. This is typical of many modified mesh forms.

5. Go to the Polygon sub-object level.

6. Select all polygons within this object by pressing Ctrl+A on the keyboard.

FIGURE 4.75
Zoom in to the curved area on the backside of the tapered wall.

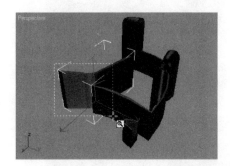

7. Scroll way down in the Modify panel and locate the Surface Properties rollout. Click the Clear All button in the Smoothing Groups area.

8. Deselect all polygons by clicking off to the side. Notice that all the smoothing information that was previously stored in the Editable Mesh has been cleared out as seen in Figure 4.77.

9. Select all polygon sub-objects again by pressing Ctrl+A.

10. Click the Auto Smooth button right below the Clear All button.

11. Deselect all polygon sub-objects and exit Polygon mode. The "seam" that was present in Figure 4.76 has been smoothed out in Figure 4.78 after you smoothed the mesh. Look carefully as the effect is subtle.

FIGURE 4.76
Smoothing
discontinuity
or "seam"

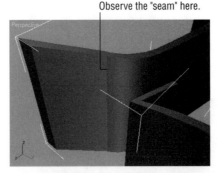

FIGURE 4.77
Editable Mesh has
been cleared of
smoothing

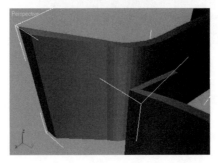

FIGURE 4.78
Resmoothed mesh

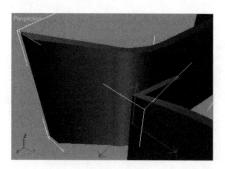

NOTE *Smoothing groups are the little numbers in the Surface Properties rollout. Each polygon sub-object can have a smoothing group number assigned. Just select a polygon and click the number button to assign a smoothing group. When adjacent polygons have the same smoothing group number, their surface normals are smoothed together. You can manually edit the smoothing groups for maximum control over the illusion.*

The Smooth Modifier

Another way of applying smoothing to any object—whether it is a mesh or not—is to use the Smooth modifier.

1. Select the Tapered wall again.

2. Apply the Smooth modifier.

3. Check Auto Smooth in the Parameters rollout.

4. Adjust the Threshold to 0 degrees. This effectively removes smoothing from the object.

5. Drag the threshold spinner upward. As you do, observe how more and more of the object gets smoothed. Set the threshold to 30 degrees as seen in Figure 4.79 where the object is properly smoothed.

6. Set the threshold at 90 degrees and observe how the illusion of smoothing extends now across the top edge. This is an example of incorrect smoothing. Figure 4.80 shows a case where the threshold value was set too high so that the crisp edges that you want to have remain are smoothed.

7. Delete the Smooth modifier after you are done experimenting by clicking the Remove Modifier from the Stack tool below the Modifier Stack List.

FIGURE 4.79
Smoothing threshold set at 30 degrees

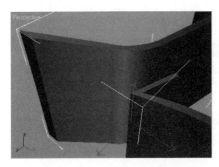

FIGURE 4.80
Smoothing threshold too high

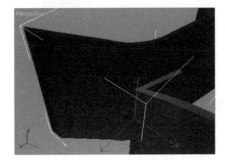

Summary

In this chapter, you learned how to get into the sub-object level of an object and make adjustments. Remember that you can use either the Modifier List drop-down list at the top of the Modify tab or the options in the Selection rollout to gain access to the sub-object level. You'll find that, no matter how your model is generated, you'll go to the sub-object level to edit vertices and edges frequently.

Along the way to creating the Chapel at Ronchamp model, you were introduced to methods that help you isolate parts of your model for easier editing. In the early stages, the Isolate tool let you see a part of your model without the surrounding parts interfering with your viewing. The Display tab of the Command Panel let you hide the ceiling of the tower to allow access to the walls. You used instance clones to your advantage when you created the towers. You also learned how to turn objects into editable meshes to fine-tune the shape of objects. You learned how to use Attach and Detach within an editable mesh. Finally, you learned how to control smoothing using the surface properties of a mesh and using the Smooth modifier.

In the next chapter, you'll continue developing the chapel model by creating the roof. There, you'll be introduced to the concept of extruding splines along a path. You'll also learn about layers and how they can be used to help organize your model.

Chapter 5

Organizing and Editing Objects

IN THE PREVIOUS CHAPTER, you began to build a fairly complex model. To continue working on that building, you'll need to employ some organizational tools, just to be able to see your work clearly.

In this chapter, you'll continue work on the Chapel at Ronchamp model. You'll be introduced to the Loft compound object that allows you to extrude a shape along a path to form complex forms. You'll also learn more ways to create and edit extruded spline shapes. Along the way, you'll learn how to organize your work through the use of object names and layers.

- ♦ Naming Objects
- ♦ Organizing Objects by Layers
- ♦ Lofting the Roof
- ♦ Creating Surfaces from Splines
- ♦ Creating Shells from Surfaces
- ♦ Completing the Roof

Naming Objects

Perhaps one of the simplest and most important things you can do to help keep your model organized is to give objects in your model meaningful names. You were introduced to this concept in Chapter 2. Let's go ahead and name all of the parts of the Chapel at Ronchamp project in preparation for creating the roof.

1. Open the chapel model in VIZ. You may also use the ch05a.max file from the companion CD.

2. If only one viewport is visible, click the Min/Max Toggle tool.

3. Click the Zoom Extents All tool to get a view of all of the parts of your model.

4. In the Top viewport, use the Select Object tool to select the south wall, as shown in Figure 5.1.

5. In the Name and Color rollout of the Create tab of the Command Panel, change the existing name to **south wall**. If you're in the Modify tab, change the name that appears just below the Modify label at the top of the tab. (In fact, you can change the name of an object in any tab except for the Utilities tab.)

6. Click the wall to the west and change its name to **west wall**, as shown in Figure 5.1.

7. Repeat this process for the north and east walls and the freestanding exterior wall in the upper right of the plan.

8. Name the tower ceiling objects as shown in Figure 5.1.

You have named just about all of the walls, except for the tower walls. Right now, it's difficult to gain access to the tower walls because the ceiling vaults are in the way in the plan view, and their arrangement in the other views is overlapping. The easiest way to get to the tower walls is to temporarily turn off the ceiling vaults. Let's do that in the next exercise.

1. Click the Select by Name tool on the main toolbar or type **H** on the keyboard.

The Select Objects dialog box appears.

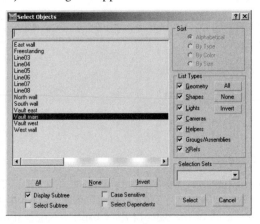

2. Ctrl+click the Vault objects to select them from the list, and then click Select. The objects are selected.

3. Click the Display tab in the Command Panel.

4. Click the Hide Selected button in the Hide rollout of the Command Panel. The ceiling vault objects disappear, as shown in Figure 5.2.

FIGURE 5.1
Selecting walls in the Top viewport

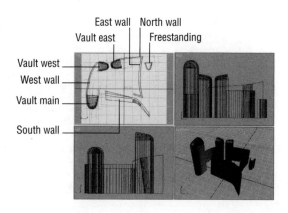

FIGURE 5.2
Naming the tower walls

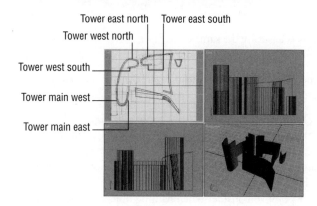

5. Rename the tower wall objects as you did with the other wall objects, using Figure 5.2 as your guide. Click the Create tab, use the Select Object tool to select a wall, and then use the Name and Color rollout to enter the new name.

TIP   *Although you can use the Modify tab to change the name of an object, the Create tab is faster for changing the names of multiple objects, since you don't need to wait for the object's parameters to load each time you make a selection.*

To finish the process, redisplay the ceiling vaults.

1. Click the Display tab in the Command Panel.

2. Click the Unhide by Name button in the Hide rollout.

The Unhide Objects dialog box displays.

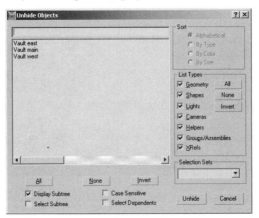

This is basically the same dialog box as the Select Objects dialog box, but instead of listing all objects that are on, it shows the objects that have been turned off.

3. Click the All button on the lower left side of the dialog box, and then click Unhide. The ceiling vault objects reappear.

If you know that you simply want to unhide objects that were hidden, you can click the Unhide All button in the Hide rollout. Here, you used the Unhide by Name dialog box just so you know that, if you need to, you can selectively unhide objects by name. This points out the usefulness of meaningful names for objects. If the object names are not descriptive, you'll have a difficult time determining which object in the list is the one you want to turn on.

Another point to consider when naming objects is their alphabetical listing. In the Sort group of the Select Objects and Unhide Objects dialog boxes, you have the option to sort the names of the objects in a variety of ways. By default, names are sorted alphabetically. To further help keep track of an object, you might consider how its name will appear in the alphabetical listing. For example, you named the Tower objects in a way that keeps them grouped together in the listing. The name Tower appears first, then the location (main, east, or west), and then the component that the object represents, such as north or south. This hierarchical naming scheme helps keep objects grouped together in a listing.

Organizing Objects by Layers

Another way to keep your model organized is through the use of layers. The idea of layers comes from drafting, where different disciplines literally drew their parts of a design on different layers of media. For example, in an architectural drawing, the mechanical engineer would draw ductwork and piping on a separate sheet, which was overlaid on the floor plan of the drawing. The different overlays were eventually combined into one sheet through reprographic techniques.

In Computer Aided Drafting (CAD), layers are used to help keep drawings organized and easier to manage. This concept is taken a step further by organizing types of graphics into walls, doors, ceiling information, and so on. In addition, notes and dimensions are usually separated into their own layers.

In VIZ, you can use layers in a similar way by organizing part of your model by the type of material you'll be applying to each object. For example, the walls that will be stucco might be placed in a layer called Stucco. If the ceiling vaults are to be given the same appearance as the walls, you might combine them into the Stucco layer as well. Roof and floor components will be given their own layers, too. You might even go further and create layers for window glass, mullions, wood detail, and so on. As you'll learn in Chapter 16, another way of working with layers is to link or import your CAD data into VIZ.

In this section, you'll begin to explore layers by using them to organize objects in the chapel model by their material assignments. You'll use these different layer/material assignments in later chapters to apply materials to objects.

Setting Up Layers

Start by setting up a few layers in your chapel model that you'll use for objects.

1. Click the Layer Manager button on the Layers toolbar.

The Layer dialog box displays.

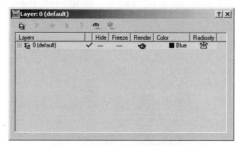

2. Click the Create New Layer button. Layer1 appears in the list box.

3. Click Layer1 to highlight the name for editing and type the name **Stucco**. It appears in place of the Layer1 name.

4. Click New again and type **Concrete roof**.

5. Click New again and type **Floor**.

6. Click New again and type **Tower walls**.

7. Close the Layer dialog box.

TIP   *If you're an AutoCAD user, you'll notice that most of the VIZ methods for creating and using layers are identical to those for AutoCAD.*

You might have noticed that one layer already exists. Layer 0 is always present and is the default layer on which all objects in a new file are created. All of the objects you've created in the chapel model, for example, reside on layer 0. You may even notice that the Color column in the Layer Properties dialog box shows a particular color for layer 0. This is the same color that you see on objects when you look at the shaded view in the Perspective viewport.

New!

The color that you see on newly created objects is the color of layer 0 by default. This is because the new nodes that are created default to a setting of By Layer, meaning an object's color is controlled by the layer that it is on, rather than having a different color assigned By Object (as is the default in 3ds max).

In VIZ 2005, layer 0's color is randomly chosen when you start a new scene. If you don't like the particular color that was chosen, you can easily change the color in the Layer manager.

Assigning Objects to Layers

Now that you have some new layers, go ahead and assign some of the walls to the Stucco layer. This is fairly easy to do: you select the object and then use the Layer drop-down list on the Layers toolbar to select a layer for the object.

New!

In VIZ 2005, the Layer tools have been completely overhauled. The way that you assign objects to different layers has changed and there are several new timesaving tools.

1. Click the Select by Name tool on the main toolbar. The Select Objects dialog box appears with a list of all of the objects in the file.

2. Ctrl+click the east wall, the north wall, the south wall, the west wall, and freestanding wall, and then click Select.

3. Click the Stucco layer in the Layer drop-down list on the Layers tool bar. This makes the Stucco layer current. Any objects you create now would be on this layer.

4. Click the Add Selection to Current Layer button in the Layers toolbar. The selected objects are now on the Stucco layer.

5. Change the current layer to Tower walls, then select the tower objects and add them to the current layer.

Another way to add objects to a layer is to create the layer with the objects preselected.

1. Select the three vault objects.

2. Click the Create New Layer button on the Layers toolbar.

3. Give the new layer the name **Vault**, make sure Move Selection to New Layer is checked, and click OK. The objects are moved to the new layer automatically as the layer is made.

Now try a little experiment to make sure that the ceiling objects are really on the Vault layer.

1. Click the Layer drop-down list.

2. Click the eyeball icon to the left of the Vault name.

The vaults disappear, and you see the towers standing alone. You've just hidden the Vault layer.

3. Open the Layer drop-down list again. Click the Vault mask symbol again to unhide the Vault layer. The vaults reappear in the viewport.

4. Click anywhere in a viewport to close the drop-down list.

Earlier, you used the Display tab of the Command Panel to hide individual objects. You can see from this exercise that you can also hide an object through its layer assignment by hiding a layer. In this exercise, you used the eyeball and mask icons in the Layer drop-down list to hide and unhide the Vault layer.

Assigning Color to Layers

Another way to help you keep track of objects and their layers is to assign a unique color to layers. This helps you visually keep track of layer assignments and can help in your everyday editing tasks by toning down the appearance of objects that you are not currently editing. Layer colors also give you a visual reference for object organization.

1. Click the Layer Manager tool to open the Layer dialog box.

2. In the Layer dialog box, click the color swatch associated with the Stucco layer.

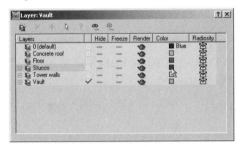

The Layer Color dialog box displays.

TIP   You can toggle to the AutoCAD Color Index (ACI) palette in the Object Color dialog box if you are more familiar with the arrangement of palette colors in AutoCAD.

3. Click the dark-brown color swatch.

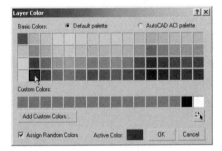

4. Click OK. The objects assigned to the Stucco layer appear in this color as shown in Figure 5.3.

5. Close the Layers dialog box.

6. Set the colors for the rest of the new layers. Use Figure 5.4 as a guide.

FIGURE 5.3
The walls display
in the color you
selected in the Layer
Color dialog box.

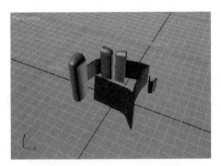

FIGURE 5.4

Use this view of the Layer Color dialog box to set the colors for the rest of the layers.

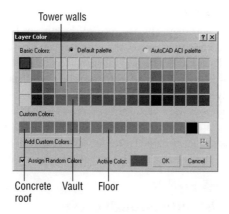

Once you have set up your layers, you can use a layer as a selection criterion.

1. Make the Stucco layer current.

2. Click the Select Objects in Current Layer button on the Layers toolbar. The objects on that layer are selected.

You can also set the current layer by selecting an object. This can be useful if you want to model additional objects on the same layer as something you see on the screen.

1. Select the Vault main object.

2. Click the Set Current Layer to Selection's Layer button on the Layers toolbar.

The Vault layer becomes current because that is the layer Vault main is on. One nice thing about this method is that you don't even have to know the name of the layer you are changing to because you are getting that information by picking the object.

The layer color or object color property you've been working with so far defines the color of the objects only as you work with them in wireframe views. These colors also appear in shaded views until you assign materials to the objects. At that point, the shaded views of objects will show a facsimile of the materials assigned to objects rather than the object's color property. The color property is only there to help you differentiate between objects and is not meant to represent the surface qualities of the material. You will learn more about materials in Chapter 7.

Setting the Current Layer

New objects you create are automatically assigned to the current layer. When you created your first box in Chapter 1, it was assigned to layer 0, the only layer in existence at the time.

New!

If you want to make a layer current, it no longer matters if objects are selected before you select a layer from the Layer drop-down list. In VIZ 2005, this behavior has changed, and you must explicitly change objects to other layers using the tools provided as buttons on the Layers toolbar. In addition to setting the current layer from the rollout of the Layers toolbar as you did in the exercise, there are several other ways to make a layer current. You may also use the Layer dialog box. Open the Layer manager and double-click the layer name from the list to make it current. You can also click in the column just to the right of the layer name, and a check mark will appear, indicating that the layer is current.

Controlling Object Visibility through Layers

In a previous exercise, you turned objects off and on using the Display tab options. If you prefer, you can control the visibility of individual objects on a layer from the Layer dialog box. The following exercise demonstrates this.

1. Open the Layer dialog box, if it isn't already open.

2. Click the plus (+) sign next to the Stucco layer. The list expands to show the objects that are assigned to the Stucco layer.

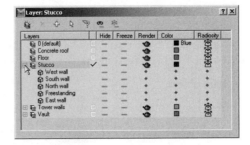

Notice that next to the object names there are dots in the Render, Color, and Radiosity columns. This tells you that those properties are controlled by the layer (By Layer) to which the objects are assigned. Dashes in the Hide and Freeze columns indicate that nothing object-specific has been set.

3. Click the dash in the Hide column for the West wall.

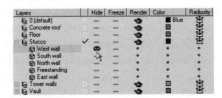

The dash changes into a mask icon to indicate that this object is hidden, even though it is on a layer that is shown.

4. Click the mask again. The dash returns. Now the object's visibility is controlled By Layer.

NOTE *You cannot show an object that is on a hidden layer in VIZ 2005. However, you can hide an object that is on a visible layer.*

This exercise shows that you can cycle through a series of settings for individual objects within a layer. When you see the mask icon, the object is hidden immediately, even while you have the Layers dialog box open. As you have just seen, you can use the Hide column to control the visibility of individual objects or layers. The other columns also allow you to control settings for layers or objects. The Render column prevents the layer or object from rendering. You can also control the color of individual objects by clicking the Color column. In fact, if you click the Color option for an object in the Layer Properties dialog box, you'll see the Object Color dialog box you saw before, but with a small and important addition. Toward the bottom of the Object Color dialog box, you'll see the By Layer option.

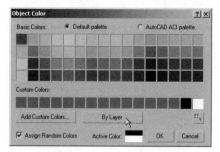

This By Layer option appears only when you select the Color option for an object in the Layer dialog box, overriding the color settings for the layer the object is on. As soon as you select a color for the individual object, the By Layer button changes to By Object to indicate the new state. If the object doesn't change to the color of its layer, you can choose By Layer to force the object to follow the layer color. You can also choose a color from the color palette to give the object a different color from its layer color.

WHAT IF AN OBJECT DOESN'T CHANGE TO ITS LAYER COLOR?

Color can be confusing if you don't understand the distinction between setting color By Layer or By Object—especially when you open up a legacy scene made in VIZ 4 or in any version of 3ds max. Some older scenes didn't use layers at all and you still have the option of taking them or leaving them in VIZ 2005. Layers are best used to organize very complex scenes and are especially appropriate to use if you import data from any AutoCAD-based application into VIZ.

If each object that you create has a different color, then your scene is set to assign color By Object. If the scene is set to By Layer, then the objects will assume the color of the layer they are on.

WHAT IF AN OBJECT DOESN'T CHANGE TO ITS LAYER COLOR? *(continued)*

There is a preference setting inside VIZ that lets you change the default creation method for new nodes to either By Layer or By Object. Choose Customize ➤ Preferences. Then select the General tab and in the Layer Defaults group, check the Default to By Layer for New Nodes check box. If you plan on using layers, then it is best to leave this setting checked (By Layer).

No matter which way you decide to set the preferences, each individual object can have its color assigned By Layer or By Object. One quick way to tell whether an object's color is assigned By Object or By Layer is to look at the color swatch next to the object's name in the Create or Modify tab of the Command Panel.

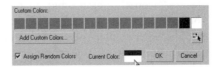

If the color swatch shows black and white, its color assignment is By Layer. If it shows a single color, its color assignment is By Object.

You can change an object's property setting from By Object to By Layer. This change causes the object to inherit its display properties from its assigned layer. To make this change, use the Select Object tool to select an object, and then right-click the object and select Properties from the quad menu. The Object Properties dialog box displays.

Click the By Layer button in the Display Properties group. This will cause the Display Properties check boxes to be enabled. The check boxes are properties that are available for each object if you enable the By Object mode.

You'll also see that the By Layer button is available for the Rendering Control and Motion Blur groups of the Object Properties dialog box. Just as with Display Properties, the By Layer button lets you determine whether the Rendering Control and Motion Blur properties are controlled by the individual object or by the layer to which the object is assigned. You'll learn more about Rendering and Motion Blur properties in later chapters.

Notice that there are also tabs in the Object Properties dialog box for Advanced Lighting (radiosity renderer) and mental ray. These tabs control specific properties for these renderers that you will be learning about in later chapters.

Lofting the Roof

Now that you have your model a bit more organized, you're ready to add the roof. In this section, you'll look at how you can use splines to create unique forms. The roof exercises will also offer an opportunity to explore the uses of layers and object names to help keep the clutter down and aid in the modeling process.

Setting Up the Shapes to Form the Roof Edge

The roof of the Chapel at Ronchamp has a unique shape. Its east and south edges form a prominent feature in the design. The shape of the roof edge looks somewhat like the hull of a boat, as shown in Figure 5.5. This shape may pose a challenge to most modeling programs, but VIZ can easily handle the creation of this unique shape.

To begin the process, you'll draw two splines. One spline will represent the cross section shape of the roof edge, and the other spline will define the shape of the roof's edge along the length of the south and east sides. The cross section shape and the shape of the roof's edge will be combined through a process called *lofting* to form the 3D roof edge.

FIGURE 5.5
A view of the chapel showing the roof feature at the southeast corner

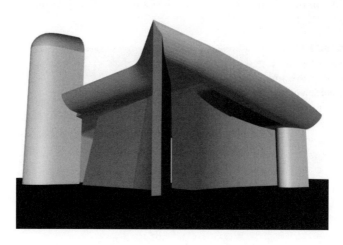

Lofting is a process whereby a cross section shape is extruded along a path. The result of this lofting is called a *Loft object*. Loft objects are a bit like Boolean objects in that they are the result of the combination of multiple objects, namely the cross section shape and the path. The term lofting comes from shipbuilding, and it refers to the method of laying out the contours of a ship's hull. Like a ship's hull, the cross sectional shape of a loft can vary along the path. As you'll see later, you can adjust the shape of the loft along the path by adjusting the profile at various points along the path.

Let's start the lofting process by turning off part of the model so that you can see your work more clearly. You'll be able to use the bitmap sketch background for some of your work, and the east wall will aid in placing the height of the roof, so turn off all of the model except for the east wall.

1. Use the Select Object tool to select the east wall. Or, if you prefer, you might practice using the Select by Name dialog box to do this.

2. Click the Display tab of the Command Panel. Then click the Hide Unselected button in the Hide rollout.

All of the walls disappear except for the east wall. Now draw the profile for the extruded roof edge.

1. Use the Region Zoom tool to zoom into the portion of the Front viewport shown in Figure 5.6.

2. Click the Create tab of the Command Panel. Then click the Shapes button and click Rectangle.

3. In the Front viewport, click and drag a rectangle from the top right corner of the east wall, as shown in Figure 5.7. You don't need to be exact about the placement or size of the rectangle.

4. In the Parameters rollout of the Command Panel, change the Length value to **1.8** and the Width value to *4*.

FIGURE 5.6

Use the Region Zoom tool to enlarge this portion of the Front viewport.

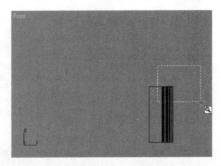

FIGURE 5.7
Drawing the rectangle for the roof edge profile

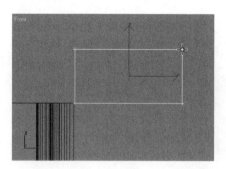

You have the basic outline of the profile drawn, but it needs a curve in the lower right corner of the rectangle, so add that next.

1. Click the Modify tab in the Command Panel, right-click the Rectangle item in the modifier stack list, and select Convert to Editable Spline. You won't need the parametric features of the rectangle, and you'll save memory by converting the rectangle to an Editable Spline.

2. Click the Vertex tool in the Selection rollout of the Command Panel (or expand the Editable Spline listing in the modifier stack list and select Vertex).

TIP You can type the following hotkeys for Editable Spline sub-object levels: 1 for Vertex, 2 for Segment, and 3 for Spline.

3. Use the Select and Move tool to right-click the vertex at the lower right corner of the rectangle. Then select Bézier Corner from the list.

4. Right-click the Select and Move tool on the main toolbar to open the Move Transform Type-In dialog box.

5. Enter −2.5↵ in the X input box of the Offset: Screen group. Then close the Move Transform Type-In dialog box. The rectangle changes shape.

6. Use the Select and Move tool to adjust the Bézier handles so that they look like the ones in Figure 5.8.

*NOTE If you find that the constraints keep jumping to the Restrict to Y setting, it's because the Bézier handle lies on top of the Y axis. When you click the handle, you're simultaneously clicking the Y axis arrow, thereby restricting your motion in the Y axis. To get around this problem, type **X** to toggle the Transform gizmo off temporarily. Type **X** again to turn it back on.*

7. Click the Vertex tool in the Selection rollout of the Command Panel (or click Editable Spline in the modifier stack list) to exit the sub-object level, or type **1** on the keyboard.

8. Right-click the Top viewport, and then move the profile upward to the north edge of the building, as shown in Figure 5.9.

FIGURE 5.8

Adjust the Bézier handles so that they look like the ones in this figure.

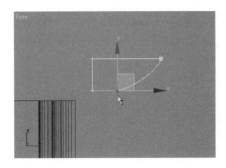

FIGURE 5.9

Move the profile to the north edge of the building.

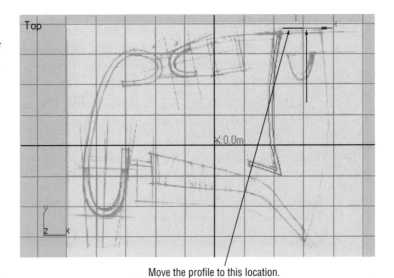

Move the profile to this location.

NOTE *You may notice that VIZ placed the profile edge on the X axis as you see it in the top view. By default, VIZ places objects on the plane defined by the X, Y, and Z axes of world space. When you draw objects in the Top or Perspective viewports, they are placed on the plane defined by the X and Y axes of the World Coordinate System. For the Front and Back viewports, objects are placed on the plane defined by the X and Z axes, and for the Left and Right viewports, objects are placed on the plane defined by the Y and Z axes.*

You have the profile ready. Now it's time to create the path over which the profile will be lofted. This time, you'll trace over the bitmap sketch to obtain the profile of the roof edge.

1. Click the Min/Max Toggle tool to enlarge the Top viewport.

2. Click the Create tab in the Command Panel. Click the Shape tool, if it isn't already active. Then click Line.

3. Draw the line shown in Figure 5.10 starting from the east end of the south wall.

4. Click the Modify tab. Then click the Vertex tool in the Selection rollout (or expand the Line item in the modifier stack list and select Vertex).

5. Convert the vertices shown in Figure 5.11 into the Bézier type by selecting them and then right-clicking and selecting Bézier from the quad menu.

You may want to zoom in temporarily to adjust the curve of the south wall. Select Views ➤ Undo View Change to return to the overall view of the plan. (The Shift+Z keystroke combination performs the same function as Views ➤ Undo View Change.)

You now have the path you want for the loft, but you need to take one more step before you use the path. The path now defines the outside edge of the loft, but you want the shape to follow the inside edge of the path. I'll explain why after you've created the loft. It will be easier to see the reason then.

To create a path that forms the inside edge of the extrusion, use the Outline tool and then delete the line segments that you don't need.

1. With the Modify tab selected, click the Spline tool in the Selection rollout of the Command Panel (or select Spline in the modifier stack list).

2. In the Outline input box near the bottom of the panel, enter 4↵ to create an outline 4 meters wide. This is the same width as the roof edge profile you created earlier.

3. Scroll up to the Selection rollout and select Segment.

4. Ctrl+click the segments shown in Figure 5.12, and then press the Delete key to delete them.

FIGURE 5.10
Draw this line, starting at the square shown at the upper right end of the line.

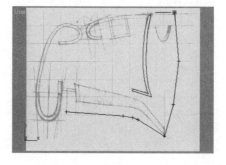

FIGURE 5.11
Convert selected vertices to Bézier type.

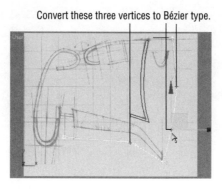

TIP   If the Outline you create in step 2 looks distorted, click Undo, then select the Reverse button, which is four buttons above the Outline button. Next, enter —4⏎ (minus four) in the Outline input box. You can also adjust the Bézier handles of the vertices to smooth out the outline.

Now you have a path that defines the inside edge of the loft. You're just about ready to perform the actual loft, but before you do that, move the path out of the floor plan area. This will allow you to make adjustments to the path later.

1. Click the Segment tool in the Selection rollout to deactivate it. Then, if it isn't already selected, click the Select and Move tool.

2. Move the spline path to the location shown in Figure 5.13.

FIGURE 5.12
Delete these spline segments.

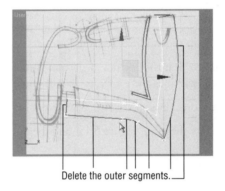

Delete the outer segments.

FIGURE 5.13
Move the spline path to the location shown here.

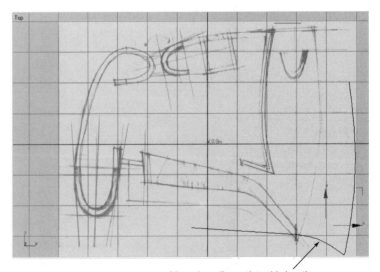

Move the spline path to this location.

Lofting an Object

Now you're ready to loft the shape you created earlier. You'll use the Loft modifier in the Modify tab to perform this maneuver.

1. Click the profile rectangle shape you created earlier to select it.

2. Click the Create tab in the Command Panel. Then click the Geometry tool.

3. In the Create tab drop-down list, select Compound Objects.

4. Click the Loft button in the Object Type rollout.

WARNING   *The Loft button will be grayed out if you do not first select a spline to act as either the loft path or shape.*

5. Click the Get Path button in the Creation Method rollout and make sure the Instance radio button is selected.

6. Move the cursor over the spline you created in the previous exercise. Notice that the cursor shows an ellipse marker. This tells you that the cursor has found an object that can be used as a path for the loft. Click the spline path you created in the previous exercise. The profile extrudes along the shape of the path, as shown in Figure 5.14.

FIGURE 5.14
The lofted shape

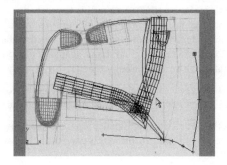

The shape is a bit crude looking. Just as with other lofted objects, you can set the number of segments used along the path. To get a smoother looking extrusion, increase the number of segments along the path. Here's how it's done:

1. Scroll down the Command Panel to the Skin Parameters rollout label and click it.

2. Change the Shape Steps value to 10 and the Path Steps value to 10.

The loft is beginning to take form, but there are still some odd results from the Loft object that need to be fixed. And this is where you see the reason for using the inside edge for the path instead of the outside edge.

Adjusting the Loft Profile in Relation to the Loft Path

In the sharp corner of the loft, you see overlap, caused by the loft bending over itself as it turns the sharp corner. Figure 5.15 shows this overlap.

This overlap can cause some undesirable results in your model later on when you apply materials and render the model. To remove the overlap, you need to adjust the location of the path in relation to the profile. Before you do that, it may help you to understand what VIZ does when you create a loft in the first place.

By default, when the loft is created, it aligns the loft path at the center of the shape. This causes the bending that you see in Figure 5.15. You want to move the loft path to the left of the shape, so that instead of the loft bending over itself, it pivots around the sharp corner. The following exercise will show you how to accomplish this.

UNDERSTANDING WHAT A LOFT DOES

When you create a loft, you are given the option of having the loft make an instance or reference copy of the shape to place at the beginning of the path. The default is to create an instance copy. This allows you to make modifications to the original profile object that will, in turn, modify the cross section shape of the loft. When you create the loft, a clone of the original shape is placed at the starting point of the path. The clone is placed in the same location as the original shape, so it isn't obvious that a clone has been created. Also, the clone of the original shape becomes a sub-object of the loft (as you'll see in the next exercise).

Another point is that the loft emerges from the profile object as if the path were perpendicular to the face of the profile shape. You can later adjust the location of the loft using the transform tools.

If you prefer, you can select the path first, and then use the Get Shape button in the Creation Method rollout to select the profile object. If you create a loft in this way, then the path will define the location of the Loft object instead of the profile.

First, set up a view so that you can see the relationship of the loft shape and the path more clearly.

1. Click the Min/Max Toggle tool, and then right-click the Front viewport.

2. Click the Arc Rotate Selected tool and adjust the view so that it looks similar to Figure 5.16. You need to be able to see the beginning of the loft shape and the corner clearly.

3. Click the Min/Max Toggle tool to enlarge the view.

Now you're ready to adjust the shape and loft alignment.

1. Click the Modify tab in the Command Panel.

2. With the Loft object selected, expand the Loft modifier in the modifier stack list and click Shape. A new rollout called Shape Commands displays. Remember that the Loft modifier creates an instance clone of the original shape and uses it as a sub-object of the lofted shape.

3. Click the top edge at the end of the loft, as shown in Figure 5.16. You'll see a partial red outline of the shape you used as the profile for the loft. The options under the Shape Commands also become active.

FIGURE 5.15
Overlap of corner

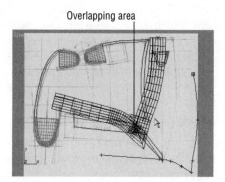

FIGURE 5.16
The view of the lofted object including the path and the shape

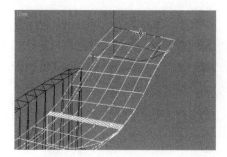

4. Click the Left button in the Align group.

The lofted shape now moves so that the path forms the inside edge of the lofted shape instead of the centerline, as shown in Figure 5.17.

5. Click the Min/Max Toggle tool to get a look at the top view. Now the overlap at the corner disappears, and you have a clean-looking corner.

Note the new relationship of the loft path to the shape in Figure 5.17. You can also see the original rectangle shape you created earlier, now that the alignment of the shape has shifted to the left side.

Clicking the Left button moved the path to the far left edge of the rectangle profile shape. Other buttons in the Align group cause the path to be aligned with different parts of the profile shape, as indicated by the button name. The Top and Bottom buttons align the path with either the top or bottom edge of the shape without affecting the current left-to-right alignment. This means that if the path is currently aligned with the left of the shape, then clicking the Top or Bottom button will align the path with the top-left or top-bottom of the shape. If the path is aligned with the center of the shape, clicking the Top or Bottom button will align the path with the center-top or center-bottom of the shape.

Fine-Tuning a Loft Object

You now have a pretty good replica of the chapel's roof edge, but suppose that you wanted to make some refinements to the shape. For example, you might want to make some slight adjustment in the relationship of the path to the shape, or perhaps you just want to adjust the curve of the path.

In this section, you'll explore some of the ways a Loft object can be fine-tuned. The changes you make to your model in this section will be for experimentation purposes only, so you'll use the temporary buffer to store your work in its current state so that you can return to it later.

FIGURE 5.17
The lofted shape after aligning the path with the left side of the rectangle profile

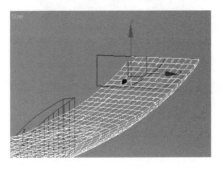

In the previous exercise, you saw how you can use a set of buttons to align the loft path with the loft shape. Now let's see how you can use the Select and Move tool to manually align the path with the shape.

1. To save the model in its current state, choose Edit ➤ Hold.

2. Click the Compare button in the Shape Commands rollout. The Compare window appears.

This window allows you to view the relationship of the path to the shape.

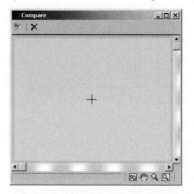

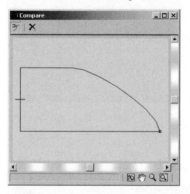

3. Click the Pick Shape tool at the top left corner of the Compare window, and then click the sub-object shape outlined in red in the User viewport. The shape appears in the Compare window.

4. With Shape selected in the modifier stack list, click the Select and Move tool and drag the red arrow at the end of the x-axis handle of the Transform gizmo of the profile to the right, as shown in Figure 5.18. You see the shape move in the Compare window. The plus (+) sign in the left half of the Compare window indicates the location of the loft path.

5. You don't really want to keep the change you just made, so click the Undo button to return the profile to its original location before you started this exercise.

Here, you see that by using the sub-object level of the Loft, you can adjust the relationship of the loft shape to the loft path by moving the loft shape. You don't actually move the original shape profile. Instead, you move the instance clone of the shape that the loft has placed at the beginning of the path. The Compare window also gives you a view that helps you align the path with the shape.

Using Different Shapes along the Loft Path

The Loft object is basically a uniform shape along its length. Suppose you want the form of the loft to change along the path. You can do this by introducing additional shapes along the path. Here, you'll begin to see the similarities between VIZ's loft feature and the lofting used in shipbuilding.

In the roof edge example, the chapel roof flattens slightly as it bends outward to the east. You can add this flattening by including a larger version of the original shape profile at the point where the flattening occurs. Try the following exercise to see how this works.

1. Click Loft in the modifier stack list to exit the sub-object level.

2. Use the Select and Move tool to select the original rectangle shape you created for the profile of the loft, as shown in Figure 5.19.

3. Shift+click and drag the red X axis arrow to the right to make a clone of the shape. In the Clone Options dialog box, make sure the Copy radio button is selected and click OK.

FIGURE 5.18
Drag the X axis arrow to the right and watch the effect on the loft shape.

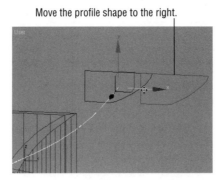

Move the profile shape to the right.

FIGURE 5.19
Create a clone of the original rectangle shape, then select its vertex.

First copy this profile shape to the left.

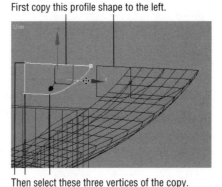

Then select these three vertices of the copy.

4. Expand the Editable Spline item in the modifier stack list, and then select Vertex (or select Vertex from the Selection rollout).

5. Click the Select and Move tool on the main toolbar and select the three vertices shown in Figure 5.19. You can either use a selection window or Ctrl+click each vertex.

6. Click and drag the selected vertices to the left along the X axis so that the shape looks like Figure 5.20.

You've created a modified version of the loft profile that you'll use to elongate the loft profile at its eastern-most point.

1. Click Editable Spline in the modifier stack list to exit the sub-object level.

2. Click the loft compound object to select it. You should see the name Loft01 at the top of the Modify tab of the Command Panel.

3. Scroll down the Command Panel to the Path Parameters rollout and click to open it. Path parameters let you select a location along the path where you can get a new shape.

4. Click and drag the Path spinner upward. As you do this, you see a small, yellow X marker move along the loft path, as shown in Figure 5.21.

5. Adjust the spinner so that the path value is 22.5. This places the yellow X marker at a point that is 22.5% of the way along the length of the entire path.

6. Scroll up the Command Panel to the Creation Method rollout and click Get Shape.

7. Place the cursor on the new, modified rectangle shape and click it. The Loft object changes to include the new shape, as shown in Figure 5.22.

FIGURE 5.20
Drag selected vertices to a new location to the left.

Drag the three selected vertices to the left along the X axis.

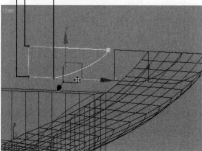

The result of the new loft isn't quite right. To get a smoother shape, you need to align the new shape with the original profile shape. Here's how it's done:

1. Select Shape from the modifier stack list.

2. With the Select and Move tool selected, move the cursor to the location of the new shape along the path, as shown in Figure 5.23. The cursor changes to a plus (+) sign when it has located the shape (it may be difficult to actually see the shape in the path).

3. Click the new shape. The new shape is now outlined in red within the loft shape.

FIGURE 5.21
The X marker on the loft path

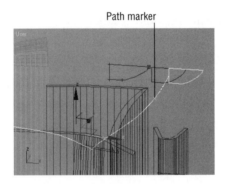

FIGURE 5.22
The new loft shape with the modified profile in place

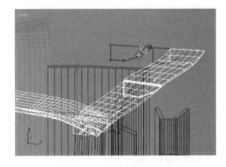

FIGURE 5.23
Click the loft shape as shown here.

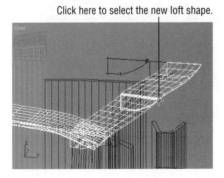

4. To help align the shapes, click the Compare button in the Shape Commands rollout.

5. Click the Pick Shape tool at the top left corner of the Compare window.

6. Click the same new shape you selected in step 3. The shape appears along with the original shape in the Compare window.

7. Click the Zoom Extents tool in the lower right corner of the Compare window to get a better view of the shapes.

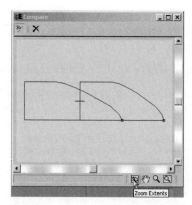

The Compare window aids in aligning the new shape to the path.

8. In the User viewport, use the Select and Move tool to move the X axis of the new shape to the right. As you move the shape, watch the Compare window and align the two shapes as shown in Figure 5.24.

With the alignment shown in Figure 5.24, the new shape is aligned to the left side and along the top edge of the loft shape.

9. Close the Compare window to get a better view of all of the viewports.

If you look at the Top viewport, you'll see that the new loft shape now uses the new shape as the profile for the rest of the loft, as shown in Figure 5.25.

FIGURE 5.24
Aligning the two shapes

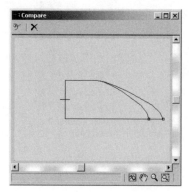

Adding a Third Shape to the Loft

The new shape is intended to occur at only one location in the loft; it's not the shape for the entire length of the loft. To bring the loft back to its original size past the flattened area, you can use the original rectangle shape. Once again, use the Get Shape tool to add another shape to the path.

1. Click Shape in the modifier stack list to deactivate it.

2. Scroll down the Command Panel to the Path Parameters rollout and click the Path Parameters label to open it.

3. Click and drag the Path spinner upward so the yellow X marker moves to the location shown in the Top viewport in Figure 5.26.

4. Go to the Creation Method rollout and click the Get Shape button.

5. In the User viewport, click the original rectangle shape, as shown in Figure 5.27. The loft changes to include the original shape at its new location.

FIGURE 5.25
The loft is now larger from the point of the new, enlarged shape addition.

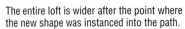

The entire loft is wider after the point where the new shape was instanced into the path.

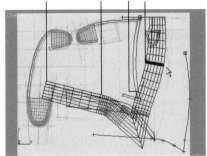

FIGURE 5.26
Move the X marker to this location using the Path spinner in the Path Parameters rollout.

Move the path marker just north of the bend in the loft path.

Just as with the enlarged shape, you need to align the new shape addition.

1. Click Shape in the modifier stack list.

2. In the User viewport, click the location of the new shape addition, as shown in Figure 5.28.

3. Click the Compare button in the Shape Commands rollout to open the Compare window.

4. Click the Pick Shape tool at the top of the Compare window, and then, in the User viewport, click the newly added shape in the loft, as shown in Figure 5.28.

5. Click the Zoom Extents tool at the bottom of the Compare window to enlarge the view of the three profiles.

6. Move the Compare window to the right so you can see all of the Top viewport.

7. In the Top viewport, use the Select and Move tool to move the shape sub-object to the right along its red X axis. Use the Compare window to align the new shape with the original loft shape, as shown in Figure 5.29.

FIGURE 5.27

The loft's new shape with the addition of the original rectangle shape in a new location

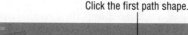
Click the first path shape.

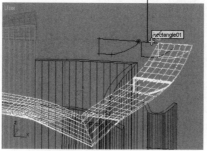

FIGURE 5.28

Click here to select the new shape addition.

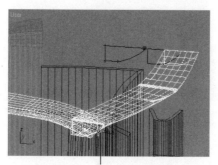
Select the new instanced shape here.

8. Close the Compare window to see all of the viewports.

You can adjust the alignment of the shapes that make up a loft at any time using the Compare window. You can also adjust the location of a shape along the path by changing the Path Level value in the Shape Commands rollout. Try the following to adjust the location of the bulge.

1. With Shape selected in the modifier stack list, click the enlarged shape in the loft, as shown in Figure 5.30.

2. In the Shape Commands rollout, click and drag the Path Level spinner downward.

Notice that the bulge shape moves toward the beginning of the loft path. When you release the mouse button, the bulge appears closer to the beginning of the loft, as shown in Figure 5.31.

3. Adjust the spinner so that the bulge is about halfway between the first and third shapes along the path. The spinner should show a value of around 25.5.

With all of the fine-tuning you've been doing, the overall shape of the roof edge has gotten a little distorted, especially near the beginning of the loft path. You can make adjustments to the loft path to compensate for minor changes in the loft by editing the original Path object.

FIGURE 5.29
Align the new shape with the other two shapes.

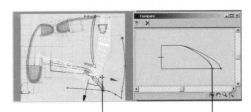

Move the loft shape to the right until it matches the view in the Compare window.

FIGURE 5.30
Click the Shape sub-object that defines the bulge of the loft.

Select the loft shape here.

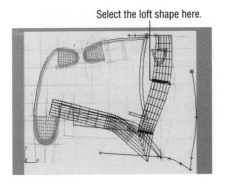

Using the Path Clone to Edit the Loft Path

Remember that in an earlier exercise, you moved the original loft path to the right of the model. You did this so that you could have a clear view of the path in order to edit it. In the next exercise, you'll make changes to the loft by editing the original line you used to define its path.

First, rotate the loft so that it is aligned with the sketch bitmap.

1. Right-click in the Top viewport. Then click the Min/Max Toggle tool to enlarge the viewport.

2. Click Shape in the modifier stack list to deactivate it. Click the Select and Rotate tool, and then click the Loft object.

3. Click the Reference Coordinate System drop-down list on the main toolbar and select View if it is not already selected.

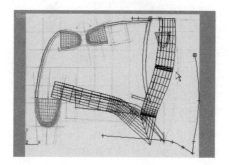

FIGURE 5.31
The Top viewport showing the bulge

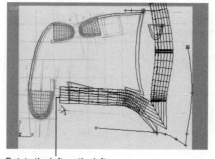

FIGURE 5.32
Align the roof with the sketch along the bottom edge.

Rotate the loft so the left
edge aligns with the sketch.

4. Click and drag the Z coordinate axis ring of the Loft object counterclockwise, so that the left edge of the Loft object aligns with the edge of the roof in the sketch, as shown in Figure 5.32.

5. Click the Select and Move tool and move the roof so that its corner is aligned with the corner of the bitmap sketch, as shown in Figure 5.33.

Now you can use the bitmap sketch as a guide to adjusting the curve of the loft. The south edge doesn't need to be edited in any way, because it is fairly well aligned with the sketch. The east edge of the roof needs to be tweaked a bit to conform to the outline in the sketch.

Start by adjusting the curve of the roof from the northern-most end.

1. Click the curve you created to define the path of the loft, as shown in Figure 5.34, and then click Vertex in the modifier stack list.

2. Click the beginning vertex at the top of the curve, as shown in Figure 5.34.

3. Make sure the View option is selected in the Reference Coordinate System drop-down list. Then click the Select and Rotate tool and rotate the vertex counter-clockwise in the Z direction so that the curve looks similar to the one shown in Figure 5.35. You need to rotate the curve only a little. If you rotate the curve too much, you can click the Undo tool and start over.

FIGURE 5.33

Align the roof corner with the corner in the sketch.

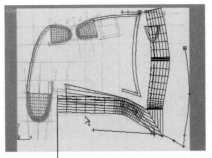

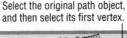

Move the loft to align with sketch as shown.

FIGURE 5.34

Select the curve, select Vertex from the modifier stack list, and then click the beginning vertex.

Select the original path object, and then select its first vertex.

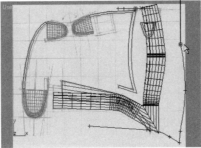

FIGURE 5.35
Rotating the vertex

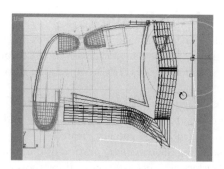

4. Click the Select and Move tool and move the vertex so the north edge of the roof extends slightly beyond the north wall.

5. Click Vertex in the modifier stack list to deactivate it.

The roof edge is now aligned with the roof sketch, and you've completed the south and east edges of the roof. You can see how editing the original path affects the Loft object. The Loft modifier created an instance clone of the original Path object and incorporated the clone into the loft. This allowed you to make changes to the original and have those changes affect the loft.

You may want to save the original loft shapes in case you want to edit the loft later, but you may not want them appearing in your model, since they can contribute to the visual clutter of the viewports. Instead of deleting them, you can place them on their own layer for safekeeping, and then hide that layer.

1. Select the original path object if it is not already selected.

2. Click the Create New Layer button in the Layers toolbar.

3. Type **Layout** for the new layer name and make sure Move Selection to New Layer is checked before clicking OK. This is the layer in which you'll store your shapes and path.

4. Click the Min/Max Toggle tool to show all the viewports and right-click in the user viewport. Click the Select Object tool on the main toolbar, and then Ctrl+click the two loft shapes you used to create the loft, as shown in Figure 5.36.

5. Click the Add Selection to Current Layer button on the Layers toolbar.

6. Open the Layer drop-down list and click the eyeball icon associated with the Layout name. The shapes disappear.

Creating Surfaces from Splines

A good portion of the roof still needs to be built. It would be simple to just fill in the remaining portion with a flat, extruded shape, but the design calls for a *trough* through the center of the roof. This trough starts out at the west end and gradually flattens to meet the east end that you just created, as shown in Figure 5.37.

There are a number of challenges in adding this part of the roof. You need to create a shape that transitions from a fairly steep curve to a shallow one at the east end of the roof. You also need to merge this roof addition to the roof edge you just created.

You might go about modeling the remaining portion of the roof in several ways. One method might be to extrude a flat surface and then use mesh editing tools to add the desired trough form to the mesh.

FIGURE 5.36
Selecting the loft shapes

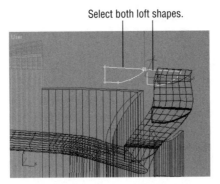

FIGURE 5.37
The remaining portion of the roof

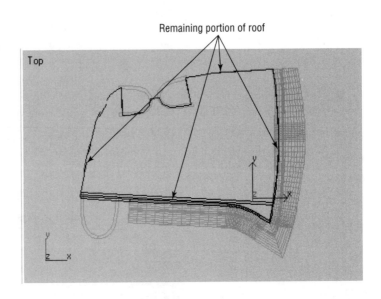

TIP   *You might want to experiment on your own with different modeling techniques. There are usually several ways to achieve the same three-dimensional form.*

New!

A new modeling approach takes the Editable Spline a few steps further to achieve the desired roof form in three dimensions. The shell modifier is new in VIZ 2005, and makes this entire modeling technique possible.

This approach begins by first creating a spline *armature*. This armature is nothing more than a set of interconnected spline segments, all within a single Editable Spline object. The vertices where segments in the armature intersect must be touching (fused) but not joined together (welded).

The next step in the modeling process is to generate a thin three-dimensional surface from the spline armature. In order for the surface to be properly generated, each part of the spline armature must be enclosed by either three or four edges as you will see later in this section.

In the next section you will give depth to the roof when you create a solid shell model from the surface you make here.

Building the Spline Armature

You can create a simple armature by laying out a grid of splines. New tools within the Editable Spline make this process easy. Drawing a rectangular grid of splines is a sure way of creating a usable armature, because each "cell" of the grid has four edges.

TIP   *You can make any manner of 3D freeform spline armature as long as the "cells" within the armature have either three or four edges between interconnected vertices. The vertices must be fused, not welded. Finally, the entire armature must be part of a single Editable Spline object.*

THE CROSS SECTION TOOL

You will use the Cross Section tool to create an armature grid that will be the basis of the main portion of the roof.

1. Open the Layer drop-down list and click layer 0. Using the Line tool, click your first vertex above and to the right of the lofted roof you made earlier.

2. Hold down the Shift key to constrain the line vertically and click the opposite endpoint of the line straight down from the first endpoint. Right-click to complete the line as shown in Figure 5.38.

3. Click the Modify panel, expand Line in the stack, and enter the Segment sub-object level.

4. Select the single segment of the Line object. Scroll down in the Modify panel and locate the Divide button. Enter **7** in the adjacent spinner and click the Divide button. There are 7 new vertices resulting in 8 segments total.

FIGURE 5.38
Draw a vertical line that is longer than the roof.

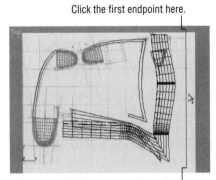

Click the first endpoint here.

Click the opposite endpoint here.

> **TIP** *In some situations, you may find that the Divide tool creates unequal divisions. This is usually due to having Bézier vertices at the endpoints of the line segment you are dividing. To obtain even divisions, go into the Vertex sub-object level, select the endpoint vertices, right-click and then select Corner from the quad menu. Once this is done, the Divide tool will divide the segment into equal divisions.*

5. Go to the Spline sub-object level by typing **3** on the keyboard.

6. Select the single sub-spline. While holding down the Shift key, use the Select and Move tool to drag the spline to the left along the X axis. Repeat this process and make several copies, lining each spline up approximately with the grid in the background image as shown in Figure 5.39. Don't worry about being overly precise—close is good enough.

New!

7. Click the Cross Section button in the Geometry rollout. This button is new in VIZ 2005. This tool integrates the functionality of the CrossSection modifier into the Editable Spline object for added convenience.

FIGURE 5.39

Copying a few
sub-splines

Make copies of the sub-splines
aligning with the background grid.

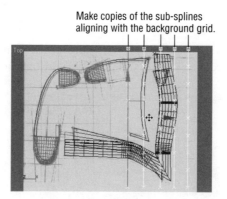

WARNING   *Before you copy the spline, make sure you are in the Spline sub-object level. That way you will be sure that you are cloning sub-splines, rather than new objects. Spline armatures will not create surfaces if they are not contained within a single object.*

8. Observe that your cursor shows the cross section icon while you hold it over the splines. Click the spline on the right first, and then click its neighbor to the left. Rubber-banding lines appear. After you click the second spline, cross section splines appear.

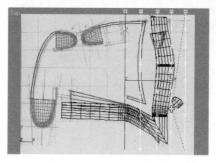

9. Click each of the remaining splines in turn, continuing from the right to the left. Right-click when you are finished. When you are done, you will have created a grid of intersecting sub-splines as shown in Figure 5.40.

THE CONNECT COPY TOOL

New!

Another new tool in VIZ 2005 that aids you in creating a spline armature is the Copy Connect tool within the Editable Spline.

1. Make sure you are still in spline sub-object mode with the leftmost sub-spline selected.

2. Scroll down the Modify panel and check Connect in the Connect Copy group.

3. Hold down the Shift key and use Select and Move to drag out a new copy of the selected sub-spline to the left along the X axis as shown in Figure 5.41.

4. Observe that cross section sub-splines were automatically added when you used connect copy. Continue making connect copies until your armature matches Figure 5.42.

FIGURE 5.40
Using Cross Section to generate sub-splines

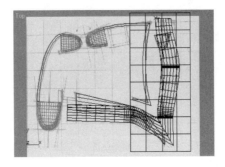

FIGURE 5.41
Making connect copies of sub-splines

As you make a connect copy, observe the automatic cross section sub-splines.

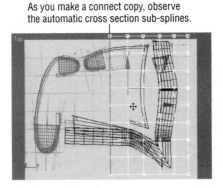

FIGURE 5.42
Completed grid armature

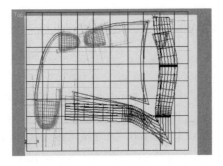

Deforming the Armature

So far you have created a flat grid. However, this is not an ordinary grid because of its unique structure. The grid you have created is a spline armature because it is composed of three or four edged cells (four in this case), is a single Editable Spline (Line in this case), and has its intersecting vertices that are fused but not welded (Cross Section and Connect Copy do this automatically).

This technique gets interesting when you start to deform this armature to create a three-dimensional surface.

1. Select the spline you have been working with and right-click. Select Hide Unselected from the display quad.

2. Hit the Min/Max Toggle or press Alt+W on the keyboard and right-click the Perspective viewport to select it. Press Alt+W again to maximize the Perspective viewport.

3. Right-click the object once again and select Properties from the transform quad. The Object Properties dialog appears.

4. Click the By Layer button in the Display Properties group to toggle into By Object mode. Check Vertex Ticks as shown in Figure 5.43 and click OK.

5. Enter the Vertex sub-object mode or type 1.

6. Click a single vertex somewhere on the armature and move it up in the Z direction.

FIGURE 5.43

Object Properties
Vertex Ticks

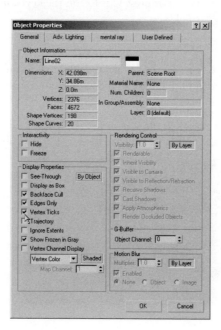

FIGURE 5.44

Beware of disturbing
fused vertices

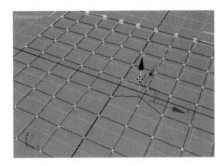

Observe that as you move the single vertex up (Figure 5.44), it is sharing the exact same position with another vertex. This is what it means to have fused vertices. Each vertex belongs to different vertical or horizontal sub-splines. If they were welded, there would be only one vertex at this location in the grid.

If you want to move this intersection point off the grid, you must drag a selection window to encompass both vertices, so that it selects them both. You do not want to disturb the pair of fused vertices relative to each other if you want to maintain this grid as a valid armature.

7. Click the Undo button once or press Ctrl+Z on the keyboard. You don't want to alter the armature by moving a single vertex.

USING SOFT SELECTION

Soft Selection gives you a way to gently deform the armature to model a gentle trough form in the roof. You can partially select multiple vertices and apply your transform gently across the entire selection set.

1. Deselect all by clicking off to the side of the viewport. Then select the pair of vertices along the eastern edge in the middle of the grid by dragging a small selection window around them.

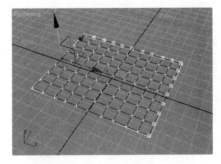

2. Open the Soft Selection rollout and check Use Soft Selection.

3. Adjust the falloff to 23 meters to affect a larger region around the two selected vertices.

Notice how the vertices in the armature are color coded. White vertices are not selected. As the falloff value of Soft Selection increases, vertices adjacent to the selected ones first turn blue, then yellow, and then orange to indicate the degree to which they are selected.

NOTE   *You can adjust the way that the Soft Selection options affect the vertices by making changes to the Pinch and Bubble settings just below the Falloff setting. Pinch causes the selection to create a spiked form when a set of vertices is transformed. Bubble causes the selection to create a wave-like form. The graphic below these settings displays a visual sample of their effect.*

4. Drag the two selected vertices down along the Z axis. Watch as the softly selected vertices get pulled along according to the degree to which they were selected (Figure 5.45).

5. Select another pair of vertices along the center of the grid along the east-west axis and move them down slightly in the Z direction. Repeat this process until you have a very gentle roof slope in the Front view as shown in Figure 5.46.

6. Exit the Vertex sub-object level by typing **1**.

FIGURE 5.45
Moving spline vertices with Soft Selection

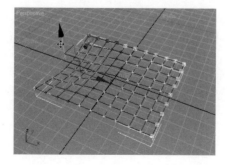

FIGURE 5.46
Forming a gradual trough

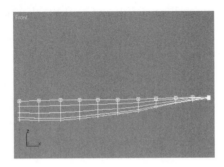

SURFACING THE SPLINE ARMATURE

Generating a surface from your spline armature is definitely the easy part of this modeling technique, assuming you already have a valid armature.

1. Select your spline armature and apply the Surface modifier.

2. You may have to check Flip Normals in the Parameters rollout in order to see the surface. The surface will only face in one direction, so check or uncheck Flip Normals until you can see the surface from the top.

3. If you still can't see the surface, you may have to adjust the Threshold spinner, also in the Parameters rollout. Change the Threshold value until you can see a surface covering the entire armature as shown in Figure 5.47.

WARNING *If parts of your armature do not display a surface, the problem is with the armature. Surfaces will only be generated where the armature encloses three or four segments because the Surface modifier can only create Tri and Quad Patch Grids to stretch over your armature.*

Creating Shells from Surfaces

After you have made a surface from splines, it is now possible to extrude this 3D surface into a volume by using the new Shell modifier.

1. Select the surface you have been working on if it is not already selected.

2. Apply the Shell modifier.

3. In the Parameters rollout, increase the Inner Amount to 100. The surface extrudes into a three-dimensional shell. You would use the Outer Amount spinner if you wanted the shell to extrude in the opposite direction.

4. If you are not satisfied with the form, you can go down the stack and edit the Vertex sub-object level of your spline armature. Click the Show End Result button in the stack controls to see the shell while you are editing the armature.

5. When you are done editing the form, right-click in the viewport and choose Properties from the transform quad. Change the Display Properties to By Layer to get rid of Vertex Ticks.

In the end, you will have modeled a gently sloping trough in the roof form as shown in Figure 5.48.

FIGURE 5.47
Surface made from splines

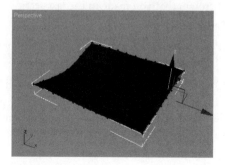

FIGURE 5.48
Roof trough

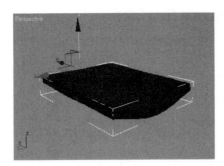

Completing the Roof

The next step in the modeling process is to find a way to cut away the parts of the roof that extend beyond the perimeter border as seen in the background sketch. You will be using Booleans creatively to achieve the ultimate form for this roof. Your first task is to trace the border for the roof trough in plan.

Tracing the Border

You will trace the border of the roof with a spline that you will use to cut away excess potions of the roof trough.

1. Right-click in a viewport and choose Unhide All from the display quad. A dialog box appears and asks you a question.

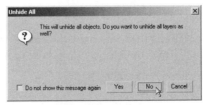

2. Choose No to unhide all objects without unhiding any layers.

3. Select the new roof trough that you made in the last section. Right-click and choose Hide Selection from the display quad.

4. Right-click in the Perspective viewport to activate it. Arc Rotate and zoom in to focus on the corner of the lofted roof as shown in Figure 5.49.

    To prepare for tracing the border of the lofted roof, you will be using a user grid to help you trace everything at the same elevation. Without using a user grid, the spline you trace would contain multiple elevations in the Z direction—in other words it would be a 3D spline. To make an effective border, we will strive to create a flat 2D spline.

FIGURE 5.49

Focus on lofted roof corner

5. Switch to 3D snap in the toolbar flyout and then right-click the Snap button.

Click the Clear All button. Check Vertex only in the Grid and Snap Settings dialog box before closing it.

6. Click the Create panel, and then click the Helpers category button. Under Standard in the drop-down list, you will see the Grid tool in the Object Type rollout below. Choose the Grid tool.

7. Drag out a user grid that snaps its first point to the top corner of the lofted roof. It doesn't matter how large you make the user grid because it simply defines a plane at the elevation you 3D snapped to as shown in Figure 5.50.

8. Click the Select Object tool. Select the lofted roof object. Right-click and choose Hide Unselected from the display quad. The user grid, along with all the other unselected objects, is hidden.

NOTE   *A user grid is still active even when hidden.*

FIGURE 5.50
Creating a user
grid at a snapped
elevation

Snap your user grid's first corner here.

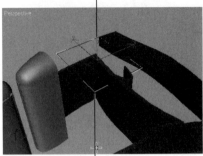

Drag out the grid to an arbitrary size.

9. Switch to 2D snap mode. This mode allows you to snap to objects that lie on the grid, namely, the top edge of the lofted roof (this is where you snapped the user grid earlier).

10. Carefully sketch out the border shown in Figure 5.51 with the Line tool using corner vertices everywhere. Snap the border to existing vertices along the east and south inner edges of the lofted roof. Continue clicking vertices around the remaining portions of the border and close the spline by clicking the last vertex on top of the first.

TIP *If you make a mistake while drawing a Line, hit the Backspace key to undo one vertex without canceling the tool. You can keep hitting the Backspace key to successively undo the placement of your vertices while you are drawing.*

FIGURE 5.51
Border spline

Draw this border.

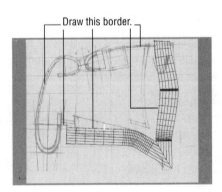

Working with Booleans

You now have a closed spline that represents the outer border of the roof trough object. That border is contained within the solid form of the roof trough object in the top or plan view. If you used the border shape now, you might extrude it and then use the resulting mesh to cut a hole into the roof trough, but this is not the desired form. When you think through your options at this point, you have exactly the opposite of what you will need to cut away the excess volume of the roof trough.

1. In the Top view, right-click and choose Unhide All from the display quad.

2. Only select the border spline you just drew and the roof trough object. Then right-click and choose Hide Unselected.

3. Draw a Rectangle around the roof trough. This rectangle must be larger than the roof trough.

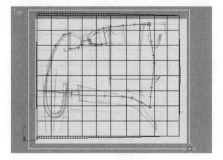

4. Select the border spline. Go to the Modify tab of the Command panel. Click the Attach button in the Geometry rollout.

5. Click the rectangle to attach it to the border spline. Turn off the Attach button.

6. Apply the Extrude modifier to the spline.

TIP   The chief reason why Boolean subtractions sometimes do not work is because of insufficient topology (internal structure). Try increasing the number of segments in your operands and try your Boolean operation again if you are having problems.

7. In the Properties rollout, change the extrusion Amount to –25 meters. The actual distance does not matter as long as it penetrates through the roof trough object. Use a negative number to cause the extrusion to go downward. Switch to the Perspective view to get a better view.

8. Change the Segments parameter of the Extrusion to 20.

9. Select the roof trough object. You are selecting this first to act as Operand A of a Boolean operation.

10. Click the Create tab, then click Geometry category button. Choose Compound Objects from the pop-up and then click Boolean in the Object Type rollout.

11. Click the Pick Operand B button and then click the object you just extruded. The A–B subtraction is performed and the roof trough form is complete (Figure 5.52).

FIGURE 5.52
Completed roof
trough

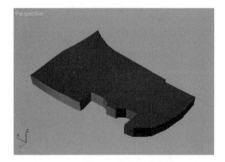

Putting It All Together

You have learned many important modeling techniques in this chapter. The roof was made in pieces to help illustrate various ways you can approach modeling tasks. Before the roof is done, you can make the lofted roof fit together with the roof trough.

NOTE *If you like, you can go back and make adjustments to the various parts of the model to make them fit together a bit better. However, you don't need to try to perfect the model since the goal of this example has been to help you become familiar with VIZ's tools through the use of a fairly complex model.*

1. Right-click in a viewport and choose Unhide All from the display quad.

2. Select the user grid object and press the Delete key to erase it. This grid was needed only to trace the border earlier.

3. Move the roof trough up in the Z direction and observe that the two pieces do not fit together properly as shown in Figure 5.53.

4. Select the roof trough and switch to the Modify panel. Boolean will be at the top of the stack. This compound object contains two operands and you can access both objects' parameters in the stack for later editing.

5. Click Operand A in the Parameters rollout in the Operands group.

6. Observe how the stack immediately changes. The stack of Operand A now appears below Boolean in the stack.

7. Click the Vertex sub-object level of Operand A within the Boolean. Here you can access the vertices of the spline armature that control this object's form.

Now that you understand how to work with Boolean operands in the stack, you can edit the armature of the roof trough to adjust it to better fit with the lofted roof. On the other hand, you can also adjust the loft path on the Layout layer to adjust the way the lofted roof fits with the roof trough. I'll leave you to practice these exercises on your own.

There is still much you could do to this model to flesh out the details. The window openings in the north and south walls need to be added. For that, you can create the form of the openings, and then use the Boolean tools to subtract those volumes from the walls. Meanwhile, you can enjoy the fruits of your labor by examining the model in the Perspective viewport. Figure 5.54 shows the Chapel at Ronchamp after some additional adjustments.

FIGURE 5.53
Roof pieces need adjusting.

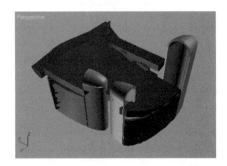

FIGURE 5.54
The chapel so far

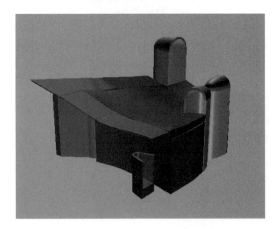

Summary

The Chapel at Ronchamp is a fairly complex building, full of unusual forms. In Chapter 4 and in this chapter, the chapel model has given you the opportunity to explore many of the modeling features of VIZ without being constrained by rectangular boxes. In fact, VIZ has the potential to free the designer from at least a few of the limitations that have restrained the design process in the past.

This concludes your use of the Chapel at Ronchamp design. In Chapter 6, you'll use another Le Corbusier design to explore cameras and lighting. You'll use the Villa Savoye design to set up a scene, including lighting and shadow.

Chapter 6

Light and Shadow

UP UNTIL NOW, YOU'VE been concentrating on methods of constructing forms in VIZ. In this chapter, you'll learn some of the ways you can control the appearance of the objects you build by manipulating light and shadow.

Three main elements affect the look of your model: materials, cameras, and lighting. This chapter will introduce you to the influence of lighting.

Lighting is one of the more interesting subjects in VIZ. You can use lighting to create effects, emphasize parts of your model, or simply set up a daytime scene. Through lighting, you can control shadows, manipulate reflective color, calculate the bending of light passing though a transparent material, and simulate lighting fixtures, based on specifications from a lighting manufacturer. It's best to think of lighting in VIZ as a kind of paint tool to add emphasis, color, or a sense of realism to your model.

- ◆ Lighting Your Model
- ◆ Rendering a View
- ◆ Ambient Light
- ◆ Adding Shadow Effects
- ◆ Playing in the Shadows
- ◆ Using the Light Lister

Lighting Your Model

Lighting is one of the most important tools at your disposal. Whether you are able to render your model successfully will depend largely on your ability to control and manipulate lighting in your model. There's a lot to cover in this topic, so let's start with an overview of the different types of lights available in VIZ.

Understanding the Types of Lights

So far, you've been depending on the default lighting in VIZ. In a Perspective viewport with Smooth + Highlights turned on, the light source is from the viewer location. In a Camera viewport, the default light source is in the same location as the camera.

VIZ offers a bewildering array of light types. There are five standard light types, two lighting systems (Daylight and Sunlight), eight photometric lights, two mental ray lights, and the Skylight. The Skylight, lighting systems, Photometric, and mental ray lights are fairly complex, so, as a gentle introduction, you'll concentrate on the standard lights first. The reason there are so many light types is partly historical and has to do with the various ways that you can render your model, as you will learn in Chapters 10 and 11.

The standard lights are Target Spot, Target Direct, Free Spot, Free Direct, and Omni. As you might guess from their names, the spot and directed lights come in two versions.

The lights that have *Target* in their name use a target point that is linked to the light source, but which can be moved separately from the light source. A light source always points at its own target, so you can reorient the light by moving the target.

Lights that have *Free* in their name are light sources that don't require the placement of a target point. You can freely rotate and move Free lights without having to transform a target location. The drawback to Free lights is that they're a bit more difficult to aim because you must rotate the sources to orient these lights. The advantage is that they're a bit easier to move because you do not have to also move their targets.

Here's a brief rundown of these different types of lights:

Target Spot Like a spotlight in a theater, a Target Spot projects a focused beam of light that can be aimed in a specific direction. The Target Spot is perhaps one of the most versatile light sources offered in VIZ.

Target Direct Otherwise known as directional lighting, a Target Direct is a source whose light rays are parallel. The main difference is that a spotlight is a concentrated source, like a flashlight, while a directional light acts more like the sun. A Target Direct is like a single, very distant light source, like our sun whose rays are nearly parallel when they reach the earth.

Free Spot The Free Spot is similar to the Target Spot, except that it has no target point. With a Target Spot, you must move the target location to rotate the light. A Free Spot can be freely rotated in any direction using the transform tools.

Free Direct This light is the same as the Target Direct light, except that it doesn't use a target point. Like the Free Spot, the Free Direct can be rotated freely without involving a target point.

Omni The Omni light acts like a lightbulb, radiating light in all directions. Like the Target Spot, Omni is a versatile light source that you'll use frequently. Since an Omni light has no particular direction, it doesn't have a target version.

Another lighting feature you'll grow to understand and use is *ambient lighting* (also called global lighting or indirect lighting). Ambient lighting can best be described as the secondary, indirect light that doesn't come directly from a particular source. You can think of ambient light as the light you get on an overcast day, when the light source seems to be from all directions. You can use ambient lighting to bring out hidden detail or, conversely, to suppress detail. Ambient light contributes a great deal towards photo-realism. In Chapter 10, you will use the radiosity renderer to accurately simulate ambient light. In Chapter 11 you will use mental ray to calculate global illumination. In this chapter you will begin your ambient journey by learning how to make quick approximations of indirect light. But first, let's learn about the obvious light in the scene—the light that comes directly from illumination sources.

Adding a Spotlight to Simulate the Sun

VIZ offers a way to accurately simulate the sun, including the correct sun angle, depending on the time of day and the location of the illuminated object on the earth. You'll see how you can accurately place the sun in your scene in the sidebar titled "Creating an Accurate Daylight Environment with the Daylight and Sunlight Systems." (A complete tutorial on placing the sun in your scene can be found in Chapter 10.) First, to get a feel for how lighting works in general, you'll use a spotlight to simulate the sun.

NOTE *Although a spotlight may not be the best type of light to simulate the sun, it's a type of light that you'll use often; so it makes a good introduction to lighting.*

VIZ lets you control the intensity as well as the *spread* of the spotlight. You can focus the light down to a very narrow beam like the headlights of a car, or you can spread the light out in a wide angle like the light from a desk lamp. To simulate the sun with a spotlight, you can place a standard Target Spot in your model at the relatively large distance from the model of about 250 feet. Like the Target Spot camera you created earlier, this Target Spot requires the placement of both the light source and the target of the light.

NOTE *The process for adding an Omni or Free light is nearly identical to that for adding a spotlight. The main difference is that an Omni or Free light doesn't require a target point.*

1. Open the Savoye6.max file from the CD. This is an early 20th century design by the world famous architect Le Corbusier.

NOTE *If you're an AutoCAD user and would like to know how the Villa Savoye model was created in AutoCAD, you can find a full tutorial on the companion CD for* Mastering AutoCAD 2005 and AutoCAD LT 2005 *by George Omura (Sybex, 2004).*

2. Right-click the Top viewport; then use the Zoom tool to zoom out so that your top view looks similar to the one in Figure 6.1.

3. Click the Create tab of the Command Panel; then click the Lights category button.

4. Leave the light type drop-down list set to Standard and click the Target Spot button in the Object Type rollout to activate it.

FIGURE 6.1
Placing the target
spotlight

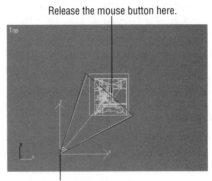

Release the mouse button here.

Start dragging the spotlight here.

5. Click and hold at a point in the lower left corner of the viewport as shown in Figure 6.1.

   As you move the cursor, you see the light appear at the point where you clicked, and the spotlight target follows your cursor. A rubber-banding line joins the light and the target.

6. Move the cursor to a point in the center of the model plan as shown in Figure 6.1. Then release the mouse button.

   Once the Target Spot is placed, it takes over as the light source in the model. Your Perspective viewport changes in appearance to show the new lighting conditions.

NOTE   When you place your first light in the scene, the hidden default lights that were illuminating the scene previously automatically turn off. The light that you see in the shaded viewports now comes completely from the sources you have placed.

7. Type **SUN** in the Name and Color rollout input box so that you can identify this new light source.

As you can see from the options in the Command Panel, you have quite a few alternatives available for controlling the characteristics of a spotlight. You can always go back and make changes to a spotlight. For now, though, you've accepted the default light settings by creating the spotlight.

Moving a Light

Notice that in the Front viewport, the spotlight displays horizontally. VIZ places the light and light target points flat along the XY plane. You must then move the light into position, to simulate the sun high in the sky. Let's move the light to a point high in Z direction.

1. Right-click the Front viewport to make it active.

2. Use the Zoom and Pan tools to adjust the front view so that it looks similar to Figure 6.2.

FIGURE 6.2

Moving the spotlight
and spotlight target

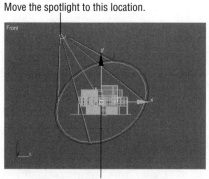

Move the spotlight to this location.

Move the target up to this point.

3. Click the Select and Move tool on the main toolbar. Then click and drag the Y axis handle of the Transform gizmo of the SUN light into the position shown in Figure 6.2. Once you've moved the light source, you see a change in the lighting of the Perspective viewport.

4. Click the Select by Name tool on the main toolbar. Then click SUN.Target in the list and click Select.

5. With the Select and Move tool active, click and drag the light's target location upward as shown in Figure 6.2. You can use the SUN light cone in the Perspective viewport to help match the target position.

The light source and its target move independently yet they are linked to each other. You also see that the Perspective viewport gives you immediate feedback regarding the light's effect on your model.

CREATING AN ACCURATE DAYLIGHT ENVIRONMENT WITH THE DAYLIGHT AND SUNLIGHT SYSTEMS

The Daylight system can be useful for shadow studies and for creating an accurate daylight representation of your design. It simulates the color, intensity, and surface reflections of a scene, and it takes into account the "sky glow" or general diffuse lighting from the sky. The Daylight system places a special light source called an IES (Illuminating Engineering Society) Sun that more accurately simulates the position and intensity of sunlight according to geographic location, time of year, and time of day. The Daylight system is intended for use with the radiosity renderer. Another lighting system called Sunlight works very much like the Daylight system. The Sunlight system is meant to be used with the Default Scanline renderer because it uses a direct light source instead of an IES Sun.

To get the most from the Daylight and Sunlight systems, you need to set a North Direction parameter to accurately orient your model in the north-south direction. You'll also need to know the location of your building or site and the date and time you wish to use for the sun's position. Once you've established these criteria, you can set up your system of choice fairly easily. You'll learn more about this feature in Chapter 10.

Editing a Spotlight

Many settings are available for your new spotlight. You can set the intensity, the color, and even the shape of the light, just to mention a few. But the two settings you'll be using the most are the light intensity and the light cone. The light intensity is set in the Intensity/Color/Attenuation Parameters rollout, and the light cone is set in the Spotlight Parameters rollout.

Let's start by looking at the Hotspot and Falloff settings.

1. First, use the Select Object tool to select the SUN Spotlight object (not its target).

2. Click the Modify tab in the Command Panel; then scroll down and click the Spotlight Parameters rollout button to open the Spotlight Parameters rollout.

3. Click and drag the Falloff/Field spinner downward until its value reaches 12 degrees. Notice that the light is reduced in size, shining on only a very small part of the model. Also notice that when you reduce the Falloff/Field value, the Hotspot/Beam value also drops. The Hotspot/Beam will always be smaller than the Falloff/Field value.

4. Click and drag the Hotspot/Beam spinner upward until it reaches a value of about 50. The light spreads out to cover a larger area. Notice that the Falloff/Field value also increases, staying slightly larger in value.

5. Now, click and drag the Hotspot/Beam spinner downward to about 20. This time the Falloff/Field value remained where it was last set while the hotspot got smaller.

6. Set the Hotspot/Beam value to about 34 and the Falloff/Field value to about 36.

The Hotspot/Beam and Falloff/Field spinners control the *spread* of the Target Spot. The Hotspot/Beam value controls the area covered by the most intense portion of the light, while the Falloff/Field value controls where the light falls off to zero intensity. There is a continuous gradient between the maximum intensity of the light within the hotspot and the zero intensity at the edge of the falloff cone. This is difficult to see in the Perspective viewport, but it will be more obvious in a rendered view. You'll see this better when you learn to make a quick rendering later in this chapter.

Now, try setting the light intensity. This is done through the Multiplier.

1. On the Modify tab of the Command Panel, scroll to the top of the Intensity/Color/Attenuation rollout; then click and drag the Multiplier spinner downward.

As you reduce the Multiplier value, the view in the Perspective viewport dims. Remember this is because the SUN Target Spot is now the only light illuminating the scene. If you set this light's multiplier to zero there will be no light at all.

2. Click the Undo tool on the main toolbar to return the Multiplier value to 1.

The Multiplier spinner controls the overall intensity of the light source. Technically, this parameter is multiplied by the color value to result in the total output intensity. You can change the color of the light source using RGB (Red, Green and Blue) or HSV (Hue, Saturation, and Value) values. You select a color using the Color Selector shown in Figure 6.3. To open the Color Selector dialog box, click the color swatch next to the Multiplier spinner in the Intensity/Color/Attenuation rollout.

The Color Selector dialog box lets you see your chosen color as a sample in the lower right corner of the dialog box. Adjacent to this on the left is the original color that was in the swatch when you opened the color selector. This feature can be helpful when you want to compare the new with the old.

Finally, if you decide that the light you selected originally isn't appropriate for the task at hand, you can use the Light Type drop-down list in the General Parameters rollout to change the type of light used.

This tool, along with the Targeted option in the same group, offers a convenient way to change a light type without having to erase the light and create another one.

FIGURE 6.3
Color Selector
dialog box

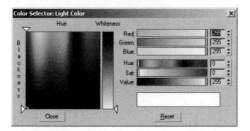

Changing the Light Type

As I mentioned in the preceding section, once you've placed a light in your model, you're not stuck with your choice of light type. You can change it in the Modify tab of the Command Panel.

You were asked to create a sunlight source using a Target Spot. There isn't anything wrong with using such a light for the sun, but the Target Direct is actually a more appropriate standard light source for the sun.

NOTE *The light rays from a VIZ Target Direct or Free Direct light are parallel, just as the rays from the real sun are basically parallel in relation to the earth. The rays from the sun are almost parallel due to the relative sizes of the sun and the earth and the vast distance between them. Even though the sun appears to be a point light source, it is about 93 million miles from earth, so from our perspective, the rays of light from the sun striking earth are essentially parallel, even though the sun is essentially an Omni light, casting light into space in all directions.*

Here's how you can change from Target Spot to Target Direct:

1. Click the Light Type drop-down list in the General Parameters rollout and select Directional. Also make sure that the Targeted option is checked.

Notice that the light changes its icon in the viewports to indicate a Target Direct light object. You might also notice that, instead of showing a cone, the light shows a narrow cylinder to indicate the direction and parallel spread of the light rays. You can see this cylinder most clearly in the Left viewport.

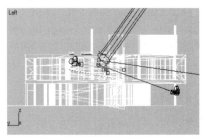

2. Scroll down the Command Panel and open the Directional Parameters rollout.

3. Click and drag the Hotspot/Beam spinner upward until its value reads around 18m and click and drag the Falloff/Field spinner until its value reads 19m. You see the light enlarge to form a large cylinder, as shown in Figure 6.4.

As described earlier, the Target Direct light source produces a light whose rays are parallel, so the light appears as a cylinder. The light rays from a Target Spot diverge, so the light forms a cone. Both light sources offer a Falloff option to soften the edge of the light.

Many other parameters are associated with the light objects, and you'll get to use a few more in later chapters. For now, let's move on to see how lighting and camera locations affect your rendering.

Rendering a View

One of the main reasons for using VIZ in the first place is to get an idea of how your design will look before it is actually built. Although you can get a fairly decent idea of how it looks in the Perspective viewport, you need to render your model to get a finished image.

FIGURE 6.4
The light falloff
increased

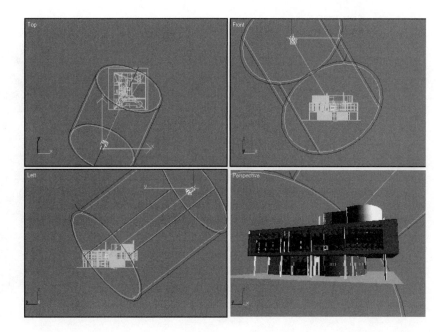

The rendering facility that VIZ offers lets you create a wide range of images, from quick-study renderings to photo-realistic images. You can also generate animated walkthroughs or virtual-reality environments.

NOTE *You'll learn how to export QuickTime virtual reality (VR) panoramas, Virtual Reality Modeling Language (VRML) worlds, and Shockwave 3D in Chapter 17.*

All of these types of output are produced through the Render Scene tool and the Quick Render tool. In this section, you'll get a look at some of the ways you can control your rendered output through Quick Render tool. The Render Scene dialog box will be covered in Chapters 10 and 13.

Try the following exercise to get a good look at the rendering options you have available.

1. Make sure the Perspective viewport is active; Arc Rotate to get a better view if desired, then click Quick Render on the main toolbar.

The Rendered Frame Window appears s as seen in Figure 6.5.

NOTE *The Rendered Frame Window used to be called the Virtual Frame Buffer in all previous versions of VIZ. The features are the same—only the name has changed.*

FIGURE 6.5
The Rendered
Frame Window

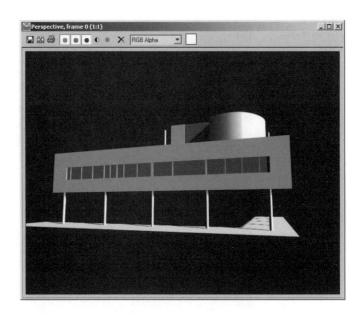

Perhaps for the first time you are creating a rendered frame. *Rendering* is the process of calculating image pixels from mathematical vectors, or in other words, making pretty pictures. A *frame* is a single still image (animations are composed of numerous frames). Notice that the lighting looks a bit more realistic in the Rendered Frame window when compared with the viewport, and it includes shadows.

2. In the Rendered Frame Window, click the Save Bitmap button.

3. The Browse Images for Output dialog box appears as seen in Figure 6.6. Click the Save as type drop-down list. Notice that a wide variety of output formats are available. Scroll through the drop-down list to get an idea of what formats are available.

4. Select PNG Image File (*.png) from the drop-down menu (pronounced "ping"). Type in the filename of **FirstRendering** and click the Save button. The .png file extension is automatically appended to the output file.

FIGURE 6.6

The Browse
Images for Output
dialog box

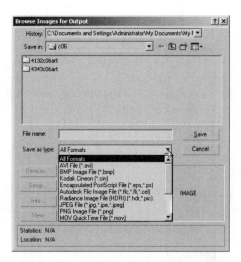

5. The PNG Configuration dialog appears. Click OK to accept the defaults and the file is saved to your hard drive. Each one of the output formats will have its own configuration dialog box with information that must be selected that is specific to each format. You will learn more about image and video formats in later chapters.

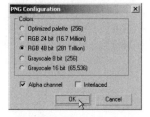

6. Close the Rendered Frame Window.

7. Choose Rendering ➤ Show Last Rendering from the menu bar. You can always view the last rendering you made in your scene by using this menu selection. The next time you make a rendering, the contents of the Rendered Frame Window will be overwritten.

Since you haven't yet added materials to the model, the rendering displays with the default colors assigned to all surfaces. Your rendering has the appearance of a cardboard model. Although it may not be the greatest rendering, it does offer a fairly accurate portrait of how the design looks. This is really just a start. The process of creating a finished rendering or animation involves a repeated cycle of rendering, adjusting, and rendering again (and again) until you've reached a look that you are pleased with. There are many *renderers* (rendering algorithms) to choose from in VIZ 2005, and learning the complexities of rendering will take you years to master. Rendering is symbolic of the magic of computer graphics—seeing your beautiful renderings appear can be quite fulfilling to you as a designer and to your clients as well.

As you progress through the chapters in this part of the book, you'll learn this process firsthand. In the next chapter, I'll explain the method for adding materials and for further enhancing the rendered image. But for now, let's continue with more on light and shadow.

NOTE *If you're familiar with the Villa Savoye design, you may notice that some parts of the building are missing or suffer from overlapping surfaces called* display artifacts. *All of the parts are there, but because their normals aren't aligned properly, they disappear when the model is rendered. You'll learn how you can set up VIZ to render both sides of a surface, regardless of the direction of the normals.*

Ambient Light

The rendering shows a picture with lots of contrast. The lighted areas are bright enough so that you cannot see any detail in the shadows. This is because there is no ambient light in the model. In the real world, there is usually some ambient light that is bounced off the surrounding objects. Indoor ambient light comes from light that is bounced off walls, floors, and ceilings, while outdoor ambient light comes from clouds and the general sky glow.

If you add ambient light to your scene, you'll begin to see more of the objects in the shadows, and you'll give your rendering a little friendlier appearance. As I mentioned earlier, there are many ways that ambient light can be calculated. The more realistic methods for calculating ambient light (radiosity and mental ray) generally take much longer to process. Here's how you increase the ambient light while using the quick and dirty Default Scanline Renderer:

1. Close the Rendered Frame Window to make more room on the screen.

New!

2. Choose Rendering ➤ Environment from the menu bar or type **8** on the keyboard. The Environment and Effects dialog box displays. This dialog box has been redesigned in VIZ 2005 and includes a tabbed interface showing the Effects tab (which was formerly in a separate dialog box).

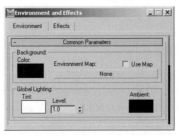

3. For now, you will just be dealing with the Common Parameters rollout on the Environment tab. Click the Ambient color swatch in the Global Lighting group.

The Color Selector displays (see Figure 6.7).

4. Click and drag the triangular slider in the Whiteness column downward as shown in Figure 6.7. This adjusts the general brightness of the ambient light.

5. As you move the triangular slider, notice that the Value spinner changes. Adjust the Value setting to 100; then click Close.

6. Click the Color swatch in the Background group; then, in the Color Selector, adjust the Whiteness slider so that the Value setting shows 200. This will make the background brighter.

7. Close the Color Selector; then close the Environment and Effects dialog box.

You've increased the ambient light so that objects in shadow will be more visible. To see the results, you'll have to render the model.

8. Click the Quick Render button in the main toolbar. The Default Scanline Renderer quickly calculates the new rendering as shown in Figure 6.8.

FIGURE 6.7
Adjusting the Whiteness value

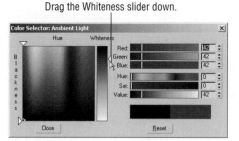

FIGURE 6.8
The model with ambient lighting increased

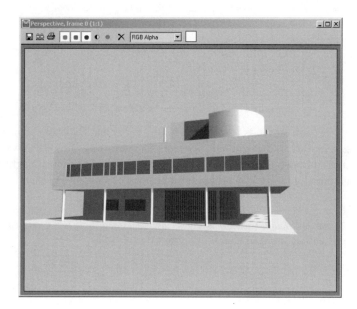

In this exercise, you only increased the amount of ambient light in your model and changed the brightness of the background. This is clearly the most simplistic approach to ambient lighting—that of approximating all the indirect light with a single color. As you can see from the Color Selector dialog box, you can also tint the ambient light with hue and saturation if you so choose. This can be useful for interior views of rooms that have a predominant color, or for sunset exterior views.

Since artificial lighting usually has a slight orange cast, as a general rule, adding an orange cast to interior scenes helps give them a more natural appearance. Likewise, outdoor scenes can be improved by adding a bit of blue to the light source to simulate the ambient light in the sky. Keep the color saturation levels very low to avoid strange results. You can imagine that if you increased the ambient color value to 255 or pure white, all the darker areas in the rendering would disappear as the contrast is eliminated. Using a particularly bright ambient color washes out the rendering and makes lighting irrelevant, as all surfaces seem to emit their own brightness. Therefore, avoid using an overly bright ambient color or there will be no point to making a rendering at all.

Faking Radiosity

As you will learn in Chapter 10, radiosity is a much more sophisticated way of calculating ambient light as compared to the method you have seen so far. Using radiosity can help you generate photorealistic renderings. The downside to using radiosity is the greatly increased render time.

In order to save time, you might find it useful to learn to fake the look of radiosity ("fakiosity") using standard lights and the scanline renderer. The downside of using the fakiosity method is that it isn't nearly as realistic or convincing as radiosity or mental ray for simulating ambient light.

NOTE *It is relatively easy to simulate "direct light"—that is, light striking surfaces on a beeline from the light source. What is really difficult in computer graphics is efficiently simulating all light striking the surfaces in a space, known as ambient light. Ambient light is influenced by light bouncing everywhere in a space from every angle and represents a huge volume of calculation.*

1. You will continue using the Villa Savoye model. Open another version of this model as `Savoye6c.max` from the CD.

2. Right-click in the perspective view. Click Quick Render. A view of the internal courtyard appears in the Rendered Frame Window as seen in Figure 6.9.

The courtyard looks flat and cartoon-like because the entire scene is lit only with the SUN direct light. In real life, the light reflected from the floor would bounce upward and illuminate the courtyard walls. Although the Default Scanline Renderer doesn't simulate light this way, you can add some lighting of your own to aid in the simulation of ambient light.

TIP *The Default Scanline Renderer is what you get out of the box when you click Quick Render. It is historically the oldest and least realistic rendering algorithm, although it is fast. In later chapters, you will be learning how to use the raytracer, radiosity, and mental ray renderers for increased realism.*

In the next exercise, you'll add some Omni lights and adjust their color settings to fake your own "bounced light" from the courtyard floor.

1. Right-click the Top viewport to make it active.

2. Click the Min/Max viewport tool to enlarge the Top viewport.

3. Click the Create tab in the Command Panel; then click the Lights tool.

4. Click the Omni button; then click the location shown in Figure 6.10 to place an Omni light in the courtyard.

5. Give this new omni light the name **Omni-court** in the name and color rollout input box.

FIGURE 6.9
Courtyard rendering

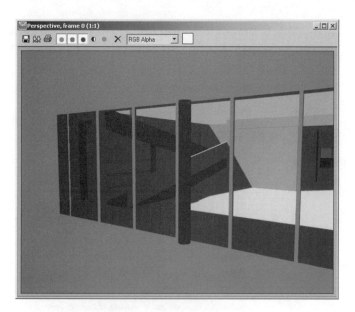

FIGURE 6.10
Placing an Omni light in the courtyard

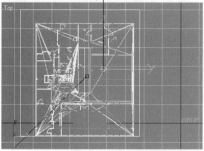

The Omni light is at 0 elevation. You'll want to raise it to a location that's just above the second-floor surface in order to simulate the light bouncing off that surface.

1. With the Omni-court light selected, click the Select and Move tool on the main toolbar.

2. In the coordinate readout, make sure the Absolute/Offset Mode Transform Type-In tool is set to Absolute; then change the Z value to 3.81 meters. This will raise the Omni light from the ground level to a level just above the floor of the courtyard.

Since the light bouncing off the courtyard floor represents a broad area, in the real world, it would throw off a very diffuse light. The Omni light, on the other hand, is a point source. You'll want to spread the bounced light source around a bit to create a more diffuse appearance. To do this, make a few clones of the Omni light.

1. With the Select and Move tool still active, Shift+drag the X axis of the Omni light's Transform gizmo and make a clone just to the right of the current Omni light's position (see Figure 6.11).

2. In the Clone Options dialog box, click Instance. You'll see the importance of making the clone an Instance in the next few exercises.

3. Click OK to close the Clone Options dialog box.

4. Make two more Instance clones as shown in Figure 6.12.

FIGURE 6.11
Cloning the
Omni light

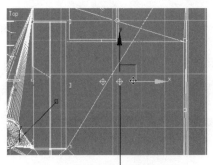

Drag an instance to the right.

FIGURE 6.12
Adding more
Omni light instances

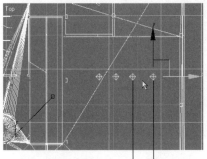

Make two more Omni instances.

With the lights in place, you can make a few adjustments to them to simulate the bounced light from the floor. First of all, you'll want to reduce the intensity of the light. Right now, the Omni lights are at full intensity. You can adjust the intensity of all four of the lights simultaneously by adjusting any one of the clones. This is because you created Instance clones. Just as with primitive objects, lights can be instanced so that the edits made to one clone are simultaneously made to all the other clones.

1. Select one of the courtyard Omni lights; then click the Modify tab in the Command Panel.

2. Go to the Intensity/Color/Attenuation rollout; then set the Multiplier spinner to **0.14**.

3. Click the color swatch next to the Multiplier spinner to open the Color Selector: Light Color dialog box.

4. Set the Hue to **20** and the Saturation to **60**; then close the dialog box. This will give the light a slight orange cast, as if it were picking up the color of the floor.

WARNING   Do not use highly saturated lights or you will overly influence the materials used. For example, if you shine a saturated red light on a blue surface, it will appear red (drowning out the blue material) because of the strong influence of the light.

5. Click the Min/Max Toggle tool; then right-click the Perspective viewport to make it active.

6. Click the Quick Render tool to get a view of your model so far. Your view will be similar to Figure 6.13.

FIGURE 6.13

A rendered view of the courtyard after adding the simulated bounced light

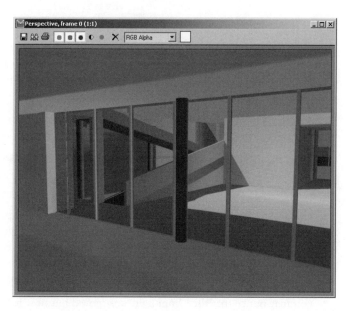

Now you begin to see more detail in the courtyard. The area around the ramps is better defined, and the alcove to the right shows more depth. You see the ceiling of the room in the foreground beginning to appear. Using colored lights can be an effective way of simulating color bleeding off large surfaces, like the courtyard or the ceiling. It is a little like color painting with light.

TIP When faking ambient light, don't be afraid to place lights in physically impossible places, like under the floor, behind a solid wall, or above the ceiling. As you'll learn later in this chapter, lights that do not cast shadows penetrate through surfaces and illuminate what lies beyond. The best "fakiosity" results come from using multiple strategically placed low-intensity lights to simulate the light bounced off large surfaces.

Adding a Highlight with an Omni Light

Next you'll learn how to add a highlight to the glass. By adding a highlight, you will be able to see that there is indeed glass in the windows, and it adds a bit of interest to the rendering. You'll also get a chance to see some of the advanced features of Omni light.

1. Go to the Create tab in the Command Panel and click the Lights tool. Then click the Omni tool in the Object Type rollout.

2. In the Perspective viewport click to place an Omni light anywhere. You don't need to be exact about the location, because the Highlight tool you'll use later will place the light accurately for you. You might notice that the shaded Perspective viewport lightens thanks to the addition of a new light source.

3. With the Omni light selected, choose Tools ➢ Place Highlight or press Ctrl+H on the keyboard. The cursor changes to the Place Highlight icon.

4. Go to the Perspective viewport and click and hold the location shown in Figure 6.14. You'll see a blue normal arrow appear at your cursor position. Release the mouse button when you see the normal pointing near the middle of the column.

The blue normal arrow represents a direction vector that is perpendicular to the surface over which the Place Highlight tool is positioned. The Place Highlight tool's job is to relocate the selected light somewhere along the normal vector. In other words, you will find the new Omni light some distance in a straight line away from the normal vector. This is helpful because it provides you with a quick way of orienting a light source in relation to a surface.

You may notice that the Omni light was moved but now it lies outside of the room. As long as the Omni is set to cast a shadow, it will be blocked from entering this room.

5. With the new Omni still selected, click the Modify panel and uncheck On in the Shadows group of the General Parameters rollout. Now the light will illuminate but not cast shadows (not possible in the real world).

6. Click the Quick Render button on the main toolbar and observe the highlight that appears on the glass as shown in Figure 6.15.

FIGURE 6.14
Click here to place the highlight on the column.

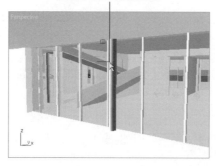

FIGURE 6.15
Rendered highlight on glass

The Place Highlight command places the currently selected light in a location that produces a highlight reflection at the location you selected in step 5. But the Omni light also shines on the rest of the building, washing out some detail. Fortunately, you can set VIZ's lights to shine only on the selected object instead of the entire model.

1. With the Omni light selected, click the Modify tab of the Command Panel.

2. In the General Parameters of the Omni light, click the Exclude button.

3. In the Exclude/Include dialog box, click the Include radio button in the upper right corner of the dialog box.

4. In the Scene Objects list, click Glass.03 to select it; then click the transfer button that points right as shown in Figure 6.16. Glass.03 moves from the list on the left to the list on the right.

TIP   *You could have instead excluded all the objects except for Glass.03 for the same effect.*

5. Click OK to close the Exclude/Include dialog box; then click the Quick Render tool. Now the highlight is limited to the glass, as shown in Figure 6.17.

At times, you may be requested to stretch reality a bit when producing renderings. The highlighted glass adds some interest to the rendering, even though it isn't necessarily a realistic portrayal of the lighting in the model. The highlight effect is not exclusive to the Omni light. The same effect can be achieved using virtually any type of light you choose.

The ability to select the objects that individual lights affect, although not possible in the real world, gives you some freedom to play with a scene, adding emphasis to some areas while downplaying others.

FIGURE 6.16

The Exclude/Include dialog box, showing the settings to include only the glass in the Omni light's list of objects

Select the Glass.03 group and then click the right arrow transfer button.

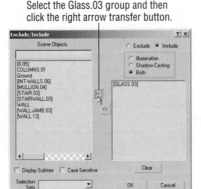

FIGURE 6.17
The villa rendered with a highlight on the glass

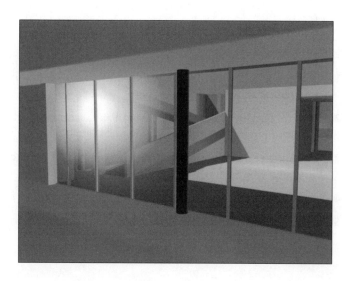

Looking at Omni Light Options

Since you're working with Omni lights, let's take a look at some of the other Omni light parameters that control its functions. You've seen how you can choose which objects the Omni light affects. The Include/Exclude dialog box is a feature common to all lights. And, just as with all other lights, you can include or exclude shadows in the manner described in the previous exercise. You can also control the Attenuation of the Omni light. The Attenuation settings let you control the distance of the light's reach.

NOTE *Attenuation is another physically impossible concept. Think of it as the ability to control where a light turns on and off as a function of how far the light is away from its source.*

By default, Attenuation is turned off. Try the following exercise to see how you can control an Omni light.

1. First, save the villa model as `MyVilla1.max`.

2. Open the `Omni.max` file. This is the file shown in Figure 6.18, and it is one of the files you can copy from the companion CD.

3. Right-click the Perspective viewport. You see an image that looks like Figure 6.18.

The `Omni.max` model is a simple scene of a light pole, a ground plane, and a wall. The light pole has an Omni light at the center of its globe. The globe itself has been excluded from the effects of the Omni light so that the light is unrestrained beyond the globe. The Omni light in this rendering has been inserted into the scene with its default settings unchanged.

The light from the Omni light casts a shadow from the pole, but is otherwise unrestrained. You can adjust the attenuation, however, to limit the range of the light. Try the following exercise to get a feel for the Attenuation settings.

1. Click the Select Objects By Name tool; then, in the Select Objects dialog box, choose Omni01 from the list and click Select.

2. Click the Modify tab of the Command Panel, scroll down the panel to the Intensity/Color/ Attenuation rollout and click to open the rollout.

3. Click the Use check box in the Far Attenuation group. A pair of Sphere gizmos appears around the Omni light, as shown in Figure 6.19.

4. Click and drag the Far Attenuation End spinner upward so that its value reads 37 feet.

5. Click and drag the Far Attenuation Start spinner upward so that its value reads 10 feet.

6. Click the Quick Render tool. You now see the light attenuated to a distance of 37 feet. It casts a dim light against the wall (see Figure 6.20).

FIGURE 6.18
An Omni light used to light a simple scene

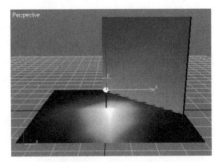

FIGURE 6.19
The perspective viewport showing the Far Attenuation spheres

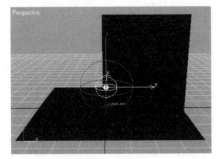

The End distance setting controls the farthest reach of the light. You can also set the distance of maximum brightness, using Far Attenuation's Start setting.

1. Click and drag the Far Attenuation Start setting spinner upward so that its value reads 28 feet. At this distance, the center white gizmo just touches the wall.

2. Click the Quick Render tool. Now the light on the wall is much brighter (see Figure 6.21).

The Start and Far Attenuation settings act a bit like the Hotspot and Falloff settings in direct lights and spotlights, only they act according to distance away from the source.

FIGURE 6.20
The rendering with Attenuation turned on and the End distance set to 37 feet

FIGURE 6.21
The rendering with the Far Attenuation Start setting at 28 feet

You've probably noticed that Attenuation Parameters also offers a Near Attenuation group. The settings in this group give you control where the Omni light begins to take effect as demonstrated in the following exercise.

1. Click the Use check box in the Near Attenuation group. Blue Attenuation gizmos display in the viewport.

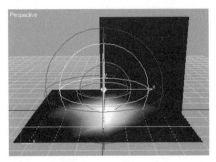

2. Set the Near Attenuation Start value to 15 feet and the Near Attenuation End value to 17 feet.

3. Click the Quick Render tool. Notice that the shadow of the pole appears to expand and soften, as shown in Figure 6.22.

This time, the Near Attenuation settings are limiting the near distance that the light begins to affect. In this scene, we've created the effect of a larger, softer shadow being cast by the pole, even though the dark area is actually the result of the Near Attenuation setting limiting the near range of the light cast by the Omni light.

FIGURE 6.22
The scene rendered using the Near Attenuation parameters

Adding Shadow Effects

You've seen how a single direct light can be used to simulate the sun. You can also use lighting to add emphasis or to provide a sense of drama. Shadows can be controlled to provide a seemingly sharp, strong light source or a softer, more diffuse interior light. In this section, you'll take a look at some of the more commonly used lighting options, starting with shadows.

By default, the shadow option for lights is turned on so that when you render your model, you see shadows cast.

NOTE The default shadow settings are controlled by the new Custom UI and Defaults Switcher.

1. Open the file `Savoye6e.max` from the CD.

2. Click Quick Render on the main toolbar. The front of the Villa Savoye is rendered with shadows as shown in Figure 6.23.

If you look carefully at your last rendering, you'll see that there are indeed shadows from the columns and the rest of the building. The shadows are not exactly right, however. There are parts of the model that show light *leaking* through the shadows as shown in Figure 6.23. You might also notice that the shadows from the columns don't quite start at the column bases.

There are a few options you can use to correct these problems. Let's start with the Shadow Map parameters of the Target Direct light object you're using to simulate the sun.

1. Click the Target Direct light object named SUN. This is the light in the lower corner of the building in the top viewport.

2. Click the Modify tab in the Command Panel to view the parameters for the Sun.

FIGURE 6.23
With the current shadow settings, the shadow is not completely correct, as shown in this picture.

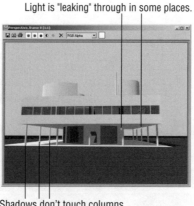

Light is "leaking" through in some places.

Shadows don't touch columns.

3. Scroll down the panel to the Shadow Map Params rollout and click it to open. You see the Bias, Size, and Sample Range settings.

4. Click the Bias setting and enter **0.2**↵ to change its value from 1 to 0.2. By reducing this number, you bring the shadow closer to the object that is casting the shadow.

5. Right-click the Perspective viewport and then click the Quick Render tool in the main toolbar. This time the shadow is rendered more accurately, filling in those portions it missed in the previous rendering (see Figure 6.24).

Softening Shadow Edges

Another option that lets you control the softness of the shadow edge is Sample Range. In some situations, you may want the edge of the shadow softer for partially cloudy outdoor scenes or for interior views with combined diffuse and direct lighting. The following exercise shows the effect of Sample Range.

1. Set the Sample Range for the SUN direct light to 10.

2. Click the Quick Render tool to see the effects of the new Sample Range setting as shown in Figure 6.25.

You can see the subtle effects of a softer shadow by looking at the shadows of the columns. Also notice that the shadows of the columns disappear on the ground below the building. The Sample Range setting is high enough to obliterate the thin column shadows.

FIGURE 6.24
The new rendering with the shadows filled in

FIGURE 6.25

The shadow edges are softened with a greater Sample Range setting.

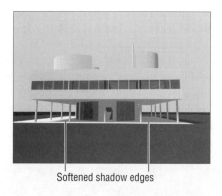

Softened shadow edges

A soft shadow edge lends realism to objects in indoor settings and in close-up views of outdoor objects, but in some situations, a sharp, crisp shadow edge is more desirable. There are two ways to achieve a sharp shadow edge. You can manipulate shadow settings in VIZ to obtain a high degree of accuracy in the shadow representation, or you can go with an entirely different shadow rendering method offered by VIZ, called *ray tracing*. This method models the actual path of light to generate shadows. Ray-Traced Shadows are more accurate, but they can add a lot of time to the rendering process. They also produce a sharp shadow edge, so in situations where a soft shadow is desired, you will have to use the default shadow mapped type of shadow or some combination of both Ray-Traced and Shadow Map Shadows.

In the next section, you'll look at how you can set up a shadow map to create a sharper shadow edge.

Understanding Shadow Maps

So far, you've been using the default *shadow mapping* method for casting shadows. A shadow map is a temporary *bitmap* image (made of pixels) of the shadows cast by objects in the model. You never actually see this bitmap. VIZ uses it to determine the shape and location of the shadow in a model. Since the shadow map is really a bitmap image, a shadow's sharpness depends on the resolution of the shadow map. If the shadow map has a small size setting, it creates a shadow that is rough around the edges, like a low-resolution rendering. Figure 6.26 shows a sample model with a very low-resolution shadow map that clearly displays the shadow map pixels around the shadow edge.

You can increase the Shadow Map Size setting to reduce the stairstepping effect of the shadow edge. This stairstepping comes directly from the pixels that make up the shadow map. Figure 6.27 shows the sample image again with the Size setting doubled from the previous figure.

A larger shadow map makes for a more even shadow edge. If the shadow map size is too great, however, it will consume greater amounts of memory and increase rendering time.

Another setting that is directly related to shadow map size is the spread of the light source. The shadow map is directly related to the area that is lit by the light source casting the shadow. If the area or spread of the light is decreased, the shadow map must also include a smaller area. If the shadow map size is reduced relative to the object casting the shadow, then more of the shadow map area can be devoted to the shadow outline. This has the effect of reducing the jagged edge of the shadow. Figure 6.28 shows the same model and light source as shown in Figure 6.27, but the hotspot has been reduced in size so the light is focused on a smaller area. Notice that the edges of the shadow appear less jagged because the shadow map isn't as stretched as it was in Figure 6.27.

You can control the jagged edge of the shadow to some degree by using the Sample Range setting. In the last exercise, you saw how the map sample range controls the softness of the edge of the shadow. A smaller map sample value makes for a sharper shadow but also reveals more of the shadow map's bitmap edge. If the Sample Range setting is too low, you begin to see the stairstep edges of the pixels of the shadow map, as shown in Figure 6.26.

FIGURE 6.26
This image shows a shadow with a low Shadow Map Size setting coupled with a low Sample Range setting of 0.1.

FIGURE 6.27
Increase the map size setting to reduce the stairstep effect.

The sample range value is actually the number of pixels in the rendered image that are blended to soften the edge of the shadow. This has the effect of hiding the pixelated shadow edges, as shown in Figure 6.29. Here you see the same image as shown in Figure 6.29 but with an increased sample range.

If you look carefully at the vertical edge shadow to the right, you can still detect the stairstep edge of the pixelated shadow map (it appears as a slightly wavy edge). But if you aren't looking for it, you may not notice it. You can also further increase the softness of the shadow edge by increasing the difference between the Hotspot and Falloff settings. As the Sample Range setting decreases, however, the hotspot/falloff difference has less effect.

FIGURE 6.28

The box and light with a decreased hotspot and falloff area

FIGURE 6.29

The same image as in Figure 6.28, but with a sample range of 6

Taking all of this into account, you need to increase the shadow map size and reduce the sample range to sharpen the shadow edge. You also need to keep the lighted area as narrow as possible while still keeping all of the objects in your scene lighted. So to get the sharpest shadow with a shadow map, you need to find a balance between the map size, sample range, light spread, and to some degree, the hotspot/falloff difference. Figure 6.30 shows the sample box and light with a sample range of 1, a map size of 2048, and a Falloff setting as close to the hotspot setting as possible.

To see firsthand the effects of these settings, try sharpening the shadows on the villa model.

1. In the Shadow Map Params rollout for the SUN light source, change the Size value to 3000.

2. Change the sample range to 1.

3. Make sure that the Perspective view is selected and then click the Quick Render button. Notice how the shadow appears to be sharper. You may also notice that the shadow is indeed more jagged around the edges in some locations (see Figure 6.31).

4. Save the villa model as MyVilla2.max.

Using Ray Traced Shadows

You may feel that using the Shadow Map settings in the last exercise requires too many compromises to achieve the sharpest shadows. If you want the sharpest, most accurate shadows possible, you'll want to use ray tracing.

Ray-Traced Shadows derive the shadow boundary by modeling the path of light from the light source to the shadow surface. The benefits are a very accurate shadow with no stairstep edges, because ray tracing is not based on a bitmap. You do pay a penalty in increased rendering time, but in many cases, the time is well worth it. Figure 6.32 shows two images of a fairly complex model that contains transparent elements as well as some detailed structural elements. The top image is the model rendered with a shadow map, whereas the second is rendered using Ray-Traced Shadows. The Ray-Traced Shadows show much more detail.

FIGURE 6.30
A fairly sharp shadow achieved with a high size setting and a low sample range

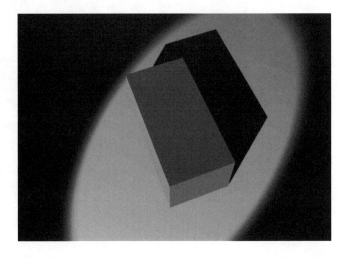

FIGURE 6.31
The villa rendered with a sharper shadow map

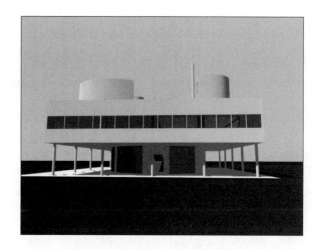

FIGURE 6.32
(Top) An image using Shadow Map shadows (Bottom) The same image using Ray Traced Shadows

With Ray-Traced Shadows, you don't have to be concerned with map sizes and sample ranges. Try the following exercise to see how Ray-Traced Shadows affect the villa model.

1. In the Modify tab of the Command Panel, scroll up to the General Parameters rollout.

2. Click the Shadow Map drop-down menu in the Shadows group and select Ray Traced Shadows.

3. Click the Quick Render tool on the Render toolbar. The villa is rendered with smoother looking shadows, as seen in Figure 6.33.

While the differences are not as dramatic as those shown in Figure 6.31, the Ray Traced Shadows rendering of the villa does show smoother shadows, particularly on the lower right side of the image. You can also see more detail in the shadow behind the window at the right side of the image. You can increase the spread of the light source now without affecting the sharpness of the shadows.

Using Advanced Ray Traced Shadows and Area Shadows

Both the Advanced Ray Traced and Area Shadows options create Ray-Traced Shadows, but they offer a few additional properties that the standard Ray-Traced Shadows do not have.

BLURRING SHADOW EDGES

Advanced Ray Traced Shadows allow you to add a softer edge, or *penumbra*, to shadows, which is a feature absent in the standard Ray-Traced Shadow.

To use it, you can select Advanced Ray-Traced Shadow from the Shadows group of the General Parameters rollout of any light.

This selection displays the Adv. Ray-Traced Params rollout, where you can control the quality with the Basic Options pop-up. Select 2-Pass Antialias for maximum quality.

FIGURE 6.33

The villa rendered using the Ray Traced Shadows option

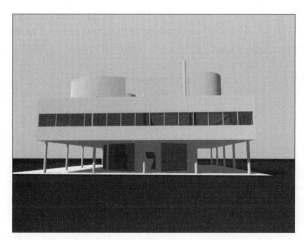

The Shadow Bias option works like the Bias option for map shadows. If the shadow appears to "bleed" around the edge of the object casting the shadow, forming a dark edge, you can increase the Shadow Bias setting to remove the dark edge. Or if the shadow appears to begin too far from the object, you can decrease the Shadow Bias setting.

The Jitter Amount setting smoothes out the effect of the blurred shadow edge. If you look carefully at a blurred shadow, you will see that it is made up of several gradations of values, each with its own distinct edge. The Jitter Amount setting will blend the gradations together to further soften the shadow edge.

CONTROLLING SHADOW SHARPNESS OVER DISTANCE

If you look at the shadow of a tree on a bright, sunlit day, you notice that parts of the tree closer to the ground cast sharper shadows than those farther away. This is caused by the combined effect of direct sunlight and the general ambient glow given off by the sky. You can simulate this effect using the Area Shadows option. Area shadows will vary the width of shadow edge blurring or penumbra, depending on the distance between the object casting the shadow and the surface on which the shadow falls.

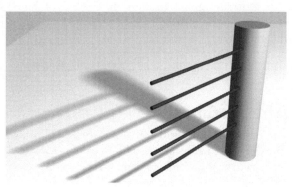

To use Area Shadows, select it from the Shadows group of the General Parameters rollout of any light. Once you've selected it, you can add the shadow penumbra effect to the shadow edge by increasing the Shadow Quality under the Area Shadows rollout in the Antialiasing Options group.

As with the Advanced Ray-Traced Shadow settings, Shadow Bias controls how close or far away the shadow starts from its object, and Jitter Amount smoothes the effect of the blurred shadow edge.

A couple of other options in the Area Shadows rollout are important in controlling shadows. The first is the Basic Options pop-up.

These options—Simple, Rectangle Light, Disk Light, Box Light, and Sphere Light—affect the shape and quality of the shadow being cast. For example, a Rectangle Light casts a shadow in the manner of a flat ceiling light fixture. A Sphere Light casts a shadow like a globe. The light itself does not take on any of these shapes, but you can think of these Area Shadow modes as the "virtual" shape of the light fixture.

In conjunction with the Mode settings are the Area Light Dimensions settings at the bottom of the Area Shadows rollout. These options control the size of the "virtual" shape of the light as set by the Mode setting. A larger Area Light Dimension tends to increase the spread of the shadow edge blur, just as a larger light fixture would tend to spread shadow edges in the real world.

You won't use these shadow options in any of the exercises of this book, so you may want to experiment with them on your own by creating a simple scene with a box, a plane for a ground surface, and a single, standard light source.

NOTE *There is a new shadow type called the mental ray Shadow Map that will be covered in Chapter 11.*

Playing in the Shadows

You've seen how you can bring out the depth of a space by adding lights to simulate reflected light. In the villa example you looked at before, you had a combination of direct light simulating the sun and a set of Omni lights to simulate ambient light. In this section, you'll learn how to play with shadows by using a combination of lights and objects.

In the last section, I mentioned that, if you use a bitmap shadow, you can soften the edge of your shadows and that Ray Traced Shadows brings out detail. Obtaining both effects in the same rendering can be a little tricky, but you may find that you need to do just that in some situations. The following series of exercises will show you how you can mix these two types of shadows to control the composition and appearance of a rendering.

Using Two Suns

You'll use a model that was created for the Avery Aquatic Center on the Stanford campus in Palo Alto, California. You'll be working on a view of the entrance to the center. The entrance consists of a tree-lined, paved walkway with a sign and a set of monuments. Let's take a look at the file and a first rendering.

1. Open the Aquatic.max file.

NOTE   *The sample file contains many materials that you will learn how to make in the next chapter.*

2. Make sure that the Perspective viewport is selected; then click the Quick Render button on the main toolbar. The rendering appears as shown in Figure 6.34.

Notice the large, square shadow in the foreground. This is a shadow of the tree in the foreground. You can see a small part of this tree in the upper left corner of the rendering. All the trees project rectangular shadows, although this is less obvious in the trees toward the back. Also notice the odd shadows of the Avery Aquatic Center sign. The sawtooth pattern on the shadow is the result of the low resolution of the shadow map used by the direct light that simulates the sun. To give you a better idea of what the sign is supposed to look like, Figure 6.35 shows a diagram of the sign's design.

FIGURE 6.34
The Avery Aquatic
Center rendered

This sign poses an unusual problem in lighting, because it contains a wavy, perforated screen. At a distance, this screen looks like a translucent material, so it is given a material that is partially transparent. Even so, a Shadow Mask shadow doesn't work well with this design, nor does it work well with the trees.

You can improve the look of the sign by using a Ray Traced Shadow for the sun, but the complexity of the model combined with a Ray Traced Shadow will substantially increase the rendering time. You want to minimize the rendering time if you can, especially if you are working toward a deadline. Figure 6.36 shows the same rendering with the sun's shadow parameter changed to a Ray Traced Shadow.

FIGURE 6.35
The design of the Avery Aquatic Center sign

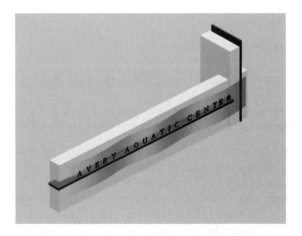

FIGURE 6.36
A second rendering with a Ray Traced Shadow setting

With a Ray Traced Shadow, the sign looks fine, but the tree shadow looks a bit odd because the trees in the scene are really just flat, vertical planes. In reality, the tree would cast a larger shadow. The tree shadow in the foreground would also have a softer edge.

To obtain a fast rendering speed and still maintain a crisp shadow on the sign, you can use two different light sources for the sun. One light will project a Ray Traced Shadow specifically for the sign and trees, while the other will project a Shadow Map shadow for the rest of the model.

Adding a Second Sun

You saw in previous chapters that you can select objects for illumination and shadow casting for each light in your model. In the following exercise, you'll remove the sign and trees from the effects of the current sunlight; then you'll create a second sun that will affect only the trees and the sign. This second sun will be set to use a Ray Traced Shadow.

1. Close the Rendered Frame Window; then select the target directional light in the User viewport. This is the light used to simulate the sun.

2. In the Modify tab of the Command Panel, click the Exclude button in the General Parameters rollout. The Exclude/Include dialog box displays.

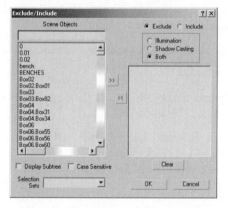

3. Scroll down the Scene Objects list box to the left and select each object whose name begins with SIGN: SIGNbody, SIGNmetal, SIGNmetal2, SIGNscreen, SIGNtext01, and SIGNtower.

4. Click the right-pointing double arrow to move the selected items to the list box to the right.

5. Scroll farther down the list on the left and select each item whose name begins with Tree except Treeshadow. These are Tree01 through Tree04 and the three Treecamphor items.

6. Click the right-pointing arrow again to include these trees in the list box on the right. This has the effect of excluding these objects from both illumination and shadow casting.

7. Click OK to exit the dialog box.

8. Right-click the Perspective viewport to activate it and click the Quick Render tool. Now you see the rendering with the trees and sign appearing rather dark, as shown in Figure 6.37.

FIGURE 6.37
The rendering with
the trees and sign
excluded from the
sunlight object

You need to illuminate the sign and trees with a light. To do this, make a copy of the existing sun and change its shadow parameter to Ray Traced.

1. If it isn't selected already, select the SUN directed light in the User viewport.

2. Choose Edit ➢ Clone.

3. In the Clone Options dialog box, choose the Copy radio button and enter **SUNraytraced** for the name. Click OK to close the dialog box.

4. In the Modify tab, click the Exclude button in the General Parameters rollout. The Exclude/ Include dialog box displays. Notice that the list on the right includes the same items that you excluded from the original SUN light object.

5. Click the Include radio button in the top right of the dialog box. This causes the new light to include only the items listed in the list box to the right, instead of excluding those items.

6. Click OK to close the dialog box.

You've created a second sun that illuminates only the sign and the trees. The original SUN directed light illuminates everything else. Now you've got one more important step to take: you need to set the new sun to cast a Ray Traced Shadow.

1. Scroll in the Command Panel to the General Parameters rollout and open it if it isn't already open.

2. Click the Object Shadows drop-down list and select Ray Traced Shadows.

3. Make sure the Perspective viewport is selected; then click the Quick Render tool. The rendering will take a bit more time when it gets to the sign. Once it's done, you'll see a view similar to Figure 6.38.

Although the view took longer to render, it still rendered considerably faster than if you had used a Ray Traced Shadow for the entire scene. But there is something missing: the sign and trees don't cast shadows. This is because the ground plane isn't included in the set of objects affected by the SUNraytraced sun object. You could include the ground in the SUNraytraced light, but you'd greatly increase the rendering time, and you'd have the same effect as you would if you had simply changed the original sun to project a Ray Traced Shadow.

To get around this problem, you can add some additional props that will cast shadows from the original SUN directed light that is casting a Shadow Map shadow.

Using Invisible Objects to Cast Shadows

The trees in this model produce a good deal of shade—considerably more than even the shadows created by the Ray Traced Shadow version of the rendered Perspective view you saw earlier. To simulate the shade from the trees, you can employ 2D shapes in the form of a tree shadow. These shapes can be used to cast shadows from the SUN directed light that uses a Shadow Map shadow. This combination will produce a softer shadow, which offers a somewhat more pleasing effect, especially for shadows in the foreground.

To save some time, these shadow shapes have already been added to the Avery Aquatic model. In the next exercise, you'll turn these shadow objects on and render the view to see how they work.

1. Click the Display tab in the Command Panel.

2. Click Unhide All in the Hide rollout. You'll see the 2D shadow object appear in the model, as shown in Figure 6.39.

3. Click the Quick Render tool. The view is rendered with the additional shadows being cast by the 2D shadow objects, as shown in Figure 6.40.

FIGURE 6.39

The 2D shadow objects appear in the model.

The 2D tree shadow objects

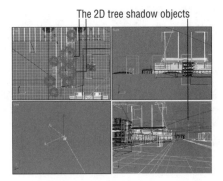

FIGURE 6.40

The scene rendered with tree shadows

The character of the rendering changes dramatically with the addition of shadows. The walkway has a more inviting appearance, instead of the somewhat harsh, sunlit open space. Also, the shadow in the foreground helps soften the composition by introducing a change in the ground plane.

Since you were spared the work of actually building and placing the shadow objects, you'll want to know some of the details of their construction. The shadow objects, named Treeshadow in the model, are 2D surfaces formed into the shape of a tree shadow. If you look in the Perspective viewport, you'll see that they are placed at about the height of the bottom of the tree canopy (see Figure 6.41). This location offers a more accurate placement for the shadow on the ground plane.

If you look carefully at the Top viewport, you'll see that the Treeshadow objects aren't centered on the trees for which they cast shadows. Instead, they are offset to the left and downward in the direction away from the light source. This simulates the way a tree shadow might be cast, given the relationship it has to the sun angle in the design.

FIGURE 6.41

The Perspective viewport with the Treeshadow objects at the level of the bottom of the tree canopy

Treeshadow objects

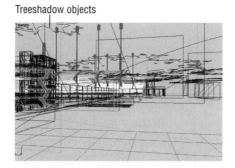

There's something else that's also quite unusual about the Treeshadow objects. Although they cast shadows in the Perspective rendering and are plainly visible in the Perspective viewport, they don't appear in the rendered view. You may recall that when you created a wineglass in an earlier chapter, parts of the glass disappeared when it was rendered. This was due to the alignment of the normals on a single surface. Remember that a surface really has only one visible side. The Treeshadow object takes advantage of this fact by orienting its normals toward the sky and away from our point of view. The end result is that VIZ doesn't render the Treeshadow object, but the trees still cast shadows.

You can create a Treeshadow object by starting with a plane or a star spline shape, editing its vertices to form a shape like the shadow of a tree. You can also form one random shape, then make multiple copies and join the copies into one object.

TIP *Another technique for creating shadows is called a* gobo light. *In this technique, you assign a projector map (a bitmap usually) to a light, and the light will cast a shadow in the shape of the bitmap. A projector map can be added to a light through the Projector Map group of its Advanced Effects rollout. Projector maps can also be animated to simulate the shadows of trees being blown by the wind, or a movie being projected upon the big screen.*

Using a Clone to Cast Shadows

The Avery Aquatic rendering is just about finished. Unfortunately, the sign itself looks as if it were floating in the rendering—as though it were pasted in. It appears to be dislocated because it doesn't cast a shadow.

You want the sign to cast a shadow using the original SUN direct light that uses a Shadow Map shadow. To do this, you'll make a copy of the main sign components that cast shadows. Those copies will be included in the set of objects that cast shadows from the original SUN directed light.

1. Click the Select by Name tool on the main toolbar.

2. In the Select Objects dialog box, select the SIGNbody and SIGNtower objects from the list; then click Select. These are the two main components of the sign.

3. Choose Edit ➤ Clone; then in the Clone Options dialog box, make sure that Copy is selected and click OK. VIZ creates copies of the objects you've selected, appending the number *01* to the name of each object.

You don't want these new objects to affect the rendered scene in any way other than to cast a shadow from the SUN directed light. To avoid any interference with other objects, you can reduce the size of these new objects so that they are smaller than the objects from which they were cloned.

1. Click the Select by Name tool again; then in the Select Objects dialog box, select SIGNbody01.

2. Click the Select and Uniform Scale tool on the main toolbar.

3. In the Transform pivot point flyout, select Use Pivot Point Center. This will cause the SIGNbody01 object to stay centered within the original SIGNbody object as it is scaled down, thereby keeping the SIGNbody01 object completely nested within the SIGNbody object (see Figure 6.42).

4. In the coordinate readout, change the X spinner value to **98%**.

You've now made the SIGNbody01 object smaller than the original object from which it was cloned. Repeat the process for the SIGNtower01 object.

1. Click the Select by Name tool again; then in the Select Objects dialog box, select SIGNtower01.

2. In the Scale Transform Type-In dialog box, change the coordinate readout's X spinner value to **98%**. VIZ maintains the Use Selection Center Transform flyout option.

3. Click the Select by Name tool once again and select SIGNbody01 and SIGNtower01.

4. Choose Group ➢ Group.

5. In the Group dialog box, enter **Signshadow** and then click OK. By grouping the newly created objects, you can keep them together and manage them more easily. From now on, you'll see the pair of objects listed as a single group surround by square brackets called [Signshadow] in the Select Objects dialog box.

FIGURE 6.42
The SIGNbody01 object is nested within the SIGN-body object.

The dark outline shows the SIGNbody01 clone.

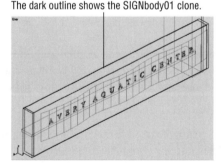

The new objects are automatically included to cast shadows from the original light source, and since you haven't explicitly included them with the objects lit by the SUNraytraced directed light, they aren't affected by that light.

TIP   It is possible to use lights that have negative multipliers. This has the amazing effect of removing light from the scene—something that is clearly not possible in the real world. Try using negative lights to soak up light from washed out areas in scenes that use the scanline renderer. Negative lights will not be effective in physically based lighting simulations with the radiosity or mental ray renderers.

Using the Light Lister

In more complex scenes you will find that you need to have dozens or perhaps even hundreds of lights. Managing these lights can become a huge problem if you have to edit the parameters for each light source—one at a time.

As you do test renderings you will undoubtedly see problems in the levels of illumination, light color, shadow casting, and so on that require you to edit many light parameters. Fortunately there is a special tool that is designed to help you with light management called the Light Lister.

TIP   Be sure to instance lights that are meant to be wired together in the real world. For example, you'll save quite a bit of time by making instance clones of downlights in the same room. That way, changes that you make to one instance are immediately updated in all of its siblings.

1. Reset the scene and create a direct light, two instanced Omnis, and a spotlight.

2. Choose Tools ➤ Light Lister….

   The Light Lister is shown in Figure 6.43. It lists each one of the light sources in your scene, and allows you to change almost all of the relevant parameters in one convenient dialog.

FIGURE 6.43
The Light Lister

Instanced lights are grouped together in a single pop-up.

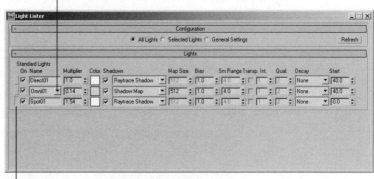

This vertical bar indicates the selected object.

Reading from left to right in Figure 6.43, you can select a light object, turn each light on or off; change the name, the multiplier, or the color; toggle shadows on or off; change shadow type; and alter all the relevant shadow parameters in the Light Lister dialog box. This is obviously much faster than individually selecting each light and changing its parameters in the Modify panel.

3. It is possible to make changes to selections of lights all at the same time by using the General Settings feature. Click the General Settings radio button in the Configuration rollout (Figure 6.44).

FIGURE 6.44

General Settings in the Light Lister

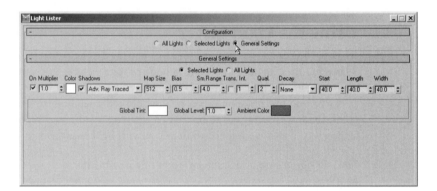

4. In the General Settings rollout, click the All Lights radio button. Any changes you make here will now affect all the lights in the scene.

TIP   You can make changes to a series of lights (but not to all of the lights in the scene) by first selecting those light objects you want to change, and then using the Selected Lights radio button in the General Settings rollout.

5. Change the shadow type to Area Shadows. This should affect all the lights in the scene.

WARNING   It may be a bit confusing, but only the things you change in the General Settings rollout will take effect. For example, even though the Multiplier may read as 1.0, it will not apply to your selected lights unless you actively change this value in the Light Lister dialog box.

6. Click the All Lights radio button in the Configuration rollout to return to the initial view. Notice that all the lights now are set to cast Area Shadows.

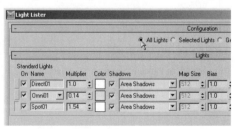

Summary

Lighting tools give you a great degree of control over a design's appearance. With lighting, you can add shadows that enhance a scene with realism and depth. Ambient light lets you bring out detail in the darker regions of a scene. You have learned many techniques for quickly approximating ambient light in this chapter. It takes some practice and experience to use these tools with confidence, but with the knowledge you've gained in this chapter, you'll be off to a good start in using them.

In the next chapter, you'll begin to explore another major tool in building your designs: the Material Editor. With the Material Editor, you can add texture and lifelike detail to your model. Materials can provide a quick way to enliven your design and provide a sense of realism. You'll see firsthand how you can quickly add interest to a design by adding materials to the Villa Savoye model.

Chapter 7

Enhancing Models with Materials

THE MATERIALS FEATURE OF VIZ lets you simulate surface color, texture, transparency, and even reflectance and roughness or bumpiness. The Material Editor in VIZ lets you create and modify materials that you can then apply to objects to achieve a realistic effect.

This chapter will introduce you to the Material Editor and how to use, design, and edit materials. You'll see how materials can be used to add color and realism to your models.

◆ Understanding Bitmap Texture Maps

◆ Adding Materials to Objects

◆ Understanding Mapping Coordinates

◆ Editing Materials

◆ Selecting Shaders

◆ Mapping Scalar Modifiers

◆ Using Bump Maps

◆ Adding Entourage

◆ Raytracing Reflection and Refraction

◆ Assigning Materials to Parts of an Object

◆ Using the Architectural Material

◆ Material Utilities

Understanding Bitmap Texture Maps

To simulate a surface material, VIZ offers preset material libraries. These are libraries of simulated materials that you can assign to objects. Each material contains properties such as color, reflectance, transparency, and roughness. Many materials also use images, or *bitmaps*, to simulate the look of complex surfaces such as marble, wood, or brick. Other materials use *procedural* maps, which are a bit like mathematical simulations of the actual material.

A bitmap is an image file composed of pixels that shows a graphic sample of the material. One common bitmap image is marble; another is brick. You might think of a material that uses bitmaps as a kind of decal or sticker that is placed on a surface. You can use bitmaps in the properties of a material in several ways: texture maps, bump maps, opacity maps, specular maps, shininess maps, self-illumination maps, and reflection maps, to name a few. Diffuse maps are the most common use of bitmaps and are the easiest to understand.

Procedural maps use mathematical formulas instead of bitmap images to simulate a texture. Unlike bitmaps, procedural maps often have parameters that can be set to control their visual effects; they also have a more uniform appearance when applied to objects that have unusual shapes or that are sliced or cut open in some way. For example, you can use the wood procedural map to create an elaborate carved wood sculpture, and the wood grain is mathematically defined three dimensionally so you can see the grain running throughout the carved regions. Phenomena such as smoke, which might normally be difficult to simulate, can also be simulated effectively using a procedural map.

In this introduction to materials, you'll be focusing on bitmap texture maps.

Diffuse Color Maps

One of the many predefined materials that VIZ offers is brick. Brick is an example of a texture map. Whenever you assign the brick material to an object, VIZ *pastes* a bitmap image of a brick wall onto the object when it is rendered so that the object looks like a brick surface (see Figure 7.1).

FIGURE 7.1
An example of a bitmap image (left) used as a texture map to simulate a brick wall

AMBIENT/DIFFUSE MAPS

VIZ calls texture maps such as the brick example in Figure 7.1 *ambient/diffuse* color maps because the bitmap is reflected in ambient and diffuse light. You can use different bitmaps for the ambient and diffuse components of a material, but generally these two are tied together. To get a better idea of the different types of light an object reflects, look at Figure 7.2. It shows a sphere that indicates the different ways light is reflected off an object.

FIGURE 7.2
A sample sphere showing different types of reflected light

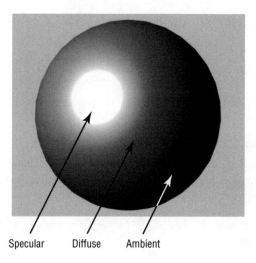

Specular   Diffuse   Ambient

    When the ambient light in a model is increased, you begin to see the dim portions of an object or those parts that are in shadows. The ambient map appears in these areas where indirect light strikes the surface. The diffuse map appears in the brighter portions of a model, which are lit by light directly emanating from light sources in the scene. The ambient and diffuse maps blend together so that, as the ambient light increases, the ambient maps seamlessly merge with the diffuse maps.

SPECULAR MAPS

Specular maps that are full-color image bitmaps appear only in specular highlights of a surface. On a shiny object, the specular portion of the object would normally appear white, as shown in Figure 7.2. You can have the specular region of an object display a surface feature by using specular maps as shown in Figure 7.3.

NOTE *Shaders control how the ambient, diffuse, and specular components of a material blend together. You will learn more about shaders later in this chapter.*

GLOSSINESS MAPS

Glossiness maps also affect the specular region of a shiny object, but instead of displaying a colored texture, a glossiness map controls the level of glossiness on a surface. You would use a glossiness map on an object whose surface is not uniformly glossy but rather is alternately rough and shiny, perhaps like a troweled stucco wall where the flat areas appear to be glossy and the depressions matte.

FIGURE 7.3
A sphere with a specular map displaying a shiny pattern

SELF-ILLUMINATION MAPS

Using the self-illumination feature, you can create materials that appear to glow or emit their own light. A self-illumination map is a grayscale bitmap image that determines the *glow* of a surface based on the bitmap's grayscale intensity. White is the brightest glow, whereas black is no glow at all.

TIP   You will learn other more advanced ways to make objects emit light when using the radiosity and mental ray renderers in Chapters 10 and 11.

OPACITY MAPS

Opacity maps use grayscale bitmap images to control opacity and transparency. For example, you can turn a solid surface into an intricate filigree using an opacity map, as shown in Figure 7.4.

FIGURE 7.4
A single, blank surface can be made to appear quite intricate by using opacity maps. The bitmap image to the left was used to turn a simple rectangular object into an intricate screen.

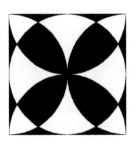

BUMP MAPS

You can also simulate a bumpy texture using grayscale bitmap images. Figure 7.5 shows a 2D bitmap image and objects rendered with a material that uses the bitmap to simulate a bumpy surface. VIZ converts the different intensities of light and dark tones of the grayscale bitmap into high and low points on the bumpy surface. The bump effect is an illusion that manipulates surface normals so that the surface seems to be in low relief.

TIP   Maps accept both grayscale and color images as input. However, most maps only use the grayscale information to affect a material. The exceptions where color information is actually used by the maps are the diffuse, ambient, and reflection maps.

FIGURE 7.5

A bumpy surface can be simulated, using a grayscale bitmap shown at left. The light portions of the bitmap translate to high points in the bumpy surface, while the darker portions of the bitmap translate to low points.

REFLECTION MAPS

A reflection map is a special type of bitmap assignment. It is used where you want a material that appears to be reflective, such as the glass in an office building or a lake or pond (see Figure 7.6). In an animated scene, the reflection map you use can move (if you select an animated image format), just as reflections move when you pass by a reflective surface.

REFRACTION MAPS

A refraction map is similar to a reflection map, but instead of giving the appearance of a reflection, such as a chrome ball, it gives the appearance of a refracted image, such as a crystal ball. A refraction map simulates the properties of glass, water, or other transparent material that bends light.

FIGURE 7.6
Reflection maps give
the impression of a
reflective surface
such as the glass
and floor in this
rendering.

FIGURE 7.6
Reflection maps give
the impression of a
reflective surface
such as the glass
and floor in this
rendering.

DISPLACEMENT MAPS

A bump map simulates a bumpy surface, but it doesn't actually change the geometry of the model. Displacement maps are similar to bump maps in that they seem to alter the shape of a surface, but displacement maps go one step further and actually modify the geometry of the object to which they are applied. You can, for example, turn a flat surface into a dome by using a displacement map. You need to be cautious when you use a displacement map, as it can generate a large number of faces on an object, thereby increasing the file size and rendering time. You can think of displacement maps as a modeling technique based on materials.

Surface Properties

There are some materials that rely solely on the properties of color, specularity, and opacity and don't use maps of any kind. Instead, they use color and specular levels to simulate the appearance of a substance (see Figure 7.7).

FIGURE 7.7
Examples of surface
materials that don't
require bitmaps

Most materials are a mixture of texture, bump, or opacity maps and color, specular levels, or transparency. Bitmaps and material properties are combined to simulate detail you would otherwise find impossible to re-create through surface or solid modeling alone (see Figure 7.8).

FIGURE 7.8

A simple sphere object with a single surface material that makes use of many of the different types of maps and properties available in VIZ

Adding Materials to Objects

For our tutorial, you'll start by selecting a few standard materials from a list and applying them to the model. Then, after checking the appearance of the materials with a test rendering, you'll look at ways to adjust the materials to better suit your model.

Before you dive in, it is important to let VIZ know where the dependent files are that you plan to use in your project.

Adding a Map Path to Help VIZ Find Bitmaps

VIZ needs to know where different types of files are kept for its use. VIZ stores its bitmap images in subfolders under Maps within the main VIZ folder. When you start to create your own materials, it may be a good idea to keep your own bitmap files in folders that are separate from the standard VIZ Map folder. For example, you might create a folder under the VIZ folder called Custom Maps to store your own bitmap files, or you might make a series of subfolders on your server so that the same set of maps can be shared within your office.

In the exercises in this chapter, you'll use bitmap files from the companion CD. The first step is to let VIZ know where to look for the files from the CD.

1. Choose Customize ➢ Configure Paths. The Configure Paths dialog box appears.

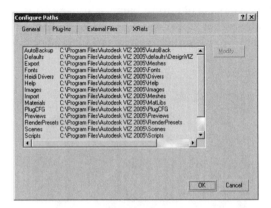

2. Click the External Files tab. You see a list showing the current path where VIZ searches for bitmap files and photometric files, among others.

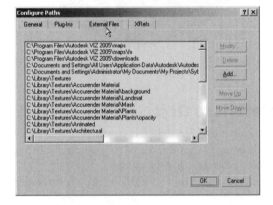

NOTE *The paths shown will likely differ from those on your system.*

3. Click the Add button to the far right. The Choose New Bitmap Path dialog box appears. This is a typical file dialog box that lets you search for and select a folder.

4. Locate and select the folder that contains the bitmaps from the companion CD; Check Include Subpaths to add multiple paths and then click Use Path.

5. Click OK in the Configure Paths dialog box.

Now you're ready to start using the bitmap files from the companion CD. You may have noticed other tabs in the Configure Paths dialog box. As you might guess, these other tabs let you indicate additional places to search: *General, Plug-Ins,* and *XRefs,* as the names of the tabs indicate. The General tab lets you determine where VIZ should look for various components of the program. Plug-Ins lets you add additional paths for plug-ins to VIZ. The XRefs tabs lets you indicate where VIZ should look when searching for XRef files. (XRefs are model files that have been externally referenced into a file. XRefs do not become part of the file into which they are imported, but remain separate files that are merely referenced when needed. In Chapter 9 you'll get a chance to learn more about XRefs.)

There are several utility programs that help you work with paths that you'll learn more about at the end of this chapter. Now that VIZ knows where to find the dependent files, you are now ready to begin the tutorial.

In this exercise, you'll open a model of the Villa Savoye and see that the glass in the model appears as an opaque blue material. The blue color is inherited from the AutoCAD layer color of the original DWG file. VIZ offers a glass material that's both transparent and shiny, and it includes a bitmap reflection that simulates the reflection of a partially cloudy sky. In the exercise, you'll add this glass material to the model.

TIP   There is a new material type in VIZ 2005 called the Architectural material. This new material greatly simplifies material creation. You may want to jump ahead in this chapter to read about how to use this new material. However, it is still important that you learn the Standard material and its associated concepts to gain a well-rounded understanding of how materials work in VIZ.

1. Open the ch07a.max file from the sample files on the companion CD.

2. Click the Material Editor tool on the main toolbar or type **M** on the keyboard.

The Material Editor window appears.

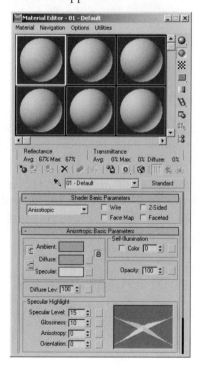

At the top, you see a set of sample slots, which are preview images of materials. Right now, there are no custom designed materials in the Material Editor, so all the slots show the same blank sphere representing the Standard material. Also notice that the top left slot is outlined with a thick, white border. This tells you that it is currently the active slot.

3. Click the Get Material button on the toolbar just below the sample images of spheres.

The Material/Map Browser appears.

4. In the Browse From radio button group, click Mtl Library. This lets you open a material library. Once you've opened a material library file, the list box to the right will change to display a set of materials.

5. Click the Open button in the File group near the bottom of the Material/Map Browser. The Open Material Library dialog box displays, listing the different material library files that are available.

You can create your own library files as you become more familiar with VIZ. For now, you'll use a predefined material library and make a few simple adjustments.

1. Select 3dsviz from the list; then click Open. A list of materials appears in the list box on the right side of the Material/Map Browser.

2. Scroll down the list and click Reflection_Outside. Once you've made your selection, you see a sample of the material in the sample viewer in the upper left corner of the window.

3. Double-click Reflection_Outside. The Relection_Outside material appears in the Material Editor in the upper left sample slot. Also notice that the name Relection_Outside appears in the drop-down list just below the row of tools.

4. Change the Opacity of the Relection_Outside material to 20%.

TIP *Glass is never completely transparent. It must have some opacity or you wouldn't be able to see it.*

5. Scroll down in the Material Editor and open the Maps rollout. Change the Reflection Amount spinner to 10%. You are toning down the amount of reflection on the glass.

6. Close the Material/Map Browser.

You've just loaded a material from one of the many VIZ material library files and placed it in the Material Editor. This is the first step in assigning a material to an object. Now, go ahead and assign the Glass-Clear material to the glass in your model.

1. Click the Select by Name tool on the main toolbar. You may need to move the Material Editor window to get to this tool.

2. Click the [Glass.03] item in the list; then click Select. The brackets denote groups in VIZ.

3. Go back to the Material Editor and click the Assign Material to Selection tool.

It may not be obvious that the glass is present in your model, so let's take a quick look at a rendered view to see the results of adding the glass.

1. Close the Material Editor and right-click the Perspective viewport to make it active.

2. Click the Quick Render tool on the main toolbar.

You see a rendered view of the building with the glass appearing as a transparent material, as shown in Figure 7.9.

FIGURE 7.9
The rendered view
with glass in place

It's difficult to tell whether the glass is really there. Next, you'll modify the parameters of the glass material to give it a bit more substance so that it will be easier to see in the rendering.

1. Click the Material Editor tool in the Material toolbar to open the Material Editor window.

2. Notice that the Glass-Clear material is still selected and is the current material in the window.

3. In the Anisotropic Basic Parameters rollout, change the Opacity spinner setting to **50**. Notice that the sample slot showing the glass darkens.

4. Click the Quick Render tool. This time the glass is more apparent in the rendering (see Figure 7.10).

FIGURE 7.10
The rendering with a
more opaque glass

You've just added a material to an object and then modified the material. Through the method just shown, you can add materials based on the object's name, as in the Glass.03 object. Be aware that, although you changed the glass transparency parameter in the model, the change didn't affect the Glass-Clear material in the RayTraced_01 VIZ material library. The parameter change affected only the material within the Material Editor and thus the model. You can save changes back to the VIZ material library using the Put to Library tool on the Material Editor's toolbar. This copies the current material to the library from which it came and saves the library to disc.

You've added a glass material to your model, and you've made a few modifications. In this section, you'll apply a material to the walls of the villa, but instead of using a pre-existing material, you'll create an entirely new one. The material you create will be fairly simple, but the exercises here will give you a chance to play with some of the settings you haven't tried yet.

1. Open the Material Editor if it is not already open; then click the lower left sample slot. You'll use this slot for your new wall material.

2. In the Material Name drop-down list, change the name to **wall**.

3. In the Shader Basic Parameters rollout, click the drop-down list and select Oren-Nayar-Blinn from the list.

4. Click the 2-Sided check box to force this material to render two-sided. If some of the surface materials seem to disappear, this will force them to appear correctly in the rendering.

NOTE *The 2-Sided option is sometimes needed in models that have been imported from AutoCAD because of improper normal orientation. This option isn't usually as critical for models built entirely within VIZ because the surfaces are facing in the correct orientation and 1-Sided surfaces generally are sufficient.*

Notice how the wall sample slot changes. It looks like a sphere with a dull surface. The options in the Basic Parameters rollout also change. In fact, the name of the rollout changes from Anisotropic Basic Parameters to Oren-Nayar-Blinn Basic Parameters, and you see additional parameters in the rollout. You can increase the matte appearance of the material by increasing the Roughness value.

Next, apply the new material to the walls and render the model.

1. Click the Select by Name tool on the main toolbar or type **H** on the keyboard.

2. In the Select Objects dialog box, Ctrl+click all the items that have WALL in their name, such as INT-WALLS and WALL-JAMB, then click Select.

3. With the wall sample selected, click the Assign Material to Selection tool.

4. Click the Quick Render tool on the Rendering toolbar. The building is rendered in a darker color.

Here you see that, by changing the type of shader you use, you actually change the value of the material. In this case, the material gets darker. This is because the Oren-Nayar-Blinn shader puts emphasis on the ambient and diffuse range of color parameters.

TIP Try changing the lighting in the scene and see how it affects the materials. Remember that surfaces render as a combination of geometry, lighting, and materials.

Fine-Tuning Color

The building is too dark, so you'll want to brighten the color of the wall material.

1. Close the Rendered Frame Window and open the Material Editor.

2. Click the Diffuse color swatch in the Oren-Nayar-Blinn Basic Parameters rollout. The Color Selector dialog box displays.

3. Change the Value setting to 230, a bit brighter. Notice that you can also drag the Whiteness slider down to achieve the same effect.

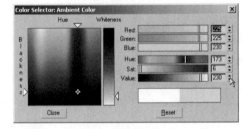

Both the Ambient and Diffuse color swatches now appear to be brighter. In the Oren-Nayar-Blinn shader, Ambient and Diffuse are linked, so changes in one color are mimicked by the other. Using the links is a quick way of ensuring you have identical hues in both swatches.

4. In the Material Editor, click the link symbol in between the Ambient and Diffuse color components. When this button is up, it means that the components are unlinked.

5. Click the Ambient color swatch to open the Color Selector. Drag the Whiteness slider up to decrease the color value. Stop dragging when the value parameter reads 180.

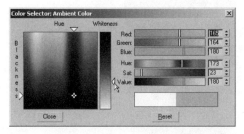

6. Close the Color Selector dialog box; then click the Quick Render tool again to see the results.

TIP   The Ambient color component of a material should be the same hue as the Diffuse color but a bit darker. This gives the material a bit more depth because the areas of the material that are indirectly lit appear darker. This may not be apparent on flat surfaces, but it has a more pronounced effect on curved surfaces.

Understanding Material Libraries

You imported the GlassClear material from the RayTraced_01 VIZ material library. This and other material library files can be found in the `matlibs` subfolder of the Autodesk VIZ 2005 folder. You aren't limited to this one material library. You can use all the files with the `.mat` extension in this folder, you can create your own library from materials you create in the Material Editor, or you can even use libraries from third-party producers. To open a different library, you need to be in the Material/Map Browser window. From there, you can select the Mtl Library radio button in the Browse From group and then select the Open button in the File group. You then see the Open Material Library dialog box.

To create a new library, click the Mtl Editor option in the Browse From group of the Material/Map Browser, then click Save As in the File group. You see the Save Material Library dialog box, which is a typical file dialog box. You can then enter a name for your library and click Save. The materials in the sample slots of the Material Editor will be saved in your new material library file.

You can also save selected materials by using the Selected radio button, or you can save all the materials in a model by choosing the Scene radio button. Both of these options in the Material/Map Browser expose the Save As button in the File group, allowing you to save an existing or create a new material library.

Adding Material Mapping Coordinates

If you just want to manipulate the color, transparency, and shininess of an object, you can usually create or use a material that doesn't use bitmaps to simulate a texture. Once you start to add a texture using bitmaps, you'll need to specify how that texture is applied to the object. You'll want to tell VIZ the size of the texture in relation to the object, as well as its orientation on the object. For example, you wouldn't want the brick pattern to appear with its courses running vertically, as in the example shown in Figure 7.11, nor would you want the brick pattern to be quite so large.

FIGURE 7.11
A brick wall with the brick course running vertically and at a large scale

To control how materials are applied to objects, you'll want to know how to use the *UVW Map* modifier. This modifier lets you precisely control the way a material is placed on an object. In the next exercise, you'll create a ground object and add a grass surface. The material you'll use, Ground-Grass, uses a bitmap image to give the appearance of grass. As part of the exercise, you'll use the UVW Map modifier to establish the orientation and size of the Ground-Grass material in relation to the object.

WHAT DOES UVW MEAN?

The *UVW* in the name UVW map refers to the coordinates of a material map. They indicate the direction of a map in a way similar to the XYZ Cartesian coordinates that you're already familiar with. The letters *UVW* are used to differentiate map coordinates from the standard XYZ coordinate designation and were chosen simply because they precede XYZ in the alphabet.

UVW map coordinates need to be differentiated from XYZ coordinates because, although they indicate direction in a way similar to XYZ coordinates, they don't treat measured distances in the same way. In a Cartesian coordinate system, distances are measured at specific intervals of feet, meters, or whatever measurement system you're using. UVW map coordinates, on the other hand, are measured as a percentage of width and height of a surface. Instead of feet or meters, UVW maps use real values from 0 to 1. The value used represents a percentage of the overall width of the surface being mapped, with 1 being equal to 100% of the surface width.

Because the coordinate values in a UVW map are based on a percentage, a U value of 0.5 can represent a measured distance that's different from a V value of 0.5. For example, imagine a rectangular surface with a UVW coordinate system whose origin is the lower left corner of the rectangle. The upper right corner of the rectangle would then be the coordinate 1,1, even though the length and width of the rectangle are not equal to each other. This may seem a bit odd at first, but if you consider that material maps are used to match an image to a surface, you begin to see the rationale behind the UVW map system. The relationship between a map and a surface is more important than their actual dimensions. You can think in terms of "What percentage of the surface does the map cover?" rather than "How many square inches does the map cover?"

First, you need to create an object to represent the ground. Use a simple box for this purpose.

1. Right-click the Top viewport; then use the Zoom tool to zoom out so that your view looks similar to Figure 7.12. Use the Pan tool to center the building in the viewport.

FIGURE 7.12

The top view

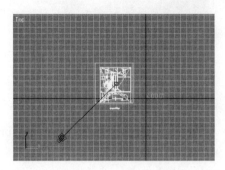

You want to zoom out so that you can create a large enough box to fill the scene without showing any obvious edges in your perspective view.

2. Click the Create tab of the Command Panel, click the Geometry tool, and then click Plane.

3. Place the plane shown in Figure 7.13 in the Top viewport.

FIGURE 7.13

Placing the plane in the Top viewport

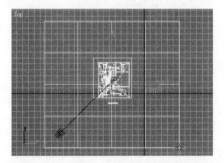

4. Give the new plane the name **Ground** in the Name and Color rollout input box.

Now you're ready to apply a material to the ground object. Just as with the glass, you'll use the Material Editor and Material/Map Browser to select a material from VIZ's Standard material library.

1. Click the Material Editor tool on the main toolbar. Then, in the Material Editor window, click the sample image in the middle of the top row of samples.

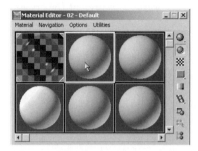

2. Click the Get Material tool just below the samples.

3. In the Material/Map Browser window, make sure the Mtl Library radio button is selected and then click the Open button in the File group.

4. In the Open Material Library File dialog box, select Ground and click Open.

5. Back in the Material/Map Browser, scroll down the list to locate the Ground-Grass listing; then double-click it. You'll see the sample slot in the Material Editor change to show the Ground-Grass material.

6. Close the Material/Map Browser.

7. Make sure that the Ground object is selected in your model; then click the Assign Material to Selection button in the Material Editor window.

8. To see the result of the new Ground object and its material, right-click the Perspective viewport, then click the Quick Render tool on the main toolbar (see Figure 7.14).

FIGURE 7.14
The rendered view with the Ground object added

Although the ground is there, it may not be what you expected. Instead of a ground plane that looks like grass, you see a green surface that varies in color but with no distinct pattern. The reason for this is that the bitmap image is stretched to fill the entire ground object. The camera view sees the grass as if it were a very near close-up view. The pixels that make up the bitmap are so stretched out that the ground looks like splotches of color.

You'll want to scale the Ground-Grass material to a size that's more in line with the Ground object's size. This can be done with the UVW Map modifier.

1. Close the Rendered Frame Window and make sure the Ground object is selected.

2. Click the Modify tab in the Command Panel.

3. Select UVW Mapping from the Modifier List drop-down list. You'll find it under the Object-Space Modifiers heading in the drop-down list.

The outline of the Ground object changes color in the Top viewport. What you are seeing is the UVW Map gizmo outlining the Ground object.

4. Expand the UVW Mapping listing in the Modifier Stack list; then select Gizmo. The UVW Map gizmo changes color to indicate its orientation. You see a green edge on the right side of the gizmo.

Let's take a moment to study the UVW Map gizmo. It has one green edge and has a small line sticking out on one side. Figure 7.15 gives you a clear picture of what the gizmo looks like.

FIGURE 7.15
The UVW
Map gizmo

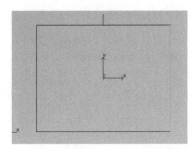

The color and the small line help you orient the UVW Map gizmo on an object by showing you which way is up and which ways are left and right. You'll get a more detailed look at the UVW Map gizmo after the current exercise. Let's continue by adjusting the gizmo to reduce the size of the material on the Ground object.

The UVW Map gizmo is now selected. To change the scale of the Ground-Grass material in relation to the Ground object, you need to scale down the gizmo.

1. Click the Select and Scale tool on the main toolbar.

2. In the coordinate readout, click the Absolute/Offset Mode Transform Type-In tool so that it's in Offset mode. Then change the X coordinate readout to **5**.

The gizmo is now very small compared to the viewport, and it is lost in the building at the center of the viewport. You'll want to move it so that you can see it again.

1. Click the Select and Move tool and click and drag the axis handle of the Transform gizmo to the right until you can see the UVW Map gizmo. It will look like a very small square, as shown in Figure 7.16.

FIGURE 7.16
Move the gizmo to
this location.

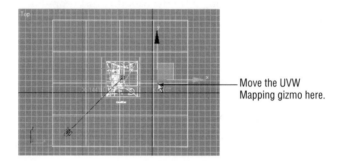

Move the UVW
Mapping gizmo here.

To see the effect of scaling the gizmo down, follow the remaining steps.

2. Click the gizmo listing in the Modifier Stack list to deactivate it. Then select the SUN light source.

3. In the Modify tab of the Command Panel, change the Hotspot/Beam parameter in the Directional Parameters rollout to **120 feet**. This will increase the area that the SUN light source covers.

4. Right-click the Perspective viewport and then click the Quick Render tool.

Now you can see the grass patterns emerging. When a texture map is smaller than the object it is assigned to, VIZ *tiles* the map to fill the object. This means that the map is repeated in a row-and-column array to fill the object's surface (see Figure 7.17).

Because the material is repeated, or *tiled*, over the Ground object, a pattern emerges, giving the ground the appearance of a manicured baseball field.

Understanding Mapping Coordinates

The UVW Map modifier you added in the last exercise told VIZ the size, location, and orientation of the material on the object it is assigned to. At render time, the image is usually applied to the object in a repeated, or tiled, fashion. You can also set a material to apply the bitmap just once. In this section, you'll take a closer look at the UVW Map modifier.

FIGURE 7.17
The rendered view of
the villa with the
Ground-Grass
UVW map altered

FIGURE 7.17
The rendered view of
the villa with the
Ground-Grass
UVW map altered

What Happens When You Add the Mapping Coordinates

The UVW Map gizmo you saw in the last exercise is a visual representation of the mapping coordinates. Its shape and color are aids in helping you see the bitmap's orientation more clearly. As mentioned earlier, the small line at the top of the icon represents the top of the bitmap, while the green shows the right side. These indicators can tell you at a glance whether the bitmap image of the material you are using is upside down, mirrored, or backward in relation to the object to which the coordinates are being applied, as shown in Figure 7.18.

FIGURE 7.18
The UVW Map gizmo in relation to a material bitmap

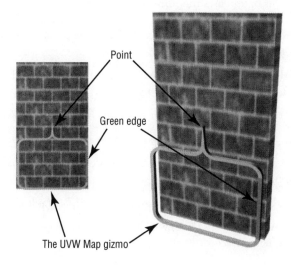

Point

Green edge

The UVW Map gizmo

The orientation of the bitmap in the preceding exercise is really not that important, but it can be important for texture maps that do have a specific orientation such as a brick pattern, or a single image such as a wine label or a road sign.

Figure 7.19 shows the UVW Map gizmo in relation to the Ground object as it appears in step 1 of the previous exercise. The gizmo represents the outline of the bitmap image associated with the Ground-Grass material. Figure 7.19 shows the relationship of the gizmo to the bitmap image, as well as the resulting rendered Ground object as seen from the top view.

Notice that the gizmo shows the approximate size of the bitmap in relation to the object to which it is being applied. When the model is rendered, multiple copies of the image are applied over the entire surface of the object, like tiles on a kitchen counter.

Figure 7.20 shows another way that the gizmo affects the appearance of a material. You see a brick wall with the gizmo rotated. The bricks are angled and aligned with the UVW Map gizmo.

Adjusting the UVW Map Gizmo

You have a number of options for controlling the size, shape, and orientation of the UVW Map gizmo. These will be crucial to your ability to place materials accurately on an object or face. Here are descriptions of the Alignment group options as they appear in the Command Panel.

Region Fit   Lets you fit the UVW Map gizmo to a specific rectangular area. This is useful for situations where you want a texture map to fit exactly over a specific region of an object. When you choose this option, you can select two points to define the two diagonal corners of the UVW Map gizmo. The process is similar to selecting a zoom region or creating a rectangle. Since this option lets you select any two points, it will stretch and distort the UVW Map gizmo in either the X or Y axis. To orient the UVW Map gizmo right side up, pick two points over the region starting with the lower left corner (see Figure 7.21).

Bitmap Fit   Adjusts the UVW Map gizmo's proportion to fit the shape of a particular bitmap image. This option uses the current UVW map size and alters the proportions to fit the bitmap proportions. The option is helpful if you want the bitmap to be displayed accurately in its original form. It also helps if you want a better idea of the bitmap's shape as you assign the mapping coordinates to objects.

View Align   Aligns the UVW Map gizmo to a viewport. This option can help you locate a UVW map or quickly align it to a viewport.

Fit   Stretches the UVW Map gizmo over the surface of an object to make it fit exactly.

Center   Centers the UVW Map gizmo on an object's surface.

Acquire   Sets the UVW Map gizmo to match the mapping coordinates of an object that already has mapping coordinates assigned to it.

Reset   Resets the UVW Map gizmo to the VIZ default size and orientation.

Normal Align   Aligns the UVW Map gizmo to the normal of a surface of the object to which the mapping is attached.

FIGURE 7.19

A comparison of the UVW Map gizmo and the actual bitmap image as it is applied to the Ground object

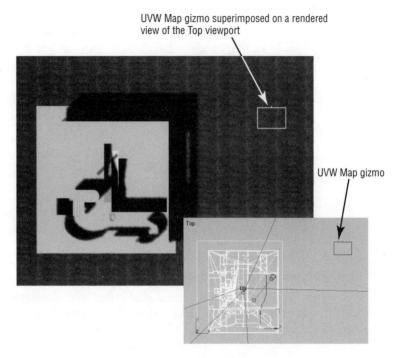

UVW Map gizmo superimposed on a rendered view of the Top viewport

UVW Map gizmo

FIGURE 7.20

A sample brick wall with the UVW Map gizmo rotated 30 degrees

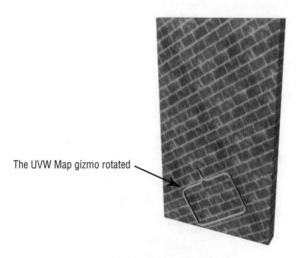

The UVW Map gizmo rotated

FIGURE 7.21

To the left, a Region Fit UVW map is placed on a wall in the Front viewport. To the right, a rendered view with the UVW map is superimposed on the view.

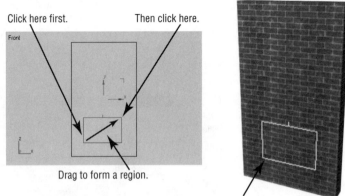

The location of the UVW Map gizmo in relation to the final rendered surface.

CONTROLLING THE TILING EFFECT

When you added the Ground-Grass material to the Ground object and reduced the size of the UVW map, the grass appeared at a smaller scale and was repeated over the entire surface of the ground in a rectangular array. This repetition of the map is called tiling. If you've ever played with the Windows desktop, you may already be familiar with the idea of tiling.

Tiling is on by default, but you can turn it off for situations when you want only a single image to appear over the surface. Figure 7.22 portrays the same brick wall shown in Figure 7.21, but this time the tiling is turned off. The brick pattern appears only in the region defined by the UVW Map gizmo. The rest of the wall surface is rendered based on the Basic Parameters rollout settings of Ambient, Diffuse, and Specular color.

FIGURE 7.22

The brick wall rendered with the tile setting turned off

The tile settings are located in the Material Editor window. Here's how to locate the tiling parameters.

1. Open the Material Editor.

2. With the Ground-Grass 1 material selected, scroll down the list of rollouts to the Maps rollout and open the Maps rollout if it isn't already open.

3. Locate the map you want to adjust; then click its button. For example, for the Ground-Grass material, click the Diffuse Color Map button labeled Map #8 (`grass.JPG`). The parameters for that particular map display in the Material Editor.

4. Open the Coordinates rollout and locate the Tile check boxes. You can click the U and V Tile check boxes to turn tiling off. Don't change this setting for your villa model, however; you want to keep the tile setting turned on.

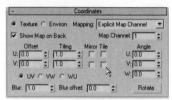

UNDERSTANDING THE DIFFERENT TYPES OF MAPPING

When you first apply a material to an object, VIZ uses its default *planar* map. As you might guess from its name, this map type maps the bitmap image to a plane, or flat surface, as shown in Figure 7.22. This option projects a flat image onto a surface. The orientation of the UVW Map gizmo in relation to the object affects the appearance of the material. Figure 7.23 shows how the same texture map can be projected onto a box with different effects.

As you can see from Figure 7.23, you aren't limited to using a planar map that's parallel to the surface you are mapping to. You can create some interesting effects by reorienting the UVW Map gizmo.

But what do you do if you want to map an image to a cylindrical or spherical object? VIZ offers several other mapping types to facilitate mapping to nonplanar surfaces.

If you look at the Parameters rollout for the UVW Map modifier, you see the radio button options shown in Figure 7.24.

The *cylindrical* map curves the bitmap into a cylindrical shape and then projects the map outward from the center of the cylinder. Naturally, you would use this type of mapping on cylindrical objects. You will want to place such a map in the center of the object.

When you choose this map, the UVW Map gizmo changes to a cylindrical one, as shown in Figure 7.25. You would then place this map in the center of a cylindrical object and assign it to the object. You can also distort the map by moving the UVW Map gizmo closer to one side or the other or rotating the map so it isn't aligned with the object.

FIGURE 7.23

A box with mapping coordinates oriented in different ways. The texture map is identical in each example.

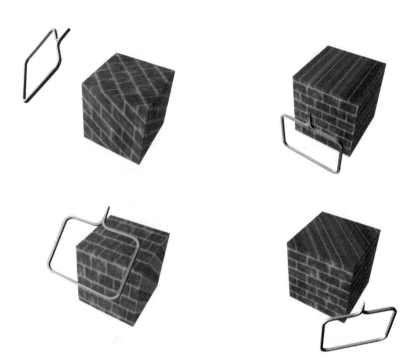

FIGURE 7.24

Mapping options

FIGURE 7.25

A view of the UVW Map gizmo when using the cylindrical mapping type, along with a sample of an object that uses this mapping type

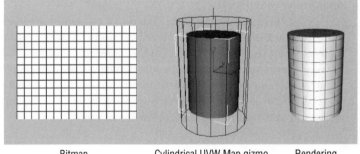

Bitmap   Cylindrical UVW Map gizmo   Rendering

The *spherical* map curves the bitmap into a spherical shape. To understand how it works, imagine taking the rectangular bitmap image and curling it around a spherical shape; then squeeze the top and bottom ends of the bitmap like a candy wrapper (see Figure 7.26). One use of this mapping type is to portray a model of the earth. You could use the spherical mapping type to place a flat map of the earth on a sphere.

FIGURE 7.26

The spherical map wraps the bitmap around a sphere.

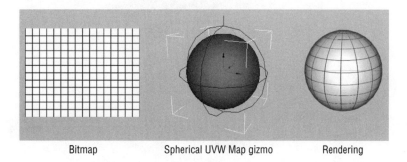

Bitmap   Spherical UVW Map gizmo   Rendering

As with the cylindrical mapping type, the UVW Map gizmo changes to a different shape when the spherical mapping type is chosen, as shown in Figure 7.26. You would place this map in the center of the spherical shape that requires mapping.

Shrink Wrap is similar to spherical, but instead of wrapping the image around a sphere, as shown in Figure 7.26, imagine wrapping a sphere in plastic wrap with the bitmap image tied at one end. Figure 7.27 shows a rendering using the same sphere and UVW Map gizmo shown in Figure 7.26. The only difference is that the sphere in Figure 7.27 uses shrink-wrap mapping instead of the spherical mapping of Figure 7.26.

FIGURE 7.27

A sample of shrink-wrap mapping

Box mapping is similar to planar, but it projects the image onto four sides, as shown in Figure 7.28, instead of a single plane. You may find that you use box mapping the most, especially if your work involves buildings.

Face mapping is similar to box mapping, but instead of projecting the image onto the sides of a box, face mapping projects the image onto each individual face of an object. This is easiest to see in a faceted object such as the 12-sided sphere shown in Figure 7.29.

FIGURE 7.28
Example of box
mapping

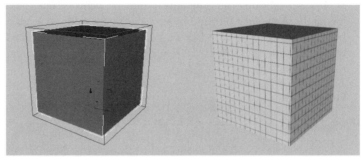

Box UVW Map gizmo   Rendering with a grid bitmap

FIGURE 7.29
Using face mapping
on a sphere

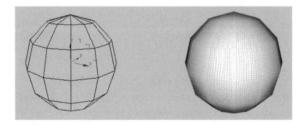

Even if smoothing is used to smooth out the surface of the sphere, face mapping will project the image onto the individual faces of the object.

XYZ to UVW mapping is mainly used for *procedural maps.* A procedural map is a map that relies on a mathematical formula rather than a bitmap image. The XYZ to UVW map aligns a procedural map to the local coordinates of the object to which it is assigned. This has the effect of *sticking* the map to the object so that if the object is stretched nonuniformly; the map will stretch with the object as if the map were a rubber sheet stretched over the object.

Although I've suggested that you use each map type with its corresponding object shape, you can achieve some unusual effects by mixing map types with different surfaces. For example, if you use a planar map on a cylinder, the image is stretched as it is projected toward the edge of the cylinder, as shown in Figure 7.30.

FIGURE 7.30
A sample of a planar
map used on a cylin-
drical surface

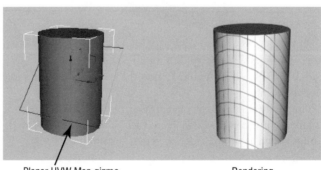

Planar UVW Map gizmo   Rendering

Just below the Mapping radio buttons in the Parameters rollout are the Length, Width, and Height input boxes. As you might guess, these options let you enter a numeric value for the length, width, and height of the UVW Map gizmo. Their spinners also let you graphically adjust the size of the gizmo.

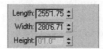

Finally, if you want to increase the tiling of the bitmap image within the area defined by the UVW Map gizmo, you can do so using the U Tile, V Tile, and W Tile input boxes at the bottom of the Parameters rollout.

These options are set by default to 1.0, causing a single image to appear within the area of the UVW Map gizmo. You can produce multiple images within the gizmo area by increasing the values in these input boxes. This offers a quick way of increasing the density of the tiled image without having to enter the Material Editor window. Figure 7.31 shows the same brick wall displayed in Figure 7.21, but this time the U and V tile settings have been changed to 2.

FIGURE 7.31

The brick wall sample shown with the U and V tile parameters set to 2

TIP   *You can also increase the tiling within the Coordinates rollout of the bitmap in the Material Editor. Changes made there affect all objects with the material assigned. In contrast, changes made in the Parameters rollout of the UVW Mapping modifier only affect the selected object.*

The mapping coordinate tools I've been discussing give you a high degree of control over the way your material assignments affect your model. As is the case with many VIZ tools, your skill in using them will develop over time. As with any craft, practice makes perfect.

THE GENERATE MAPPING COORDINATES OPTION

Many of the VIZ objects you encounter will have a check box labeled Generate Map Coords as one of their parameters. This offers another method for applying mapping coordinates.

The Generate Mapping Coords option applies a sort of custom mapping coordinate to standard primitives. For example, if you create a Box standard primitive and select Generate Mapping Coords in the box's parameter rollout, materials mapped to the box will behave as if the Box UVW Mapping modifier were applied to the box. A Sphere primitive with the Generate Mapping Coords option selected will behave as if a spherical mapping were applied. As an added benefit, the mapping will conform to any changes applied to the shape of the object. If a box's width is increased, the mapping coordinates will automatically follow the width change (although this may actually be undesirable for some types of material, such as brick or tile).

You have less control over the mapping coordinates with the Generate Mapping Coords option, because objects that use it don't have an adjustable UVW Map gizmo. However, you can still control the UVW tiling to adjust the density of the map over the object. This can be done using the Material Editor window in the Coordinates rollout for the material map you are working with.

In the case of a lofted object, the Generate Mapping Coords option is the only way to apply a material that will conform to a loft's unusual shape. If you apply a UVW Map modifier, the modifier will take control over the mapping coordinates.

Note that imported objects, such as those found in AutoCAD models, don't have a Generate Mapping Coords option. They require a UVW Map modifier whenever bitmap materials are applied.

Editing Materials

The last time you rendered your Villa Savoye model, the glass was virtually invisible, and the ground color and texture looked too strong and unnatural. In this section, you'll learn how to use the Material Editor to adjust both the glass and Ground-Grass materials to improve your image.

Adjusting Bitmap Strength

We'll start our exploration of the Material Editor by making a few changes to the Ground-Grass material. The grass pattern is repeated regularly, so that it looks almost like a manicured baseball field. Also, the ground surface is quite flat. Let's adjust the material so that it looks a bit more like a natural grass surface.

1. Click the Material Editor tool in the main toolbar to open the Material Editor window.

   The sample of the Ground-Grass material is shown on a sphere, but the surface to which you are applying the material is flat. You can get a preview image on a cube instead of on a sphere to get a sample view that's more in line with the object you are mapping to.

2. Click and hold the Sample Type tool in the set of tools to the right of the window. You see a flyout containing two additional sample types.

3. Drag the mouse over to the cube. Release the mouse. The sample changes to a cube shape.

Now the sample gives us a better idea of what the Ground-Grass material looks like, and it certainly looks similar to the sample in our model. In the rendering of the model, the Ground-Grass material is a bit too strong, so you need to tone it down for your Ground object. Here's how to do it:

1. Click and drag the sample Ground-Grass slot from the middle of the top row to the next box to the right. You see a copy of the material in the upper right box. This gives us a copy of the material settings that we can play with without affecting the original settings. It also lets us compare two settings side by side. As you can see from all the slots available, you can make many copies and variations.

2. Click the original Ground-Grass slot in the middle of the top row to make it active.

3. Click the Go to Parent tool to return to the parent material. You see the map options as a list with check boxes that you can use to turn a map feature on or off. Each feature also has an Amount spinner you can use to set the strength of the map, and map buttons you can use to select the type of map (see Figure 7.32).

FIGURE 7.32
The Maps rollout with map options

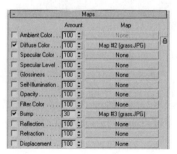

4. Adjust the Amount spinner in the Diffuse Color row to read **30**. This decreases the strength of the `grass.JPG` texture bitmap to 30%.

5. Click the Quick Render tool. The pattern on the ground of the rendered view is less apparent.

The sample slot now shows that the grass pattern isn't so strong. The grass is greener and the regular pattern of the bitmap tiling isn't quite so obvious.

When you reduced the strength of the texture map in step 4, you reduced the strength of the bitmap image. This caused the colors in the Blinn Basic Parameters rollout to have a stronger effect.

Before we go on, look over the other options in the Maps rollout (see Figure 7.32). You've just seen how the Amount spinner affects the strength of a map. The buttons in the Map column to the far right let you select a map type, which can be a bitmap or a procedural map. If you click a button that's labeled None, you'll open the Material/Map Browser, which offers the selection of maps shown in Figure 7.33.

FIGURE 7.33

The Material/Map Browser appears when you click any None button in the Maps rollout.

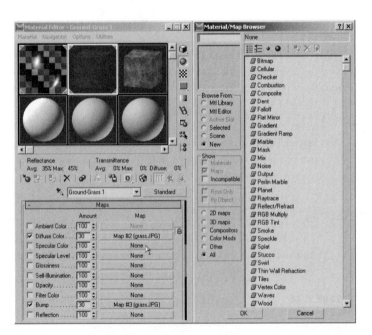

If you select Bitmap from the top of the list, you will then have the opportunity to select a bitmap image file. The other options are procedural maps.

Back in the Maps rollout, if you click a button that already has a map assigned to it, such as the Map #2 (`grass.JPG`) button, the Material Editor changes to show the parameters associated with that map (see Figure 7.34).

FIGURE 7.34

A view of the options for the Map #2 (grass.JPG) button

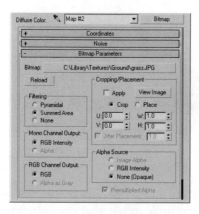

You might think of these options as being similar to sub-object levels. They are components of the material currently selected in the Material Editor. From here, you click the Go to Parent button on the Material toolbar to return to the Maps rollout.

You'll get a chance to work with these settings a bit more in the next chapter. For now, let's continue by looking at how you can adjust the color of a material.

Adjusting the Material Color

With the strength of the texture map diminished, you can begin to make some color adjustments using the Blinn Basic Parameters rollout. *Blinn*, by the way, is the name given to a method of shading that VIZ uses, and it is one of several shading methods (see "Selecting Shaders" later in this chapter).

1. In the Material Editor, scroll back up to the Blinn Basic Parameters rollout.

2. Click the dark color swatch labeled Ambient. The Color Selector dialog box displays (see Figure 7.35).

3. Change the Hue value to **116**. This changes the color to a blue-green hue.

4. Click and drag the Sat (Saturation) spinner all the way up so that its value is 255. This spinner controls the intensity of the color.

5. Click and drag the Value spinner down until its value is 80. This controls the lightness of the color.

FIGURE 7.35

The Color Selector dialog box showing the new settings. Note the sample color swatch at the lower right corner of the dialog box.

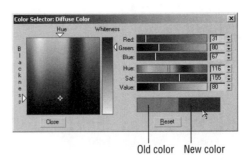

Old color   New color

Right now, you see a dark green on the right side of the color swatch. If, for some reason, you decide that the changes you've just made are not what you want, you can click the Reset button below the swatch to return the settings to what they were before you made any changes. The Reset button allows you to experiment with colors while the Color Selector dialog box is open.

Let's see the results of your color modification:

1. Click the Close button in the Color Selector.

2. Click the Quick Render tool in the Rendering toolbar and watch carefully as the renderer renders the Ground object.

The color difference is subtle, but the ground is definitely greener with the increase in the saturation of the Material Editor's Ambient setting.

You've seen how you can adjust color in the Color Selector dialog box by making changes to the Sat and Value spinners. The Hue spinner lets you select the color or hue from a slider or spinner.

If you prefer, you can also control color using the R, G, and B (red, green, and blue) sliders and spinners. You may notice that these settings automatically change as you adjust the H, S, and V (Hue, Sat, and Value) settings.

Copying Color Settings

The Blinn Basic Parameters rollout offers three color settings: Ambient, Diffuse, and Specular. The Ambient color you just experimented with is the color of an object in a shadow or in very low lighting conditions; the Diffuse color is the color of an object under normal or good lighting conditions; and the Specular color is the color of an object with a very bright light shining on it (see Figure 7.36).

VIZ offers you the ability to adjust the color of an object under these three basic lighting conditions so that you can make subtle variations in the appearance of an object. Each of these three color types can be set just as you set the Ambient color in the last exercise. You can also copy or swap colors between these settings just by clicking and dragging the color swatch. Try the following exercise to copy the Ambient color to the diffuse color setting.

1. In the Blinn Basic Parameters rollout, click and hold the color bar next to the Ambient button.

2. Drag the cursor away from the bar. Notice that a rectangle appears and moves with the cursor.

FIGURE 7.36

The basic areas defined by the Ambient, Diffuse, and Specular settings

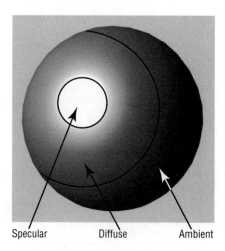

Specular   Diffuse   Ambient

3. Place your cursor on the bar next to the Diffuse button; then release the mouse button. You see the Copy or Swap Colors dialog box.

4. Click Copy. The Ambient color now appears in the Diffuse color swatch.

5. Save your work as ch07b.max.

If you had selected the Swap option in the Copy or Swap Colors dialog box, you would see the Ambient and Diffuse colors exchange places. By clicking and dragging color swatches, you can quickly match a color. In many situations, you may want to tone down an object's appearance. Making the Ambient and Diffuse colors the same can easily do this.

TIP   *In general, it's a good idea to have the hue and saturation of the Ambient color match those of the Diffuse color. You can lower the Value setting of the Ambient color to determine the darkness of areas in shadow.*

Selecting Shaders

Shaders are a set of methods VIZ uses to render materials. When you create a new material, one of the main things you need to determine is which shader to use. Walls are usually matte surfaces, so the wall material should use a shader that's best suited to such a surface. Baseboard trim might have a semigloss paint, in which case you'd best select a different shader to simulate the shiny surface.

As you work with the Material Editor, you'll notice that you have a set of options under the Shader Basic Parameters rollout. You can think of shaders as different rendering methods applied to objects when they are rendered. Each shader provides a different way that the primary components of a material (the Ambient, Diffuse, and Specular colors, for example) are blended together. The primary shader options are found in the Shader Basic Parameters drop-down list. This list offers eight shaders: Anisotropic, Blinn, Metal, Multi-Layer, Oren-Nayar-Blinn, Phong, Strauss, and Translucent Shader.

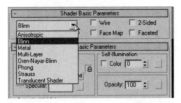

Don't let these strange-sounding names scare you off. They are just different methods that VIZ uses to render Specular highlights and Diffuse and Ambient lighting on objects. You choose a shader depending on the type of material to which you are assigning the highlights or lighting. Here's a run-down of the shaders and their specialties:

Anisotropic   Measures the difference of shininess from different angles and renders highlights accordingly. This shader is best used for very shiny objects.

Blinn   Offers a softer highlight than Phong, particularly for objects with which you want to show highlights from lights bouncing off at low angles.

Metal   As the name suggests, Metal is a shader designed for metallic objects. It's specifically designed to simulate the characteristics of light bouncing off a metallic surface.

Multi-Layer   Similar to Anisotropic, but it offers more control. It's especially useful in controlling highlight effects, which makes it highly appropriate for shiny objects.

Oren-Nayar-Blinn   Offers a high degree of control over the effects of Diffuse lighting on an object. It's especially useful for matte or rough objects.

Phong   Offers a general shader for smooth, uniform surfaces and can be used as an all-purpose shader.

Strauss   Similar to the Metal shader but with simpler controls.

Translucent Shader   Similar to the Blinn shader with the additional option of translucency. You can use this shader to simulate frosted glass.

When you select one of these shaders from the Shader Basic Parameters drop-down list, the Basic Parameters rollout will change to offer options specifically geared toward that shader. You may want to stick with one or two of these shaders to start out, then experiment with others as you become more familiar with VIZ. By offering these shaders, VIZ gives you more control over the way objects look and also makes its own rendering faster.

In addition, there are four check boxes that control how a material is rendered:

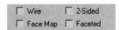

Wire   Renders a material in wireframe view.

2-Sided   Forces a material to be two-sided so that the appearance of a surface is not dependent on its normal.

Face Map   Causes a mapped bitmap to appear on the faces of an object in a way similar to the Face Map parameter for the UVW Map gizmo.

Faceted   Forces smoothed objects to be rendered as faceted.

Map Scalar Modifiers

You have seen how you can map materials to objects by generating mapping coordinates (in the case of Primitives this is built-in), and by applying the UVW Mapping modifier. You have also seen how to fine-tune the tiling of a bitmap in the Coordinates rollout in the Material Editor. However, there is another way to approach the issue of mapping materials—that is to use one of the Map Scalar modifiers.

TIP   *In most cases, Map Scalars can be used to simplify the issue of mapping. Use the other options if you want greater control.*

New!   The Map Scalar Object Space modifier (OSM) is new in VIZ 2005. It provides a simplified way to map materials that will scale with the object. The older Map Scalar World-Space modifier (WSM) is still available for those occasions when you want the map size to be bound to absolute world scale.

1. Open the sample file `Mapping.max` (Figure 7.37) from the CD.

FIGURE 7.37
Mapping sample cubes

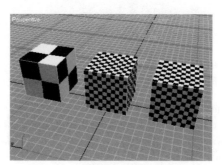

The sample file contains three 5′ cubes that all share the same material. The applied material is using a Checkers diffuse color map that is set to tile once in each texture direction, U and V. The pattern that is mapped then consists of four squares, alternating white and black, that make a larger square as seen in Figure 7.38.

FIGURE 7.38
The mapped pattern

2. Select the first cube on the left and switch to the Modify panel. Observe that the stack shows that this Box object has a UVW Mapping modifier applied with the Box mapping type selected.

3. The pattern shown in Figure 7.38 appears on each one of the six faces of the cube because Box mapping was selected in the UVW Mapping modifier. Change the V Tile parameter to 3.

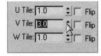

TIP   Use the UVW Mapping modifier when you want to have nonuniform tiling or finer control over the mapping type.

4. Select the middle cube. Observe how its stack shows a Box object with a Map Scalar Binding (WSM) applied. In this case, WSM stands for World-Space modifier, meaning that the effects of the map scalar are bound to the absolute size of the Home Grid. Both Map Scalar modifiers apply Box type mapping automatically, so you see the pattern tiling on each of the six faces of the cubes.

5. Change the Scale parameter of the Map Scalar Binding WSM to 2'6".

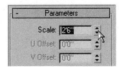

Observe how the pattern from Figure 7.38 is tiled exactly twice on each surface of the middle cube as shown in Figure 7.39. This occurs because the cube's edges measure 5' and the pattern is bound to precisely half that size in world space of 2'6".

TIP   *Use one of the Map Scalar modifiers when you want to bind your mapping to a specific size.*

FIGURE 7.39
Map Scalar tiles to
specific size

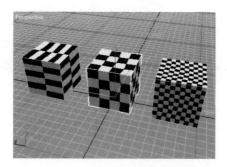

6. Select the cube on the right. Observe how its stack shows a box with the Map Scalar OSM applied. OSM is an object-space modifier, meaning its scale is based upon the object's transform scale.

7. Change the Scale parameter of the Map Scalar OSM to 2′6″. The pattern tiles twice, just like the WSM version did earlier.

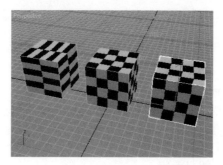

NOTE   *The difference between the Map Scalar OSM and WSM becomes apparent when you scale the objects to which they are applied.*

8. Select all three cubes and scale them down to 50%.

Figure 7.40 shows the result. The left cube's pattern gets smaller with the object but it maintains the same nonuniform tiling. The middle cube's pattern remains the same size as the object gets smaller because its Map Scalar is bound to world space. The right cube's pattern gets smaller as the object is scaled because its Map Scalar works in object space and is subject to the same transforms as the object itself.

FIGURE 7.40
Scaling the objects reveals the difference between WSM and OSM

UVW Mapping maintains nonuniform tiling when it is scaled.

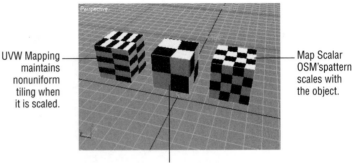

Map Scalar OSM'spattern scales with the object.

Map Scalar WSM maintains the size of the pattern when it is scaled.

Using Bump Maps

Earlier in this chapter, you saw a sample of a bump map (Figure 7.5). It showed how a grayscale image creates the impression of a bumpy surface. Bump maps can also generate other types of surface textures.

In the following exercise, you'll modify the ground material to make the ground appear more like a rolling surface than a flat one.

1. Open the file you saved earlier as ch07b.max.

2. Click the Material Editor tool on the main toolbar to open the Material Editor.

3. In the Material Editor, click the Ground-Grass sample slot in the middle of the top row.

4. Scroll down the Material parameters to the Maps rollout and open it.

5. Click and drag one of the None buttons onto the Grass2.jpg button that is currently shown in the bump channel. This will clear the bump map selection. Then click the Bump Map button.

6. In the Material/Map Browser, make sure that the New radio button is selected in the Browse From group and then click Noise from the list. You'll see a sample of Noise in the upper left corner of the dialog box.

7. With Noise selected, click OK. The parameters for Noise appear in the Material Editor.

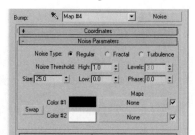

You may recall that a bump map uses varying shades of gray to determine the highs and lows of the bumps on a surface. The Noise material is a procedural map that generates a random pattern of gray tones. As a bump map, Noise will produce a random bumpy surface.

With the Noise map added, let's take a look at the ground as it is rendered.

1. Click the Select Object tool and then click the Ground object.

2. Right-click the Perspective viewport, and then click the Quick Render tool. You see the ground rendered in the Rendered Frame Window.

The ground renders in a bumpy texture that looks more like the sandy surface of a beach. You'll want to spread the bumps over a greater surface to give the impression of a rolling, grassy surface.

1. Open the Material Editor dialog box.

2. In the Noise Parameters rollout, change the Size value to 150. This spreads the noise over a greater area of the surface to which it is applied.

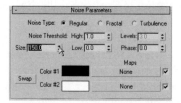

3. Click the Quick Render tool again. This time the ground appears smoother.

Now try another Noise option to give the ground a more random appearance.

4. Go back to the Material Editor, and click the Fractal radio button for Noise Type.

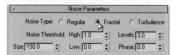

5. Click the Quick Render tool. You'll see the entire scene rendered with the ground appearing as an uneven, grassy surface, as shown in Figure 7.41.

FIGURE 7.41
The ground rendered with a bump map

The ground has a more natural appearance, and the Noise bump map reduces the regular tiled appearance of the `Grass.jpg` bitmap.

Adding Entourage

Entourage is a term taken from traditional architectural rendering. It refers to photographic "extras" that are added to a rendering to make it appear more realistic. You can think of entourage as cutouts or props that are added to the scene to make it more lifelike. Examples of entourage are people, trees, cars, street furniture, and signs. Entourage is not really 3D models, however. As 2D photographic elements, they are handled mainly through materials.

The key to designing an entourage material is to use an opacity map to hide unwanted portions of the surface to which the texture is mapped. Generally entourage materials are applied to Plane or Box primitives that act like flat billboards, displaying their contents for the world to see. Once you apply an opacity-mapped material to an object, it is also important to adjust the object to fit the bitmap's aspect ratio or undesirable stretching will occur.

Hiding Unwanted Surfaces with Opacity Maps

An opacity map is a grayscale bitmap image that tells VIZ which part of the surface is opaque and which part is transparent. The black portions of an opacity map become completely transparent, whereas white is completely opaque. Shades of gray create varying degrees of opacity.

To see how this works, look at Figure 7.42. To the left you see an opacity map. The middle figure shows a simple box in VIZ without a material assigned to it. The figure to the far right shows the same box that is assigned a material using the opacity map at left. Notice that the portions of the opacity map that are black appear invisible in the box.

FIGURE 7.42
A sample of an opacity map and an object to which it is assigned

Opacity map   Object   Object with opacity map material applied

You can also use shades of gray to simulate a semitransparent material or to gradually change the transparency of a surface. Color images can be used for opacity maps as well, though the color information is not used, only the pixel grayscale value.

Now that you have an understanding of what opacity maps are, let's design the entourage material of a tree.

1. Open the Material Editor by typing **M** on the keyboard.

2. Click the middle left sample slot to work on a new material.

3. Click the small square button next to the Diffuse color swatch. This is a shortcut button that accesses the Diffuse color map in the Maps rollout. It should have a tool tip that reads "None" because there is no map assigned yet.

4. Select Bitmap from the Material/Map Browser.

5. Click the `magnoliaIM.jpg` file from the CD `maps` folder as your diffuse color image.

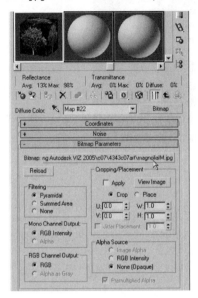

6. Click the Go to Parent tool on the Material Editor toolbar.

The diffuse color bitmap is considered a "child" of the material. When you added the bitmap file to the Magnolia material, you entered a type of sublevel for the material. The Go to Parent tool brings you back up to the "main" level of the material's parameters.

7. Click the small square button next to the Opacity spinner. This is another shortcut for the Opacity map in the Maps rollout.

Once again, you see the Material/Map Browser dialog box.

8. With the New radio button selected in the Browse From group, double-click the Bitmap listing in the right column.

9. In the Select Bitmap Image file, select `magnoliaOP.jpg`. You see the sample image of the `magnoliaOP.jpg` file in the lower right corner.

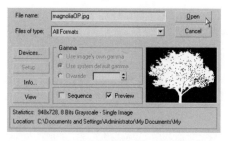

This file is similar to the `magnoliaIM.jpg` file, but it has been reduced to black and white and shows only the silhouette of the tree. The tree is white and everything else is black.

10. Click Open. Notice what happens to the sample image. Now you see the tree without the black background. The change in the sample is very subtle.

You've just created a material that, when applied to an object, will appear as a tree. At this point, you can apply your material to an object, but before you do that, let's look at a few of the tools on the Material Editor toolbar that can help you work with and understand materials.

TIP   You can also use the alpha channel of some image formats to store the grayscale opacity data. Chapter 14 discusses this technique using Adobe Photoshop.

1. Click the Material/Map Navigator tool on the Material Editor toolbar.

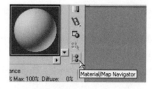

The Material/Map Navigator dialog box appears.

This dialog box gives you a clear picture of the way your new material is organized. You see the name at the top with two branches under it. Each branch is a child map that you've added to your material.

2. Click the Diffuse Color listing in the Material/Map Navigator. The parameters in the Material Editor change to those for the selected map.

3. Click the View List + Icons tool in the Material/Map Navigator.

Now you see the actual images used for the maps, plus the resulting material at the top of the list. The arrangement of images shows you the material hierarchy. You can click and drag the right edge of the dialog box to resize it.

4. Click the Go Forward to Sibling button in the Material Editor dialog box. This moves you to the next material or map at the same level in the material hierarchy.

NOTE *The family analogy of parent/child/sibling helps you to visualize the material hierarchy.*

The parameters in the Material Editor dialog box change to the Opacity map parameters, and the Opacity map parameter listing in the Material/Map Navigator is highlighted. The Go Forward to Sibling button lets you advance through the different child levels.

5. Click the Show End Result tool on the Material Editor toolbar to turn it off.

The Opacity map bitmap appears in the sample slot for the Magnolia material. This tool lets you see the results of any change you make to the child parameters.

6. Close the Material/Map Navigator and click the Go to Parent tool on the Material Editor toolbar to go up to the main parameter level.

7. Name this material Magnolia in the Material Editor.

Now let's add geometry for the tree to the model. First, you'll need to create an object to which to apply the Magnolia material. This will be a simple, flat, vertical box.

1. Close the Material Editor to get a clear view of your viewports.

2. Right-click the Top viewport and click the Min/Max Toggle tool to enlarge it.

3. Click the Create tab in the Command Panel; then click the Geometry tool.

4. Click Box, and then create the box shown in Figure 7.43. Use the Length, Width, and Height parameters options to set the length to 0, the width to 24 feet, and the height to 24 feet. You want the box to be as thin as possible so its edge does not appear in any view.

FIGURE 7.43
Placing the box for the tree material

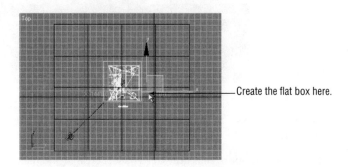

Create the flat box here.

5. Give the box the name **Tree01**.

6. Click the Min/Max Toggle tool to view all of the viewports.

TIP   You can also use Plane primitives for entourage elements, but be aware that planes are only visible from one side.

Now that you have created the thin box, it is time to apply the entourage material that you designed earlier.

1. Open the Material Editor dialog box.

2. With the Magnolia material selected, click the Assign Material to Selection tool. The Magnolia material is now assigned to the box you just created.

3. Click the Show Map in Viewport button in the Material Editor.

4. Right-click the Perspective viewport, and then click the Quick Render tool in the main toolbar. The model is rendered with a tree in the background as shown in Figure 7.44.

The scene still looks a bit bare, so make a few copies of the tree to give the impression that the building is surrounded by a grove of trees.

1. In the Top viewport, select the tree you just created and make the clones shown in Figure 7.45.

FIGURE 7.45
Making clones
of the tree

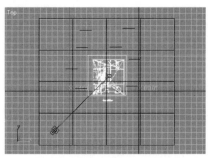

Instance trees around the building.

2. Open the Material Editor and change the Magnolia material's Specular color to pure black. If you do not change this, you will be able to faintly see the hidden areas of the Box in a rendering.

WARNING *Objects with opacity maps, such as the trees you just created, will cast a shadow that matches the opacity map when you use Ray-Traced Shadows. If you use a shadow-mapped shadow, objects with opacity maps will cast a shadow in the shape of the object to which the material is mapped. In the case of the trees, the use of shadow maps would give you a rectangular shadow instead of a shadow in the shape of the tree. Therefore, Ray-Traced Shadows are preferable for entourage.*

3. Render the Perspective view again.

3D Plants

VIZ offers a set of fairly detailed 3D trees and shrubs that you can easily add to any model. To access them, click the Geometry button in the Create tab of the Command Panel.

From there, select AEC Extended from the drop-down list. You'll see the Foliage button in the Object Type rollout.

Click the Foliage button. You'll see the different types of foliage appear in the Create tab of the Command Panel.

You can click the plant you want in the Command Panel and then click in the viewport to place it. Once the plant has been placed, you can use the transform tools in the main toolbar to move, rotate, or scale the plant. You can also use the Modify tab to alter other foliage parameters such as leaf density, plant height, or even the shape of the plant.

The trees really help give the rendering a realistic appearance (see Figure 7.46). You can further enhance the rendering by varying the size of the trees and mirroring them so that some of the trees appear as reversed images. This adds a bit more variety and makes it a little less obvious that the trees are identical. Of course, you can create different types of tree entourage in the Material Editor and add them to the scene.

FIGURE 7.46
The rendered view
with more trees

NOTE In the preceding exercise, you created the tree material in the Material Editor, using two existing bitmap images for the texture map and opacity map. Chapter 14 describes how you can use Adobe Photoshop to create your own bitmap images for texture maps and opacity maps. You can even use Photoshop to create other textures such as granite, stucco, or marble.

WARNING Beware that 3D foliage can consume huge amounts of memory and render time because each leaf is modeled as geometry. Opacity-mapped entourage is much more efficient but remains flat. In animations where the camera is moving, 3D foliage can be more convincing.

The method I've shown you here for creating and adding opacity-mapped trees also works for adding people. You can also use this method to quickly add text or signage to a model for which the proper fonts are not available in Windows. Adobe Photoshop or another similar program can aid you in creating the texture and opacity maps for people. If you don't want to create your own, there are many third-party sources for texture maps and models. Here is a partial list of companies that provide texture maps and models for VIZ.

Buy Creative www.buycreative.com

Marlin Studios www.marlinstudios.com

Scott Onstott's 3D Models www.scottonstott.com

Turbo Squid www.turbosquid.com

In addition to texture maps, some of these companies also offer prebuilt 3D objects such as furniture, cars, appliances, cabinetry, and animals. If you are in a hurry to build scenes quickly, check out the library of objects offered by these and other companies.

Adjusting an Object to a Bitmap Shape

Sometimes you may find it necessary to match the object's shape to a bitmap's shape. For example, you may create a material that uses bitmap images of people standing. To avoid distorting the shape of the people, you would want to match the object as closely as possible to the aspect ratio of the bitmap image (see Figure 7.47).

FIGURE 7.47
Two renderings with people used as bitmaps. The image to the left has distorted the people.

To do this, choose the Bitmap Fit Alignment option under the Parameters rollout of the UVW Mapping Modifier.

Locate the bitmap file associated with the material that uses the bitmap. Once the file has been selected, return to the VIZ screen, and the Map gizmo will be adjusted to fit the aspect ratio of the selected bitmap.

Once you have the new Map gizmo, you can adjust your object to fit as closely as possible to the Map gizmo proportions. You may not be able to get an absolutely accurate match, but you can get close. Then, once you've gotten the object to the right proportions, use the UVW Mapping option described earlier in this chapter to align the map exactly to the object.

In the beginning of this chapter you have been working with the exterior of the villa model. Let's explore the model's interior to investigate ray tracing concepts.

REMOVING OR CHANGING A MAP

At some point, you may decide that you want to remove or change a map in a material definition. You can remove a map by following these simple steps.

1. Open the Material Editor.

2. In the Maps rollout, click the button that corresponds to the map you want to remove.

3. Click the Type button (typically labeled Bitmap) on the Material Editor toolbar.

4. In the Material/Map Browser dialog box, click None, and then click OK to close the dialog box.

The map assignment will be removed for the selected map, and the Map button will show None. The Type button in step 3 can also be used to change a map from one type to another.

Alternatively, you can drag a button in the Maps rollout marked None on top of a button containing a map and it will be replaced with None.

Ray Tracing Reflection and Refraction

So far you haven't seen convincing glass surfaces in your renderings. This is because the materials you have made do not account for light reflecting off surfaces or passing through translucent surfaces (refraction). To simulate such phenomenon, you will use the ray tracing renderer. The raytracer has been built into VIZ for several versions and it is used in the form of the Raytrace map or the Raytrace material). You cannot see ray traced effects in the viewports—they must be rendered.

You will now create accurate reflections on a surface by using ray tracing.

An element in the interior that can use some attention is the glass itself. Right now, the glass appears totally transparent, but in real life, the glass would reflect the scene around it. A quick way to make shiny objects look better is to use bitmaps in the reflection channel, but since they reflect a generic photo, they leave something to be desired. Bitmaps used in the reflection channel reflect the bitmap itself in the shiny parts of the object to which the material is assigned. In the real world objects do not reflect a generic image (of the sky, or of a building for example); they reflect the actual objects in the room.

If you are looking to produce the greatest accuracy, you'll be happy to know that it is possible to reflect what is actually in the room. To produce such an effect on the glass, you can use what is called a Raytrace map. A Raytrace map is a procedural map that produces an accurate reflection based on a combination of the information it gets from the viewing position, the reflective surface, and the objects in the immediate environment.

NOTE *Alternatively, you can use the Raytrace material instead of the Raytrace map within the Standard material. The effect will be the same either way.*

In the current Villa Savoye model, the glass was created from a Standard material using a reflection bitmap. Here you will have the opportunity to learn how to add the Raytrace map to a Standard material. In the following exercise, you'll alter the glass material with a Raytrace reflective map, then you'll see the results with another quick render.

1. Open the file Savoye7a.max from the CD.

2. Open the Material Editor; then click the Reflection_Outside material.

3. Scroll down to the Maps rollout and observe that this material already has a bitmap in the reflection channel called Lake_mt.jpg. Click the Map#19 button in the Reflection channel to enter the child map controls.

4. Click the Bitmap map type button. You will be changing the map type in step 5.

The Material/Map Browser displays.

5. Select New in the Browse From group; then Select Raytrace from the list and click OK.

6. The Replace Map dialog box displays. Click the Discard old map radio button and then click OK. The Ray Traced parameters replace those of the bitmap parameters.

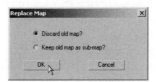

7. Go back up to the Maps level by clicking the Go to Parent tool on the Material Editor toolbar.

8. Change the Amount value of the reflection map to **15**. A low value will reduce the strength of the reflection; otherwise, the glass will look more like a mirror than a piece of glass.

You've now got a Ray Traced reflection map assigned to your glass material.

9. Close the Material Editor again; then click the Quick Render button. The finished rendering will show a reflection of the building interior from the glass, as shown in Figure 7.48. You'll also notice that the rendering takes a bit longer to complete.

FIGURE 7.48
Rendered view with reflective map on glass

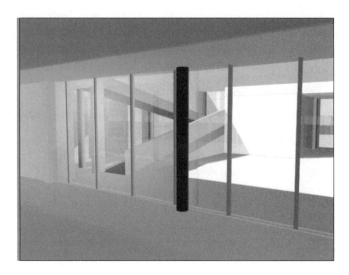

Now the courtyard is really beginning to look a bit more realistic. The simulated bounced light reveals some of the detail in the ramp and alcove areas, and the reflective glass adds to the sense of realism.

In the next section, you'll take a look at how the tools you've learned about so far can help improve the interior view of the villa.

Assigning Materials to Parts of an Object

As you work with imported AutoCAD files in VIZ, you'll almost certainly find yourself faced with the situation where you want to add a material to a single surface of an object. This is the situation on the second floor of the villa. You could enter the sub-object level of the second floor to detach the floor surface, and then treat the floor as a separate object. This works fine for some situations, but once the floor is detached from the rest of the second floor, any transformations you perform to the second-floor mesh won't be synchronized with the floor pattern.

To maintain the connection of the second-floor surface with the rest of the second-floor object and to add a separate material to the floor surface, you'll need to use another method of applying materials. A type of material called a Multi/Sub-Object material allows you to apply multiple materials to a single object. In the villa example, you can use a Multi/Sub-Object material to apply a floor material to the second-floor surface without affecting the walls and ceilings to which the floor is attached.

Opening a Group

The Savoye model's objects are organized into groups. You may remember from Chapter 2 that a group is like a collection of objects that have been bound together to act like a single object. When you select a group, all the objects in the group act like one object. You can temporarily open a group to edit individual objects, or you can permanently break up the group.

Before you can start to work on the second-floor object to add a material, you'll need to gain access by opening the group to which the second-floor object belongs. The following exercise will step you through the process.

1. Click the Select Object tool on the main toolbar.

2. In the Select Objects dialog box, click [INT-WALLS.06] and then click Select. (The items in the dialog box shown in square brackets are actually groups of objects.)

3. Choose Group ➢ Open.

NOTE *To close a group, select a member of the group and then choose Group ➢ Close.*

With the group open, you now have access to the individual objects within the group. You may notice that opened groups display a pink bounding box. The next step is to select the second-floor object so that you can start to work with its material assignment.

1. Right-click in the Left viewport; then use the Region Zoom tool to zoom into the area shown in Figure 7.49. You want to see as much of the building as possible.

2. Click the Min/Max Toggle tool to enlarge the Left viewport. Your view should look similar to Figure 7.49.

3. Click the Select Object tool; then select the building at the second-floor level at the point shown in Figure 7.49.

FIGURE 7.49
Select the building by clicking at the point shown here.

Click here to select the building walls and floors.

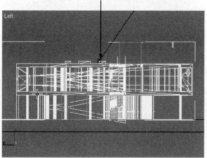

You should see the name INT-WALLS.05 for the object name in the Command Panel. If you don't see this object selected, use the Select by Name tool and select it. Now you're ready to start working with Multi/Sub-Object materials.

Creating a Multi/Sub-Object Material

A Multi/Sub-Object material is like a group of materials collected under one material definition. Each material in this group is assigned a number to identify it within the collection of materials. It's easiest to understand when you've worked with it first hand, so let's get started.

You'll start by acquiring the material that's assigned to the INT-WALLS.05 object.

1. Click the Material Editor tool on the main toolbar to open the Material Editor window.

2. Use the scroll bar to the right of the sample slots to scroll down to a row of free slots below the ones that are currently occupied.

3. Click a slot containing an unused, default Standard material.

4. Click the Get Material button on the Material toolbar.

5. In the Material/Map Browser, click the Selected radio button in the Browse From group. You'll see the material that is assigned to the INT-WALLS.05 object in the list box.

6. Double-click the material in the list box; then close the Material/Map Browser.

The Wall material now appears in the selected sample slot. This is the material you assigned to the walls of the villa earlier in the book. For this exercise, you'll create a new Multi/Sub-Object material using the existing Wall material as a starting point.

The next step is to change the material from a Standard one to a Multi/Sub-Object material.

1. Enter the name **Wall Second Floor** in the Material Name input box. This assigns a new name to the material in the active slot.

2. To the right of the Material Name input box, click the Type button labeled Standard.

3. In the Material/Map Browser, make sure that the New radio button in the Browse From group is selected; then select Multi/Sub-Object from the list box. Click OK.

4. The Replace Material warning displays.

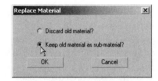

Make sure the Keep old material as sub-material? option is selected, then click OK. You return to the Material Editor with the Multi/Sub-Object Basic Parameters rollout.

As you can see from the Material Editor, the Multi/Sub-Object material offers several listings for additional materials. Each material is a sub-material of the main, parent material. In this exercise, you need only two sub-materials, so go ahead and reduce the number of available listings to two.

1. Click the Set Number button in the Multi/Sub-Object Basic Parameters rollout.

2. In the Set Number of Materials dialog box, enter **2** and then click OK.

When you return to the Material Editor, you see only two sub-material listings. The existing Wall material is number 1, and a yet-undefined material is number 2. Now let's add the material that will become the floor surface of the second floor.

1. Click the material button that's in the number 2 position in the Multi/Sub-Object Basic Parameters rollout. The Material Editor window changes to show the parameters for a Standard material. It may be difficult to tell that you're working with a Multi/Sub-Object material from the looks of the window, but one clue is the Go to Parent tool that's on the toolbar.

NOTE   *While the rest of the window may look like a standard material, the presence of the Go to Parent tool tells you that you are really in a child level of a multilevel material definition.*

2. Click the Type button that's labeled Standard. The Material/Map Browser appears.

You'll use a granite tile material for the floor, so you'll want to open the appropriate material from the editor.

1. In the Material/Map Browser, click the Mtl Editor radio button in the Browse From group.

2. Scroll down the list and double-click Stone-Granite Tiles (Standard).

3. A small dialog box appears with the question, Instance or Copy? Select Copy and click OK.

TIP   *You can instance material nodes in much the same way as geometry nodes. Instances share the same parameters whereas copies are always unique.*

4. Back in the Material Editor window, click the Go to Parent tool on the toolbar.

5. In the Names column of the Multi/Sub-Object material, type in the following names for the sub-materials: **walls** and **floor2**.

6. Click the Assign Material to Selection tool to assign the new Multi/Sub-Object material to the second-floor object.

The new material is now applied to the second floor object, though nothing appears to have changed. Since the Wall sub-material is the same as the old Wall material originally assigned to the second floor, the villa's appearance hasn't really changed. You need to take a few more steps before the Stone-Granite Tiles sub-material will appear on the floor of the villa.

Applying a Sub-Material to an Object's Surface

The second-floor object of the villa, named INT-WALLS.05, was created from 3D Solids in AutoCAD, so in VIZ, it's an editable mesh. To apply a sub-material to the polygons of an editable mesh, you'll need to select the polygons to which the sub-material is to be applied.

1. Click the Modify tab on the Command Panel.

2. Expand Editable Mesh in the stack and then click the Polygon sub-object level.

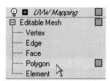

3. Click the Crossing Selection tool on the main toolbar so that it changes to the Window Selection tool if it is not already set to Window Selection. Change the selection type to Rectangular if it is not already set that way. You only want to select polygons that are completely within a selection window.

4. Type **Q** on the keyboard to enter Select Objects mode; then carefully place a rectangular selection region around the top surface of the second floor, as shown in Figure 7.50.

FIGURE 7.50
Place a rectangular selection region around the area shown in this figure.

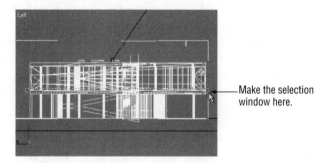

You now have the floor surface polygons of the second-floor object selected. The next step is to assign the number 2 sub-material to this selected surface.

1. Scroll down the Modify tab to the Surface Properties rollout.

2. In the Material group, change the Set ID value to 2.

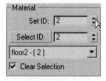

Remember that the granite tile sub-material is the number 2 material in the Multi/Sub-Object Basic Parameters rollout, so by entering 2 for the Material ID, you are assigning the granite tile sub-material to the selected surface. You can also verify this because the pop-up in the Material group says floor2, which is the second sub-material.

NOTE *An alternate method for assigning a sub-material to an object is to use the Material modifier. This modifier offers a single parameter—the Material ID number.*

You need to take a few more steps to complete the floor material assignment. Since the granite tile sub-material uses maps, you'll need to apply a UVW Map modifier to the second-floor object.

1. Scroll up to the top of the Command Panel; then click the yellow Polygon level to return to the Object level.

2. Click the UVW Mapping modifier at the top of the stack.

By default, a planar UVW map is applied to the second-floor object, and it is adjusted to fit the outline of the object. Because the outline isn't an exact square, you'll want to adjust the UVW map proportions to a square so that the granite tile material map won't be distorted.

1. Scroll down the Modify tab to the UVW Mapping Parameters rollout.

2. Change the Length and Width parameters to 60 feet each. This will place a single instance of the tile pattern on a square area that measures 60 feet on each side. Since the granite tile map is a 4-by-4 tile pattern, this will place a single 4-by-4 tile array on the entire floor area of the villa. If you look at the Perspective viewport now, you'll see that the floor contains a set of very large tiles that may also be distorted and pixelated.

NOTE *Textures are often distorted in the viewports because they are rendered with the Interactive Viewport Renderer (IVR). This renderer sacrifices quality for speed, so what you see isn't always perfect. You must render the scene to view the "real" material.*

Since a single 4-by-4 array of tiles is currently spread over a 60-foot by 60-foot area, you can calculate that a single tile is exactly 15 feet on each side (60 feet divided by 4). To get the tiles down to a reasonable size, you can adjust the U Tile and V Tile settings in the UVW Mapping Parameters to a value that increases the number of tiles within the 60-foot square area. If you want the tiles to be 1 foot square, for example, you would set the U Tile and V Tile settings to 15.

1. Go ahead and change the U and V Tile settings in the UVW Mapping Parameters rollout to **15**.

2. Click the Min/Max Toggle tool to view all four viewports.

3. Right-click the Perspective viewport; then click the Quick Render tool on the Rendering toolbar. Your rendering will look similar to Figure 7.51.

4. Save your work as Savoye7c.max.

TIP   You could have used the Map Scalar WSM instead of the UVW Map modifier to bind the actual size of the tiles to world scale.

In these last few exercises, you can see how you can control the exact size of the granite tiles through the use of the UVW mapping parameters. This is an important feature of VIZ, so let's take a moment to review what happened. First, you applied the UVW mapping to the second-floor object. You then set the mapping to an exact value of 60 square feet. Once the exact dimension of the map is established, you can determine the size of the individual tiles of the granite tile by correlating the U and V Tile settings to the size of the UVW mapping dimension. The default value of 1 for the U and V Tile setting means that one copy of the map is placed within the UVW mapping area. By changing the U and V Tile values to 15, you've created a 15-by-15 array of the granite tile map.

You can have as many as 99 map channels in a design, although you'll probably use only two or three in a project. You may have also guessed that you can use a different channel for each different map of a material. In the example given here, the same map channel is applied to all of the maps of the material. You can, however, apply a different UVW mapping to the bump map or the diffuse map, thereby creating a different surface effect.

USING MULTIPLE UVW MAPS ON A SINGLE OBJECT

If you're able to apply multiple materials to a single object, you may be wondering whether you can apply multiple UVW maps to an object as well. After all, different surfaces may require different UVW mapping settings. You can indeed apply multiple UVW Map modifiers to a single object. You can then correlate the different UVW Map modifiers to individual sub-materials through *map channels*. You can think of a map channel as a number that links a sub-material to a UVW Map modifier. The concept is simple, but the execution is a bit obscure. Here are the steps that you take to link a sub-material to a UVW map. (These steps aren't part of the main exercise of this book and are provided only to explain the process for linking multiple UVW maps to multiple material maps.)

1. Open the Material Editor; then select the Multi/Sub-Object material you want to work with. For this example, let's assume you are using the Wall Second Floor material.

2. Click the sub-material button from the listing in the Multi/Sub-Object Basic Parameters. For the Wall Second Floor material, click the Granite Tiles button.

3. Go to the Maps rollout and click the Map button for any active map.

4. In the Coordinates rollout, set the Map Channel to 2.

5. Click the Go to Parent tool in the Material Editor toolbar; then repeat steps 3 and 4 for the next active Map button.

6. Set the Map Channel value for each map in the material.

Once you've assigned a map channel to the maps in a material, you can then assign a UVW Map modifier to the channel you assigned to the material.

1. Select the object to which the sub-material has been assigned. In our villa example, you would select the INT-WALLS.05 object.

2. Add the UVW Map modifier; then scroll down the UVW Mapping Parameters rollout to the Channel group.

3. Enter **2** in the Map Channel input box.

Map Channel 2 then links the current UVW Map modifier to the granite tile maps that have been assigned to Map Channel 2.

1. Adjust the other UVW mapping parameters according to your needs.

Using the Architectural Material

New!

The Architectural material is new to VIZ 2005. It greatly simplifies material creation with a series of commonly used real-world templates. You may find this material easier to use than the Standard material covered thus far. Almost every real material can be simulated with this feature.

NOTE   You can use the Architectural material with all types of renderers: scanline, ray tracing, radiosity, and mental ray. Reflection, refraction, radiosity, and global illumination parameters are automatically set with this material type.

1. Choose File ➤ Reset.

2. Type **M** to open the Material Editor.

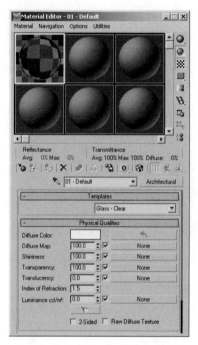

Notice how all the blank materials in the editor are now of the Architectural type in VIZ 2005. The material in the first sample slot has a Glass - Clear template applied, just to get you thinking about the possibilities. Feel free to change this sample slot at any time.

3. Open the Templates drop-down list and scroll through it to get an idea of what comes pre-configured as a template.

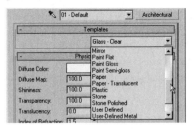

4. Select Paint Gloss from the Templates drop-down list.

Observe how some of the parameters in the Physical Qualities rollout changed when you selected a new material template within the Architectural material. Each template contains settings that populate these parameters. Figure 7.52 shows the Physical Qualities rollout and all the available parameters that can be set by the templates.

FIGURE 7.52

Physical Qualities of the Architectural material

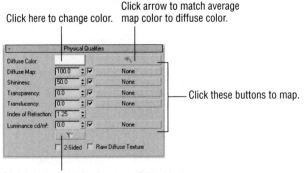

TIP You can change the parameters contained in the templates by editing the `ArchitecturalMaterialTemplates.ini` *file that's located in the* `plugcfg` *subfolder under the main VIZ folder on your hard drive. However, be careful to make a backup of this file before editing it in case something goes wrong. You will have to restart VIZ before changes of this type take effect.*

In general, using the Architectural material is very easy. At the minimum, simply select a template, change the diffuse color, and assign the material to your selection. This is great for those of you just starting to use VIZ 2005.

When you want finer control, go ahead and customize the settings in the Physical Qualities and Special Effects rollouts as you will read about in the next two sections. Intermediate and Advanced users will want to know the finer points to better simulate real world surfaces.

The Physical Qualities Rollout

This rollout contains the most important and most obvious aspects of the Architectural material. Use the Physical Qualities rollout to accurately simulate the character of the material with the following controls:

Diffuse Color   Use this swatch to open the color picker so you can select the Diffuse color, often the most important aspect of a material. The Ambient color is managed automatically so you don't have to think about it.

Diffuse Map   Click the None button in this channel to open the Material/Map Browser to assign a map. There is an Amount spinner that varies as a percentage from 0 to 100. The Amount spinner controls what percentage of the map is used in the diffuse channel. Whatever percentage remains (out of 100) is blended with the Diffuse color.

Next to the Amount spinner there is a check box that allows you to quickly toggle the map on and off. This helps when you are doing test renders and wish to accelerate a rendering by temporarily leaving out certain maps (especially the time-consuming Raytrace map).

The Arrow button next to the diffuse color swatch becomes enabled whenever you assign a diffuse map. Clicking this arrow calculates the average pixel color of the diffuse map and copies it into the diffuse color swatch. This is especially helpful in radiosity renderings (see Chapter 10) as the Diffuse Color controls what color surfaces will emit in light bouncing.

Shininess   This parameter controls both the specular level and glossiness parameters that you may have used before in the Standard material. You may also notice that you do not have to select any shaders with the Architectural material. The shaders used are automatically handled based upon the template that you choose.

The percentage used in the Shininess amount is entered automatically by the template, so you don't have to alter it unless you wish to further customize your material.

TIP   Instance the diffuse map in the Shininess channel when you want the bright areas of the map to represent the shiny areas as well.

Transparency   Transparency is the opposite of Opacity (from the Standard material). Transparency is the amount of light that passes through the material without illuminating it (as with most kinds of architectural glass).

You won't be able to see any diffuse color on objects that are 100% transparent, but you will still be able to see the shiny areas.

Translucency   Use this channel when you are simulating objects that allow some light through, but scatter it within the object. Art glass or frosted privacy glass are some examples of translucent materials.

Index of Refraction   The Index of Refraction (IOR) is a physical optics property that all translucent and transparent materials naturally have. Light reflects and/or refracts at the interface between two materials with different IOR. The template will set this value for you. There are no units with this spinner, but be aware that it is not a percentage.

Material	IOR
Vacuum	1 exactly
Air	1.0003
Water	1.33
Glass	1.50 to 1.70
Diamond	2.41

Luminance   Set this value if you want the material to glow with its own light. The units are in candelas per square meter. You can think of one candela as roughly the light emitted from one wax candle.

Set Luminance from Light   If you are using the radiosity renderer (see Chapter 10), chances are you are using photometric lights that simulate real-world intensities. Click the button with the spotlight icon near the bottom of the Physical Qualities rollout and then click a photometric light to copy its intensity into the Luminance Amount spinner. This is a quick way to make your material emit the light intensity of a known luminaire without having to remember the numerical intensity values.

Check Boxes   The 2-Sided check box is useful when you are rendering imported surfaces that have their normals facing in the wrong direction. Be aware that your rendering may take longer (especially if you are ray tracing).

The Raw Diffuse Texture check box is used only in radiosity rendering (see Chapter 10). It excludes the surface from illumination and exposure control, so your whites stay pure white. This is helpful when you are simulating the surface of a luminaire and want it to read as pure white but don't want the surface itself to emit light.

The Special Effects Rollout

The Special Effects rollout contains four channels that simulate advanced features. You have already seen how to use a Bump map earlier in this chapter, and this channel is the same as the Bump channel found in the Standard material.

Bump   Bump simulates low relief by manipulating surface normals (similar to how smoothing works). Any type of map will work in this channel. Noise is often used to make a rough, uneven surface. On the other hand, you can instance the diffuse map into this channel, and only the grayscale component of a color image will be used to lift, or bump, the surface upward.

Displacement   Displacement differs from Bump in that this channel actually alters the geometry that it is applied to at render time. Displacement can be used to simulate surfaces that are difficult to model with other techniques. Typically bitmaps are used in this channel although most map types are supported.

Intensity This is a new channel that simulates the brightness or *intensity* of a material. It can be used for positive effect to simulate roughness, which you can think of as variable brightness across a surface.

TIP *Try using a Noise map in the Intensity channel to make your material more realistic and to avoid that flat look that is so common in computer graphics.*

Cutout This is similar to the Opacity channel in the Standard material but better. When you place a Bitmap in the Cutout channel, not only are the black areas of the bitmap transparent, but the *cutout* area will not have any reflections, refractions, or shininess. In other words, the black areas of a map in this channel are completely and utterly cut out. This is perfect for entourage, covered earlier in this chapter.

Other rollouts The Advanced Lighting Override rollout is used only for tweaking radiosity solutions and works the same as the Advanced Lighting Override material from VIZ 4 (see Chapter 10).

The Supersampling rollout allows you to apply anti-aliasing at the material level. You can opt to control supersampling at the global or local levels. In other words, you can enable supersampling within one material if you want its settings to differ from the global supersampling options.

The mental ray Connection rollout is to be used only with the mental ray renderer (see Chapter 11).

The Material Utilities

There are many utilities that help with materials and two are new in VIZ 2005. Utilities are like separate programs that run inside VIZ. Each of the utilities was designed to do a very specific job and they extend the functionality of VIZ. Here is how you can access the relevant utilities that help when you are designing, editing, and managing materials:

1. Click the Utilities tab of the Command panel.

A list of utilities is shown as buttons in the Utilities rollout. You can run each of these utility programs by clicking the appropriate button. Be aware that there are many more utilities that are not shown as buttons by default.

2. Click the More… button in the Utilities rollout. The Utilities dialog box (see Figure 7.53) appears showing any utilities that are not already shown as buttons in the Command Panel.

FIGURE 7.53

Utilities dialog box

Each of the utilities was designed to do a very specific job and to extend the functionality of VIZ. The relevant utilities that help when you are designing, editing, and managing materials are as follows:

Bitmap/Photometric Paths   Use the utility shown in Figure 7.54 to change the hard-coded paths that are referenced by your bitmaps. Often incredibly helpful when you open a VIZ file made by a person in a different organization or department, this utility lets you repath all the missing bitmaps in one interface. This can be a timesaver when compared to searching each material in the scene for its missing bitmaps.

FIGURE 7.54

Bitmap/Photo-metric Path utility

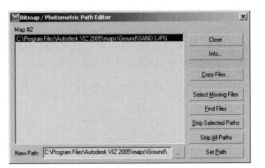

New!

Clean Multi-Materials   This utility program fixes a problem with the Multi/Sub-Object material—the fact that there are often "extra" sub-materials that aren't referenced anywhere in the scene. Use the utility shown in Figure 7.55 to remove unused sub-materials without affecting material IDs or sub-materials that are in use.

FIGURE 7.55
Clean Multi-
Materials utility

FIGURE 7.55
Clean Multi-
Materials utility

Color Clipboard   Use the Color Clipboard as shown in Figure 7.56 to hold color information in four convenient swatches. Drag a color swatch from anywhere in Material Editor onto any one of the four swatches in the Color Clipboard rollout and the color will be stored there during your session.

You can also click the New Floater button to open a separate floating dialog box that has additional color swatches. Click one of the Save buttons to store your favorite 12 colors in a CCB file for later reuse.

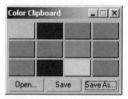

FIGURE 7.56
Color Clipboard

Fix Ambient   Use this simple program to change any materials that have different colors in the ambient and diffuse color channels. The utility shown in Figure 7.57 will copy the diffuse color into the ambient color for all materials that you select.

FIGURE 7.57

Fix Ambient utility

Instance Duplicate Maps   Figure 7.58 shows the Instance Duplicate Maps dialog box. Use this utility in your projects when you want to convert unique maps that are identical into instanced maps. This is more efficient and may save some memory in addition to giving you more coordinated control over the shared parameters in the instanced maps.

New!

FIGURE 7.58

Instance Duplicate Maps utility

Lightscape Materials   Use this utility (Figure 7.59) only if you are importing radiosity solutions from Discreet Lightscape into VIZ. Lightscape is a classic program that brought radiosity to the masses and may still be in use in some quarters.

Material XML Exporter   The Material XML utility (see Figure 7.60) can be used to export the materials in your scene to an XML file that can be used in Autodesk Architectural Desktop 2004.

You can drag and drop these XML files from a web page into VIZ or Architectural Desktop (ADT). Use this as an alternative to material libraries within VIZ and as a new way to communicate with ADT users.

Resource Collector   Use the Resource Collector shown in Figure 7.61 to copy and optionally compress all your scene's bitmaps (and photometric files) into a single folder. This makes it much easier to send scenes to other organizations because all the associated bitmaps will be included.

FIGURE 7.59
Lightscape Materials utility

FIGURE 7.60
Material XML Exporter

FIGURE 7.61
Resource Collector

NOTE   *The Resource Collector is very similar to AutoCAD's Express tool called Pack 'n Go.*

Summary

This chapter introduced you to the different ways you can design and use materials in your model. You've also seen that, by making changes to materials, you can greatly alter the appearance of your rendering. The Material Editor is a powerful tool, so you will want to get as familiar as possible with it.

Chapter 8 delves deeper into the use of cameras and the environment. In addition to a continued look at materials, you'll learn more about lighting and how to add a backdrop to your design.

Chapter 8

Staging Your Design

IF YOU'VE EVER TAKEN a presentation drawing class, you've probably been shown the importance of carefully observing the subject of your drawing. It's important to be aware of the details of a scene or landscape that might otherwise go unnoticed. By recording those details in your sketches and drawings, you create a sense of depth and realism.

When you create a scene in VIZ, it helps to recall those lessons in observation, even though you aren't creating a scene from real life. If you're creating a rendering of a building with lots of glass, it helps to go out and take a look at buildings and carefully study how glass reflects the surrounding landscape. If you're doing an interior rendering, you may find it helpful to find a room that's similar to the one you are rendering and carefully examine how the light is reflected throughout the room from various sources. By understanding the behavior of materials and light in the real world, you are better equipped to create realistic scenes in VIZ.

In this chapter, you'll take a look at what I call *staging*. Staging is the process of setting up your scene for a shoot, and that includes placing the camera and thus setting up the relationship between the subject being shot and its surrounding environment.

- ◆ Understanding the VIZ Camera
- ◆ Setting Up an Interior View
- ◆ Creating an Environment
- ◆ Using a Matte Painting
- ◆ Immersive Environments for Animation
- ◆ Skydome Model with Seamless Texture
- ◆ Ray Tracing Reflections and Refraction
- ◆ Using Render Types
- ◆ Render Elements for Compositing

Understanding the VIZ Camera

So far, you have been working with the standard views including Top, Left, Right, and Perspective viewports. By constantly changing the standard views by zooming, panning, and rotating, you have learned to see objects from all angles as you modeled them. When you place a VIZ camera, that camera holds a particular point of view that you can use to frame a composition or to get inside an interior space for a rendering.

VIZ cameras follow the Single Lens Reflex (SLR) film camera metaphor, where you can make adjustments like changing the focal length of the lens from telephoto to wide angle, or changing the focal depth, which is akin to changing the f-stop on the lens to capture depth-of-field effects. Once you carefully place your camera in the scene, you can switch into this composed point of view and render the scene from within the camera.

Adding a Camera

In this exercise, you'll add a new camera in VIZ. You'll add a camera that shows an interior view of the courtyard on the second floor of the model.

1. Open the Savoye8a.max file from the CD.

2. Right-click the Top viewport to make it active; then use the Zoom Region tool to enlarge the view so that it looks similar to Figure 8.1. Make sure the Top viewport is displaying in the wireframe by right-clicking the Top label and selecting Wireframe.

FIGURE 8.1
Click and drag this point to place the camera.

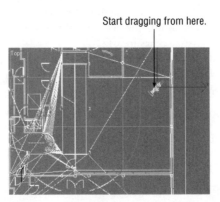

Start dragging from here.

3. Click the Cameras tool in the Create tab of the Command Panel.

4. Click the Target button in the Object Type rollout.

5. In the Top viewport, click and drag the point shown in Figure 8.1.

6. Move the cursor toward the lower left of the viewport. As you do, you see a rubber-banding line from the point you selected in step 4. Click the point shown in Figure 8.2.

FIGURE 8.2
The target location

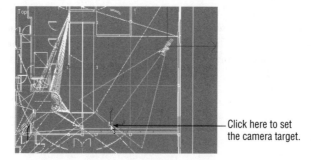

Click here to set the camera target.

7. You've just created a camera as shown in Figure 8.3. Now give your new camera a name. In the Name and Color rollout in the Command Panel, change the name from Camera01 to **Mycamera**.

FIGURE 8.3
The new camera

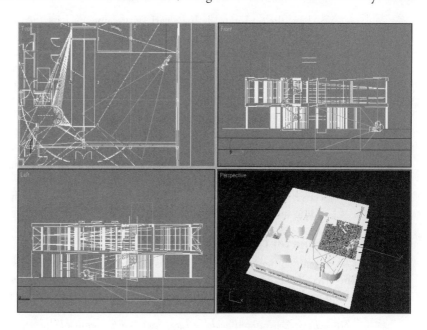

8. Right-click the Perspective viewport; then type **C**. The viewport changes to show the view from your new camera.

NOTE *VIZ automatically assigns the name Camera01 to the first camera created in a design. Additional cameras are called Camera02, Camera03, and so on. To help associate a camera with a view, you might consider naming your cameras with meaningful view names, just as you would name geometry in your model.*

Your new camera displays as a simplified camera shape, while the camera target simply displays as a small cube helper. The camera's field of view is also shown as a cyan pyramid. Notice that the camera displays on the ground plane defined by the XY coordinates. As with all newly created objects, the camera and target originate by default on the XY plane of world space. The camera's current location won't give you a view of the courtyard, which is on the second floor. You can later move the camera into position to get a courtyard view. But first take a moment to study the camera parameters in the Command Panel.

You have the option to define a variety of camera settings. At the top of the Parameters rollout, you see the Lens setting, which adjusts the camera's focal length. A camera's focal length determines its field of view. In fact, just below the Lens setting is the FOV setting (which stands for field of view). If you prefer, you can enter the field of view in degrees instead of focal length. When you change one setting, the other setting also changes in an inverse relationship. VIZ offers a default focal length of 43, or an FOV of 45, which is close to the typical focal length found in most cameras. (A setting of 43 simulates the human eye.) Below the Lens and FOV settings, you can select from a set of Stock Lenses—predefined focal lengths.

You might also notice a check box labeled Orthographic Projection. As you might guess, this check box lets you change the view from a perspective to an orthographic projection. With this setting checked, your camera view will appear as a flat projection (like the Top or Right views) instead of a perspective view. The Orthographic Projection check box is handy for creating rendered elevations of building models.

ADJUSTING THE CAMERA LOCATION

As with any other VIZ object, cameras can be moved or rotated using the transform tools (scale has no effect). Cameras and their targets are treated as separate objects when you apply the Move transform tool. Free cameras do not have targets and can be moved by selecting the camera body only.

TIP *Target Cameras work much like Target Spots. Both have separate linked target helpers that aid in positioning and aiming.*

Even though the Camera and Target are separate objects, they are linked together, as you'll see a bit later. In this exercise, you'll see how moving your camera affects its view.

1. Right-click the Left viewport. Then use the Zoom Region tool to enlarge the view of the building as shown in the lower left corner of Figure 8.3.

2. Click the Select by Name tool on the main toolbar. Then, in the Select Objects dialog box, Ctrl+click the Mycamera.Target listing and click Select. By doing this, you include both the Mycamera camera and Mycamera.Target in the selection.

3. Click the Select and Move tool; then, in the Left viewport, click and drag the Y axis handle of the Transform gizmo. Watch the Mycamera viewport. The view looks as though you were riding an elevator up to the second floor.

4. Set the vertical camera location so that the Mycamera is approximately 18′ above ground level.

While you are moving the camera location, you get immediate visual feedback by watching the Camera viewport. In this exercise, you moved both the camera and the target together to adjust the view. Next, you'll fine-tune the camera view by moving only the target.

TIP   If you want to create a camera that matches an existing viewport, you can do so by choosing Views ➤ Create Camera from View.

ADJUSTING THE TARGET

The Mycamera camera is at an elevation that roughly approximates the height of a person. Both the camera and the target are at the same elevation. You'll want to drop the target location down a bit to center the view of the courtyard.

1. Click the Select by Name tool on the main toolbar, or type **H**.

2. In the Select Objects dialog box, locate and click Mycamera.Target. Then click Select.

3. In the Left viewport, click and drag the Y coordinate arrow downward about 3 feet until the Mycamera viewport looks similar to Figure 8.4.

In this exercise, you used the Select Objects dialog box because it would have been difficult to select the camera target in the middle of the model.

TIP   You can also select a camera, right-click, and then choose Select Camera Target from the Tools1 quad menu.

Editing the Camera Location with the Viewport Tools

In the previous chapters, you used the viewport navigation tools in the lower right corner of the VIZ window to control your Perspective viewport. You learned that in a perspective view, the tools offered on the Viewport toolbar changed to tools more appropriate to the perspective view. Similarly, when you have a camera view assigned to a viewport, the Viewport toolbar offers a set of tools uniquely suited to the camera. These Camera viewport tools serve not only to alter the view in the Camera viewport, but to edit the camera location and orientation.

FIGURE 8.4

Adjust the camera target location until your view looks like this one.

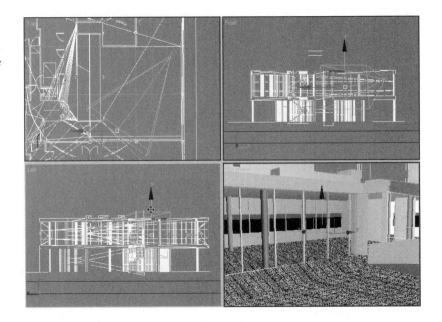

USING THE DOLLY CAMERA AND FIELD-OF-VIEW TOOLS

To get a close-up view of a particular portion of your model, you typically use the Zoom Region tool or the Zoom tool in the standard viewports. In a Camera viewport, there really isn't an equivalent to the Zoom Region tool. You do have two tools that have the same effect as the Zoom and Field-of-View tools for the Perspective viewport. The Dolly Camera tool acts exactly like the Zoom tool in a Perspective viewport. You have the added advantage of being able to see the effect of the Zoom tool on the camera location. Try the following exercise to see firsthand what Zoom does.

1. If it isn't already selected, select the Mycamera camera and then right-click the Mycamera viewport to make sure it's active.

2. Click the Dolly Camera tool in the bottom right corner of the user interface.

3. Click and drag upward in the Mycamera viewport and notice what happens in the other three viewports. The Mycamera viewport enlarges, and you can see the camera move closer to the target in the other viewports. Notice that only the camera moves; the target remains stationary.

4. Click the Undo tool to return the camera to its original location (where it was before you used the Dolly Camera tool).

5. Click the Field-of-View tool; then click and drag upward in the Mycamera viewport.

Notice what happens to the camera in the other three viewports.

6. Click the Modify tab and watch the camera parameters as you adjust the Field-of-View tool. Notice that the Lens and FOV settings change with the adjustments of Field-of-View tool.

7. Adjust the view so that the Lens parameter shows around 35 mm.

The Field-of-View tool alters the camera field of view just as it does for the Perspective viewport. The only difference is that now you can see its effect by watching the camera. As you click and drag the Field-of-View tool, you see the cyan-colored Field-of-View gizmo change in the Top, Left, and Front viewports (see Figure 8.5).

FIGURE 8.5

The field of view of a camera changes when you click and drag the Field-of-View tool.

Using Field-of-View changes the size of the Camera gizmo.

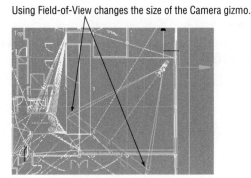

A tool that performs a function similar to that of the Field-of-View tool is the camera's Perspective tool.

The Perspective tool also changes the camera's field of view, but it simultaneously moves the camera closer to or farther away from the model. This has the effect of keeping the size of the image the same in the Camera viewport while the field of view changes.

TIP   *If you set up a camera for a wide field of view, the perspective view may begin to exaggerate the vertical taper of tall objects. You can compensate for this exaggeration by using the Camera Correction modifier, which creates the illusion of a two-point perspective. See Appendix B for more information.*

PANNING YOUR CAMERA VIEW

Like the Dolly Camera and Field-of-View tools, the Truck Camera tool moves the camera as it alters the camera view. You can see exactly how the Truck Camera tool works by the way that it moves the camera and target.

1. Click the Truck Camera tool in the Viewport toolbar.

2. In the Mycamera viewport, click and drag the Truck Camera tool and watch what the camera does in the Top, Left, and Front viewports.

3. Click the Undo tool to return the camera and target to their previous locations.

The camera and target move together in a path perpendicular to the direction that the camera is pointing.

ROTATING THE CAMERA

You've used the Arc Rotate tool to move your point of view in the Perspective viewport. When you're working with a Camera viewport, the function of the Arc Rotate tool is divided into two tools: the Orbit Camera tool and the Roll Camera tool.

The Orbit Camera tool performs the same function as clicking in the center of the green circle of the Arc Rotate tool. Your camera location orbits about the camera target location as you drag, remaining at a fixed distance from the target. You won't see the green circle that you see with the Arc Rotate tool. If you want to limit the camera motion to horizontal or vertical, you can hold the Shift key down as you click and drag the mouse.

The Roll Camera tool performs the same function as clicking and dragging the outside of the green circle of the Arc Rotate tool. The camera view rotates, remaining at a fixed location.

There is also a flyout option under the Orbit Camera tool. You can click and hold the Orbit Camera tool to reveal the Pan Camera tool.

The Pan Camera tool lets you change the direction in which the camera is pointing as if it were on a fixed tripod, without changing the camera's position. Holding down the Shift key while using the Pan Camera tool constrains the motion to either a vertical or horizontal plane, while moving the camera.

Setting Up an Interior View

Now let's focus our attention on the interior space. You may notice that it is difficult to see into an interior space when you are using the Perspective view. Placing a camera into an interior is a great way to see inside. You will switch back to a Perspective view to continue modeling after you have placed an interior camera. First, set up the camera to view more of the interior and less of the courtyard.

1. Right-click the Top viewport and click the Min/Max Toggle tool to enlarge it.

2. If you need to, adjust the view so that you can get a good look at the room toward the bottom of the viewport, as shown in Figure 8.6.

FIGURE 8.6
Moving the
Mycamera camera

Copy Mycamera from here.

Drag the copy to here.

3. Click the Select and Move tool; then click the Mycamera camera that you made in the previous section.

4. Hit the spacebar to toggle the Selection Lock on.

NOTE You will find it easier to move objects with Selection Lock on because you can't inadvertently select anything else in this mode.

5. Shift+click and drag the camera in the XY plane to the location shown in Figure 8.6.

6. In the Clone Options dialog box, make sure the Copy radio button is selected; then click OK. Note that the name of the new camera is Mycamera01.

You now have a new camera for your interior view. Next, rotate the camera so that you are looking down the room instead of out the window.

1. Click the Min/Max Toggle tool to get a view of all four viewports.

2. Right-click the Mycamera label in the Camera viewport; then select View ≻ Mycamera01.

3. Click and hold the Orbit Camera tool in the Viewport Navigation Control toolbar; then select Pan Camera from the flyout.

4. Start dragging the cursor horizontally from left to right in the Mycamera01 viewport and then hold down the Shift key to adjust the view so that it looks like Figure 8.7.

FIGURE 8.7
The new
Mycamera01
viewport

By holding the Shift key while dragging the mouse, the Pan Camera tool is constrained to a horizontal motion.

NOTE *In VIZ, the Shift key usually brings up the Clone Options dialog box, but in this context, the Shift key is being used as a constraint by holding it after you start dragging, as in many other software programs.*

5. Click the Quick Render tool to get a look at the room. Your view should look similar to Figure 8.8. Notice that there is a light source that illuminates the courtyard.

FIGURE 8.8
A rendered view of
the interior

Creating an Environment

In the movie industry, artists are employed to produce background images (called mats or matte paintings) to simulate special environments, such as mountainous terrain, a canyon, or the interior of a space station. You can employ a similar technique using VIZ's environment background option. The *environment* in VIZ is everything surrounding the objects in your scene.

The following exercise will show you how to quickly add a sky to the villa model by adding a bitmap image for a background.

1. Open Savoye8b.max from the sample files on the companion CD.

2. Choose Rendering ➢ Environment or type **8** on the keyboard. The Environment and Effects dialog box displays.

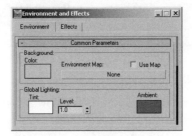

3. Click the Environment Map button labeled None just below the Use Map check box. The Material/Map browser appears, showing a list of new material types.

4. Click the Bitmap option in the list of maps, and then click OK.

The Select Bitmap Image File dialog box displays. By default, the Select Bitmap Image File dialog box shows the contents of the VIZ 2005/Maps folder.

5. Locate the Maps folder under the VIZ program folder. Double-click the Backgrounds subfolder and select the SUNSET90.JPG file. You'll see a preview of the selected file in the lower right corner of the dialog box, as shown in Figure 8.9. At the bottom of the dialog box, you'll also see statistics about the file.

FIGURE 8.9
The Select Bitmap
image file with a pre-
view in the lower
right corner

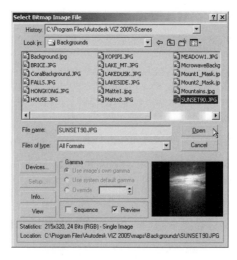

6. Click Open. Note that the name of the file now appears on the Environment Map button.

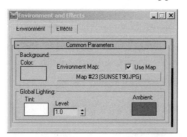

7. Close the Environment dialog box. Make sure that the Mycamera01 viewport is currently active and then click the Quick Render button to see the result of your background addition. The model is rendered with a sky in the background, as shown in Figure 8.10.

WARNING *Figure 8.10 highlights a mismatch that often occurs between the lighting in the scene and the environment. Because light sources are independent of environment bitmaps, it is easy to set up lighting in your scene that doesn't necessarily go with the implied lighting in an environment image. In Figure 8.10 the environment shows a sunset while the lighting in the scene suggests midday sun. Clearly, one or the other of these two variables could be adjusted for a more realistic image. Keep this potential mismatch in mind when you design environments.*

NOTE *Now in VIZ 2005, the environment background automatically displays in the viewport.*

FIGURE 8.10
The sky in the rendering

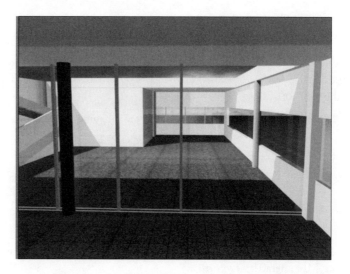

FIGURE 8.10
The sky in the rendering

Making Adjustments to the Background

In many cases, the background image will need to be adjusted to fit the scene. The background image may not fit the rendering correctly, or it may be too dark or light. You might notice that our sunset background is a bit below the horizon and is a bit dark overall. In this section, you'll learn how to use the Material Editor to make adjustments to the background.

1. Click the Material Editor tool in the main toolbar.

2. In the Material Editor dialog box, click the sample slot on the right of the bottom row. Then click the Get Material tool.

3. In the Material/Map Browser dialog box, click the Scene radio button in the Browse From group.

   The materials list changes to show all of the materials currently in the model.

4. Select the listing that shows (SUNSET90.JPG) in its title. You see a sample of the material in the preview window in the upper left corner of the dialog box.

5. Double-click the (SUNSET90.JPG) listing. The sunset image appears in the selected sample in the Material Editor. Options for the background bitmap also display in the lower half of the Material Editor.

WARNING *This may be the first time you have seen a map appear by itself in the Material Editor. Remember that you can't apply maps by themselves to objects—maps are usually children of materials.*

Once you've got the background image in the Material Editor, you have access to parameters that control its appearance. Next you'll use the Coordinates rollout to offset the environment background in the viewport.

1. Go to the Coordinates rollout and try dragging the U and V Offset spinners.

The environment background image moves in relation to the stationary geometry in the Mycamera01 viewport.

2. Right-click the label of the camera viewport and select Views ➤ Mycamera from the context menu.

3. Right-click the Mycamera viewport to activate it. Using the Pan Camera tool, drag upward in the viewport to aim the camera upward.

You now have a better view of the sky above the courtyard.

4. Click the Mapping drop-down list in the Coordinates rollout. Change the mapping type to Spherical Environment.

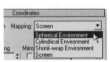

NOTE *Cylindrical and spherical mapping wraps the environment bitmap around the inside of these two corresponding shapes. Shrink-wrap mapping conforms the map to a complex concave surface. Screen wrapping is probably the most often-used choice because it simply pastes the bitmap flat on the background screen like a matte painting.*

Notice that the image distorts as it stretches around the inside of a large sphere that surrounds the model, as shown in Figure 8.11. You can see the clouds curving slightly as they wrap around the sphere.

Fisheye camera lenses have spherical distortion appropriate to a spherical environment mapping. You will learn how to make both spherical and cylindrical wraparound panoramas of your virtual scenes in Chapter 17. In order to effectively use spherical, cylindrical, or shrink-wrap environment mapping, the bitmap used must be distorted in the same way. Otherwise, a "normal" bitmap would appear stretched if used in this way.

FIGURE 8.11
Spherical environment mapping

Since you will be using the SUNSET90.jpg bitmap, you should use screen mapping to directly paste the image into the environment without distortion.

1. Change the mapping type back to Screen.

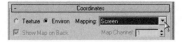

2. In the Coordinates rollout, set the U and V Offset amounts back to 0. The bitmap will now be pasted directly into the background as shown in Figure 8.12.

FIGURE 8.12
Screen environment mapping

You can adjust the Offset and Tiling spinners as desired to move and stretch the setting sun around in the background until it is in an aesthetically pleasing location in relation to the building. Now let's see how to adjust the brightness of the background image.

1. Open the Material Editor again.

2. Scroll down to the Output rollout and click the Output button to open the rollout at the very bottom. You'll see a graph and a set of check boxes and spinners.

3. Click the Enable Color Map check box in the Output rollout. The graph is highlighted so that you are able to adjust its settings.

If you're an Adobe Photoshop user, the Color Map graph should be somewhat familiar as it is similar to Curves in Photoshop. The Color Map lets you adjust the tonal range of an image by manipulating the line in the graph. Right now, the line goes straight from 0,0 in the lower left corner to 1,1 in the upper right. You can adjust brightness, contrast, and tonal range of an image by adding control points to the line and then moving the control points. The next exercise will show you some of the Color Map functions.

1. Scroll the Output rollout upward so that you can see all of the Color Map group and then click the Add Point tool on the Curve toolbar.

2. Click the color map graph line at its midpoint, as shown in Figure 8.13. A square handle appears on the line.

3. Click the Move tool on the Curve toolbar.

FIGURE 8.13
Click the midpoint
of the line.

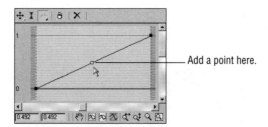

Add a point here.

4. Click the handle you just created and drag it upward and then release. Notice what happens to the sample slot image in the Material Editor. It gets brighter.

By adjusting the line upward at its midpoint, you've increased the amount of the midtones in the image. Let's see what other options you have to edit the curve. You can get direct feedback on the effect of your changes by viewing the sample bar at the bottom of the Output rollout.

1. Scroll the Material Editor panel upward so you have a good view of the sample gradient bar, as shown in Figure 8.14.

FIGURE 8.14
Scroll the output
rollout of the Mate-
rial Editor panel so
that you can see a
view similar to
this one.

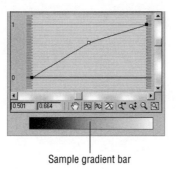

Sample gradient bar

2. Right-click the handle you moved in the last exercise, and then select Bézier Smooth from the pop-up list.

3. Move the handle back to its midpoint position; then adjust the Bézier handles so they look like those in Figure 8.15. The sample image fades in contrast, and the gray area of the sample tonal range at the bottom of the graph widens.

4. Now adjust the handles to look like Figure 8.16. The sample image increases in contrast.

5. Finally, reposition the curve handle to the left so it looks like Figure 8.17.

FIGURE 8.15
The Bézier handles
in a new orientation

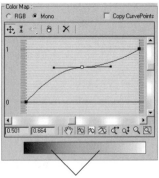

The gray tones widen.

FIGURE 8.16
The Bézier handles
set to increase
contrast

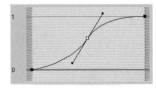

FIGURE 8.17
Move the handle to
the left to brighten
the image.

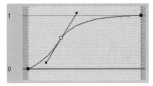

6. To apply the image changes to your model, right-click in the Mycamera viewport. The background in the Mycamera viewport changes to match the sample in the Material Editor.

Besides the overall tone of the image, you can also manipulate the curves for each of the red, green, and blue color components. For example, suppose you want to increase the blue and downplay the red in the background. You can use the R, G, and B tools to isolate each color.

1. Click the Copy CurvePoints check box and then click the RGB radio button at the top of the Color Map group. Copy CurvePoints forces the RGB settings to use the current curve settings.

2. Click the R and G tools on the Output toolbar to deactivate them.

The tools should look as if they are in an up position. The line is now blue to indicate that only the blue component of the curve is active.

3. Now move the curve handle to the left. The sample image becomes bluer.

4. Click the R button to activate the red component. Now you see two curves, one red and one blue.

5. Click the B button to deactivate the blue component. Then click and drag the handle on the red curve to the right just a little to reduce its strength.

6. Click in the Mycamera viewport to update the background in your model.

Now the sky is bluer and a little less ominous looking.
You've seen that you have a lot of control over the background image.

TIP   *You can use the Output options on any material that uses a bitmap. You can even apply an Output map as a parent to those map types that do not already have an Output rollout built in. Use the Output rollout in VIZ as a quick alternative to doing color correction in Adobe Photoshop.*

For example, you can edit the Ground-Grass bitmap for the ground using the same tools you just used on the background. To gain access to the Output rollout for Maps, go to the Maps rollout and click the button for the map you want to edit. For example, you can click the GRASS2.jpg Diffuse map for the Ground-Grass material. You'll find the Output rollout at the bottom of the Map parameters that appear in the Material Editor.

Immersive Environments for Animation

One of the limitations of using a matte painting is that the illusion breaks down if the camera moves more than just a little. You can perceive the flatness of the background especially if the camera turns because the environment bitmap does not turn with the rest of the scene.

In animations where the camera moves, you must devise immersive environments where the background remains credible. One way to accomplish this is to use an abstract background that looks the same no matter where the camera turns. Another more complex method is to actually model the environment with a large skydome object that envelops the rest of the scene. You will be learning how to create immersive environments that can be used in animated scenes here, but you will hold off on diving into the subject of animation until Chapter 12.

Creating a Credible Background

In animations where you are showing an outdoor flyby of a building, the background can be a simple gradient from bottom to top. Such a background will not appear to be static, because no objects in the background define a point of reference as the camera moves.

1. Choose Rendering ➤ Environment or type **8** on the keyboard. The Environment dialog box appears.

2. Click the Map #23 (SUNSET90.jpg) button to change the map type.

3. The Material/Map browser appears. Select Gradient from the list and notice the sample in the upper left of the dialog box. It shows a grayscale gradient from black at the top to white at the bottom.

4. Click OK to select the gradient map.

You've switched to a gradient map for the background, but you will want to add some colors to the gradient.

1. Click the Material Editor tool on the main toolbar to open the Material Editor.

2. Use the slide bar on the right to view the third row of sample slots just below the ones visible in the dialog box.

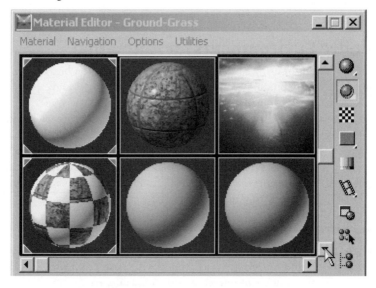

 3. Click the undefined slot at the bottom right to select it; then click the Get Material tool.

4. In the Material Map dialog box, click the Scene radio button in the Browse From group, and then double-click the Map listing that shows Map #24 (Gradient)[Environment] in the name. The slot now shows the gradient.

Once you've got the gradient in the sample slot, you can begin to play with its parameters.

1. Scroll down Material Editor to the Gradient Parameters rollout, and click the color swatch labeled Color #1.

2. In the Color Selector dialog box, set the Hue setting to 155, the Saturation (Sat) setting to 220, and the Value setting to 100.

3. Click Close. In Gradient Parameters, click the color swatch for Color #2.

4. At the Color selector, set the Hue setting to 155, the Saturation to 125, and the Value to 255.

5. Click Close when you're done, and then close all of the other dialog boxes. Now you see a color gradient background in the Mycamera viewport.

The new background looks like a typical clear sky with a gray horizon. It won't matter that the background remains the same throughout an animation, since the gradient colors won't give away the fact that they are not moving with the camera. Of course, you can use the gradient background for still images as well.

TIP   You can create an animated background by using an animated AVI or MOV file for background image. Likewise, you can create an animated texture by using an AVI or MOV file for a texture map.

Using a Texture Map and Hemisphere for the Sky

The gradient background offers the illusion of a clear sky, but what if you want to add some clouds? You can simulate a cloudy sky by adding a flattened dome over your model and then assigning a texture map that uses a bitmap of a cloudy sky to the dome. Here's how it's done.

First you'll add the hemisphere object.

1. Right-click the Top viewport, and then click the Zoom Extents tool in the lower right corner of the VIZ window.

2. In the Create tab of the Command Panel, click the Geometry button and select Sphere.

3. In the Top viewport, click and drag a sphere from the center of the building as shown in Figure 8.18. Make the sphere extend to the corner of the Ground plane with a radius of about 1,060 feet.

FIGURE 8.18
Create a sphere with a radius of 1,060 feet.

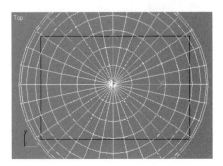

4. Right-click the Front viewport, and click the Zoom Extents tool.

5. In the Command Panel, change the Hemisphere parameter for the sphere to 0.7. Most of the sphere will disappear, leaving the topmost portion. Change the name of the sphere from Sphere01 to **Skydome** so that you can keep track of its function.

6. Move the Hemisphere so that its base is just below the ground plane as shown in Figure 8.19.

FIGURE 8.19
Move the hemisphere downward in the Z axis so that its base is just below the ground plane.

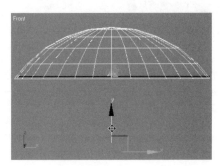

When you adjust the Hemisphere parameter, VIZ flattens the bottom of the sphere and places a surface on the flattened area. You need to place the bottom of the flattened sphere below the ground plane so that the sphere's flattened surface doesn't appear in your camera view.

Now you've got a dome over your model, which will become the sky. Spheres are normally intended to be viewed from the outside, so when VIZ creates a sphere, the normals are pointing outward. In this situation, you want your sphere to be viewable from the inside, so you need to invert the direction of the skydome's normals.

1. With the skydome hemisphere selected, click the Modify tab.

2. Right-click Sphere in the Modifier Stack list, then select Editable Mesh. You won't need to make changes to the skydome's parameters, so this operation will help conserve memory and simplify the object.

3. Click the Element button in the Selection rollout to enter the element sub-object level.

4. Click the skydome to select it at the element sub-object level.

5. Scroll down to the Surface Properties rollout, and click the Flip button in the Normals group. You'll notice that the Camera view will change so that you no longer see the background gradient. Instead you see the inside of the skydome, showing you that the normals really are flipped.

6. Back in the Modifier Stack list, click Editable Mesh to return to the Object level.

The skydome is just about ready. You now need to create a material to apply to the skydome to simulate the clouds. The material will also require a UVW Map applied to the skydome.

1. Open the Material Editor, then scroll down the Sample slots and click an unused slot.

2. Rename the selected slot's material name as **Skydome**, then open the Map rollout at the bottom of the dialog box.

3. Click the Diffuse Color Map button. Then, in the Material/Map browser, double-click Bitmap.

4. In the Select Bitmap image file dialog box, open the `\Program Files\Autodesk VIZ 2005\Maps\Skies` folder. Then locate and select `Cloud2.jpg`. This is a fairly generic sky with a few clouds.

5. Click Open. Return to the Material Editor, and you see the sky bitmap in the sample slot.

6. With the skydome object selected, go ahead and click the Assign Material to Selection button on the Material Editor toolbar.

7. Click the Show Map in Viewport button in the Material Editor.

The sky in the Camera viewport will change color but won't display the sky bitmap properly. This is because the skydome material requires a UVW map, which doesn't exist yet.

You're just about finished creating the sky. The last item you need to take care of is the UVW map. For this situation, the best map will be the Planar map. You want as much of the material map as possible to fit on the skydome. You'll get the most natural-looking sky by mapping the skydome material as a flat plane against the skydome object.

1. In the Modify tab, click the UVW Map modifier from the Modifier drop-down list. The Planar map is the default, so you don't really need to do much else. VIZ automatically aligns the map to the skydome object and adjusts the UVW map to fit the skydome.

2. Right-click the Top viewport and click the Zoom Extents tool to get a better view of the UVW Map gizmo.

3. Switch to the Mycamera01 viewport, then click the Quick Render tool to see the results. The sky appears out the window, but it is too dark.

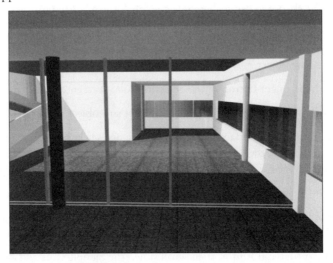

TIP You can simulate clouds blowing in the wind by very slowly rotating the skydome in an animation. Read more about animation in Chapter 12.

Since there are no lights directed toward the skydome, it appears as a dark background. You can add an Omni light, whose only purpose is to light the skydome.

1. Close the Rendered Frame Window and right-click the Top viewport.

2. Go to the Create tab in the Command Panel, select the Lights button, and then click the Omni button.

3. Click the center of the dome to place an Omni light there.

4. In the Command Panel, change the name of the new Omni light to **skydomelight** and turn off its On option in the Shadows group of the General Parameters rollout.

5. Open the Intensity/Color/Attenuation rollout and set the Multiplier input box to 1.

Now you've got a light for the skydome. You'll want to make sure that it illuminates only the sky.

1. In the General Parameters, click the Exclude button.

2. In the Exclude/Include dialog box, click the Include radio button in the upper right corner.

3. Select Skydome from the list box to the left; then click the right-pointing arrow to move the selection to the list box on the right.

>>

4. Click OK to close the dialog box.

5. Right-click the Camera viewport, and click the Quick Render tool again. This time the sky appears brighter.

NOTE Objects that are excluded from illumination render correctly but still appear illuminated in the viewport. The Interactive Viewport Renderer doesn't handle this aspect of illumination as well as the other renderers, but it does display in real-time.

Now you have a sky that will stay in one place as the animation moves through the scene. Since the sky bitmap is now assigned to an object in the model, it will remain fixed in relation to the rest of the model. The net effect will be that the sky will appropriately follow the rest of the objects in the scene as the camera moves along its path.

TIP You can also create an interesting effect by combining the gradient background with the skydome sky. If you adjust the Opacity setting for the skydome material to a value less than 70, the gradient background will begin to show through the skydome object.

Using Render Types

Rendering in VIZ is often a cyclical process of rendering, adjusting, and then rendering again. By rendering just a portion of your model, you can save time by reducing the time you spend in these revision cycles. Try rerendering your model with the changes in the diffuse color, but this time, render only the Ground object.

1. Type **P** to switch into a Perspective viewport.

2. Click the Zoom Extents button to get a view of the whole model and then use the Zoom and Pan tools so you are inside the skydome and can see the exterior of the building.

3. Click the Ground object to select it.

4. Click the Render Type drop-down list on the Rendering toolbar; then click Selected from the list.

5. Click the Quick Render tool. Your camera view is rendered with just the Ground object re-rendered.

The Rendered Frame Window is overwritten with the new pixels from the selected object. In this instance, the rendering process was much faster. By rendering a selected object or set of objects, you can save some time if you're rendering just to see the results of some changes you've made to your model. There are other options in the Render Type drop-down list that you'll want to know about. Here's a rundown of those options and what they do:

View Renders the current viewport in its entirety. This is the option you've used for most of the exercises so far.

Selected Renders just the objects selected.

Region Renders a selected region of the viewport. When you choose this option, you are asked to select a region in the currently active viewport. An adjustable marquee that displays in the viewport allows you to select a rectangular area of the viewport (see Figure 8.20). Once you select an area and click OK in the lower right corner of the active viewport, VIZ renders only the selected portion of the viewport and nothing else. If you've previously rendered the full viewport, the region you select will be overlaid onto the last rendered view in the render window. This can save lots of time if you need to rerender only a part of a view. To rerender a region, you may use the Region Selected option.

Crop Lets you crop an area for rendering. It works just like the Region option, but instead of leaving any previous rendering in the render window, it crops the rendering to the area you selected. To rerender a cropped view, you may use the Crop Selected option.

FIGURE 8.20

Selecting a region for the Region, Crop, and Blowup options

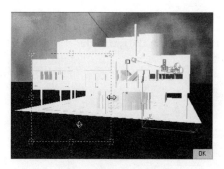

Blowup   Works like the Region and Crop options, but instead of keeping the view size the same as the overall viewport, Blowup enlarges the selected region to fill the render window.

Box Selected   Calculates the width and height of the current selection's bounding box, then offers a dialog box that lets you specify the width and height of the rendered image size. The default size that VIZ offers is based on the bounding box. The area of the bounding box expands to fill the entire rendered view.

Region Selected   Renders a view using the last region selected with the Region option. The Region Selected option bypasses the marquee/OK button step.

Crop Selected   Renders a view using the last cropped view selected with the Crop option. The Crop Selected option bypasses the marquee/OK button step.

Of all the options listed, View, Selected, and Region are the ones you'll use the most. Region, in particular, can be especially useful if you want to change part of a rendering that takes a lot of time to process.

TIP   If you decide you don't want to continue with a rendering, you can press the Escape key to cancel at any time.

Render Elements for Compositing

Another way of rendering just a portion of your scene is to use render elements. These elements are quite different than render types in what they render. Rather than rendering selected objects or parts of the whole image, render elements break the image into its visual components that can be used later in compositing programs like Adobe Photoshop for still images or Discreet combustion for animations.

Elements that can be rendered separately are the alpha, atmosphere, background, reflection, refraction, self-illumination, shadow, specular, z-depth, or a blend of any of these image channels. To get a sense of how this works, let's try an example.

1. Click the Render Scene button on the right side of the main toolbar. The Render Scene dialog box appears.

NOTE *You will learn more about the Render Scene dialog box in Chapter 10.*

2. Click the Render Elements tab at the top of this dialog box. The Render Elements tab appears as shown in Figure 8.21.

FIGURE 8.21

Render Elements tab of the Render Scene dialog box

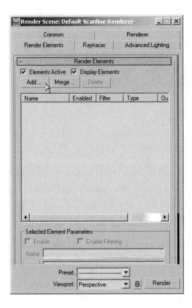

3. Open the Render Elements rollout and click the Add button.

4. Select Z Depth and click OK. Scroll down the panel to the bottom.

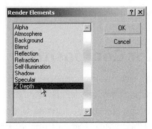

NOTE *The Z Depth element renders as a grayscale image in shades of gray representing the distance away from the picture plane (known in compositing as the camera's Z direction).*

If you wanted to save this render element as an image file, you would enter the filename and folder in the Selected Element Parameters group. Save render elements as RLA or RPF image formats.

If you wanted to output your render elements to Discreet combustion compositing software, you would enable that link and save a file as shown here.

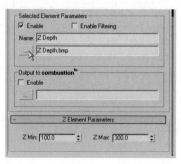

Note that each element's parameters will appear in specialized rollouts at the bottom of the dialog box, like the Z Element Parameters rollout in this example.

5. Click the Render button at the bottom right of the dialog box. Two separate Rendered Frame Windows will appear. The first one shows the usual rendering while the second contains the chosen render element as shown in Figure 8.22.

The render element images can be brought into a compositing program where special effects can be applied based upon the visual information that has been separated out as elements.

FIGURE 8.22
Z Depth Render
element

Summary

Cameras provide the ability to create the exact view you want by giving you control over camera and target placement. You have seen how cameras make it easier to visualize interior spaces. As you are staging your design, you have become aware of the importance of the surrounding environment in setting up a realistic rendering.

Several different techniques were explored in creating realistic environments, including the often-used screen bitmap, spherical, and cylindrical environment maps, a gradient background, and the truly immersive skydome environment. You have also learned how to save time by using render types and learned about compositing with render elements. In the next chapter, you see the possibilities for working with materials and objects from external files.

Chapter 9

Working with Files

THE TERM *SCENE* IN VIZ refers to your model files. In this chapter, you'll look at ways that you can access and utilize your scenes while developing your renderings and animations. VIZ offers a variety of ways that can help you improve your workflow. You can divide a file into smaller pieces and recombine them while keeping those pieces unique. This can help you manage large scenes that require the work of several people. Other tools let you quickly update objects in your scene or perform what-if scenarios to try out different options.

In this chapter, you'll experiment with different ways of bringing in some additional furniture from the companion CD. In the process, you'll lean about the different ways that you can combine and access your scenes.

- ◆ Gaining Access to Materials and Objects from Other Files
- ◆ Arranging Furniture with XRefs and the Asset Browser
- ◆ Replacing Objects with Objects from an External File
- ◆ Arranging Furniture with XRef Scenes
- ◆ Using Rendered Frame Windows
- ◆ Using the Asset Browser on the Internet

Gaining Access to Materials and Objects from Other Files

In this section, you'll be working with groups as you did in Chapter 2. You'll also use a tool called an XRef to transfer the modified fabric material from the `Mybigchair.max` file to the `MyCouch.max` file.

XRefs are a way to include other VIZ files in your scenes without having to actually combine file data into a single file. For example, you may want to create a file that contains the furniture arrangement for an office, but you want to keep that furniture data separate from the actual office design file. You can XRef the office design into your furniture file so that you can accurately locate the furniture.

Since the furniture data is stored as another file, changes made to the furniture file will be automatically updated in the office file when you reload the XRef. Then, when you're done, you can remove the XRef of the office design in a single step. The furniture file then maintains its independence from the office design file. This avoids duplication of data and reduces your disk storage space requirements. You can then XRef the furniture file into the office design file whenever you need to show furniture.

XRefs can be used as an organizational tool to help reduce the complexity of large models by segregating similar types of objects into separate files. XRefs are also useful for dividing work between members of a design team. In an interiors project, for example, you can have one designer working on a floor layout, while another designer works on floor patterns or lighting.

VIZ offers two ways to use XRefs. The XRef Scenes dialog box lets you combine whole scene files into a single file. It also allows you to divide portions of a scene into separate files so that they can be edited by several individuals.

WARNING   *Only one individual may read and write a VIZ file on a local area network (LAN) at any given time. External references are a way of combining the files from several people into a master scene.*

If you think you may need to edit objects brought in as XRefs, you can use the XRef Objects dialog box. You can apply transforms and modifiers to individual objects that have been imported using this dialog box, although such changes won't affect the source file.

As an introduction to XRefs, you'll use the XRef Objects dialog box in the following exercise to import a material into the MyCouch.max file. XRefs aren't necessarily the only way to import materials, but you'll use the XRef Objects dialog box in this way to see firsthand how this dialog box works.

NOTE   *If you are an AutoCAD user, you will find that the VIZ XRef tools perform the same functions as the AutoCAD XRef tools, though VIZ uses a different set of dialog boxes.*

1. Open the MyCouch.max file from the CD or from your own working folder from Chapter 2.

2. Select the couch and type **H** on the keyboard.

In the Select Objects dialog box, Couch01 is surrounded by square brackets indicating that it is a group.

This will make it easy to apply a material to the entire piece of furniture because all the objects that compose the group are managed as a single object. The next job is to add the material. You used the Fabric-Blue Nap 2 material from the standard material library, but it has been modified in the Mybigchair.max file. You could reconstruct the modifications made to the material in this file, but that would be time consuming. Instead, try using the XRef Objects command to import the material and the changes that were made to it from the Mybigchair.max file.

3. Choose File ➤ XRef Objects. The XRef Objects dialog box displays.

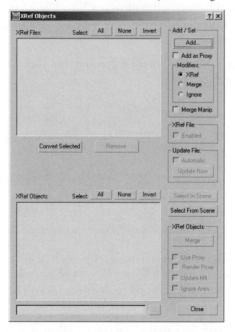

4. In the XRef Objects dialog box, click the Add button in the upper right corner.

5. In the Open File dialog box, locate and open the `Mybigchair.max` file from the CD. The XRef Merge–Mybigchair.max dialog box displays.

6. Click [Bigchair01] from the list; then click OK. The XRef Objects dialog box now shows the `Mybigchair.max` file in the XRef Objects list box and a listing of objects from the file in the XRef Objects list box.

7. Select Bigchair01 from the lower list box and then click Close. The dialog box closes, and the chair displays in the drawing.

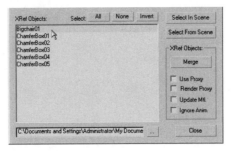

The chair now displays in the couch model. The chair hasn't really become a complete part of the couch model. You might think of an XRef as a kind of *guest* that is visiting but doesn't really belong to the file. Still, you can use the transform tools on the "guest" XRef or acquire materials and objects from the XRef.

1. Click the Material Editor tool in the main toolbar.

2. In the Material Editor window, click the Get Material tool.

3. In the Material/Map Browser, click the Scene radio button in the Browse From group; then double-click the Fabric-Blue Nap 2 listing.

4. Close all of the open windows and dialog boxes.

You've just imported a material from the Mybigchair.max file. You don't need the chair in your couch file, so let's remove it.

5. Choose File ➢ XRef Objects; then, in the XRef Objects dialog box, click the path for Mybigchair.max, listed in the top list box.

6. Click Remove in the middle of the dialog box. You see a warning message asking whether you really want to remove the selected XRefs from the scene.

7. Click OK. Close the XRef Objects dialog box.

The chair disappears, leaving your couch file as it was before you imported the chair. Now you can apply the newly acquired material to the couch.

8. Select the Couch group.

9. Open the Material Editor window.

10. With the Fabric-Blue Nap 2 material selected, click the Assign Material to Selection tool.

11. Close the Material Editor.

For the final step, you'll need to make sure the couch has the same mapping coordinate scale as the other chair.

12. Click the Modify tab; then select UVW Map from the Modifier list.

13. In the Mapping group of the Parameters rollout, select the Box radio button; then change the U, V, and W Tile values to **0.7**.

14. Save the file as **Couch01**.

15. Do a quick rendering of the couch.

OPTIONS FOR IMPORTING MATERIALS

You have several other options for importing materials from another file. First, you can go to the Mybigchair.max file and save the fabric to the standard material library under a new name. To do this, click the Put to Library tool in the Material Editor window. You can also set up a new material library and place the fabric there. Here are the steps for creating a new material library:

1. Click the Material/Map Browser tool in the Rendering toolbar.

2. In the Material/Map Browser window, click the Mtl Editor radio button in the Browse From group.

3. Click the Save As button in the File group.

4. Enter a name for your new material library file.

You can then retrieve the fabric from the new library, using the Material/Map Browser. This method is helpful when you are working on a team that needs to have access to a common set of materials.

A third option is to use a VIZ scene file as if it were a material library. Here are the steps to do this:

1. Click the Material Editor tool on the Rendering toolbar.

2. In the Material Editor window, click the Get Material tool.

3. In the Material/Map Browser, select the Mtl Library radio button in the Browse From group.

4. Click the Open button in the File group.

5. In the Open Material Library dialog box, select Autodesk VIZ (*.max) from the File of Type drop-down list.

6. Locate and open the Mybigchair.max file.

7. In the Material/Map Browser, double-click Fabric-Blue Nap 2 in the list box. The imported material appears in the Material Editor window's sample slot.

This is the fastest method for obtaining a material from another file.

You are able to import a material from another file using the XRef Objects dialog box. As you might guess, materials aren't the only things you can import. For example, if you want to import the seat back from `Mybigchair.max`, you can do so by selecting the object from the bottom list of the XRef Objects dialog box and selecting Merge. Once an object is merged, it becomes part of the current file's database (no longer an XRef). Here is a listing of the options available in the XRef Objects dialog box:

Add   Opens a file dialog box, allowing you to select a file containing objects to XRef.

Add as Proxy   Lets you use XRef objects as *stand-ins* for other XRef objects in the current file. This is useful for study renderings and animations because it allows you to temporarily substitute simplified geometry for complex geometry in a scene.

New!   **Modifiers**   Special handling of modifiers from XRef files is new in VIZ 2005. There is a radio button in the Modifiers group that can be set to XRef, Merge, or Ignore. When it is set to XRef, it means that the modifiers are contained within the XRef file and cannot be changed. Merge means the modifiers assigned to the XRef objects can be changed but are not reflected back into the XRef file. Ignore means the modifiers from the XRef file are disregarded.

New!   **Merge Manipulators**   This check box is new in VIZ 2005 and allows you to control whether you have local control over manipulators. When checked, any manipulator applied to the XRefed object is merged into the scene. The manipulators coming from the XRef cannot be altered when this is unchecked.

Convert Selected   Converts a selected object in the current scene into an XRef object. The selected object or objects are removed from the current scene and saved as MAX files; then they are reinserted into the current file as XRef objects.

Remove   Removes all XRef objects from the current scene.

XRef File   Turns off selected objects.

Update File   Controls how XRef objects are updated.

- ◆ *Automatic* updates XRef objects whenever the source file is saved.

- ◆ *Update Now* lets you manually update XRef objects. It updates objects from the current state of the source file.

Select in Scene   Lets you select objects in the viewports based on the objects selected in the XRef Objects list box.

Select from Scene   Lets you highlight objects in the XRef Objects list box based on selected objects in the viewports.

XRef Objects   Gives you additional control over the XRef objects that are selected in the XRef Objects list box.

- ◆ *Merge* converts selected XRef objects into actual objects in the current scene.

- ◆ *Use Proxy* displays the proxy version of the selected object.

◆ *Render Proxy* renders proxy objects in place of the selected object.

◆ *Update Mtl* updates the material assignment of the selected object from the source object whenever a file update occurs. With this option turned off, the object's geometry is updated but the material doesn't change. It's important to note that you can edit the material assigned to an XRef object; so if you turn the Update Mtl option on, you run the risk of reversing any material changes you've made to XRef objects.

◆ *Ignore Anim* causes VIZ to ignore animations applied to XRef objects.

Once you've imported an XRef object, you can use the transform tools to edit it. You can also modify an XRef object using the Modify tab in the Command Panel. With an XRef object selected, the Modify tab gives you control over the way XRef proxy objects behave and are displayed. The options found in the Modify tab correspond to the XRef Objects area of the XRef Objects dialog box.

Arranging Furniture with XRefs and the Asset Browser

Now that you've got a chair and a couch, you can begin to use them to create a setting for the interior of the villa model. In this section, you'll use the chair—plus some other furniture that's available on the companion CD—to create the interior setting.

In the process of arranging the furniture, you'll get a chance to explore another way of using XRefs. This time you'll use the XRef Scenes option to temporarily combine the villa model with a new furniture file to help lay out the furniture. You'll also look at how you can import geometry from one VIZ file to another through the Merge command and the Asset Browser. The Asset Browser is a tool that helps you manage your projects by giving you a seamless way to access data from your own computer, your network, and the Web.

Let's start by taking a look at how the Merge command can be used to import VIZ file data.

1. Choose File ➤ Reset to create a new file and reset the new file to VIZ's default settings.

2. The Reset Warning message displays. Click Yes.

3. Choose File ➤ Merge. The Merge File dialog box displays. This is a typical file dialog box.

4. Locate and open the Couch01.max file you just created. The Merge dialog box appears.

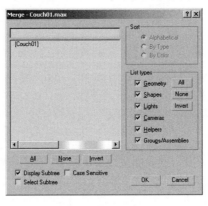

The Merge dialog box shows a listing of objects from the file you selected. Since the Couch01.max file contains only a single group, you see the group name in the list. Had you not grouped the objects in the Couch01.max file, you would see the individual object names listed.

5. Select [Couch01] from the list; then click OK. The couch displays at the origin of the model.

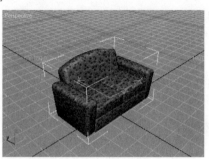

As you saw in steps 3 and 4, Merge gives you the opportunity to select specific objects to import from other VIZ files—although in the case of the couch, you really had only one object to choose from. You can also use Merge to import cameras or geometry from other models. Unlike XRef objects, the objects you import using Merge become a part of the database of current files and have no link to the source file.

Let's try the Merge command again by adding the chair you created earlier.

1. Move the couch to the right 5 feet 2 inches so that it's at the far right side of the viewport.

TIP You may have to change your units to U.S. Standard feet and inches after resetting the scene earlier.

2. Choose File ➤ Merge.

3. In the Merge File dialog box, locate and select mybigchair.max and then click Open.

4. In the Merge dialog box, click [Bigchair01] and then click OK. This time you see a dialog box warning you that a duplicate material name exists in the current scene.

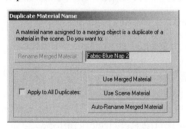

You have four options at this point:

◆ You can rename the imported duplicate material by entering a new name in the input box near the top of the dialog box. This will maintain both the merged material and the material in the current scene as unique materials.

◆ You can click Use Merged Material to replace the material in the current file with the material of the merged file.

◆ You can click Use Scene Material to maintain the current material and discard the duplicate in the merged file.

◆ You can click Auto-Rename Merged Material to have VIZ rename the merged material to maintain it as a unique material.

5. Click Use Scene Material. The chair displays at the origin of the file.

Choosing this option causes VIZ to use the Fabric-Blue Nap 2 material currently in the file for both the chair and the couch.

6. Click the Select and Move tool from the main toolbar; then Shift+click and drag the chair to the left 5 feet 2 inches.

7. In the Clone Options dialog box, click the Instance option; then click OK.

Replacing Objects with Objects from an External File

You've just seen how you can use the Merge command to import parts of a scene into the current scene. Another command, called *Replace*, is similar to Merge, but it lets you replace objects in the current scene with similarly named objects from external files. This can be useful in updating scene design elements. You can also use Replace to temporarily substitute complex geometry with simple *stand-in* geometry for quick-study renderings. The following exercise will demonstrate how Replace works.

1. Save the current scene as **VillaFurniture.max**.

2. Open the Mybigchair.max file.

3. Click the chair; then choose Group ➢ Open. This gives you access to the individual objects that make up the chair's group.

4. Click the chair back to select it; then click the Modify tab of the Command Panel.

5. Select ChamferBox from the modifier stack list.

6. Modify the Width parameter so that it's **24** inches.

7. Choose Group ➢ Close to close the group; then save the file.

You've made a slight modification to the chair. Now you can use Replace to see how you can update the chair in the VillaFurniture.max file to the new chair design.

Before you actually perform the Replace operation, you need to change the name of the object that forms the back of the couch. Remember that you created the Bigchair01 file from the Couch01 file, so both the couch and chair share objects of the same name, even though they may not all be the same shape. The Replace command works by replacing objects in one file with objects of the same name from another file. Since you don't want to replace the back of the couch, you'll have to change the couch back object's name first.

1. Open the VillaFurniture.max file.

2. Select Couch01; then choose Group ➢ Open.

3. Click the Couch01 back. When you place the selection cursor on the back, you should see the name [Couch01] ChamferBox02. If not, type **H** on the keyboard and select it by name.

4. In the Modify tab of the Command Panel, change the name of the object, ChamferBox02, to **Couchback01**.

5. Choose Group ➢ Close.

Now you're ready to replace the back of the chair with the one you modified earlier.

1. Choose File ➢ Replace.

2. In the Replace File dialog box, locate and select Mybigchair.max and then click Open. The Replace dialog box displays.

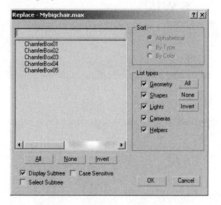

3. Select ChamferBox02; then click OK. You'll see a warning message.

4. Click Yes. The chair back will be replaced with the new chair back you edited in the Mybigchair.max file.

Notice that the back was replaced in both the original chair and in the instance clone of the chair. Had you made a copy instead of an instance clone, only the original chair back with the same name, ChamferBox14, would have been replaced. This demonstrates that instance clones are replaced along with the original objects.

Importing Files from the Asset Browser

Like the Merge command, the Asset Browser lets you import a file into the current file. It doesn't let you pick and choose which parts of a file are imported, but it does perform other functions, such as opening VIZ files in a second VIZ session or browsing the Web for materials and geometry.

As an introduction to the Asset Browser, try the following exercise. You'll use the Asset Browser to import another copy of the chair.

1. Move the chair to the back of the view.

2. In the Command Panel, select the Utilities tab and then click the Asset Browser button.

You see the following message:

3. Click OK. The Asset Browser displays.

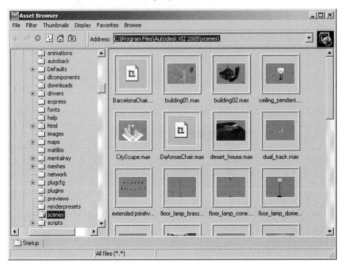

You can browse the contents of your computer and view thumbnail images of VIZ files and image files. You can then drag and drop files into VIZ, just as you would from Windows Explorer. One special feature of the Asset Browser is its ability to let you drag and drop VIZ components from websites that contain what is called i-drop content, just like you can from any browser. In fact the Asset Browser is an Internet browser that is built into VIZ.

Before you look at the Asset Browser's Internet capabilities, continue with the chair exercise to see how it works within your own computer.

4. On the explorer bar on the left side of the Asset Browser, locate the `\Autodesk VIZ 2005\Maps` folder and click it. The window to the right displays the image files contained in that folder.

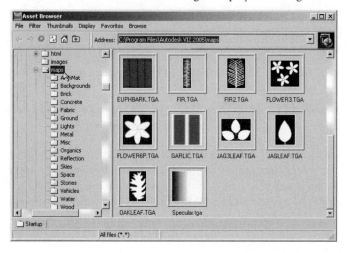

5. Choose Thumbnails ➢ Small (50 × 50). The images become smaller, allowing you to see more of them.

6. Click the `\Autodesk VIZ 2005\maps\ArchMat` folder. Again, you see a set of thumbnail views of the files. Note that the Asset Browser shows you the content of the image files as well as the MAX files.

NOTE *If all you see is a set of blank boxes, you can turn on the thumbnail views by choosing Thumbnails ➢ Create Thumbnails.*

You can drag and drop image files from the Asset Browser into a VIZ file. If you drag and drop an image into a viewport, it becomes a background. You get a message asking whether you really want the image to be used as a background. If you drag and drop an image onto an object, the image will be mapped to the diffuse color channel of the object.

You can also drag and drop image files into a map slot in the Maps rollout of the Material Editor as an alternative way of importing image maps for materials. And as mentioned earlier, you can import VIZ (MAX) files through the Asset Browser. Try importing your chair into the current scene using the Asset Browser.

7. In the Asset Browser, use the list box to the left to locate the folder containing the sample files from the companion CD.

8. Locate the `mybigchair.max` file and select it.

9. Move the Asset Browser so that you have a clear view of the center of the VIZ viewport. Then click and drag the `mybigchair.max` file from the Asset Browser into the VIZ Perspective viewport. A shortcut menu appears offering the Open, Merge, XRef, and Cancel options.

10. Select Merge. Once again, you see the Duplicate Material Name dialog box.

11. Click Use Scene Material. The chair displays in the viewport. As you move the cursor, the chair follows.

12. Place the chair roughly in the center of the view and click this new chair location.

TIP *You can use the Asset Browser to open a VIZ file in a second session by double-clicking the file's thumbnail. You may want to refrain from doing this if your system has limited memory.*

If you have the four standard viewports open in VIZ, the orientation of the imported object will depend on the viewport into which the object is dragged. If you drag the imported object into the Top viewport, the object will be oriented in the normal orientation. If you drag the object into the Left or Front viewport, the object will be oriented sideways with its Z axis pointing toward you from the viewport.

Let's insert a few more items using the Asset Browser. This time try inserting a lamp from the companion CD into a Top viewport in VIZ.

1. In VIZ, click the Min/Max Toggle tool to view all four viewports; then right-click the Top viewport and click the Min/Max Toggle tool again to enlarge it.

2. Go to the Asset Browser and locate the file called `torch1.max`. This is a file from the companion CD.

3. Click and drag the `torch1.max` file into the VIZ Top viewport; then select Merge from the shortcut menu.

4. Adjust the location of the Torch1 lamp so that it displays in the left side of the viewport, as shown in Figure 9.1.

5. Repeat steps 1 through 4 to insert the files named `lamp01.max`, `tablelarge.max`, `tablesmall.max`, and `bruer.max`. All these files are from the companion CD. Use Figure 9.1 to position the inserted objects.

FIGURE 9.1
Inserting objects
from the Asset
Browser

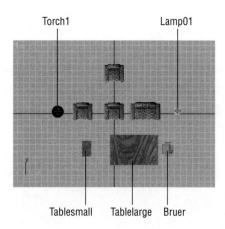

As a rule, you can click and drag objects easily from the Asset Browser to VIZ, using the Windows taskbar, as long as you insert the objects into a non-Perspective viewport. If you must insert an object into a Perspective viewport, you can do so under two conditions. You can click and drag into the VIZ button of the Windows taskbar if the Perspective viewport is expanded to fill the entire VIZ window. If several viewports are displayed, you must click and drag directly from the Asset Browser to the Perspective viewport, bypassing the Windows taskbar. This requires that the Perspective viewport be at least partially visible, with the Asset Browser window overlapping VIZ. You must follow this same procedure to click and drag bitmaps into the VIZ Material Editor.

Arranging Furniture with XRef Scenes

Now that you've got some furniture to work with, the next step is to lay out that furniture. Start by putting together a basic arrangement.

1. Go to the Top viewport and arrange the furniture in a way similar to that shown in Figure 9.2.

FIGURE 9.2
The furniture
arrangement

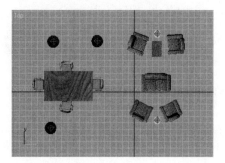

2. Next, attach the villa model as an XRef. This will give you a point of reference for the actual location of the furniture. Choose File ➤ XRef Scenes. The XRef Scenes dialog box displays.

3. Click the Add button. The Open File dialog box displays. Locate and select the mysavoye.max file; then click Open. You may also use mysavoye9.max from the companion CD. The filename displays in the XRef Scenes dialog box as well as in the current scene.

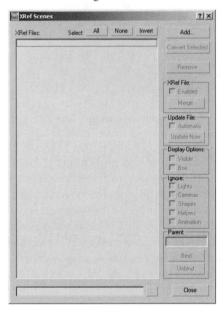

4. Click Close. You now see the villa in the furniture layout.

5. Change to a wireframe view; then zoom out and adjust your view so that it looks similar to Figure 9.3.

You see that the building is to the left of the furniture in the Top viewport. You want to move the furniture into the living room of the XRef villa scene.

1. Click the Select Object tool in the main toolbar; then place a selection region around all the furniture in the Top viewport. You may notice that VIZ ignores the XRef scene in the selection.

2. In the Top viewport, use the Select and Move tool to move the furniture into the living room area shown in Figure 9.3.

3. Click the Min/Max Toggle tool and adjust the Front viewport so that you can see the furniture and the second floor of the villa, as shown in Figure 9.4.

4. Move the furniture to the second floor. Do a rough placement in the Front viewport; then zoom in and make a finer adjustment to the vertical location of the furniture.

5. Go to the Top viewport and fine-tune the furniture arrangement to fit the room, as shown in Figure 9.5.

You might notice that the XRef objects are inaccessible. They are visible and will render, complete with lighting, but you cannot manipulate any of the objects in the XRef scene.

FIGURE 9.3
Move the furniture into the living room in the Top viewport.

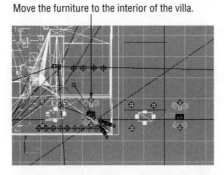

FIGURE 9.4
The Front viewport showing the furniture and the villa's second floor

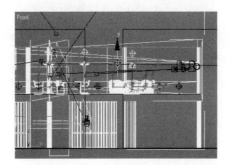

FIGURE 9.5
Making final adjustments to the furniture placement

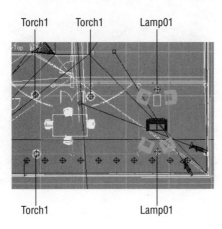

The important thing to note here is that the coordinate system of the XRef file is aligned with the coordinate system of the current scene; so when you move the furniture to fit the XRef scene, you are placing the furniture in the appropriate location relative to the XRef scene coordinate system.

Next you'll switch the relationship of the two files you are working with. You'll close the furniture file, open the villa file, and import the furniture file as an XRef.

1. First, remove the XRef of the villa file.

2. Choose File ➢ XRef Scenes.

3. In the XRef Scenes dialog box, select the villa file in the list box and then click Remove.

4. Click Close to exit the XRef Scenes dialog box.

5. Save the current file as **VillaFurniture2.max**.

Now you're ready to place the furniture in your villa file.

1. Open the mysavoye9.max file.

2. Choose File ➢ XRef Scenes.

3. In the XRef Scenes dialog box, click the Add button.

4. Locate and select the VillaFurniture2.max file; then click Open.

5. Close the XRef Scenes dialog box.

6. Right-Click the Mycamera01 viewport and render it. Your rendering should look similar to Figure 9.6.

FIGURE 9.6

A rendered view of the interior of the villa's living room with furniture

XRefs are useful, especially when your models become very complex. You can divide a model into several files and XRef them together, for example, to help keep objects organized. This can also aid in situations where you must divide design tasks between several people. You can also nest XRef files where an XRef contains other XRefs. There are other settings offered by the XRef Scenes dialog box. Here is a listing of those options for your reference:

Add   Lets you locate and select an XRef scene.

Convert Selected   Lets you convert objects in your current scene into XRef scenes. The selected objects are saved as MAX files and are removed from the current scene. They are then imported as XRef scenes back into the current scene.

Remove   Completely removes a selected XRef scene from the current scene.

XRef File   Gives you control over the way XRef scenes are linked to the current scene.

- ◆ *Enabled* lets you turn a selected XRef scene on or off. This is useful if you want to temporarily remove an XRef scene from the current scene without completely removing the link to the XRef scene. This option also removes the XRef scene from memory, making more memory available for other operations.

- ◆ *Merge* merges an XRef scene into the current scene, thereby ending the XRef relationship.

Update File   Controls how XRef scenes are updated.

- ◆ *Automatic* updates XRef objects whenever the source file is edited and saved.

- ◆ *Update Now* lets you manually update XRef objects from the current state of the source file.

Display Options   Controls the visibility of XRef scenes in the viewports. They have no effect on how XRef scenes are rendered.

- ◆ *Visible* turns the display of XRef scenes on or off.

- ◆ *Box* converts the display of XRefs into bounding boxes.

Ignore   Lets you control the inclusion of specific types of objects from an XRef scene. Items that are turned off won't be imported into the current scene if Merge is used.

Parent   Gives you control over the position and animation of an XRef scene by associating, or *binding*, an XRef scene to an object in the current scene.

- ◆ *Bind* is the mechanism by which you make the association. First click Bind; then select the object that you want the selected XRef scene to be bound to. The XRef scene's origin will be aligned with the selected object's pivot point. You can use a dummy object as a Bind parent object. You may then animate the bound object to animate the XRef scene.

- ◆ *Unbind* will unbind the selected XRef scene from the object to which it is bound. The Name field box at the top of the Parent group displays the name of the object to which a selected XRef scene is bound.

Using the Rendered Frame Windows

While we're on the subject of file usage, you'll want to know how you can save, compare, and print rendered views from the Rendered Frame Window. The toolbar that appears when you render a view lets you do all of these tasks. If you decide that you want to save the result from the Rendered Frame Window to a file, you can do so by clicking the Save Bitmap tool on the Rendered Frame Window's toolbar.

This tool opens the Browse Images for Output dialog box.

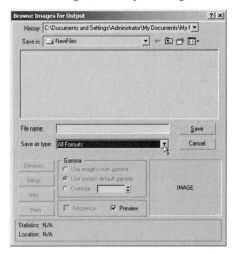

In this dialog box, you can enter a filename and then select a file type for the image. You can choose from a fairly extensive list of bitmap image file types, as listed here:

File Type	Extension
Audio-Video Interleaved	`.avi`
Windows Bitmap	`.bmp`
Kodak Cineon	`.cin`
Encapsulated PostScript	`.eps, .ps`
Autodesk Flic	`.flc, .fli, .cel`
High Dynamic Range Image	`.hdi, .pic`
Joint Photographic Experts Group	`.jpg, .jpe, .jpeg`
Portable Network Graphics	`.png`

File Type	Extension
QuickTime	`.mov`; requires Apple QuickTime
Silicon Graphics image	`.rgb`
RLA	`.rla`
Rich Pixel Format file	`.rpf`
Truevision Targa	`.tga`, `.vda`, `.icb`, `.vst`
Tagged Image File Format	`.tif`, `.tiff`

New!

The HDRI Image File format is new in VIZ 2005. These files support files a wide exposure range that stores far more information than normal images.

NOTE   *See Chapter 11 for more discussion of HDRI.*

The Browse Images for Output dialog box also lets you set some of the parameters for the chosen image file by using the Setup button. For example, if you select TIF Image File as the Save As Type file option, the Setup button will open a dialog box that lets you choose between a color and a monochrome TIFF file.

NOTE   *The RPF file format offers support for arbitrary image channels beyond the standard RGB and alpha channels. These additional channels can be used during post-production compositing of animations for the inclusion of special effects. When you select the RPF file format at rendering time, VIZ will open the RPF Image File Format dialog box, which allows you to select from a set of Optional Channels options. The RPF format is similar to the RLA format that's popular with SGI computers.*

Printing Images

In addition to viewing and saving files, the Rendered Frame Window lets you print your renderings. You can print directly from the window by clicking the Print Bitmap tool on the toolbar. This will send the print to the default printer you have set up on your computer.

If you want to print an existing image file that you've saved to disk, you can do so from the Browse Images for Output dialog box. Click the Save Bitmap tool in the Rendered Frame window; then, in the Browse Images for Output dialog box, locate and select an image file. If the Preview check box is checked, you'll see a thumbnail version of the file in the lower right corner of the dialog box. You can then click the View button in the lower left corner. VIZ opens another Rendered Frame Window displaying the selected image. From this new window, you can click the Print Bitmap tool to print the image.

TIP   *You can open an image that you have already rendered by choosing File ➤ View Image. The image will open in its own Rendered Frame Window that you can use to print it out. Otherwise, open your rendered images in Adobe Photoshop for greater control over cropping, print size, resolution, and so on.*

Opening Multiple Rendered Frame Windows for Comparisons

The View button in the Browse Images for Output dialog box can be a handy tool if you want to compare a current rendering with a rendering that you have saved as a file. You can also open multiple frame buffer windows to view several versions of your scene at once while you're rendering it. To do this, use the Clone Rendered Frame Window tool.

This tool will open a copy of the current window contents. You can then modify your scene and render again. The cloned Rendered Frame window will retain the original rendering, whereas the main RFW will display the revised scene. You can make several clones—one for each scene variation you want to try. You can minimize the windows while you are working and then maximize them later to view their contents.

Zooming, Panning, and Controlling Channels in the Rendered Frame Window

The Rendered Frame Window also provides a set of functions that let you control various aspects of the window display. For example, you can enlarge an area of the window to get a closer look at a detail in your rendering. To do this, hold the Ctrl key down while you click the mouse. When you press the Ctrl key, the cursor changes to a magnifying glass. Clicking the mouse zooms in on the view. Once it is zoomed in, you can pan by holding down the Shift key and clicking and dragging the mouse. Right-clicking while holding the Ctrl key zooms the view back out.

If you want to view the red, green, blue, or alpha channel of the Rendered Frame Window, you can use the Enable Channel buttons on the window's toolbar, as shown in Figure 9.7. Typically, all three of the channel buttons are on. To view a single color, click the two channel buttons you do *not* want displayed. This turns them off. The Channel Display list is for RPF images. This drop-down list lets you display additional channels rendered when using the RPF file type that offers the special-effects channels.

You can also view a monochrome version of the rendering by using the Monochrome tool. Finally, you can clear the contents of the Rendered Frame Window by clicking the X button.

Obtaining Colors from External Bitmap Files

Perhaps one of the more interesting features of the Rendered Frame Window is the seemingly innocuous color swatch, located at the right end of the window's toolbar. If you right-click in the Rendered Frame Window, VIZ will record the color at the location of your cursor in the color swatch. If you right-click and drag the cursor over the contents of the Rendered Frame Window, you'll see a readout of the color over which the cursor passes.

Once a color is selected and placed in the color swatch, you can click and drag this color swatch to any other color swatch in VIZ.

This feature of the Rendered Frame Window color swatch is significant, because with it, you can import colors from a saved bitmap image file. You may, for example, be asked to match a specific color from a color chip. You can scan the color chip and save it as a bitmap file. Then, using the Rendered Frame Window, you can open the scanned color chip file, right-click the color, and then click and drag the color from the Rendered Frame Window color swatch to the Material Editor. You can then apply the material with the imported color to an object such as an interior wall.

FIGURE 9.7
The Red, Green, Blue, and Alpha Channel tools

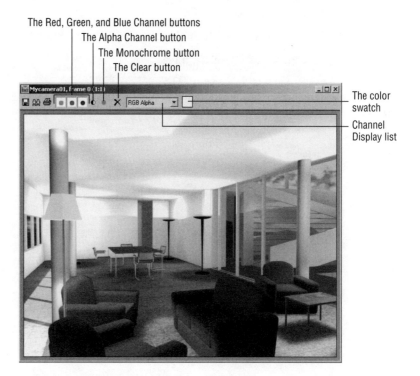

NOTE *If you intend to use your scanner to match colors, make sure that your scanner and printer or other output device have been calibrated for accurate color reproduction.*

Using the Asset Browser on the Internet

You've seen how you have quite a few methods at your disposal for gaining access to files on your computer. The Asset Browser offers an additional capability of importing files from the Internet or from your company's intranet.

The methods for doing this are similar to those for importing local files. The main difference is that, instead of using the list of file folders on the left side of the Asset Browser, you use the browser functions.

You can use the Asset Browser as you would other web browsers to locate information on the Web. And as mentioned earlier, you can import materials, bitmap images, model geometry, and light objects from sites that offer such items. Or, if you prefer, you can use your favorite web browser to perform the same functions.

TIP *You can access a free i-drop catalog of classic designer furniture at ScottOnstott.com. These are free 3D models that you can use in your own designs that you drag and drop from the Internet directly into VIZ using i-drop technology.*

1. Open the Asset Browser or your favorite web browser and point it to `http://ScottOnstott.com`.

2. Using the navigator bar on the left side, click Free Stuff ➤ 3D Models ➤ Catalog 1.

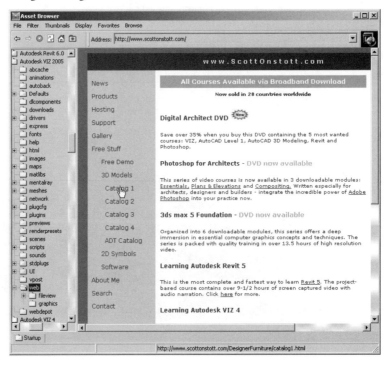

3. Select a piece of furniture that you want to download. In this example, click the thumbnail image of the red office chair.

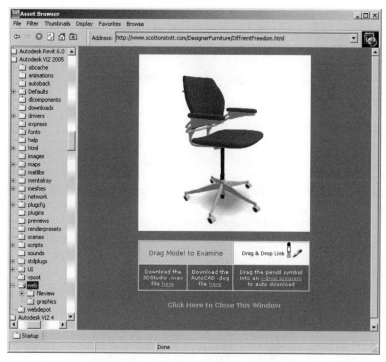

If you are using your favorite Internet browser, a small pop-up window will appear. If you are using the Asset Browser within VIZ, the page will appear in the same window.

4. Drag the i-drop pencil symbol from the Asset Browser to the Top viewport in VIZ as shown in Figure 9.8. You'll have to carefully position the Asset Browser first before you drag and drop so that you can see both the i-drop pencil icon and a portion of the top viewport.

FIGURE 9.8

Drag i-drop content from the Asset Browser into the VIZ viewport.

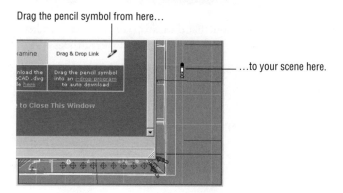

Drag the pencil symbol from here…

…to your scene here.

5. After you drag, a dialog will appear showing the download progress.

6. A small context menu will appear in the viewport after the download is complete with options for Open, Merge, or XRef. Select Merge for this example. An Obsolete File dialog box may appear indicating that the file you are merging was created in a previous version of VIZ. If the dialog box appears, click OK. There is nothing wrong with so-called "obsolete" files; many websites offer older versions of VIZ files to offer backward compatibility with those still using VIZ 4.

7. Move the new chair up to the second floor in the Left viewport and position it in the room. The MyCamera01 viewport will show the 3D model you downloaded.

When you are done, note that the i-drop content you downloaded off the Internet is automatically stored in the `downloads` subfolder under the main `Autodesk VIZ 2005` folder.

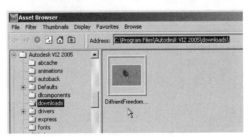

TIP   *You'll be able to access i-drop content with the Asset Browser in the future without having to download it again because it is stored locally on your computer.*

Summary

You've looked at the many different ways that you can use your VIZ files to construct and edit your scenes. Some file options, such as saving and importing files, are fairly straightforward in their use. Others, such as XRef scenes, are open to any number of uses. The Asset Browser offers you the ability to manage your files more easily, and doubles as a Web browser with which you can import items from the Web. You also took a closer look at the Rendered Frame Window to see how rendered images can be stored, viewed, and printed.

In the next chapter, you'll explore the radiosity renderer and learn how to make photometric luminaries.

Chapter 10

Using Radiosity

IN CHAPTER 6, YOU added lights to simulate a realistic view of the Villa Savoye model. You added a standard directed light to simulate the sun; then you added Omni lights to simulate light that's reflected off the building surfaces as indirect light. This method of simulating the natural behavior of light is sometimes referred to as "fakiosity" and can be quite useful when you are in a hurry to get a rendering out. In this chapter, you'll create the same scene as in Chapter 6, but this time you'll use a VIZ feature known as *radiosity*.

As mentioned in Chapter 1, radiosity rendering is a method whereby the behavior of light is more accurately modeled to create an almost lifelike representation of a scene. Radiosity takes into account the way light bounces off surfaces, and it picks up and reflects the color and intensity of this bounced light. Instead of having to add Omni lights as you did in Chapter 9, you can add a single Sun light and have VIZ determine the way light bounces off surfaces and illuminates the scene. Another tool, called *ray tracing rendering*, also models the behavior of light, but in a different way. Ray trace rendering is best suited for rendering very shiny or transparent material such as glass or mirrors. Radiosity and ray trace rendering together are considered to be a class of rendering called *global illumination.*

In this chapter, you'll concentrate on radiosity rendering. Radiosity simplifies your work in many ways and complicates it in others, but the ultimate result is a more accurate rendition of a scene.

- ◆ Adding Daylight to Your Model
- ◆ Understanding the Radiosity Workflow
- ◆ Creating a Finished Rendering
- ◆ Working with Artificial Lights
- ◆ Using Photometric Lights
- ◆ Understanding Dynamic Range
- ◆ Assembling an Articulated Luminaire

Adding Daylight to Your Model

You'll start this chapter, as in Chapter 6, by adding a sun to your model. But the sun you are going to add is a little different.

New!

To help simplify your work, VIZ provides a tool called the *Daylight system*. The Daylight System includes a light source, called an *IES Sun*, which accurately reproduces the color and intensity of sunlight. IES stands for the Illuminating Engineering Society, an organization devoted to the lighting industry. Among other things, the IES establishes methods for quantifying and standardizing the way light sources are specified.

In addition to the IES Sun, the Daylight System incorporates an *IES Sky* that simulates the general glow of the sky. This sky glow is the result of sunlight being scattered by the earth's atmosphere. We don't often think about it since it's always present during the day, but the sky glow contributes a great deal to the quality and behavior of daytime light. A third feature of the Daylight System is its ability to accurately locate the direction of the sun based on the location and orientation of your model and the time and date for your rendering. This feature is helpful for creating sun shadow studies, as you'll see in Chapter 13.

So let's start by adding a Daylight System to the Villa Savoye model.

1. Open the `Savoye10.max` file from the companion CD. This is basically the same file as `Savoye6.max`, which you used earlier, with all the lights turned off and hidden.

2. Adjust the top view so that it looks similar to Figure 10.1.

FIGURE 10.1

Adjust the top view so that it shows a view similar to this one.

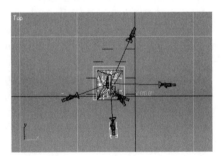

3. Click the Create tab in the Command Panel; then click the Systems tool.

4. Click the Daylight button in the Object Type rollout.

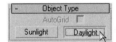

TIP   *In addition to Daylight, VIZ has another option called Sunlight. Sunlight is an older system that uses a direct light to simulate the Sun. Sunlight works much like Daylight with the light source being linked to a compass and a Sun angle calculator. If you are planning on only using the scanline renderer, then Sunlight is the best choice. If you are planning on doing radiosity rendering, choose Daylight instead.*

The Command Panel changes to show the Daylight System's options.

The Daylight System is a bit hidden in the VIZ Command Panel, but once you find it, you'll see that it offers a lot of options, mostly related to time, date, and location. Before you actually place the sun in your model, you'll first establish a location, then the date and time. This will help keep the results you get from later exercises consistent with those in this book.

1. In the Command Panel, click the Get Location button in the Location group of the Control Parameters rollout.

The Geographic Location dialog box displays.

2. Select Europe from the Map drop-down list. A simple map of Europe displays in the dialog box, and the list of city names in the list box to the left changes.

3. In the City list, locate and select Paris, France. A cross displays the location of Paris in the map.

TIP   You can also click on the map near the center of France and if Nearest Big City is checked, Paris should be highlighted in the City list.

4. Click OK.

The Villa Savoye is located in a town called Poissy, whose nearest major city is Paris. For the purposes of this exercise, Paris will be close enough; but if you wanted to be absolutely precise, you could use the Latitude and Longitude settings in the Location group of the Control Parameters rollout to enter the exact location of Poissy.

Now let's set the time and date. You'll set the time and date so that the sun will appear in roughly the same position as the sun you used in Chapter 6.

1. In the Time group of the Control Parameters rollout, change the hours to **13** and the minutes to **50**.

2. Change the month to **4** and the day to **17**.

Now you are ready to place the sun in your model.

1. In the Top viewport, click and drag the mouse from the center of the building, as shown in Figure 10.2, but don't release the mouse button just yet. As you drag the mouse, you see a compass rose appear.

2. Adjust the compass rose so that it's about the size shown in Figure 10.2. It doesn't need to be exact in size—just large enough for you to see it.

FIGURE 10.2

Placing the sun in your model

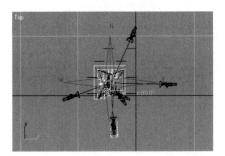

3. Now drag the mouse downward. You see the IES Sun drag with your mouse (see Figure 10.2). If you made the correct settings in the control panel, the sun will appear in the lower-left corner of the viewport.

4. Adjust the mouse so that the sun is at the edge of the viewport; then click to place it.

Although you spent some time setting up the date, time, and location for the sun, these settings aren't set in stone. You can change any of the these settings at any time.

NOTE *You can access the date, time, and location controls on the Motion tab of the Command Panel.*

In addition, you can change the orientation of the compass rose in relation to the model in order to get the most accurate sun angles. You can also animate the sun as it crosses the sky for any given day. You'll learn more about animating the sun in Chapter 13. For now, let's continue by taking a look at the rendered results of your new sun.

When you added the Daylight System, you may have noticed that the Mycamera perspective viewport brightened quite a bit. Now let's see how the new sun affects a rendered view of the building.

1. Choose Rendering ➤ Environment.

2. Click the Ambient color swatch in the Global Lighting group.

3. At the Color Selector, change the Value setting to **0**; then close the Color Selector. You want to let the Daylight System light the scene without the influence of the Ambient lighting setting because radiosity will calculate the ambient light much more accurately than using a simple color.

4. Back at the Environment dialog box, go to the Exposure Control rollout and select Logarithmic Exposure Control from the drop-down list; then close the dialog box.

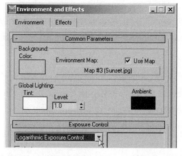

NOTE *You'll learn more about Exposure Control later in this chapter under "Refining Your Radiosity Solution."*

Now, take a look at the results so far.

1. Switch to the Mycamera viewport.

2. Click the Quick Render tool in the main toolbar. The rendering will take a bit longer than previous renderings. When it's finished, you'll see a view similar to Figure 10.3.

FIGURE 10.3

The first rendering after placing the Daylight System in your model

The rendering appears very rough, with saturated colors, too much contrast, burned out lighting, and very little detail, but it gives you a general idea of how the lighting affects the scene in a scanline rendering. There are still a number of settings you'll have to work with to get a good rendering from the Daylight System and the radiosity renderer. But before you go any further, you'll want to know about the concept of the *radiosity workflow.*

Understanding the Radiosity Workflow

The radiosity workflow is the series of steps you need to take to get good results from VIZ's radiosity renderer. By now, you have probably come to see that any rendering in VIZ requires a series of procedures that you often repeat to refine your rendering. For radiosity rendering, those steps are a bit more specific.

You've already taken a few of those steps by following the tutorials in this book. The first step is to establish a consistent unit of measure, which you did in earlier chapters. Here is a listing of the steps in the radiosity workflow:

1. Establish consistent units within the scene. For example, in the Units Setup dialog box, make sure that the Scene Unit Scale setting is the same as the Display Unit Scale. This is important because many of the settings related to radiosity are dependent on the Scene Unit Scale.

2. For best results, place photometric lights in your scene, rather than standard lights.

3. Make sure the exposure controls are set properly. In most cases, you would use either the Automatic or the Logarithmic Exposure Control option in the Environment dialog box.

4. Render your view to get a general idea of how much illumination there is in the scene.

5. Use the radiosity control panel to generate a radiosity solution.

6. Render your view again to see how it looks based on the solution data.

7. Adjust the reflectance value of materials, brightness levels of the environment, and other settings to "hone" your view.

8. Render again and make further adjustments.

You've already done the first four steps of the workflow. Those steps are crucial to establishing the basis for your radiosity renderings, because the other steps are built on them. Steps 5–8 are really the heart of the radiosity workflow, and they take the most time. Don't worry if you don't quite understand what all these steps mean. In the next section, you'll work through these steps to get firsthand experience with the radiosity workflow.

Refining Your Radiosity Solution

So far, you've set up the radiosity rendering, but there are still a few things you need to take care of. Next, you'll work on the materials and use some radiosity tools to start to understand how the light interacts with the materials in your model. VIZ calculates how light interacts with your model by generating a *radiosity solution.* Once this solution is established, VIZ can create a realistic rendering based on the solution data. Start by generating a simple radiosity solution, which will give you a general idea of the color and lighting in your design.

New!

1. Choose Rendering ➢ Render… or hit the F10 key to open the Render Scene dialog box and then click the Advanced Lighting tab. The Render Scene dialog box has been redesigned in VIZ 2005.

2. Click the drop-down list in the Select Advanced Lighting rollout. Select Radiosity to select this renderer from the list. A set of rollouts appears lower down in the Render Scene dialog box.

NOTE   *VIZ is written in a modular way that allows future rendering plug-ins to be selected from the Advanced Lighting pop-up.*

3. In the Radiosity Processing Parameters rollout, click the Start button. The processing bar now displays VIZ's activity as it processes the model to determine how the light is reflected off the model's surfaces.

4. Once the processing is completed, make sure the Display Radiosity in Viewport option is checked in the Interactive Tools group.

A sample of the radiosity solution appears in the Mycamera viewport.

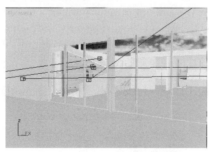

The sample in the Mycamera viewport is too bright, saturated, and washed out. You can adjust the brightness using the Brightness setting for the exposure. This is done in the Environment dialog box.

1. Choose Rendering ➢ Environment or click the Setup button in the Interactive Tools group of the Radiosity dialog box.

2. The Environment and Effects dialog box appears. In the Logarithmic Exposure Control Parameters rollout, click and drag the Brightness spinner downward and watch the result in the Mycamera viewport. The viewport begins to dim.

3. Set the Brightness value to **10**.

The Display Radiosity in Viewport option lets you get a general idea of the lighting in your scene without resorting to a full rendering. In this particular instance, you are able to see the effects of color in your scene. You also have control over the brightness and contrast.

The view now appears to be quite orange in color, which isn't exactly what you might have expected or wanted. The reason for the orange cast is the high reflectance value of the materials in the model. You'll need to make some adjustments to your materials for radiosity rendering.

Setting the Material Reflectivity

In earlier chapters, you created materials and applied them to parts of your model without any concern for the reflectance value of materials. The standard rendering methods you used didn't make use of those reflectance values.

Now that you are using radiosity, you'll want to go back and make some adjustments to the wall and floor materials to take their reflectance values into account. Those reflectance values affect the radiosity solution because the amount of reflectivity of a material affects the appearance of other materials in the scene. In the case of your current view, the high reflectance of the wall and floor materials causes the scene to exaggerate the predominant color of the scene.

1. Click the Material Editor tool in the main toolbar to open the Material Editor.

2. Select the Wall material sample slot, which is just below the glass on the left side of the window.

3. Select Blinn from the Shader Basic Parameters rollout.

4. Click the Diffuse color swatch in the Blinn Basic Parameters rollout.

5. In the Color Selector dialog box, change the Value setting to **155**. Notice what happens to the Reflectance values shown just above the Material Editor toolbar.

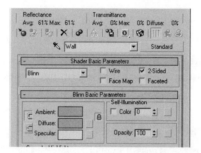

The Reflectance values change from 100% to 61%, which is more in line with a light-colored wall surface. Next, change the reflectance value of the floor material.

1. Scroll down the sample panel to the Stone-Granite Tiles material and select it. Stone-Granite Tiles is just below the Wall material in the sample slots.

2. Select Anisotropic from the Shader Basic Parameters rollout; then select the Diffuse color swatch in the Anisotropic Basic Parameters rollout.

3. In the Color Selector dialog box, change the Value setting to **60** and the Saturation value to **150**. Once again, notice what happens to the Reflectance value in the Material Editor; it drops to an average of 38% and a maximum of 62%. There is a difference between average and maximum reflectance values because the diffuse channel is mapped with a bitmap that varies in color. Areas where the bitmap is brighter have a higher reflectance value.

4. Close the Color Selector and the Material Editor.

You were able to reduce the reflectance value of the materials by changing the materials' color value. For materials that use bitmaps, you can also adjust the reflectance by reducing the RGB value of the bitmap in the Output rollout for the bitmap (see "Making Adjustments to the Background" in Chapter 8 for more information on the Output rollout). You also changed the shader for each material to one that's more appropriate to the material.

WARNING *You may have noticed that in this model of the Villa Savoye, the floor material isn't the same multi/sub-object material that you created in Chapter 6. The floor surface and walls were separated into individual objects to help simplify this tutorial. If you are working with multi/sub-object materials, you need to go one level deeper into the material to make the adjustments to the shader parameters. Otherwise, the process of adjusting material reflectance is the same.*

Now let's see the results of the changes you made.

1. Back in the Radiosity Processing Parameters rollout of the Render Scene dialog box, click Reset All. You'll see the Reset Radiosity Solution warning message.

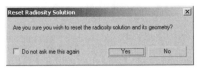

2. Click Yes. The preview in the Mycamera viewport reverts to a display that doesn't include the radiosity solution.

3. Click the Start button in the Radiosity dialog box. After a minute or two, a new view appears in the Mycamera viewport. Click the Logarithmic Exposure Control button and set the brightness to about 30.

This new view looks a bit more reasonable, with less of the orange cast that you saw the first time.

4. Click the Quick Render tool in the main toolbar to see how the model looks so far.

In this last set of exercises, you modified the reflectance values of the walls and floor to something more in line with the materials' actual values. You used a value of about 60%. Table 10.1 gives you some general guidelines for reflectance values of materials.

TABLE 10.1: REFLECTANCE VALUES OF MATERIALS*	
MATERIAL	**REFLECTANCE (%)**
Some Sample Materials	
Soot, coal	5
Black felt	18
Plowed field	25
Tarnished copper	36
White marble	54
Polished stainless steel	63
White oil paint	70
White paper	72
Polished aluminum	80
Highly polished copper	82
Highly polished aluminum	90
Highly polished silver	93
Material Types	
Masonry	20–50
Wood	20–50
Ceramic	20–70
Fabric	20–70
Stone	20–70
Paper	30–70
Plastic	20–80
Paint	30–80
Metal	30–90

* Adapted from Autodesk Lightscape and Autodesk VIZ 2005 User's Guide

Understanding the Radiosity Mesh

If you compare this latest rendering to the early renderings you did in Chapter 6, you'll see that more of the subtle detail is visible, especially around the ramp. But there are some odd colors, and the scene looks far from realistic. To add more realism, you'll need to apply a *radiosity mesh* to your model. To understand the radiosity mesh, you need to know a little bit about how VIZ's radiosity feature works in a general way.

You've learned that radiosity is a method whereby the behavior of light is modeled in the computer. More specifically, it is the method that simulates the reflective quality of the materials in a model. For this to happen, surfaces in the model are broken down into small sections called *elements*. VIZ uses these elements to calculate the way light bounces from one surface to another. Figure 10.4 gives you an idea of how the behavior of reflected light is mimicked by elements in the model.

FIGURE 10.4

Radiosity rendering uses elements of a mesh to help determine the reflection of light within a model. Light that's reflected from one element illuminates other elements.

VIZ creates the mesh of elements, then it calculates the reflective quality of each element. When a final rendering is created, the reflective characteristics of the mesh elements are taken into account to create the subtle lighting features over the surfaces of your model.

The collection of these elements in a radiosity solution is called a radiosity mesh. When you create a radiosity mesh, you can see the results as a series of triangular faces in a wireframe view. These meshes are not to be confused with the actual faces that make up the geometry of objects; they reside in the model only as part of the radiosity solution.

The size of the mesh elements can be controlled, as you'll see a bit later. You want control over the mesh size because if the elements are too frequent, the radiosity solution will take too long to calculate. If they are too large, the radiosity solution will be too inaccurate to generate a good rendering. You need to determine an element size that's a good balance between the time it takes to generate a radiosity solution and the quality of the solution. The default size of 1 meter, or about 39 inches, is a good, general-purpose size.

Another feature of the radiosity mesh is that you can determine which objects in your model are assigned the mesh data. You don't have to assign a radiosity mesh to the entire model; in fact, you don't want to apply a mesh to everything, because that would slow the radiosity solution process. As a rule of thumb, you want to apply a radiosity mesh to objects that have the greatest impact on the reflected light in a scene. Floors and walls are certainly good candidates for the mesh, while handrails, window mullions, and small objects are not.

SELECTING OBJECTS FOR THE MESH

To determine which objects are applied to the radiosity solution, you need to use the Layer Manager dialog box. You may recall from Chapter 5 that you can control the organization, color, and visibility of objects through the Layer Manager dialog box. This is also where you control which objects are used in the radiosity solution. The following exercise shows you how. In order to get a more realistic simulation of the reflected light in the scene, you'll apply a global mesh. First, though, you'll exclude the smaller objects that have the least impact on reflected light in the scene. Excluding these smaller objects from the mesh will save time during radiosity processing.

1. Click the Layer Manager tool in the main toolbar.

2. In the Layer Manager dialog box, click the plus (+) sign just to the left of the layer 0. The list expands to show the name of all the objects in the scene.

3. Select the Mullion layer. The layer should appear yellow in the list.

4. For the Mullion layer, click the corresponding radiosity icon twice in the Radiosity column. The icon turns into a dot the first time you click; then it changes to a gray icon on the second click. This removes the selected objects from the radiosity solution.

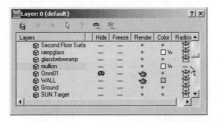

WARNING   *It's important that you click the icon twice so that the gray radiosity icon appears. If you leave it as a dot, the main layer setting at the top of the list will control the behavior of the indented objects.*

5. Scroll down the list and select Ground; then turn off the radiosity setting for the Ground object, just as you did for the Mullion layer. This is an important layer to remove from the radiosity solution, since it would greatly increase the time it takes to derive a solution, due to its size.

6. Finally, turn off the radiosity setting for the MULLION.0x objects and the STAIR objects.

7. Close the Layer Manager dialog box.

OBTAINING A RADIOSITY SOLUTION USING THE MESHING OPTION

You've just turned off the radiosity setting for several objects. The next step is to generate another radiosity solution, but this time you'll turn on the global mesh option.

1. Go back to the Render Scene dialog box on the Advanced Lighting tab; then open the Radiosity Meshing Parameters rollout.

2. Click the Enabled check box to enable the radiosity meshing.

3. Click the Reset All button near the top of the Radiosity Processing Parameters rollout.

4. Change the Initial Quality setting to **65%**. This will help reduce the time it takes for VIZ to generate a radiosity solution, although it will also reduce the quality of the solution.

5. Click the Start button.

This time VIZ will take considerably more time to generate a solution, so you may want to take a short break here. As the solution is generated, you'll see the Processing graph display VIZ's activity.

In step 4, you reduced the Initial Quality setting. At this point, you're testing your settings, so you'll want to get a rough idea of how the radiosity solution will look. By reducing the Initial Quality setting, you'll get a good idea of how it will look without a huge impact on time. When the radiosity solution is complete, you'll see the results in the Mycamera viewport (see Figure 10.5). You can see that the scene is beginning to look much better. In addition, if you look carefully, you'll see that the other wireframe viewport shows the radiosity mesh over the building.

FIGURE 10.5
The viewport views after the radiosity solution is generated with the meshing option turned on

The sample Mycamera viewport looks better, but there are a few distortions in the image. Try the following to get a better look at the current results.

1. With the Mycamera viewport selected, click the Min/Max Toggle tool to enlarge it. The columns and mullions look distorted, and the ceiling shows a mottled effect.

2. Click the Quick Render tool in the main toolbar. The rendering also has similar distortions, as shown in Figure 10.6.

FIGURE 10.6

The rendering shows distortions in the columns and the ceiling.

IMPROVING THE RADIOSITY SOLUTION

The distortions you see are the result of a low quality setting. Also notice that the rendered view is a bit darker than the sample viewport view. In the next exercise, you'll refine the radiosity solution to get an improved rendering. While you're at it, you can brighten the scene to show more of the interior space.

1. Open the Environment and Effects dialog box by pressing the 8 key on the keyboard and in the Logarithmic Exposure Control Parameters rollout, change the Brightness setting to **40**.

2. In the Radiosity portion of the Render Scene dialog box, change the Initial Quality setting to **80**; then click the Continue button. You don't have to reset anything because none of the model's geometry has changed. Once the process is finished, you'll find that the Mycamera viewport doesn't appear to have changed much.

3. Render the view again. This time the ceiling begins to even out, but the columns are still not right.

4. Back in the Radiosity dialog box, change the Refine Iterations (All Objects) setting to **1**; then click the Continue button.

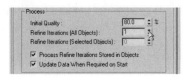

This time, the sample image begins to improve noticeably.

5. Render the view again. Now the scene looks more realistic, and the columns appear smooth. The ceiling, however, still looks a bit splotchy.

6. In the Interactive Tools group of the Radiosity dialog box, change the Filtering option to **1**. This option evens out the lighting on surfaces.

Notice that you see the result of this setting immediately in the Mycamera sample viewport.

7. Render the view a third time. Now the rendering contains fewer distortions, as shown in Figure 10.7.

FIGURE 10.7

The rendered view with Refine Iterations and Filtering settings set to a value of 1

This time you used a few new settings in the Radiosity portion of the Render Scene dialog box. First, you changed the Initial Quality setting to 80. This is a good setting for most renderings; you probably won't want to make it much higher except for your most demanding presentations.

Next, you changed the Refine Iterations (All Objects) setting to 1. This option improves surface lighting smoothness by taking into account the light energy of the surrounding environment. The option just below Refine Iterations (All Objects) is Refine Iterations (Selected Objects). As the name suggests, this option works on selected objects instead of the entire scene. To use it, select the objects in the scene for which you want to refine iterations, then set the Refine Iterations (Select Objects) option. In complex scenes, this can help save time because you can additionally refine only those objects that you select.

The third setting you made was to increase the Filtering setting in the Interactive Tools group. This setting averages the light levels between elements to reduce the mottled effect of the radiosity solution. You can increase this value to 3 or 4, but higher values are not recommended.

You may have also noticed that you didn't have to reset the radiosity solution for your scene after making changes to the Refine Iterations and Filtering options. That's because these changes don't affect the materials in the scene.

CONTROLLING THE RADIOSITY MESH SIZE OF INDIVIDUAL OBJECTS

When you included the radiosity meshing option in an earlier exercise, VIZ applied the mesh size globally—that is, to all the objects selected for the radiosity solution. If you need to, you can set the mesh size for individual objects. To do this, take the following steps:

1. Select the object you want to set.

2. Right-click the object; then select Properties from the Transform group of the Quad menu.

3. In the Object Properties dialog box, select the Adv. Lighting tab.

4. In the Geometric Object Properties group, turn off the Use Global Subdivision Settings option. You'll see the Meshing Size and Subdivide options turn from gray to black, indicating their availability.

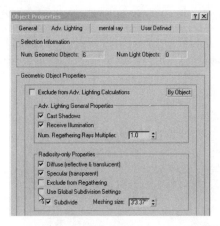

5. Set the Meshing Size option to the value you desire, and make sure the Subdivide option is checked.

6. Close the Object Properties dialog box.

You can then reset your radiosity solution and start a new one. The selected object will subdivide into the size elements you specified in step 5, while all other objects will use the global setting.

USING THE SUBDIVIDE MODIFIER

Another way to control the radiosity mesh size of individual objects is to apply the Subdivide modifier. One advantage of using this method, as opposed to using the Object Properties dialog box, is that you will see visual feedback in the viewport before calculating the radiosity solution. This added visual feedback is crucial, since you don't want to spend time calculating a solution only to discover that the mesh size isn't what you intended. To try this method, take the following steps:

1. Select the object you want to subdivide.

2. Apply the Subdivide modifier. You will see its Parameters rollout appear on the Modify tab of the Command Panel.

3. Right-click on the viewport menu and switch to Wireframe or Edged Faces display mode and adjust the Size parameter to interactively subdivide the selected object.

   The smaller the size, the more complex the radiosity mesh becomes. Areas with greater curvature also receive more subdivision. The Subdivide modifier's algorithm automatically determines where on an object the radiosity mesh gets added based upon the maximum size parameter that you set as shown on a Teapot in Figure 10.8.

FIGURE 10.8
The Subdivide modifier increases mesh complexity.

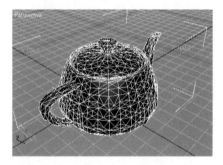

TIP   Smaller meshes give better lighting detail when you calculate a radiosity solution, but they will take longer to process. In general, it is best to subdivide only in problem areas where you notice distortions in your test radiosity solutions.

Creating a Finished Rendering

Up until now, you've been working with the process of refining your image and making adjustments until you have a fairly good representation of the space. In many cases, you might find that the results you get from the process you've learned so far are good enough. But if you really want to get the very best rendering possible, you can take a few more steps that can dramatically improve your final rendering output.

You were introduced to the Quick Render tool in Chapter 6. In this section, you'll get a closer look at some of the ways you can control your rendered output through the new Render Scene dialog box.

New!

The Render Scene dialog box has been redesigned in VIZ 2005. The old Raytrace Globals and Radiosity dialog boxes have been integrated via a tabbed interface into the new Render Scene dialog box. Try the following exercise to get a good look at the rendering options you have available.

1. Make sure the Mycamera viewport is active; then click the Render Scene tool on the main toolbar. The Render Scene dialog box displays.

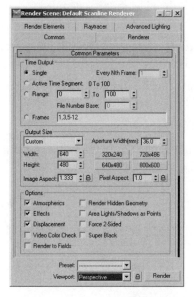

2. As you've already seen, there are tabs at the top of this dialog box, and each tab represents a different page within the dialog box. Click the Common tab now.

   Like the Command Panel, the Render Scene dialog box offers a vertical scrolling panel with rollouts. The main rollout on the Common tab is called Common Parameters, and it offers the most used settings that you'll encounter in your work.

3. Place the cursor over a blank area in the dialog box until you see the hand cursor. Then click and drag upward. You'll see additional rollouts with more settings. You can also right-click within a rollout and you'll see a context menu listing all the rollouts that are available there.

4. Scroll back to the top so that you can view the top of the Common Parameters rollout. Then resize the dialog by dragging its lower right corner so that you can see the entire rollout (assuming you have enough resolution on your screen to display such a tall dialog box).

Let's take a moment to examine the Common Parameters rollout and the groups it includes.

Time Output group   At the top, you see a group labeled Time Output. These settings offer control over animation output, although their use isn't necessarily limited to animation work. You'll see later how these settings can be used for automating the rendering of several views of a model such as the elevations of a building.

Output Size group   This group offers control over the size of the image file that Render generates. You can control the width and height in pixels, or select from a set of predefined, standard image sizes if you are outputting to a traditional medium.

Options group   This group offers control over special effects and rendering tools. Some of these options are concerned with animation files destined for video, while others control more general effects of the renderer.

Advanced Lighting group   Below the Options group, you see the Advanced Lighting group, which lets you turn radiosity rendering on or off with one check.

Render Output group   Finally, this group lets you determine the type of file output to be generated and how it will be rendered.

Let's create an image file.

1. Click the Files button in the Render Output group of the Render Scene dialog box. The Render Output File dialog box displays.

NOTE   *You may see a list of files in your view of the Render Output File dialog box, even though none are shown here.*

With the exception of a set of options in the lower half of the dialog box, the Render Output File dialog box is a typical File dialog box.

2. Enter **Myfirstrender** in the File Name input box and select a folder to save the file on your hard drive.

3. Click the Save as Type drop-down list and select BMP Image File (*bmp).

4. Click the Save button. The BMP Configuration dialog box displays.

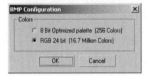

TIP   *Each image file format has its own configuration dialog with settings specific to that type. You can edit these settings later by clicking on the Setup button in the Render Output File dialog.*

5. Select RGB 24 bit and click OK. You return to the Render Scene dialog box. The filename you entered displays in the file listing below the Files button.

6. Click the Render button. The Rendered Frame Window opens and shows the progress of the rendering. There is no need to save the rendering from the Rendered Frame Window because a file has already been saved to disk as you requested in the Render Scene dialog box.

7. When the rendering is complete, uncheck the Save File check box in the Render Scene dialog box. There are two new drop-down lists along the bottom edge of the Render Scene dialog box. The Viewport drop-down list allows you to select a viewport to render that can be different from the currently active viewport.

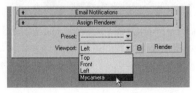

The Preset drop-down list contains a list of preset settings that you can choose from. It also has the provision to load and save your own preset lists of settings.

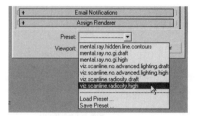

When you select a preset from the drop-down list, the Select Preset Categories dialog box appears from which you can choose what categories you would like to load presets into. The presets you load will alter whatever settings were in the appropriate categories previously.

If you choose to save a preset, a standard File Save dialog box appears. Presets have the `.rps` file extension and are normally saved in the `RenderPresets` folder within the `Autodesk VIZ 2005` program folder.

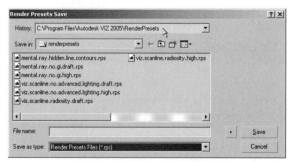

You will find that render presets save you a lot of time and make it easy to share your rendering settings with a colleague just by copying your custom `.rps` file for them. You no longer need to make detailed notes of all the settings you used because you can now exchange a render presets file.

In this section, you'll make some final adjustments to your scene to produce a truly lifelike rendering of the Villa Savoye interior space. But be prepared for some long rendering times in this section. With the improved image quality comes much longer rendering times.

TIP   If you have a slow computer, you may want to just look at the sample renderings on the companion CD instead of starting the renderings as the exercises ask. This will save you from having to wait for hours to view the results of a rendering. The exercises will explain which files to view at the appropriate points in the exercises.

You'll start by changing your view to show more of the interior; then you'll render the view with the current settings to get an idea of how the interior will look.

1. Right-click the Mycamera label in the upper left corner of the Mycamera viewport and select View ➢ Mycamera01. The view changes to show more of the interior.

2. Click the Quick Render tool in the main toolbar. You get a view similar to the one shown in Figure 10.9.

FIGURE 10.9
A rendered view of the interior space

With this new rendering, you begin to see some flaws in the shading. There are some light leaks in the back corner of the room on the ceiling, and the columns and mullions on the right side of the room don't cast shadows on the ceiling where you would expect to see them. You can solve most of the shadow problems by using the Regather Indirect Illumination option.

1. On the Advanced Lighting tab of the Render Scene dialog box, scroll down and open the Rendering Parameters rollout. Turn on the Regather Indirect Illumination option.

2. Click the Quick Render tool in the main toolbar—but before you do, be aware that this rendering will take nearly an hour to complete. If you're in a hurry, take a look at the file named `Figure10-10.tif` on the companion CD, as shown in Figure 10.10.

FIGURE 10.10

The interior view rendered with the Regather Indirect Illumination option turned on

In previous renderings, the shadows weren't quite right, and in some places they didn't appear at all. In this latest rendering, you see that the shadows of the columns on the ceiling are clearly defined. The shadows from the wall are also more accurate. You can even see light reflected from the windowsill toward the left of the view. It is a very realistic and lifelike view. This is because the Regather Indirect Illumination option calculates shadows from all the light in the scene and fixes any shadow areas that may have been missed. In one sense, this single option is the heart of radiosity rendering because the regathering of indirect illumination best simulates the natural lighting of a scene. Unfortunately, regathering usually takes a very long time to render.

There is one feature of the image that is not very realistic. If you look at the darker areas, you see that the image is rough and grainy. You can improve the accuracy of the rendering by increasing the Rays per Sample and Filter Radius options in the Rendering Parameters rollout.

1. In the Rendering Parameters rollout of the Radiosity dialog box, change the Rays per Sample value to **128** and the Filter Radius value to **4**.

2. Render the view again. If you are in a hurry, look at the file named `Figure10-11.tif` on the companion CD, as shown in Figure 10.11.

3. Save the file as `Myradiosity.max`.

FIGURE 10.11

The interior view with the Rays per Sample and Filter Radius settings increased

If you look carefully at the latest rendering, you'll see that the graininess is reduced but not completely eliminated. By increasing the Rays per Sample setting, VIZ uses more sample rays in its calculation of indirect light. You might think of these sample rays as the simulated light rays or photons bouncing around in the scene. The increased number of rays improves the smoothness of the shaded areas.

The Filter Radius setting is similar to the Filtering setting in the Interactive Tools group. It averages ray samples with neighboring samples to even out the grainy appearance.

These final renderings take a long time for VIZ to produce, but the results are often worth the wait. You've seen how you can build up to the final rendering by making adjustments to the scene and the radiosity settings. By testing your settings, you can get a fairly good idea of how the scene will appear before you commit VIZ to a final rendering using the Regather Indirect Illumination option.

Working with Artificial Lights

You've seen how the Daylight System in conjunction with the radiosity feature can create some realistic views of a scene. The Daylight System is great for daylight illumination, but in a lot of situations, you'll be working with artificial lighting.

In prior chapters, you used standard lights to illuminate interior spaces, but if you intend to use VIZ's radiosity features, you'll want to use photometric lights for best results. Photometric lights let you set their intensity, distribution, and color to real world equivalents for radiosity processing of the accurate physically based lighting simulation. Photometric lights work in concert with radiosity to provide a more accurate rendition of a scene. In this section, you'll start to add some photometric lights to the Villa Savoye interior view to see how they interact with the radiosity settings you've become familiar with.

Just as with the first example in this chapter, you'll perform some operations similar to those you did in Chapter 9. You'll add furniture and lights to the interior of the Villa Savoye model, but this time, the

TOUCHING UP A RENDERING TO SAVE TIME

If you performed a full rendering using the Regather Indirect Illumination setting, you know that it takes a very long time to render such a view. Although the regathering option produces excellent results, the cost in time may be too great for some of your projects. VIZ offers an interesting tool that can help speed up your work if you're willing to do a little "touch-up" of your rendering.

The Light Painting rollout in the Radiosity dialog box lets you add or subtract illumination to surfaces in a scene. If light leaks through parts of a shadow, you can use the Light Painting tools to darken the areas of the shadow where the light leaks occur. If an area is too dark, you can "paint in" more light.

To use these tools, you must first select the object whose surface you wish to adjust. Once you select an object, the tools become available.

There are three main tools on the left side of the Light Painting rollout:

◆ The one that looks like a dropper is the Pick Illumination from a Surface tool. With this tool selected, you can find the illumination level of a surface in the sample radiosity viewport by clicking the surface. The illumination value appears in the Intensity input box on the right side of the rollout.

◆ To reduce the illumination on a surface, click the Subtract Illumination from a Surface tool (it looks like a paintbrush with a minus [−] sign) and then "paint over" the areas that appear too bright. You can adjust the value in the Pressure input box to control the amount of change applied to the surface as you paint over the surface.

◆ To increase illumination on a surface, use the Add Illumination to a Surface tool, which shows a paintbrush with a plus (+) sign.

If you decide that you don't like the changes you've painted in, you can click the Clear button to discard your changes.

lights will be photometric lights instead of the standard Omni lights you used in Chapter 9. You'll also examine some of the ways shadow parameters affect your rendering.

Using Photometric Lights

In this section, you'll return to the furniture layout you saw in Chapter 9. But this time, you'll add photometric lights. The file you'll be working with is basically the same as the one you used in Chapter 9, complete with light fixtures and chairs. The standard Omni lights have been removed from the light fixtures so that you can add the photometric lights and set the lighting parameters. Also, a highly reflective object has been added just inside the torchiere lamps, as shown in Figure 10.12. This material will reflect the light from the photometric lights that you will add.

FIGURE 10.12
A reflector has been added to the inside of the torchiere lamps.

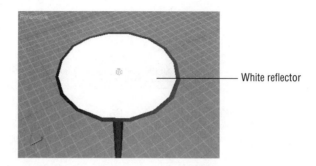

White reflector

1. Open the villaFurniture10.max file on the companion CD.

2. In the Top viewport, zoom into the three torchiere lamps and large table, as shown in Figure 10.13.

3. Select the Create tab in the Command Panel; then select the Lights tool from the Command Panel toolbar.

FIGURE 10.13
Zoom in to the lamps and table in the top view; then place the first light in the center of the torchiere in the upper right portion of the view.

Place the first photometric light here.

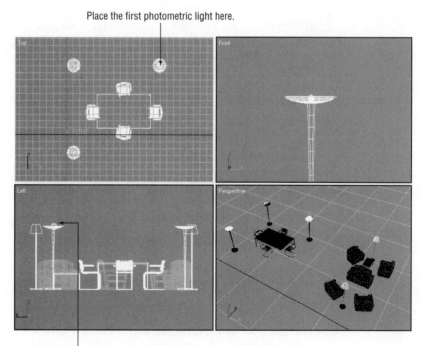

Adjust the light height so that it appears within the lamp "bowl."

4. Select Photometric from the Lights drop-down list.

5. Click the Free Point button. The Free Point options appear in the Command Panel.

You've selected a photometric light type. Before you place it in the scene, you'll want to make some adjustments to the light's parameters so that the light's character will be closer to that of a typical torchiere light source. Let's assume that you initially want a 100-watt halogen bulb for the torchiere fixtures.

1. In the Intensity/Color/Distribution rollout in the Command Panel, select Halogen from the drop-down list in the Color group.

2. In the Intensity group, click the cd radio button for measurement in candelas if it is not already selected; then enter **139** in the left input box just below the radio buttons.

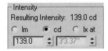

3. Turn on the Multiplier option at the bottom of the Intensity group and leave the value at 100%.

The cd radio button tells VIZ that you want to specify the light intensity in candelas (see "Understanding Photometric Lights" later in this chapter). You gave the light an intensity of 139 cd, which is equivalent to a traditional 100-watt light bulb.

You also saw how you can specify the color temperature of a light. You can choose from a list of predetermined light color types, or you can enter a color temperature in the Kelvin input box in the Color group.

Now you are ready to place the light in the scene.

1. In the Top viewport, click in the center of the torchiere in the upper right corner to place a light (see Figure 10.12). The light now appears in the other viewports.

2. The light is too low in the scene, so you'll need to raise it. Click the Select and Move tool; then change the Z axis spinner in the coordinate readout to **16′ 10″** to move the light into a position inside the torchiere bowl.

3. Shift+click and drag the X axis of the new light to a position in the center of the torchiere in the top left corner of the Top viewport, as shown in Figure 10.14.

FIGURE 10.14
Instance the light to
the other torchiere
fixtures.

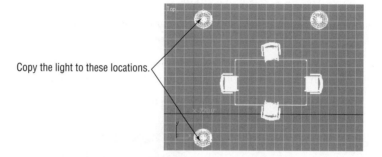

Copy the light to these locations.

4. In the Clone Options dialog box, select Instance; then click OK.

5. Shift+click and drag the Y axis of this second light downward to the center of the torchiere in the lower left corner of the Top viewport, as shown in Figure 10.14. Make this an Instance clone also.

You've got the lights added to the torchiere lamps. Next, you'll want to add the lights to the other two lamps by the chairs.

1. Pan the Top viewport to the left so that you can see the first torchiere and the other two lamps clearly, as shown in Figure 10.15.

2. Click the Select by Name tool in the main toolbar; then, in the Select Objects dialog box, select FPoint01, which is the first photometric light you added to the scene.

3. Using the XY plane on the Transform gizmo, Shift+click and drag the Fpoint01 light to the center of the lamp in the upper right corner of Top viewport, as shown in Figure 10.15.

FIGURE 10.15
Adding the photo-
metric lights to the
lamps by the chairs

Copy this light...

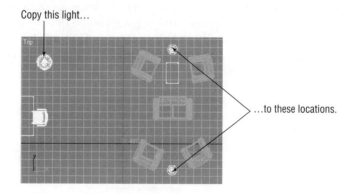

...to these locations.

4. In the Clone Options dialog box, select Copy; then click OK. You'll want the control of this light to be independent of the torchieres.

5. Use the Z axis spinner in the coordinate readout to adjust the height of the new light to **16´8˝**.

You've added a light source to the lamp, but it isn't a torchiere; thus you'll want to change the color of the light from halogen to incandescent.

1. With the new light selected, select the Modify tab of the Command Panel; then scroll down the panel to the Intensity/Color/Distribution rollout.

2. In the Color group, select Incandescent from the drop-down list.

Now, make a copy of this new light to the other lamp.

1. Shift+click and drag this new light to the lamp in the lower right corner of the Top viewport, as shown in Figure 10.15.

2. In the Clone Options dialog box, select Instance; then click OK. This will allow you to control both lamps by adjusting the settings of just one.

3. Save the file as Myphotometric.max.

You used the Instance clone option so that you can control the properties of all the torchiere lights through a single light. As you've seen from this example, adding photometric lights is no different from adding standard lights.

Using a Shortcut to Generic Light Fixtures

In the previous exercises, you were asked to set up the color and intensity of the lights you placed in the scene. This was done because it's important to know about the process of setting up lights and where to look for the appropriate settings. But if you are in a hurry and you only need some generic lights in your scene, you can select a light from a set of preset lights from the VIZ menu bar. Choose Create ➢ Lights ➢ Photometric Lights ➢ Presets. You'll see a list of generic lights that are commonly used in residential or small commercial scenes.

These lights are set up with the proper light type, color, intensity, and distribution style for the type of light they represent. Remember these lights when you only need some generic lighting in a scene.

Importing the Photometric Lights Using XRefs

So far, you've added photometric lights to a furniture layout. Next, you'll add that furniture layout, complete with lights, to the radiosity model you worked with in the first part of this chapter. You'll start by using VIZ's XRef feature to include the furniture in the Savoye interior scene.

1. Open the `Myradiosity.max` file that you saved earlier, or use the `Myradiosity.max` file from the companion CD.

2. Choose File ➢ XRef Scene.

3. In the XRef Scenes dialog box, click the Add button; then locate and select your `Myphotometric.max` file, or use the `Myphotometric.max` from the companion CD.

4. Click Close. The furniture appears in the interior of the scene.

With the addition of new geometry and lights, you'll have to reset the radiosity solution. Before you do that, though, turn off the sunlight and daylight.

1. Click the Select by Name tool in the main toolbar; then, in the Select Objects dialog box, select Daylight01.

2. In the Modify tab of the Command Panel, turn off the Active setting for both the Sunlight and Skylight groups of the Daylight Parameters rollout.

With the sun and daylight inactive, you're ready to generate a radiosity solution. Since you've added some lights and more complexity to the scene, you can reduce the quality setting and turn off the Refine Iterations setting to speed up the process.

1. Open the Radiosity portion of the Render Scene dialog box; then click Reset All. In the warning message, click Yes.

2. Change the Initial Quality setting to **60**.

3. Change the Refine Iterations setting to **0** and the Filtering option in the Interactive Tools group to **0**.

4. Click the Start button and wait. You can take a break at this point while the radiosity solution is being processed. Once the radiosity solution is complete, you'll see a very dark image in the Mycamera01 viewport.

The sample image is dark because the exposure setting was made for a daylight level of light intensity. You've turned off the sun and daylight, so to compensate for the change, you'll change the exposure brightness setting.

1. Choose Rendering ➤ Environment or click the Setup button in the Interactive Tools group of the Advanced Lighting tab of the Render Scene dialog box. Another alternative is to click Rendering ➤ Advanced Lighting ➤ Exposure Control.

2. In the Logarithmic Exposure Control Parameters rollout, change the Brightness setting to **100**; then close the Environment and Effects dialog box. The sample image brightens to reveal the room interior with furniture.

3. Click the Quick Render tool in the main toolbar to get a better idea of the results of the radiosity solution. The rendering reveals some problems with the solution.

The shadows and lighting show some odd patterns. They are caused by the default shadow map shadows used by the photometric lights.

Adjusting Shadows for Photometric Lights

The default shadow for the Daylight System is a ray traced shadow, which gives you an accurate, though hard-edged, shadow on surfaces. The free point photometric lights may use a shadow map shadow by default, which is limited in accuracy. Fortunately, all the lights offer the full range of shadows that VIZ offers.

IMPROVING THE SPEED OF TRIAL RENDERINGS

As you work to refine your radiosity solution, you'll probably create many trial renderings of your scene. If you're focusing on the color and light levels in your rendering and aren't too concerned with shadow accuracy, you can greatly improve rendering speed by turning on the Re-Use Direct Illumination from Radiosity Solution option in the Radiosity dialog box. You'll find this option in the Rendering Parameters rollout.

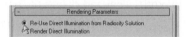

The Re-Use Direct Illumination from Radiosity Solution option uses the radiosity mesh to calculate shadows instead of using VIZ's standard renderer to generate shadows. Shadows won't be rendered accurately, but you'll get a fairly good representation of the lighting in the scene.

In this section, you'll use some other types of shadows to help improve the appearance of a rendered view. You'll use a standard ray traced shadow for the torchiere lamps, and for the lamps closest to the view camera, you'll use area shadows. You may recall from Chapter 6 that an area shadow is a type of ray traced shadow that simulates the way shadows tend to soften or show a penumbra for objects farther away from the light source. Area shadows are useful in this particular scene, because they best simulate shadows that you see in the foreground.

To gain access to the lights from the XRef file, you'll first merge the XRef file with the current scene. You can also go back to the XRef file and make the changes there, but merging the file will help simplify the exercises here.

1. Choose File ➢ XRef Scene.

2. Select the `Myphotometric.max` file in the list; then click the Merge button in the XRef File group.

3. In the warning dialog box, click OK; then close the XRef Scenes dialog box.

Now you can gain access to the lights of the lamps.

1. Click the Select by Name tool in the main toolbar.

2. In the Select Objects dialog box, locate and select the FPoint01 light in the list box.

3. In the Modify tab of the Command Panel, locate the Shadows group in the General Parameters rollout for the Fpoint01 light and change the setting to Ray Traced Shadows.

Since you made instances of the torchiere lights, you needed to change only one of them in order to change the shadow setting for all three torchieres. Now change the other two lamps.

1. Click the Select by Name tool in the main toolbar.

2. In the Select Objects dialog box, locate and select the FPoint04 light in the list box.

3. In the Modify tab of the Command Panel, locate the Shadows group in the General Parameters rollout for the FPoint01 light and change the setting to Area Shadows.

4. Open the Area Shadows rollout in the Command Panel; then change the Mode setting in the Basic Options group to Sphere Light. This causes the Fpoint04 light to simulate a light in the shape of a sphere, similar to a typical household bulb.

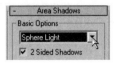

5. Scroll down a bit farther to the Area Light Dimensions group of the Area Shadows rollout, and change the Length, Width, and Height settings to **2″**, a typical lightbulb size. The area light needs this information to calculate the penumbra of the shadow.

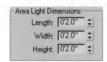

6. Go to the Radiosity portion of the Render Scene dialog box and click the Reset button. In the warning dialog box, click OK.

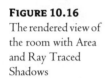

7. Click Start to create a new radiosity solution; then click the Quick Render tool in the main toolbar to see the results of the change in Shadow mode (see Figure 10.16). If you are in a hurry, take a look at the file Figure10-16.tif from the companion CD.

FIGURE 10.16

The rendered view of the room with Area and Ray Traced Shadows

TIP   If you just want to blur the edge of Ray Traced Shadows, you can use the Advanced Ray Traced Shadow mode. This mode offers a Blur setting in its Advanced Ray Traced Shadow rollout that allows you to control the amount of blur applied to the shadow edge.

This last exercise shows that in some cases, you'll have to do a full rendering to see how shadows will appear. The Area Shadows mode greatly increases the rendering time, but it adds a higher degree of realism to the scene. If your scene involves only shadows seen from a distance, you can probably avoid using area shadows. But if your scene includes shadows that are close to the foreground, area shadows will help improve the realism of the scene.

To get a better idea of the advantages of area shadows, compare Figure 10.17, which uses Ray Traced Shadows for all the lights, with Figure 10.16. In Figure 10.17, the shadows of the objects in the foreground are rendered with hard edges, creating an unnatural look.

FIGURE 10.17
The interior rendered using Ray Traced Shadows throughout

Figure 10.18 shows a final rendering of the interior using the Regather Indirect Illumination setting. If you compare this image with a very quick shadow mapped scanline rendering, you see that greater detail is revealed in the scene, and the shadows are rendered with more subtle variation. Colors are also varied. But the biggest difference is that the radiosity rendering shows you a very close facsimile to the realistic appearance of the space, given the lighting you've applied and the materials you've used. However, it takes quite a bit more time to render as you have seen here.

For a comparison, Figure 10.19 shows the interior view with a regathered rendering, using the Daylight lighting scheme.

FIGURE 10.19

The Savoye interior with furniture, using the Daylight System and radiosity

When you use the Regather Direct Illumination rendering option, rendering times go way up. You can reduce rendering times a bit by controlling the Mesh Size option for individual objects. Reduce the Mesh Size option in the Object Properties dialog box for objects in the foreground of the scene and increase the Mesh Size option for objects farther away in the background. See the section entitled "Controlling the Radiosity Mesh Size of Individual Objects" earlier in this chapter.

Understanding Photometric Lights

The real benefit of radiosity rendering is its ability to show you how your design will look in real life, given very specific lighting conditions. Because lighting plays a major role in the fidelity of your rendering, it's important to understand how to control lighting in your model. This section gives you an overview of the photometric lighting tools that are available to you in VIZ.

Points Are Bulbs, Linears Are Tubes, and Areas Are Rectangles

In the exercises of this chapter, you've used a free point photometric light. A free point light can behave in a way similar to a simple, household lightbulb. You also have the option of using a linear light, which behaves like a single, straight fluorescent tube, or an area light, which behaves like a square or rectangular fluorescent fixture such as those commonly found in kitchen and office ceilings. If you look at the Object Type rollout for photometric lights in the Create tab of the Command Panel, you see eight types.

There are really just three types of photometric lights in common usage: point, linear, and area (plus the IES Sun and Sky that are used within the Daylight system). Each common light is presented twice, with the Target option turned on or off. You may recall from Chapter 6 that a target light allows you to indicate a precise direction for the light by adding a target point to the light object. The target point can be moved independently from the light source. The Target option is significant for lights that can be pointed in a particular direction. Figure 10.20 shows the three common photometric light types with their Target options turned on, as they appear in a user viewport.

FIGURE 10.20

The three photometric light types with their Target options turned on

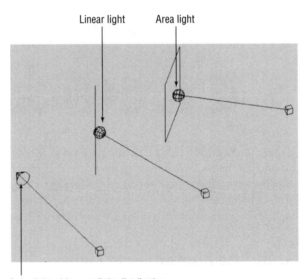

Point light with a spotlight distribution

After you place a photometric light in a scene, you're not fixed to the type of light you inserted. You can alter its type by selecting a different one from the Light Type group of the General Parameters for the light. You can also turn the Target option on or off in this group.

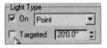

TIP One specific type of light, the isotropic point light, doesn't have a need for a target, since it behaves like a point source, casting light in all directions. Still, you can include a target with an isotropic point light to "aim" the intensity distribution (called a photometric web) in a particular direction.

Controlling the Direction of Lights

Each one of these light types can have a different type of *distribution*, which is the way the light is cast from its source. The distribution options differ, depending on the type of light you are using. Point light sources can have an isotropic, spotlight, or web distribution. An isotropic distribution mimics the behavior of a point light source, directing light equally in all directions. A spotlight distribution behaves just as the name indicates, like a spotlight directing light in a cone. Figure 10.20 shows a point light with a spotlight distribution. A web distribution varies the intensity of light in different directions. You'll learn more about web distribution in the next section.

Both the linear and area lights offer a diffuse distribution and a web distribution. A diffuse distribution throws the most intense light in a direction that's perpendicular to the light surface. For example, for an area light mounted on a ceiling, such as a square florescent fixture, light intensity is greatest in the directly downward direction. The intensity falls off at oblique angles to the fixture.

To select a distribution type, look for the Distribution drop-down list in the Intensity/Color/Distribution rollout.

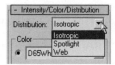

Understanding Web Distribution

Most of the distribution modes are easily understood because you can relate them to fixtures you are familiar with. For a simple lightbulb, you would use a point light with an isotropic distribution; and for a bare fluorescent tube, you would use a linear light with a diffuse distribution. The web distribution is a bit more esoteric, but in the simplest terms, it is a 3D representation of the varying light intensity from a light source.

To help you understand a web distribution, you can think of a simple lightbulb as having a web distribution where light intensity is the same in all directions. This is represented graphically as a simple sphere similar to the graphic that represents a point isotropic light in VIZ (see the image on the left in Figure 10.21).

Now, imagine that a light source distributes light with varying intensity, depending on the direction of the light. For example, imagine a light source that casts very low intensity directly upward, its highest intensity directly downward, and a medium intensity out the sides. A web distribution for such a light would look like the image on the right in Figure 10.21.

FIGURE 10.21
On the left: an isotropic distribution. On the right: a fictitious web distribution, with low intensity upward and high intensity downward.

If you've ever looked at the specifications for light fixtures, chances are you've seen a 2D form of a web distribution called a *goniometric* diagram. The web distribution is a 3D representation of a 2D goniometric diagram.

The main feature of the web distribution is that it's customizable. Many lighting manufacturers can supply web distribution data for their light fixtures in the form of files that can be downloaded and used by VIZ. By using such files, you can get a very accurate simulation of the specific lighting fixture that you have specified for your scene.

VIZ can read the three major web distribution file types, which are IES (Illuminating Enginnering Society), CIBSE (Chartered Institution of Building Services Engineers—used in the United Kingdom), and LTLI (Danish Illuminating Laboratory—acronym from the Danish). There are some sample IES web distribution files in the Maps folder within the Autodesk VIZ 2005 main folder; you might want to experiment with these.

Once you've obtained the web distribution file, you can apply it to a light.

1. Select a photometric light; then, in the Modify tab of the Command Panel, select Web from the Distribution setting of the Intensity/Color/Distribution rollout.

2. Set the Color and Intensity settings appropriately.

3. Scroll down the Command Panel to the Web Parameters and open it.

4. Click the Web File button; then locate and select the web distribution file that you obtained from the lighting manufacturer.

When you insert the light, you see that it has a unique shape. This is the graphic representation of the web distribution. Figure 10.22 shows a sample web distribution called Cooper (sample on the CD) that has been applied to a target point photometric light. Figure 10.23 shows the same light superimposed on a rendering of the light as it is reflected off nearby surfaces.

FIGURE 10.22
A sample photometric web distribution applied to a point light

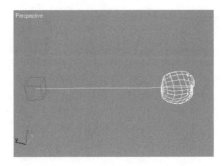

FIGURE 10.23
The Cooper light superimposed on a rendering of the light against two surfaces

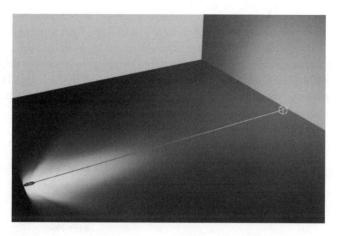

Besides being useful for specific light fixtures, web distribution files can help you approximate the behavior of other similar lights when you can't get the exact specifications from a manufacturer. If you are a lighting specialist, you can create your own, custom web distribution files. A discussion of that process would go beyond the scope of this book, but fortunately, there are many sources for web distribution files on the Web. Erco Lighting (`www.erco.com`) is an excellent source specifically for lighting data and downloadable photometric web distribution and luminaire files.

Specifying the Color Temperature and Light Intensity

The light distribution can have a great effect on the quality of your radiosity solution, but color also plays an important role. VIZ lets you control the color temperature of lights, or you can choose from a set of predetermined color settings. You'll find the color options in the Color group in the Intensity/Color/Distribution rollout.

You can choose from a drop-down list of 15 common light types, from Fluorescent to Metal Halide, or you can enter a specific color temperature in the Kelvin input box. Color temperature is an industry standard means for specifying colors associated with luminaires.

Perhaps the single greatest influence on a scene is the lighting intensity. VIZ's photometric lights let you specify a light's intensity using one of three measurement systems: lumens, candelas, or lux. You may be most familiar with lumens if you live in North America, since most household lightbulbs specify brightness in terms of lumens. For example, a typical 100-watt incandescent bulb may be specified to produce 1,750 lumens. As you look at the specifications for light fixtures, you will also find lights rated in candelas, or cd. A third method for measuring intensity is lux, which takes distance from a light source into account.

These three different units of measure express different aspects of light intensity. Lumens indicate total light intensity from a source. Candelas indicate light intensity to a point, rather than the overall light output. Lux measures intensity over an area at a specific distance from a source.

You can obtain intensity specifications from lighting manufacturers, and there are many websites that offer general intensity values for various types of lights. Table 10.2 provides a listing of some of the more common light intensities. You can specify light intensity parameters in the Intensity group of the Intensity/Color/Distribution rollout for any photometric light.

TABLE 10.2: LIGHT INTENSITY FOR COMMON LIGHTS

WATTS	LUMENS
Household Lightbulbs	
15	105
40	445–490
60	555–890
75	1,080–1,200
100	1,420–1,750
150	2,650–2,850
200	3,250–3,930
Household Halogen Lamps	
40	410
50	530
60	880
75	940
100	1,400
Mercury Vapor Lamps	
100	4,200
125	5,000
250	11,000
400	20,000
1,000	55,000
High-Pressure Sodium Vapor Lamps	
100	9,500
250	30,000
400	50,000
1,000	130,000

Specifying Linear and Area Light Dimensions

Two of the light types, linear and area, have some dimension beyond a single point. For this reason, linear and area lights have special rollouts that allow you to specify their size. For a linear light, you need to specify only the length of the light, such as a 2- or 4-foot fluorescent tube. Area lights need a length and a width.

When you choose a linear light, you will see a parameter rollout in the Command Panel named Linear Light Parameters. It contains a single setting that lets you set the length of the linear light. Similarly, the area light offers the Area Light Parameters rollout; its length and width settings allow you to adjust the size of the area light.

In addition to these settings, you will want to be aware of the Area Shadows options that relate to these types of lights. For example, if you have an interior scene with an area light close to the foreground, you should specify an area shadow for this light. You can then choose a rectangle light from the Modes drop-down list of the Area Shadows rollout. This option simulates a flat, rectangular light source to produce the shadows. You can then enter the size of the area light in the Area Light Dimensions rollout.

Understanding Dynamic Range

You have already experimented a bit with dynamic range in VIZ, even if you were unaware of the adjustments you were making earlier in this chapter. Within the Environment and Effects dialog box in the Logarithmic Exposure Control Parameters rollout, you adjusted the Brightness parameter to control the *dynamic range*.

To understand dynamic range, it is helpful to consider traditional film photography. The camera's shutter speed and the f-stop of the lens are used to control how much light reaches the film over the period of time the shutter is open to the environment. On a bright sunny day, the shutter speed will have to be very rapid to capture an image without overexposing the light sensitive chemicals on the film. On the other hand, a photographer might have to use a tripod to take steady photos at twilight because the exposure times must be very long to allow enough light to expose the film. These methods were developed to deal with exposing sensitive film to the large dynamic range of light in the real world.

Our eyes have pupils that dilate and many other mechanisms to control the amount of light our retinas are exposed to. Human eyes can distinguish light that is 10 million-billion times brighter than the dimmest light we can perceive. We perceive a wide dynamic range of visible light, but this is still a narrow range within the entire electromagnetic spectrum.

Computer monitors display white only about one hundred times brighter than they display black. Therefore, monitors have a very limited dynamic range. When you make a radiosity lighting simulation based upon real-world photometric light sources, the lighting data covers a wide dynamic range suitable for perception by our eyes. Unfortunately, we must display this data on a computer monitor and a huge amount of information is lost. To compensate, we use exposure control in VIZ to match the large lighting dataset to the limited dynamic range that the monitor is capable of displaying.

As you'll learn in Chapter 11, HDRIs (High Dynamic Range Images) are a new way to store raster images with much more information representing a great range of light intensity. All the data in an HDRI cannot be displayed on the monitor at one time, since this would exceed the monitor's narrow dynamic range. However, HDRI data can be used with more accuracy in a radiosity lighting simulation and can be reused in scenes that are lit by candlelight and again in daylight.

Exposure control is the way VIZ moves through the larger dynamic range of visible light and maps it to what can be displayed on a monitor. There are several exposure control algorithms to choose from in VIZ. Let's explore the options:

Type **8** on the keyboard or choose Rendering ➤ Environment and open the pop-up in the Exposure Control rollout to explore the various exposure control algorithms.

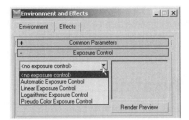

Automatic Exposure Control   As the name implies, this algorithm automatically samples the image and builds a histogram to give reasonable color separation in the rendered image. It excels at displaying very dim lighting in stills and scenes with low dynamic range. Automatic Exposure Control should never be used in an animation because each frame would have a different histogram and would cause the movie to flicker.

WARNING   *Automatic Exposure Control does not work with mental ray (see Chapter 11).*

Logarithmic Exposure Control   This is your general-purpose exposure control algorithm, and it is good for stills and animations. It is best for scenes with very high dynamic range (where there are very bright as well as very dark areas in the image). Exposure control maps the lighting data from the radiosity solution (which has high dynamic range) to RGB values on the monitor (very limited dynamic range). Figure 10.24 shows the interface. Here are its controls:

Brightness, Contrast, and Mid Tones   These are the main controls that give you visual feedback in the viewport without requiring you to render or recalculate the radiosity solution.

Physical Scale   Use this parameter to specify a physical scale for standard lights. Normally you would be using photometric light sources in a radiosity rendering, but this feature is provided in case you have a legacy scene that uses standard lights. The units are in candelas. Set the value to the brightest light source in your scene to give your radiosity solution some basis for realism.

NOTE   *Each standard light's Multiplier parameter is multiplied by the Physical Scale to arrive at a light intensity in candelas. Photometric lights are unaffected by the Physical Scale parameter.*

Color Correction   The color that you put into the color swatch will be pure white in the rendering. All the other colors are shifted to compensate when this parameter is checked. Color Correction can remove the color cast that comes from light sources if desired.

Desaturate Low Levels   This feature simulates how the human eye switches from cone to rod vision in dim lighting conditions. You see very dim areas without any color (desaturated) because you perceive this light information with the rods in your eyes, which only sense intensity levels. This feature is only apparent in very dim areas where less than 50 lux illuminate the scene.

Affect Indirect Only   Turn this on only if you are using standard lights in a radiosity rendering. When this is checked, it overrides the Physical Scale parameter and the image is rendered much like a scanline rendering. This is helpful for comparisons between scanline and radiosity renderings.

Exterior Daylight   Check Exterior Daylight to compensate for the extreme intensity of sunny outdoor scenes. You still can adjust Brightness, Contrast, and Midtones as usual, but everything is shifted several orders of magnitude so the image is not overexposed.

FIGURE 10.24

Logarithmic Exposure Control

Pseudo Color Exposure Control   Pseudo Color is only used to analyze the lighting data from your radiosity solution. This analysis can be invaluable to lighting designers who benefit from the real-world data that is generated from such a simulation. The interface is quite different from the other exposure control algorithms because its purpose is also quite different.

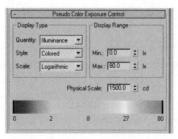

The viewport displays the scene in vibrant hues, obviously not how the scene looks to the eye. The hues are there to help you visualize the lighting data's illuminance or Luminance values.

NOTE   *Luminance is a measure of how bright or dark we perceive a surface because it's based on the value of light reflected. Illuminance is the quantity of light energy per unit time per unit area, and it is a measure of how much energy has fallen on a surface without the measurement being dependent on the size of the surface.*

You can shift the hues by adjusting the Min and Max display range parameters. They affect the color ramp scale units that are shown both in the Environment and Effects dialog box as well as the rendered image.

New!

When you make a rendering using Pseudo Color Exposure Control, the image will have a calibration scale that is automatically added to the bottom of the image as shown in Figure 10.25. This visual data can help you (or your lighting consultant) select the proper luminaires for the fixtures that are based upon your lighting design intent.

FIGURE 10.25
Illuminance pseudo color rendering

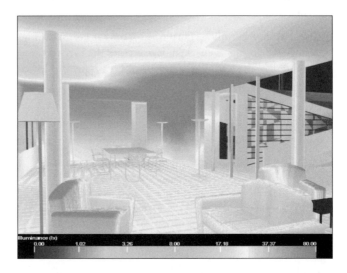

There is a special tool, geared toward lighting engineers and designers, that is meant to be used in conjunction with Pseudo Color Exposure Control called Lighting Analysis. Let's see how it works:

1. In your scene that already has a radiosity solution displayed with pseudo color, choose Rendering ➤ Advanced Lighting ➤ Lighting Analysis....

2. Your cursor shows the eyedropper symbol. Drag the cursor across a viewport showing the shaded pseudo color data. The Lighting Analysis dialog box will display dynamic numerical data at the point on the surface you select in the scene (Figure 10.26).

Using this tool, you can obtain real-world lighting data including average, min, and max numbers for luminance, illuminance, reflectance, and transmittance at any point you select based upon your radiosity simulation.

Assembling an Articulated Luminaire

In this section, you will learn how to make an *assembly* that wires important parameters from a light source together with a light fixture shown with a streamlined user interface. The assembled structure is called a *luminaire* in VIZ.

FIGURE 10.26
Lighting Analysis
numerical data

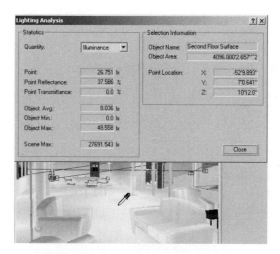

You will also learn the basics of *kinematics* in this section in order to link the joints of an articulated desk lamp in a realistic fashion. Kinematics is the study of articulated motion, and you will be learning the differences between forward and inverse kinematics with the desk lamp model. When you are done, you will have a luminaire that you can quickly drop into a working scene and adjust in a user-friendly way.

Transforming Pivot Points

You begin by adjusting the pivot points of the sample model in preparation for linking its joints together in a hierarchy. Each one of these objects (except the Base) has a joint where two parts meet. The pivot point of each part must coincide with that object's axis of rotation.

1. Open the file `Luminaire01.max` from the CD.

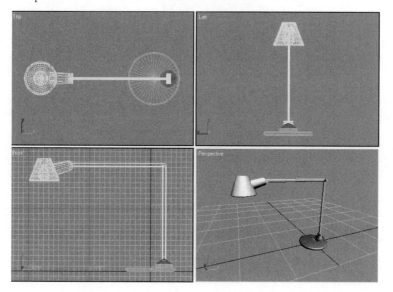

2. Examine the parts of this simple desk lamp model. Type **H** on the keyboard to open the Select Objects dialog box. There are five parts to this lamp: Arm01, Arm02, Base, Hood, and Swivel. Select each object in turn and identify it on the screen.

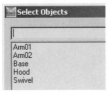

3. Switch to the Front viewport and select the Hood object. Zoom into the area where Hood meets Arm2.

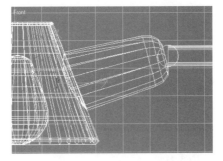

4. Click the Hierarchy tab of the Command Panel. Click the Pivot button and turn on Affect Pivot Only in the Move/Rotate/Scale group.

5. Click the Select and Move tool. Move Hood's pivot to the center of the round joint on the right by dragging the Transform gizmo. Turn off the Affect Pivot Only button when you're done.

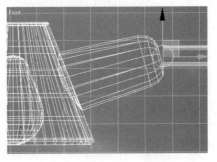

6. Repeat steps 3–5 for Arm01 and Arm02 by moving their respective pivots to the center of each of their round joints.

Aligning the Light Source with the Fixture

You may notice that a lightbulb geometry has been modeled to fit inside the desk lamp's hood. Next you'll add the light source.

1. Click the Create tab of the Command Panel and select the Lights category button. Change the pop-up to Photometric and click Target Point in the Object Type rollout.

2. Drag out a target point light in the Top viewport without regard to its position.

3. Move the point source itself inside the lightbulb in both the Top and Front viewports.

4. Right-click the Top viewport to activate it; then select the Point01.Target and press Alt+A to invoke the Align command.

5. Instead of trying to click the alignment object, type **H** to use the Select Objects dialog box and select the Point01 from the list.

6. In the Align Selection dialog box, check X Position and Y Position. Choose Center for both Current and Target radio buttons to align the target directly below its source, as shown in Figure 10.27. Click OK to close the dialog box when you're finished.

7. Select Point01 and switch to the Modify tab of the Command Panel.

8. In the Intensity/Color/Distribution rollout, click the pop-up and change the distribution to Spotlight. Change the bulb color to Halogen.

9. Change the intensity to 3,000 candelas and click the Multiplier check box to activate this feature. One hundred percent is now 100% of 3,000 candelas.

FIGURE 10.27
Aligning the Target
Point

Move the point source here.

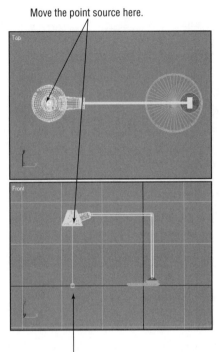

Align the target directly below the source.

Using Schematic View

Schematic View is a program within VIZ that helps you visualize the relationships between *nodes* in a scene. Nodes are containers for objects' geometry, transforms, modifiers, materials, relationships, and so on. Visualizing nodes can be especially helpful when establishing parent-child hierarchical links like you are about to do with the desk lamp.

Link and Unlink tools are available in Schematic View, allowing you to set up hierarchies. You can arrange nodes in a structure that resembles the model you are linking, which gives you a visual reference to the kinematic chain you want to animate.

NOTE *Schematic View was designed for complex character animation and comes to VIZ from 3ds max. A full exploration of Schematic View is beyond the scope of this book.*

1. Click the Open Schematic View button on the main toolbar.

2. Click the Connect button on the Schematic View toolbar.

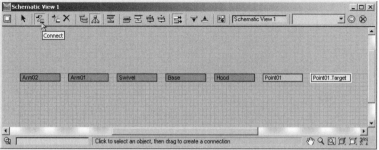

3. Drag a link between the Point01 and Hood nodes in Schematic View. Your cursor will change to the Connect icon while you are dragging and a rubber band will connect your cursor and the Point01 node.

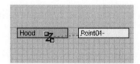

TIP   *Always drag nodes from child to parent in Schematic View.*

4. Connect Point01.Target with Hood also by dragging a link between these two nodes. The Hood is now said to be the parent of the point light and its target (Point01 and Point01.Target are siblings in this family hierarchy metaphor).

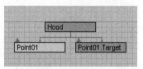

5. Continue making relationships in Schematic View by linking Hood to Arm02 next. Then connect Arm02 to Arm01. Arm01 should be linked to Swivel and finally Swivel should be the child of Base. When you are all done, your hierarchy should look like Figure 10.28. Notice that the whole family are children of Base. This is as intended so that you will be able to move the entire model with the Base.

TIP   *If you make any mistakes connecting nodes, you can use the Unlink Selected button to make corrections, or you can open the* Luminaire02.max *file from the CD.*

FIGURE 10.28
Node Hierarchy

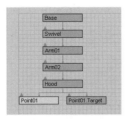

FORWARD KINEMATICS

So far you have established links between various nodes in your model. These links establish what is called a *kinematic chain*. Kinematics is the study of moving chains of linked nodes.

In forward kinematics (FK) you transform the top node in the hierarchy to affect the entire chain. Let's see what this means with an example:

1. Close the Schematic View dialog box. Choose Edit ➤ Hold to experiment without worrying about altering the scene.

2. Select the Base object and move it in the Perspective viewport. Observe that all the objects move together because they are linked to this top ancestor.

3. Select Arm02 and move it. Notice that Arm02, Hood, the Point light, and its target move as one. However, Arm01, Swivel, and Base remain behind. Only the object and its children are affected. The object's parents stay at home, if you will. Click Undo.

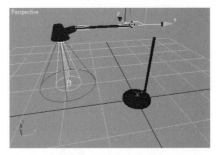

INVERSE KINEMATICS

In inverse kinematics (IK), the chain is resolved in reverse fashion. You transform the bottom node in the hierarchy and thereby affect all of its ancestors. Instead of all moving with the child, the nodes in IK try to stay connected while the top node stays behind. Again, an example is the best way to understand this concept:

1. Switch to the Hierarchy tab of the Command Panel.

2. Click the IK button and then click the Interactive IK button to turn on this mode. Any transforms you now perform are in IK mode until you turn this button off.

3. Select the Point01.Target and move it in the XY plane. Observe how all the nodes move as they need to to stay connected with all the other nodes in the chain. All nodes move except the Base, which is called the *terminator* of the IK chain.

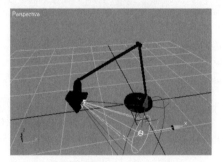

4. Turn off Interactive IK mode and choose Edit ➢ Fetch to end your experiment. A dialog box will appear asking if it's OK to restore. Click Yes.

JOINT CONSTRAINTS

You may have noticed that when you were experimenting with moving the light's target in IK mode, even though the lamp parts stayed connected, they got all twisted out of shape. We all know that in the real world, these kinds of simple mechanical joints have a limited range of motion. When you specify *joint constraints* you set up each joint with information about how it is allowed to rotate, how far, and how easily. Joint constraints help make the desk lamp's motion more realistic.

1. Switch to the Parent Reference Coordinate System in the pop-up on the main toolbar when working with joints. This is especially important if any of your objects have rotated pivots with respect to the World Coordinate System.

2. Select the Hood object and switch to the Hierarchy tab of the Command Panel. Make sure the larger IK button is still selected and Interactive IK mode is off. Scroll down to the bottom roll-out called Rotational Joints. Right-click the perspective view, do a Zoom Extents Selected on Hood, and click the Select and Rotate tool.

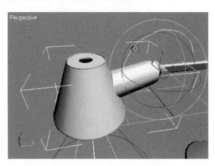

TIP *You can force the default lighting to display in a viewport, even when you have already added light sources to the model. Choose Customize ➢ Viewport Configuration. On the Rendering Method tab, in the Rendering Options group, check Default Lighting. Radio buttons underneath allow you to select default lighting with either one or two lights.*

3. Notice that the green ring of the Transform gizmo indicates the direction this joint should rotate. Uncheck the Active check boxes in the X Axis and Z Axis groups in the Rotational Joints rollout. Now this joint will only be allowed to rotate in one direction as designed.

4. In the Y Axis group, check Limited. Then drag the From spinner down to about –45 degrees. The Hood will rotate in the viewport as you set this joint limit.

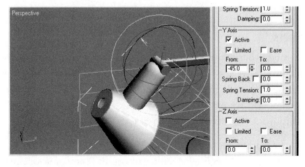

5. Drag the To spinner to about 45 degrees to set the upper rotation limit.

6. Set Damping to 0.5 to give this joint 50% resistance to being rotated.

7. Select Arm02 and uncheck Active for both the X and Z axes since this joint should also only rotate in the Y direction. Check Limited and set the limits from –45 to 45 degrees. Give this joint 50% damping also.

8. Press the PageUp key on the keyboard to move to the next ancestor up in the hierarchy (PageDn goes the other way). You should now have Arm01 selected.

9. Uncheck Active for both the X and Z axes for this joint. Limit this joint to a range of motion between –30 and 30 degrees without damping.

10. Hit the PageUp key again to advance to the Swivel object. This time, uncheck its X and Y active axes. You don't need to set limits for the swivel joint because it can spin all the way around.

11. PageUp to the Base object. Uncheck Active for all three rotational joint axes since the base shouldn't rotate at all.

12. Switch the Reference Coordinate System back from Parent to View now that you are done setting joint constraints (see step 1).

13. Finally, you must set the Base as terminator of the kinematic chain. The terminator will not move relative to the rest of the chain. Open the Object Parameters rollout near the top of the IK Hierarchy panel. Check Terminator and you are done.

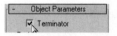

You have now set up the joint constraints for the articulated desk lamp model. The lamp moves in a realistic fashion, based upon what each one the mechanical joints range of motion allows.

TESTING IK JOINT CONSTRAINTS

Now that you have gone to all the trouble of specifying how each joint is allowed to rotate, how far, and how easily, it is time to test the model and see if it meets your expectations.

1. Choose Edit ➢ Hold whenever you are testing. There are some things in IK that cannot be undone, so holding is always a good idea.

2. Click the Hierarchy tab, then the IK category button, and turn on Interactive IK mode.

3. Select the Point01.Target object, hit the spacebar to lock your selection, and move the target around in all directions. Observe the motion of all of the parts of the desk lamp model. If you want to tweak anything in its settings, now is the time to do it.

4. When you are satisfied with the behavior of the desk lamp, turn off Interactive IK mode and perform an Edit ➢ Fetch.

The lamp should move in an accurate and realistic fashion. You can easily transform all the parts of the fixture by dragging the light's target wherever you want illumination.

USING THE HD SOLVER

One problem with investing so much time into building an articulated model is that it requires your colleagues to share the same high level of knowledge to take advantage of your work. If they don't understand IK, then they won't be able to articulate the model as you intend.

One thing you can do to make your model more user-friendly is to apply the HD (History Dependent) Solver to the IK chain. No longer will users of your model need to understand the difference between forward and inverse kinematics in order to use your functioning model.

The HD Solver makes it unnecessary to switch in and out of Interactive IK mode to transform the articulated model. All the IK calculations are applied to your model permanently, and people can articulate it right away without understanding the technicalities of IK.

1. Select the Point01.Target object. You must select the child end of the chain in this step.

2. Choose Animation ➢ IK Solvers ➢ HD Solver. A rubber band will attach to your cursor. Instead of trying to click an object, you can be more specific by selecting it by name. Be careful not to make a mistake; this step is not undoable.

3. Type **H** to open the Select Objects dialog box. Select Swivel and click Pick.

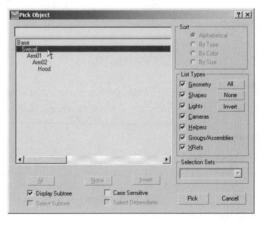

TIP *Check Display Subtree (on by default in VIZ 2005) in any Select Objects dialog box to display the hierarchy as indents in the list.*

You selected the Swivel object in step 3 and not the Base because the HD Solver should not be bound to the terminator (that's just how it works). Remember to bind it to the second object from the top of the hierarchy. Observe how the HD Solver graphically displays the limited joint constraints showing their range of motion in the viewport as shown in Figure 10.29.

FIGURE 10.29
HD Solver

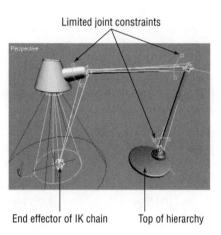

Limited joint constraints

End effector of IK chain   Top of hierarchy

BINDING THE END EFFECTOR TO ITS PARENT

The *end effector* is the object that you move to transform the chain when you're using the HD Solver. In this case, the end effector is the light's target.

You will find that you cannot move the Point01.Target away from where it was when you applied the HD Solver. This would be a serious flaw because it would mean that the lamp would be "stuck" in this position forever. Fortunately, the simple solution is to bind the end effector to its parent.

1. Select the Point01.Target object.

2. Switch to the Motion tab of the Command Panel. Click the Parameters button if it's not already selected and then scroll down near the bottom of the IK Controller Parameters rollout. Click the Link button under End Effector Parent in the End Effectors group.

3. Select the Base object from the Perspective viewport. The Base is now linked as the parent to the end effector. In other words, you have linked the bottom and top of the chain together, making a complete mathematical unit.

TESTING THE ARTICULATED CHAIN

Now that you have applied the HD Solver to the kinematic chain, and bound the end effector to its parent, it is important to test the behavior of the system to make sure it works the way you designed it. If you discover any problems in the testing, you will know you have to go back and fix them before you assemble the luminaire in the next section. If the desk lamp moves in a realistic fashion without using Interactive IK mode, it passes the test. Let's test the articulated chain now:

1. Choose Edit ➢ Hold for this test.

2. Move the Base object. The entire desk lamp hierarchy should move freely. If the light's target seems stuck in position, go back and bind the end effector to the top parent as described in Binding the End Effector to its Parent.

3. Move the light target with Interactive IK mode turned off. The parts of the desk lamp should articulate to keep up with the target object. The joints should move in a realistic way, where each joint moves within prescribed limits with damping where appropriate.

4. Type **H** on the keyboard to have a look at the object hierarchy. The Base is the terminator and is the top-level parent. Point01.Target is the end effector and is a sibling with Point01 at the bottom of the hierarchy.

5. Choose Edit ➢ Fetch after you are satisfied that your scene is working properly. If you made any mistakes, go back and correct them, or open the `Luminaire05.max` file from the CD to continue.

ASSEMBLE THE LUMINAIRE

An *assembly* is a containing data structure that organizes a light fixture and its light source into a simplified interface called a *luminaire*. You can think of an assembly much like a group, but with an added feature called a *head*. The head is a classified as a helper object that contains the simplified user interface.Let's assemble the luminaire now:

1. Select all the objects except for Point01.Target. Remember to leave the light's target out of the assembly so that you'll be able to transform it independently later on. Everything going into the assembly will be treated as one object (much like a group).

2. Choose Group ➤ Assembly ➤ Assemble. The Create Assembly dialog box appears.

3. Type **DeskLamp01** in the name box. Notice that Luminaire is the only head object listed because there is only one head helper that ships with VIZ 2005. Click OK.

TIP *It is possible to create custom assembly head helpers with the MAXScript programming language.*

4. Click the Modify tab of the Command Panel. Observe the simplified interface of the assembly object.

5. Type **H** on the keyboard and notice that the assembly shows up in square brackets, just like a group would appear in the list. There are now only two objects in the scene: the DeskLamp assembly and the target that articulates the entire rig.

WIRING PARAMETERS

The assembly's interface is very simple and contains only the Dimmer spinner and Filter color swatch. The only problem with the interface of the assembly is that it doesn't actually work yet.

Right now there is no behind-the-scenes connection between the user interface components of the assembly head and the actual parameters of the light source they represent. To make this connection, you will *wire the parameters now:*.

1. Select the DeskLamp01 assembly.

2. Choose Group ➢ Assembly ➢ Open. Red selection brackets appear around the opened assembly.

NOTE *An open assembly displays red selection brackets while an open group displays pink selection brackets. Remember these colors; they'll help you identify and differentiate between the different ways of organizing objects.*

Notice that there is a green 2D symbol of a lamp that appears on the grid near the Base. This symbol represents the assembly head itself and only appears in an opened assembly object as shown in Figure 10.30.

FIGURE 10.30
Opened Assembly

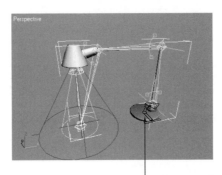

Assembly head helper symbol

3. Select the head helper symbol. Type **H** to examine the hierarchy. The assembly head is the DeskLamp01 object itself when the assembly is opened.

4. Right-click in the Perspective viewport on the assembly head and select Wire Parameters from the transform quad.

5. A small context menu will appear. The parameters are organized into two categories: Transform and Object. From this small menu select Object (Luminaire) ➢ Dimmer.

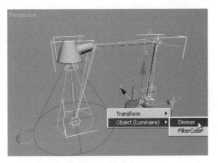

6. A rubber band will be attached to your cursor. Click the Point01 light source object.

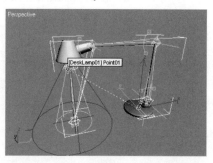

TIP *You may have to Arc Rotate so that you can see under the lamp if you can't see the spotlight symbol. If so, Arc Rotate first and then repeat steps 5 and 6.*

7. Again, from a small context menu, select Object (Target Point) ➢ Multiplier.

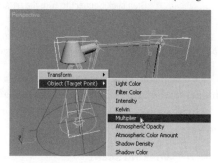

8. The Parameter Wiring dialog box appears with both the Dimmer in the head and the Multiplier in the light selected. Click the two-way arrow and then click Connect to wire these parameters together (Figure 10.31). Close the dialog box.

9. Right-click again on the head object and select Wire Parameters from the quad.

10. Select Object (Luminaire) ➢ Filter Color from the context menu.

11. Click the Point01 light with the rubber band. Select Object (Target Point) ➢ Filter Color.

12. Establish a two-way connection between the Filter Color parameters like you did in step 8. Click Connect and close the Parameter Wiring dialog box.

13. The last step is to close the assembly. With the DeskLamp01 head still selected, choose Group ➢ Assembly ➢ Close.

The parameters from the assembly head are now wired together with the light source parameters they represent.

14. Save your work as Luminaire07.max (provided also on the CD for reference).

FIGURE 10.31
Wiring Parameters

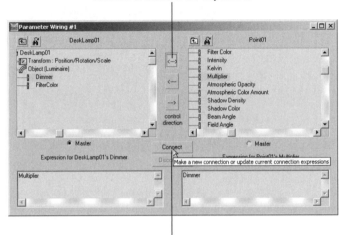

Click here to establish two-way control.

Then click Connect to wire the parameters.

NOTE *Try changing the Filter Color and Dimmer in the assembly to see how the light source responds.*

The DeskLamp model is completed. The complexities of the articulated IK hierarchy and the photometric luminaire are hidden within the user-friendly assembly where you can easily adjust the intensity and filter color of the light source. You can articulate the desk lamp by moving the light target in a very intuitive fashion.

MERGE THE DESKLAMP INTO A WORKING SCENE

To enjoy the fruits of your labor, try merging the DeskLamp into a working project or a blank scene. Take a look at this very simple example:

1. Choose File ➢ Reset or open a project you have been working on earlier.

2. Choose Customize ➢ Units Setup and change your Units to U.S. Standard feet and inches.

3. Create a box representing a desk volume about 30″ in height.

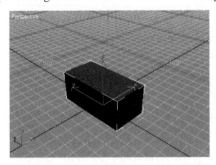

4. Switch to the Utilities tab of the Command Panel.

5. Open the Asset Browser utility as shown in Chapter 9.

6. Navigate to the folder where the DeskLamp luminaire files are stored on your hard drive (or use the files on the CD if you prefer).

7. Position and resize the Asset Browser so that you can see both the Luminaire07.max file and the box in the Perspective viewport.

8. Turn on Autogrid on the Extras toolbar.

9. Drag the thumbnail of Luminaire07.max onto the top of the desk in the viewport as shown in Figure 10.32.

FIGURE 10.32
Using the Asset Browser and Autogrid

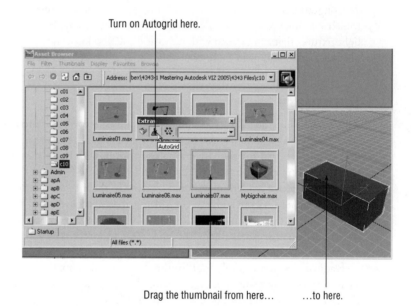

10. Release the mouse button on top of the desk surface and select Merge from the small context menu. Click OK to the Merge. The Raytrace Global Tracks dialog box, should it appear.

11. Click on top of the desk surface to locate your articulated luminaire assembly in all its glory. Autogrid ensures that the DeskLamp is placed and oriented according to the surface you select.

TIP   *Try merging light fixtures onto a ceiling with Autogrid. It works well when ceiling-mounted light fixtures are designed upside down with the pivot of the assembly on the grid at what will be the ceiling surface.*

12. Close the Asset Browser.

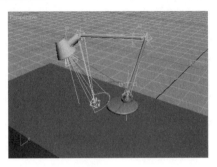

Congratulations on completing this long and complex exercise. You have seen how to build a photometric luminaire with an articulated kinematic hierarchy. In other words, you know how to make light fixtures that can be used with radiosity, and you know how to create realistic behavior in simple machines. You will need these two skills often when you are modeling real-world light fixtures.

Summary

This chapter introduced you to some of the radiosity tools and methods available in VIZ. As you've seen, there are a great number of tools and optional parameters that you can work with. Use this chapter as a springboard for your own experimentation with radiosity rendering. For example, you may want to experiment with the Initial Quality and Refine Iterations settings to see how much quality you can get from a rendering without resorting to the Regather Indirect Illumination setting. I'd also encourage you to try out some of the settings that weren't directly covered in an exercise, such as the Light Painting options in the Radiosity dialog box or the object meshing parameters for individual objects. If you need further help, the VIZ 2005 user reference offers some great information. Search for *Modeling Global Illumination with Radiosity* and *Radiosity Workflows* for general information on radiosity.

Radiosity is an incredible tool for the design professional, and VIZ offers this very complex tool in a relatively easy-to-use package. Although the rendering may take a while, the tool is still one of the faster radiosity rendering programs available. I highly recommend that you gain as much familiarity with it as you can by practicing the exercises in this chapter and experimenting on your own with projects you are familiar with. You'll be rewarded with better control over your lighting schemes, and ultimately, you'll have more confidence in your designs.

As you gain more experience with VIZ, try building your own luminaires for a worthy challenge. You can gradually build a library of luminaires to reuse in future projects.

Chapter 11

Using mental ray

IN CHAPTER 10, YOU learned how to render an advanced lighting simulation of the Villa Savoye model with the radiosity renderer. Radiosity was originally popularized in the mid '90s by Lightscape Technologies, which made a stand-alone product called Lightscape (later bought out by Autodesk). Radiosity technology was integrated into VIZ 4, and brought with it the ability to create stunningly realistic images with its physically based lighting renderer.

New!

Now in VIZ 2005, the bar has been set higher with the integration of the mental ray renderer.

In this chapter, you will learn how to use the mental ray renderer. As you learned in Chapters 9 and 10, Radiance files containing a high dynamic range are now supported in VIZ 2005. Radiance HDRI (High Dynamic Range Image) files are another hot topic in computer graphics and you will be using them in conjunction with mental ray in this chapter.

- ◆ Understanding mental ray
- ◆ Using Photon Maps
- ◆ Final Gathering
- ◆ Contour Renderings
- ◆ Skylight Global Illumination
- ◆ Using High Dynamic Range Images

TIP   It is up to you to educate yourself on the numerous minor settings that can help refine the mental ray rendering process. It is worth reading the technical details on mental ray in the VIZ User Reference if you plan to use it professionally.

Understanding mental ray

mental ray is an optional renderer that you can use in VIZ. More than just a renderer, mental ray uses special materials, lights, cameras, and rendering controls. Therefore ideally, you should decide whether to use the default scanline renderer or the mental ray renderer before you begin applying materials in your scene.

NOTE *A radiosity solution is calculated in conjunction with the default scanline renderer. As you saw in Chapter 10, the difference is that radiosity stores indirect illumination and the scanline processes direct illumination.*

Not only can mental ray create a physically correct lighting simulation, but it can also render all imaginable visual phenomena (including some not possible to simulate with radiosity) through its fully programmable libraries of shaders.

You may remember from Chapter 7 that *shaders* are the algorithms that enable the primary components of a material (the ambient, diffuse, and specular colors, for example) to be blended together in different ways. With the mental ray renderer, shaders take on the expanded definition as any algorithms used in rendering.

mental ray's shaders are used in materials, lights, cameras, and in the renderer itself. The fact that shaders are programmable allows advanced animation and effects companies to push the computer graphics bar even higher. The larger firms in the film and game markets have resources to hire programmers to write subroutines for shader libraries that feature new procedural textures, materials, new lighting models, and much more.

TIP *ShadeTree is an interactive visual shader authoring environment that supports mental ray and the popular Pixar RenderMan renderer. You can find out more about ShadeTree at* www.cinegrfx.com.

Programmers can also repackage existing shaders in new ways as mental ray phenomena (scripted shader trees). There are many shader libraries and phenomena (including the LumeTools Collection and Physics phenomena) that ship with the version of mental ray that is integrated with VIZ 2005, so you'll have a lot to choose from.

Most smaller firms (including most architects) won't have the resources to hire programmers for their projects, but they still benefit from the interest and continued shader development that mental ray enjoys in larger markets.

NOTE *In addition to VIZ 2005, mental images' mental ray has been integrated into Discreet's 3ds max, Softimage | 3D and Softimage | XSI, Alias's Maya, Side Effects Software's Houdini 5, SolidWorks PhotoWorks 2, Dassault Système's CATIA V4 and V5 products, and others. You can find out more about mental images and see their impressive architectural rendering gallery at* www.mentalimages.com.

mental ray is a complete rendering system that can calculate any visual phenomenon that you wish to simulate, including both direct and global illumination, caustics, ray traced reflections and refractions, and more. In fact, mental ray is a renderer of such power and depth that entire volumes have been written on the subject. We will concentrate on the basic features of mental ray in this chapter so that you can get started on a sample project.

TIP *Please refer to* Rendering with mental ray, book 1, *by Thomas Driemeyer (Springer Verlag, 2001) for the definitive text on using this renderer. Also refer to* Programming mental ray *(by the same author and publisher) to learn how to program shaders (C or C++ programming experienced required).*

mental ray takes great advantage of *parallelism* in information processing systems. Multiple threads can run in parallel (at the same time) on one or more processors, in one machine, or across a network to process your rendering.

In addition, only the incremental changes to the scene database are rendered in the sequential frames of an animation. This can save huge amounts of time as compared to radiosity, whose solution often needs to be entirely recalculated for each frame under changing lighting conditions.

WARNING *Contact a skilled network administrator to set up mental ray for rendering in parallel across your network. Refer to Help* ➤ *User Reference and search for Network Rendering for more information.*

When you render an image with mental ray, you'll notice a big difference in the Rendered Frame Window. You are probably used to the way the default renderer processes scanlines from the top of the frame downward. mental ray processes frames in *buckets*—small rectangular blocks of pixels.

NOTE *Processing the frame in buckets creates great modularity that allows the massive parallelism that this renderer enjoys; each bucket can be given to a different thread for processing. Therefore, mental ray can take advantage of parallel distributed processing more than most renderers.*

Figure 11.1 shows how the buckets appear in the Rendered Frame Window. You will see the buckets firsthand in the next section when you render with mental ray using the sample project.

The order that the buckets are rendered may seem like a mystery to you at first. By default, mental ray chooses the bucket order based upon minimizing the memory cost of switching to the next one. If you're rendering buckets across a network, bucket order also is influenced by the need to minimize traffic and load balance the processors, so the buckets may seem to appear in the Rendered Frame Window at random.

FIGURE 11.1
Bucket processing in
Rendered Frame
window

Buckets that have already been rendered   Buckets yet to be processed

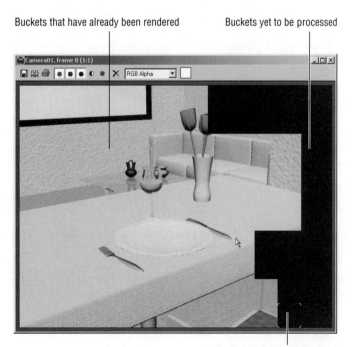

Current bucket being rendered

Setting Up mental ray

Now that you understand what mental ray can do and how it renders, there are two things you will need to do to actually start working with mental ray in VIZ. You'll need to verify a setting in the Preference Settings dialog box, and then assign the renderer in the Render Scene dialog box.

1. Open the file Room.max from the CD. The sample file contains a single room interior with furnishings. The materials have already been set up for the default scanline renderer and presently, no light sources are in the model.

2. Choose Customize ➤ Preferences. Click the mental ray tab.

   Make sure Enable mental ray Extensions is checked in the General group. This should already be checked as it is on by default. It is important to be aware that this setting exists, in case you ever encounter a scene where this has explicitly been turned off (otherwise mental ray would not work).

3. Click OK to close the Preference Settings dialog box.

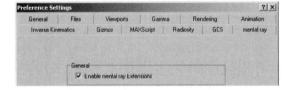

The next thing to do to enable mental ray is assign it as the production renderer in this scene.

4. Press the F10 function key to open the Render Scene dialog box. Click the Common tab and close the Common Parameters rollout. Then open the Assign Renderer rollout.

5. Click the browse (...) button next to the Production renderer, which currently is assigned to the Default Scanline Renderer.

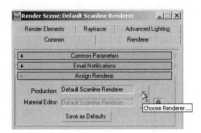

WARNING *Although it is possible to assign different Production and Material Editor renderers, it is not recommended (they are locked together by default). It makes more sense to view materials in the same way that you will render them.*

6. The Choose Renderer dialog box appears. Select mental ray Renderer from the short list and click OK.

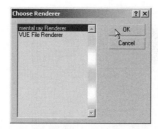

The scene is now enabled for rendering with mental ray, both for the Production renderer and in the Material Editor. Notice that the tabs in the Render Scene dialog box changed after you changed renderers. Now Indirect Illumination and Processing tabs replace the Raytracer and Advanced Lighting tabs. In addition, the controls that were on the Renderer tab have changed—they are now specific to mental ray.

7. Close the Render Scene dialog box without rendering yet.

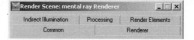

The Material Editor and mental ray

When you set up a scene to use mental ray, new materials and maps become available to you in the Material Editor. In addition, you can use lights and camera features specific to mental ray.

Let's take a quick tour of the Material Editor to see what has changed when you're using the mental ray renderer.

1. Press M to open the Material Editor.

2. Find the available gray sample slot on the lower right, scrolling through the samples if necessary, and click to select it.

Most of the sample slots have already been filled with materials from this scene, and you will be revising several of them in the next section.

3. Click the material type button as shown in Figure 11.2.

FIGURE 11.2
Changing
material types

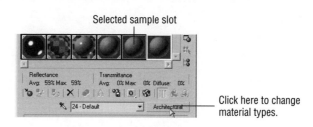

The Material/Map Browser dialog box appears as shown in Figure 11.3.

FIGURE 11.3
New material types
for mental ray

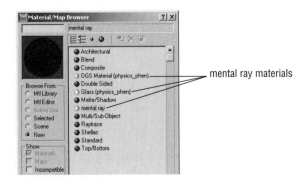

mental ray materials

Notice that the mental ray materials are represented as yellow spheres in the Material/Map Browser.

4. Double-click the mental ray material to change the material type from Architectural to this new material.

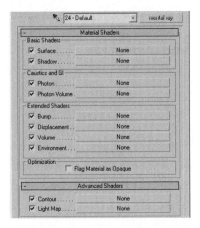

The mental ray material's shaders are grouped into categories of Basic Shaders, Caustics and GI, and Extended Shaders, and there are two more in the Advanced Shaders rollout.

5. In the Material Editor, click the sample slot to the left of the current one. Currently an Architectural material is filling this unused slot. Open the mental ray Connection rollout at the bottom of the panel.

You see shaders organized into the same categories in which they appeared in the mental ray material. The difference is that the mental ray Connection rollout provides access to these shaders from within the Architectural material.

TIP   You can also find a mental ray Connection rollout in the Standard material. Using this rollout can be helpful in legacy scenes that were created in earlier versions of VIZ.

Notice that some of the shaders are grayed out because their effects are locked to features in the hosting material. For example, the Surface shader is locked because any map or shader applied to the Diffuse Map in the Physical Qualities rollout would be automatically translated to act as a Surface shader by mental ray.

These settings were not grayed out in the mental ray material because there is no hosting material from which to translate this information. The mental ray material itself can be used to completely describe a material's surface by choosing the appropriate shaders.

6. Click back on the mental ray material's sample slot on the lower right of the Material Editor to select it again.

7. In the Material Shaders rollout, click the None button next to Surface in the Basic Shaders group.

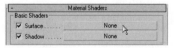

The Material/Map Browser appears again but this time it displays only compatible maps and shaders (materials and incompatible maps and shaders not shown).

8. Scroll down the list in the Material/Map Browser and see how the list goes on and on.

Notice that the mental ray shaders acting as maps are represented as yellow parallelograms in the Material/Map Browser. The green icons are the familiar maps from the default scanline renderer that you can still use with mental ray.

TIP   *mental ray shaders can act as both materials and maps in VIZ. As if that wasn't confusing enough, shaders can also be used in lights, cameras, and the Render Scene dialog box as well.*

Finally, observe the parenthetical descriptions after most of the mental ray shaders acting as maps in the Material/Map Browser. These indicate which shader library the specific shader came from.

NOTE   *Several shader libraries are included in VIZ's implementation of mental ray; you can mix and match these shaders as you see fit. There are shader libraries from Discreet (3ds max), and mental images (base, contour, and physics); and the LumeTools Collection (lume) is also included. Each shader library has its own very technical help file that you can access from links in VIZ's User Reference.*

9. Close the Material/Map Browser and the Material Editor. This completes the quick tour of the changes made to materials with mental ray.

USING VIZ MATERIALS WITH MENTAL RAY

For the most part, mental ray interprets VIZ materials and maps the same way the default scanline renderer does. However, you will get the most reliable results with mental ray by using its own purpose-built shaders, which act as both materials and maps in VIZ.

Because mental ray completely takes over from the default scanline renderer, there are many small gaps, errors, and omissions in mental ray's ability to faithfully reproduce your intentions if you are still using the "regular" materials and maps you are accustomed to from your experience with other renderers.

In order to use VIZ's materials and maps, you must translate them into mental ray's own scene description language prior to rendering—a process that's too complex to detail here.

NOTE *To learn how to deal with this, read the extensive, detailed notes in the User Reference. Choose Help ➢ User Reference. Click the Contents tab and then expand the navigation nodes for Rendering ➢ Renderers ➢ mental ray 3.2 Renderer. Read "Getting Good Results with mental ray" and "Autodesk VIZ Materials in mental ray Renderings."*

Hopefully you haven't been scared off by the warnings associated with using mental ray in VIZ. As you are beginning to see, mental ray is an extremely complex and rich renderer, and although its marriage with VIZ is a happy one, it is not without its issues. The next section discusses one of the most innovative technologies used in mental ray.

Using Photon Maps

Mental images pioneered the use of the *photon map* in mental ray. To understand what the photon map does, it helps to review how the radiosity renderer stores global illumination data. You may remember from Chapter 10 how the radiosity renderer creates a mesh overlaying the geometry in the scene. It is this mesh that stores the data from the lighting simulation. In fact, each vertex in this mesh stores a color (called the vertex color). When these vertex colors are blended together, you see the global illumination in the viewport and rendering. A denser radiosity mesh can hold greater lighting detail and also requires more memory.

Instead of using a geometrical mesh to store lighting data, mental ray can store indirect illumination in a single map that covers all the surfaces of the model that *photons* (light particles) strike.

NOTE *Chapter 17 shows how the Render to Texture feature can create a light map that covers multiple surfaces automatically. This works in much the same way that the photon map works internally within mental ray.*

Since indirect illumination can be stored in a map rather than a geometrical mesh, it requires far less memory. On the downside, a photon map cannot be displayed in the viewport like the radiosity mesh can.

In mental ray, selected light sources can emit photons, which are traced through the scene. These photons are either reflected off surfaces or, when transparent or translucent surfaces are encountered, transmitted through them. Depending on the trace depth, which controls the number of bounces to be calculated, these photons eventually strike a diffuse surface much like a paintball. The photons leave the intensity and color that is picked up in the interactions encountered in each photon's brief flight where they strike in the photon map. Very few of these photons actually hit the picture plane (think of it like the camera lens itself), but it doesn't matter because the photons leave their mark right where they strike—on the wall or floor, for example.

NOTE *Raytracing works a little like a photon map but in reverse. Particles (rays) are traced backward from the picture plane, through various bounces and transmissions through surfaces in the scene, ultimately reaching the light sources that emitted them. Unlike a photon map, only the particles that hit the picture plane are considered in raytracing. Refer to Chapter 7 for a review of raytracing.*

If you only shoot a small number of photons, the room might look like a paintball war zone. The genius of this technique is that when the photons overlap (you can also control their size), mental ray smoothes them together with a sampling algorithm. When you shoot a large number of photons (10,000 is default), a lot of smoothing will occur in the photon map, and the indirect illumination built up by the smoothed photons begins to look good.

An important consideration to keep in mind when using a photon map is that the space in your model will have to be fully enclosed by geometry. Otherwise, photons would escape, and therefore would never get recorded in the photon map. Photons must reflect or refract the number of times set by the trace depth before they are recorded in the photon map.

For example, an interior architectural space must have a ceiling to effectively use the photon map technique. For outdoor scenes, you can enclose the entire model in a skydome (see Chapter 8) and the photons will be contained in the modeled environment.

SIMULATED ILLUMINATION

Direct illumination is light emitted from a source that reflects off a surface and travels directly to the picture plane, and it is easily calculated by any renderer. Computer graphics programs have been able to simulate direct light from the earliest days of Phong shading.

Indirect illumination is much more difficult to simulate and accounts for 99% of the light in the scene, representing all the light that is emitted from sources that does not end up hitting the picture plane. However, indirect illumination influences light that does hit the picture plane (so you see its influence in your rendering) and is critical in making realistic images.

One aspect of indirect illumination is called global illumination (GI), which realistically represents the ambient light in the scene through light inter-reflection. Both mental ray and radiosity can simulate GI, although they do so in different ways. GI effects include color bleeding, which occurs everywhere but is clearly evident when a red wall is next to a white one, for example. Some red color will bleed over and give the white wall a pinkish tint. These subtle visual cues give rendered images a feeling of realism, even if you were not consciously aware of it until now.

mental ray can also simulate another aspect of indirect illumination with the photon map that radiosity cannot simulate—that of a phenomenon referred to as *caustics*. In the science of optics, caustics are the effects of light cast upon a diffuse surface via reflection off of or refraction through another surface.

You will notice caustics effects in the bright spots on the ground when you are looking through a magnifying glass, for example. Another example of caustics is the bright spots that appear on a tablecloth through a wineglass that is lit by a spot light. Caustics effects are focused, stronger light that appears on the final surface.

In the real world, light can be thought of as a wave phenomenon, rather than existing as particles, rays, or photons. All the light in a physical space is experienced simultaneously. You cannot separate a portion of light in a room (thinking of it as individual rays) and say that it doesn't influence the rest of the light at the same time. All the light in a space is actually expressed as a single wave equation in quantum physics. Light is a marvelously complex phenomenon that we can only begin to simulate with computers.

Testing the Photon Map Effects

To see the effects of photon maps, as well as global illumination and caustics, let's make our first series of mental ray renderings. As a reference point, we'll begin with a single direct light source without enabling photon maps. You will first have to add a light source to the model.

1. Open the file `MentalRay.max` from the CD. This is the same sample project you saw in the last section with its materials converted to mental ray shaders.

2. Click the Create tab of the Command Panel and click the Light category button. Click the mr Area Spot button in the Object Type rollout.

Two light sources have been designed to work with mental ray: the mr Area Spot and mr Area Omni. Although you can use the other light types with mental ray, you will get the most reliable results by using these sources.

3. Drag the mr Area Spot light out in the Top viewport as shown in Figure 11.4.

4. Press **H** to open the Select Object dialog box. Select mr Area Spot01 from the list and click Select.

FIGURE 11.4

Creating an mr Area Spot

5. Right-click the Left viewport to activate it. Using the Select and Move tool, drag the spotlight up just below the ceiling.

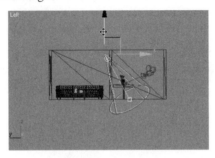

6. Right-click the Perspective viewport to activate it. Then right-click the viewport label to open the viewport menu. Select Views ➤ mr Area Spot01 from this menu to look through the new spotlight in this viewport.

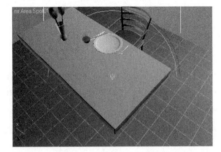

7. Using the Light Hotspot tool located in the lower-right of the user interface with the other navigation tools, drag the hotspot up to decrease its size in the mr Area Spot01 viewport. You should be able to see the hotspot gizmo decrease in size the Camera01 viewport.

8. Press **H** to open the Select Objects dialog box. Select mr Area Spit01.Target from the list and click Select.

9. Press Alt+A to invoke the Align tool and then click the dinner plate. The Align Selection (Plate) dialog box appears.

10. Click all three check boxes for the X, Y, and Z Positions and make sure that the radio buttons for the Current and Target Objects are on Center. Click OK to perform the alignment.

Now the spotlight is aiming more directly at the plate.

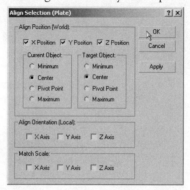

11. Using the Light Falloff navigation tool (next to the Light Hotspot tool), drag down in the mr Area Spot01 viewport to increase the size of the spot's falloff.

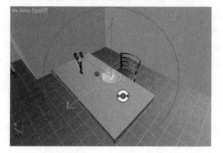

The Falloff gizmo should completely surround the table so that it will be fully illuminated.

12. Right-click the Camera01 viewport to activate it. Press the F10 function key to open the Render Scene dialog box. Click the Render button at the bottom of the dialog box to begin your first mental ray rendering.

The rendering will proceed to appear progressively in the Rendered Frame Window as buckets are processed. After a few seconds, you will see a rendering similar to Figure 11.5.

NOTE *During the rendering process, a small Raytrace Message dialog box will appear. This displays messages (and potential errors) that pertain to raytracing as they occur during rendering. As you can see, mental ray automatically performs raytracing as needed by using the RayFX raytrace engine that was developed by Blur Studio (once sold as a separate product). You can minimize this window if it obscures your view of the Rendered Frame Window.*

FIGURE 11.5
First mental ray
rendering

The rendering in Figure 11.5 is very dark because mental ray is only rendering direct illumination and raytracing the scene by default. There is only one light source in this model, and it illuminates the surfaces it directly strikes. There is no bouncing of light with direct illumination.

Let's experiment with a photon map next. This will allow us to render indirect illumination. More specifically, let's consider GI first, as it will have the largest effect.

1. Click the Indirect Illumination tab of the Render Scene dialog box. Check Enable in the Global Illumination group.

2. Check All Objects Generate and Receive Caustics & GI at the bottom of the Photons (Caustics & GI group).

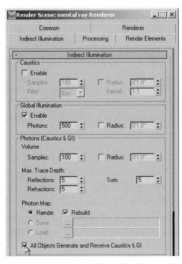

By default, no objects are set to generate Caustics and GI (although they can all receive both forms of indirect illumination). By checking the box, all objects in the scene both generate and receive both forms of indirect illumination.

WARNING *Generating photon maps is time consuming, especially in complex scenes. You can save time by specifying exactly which objects are to generate and/or receive caustics and/or GI. In general, the largest surfaces in the model are the most important participants in indirect illumination.*

3. Select the green tiled floor by clicking it in the Camera01 viewport. Right-click in the viewport to open the quad menu. Select Properties from the transform quad.

4. Click the mental ray tab of the Object Properties dialog box. Check Generate Global Illumination to enable this feature for the floor object. Click OK to close the dialog box.

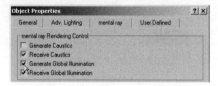

NOTE *Steps 3 and 4 are not strictly necessary in this example because you set all objects (including the floor) to generate GI in step 2. The sample project is so small that it doesn't take much time for all objects to generate GI, but this would become more important in a complex scene. There, you could save time by being selective about which objects generate and which objects receive both caustics and GI as set via Object Properties.*

5. Scroll down to the bottom of the Indirect Illumination rollout. Change the GI Photons to 1000. This reduces the number of photons that will be emitted from all the light sources in the model from the default of 10000.

TIP *It is a good idea to do test renders with fewer photons to get an idea of how they appear in the space. Greater numbers of photons take ever-greater amounts of time to render.*

6. Click the Render button at the bottom of the Render Scene dialog box. A rendering similar to Figure 11.6 will appear showing 1000 GI photons.

You are able to see indirect illumination in areas that were previously dark in Figure 11.5. These areas are being lit exclusively by the GI photons in the photon map. Notice that some of the photons on the table and walls are green, indicating that they picked up that color by being reflected off of the floor. We will need to make some changes to make this rendering look better.

By default, the photon size is set to 1/10th the size of the scene extents. This is usually close to the "right" size, but you can manually override the photon size by using the Radius parameter for better results.

FIGURE 11.6
1000 GI photons

7. Check Radius in the Global Illumination group. This enables the adjacent spinner. Change the radius size to 6″ in the spinner.

8. Do another test render by clicking the Render button at the bottom of the Render Scene dialog box. The rendering will display smaller photons as seen in Figure 11.7.

FIGURE 11.7
Smaller GI photon radius

The rendering is looking more like a paintball war zone. You can deduce that the default photon radius was approximately 1′6″ by comparing Figures 11.6 and 11.7 (based upon the fact that you know the radius was 6″ in Figure 11.7).

The best results from a photon map occur when the photons are numerous enough and sized to have about half their diameters overlapped. It is only when the photons overlap that their colors are sampled and smoothed together.

If the photons overlap too much, there will be too much smoothing and subtle variations in lighting will be lost. If the photons do not overlap enough, they won't be smoothed so they will still be apparent as photons in the rendering (as in Figure 11.7).

Choosing the right settings is usually a matter of doing a few test renders and observing carefully.

9. Change the Radius in the Global Illumination group to 2′. Change the number of GI Photons in the Global Light Properties group to 100000. Click Render and watch as the rendering appears in the Rendered Frame Window (Figure 11.8). This will take about 4 minutes to render on most computers.

This time the photons are adjusted so that they are numerous enough and sized properly to blend successfully. You are now able to see much of the room that is illuminated solely by the indirect light of the photon map. Notice the color bleeding that is happening between the saturated green floor and the white walls—a characteristic and desirable effect of global illumination. Color bleeding happens in the real world and is something GI can simulate.

FIGURE 11.8
GI photons after
adjustment

Let's take a look at caustics next. You will be adding another light source to the scene because Figure 11.8 still looks a bit dark. The room could use more general lighting.

1. Click the Create tab of the Command Panel and click the Lights category button. Click the mr Area Omni tool in the Object Type rollout.

2. Click in the middle of the room in the Top viewport to place the light source as shown in Figure 11.9.

FIGURE 11.9
Adding an mr Area Omni light

Click here to place the light.

3. Using the Select and Move tool, move the light up to a height of 7′ in the Z direction by entering this number in the Z transform spinner at the bottom of the interface.

The mr Area Omni is now positioned just below the ceiling.

4. Click the Modify tab of the Command Panel. In the General Parameters rollout, uncheck On in the Shadows group. The general light in this room shouldn't cast any shadows that might compete with the dramatic spotlight that's already set up.

TIP *In mental ray, essentially only two shadow types are available: Ray Traced Shadows, and mental ray Shadow Map. The other types still appear in the shadows drop-down list, and if selected, they are automatically converted to the two types at render time. Because this leaves room for confusion, it is best to choose one of the explicitly supported types. You will get the best results with Ray Traced Shadows in mental ray.*

5. Scroll down and open the Area Light Parameters rollout. You can choose from two types of area light types: Sphere or Cylinder. Leave Sphere selected and change the Radius parameter to 6″.

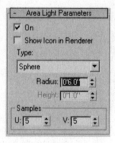

You won't be able to see any gizmo in the viewport that represents the area light shape. These effects are only seen in a rendering.

6. Scroll down further on the Modify tab of the Command Panel and open the mental ray Indirect Illumination rollout (this rollout never appears on the Create tab). Change the Energy multiplier to 0.8.

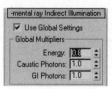

This reduces the indirect illumination energy that this particular light source will emit, by multiplying the global Energy parameter on the Indirect Illumination tab of the Render Scene dialog box by this value (50000 times 0.8).

7. Open the Intensity/Color/Attenuation rollout and change the Multiplier to 0.4. This reduces the amount of direct illumination that this light source will contribute.

WARNING *If light sources have too much direct illumination intensity, they will wash out the subtle indirect illumination effects.*

8. Back in the Render Scene dialog box, uncheck Enable in the Global Illumination group. To test caustics, it is helpful not to get distracted by other forms of indirect illumination.

9. Check Enable in the Caustics group. Change the number of Caustic Photons to 1000 in the Global Light Properties group to reduce the time required to make a test rendering. Change the Viewport drop-down list at the bottom of the Render Scene dialog box to Camera01.

10. Change the Render Type drop-down list on the right side of the main toolbar to Region. By rendering a narrow region, you will save more time by rendering fewer buckets in your test renders.

TIP *You can see what is going on with the rendering process (including any warnings) by opening the Message Window. Choose Rendering* ➢ *mental ray Message Window and leave it open when you are rendering.*

11. Click the Quick Render button. A selection region appears in the Camera01 viewport. Drag the opposite corners of this region to enclose a smaller region around the wineglass as shown in Figure 11.10.

FIGURE 11.10
Making a region in
the viewport

Drag two corner handles to enclose this region.

12. Click the OK button shown in the lower right corner of Figure 11.10 to start the rendering. The Rendered Frame Window shows only the changes made within the region you selected in the previous step (Figure 11.11).

FIGURE 11.11
Caustic region test
render

Caustic areas

The overall rendering is much brighter now that you have added the new light source (compare with Figure 11.8). Caustic effects are usually much more subtle than GI effects, so pay close attention to your test renders to perceive them.

You can see two areas exhibiting caustic indirect illumination effects in Figure 11.11. One brighter caustic area surrounds the stem and base of the wineglass, while the other caustic area is making the shadow of the wineglass on the tablecloth appear brighter.

Increasing the number of caustic photons may give the effects slightly more definition, but the results attained with 1000 caustic photons are acceptable.

TIP *If you don't see any caustic areas where you expect to see them (near glass or water usually), try increasing the number of caustic photons that your light sources emit. Be careful not to boost the number of photons too high, however, as extremely long render times may result.*

13. Now that you have tested both caustics and GI, it is time to combine them in a full rendering. Enable Global Illumination in the Render Scene dialog box. Change the render type drop-down list on the main toolbar to View (default) and click the Quick Render button. Figure 11.12 shows the results so far.

FIGURE 11.12
Rendering showing caustics and GI effects

14. Save your work as MentalrayGI.max.

TIP   You can save a lot of time in an animation (only when the lighting doesn't change in the scene) by saving the photon map as a file. That way, the photon map will not be recalculated for each frame. The controls for saving and loading photon map files (*.pmap) are in the Photons group on the Indirect Illumination tab of the Render Scene dialog box.

In this section, you have learned how to approach indirect illumination slowly by doing test renders and making the necessary adjustments to GI and caustics separately. This approach yields faster visual feedback by rendering many quick tests. Figure 11.12 shows the impressive results you have been able to achieve using a photon map in mental ray.

The next section introduces you to a technique that can improve the quality of your renderings beyond what is possible with a photon map, and you may also save rendering time.

Final Gathering

Final gathering (FG) is an optional step for improving global illumination. However, FG does not help with caustics, so you'll have to rely exclusively on the photon map to simulate that aspect of indirect illumination. Therefore, FG is useful in scenes with overall diffuse lighting, but not very helpful in scenes where caustics play a major role.

Using a photon map alone for GI often leaves dark corners where photons did not reach and patchy areas of light variation where photons did not get smoothed properly. You can smooth all these rendering artifacts by using FG.

When a scene uses FG, fewer GI photons are needed, so the GI photon map can be calculated more quickly. However, FG usually increases render time overall, because additional calculations are performed after the photon map is complete.

FG works by gathering very precise GI data for a few points and then averaging the data from these points together. The technique samples GI data that has already been calculated, so it should be used after you generate a photon map for the most accurate results.

NOTE *You'll learn how to use FG without generating a GI photon map in the section on Skylight GI. FG is conceptually very similar to regathering in radiosity (see Chapter 10).*

Let's take a look at using FG in the sample project:

1. Open `MentalRayGI.max` from the CD or continue from where you left off in the last section.

2. Open the Render Scene dialog box if it is not already open. Click the Indirect Illumination tab.

3. Disable Caustics while you are testing FG to save time by un-checking the box in the Caustics group.

4. Enable GI by checking in the Global Illumination group. Also check Radius and set the value to 1′6″.

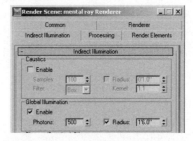

5. Enable FG by checking the box in the Final Gather group. Also check Fast Lookup, Preview, and Rebuild.

TIP *Only use the Preview (No Precalculations) setting when doing test renders. It renders much faster but leaves rendering artifacts.*

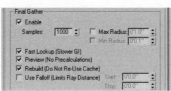

6. In the Global Light Properties group, decrease the number of GI photons to the default value of 1000. You had increased this value in the last section to get better results from the photon map. With FG, you don't need a very accurate photon map, so decreasing this parameter will save a little processing time.

7. Click the Render button at the bottom of the dialog box and then wait a few minutes for the rendering to be processed. Look closely at the rendering and you will see artifacts visible in the preview.

   If you look closely at the tablecloth, for example, you'll see Rendering artifacts, which are variations in light that are apparent at the borders of the buckets. It is usually worth doing a quick preview rendering to be sure that the overall illumination looks good before doing the lengthy final, final gathering.

   One other setting can improve the quality of your final output—*sampling*, an anti-aliasing technique.

NOTE *Anti-aliasing algorithms smooth out jagged edges that appear in grids of pixels.*

   Sampling in mental ray is equivalent to VIZ's supersampling feature that is part of materials. In mental ray, sampling is done at the scene level, so you don't have to turn on supersampling in any materials.

8. Click the Renderer tab of the Render Scene dialog box. In the Samples per Pixel group, change the Minimum drop-down list to **4**. Then change the Maximum drop-down list to **16**. Now many additional samples will be made for each pixel, most likely eliminating any jaggedness from the rendering.

TIP *Anti-aliasing is controlled by the sub-pixel sampling setting. You should always set the Maximum samples per pixel to a higher value than the Minimum setting. For test renders, try using π for the Minimum and 1 for the Maximum, as this will render much faster. π means one sample per pixel. For high-quality renderings, you can increase to 16 or more samples per pixels.*

9. Click back on the Indirect Illumination tab. Check Enable in the Caustics group. The final output will also render the caustic effects that you tested in the last section.

10. Uncheck Preview (No Precalculations) in the Final Gather group and click the Render button at the bottom of the Render Scene dialog box to do another rendering. Be prepared to wait a few hours for this to process.

11. Save your work as MentalrayFG.max. This file is also provided on the CD for your convenience.

Figure 11.13 shows the results of all your hard work in the final output.

FIGURE 11.13
Final Rendering

Reviewing the Basic mental ray Workflow

Now that you have experienced the entire rendering workflow in mental ray, let's take a moment to summarize the steps usually taken to produce final output in mental ray before we move on to more specialized topics. The first thing to do is assign mental ray materials to the objects in your scene. Next add mental ray lighting. Neither of these first two steps is strictly necessary because most of the VIZ materials and lights are automatically converted to mental ray versions by the renderer, but you should add or convert them manually for the most reliable results.

Then try a test rendering with a low number of GI photons. Adjust the size and number of the photons until you achieve acceptable results. If you expect caustics to play a role in your image, do more tests with a low number of caustic photons and adjust their size and number as necessary with further tests. If you feel that the photon map quality is acceptable, you are done.

However, if you notice darkness in the corners of your geometry, color noise, too much blurriness, patchiness in the lighting, or other rendering artifacts, you should perform final gathering. If you go the FG route, do a preview first to make sure it is worth spending the time necessary to perform the lengthy calculation without further tweaking. Adjust sampling if you notice aliasing and then process the final output.

If you can, render your job in parallel to save time. mental ray is perfect for render farming. If you plan on using it a lot professionally, it may pay to consider hiring someone to set up a network of rendering processors to insure that you get your work done by the deadline.

Contour Renderings

mental ray contour renderings are like line drawings of 3D geometry. Not to be confused with wireframe renderings that show all the objects' topology, contour renderings only show the outlines of objects, and often they can look very appealing with a hand drawn look. One of the best things about them is contour renderings generally do not take a lot of time to set up or process.

You will be using mental ray contour shaders in the Render Scene dialog box and in a single material assigned to the objects in the scene. Once the contour shaders are used, you can control their settings by instancing them into the Material Editor. Let's set up the sample project for a contour rendering.

1. Open the file `MentalRayContour.max` from the CD. This is the original Room sample project with the mental ray renderer already assigned.

2. Press the F10 key to open the Render Scene dialog box if it is not already open. Click the Renderer tab and open the Camera Effects rollout.

3. Enable contours by checking the box in the Contours group.

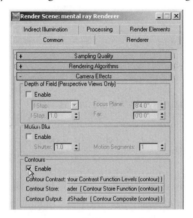

Three shaders are enabled corresponding to the channels called Contour Contrast, Contour Store, and Contour Output.

4. Click the button (marked Contour Composite) in the Contour Output channel.

    The Material/Map Browser dialog box appears.

5. Select the Contour Only (contour) shader from the list and click OK.

6. Type **M** to open the Material Editor. Drag the Contour Only shader from the button in the Contour Output channel to a blank sample slot on the lower right in the Material Editor as shown in Figure 11.14.

7. Select Instance from the small Instance (Copy) Map dialog box (also shown in Figure 11.14).

FIGURE 11.14

Instancing contour
shader in editor

Drag the shader from here...   ...to here.

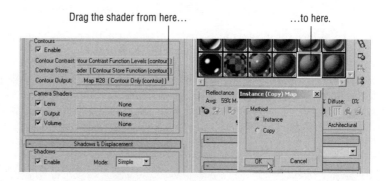

8. Click the Background Color swatch in the Contour Only (contour) Parameters rollout of the instanced map in the Material Editor.

9. Change the color to white in the Color Selector: background dialog box that appears. Close this dialog box after you select the color.

10. Drag the Contrast Function Levels (contour) shader from the Contour Contrast channel in the Render Scene dialog box into the last available sample slot in the Material Editor.

11. Choose Instance from the small Instance (Copy) Map dialog box again.

12. Change the Angle Step Threshold to 5.0 in the Contour Contrast Function Levels (contour) Parameters rollout. Also check Color Contrast contours.

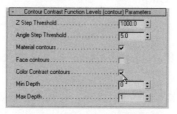

13. Press Ctrl+A to select all the objects in the scene. Click the ceiling sample slot in the Material Editor, then click the Assign Material to Selection tool. Click Replace if you are asked, "Do you want to replace or rename this material?"

Now all the materials have a single white material assigned.

14. Open the mental ray Connection rollout in the ceiling material. Click the None button in the Contour channel in the Advanced Shaders group.

15. Choose Simple (contour) from the Material/Map Browser that appears. Click OK to close the dialog box.

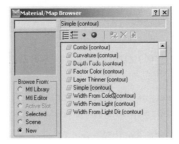

16. Change the Width to 0.1 in the Simple (contour) Parameters rollout.

17. Click Render at the bottom of the Render Scene dialog box. Figure 11.15 shows the resulting contour rendering.

The rendering is processed very quickly without complicated materials, lights, or indirect illumination to calculate. Notice that the contours appear only after the diffuse rendering is completed in the Rendered Frame Window. The contour shaders are applied after the rendering is complete based on information gathered during the rendering process.

NOTE *mental ray can render several "special effects" including depth-of-field, motion blur, displacement, plus volumetric light and fog effects. Many of these effects are also available in VIZ with the scanline renderer, but mental ray also has (often more efficient) versions of them.*

FIGURE 11.15

Contour rendering

Skylight Global Illumination

Using a Skylight to produce global illumination is a trick that has recently become quite popular in computer graphics. *Skylight* is scattered light that does not come from any particular direction, simulating the luminosity of the sky itself. Skylight emanates from a dome of infinite radius that surrounds the scene everywhere above the horizon.

WARNING *When you solely use Skylight to illuminate a scene, light will not enter interior spaces that are not open to the sky. You can still render interiors using this technique by hiding the ceiling and/or roof objects, thereby allowing the scattered light from the sky to softly illuminate the scene.*

If you remember the section on using photon maps, you know that global illumination is simulated with photons, and photons are emitted from light sources. However, no photons can be emitted from a Skylight because they cannot come from any particular direction, by definition.

Rendering GI with a Skylight is a trick because you must use (FG to provide the GI without the benefit of a photon map. From the section on FG you might recall that it was designed to be used after the photon map calculated at least some GI. It turns out that the FG algorithm itself can calculate GI but for *one bounce only*. This means that using FG exclusively to generate GI won't yield accurate results because only the first reflection of the photons can be considered. If you are striving to make an accurate lighting simulation, do not use this method. This method is great for producing beautiful abstract renderings with little fuss.

NOTE *Since generating a photon map in a complex scene can be time consuming, many of those in the film industry started using FG only and skipped the more accurate photon map process to save precious time, which is often equivalent to money.*

Remember, this trick won't work for caustics because FG doesn't consider caustic phenomena. Using the Skylight for GI guarantees that soft and gentle illumination will be everywhere. It also simplifies lighting because there are no other traditional lights in this trick. Let's see how it works in our now-familiar sample project:

1. Open the file `MentalRaySkylightGI.max` from the CD.

2. Press **H** to open the Select Objects dialog box. Select the Ceiling object and click Select.

3. Right-click in the Camera01 viewport and choose Hide Selection from the display quad.

4. Click the Create tab of the Command Panel and click the Lights category button. Select the Skylight tool in the Object Type rollout.

5. Click a point under the table in the Camera01 viewport to locate the Skylight. It doesn't matter where this object is placed as long as it is oriented dome upward. The Skylight will emanate light in all directions from the inside of a hemisphere corresponding to the form of its gizmo in the viewport.

6. Click the Modify tab of the Command Panel. In the Skylight Parameters rollout, click the Sky Color swatch.

The sky color is currently a pale blue, which is perfect for an exterior rendering. However, you are using it in an interior, so it is better to choose a pale warm color to simulate the light in the space.

7. Drag the Hue slider over into the yellow tones to warm up the scene and click Close.

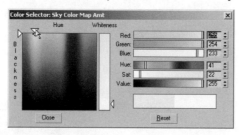

WARNING *Do not use saturated color for the sky color because it will interact strangely with the materials in the scene.*

8. Press the F10 key to open the Render Scene dialog box if it is not already open and click the Indirect Illumination tab. Enable Final Gathering and check Preview (No Precalculations).

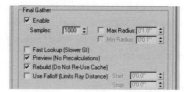

9. Click the Render button at the bottom of the Render Scene dialog box to make a test render.

10. Observe the image appear in the Rendered Frame Window. Click the Cancel button in the Rendering dialog box after a few buckets are processed once you have had a chance to verify that there is an acceptable level of illumination.

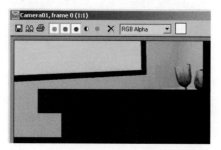

11. Uncheck Preview (No Precalculations) in the Render Scene dialog box, and then make another rendering. This rendering should take around ten minutes to process. Figure 11.16 shows the result.

FIGURE 11.16
Skylight GI

NOTE *This rendering could be improved by increasing the Samples per Pixel on the Renderer tab like you did in the last section to anti-alias the final output. You could also increase the number of Final Gather Samples on the Indirect Illumination tab. However, increasing sampling requires far more rendering time, and whether to improve the rendering depends ultimately on your computing resources and deadline.*

Image-Based Lighting and Skylight

As an alternative to using a solid color in the Skylight, you can get more varied results by using an environment map to illuminate the scene. This way, there will be variation in color and intensity in the scattered light. This technique is called Image-Based Lighting (IBL) in computer graphics circles. Let's try IBL now:

1. Press the **8** key to open the Environment and Effects dialog box. Click the None button below Environment Map.

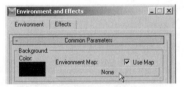

2. Select Bitmap from the Material/Map Browser and click Open.

3. In the Select Bitmap Image File dialog box, browse to the CD and select SphericalPanorama .jpg and click OK.

NOTE   You will learn how to make panoramic renderings in Chapter 17.

4. Press **M** to open the Material Editor if it is not already open. Drag the environment bitmap from the Environment and Effects dialog box to the lower right sample slot in the Material Editor as shown in Figure 11.17.

FIGURE 11.17
Instancing the environment map into the Material Editor

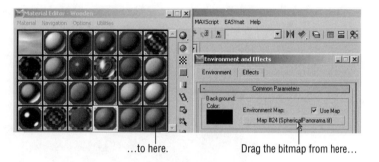

...to here.   Drag the bitmap from here...

5. Choose Instance from the small Instance (Copy) Map dialog box that appears.

6. Click the View button in the Bitmap Parameters rollout to have a look at the image you'll be using as an environment map.

7. Change the Mapping type in the drop-down list in the coordinates rollout to Spherical Environment to match the distortion in the panoramic bitmap.

Close the Environment and Effects dialog box. To make IBL, you still need to instance the environment map into the Skylight.

8. Type **H** to open the Select Objects dialog box, select Sky01 and then click Select. Click the Modify tab of the Command Panel.

9. Click the Use Scene Environment radio button in the Skylight Parameters rollout.

10. Click the Quick Render button to do another Skylight GI rendering, but this time with image based lighting. Figure 11.18 shows the result.

FIGURE 11.18
Image-based lighting

Notice how you can see part of the environment map outside the window. This map is what is lighting the scene through the Skylight, with FG providing GI.

11. Save your work as MentalRaySkylightIBL.max. This file is also provided on the CD for your convenience.

TIP You can get more realistic image-based lighting by using High Dynamic Range Images (HDRI).

Using High Dynamic Range Images

High Dynamic Range Images (HDRI) store more information than can be displayed on a computer monitor. Monitors can only display 256 variations in light intensity (from the blackest blacks to the whitest whites). In the real world, our eyes can perceive enormous dynamic range from subtle candlelight to direct sunlight that is millions of times more intense.

In Photoshop, you may have experienced data loss in your image by making various adjustments to the brightness, contrast, color balance, by sharpening, and so on. For example, when you brighten a traditional 8-bit photo, eventually you will get burnout where the pixels turn all white and there is no more tonal information. After all, how much brighter can pure white get? The answer is now many orders of magnitude brighter if you are using HDRI.

HDRI can store exposure data that varies across many orders of magnitude in brightness. You can't see all this data on the monitor at one time, but VIZ can use this information in a rendering. VIZ can also save renderings in the `.hdr` format to preserve this more extensive visual information.

WARNING   *HDRI have variable bit-depth based upon how much exposure data is stored. Images that store many f-stops of exposure can grow to massive file size that may overwhelm the available memory in your rendering pipeline.*

It is easy to use HDRI in VIZ. Simply select an `.hdr` or `.pic` image and you will see a dialog box like the one in Figure 11.19.

FIGURE 11.19
HDRI load settings

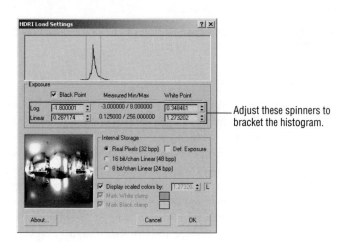

Adjust these spinners to bracket the histogram.

Use the spinners to move the vertical red bars to different positions within the histogram to bracket a narrower dynamic range that can be displayed on the monitor. The preview image will get brighter or darker depending on which portion of the dynamic range you select.

TIP   *You can use HDRI anywhere you use bitmaps in VIZ. The most common uses of HDRI are in Skylight IBL, backgrounds, and reflection maps.*

Various techniques can be used to capture HDRI data from the real world. One way is to make multiple photos with different exposure levels (f-stops) in each shot. You can then composite all this data together using special HDRI software (see the HDRI Links sidebar). There is also a camera company that makes an HDRI-friendly camera that can capture 26 f-stops of exposure in a single shot (talk about bracketing!)

HDRI LINKS

Here are a few websites to explore for more information about HDRI:

HDRView　This software is used to view HDRI on Windows and is free for not-for-profit use.
www.debevec.org/FiatLux/hdrview/

HDRShop　This is HDRI processing and manipulation software.
www.debevec.org/HDRShop/

RADIANCE　This rendering software supports HDRI and was developed by the U.S. Department of Energy with additional support from the Swiss Federal Government.
http://radsite.lbl.gov/radiance/

RealTexture　This site offers collections of HDRI on CD plus an HDRI photo shooting service.
www.realtexture.com/hdri1.htm

Spheron　This company produces the SpheroCam HDR that captures 26 f-stops in a single shot.
www.spheron.com

Industrial Light & Magic's open HDRI format　Learn about how the top-notch film effects pros use HDRI.
www.openexr.com

Some use software to stitch together panoramas that wraparound the greater part of a sphere (see Chapter 17). In still another technique, some photograph a spherical chrome ball to get an entire hemispherical panorama reflected in one shot (called a light probe).

In short, HDRI is all the rage in computer graphics today, and you can be one of the few to explore the cutting edge of technology if you so choose. The big film effects production companies are using HDRI exclusively nowadays, so it makes sense that this technology is finding its way into VIZ.

The holy grail of IBL is to use real HDRI environments to illuminate virtual models using light data from the real world. At least in theory, there is no better way to realistically illuminate a virtual scene. Now you can combine all the acronyms used in this chapter by using HDRI in IBL by FG the Skylight GI (in English that is "using High Dynamic Range Images in Image-Based Lighting by final gathering the Skylight global illumination"). Good luck!

Summary

You have been exposed to a lot in this chapter. Remember that mental ray is an optional renderer that you can grow into with time and experience. Although there is a steep learning curve associated with using mental ray, it may well be worth the effort to produce stunning state-of-the-art computer-generated imagery. In the next chapter, you will change gears and study the art of motion.

Chapter 12

Understanding Animation

PERHAPS THE MOST INTERESTING and fun part of using VIZ is creating an animated presentation of your design. Animation can really bring your designs to life by adding motion over time.

Time is really the key ingredient to animation. This may sound a bit simplistic, but it will become clear as you work through the tutorials in this chapter that you need to pay close attention to the interaction of objects in your model through time. As you gather more experience animating your work, you'll start to develop an almost intuitive sense of what I call the *spacetime* of your model; the 10 to 20 seconds of each animated segment you create. You'll become intimately familiar with this spacetime as you move and adjust the elements of your model. So as you work through this chapter, be aware of how time is always the key component of animation.

Each camera move, light intensity change, and even object movement must be carefully choreographed to create a natural flow of your vision through time. I'll show you the basic tools needed to accomplish this. You will be working primarily by *keyframing* within VIZ. This fundamental animation concept means designating critical points in the sequence (keyframes) where you want specific camera positions or lighting conditions and letting the program animate the change between those points. You'll use the building you've been working with from Chapter 6 to explore keyframing.

- ◆ Understanding the World of Video Time
- ◆ Creating a Quick-Study Animation
- ◆ Understanding Keyframes
- ◆ Increasing the Number of Frames in an Animation Segment
- ◆ Accelerating and Decelerating the Camera Motion Smoothly
- ◆ Editing Keyframes
- ◆ Adding More Frames for Additional Camera Motion
- ◆ Adding Frames to the Beginning of a Segment
- ◆ Other Options for Previewing Your Motion
- ◆ Moving the Camera Target through Time
- ◆ Controlling Lights over Time

Understanding the World of Video Time

You may recall from childhood a special type of book called a *flipbook* that showed a crude animation of a cartoon character. Flipbooks are nothing more than a series of still pictures that, when flipped through, give the impression of motion. Today, you can purchase software that will create flipbooks for you. You could probably even create a flipbook of your VIZ animation.

Flipbooks demonstrate, in a crude way, how television and film work. To give the impression of motion, your television is really flashing a series of still images at you. These still images appear so fast that your mind doesn't perceive them individually, but as a smooth stream of motion, just like the flipbooks. This process is called *flicker fusion*, where the flickering images fuse in your perception to create the illusion of continuity through time.

Flipbooks are an example of traditional *Straight Ahead* animation. They are drawn one picture at a time, straight ahead in time from the beginning to the end of the sequence. When shot with a still camera, this technique is called *Stop Motion* and is often how Claymation is done.

Traditional animators came up with a more efficient technique called *Pose-to-Pose* animation. In this technique, the most talented traditional animators would only draw the important poses for a character that tell the story. Their interns would do the tedious work to fill in all the pictures in-between the poses to produce a smooth stream of motion. Each picture is known as a *frame*.

In the U.S., we use what is called the National Television System Committee (NTSC) standard for television. This standard determines, among other things, the number of times per second these still images appear on your TV. The rate of images per second, or *frame rate* as it is more commonly called, is 29.97 frames per second (FPS). This means that your TV displays one whole picture or frame each 1/29.97th of a second. So for 10 seconds, you will see 29.97 frames or complete pictures. The European standards called Phase Alternate Line (PAL) and Système Electronique Couleur Avec Memoire (SECAM) use 24 FPS.

As you work in VIZ, you can think of each of these frames as a unit of time. For the sake of our discussion, we'll round this unit of time to 1/30th of a second. So 30 frames are equal to one second. This will become more apparent as you work through the tutorials.

Like the traditional animators of the past, you will be responsible for establishing the keyframes, known as *keys* in your sequence. VIZ will fill in all the in-between frames automatically, and you'll be able to fine-tune the way VIZ interpolates between your keys to control the nuances of motion.

Creating a Quick-Study Animation

A single image such as a rendering can show a lot of detail, but an animated view of a design can offer a better sense of form and space. If an animated view is properly done, you can also get a better sense of the scale of a design.

When you create an animation, you are literally rendering several hundred still images that are later combined to form the frames of an animated movie. Since you are generating so many mini-renderings, animations take quite a bit longer to produce than still images.

New!

Animation in VIZ begins by getting into a keyframing mode. There are two keyframing modes to choose from in VIZ 2005: Auto Key and Set Key.

NOTE *Set Key is an advanced mode designed for professional character animators. This mode allows you to try out a pose before you commit to it by saving specific keys manually.*

Auto Key mode is easier to use and replaces the old Animate button from VIZ 4. You get into this mode by simply clicking the Auto Key button at the bottom of the user interface.

1. Open the Savoye12.max file from the CD.

2. Choose Customize ➤ Show UI ➤ Show Track Bar. The track bar represents time as it flows from left to right. Keys you save will appear later on the track bar.

3. Click the Auto Key button at the bottom of the user interface.

   The button turns red to let you know that you are in Auto Key mode. The time slider and the edge of the active viewport also turn red.

4. Click and drag the time slider to the far right. The time slider sits just below the viewports and just above the track bar.

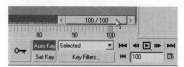

When you start to animate your model, you can think of your animation as a self-contained slice of time. That time is divided into 30 divisions per second. Each of those divisions is called a frame, and each frame is a single, still image.

The time slider shows two numbers. The first number is the current frame, and the second number is the total number of frames in your slice of time, called a *segment*. The default segment that VIZ offers is 100 frames, or a little over 3 seconds of animation at 30 frames per second. When you move the slider to the far right, you change your position in your active time segment to the last frame, or frame 100. This may seem a bit confusing right now, but the next exercise will give you a firsthand impression of how time works in VIZ.

NOTE *Longer animations may be made of multiple segments, called shots. Typically, video editing software is used to composite rendered sequences from VIZ together into shots and provides transitions and special effects. Discreet combustion and Adobe Premiere are two popular video editing packages.*

SETTING ADAPTIVE DEGRADATION

If your model is very complex or if your computer's graphics card is on the slow side, you'll see your Camera viewport reduced to Bounding Box Shading mode as you move the time slider. This reduction of quality is a feature called *adaptive degradation*, and it lets you get a sense of the motion without taxing your video hardware and slowing down the real-time preview. You can control the way adaptive degradation affects your viewport display through the Adaptive Degradation tab of the Viewport Configuration dialog box. To get to this dialog box, either choose Customize ≻ Viewport Configuration or right-click the viewport label and select Configure from the shortcut menu. The Viewport Configuration dialog box displays.

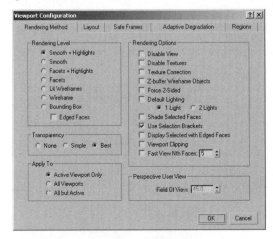

This dialog box lets you control the way objects are displayed in a viewport. The Rendering Method tab offers general settings for the way VIZ displays objects in the viewport.

If you click the Adaptive Degradation tab, you see the options that control the way VIZ displays objects as you move the time slider.

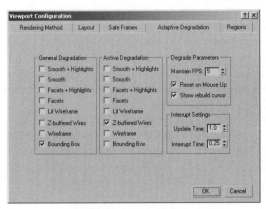

The General Degradation group controls the viewports that are not active, whereas the Active Degradation group controls the viewport that is affected by the time slider's motion.

Adding Camera Motion

VIZ starts out by giving you an active time segment of 100 frames. The time slider you just used lets you move through the frames quickly. To get a better picture of how this works, let's add some motion to the model.

1. Right-click the Perspective viewport label in the upper left corner and then select Views ➢ Camera.View.3DFRONT. You'll use this view in the animation example.

2. Right-click the Top viewport to make it active.

3. Click the Select and Move tool; then click the 3DFRONT camera object. This is the camera at the very bottom of the Top viewport, as shown in Figure 12.1.

4. Make sure the time slider is still at the far right. Move the Camera.View.3DFRONT camera to the location shown in Figure 12.2.

5. Now, right-click the Camera.View.3DFRONT viewport to activate it. Click and drag the time slider slowly from its position at the far right to the far left and back again. Notice what happens to the Camera.View.3DFRONT viewport.

   The view changes dynamically as you move the bar. Also notice that the camera in the other viewports moves, showing you its location at each frame.

FIGURE 12.1

Selecting the 3DFRONT camera.

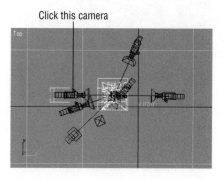

FIGURE 12.2

Moving the camera.

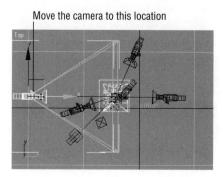

You have just created a camera motion by simply selecting a frame using the time slider, then positioning the camera in the new location for that frame. Moving objects while in Auto Key mode changes their location in time as well as within the space of the model. Had you moved the camera with Auto Key mode turned off, you would have simply moved the camera with no resulting change in the relative motion over time.

Adjusting the Camera Path

If you study the animated perspective view as you move the time slider back and forth, you may notice that you alternately move closer to the building and then farther away from it. This is so because the motion path of the camera is a straight line between the beginning camera location and the end location, as shown in Figure 12.3. As the camera moves through its path, or *trajectory* as it is called in VIZ, it also moves farther from to the model.

FIGURE 12.3

The visible trajectory

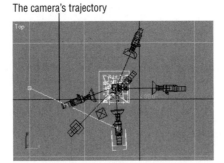

The camera's trajectory

Let's assume that you don't want that effect, and that you want the camera to stay as consistent a distance from the model as possible. To achieve that effect, you can move the time slider to position the camera at its closest position to the model, then move the camera farther away at that point in time, with Auto Key on.

1. Move the time slider to the middle of the slider position so that the slider shows 50/100. This places your camera at frame 50.

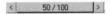

You can also enter **50** in the current frame text box.

2. While Auto Key is still on, use the Select and Move tool to move the camera away from the model to a location similar to the one shown in Figure 12.4.

FIGURE 12.4

The camera's position at a keyframe

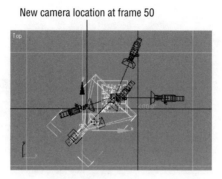

New camera location at frame 50

3. Right-click the Camera.View.3DFRONT viewport; then click the Play Animation button in the time controls.

The viewport displays the effect of the camera through the frames.

4. To stop the playback of the camera animation, click the Stop button.

5. Right-click the Top viewport; then click Play again. Notice that this time you see the camera motion in the Top viewport.

6. Click the Stop button to stop the playback.

Here you see how moving the camera at a particular frame in the time slider affects the camera motion. When you altered the camera location in this last exercise, you were actually adding what is called a *key* or *keyframe* to the camera path. A keyframe is a point along the camera path that directs its motion. You can think of the camera path as a spline and the keyframe as a control point or vertex on that spline.

There is evidence of this keyframe in the space just below the time slider, called the track bar. Look at the middle of the track bar, and you'll see a red bar at the 50/100 location, as shown in Figure 12.5. This bar tells you that a key exists at that point in time. A careful examination of the slider reveals that there are also two other red bars, one on each end of the track bar.

FIGURE 12.5
The bars below the time slider indicate the location of a keyframe.

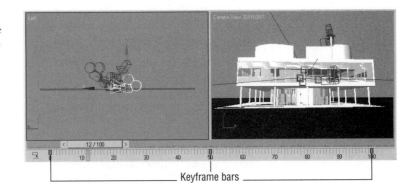

Keyframe bars

The keyframe bars in the track bar appear only when an object that is animated is selected. Since the camera is selected, you can see the keyframe bars.

1. Right-click the keyframe bar in the middle of the track bar.

2. Select Go to Time from the shortcut menu. The time slider moves to the keyframe location, and the view from that location is displayed in the Camera.View.3DFRONT viewport.

The Go to Time option offers a quick way to move the camera to a keyframe location.

Viewing the Camera Trajectory

When you're working on an animation sequence, it helps to see the animation path, or trajectory, of an object. For example, if you could see the path of the camera in the last exercise, it would be easier to determine the distance between the camera and the model throughout the animation. VIZ offers a number of tools for displaying the camera path as well as the location of the keyframes along the path. The following exercise will show you some of those tools.

1. First, make sure that the Camera.View.3DFRONT camera is still selected. Then click the Motion tab in the Command Panel.

2. Click the Trajectories button.

Now you can see the path of the camera as a dotted line in the Top viewport, as shown in Figure 12.6.

3. Right-click the Top viewport and then click the Min/Max Toggle tool to enlarge it.

4. Move the time slider to the 75/100 position to get a better view of the keyframes on the trajectory.

FIGURE 12.6

The Top viewport showing the camera path

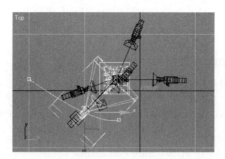

You can see the keyframes as small squares in the path. The dots in the path represent the individual frames of the animation.

5. Use the Select and Move tool to move the camera slightly to the right.

6. Move the time slider to the 25/100 position.

By moving the camera in step 5, you added another keyframe to the path. You can add a keyframe without having to move the camera by using the Parameters button in the Motion tab of the Command Panel.

1. Click the Parameters button in the Motion tab of the Command Panel.

2. With the time slider at the 25/100 position, click the Position button in the Create Key group of the Look At Parameters rollout.

You've just added another keyframe at frame 25. Note that the Position button in the Create Key group lets you add a keyframe without changing the position of the camera.

1. Right-click the keyframe bar in the track bar at the 75/100 position.

2. Select Delete Key ➢ Camera.View.3DFRONT: Position from the shortcut menu. The keyframe is removed from the camera trajectory. Repeat this step for the key frame you created at the 25/100 position.

Just as with objects in your model, you can select multiple keyframe bars that appear in the track bar by holding down the Ctrl key when you select. You can then right-click a keyframe bar and select an option from the shortcut menu to edit the selected keyframes. In the last, brief exercise, you deleted a single keyframe using the right-click shortcut menu.

Controlling the Camera Trajectory Visibility

When you clicked the Parameters button in a previous exercise, the camera trajectory disappeared. This is because the path is typically visible only when the Trajectory button is selected. You can permanently turn on the trajectory visibility through the Object Properties dialog box.

1. Right-click the Camera.View.3DFRONT camera. Then click Properties in the shortcut menu. The Object Properties dialog box displays.

2. Click the By Object button in the upper right corner of the Display Properties group twice. This turns on the options listed in the Display Properties group.

3. Click the Trajectory check box. This turns on the path trajectory display.

4. Click OK to close the dialog box.

Now you can see the camera path and keyframes for the Camera.View.3DFRONT camera object. By turning on the path trajectory display, you can more easily edit the camera path. You'll want to turn it off, however, when you're editing the model, because the path trajectory can add to the visual clutter of a complex model.

TIP   Another way to control the trajectory visibility is to select the animated object, click the Display tab, and then place a check in the Trajectory option in the Display Properties rollout. Note that this will change the display properties of the selected object from By Layer to By Object.

Once you've established the keyframes of your animation (the beginning and end frames are also keyframes), you can edit them to further refine your camera motion. You'll see how that's done later in this chapter. For now, lets get a preview of this animation.

Creating a Preview Animation

Rendering even a short animation is a time-consuming affair, so you'll want to make sure that the motion in your animation is exactly what you want before you commit to actually producing a final animation. One tool that will help you determine what your animation will look like is the *preview* animation. A preview animation is really a very crude facsimile of how your final animation will look. You should use it only to get a rough idea of whether your animation works in a general way. Still, it can reveal many of the flaws in your animation that might otherwise go unnoticed, such as a jerky camera motion or a camera-object collision that isn't obvious.

NOTE *Preview animations are made using the Interactive Viewport Renderer, which has the quality of what you see in the viewports.*

Try the following exercise to create a preview animation of your work so far.

1. Click the Min/Max Toggle tool to get a view of all the viewports if necessary. Then right-click the Camera.View.3DFRONT viewport.

2. Choose Animation ➢ Make Preview. The Make Preview dialog box displays.

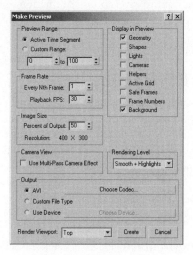

3. Click the Create button. If this is the first time you've used this feature, you'll see the Video Compression dialog box. (You'll learn more about video compression in Chapter 13.)

4. Go ahead and click OK. You'll see a small version of the model in the viewport area as the preview is created. Then the Windows Media Player opens and plays back the preview.

5. Click the Auto Key button to deactivate this mode. If you're not actually working on animation motion, it's a good idea to keep it turned off because any transforms you apply to objects would be automatically keyed.

If you have another application designated to play back AVI files, you'll see that application rather than the Windows Media Player.

The preview is crude, but it does give you a good feel for the camera motion through the model. The model itself isn't rendered, and the lighting effects aren't rendered accurately.

If you look at the Make Preview dialog box, you see that you have several options that control the preview animation. You can have the animation display the frame number, grid, or light locations, for example, by clicking the check box next to each of these items. Or you can control the size of the animation using the Percent of Output input box (100 percent is equivalent to a 640×480 image).

If you want to limit the preview to a particular range of frames, you can specify that range in the Preview Range group. The Rendering Level drop -down list lets you determine whether the preview renders a shaded view, a wireframe view, or a bounding box view, which shows the objects of the model as simple boxes. The Output group gives you control over the Audio-Video Interleaved (AVI) settings. Finally, the Render Viewport pop-up lets you select a viewport to render. By default, the preview animation is that of the currently active viewport.

When VIZ creates a preview animation, it saves the animation as a file named `_scene.avi` (the filename begins with an underline character) in the Previews folder of the main VIZ folder. Every time you create a preview, VIZ overwrites this file without asking you whether it's OK or not. If you create a scene animation that you want to save, choose Animation ➤ Rename Preview. The File dialog box that displays lets you save the last preview animation under a different name, thereby permanently saving the preview.

Understanding Keyframes

The exercise you just completed demonstrated that you can add a *keyframe* to the camera trajectory. The keyframe displays as a small square on the camera trajectory. It is a point along the camera trajectory that can be manipulated in a number of ways to adjust your camera motion. A keyframe was created in the middle of the series of frames, at frame 50, and then moved so that the camera path curved around the building.

The simplest adjustment to a keyframe is to move it. Notice that there are keyframes at the end and beginning of the camera path. These are automatically created as soon as you create motion for an object. Let's try changing the view of the last frame of this camera path by moving the end keyframe.

Right-click the top viewport to make it active. Click the Select and Move tool on the main toolbar.

6. With the time slider set to frame 100 (the far right), move the Camera.View.3DFRONT camera to the location shown in Figure 12.7. Notice what happens to the camera path.

The tiny dots on the camera path show you graphically the location of the camera at each frame. They also indicate the change in speed of your camera over time.

FIGURE 12.7

Moving the camera keyframe for frame 100, the last frame

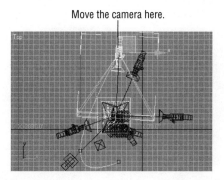

Move the camera here.

Notice that after you move the last keyframe, the dots are spread apart between the middle keyframe at frame 50 and the last frame at frame 100. This tells you that the camera motion is faster between frames 50 and 100 than it is between frames 0 and 50. You can see this because the distance between frames is greater from frame 50 to 100 than it is between frames 0 to 50. You can see another visual representation of this by creating a preview animation.

You might also notice that the camera path now crosses right through some trees. To smooth out the camera motion, and to avoid the trees, you will want to move the middle keyframe at frame 50. You can use some tools found in the Motion tab of the Command Panel to help you quickly move to keyframes.

1. With the Camera.View.3DFRONT camera still selected, click the Motion tab of the Command Panel. Click the Parameters button if is not already active.

2. In the Key Info (Basic) rollout, click the left key selector arrow so that key number 2 is displayed in the box to the right.

The camera moves to key 2, as does the time slider. This shows you that the key selection arrows can quickly place your camera on the keyframe you want.

3. Click the Select and Move tool; then move the camera to the location shown in Figure 12.8.

FIGURE 12.8
Move the camera.

Move keyframe 2 to this location.

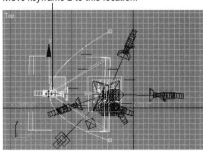

4. Right-click the Camera.View.3DFRONT viewport, and choose Animation ➢ Make Preview. The Make Preview dialog box appears.

5. Click the Create button. You see each frame of the preview animation display on the screen. When VIZ has completed rendering the animation, the preview is opened in the Windows Media Player or whatever application you have set up to play back AVI files.

6. Play the animation to see the results.

The preview shows that your camera motion is too fast. Also, the beginning and end are rather abrupt. Next you'll learn how to increase the overall number of frames in the current animation to slow the animation down.

TIP   Most beginning animators try to fit too much into too short a time segment. Slower motion is usually better in architectural animations, and that equates to rendering many more frames.

Before we move on, however, I'd like to summarize the steps involved in animating an object. You can create motion in VIZ by turning on the Auto Key button, selecting a point in time with the time slider, and then transforming the object by moving, rotating, or scaling it. This creates a keyframe and possibly an animation trajectory. Once a keyframe is created, you can alter that keyframe by returning to that point in time using the time slider, and then transforming the object. If you select a frame that is not a keyframe and then move the object, you create a new keyframe. This is easy to do accidentally, so be careful when moving cameras and objects with the Auto Key button active.

Keyframes can be deleted in a number of ways, the simplest of which is to right-click the keyframe bar in the track bar under the time slider and select Delete Key. An animated object must be selected before the keyframe bars will appear. You can also add a key at any frame without actually moving an object by right-clicking the time slider. Doing so opens the Create Key dialog box.

You can enter the type of keyframe, as well as a source and destination time other than the default time shown in the dialog box; then click OK to accept the new keyframe settings.

Increasing the Number of Frames in an Animation Segment

At the beginning of this chapter, I mentioned that the standard frame rate for video in North America is about 30 FPS. So in order to lengthen the time in our building animation, we need to increase the number of frames over the camera path. Right now, we have 100 frames, or about 3 seconds of animation. Let's see what we need to do to increase our current path to 300 frames for a 10-second animation.

1. Click the Time Configuration tool at the bottom of the user interface.

The Time Configuration dialog box displays.

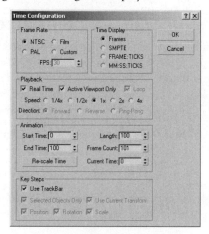

2. In the Animation group, click the Re-scale Time button. The Re-scale Time dialog box displays.

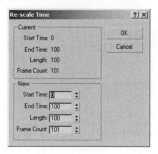

3. In the End Time input box, enter **300**. When you press ↵ the Length value changes to match the End Time value.

4. Click OK; then click OK again in the Time Configuration dialog box. Notice that the time slider now shows 300 for the total number of frames. You'll also see a greater number of dots in the Camera.View.3DFRONT trajectory.

5. Create another preview animation, making sure that you have selected the Camera.View .3DFRONT viewport as the render viewport. The animation is now three times slower.

In the Time Controls dialog box, you saw that you have an option to set the End Time as a separate value from the Length of the animation. VIZ lets you work with *active time segments*. An active time segment is a block of time, within your animation, that you are currently working on. Right now, that block of time includes the entire time of the animation, but you can set up VIZ to limit your active time segment to just a few frames of the overall time length. This feature is useful if you are working on a very large animation and want to isolate your work to a specific set of frames. You'll see how to work with active time segments in the next section. Right now, let's see how to smooth out the beginning and end of the camera path so it doesn't seem so abrupt.

Accelerating and Decelerating the Camera Motion Smoothly

You don't want the camera to suddenly start moving at its full rate, or your animation will seem jarring. You want the camera motion to start out slowly, and then increase speed as if you were in a car starting out from a stoplight. The same is true for the end of the camera path. You want to slow down gradually and not stop instantly. You can control the acceleration and deceleration of the camera by setting the key tangent properties. These are available in the Key Info (Basic) rollout of the Motion tab.

1. With the Camera.View.3DFRONT camera selected, set the time slider to the 0 frame position at the far left.

2. Select the Motion tab in the Command Panel and scroll down to the Key Info (Basic) rollout.

3. Click and hold the Out button at the bottom of the rollout. You'll see a set of buttons. These are the tangent options for the keyframe.

4. Select the Slow tangent button. This is the button that looks like the top quarter of a bell curve.

This button has the effect of slowing the camera motion as it approaches or leaves a keyframe. In this case, it will slow the motion as it leaves frame 0 because you used the Out tangent. You may notice that now the dots on the camera trajectory are closer together as they approach the first keyframe. The shape of the trajectory also changes to one that is straighter than in frame 0.

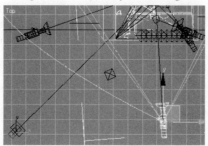

5. Create another preview animation of the camera.

You will notice that now the beginning of the animation starts out in a gradual acceleration from a stop. The bunching up of dots at the starting keyframe shows you that the frames at the beginning are closer together. As the frames move away from the starting keyframe they gradually spread apart, traversing a greater distance with each frame until a uniform frame-to-frame distance is reached. The net effect of all this is a smooth acceleration from the camera starting point.

Now adjust the ending keyframe to decelerate the camera motion gradually.

1. In the Key Info (Basic) rollout of the Motion tab, click the right key selection arrow until 3 is displayed in the key number box if it is not already displayed.

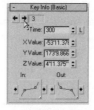

2. Click and drag the In button and select the Slow button. Since you want the camera to gradually decelerate toward the keyframe, you use the In button to make the setting. Just as with the first keyframe, you see the dots in the trajectory move closer together as they approach the last keyframe.

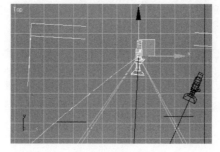

3. Create another preview to see the results.

In this second exercise, you adjusted the frame rate for the end of the camera path in a way similar to the beginning. As the frames approach the last keyframe, they gradually become closer together. The net effect is a deceleration of the camera motion.

This latest camera motion seems to move a bit faster than before. Since the frames have been moved closer to the beginning and end keyframes, they become more spread out over the rest of the trajectory, adding some speed to the camera motion. Remember that you are working with a fixed number of frames, so as you move frames closer to the beginning and end, the rest of the trajectory has fewer frames, and fewer frames means faster motion.

Let's take a moment to get to know some of the other key tangent options. You already know what the Slow tangent option does. Here is a listing of all of the tangent options for both in and out directions and what they are used for.

Smooth Creates a smooth transition through the keyframe. Smooth has a tendency to overshoot the smooth curvature beyond the key, resulting in sometimes undesirable behavior (see the Auto option).

Linear Straightens the trajectory near the keyframe. If Linear is used for the Out parameter of one keyframe and the In parameter of the next, the resulting trajectory between the two keyframes is a straight line, and the intervals between frames become uniform.

Step Causes the keyframe frame number to jump one frame to the next or prior keyframe, depending on whether Step is used for the Out or In keyframe parameter. For example, if Step is selected for the In parameter of the current keyframe, the prior keyframe's Out parameter will automatically be changed to a Step tangent, and the prior keyframe's frame number will be one less than the current keyframe's frame number.

Fast Causes the rate of change to increase around a keyframe. For example, using Fast in keyframe 2 of the previous exercise will cause the camera to appear to speed up around the keyframe. The trajectory also becomes straighter near the keyframe.

Slow   Causes the rate of change to decrease around a keyframe. This has the opposite effect from that of the Fast tangent option.

Custom   Allows you to make fine adjustments to the rate of change through a keyframe. When Custom is selected, you can edit the rate of change through a keyframe in the Function Curves of the Track View dialog box.

New!   **Auto**   The Auto Tangent Interpolation is new in VIZ 2005. It guarantees a smooth transition between keys, and avoids the problems often experienced with the Smooth type. Auto is now the default tangent type. When you edit any Auto tangent handle, the tangent type converts to Custom and no more automatic adjustments are performed.

You'll get a chance to use some of the other tangent options later in this chapter, including the Custom tangent option. Now let's continue with a look at some of the other ways a keyframe can be edited.

OTHER WAYS OF CONTROLLING SPEED

If your animation is strictly for video or film, you have no alternative for controlling speed other than increasing or decreasing the number of frames in a segment. On the other hand, if you plan to have your animation shown exclusively on a computer monitor, you have other options.

Most video playback programs for computers allow you to vary the frame rate of your animation, though you probably would not want to go below 15 FPS. Any slower and you will notice the jerkiness between frames.

There are many variables that affect the quality of computer playback of animations. Color depth, image size, and file types all affect how well an animation will appear on your computer screen. In general, an MPEG 1 file will play back nicely at 30 FPS. MPEG 1 offers full color at a frame size of 352×240. If you want a larger size, you may need specialized display hardware to get a full 30-FPS playback speed. There are a few video cards available that will perform hardware-assisted playback of MPEG 2 files that display a maximum frame size of 720×480. MPEG 2 is commonly used for satellite dish systems.

Editing Keyframes

Keyframes are not set in stone, and it's a good thing they aren't. A recurring theme in this part of the book is the cycle of editing, testing, and then editing again. This process applies to keyframes as much as it does to editing materials and lights.

In the following set of exercises, you will add more keyframes and then adjust them to further understand how they work. You'll focus on the Camera position keyframes, but as you will learn later, these changes can be applied to keyframes for other objects in your model, such as the lights and geometry. You can also keyframe certain object parameters, like a camera's Field of View (FOV), or a Door's Open parameter for example.

The camera path comes a bit too close to the trees. This in turn blocks out the view of the building. Let's add another keyframe to the camera trajectory so that we can pull the trajectory farther away from the trees without distorting it.

1. Move the time slider to frame 210. The camera should appear at the location shown in Figure 12.9.

FIGURE 12.9
The camera location

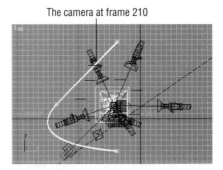
The camera at frame 210

2. Select the camera and scroll up to the Look At Parameters rollout of the Motion tab, and click Position under the Create Key group.

You may also right-click the time slider and then, in the Create Key dialog box, make sure that just the Position option is checked and click OK.

3. Right-click the Top viewport; then click the Min/Max Toggle tool to get a better look at the camera trajectory.

When you add a new keyframe, VIZ automatically applies an Auto tangent for the In and Out settings.

Now let's adjust the location of the second and third keyframes to make the trajectory a more symmetrical, curved path.

1. Move the current keyframe 3 to the location shown in Figure 12.10.

2. Click the left key number arrow in the Key Info (Basic) rollout to go to keyframe 2, and move that keyframe to the location shown in Figure 12.10.

FIGURE 12.10

Moving keyframes 2 and 3 into their new locations

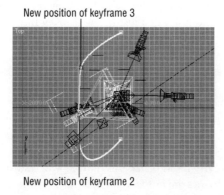

New position of keyframe 3

New position of keyframe 2

WARNING *Verify that Auto Key mode is on before you move any keyframes. If you move objects when Auto Key mode is off, changes you make apply globally to the entire animation.*

Take a moment to zoom in and study the distribution of the dots along the camera trajectory. They are no longer evenly distributed over the path, but are crowded at the beginning of the trajectory and spaced out in the latter half. This will create an animation that will start out slowly, and then suddenly speed up.

3. To adjust keyframe 2 so that it occurs a little earlier in the trajectory, change the Time value in the Key Info (Basic) rollout to **105**.

NOTE *Only the new keys will be recognized and navigable in the Key Info (Basic) rollout. The old nodes remain on the trajectory for reference.*

Notice how the trajectory changes in shape to accommodate the new setting.

4. Go to keyframe 3 and change its Time value to **200**.

Although the new frame numbers were provided to you in this exercise, in real projects you can use the Time spinner to adjust the time while watching the dots in the trajectory. As you adjust the Time spinner, the dots will change their location. When the dots appear more evenly spaced, then you know that the keyframe is in an appropriate location for a smoother camera motion.

Another way to even out the frames through a keyframe is to use the Normalize Time button in the Key Info (Advanced) rollout, located just below the Key Info (Basic) rollout.

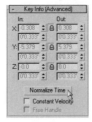

When you move to a keyframe and click this button, VIZ adjusts the location in time of the current keyframe so that the frames are more evenly spaced. The one drawback to using the Normalize Time button is that it makes the other keyframe parameters inaccessible.

Adding More Frames for Additional Camera Motion

Now let's suppose we want to add some additional camera motion to the current animation. It may seem as though you've used up all the available frames for the tour around the building. You can, however, add additional frames at the beginning or end of a segment of frames.

Adding Frames to the End of a Segment

Adding frames to the end of a segment is a fairly straightforward operation. Here's how it's done.

1. Click the Time Configuration tool at the bottom of the user interface.

2. In the Time Configuration dialog box, enter **400** in the Length input box of the Animation group; then click OK.

Notice what happens to the time slider. Position 300 now appears at about three-quarters of the distance from the left side of the time slider, and the overall frame count now shows 400.

Although you added more frames to the animation, the additional frames had no effect on the existing frames. The number of frames in the camera path did not change. You simply added more frames to the end of the animation. Those additional frames are not yet being utilized.

Now let's make use of those extra frames.

1. Move the time slider all the way to the right so that it reads 400/400.

2. Move the camera to the position shown in Figure 12.11.

3. Click the Min/Max Toggle tool to view all of the viewports.

FIGURE 12.11
Move the camera to a location somewhere in the courtyard.

The new camera location for frame 400

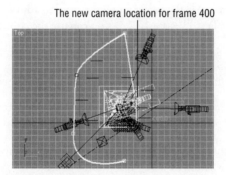

Remember that one way to create a new keyframe is to select a new frame number, and then move the camera or other VIZ object. In this case, you added more time and then set the frame slider to the new end of the segment and moved the camera while Auto Key mode was on.

Your view at frame 400 is too low in the building. You'll want to move the end location of the camera to the courtyard level. This will create an animation that will give the impression of flying over the building.

1. With the camera still selected and the Select and Move tool still active, enter **16′** in the Z input box of the coordinate readout.

The camera will move to a vertical location similar to the one shown in Figure 12.8.

FIGURE 12.12
Adjusting the camera's vertical location

The camera's new vertical location

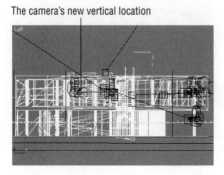

2. You'll want to have the camera slow down as it approaches this last keyframe, so in the Key Info (Basic) rollout of the Motion tab, set the keyframe to **5** and then select the Slow option for the In tangent parameter.

If you look at the Left viewport shown in Figure 12.12, you will see that your camera trajectory moves the camera through the wall of the courtyard. You'll want to adjust the vertical location of the other keyframes so that the camera motion brings you above the building.

1. Use the Zoom and Pan tools to adjust the Left viewport view so that it looks similar to Figure 12.13. You want to be able to see all of the keyframes in the camera path.

2. Go to keyframe 4 and use the Select and Move tool to adjust the vertical height of the camera so that it looks similar to Figure 12.13. You can use the coordinate readout to set the camera height to 88 feet.

3. Adjust the vertical locations of keyframes 3 and 2 so that they look similar to Figure 12.13. Keyframe 3 is at a height of 44 feet and keyframe 2 is at a height of 12 feet.

NOTE *You may have to delete the original position keys 2 and 3 to keep them from affecting the camera path. Make adjustments as needed to make your trajectory match up with Figure 12.13.*

4. Make sure the Camera viewport is currently active; then choose Animation ➤ Make Preview and make a preview animation of what you have so far.

You may also drag the frame slider from far left to right and back again. You get a sense of the motion while you watch the perspective view. This is called *scrubbing* the animation.

Adjusting the Camera Motion through a Keyframe

You'll want to refine the animation a bit more. Suppose you want to add a bit more time at keyframe 4 to pause at the bird's-eye view of the villa. You'll also want to correct the part of the animation between keyframes 4 and 5 where the camera flies through the roof.

VIZ offers a variety of tools that let you fine-tune the motion of an object through a keyframe. Each frame can hold keys on numerous animation *tracks*. Tracks are separate containers that store independent information, much like how the audio tracks on an old 8-track magnetic tape recorder each recorded a signal coming from a different microphone or instrument pickup.

FIGURE 12.13

Adjust the vertical position of the keyframes as shown here.

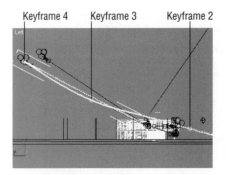

In VIZ, tracks store data from *animation controllers.* An animation controller is a specialized algorithm that is responsible for recording a specific kind of animation data onto a track (position, rotation, scale, object parameters, audio, mathematical expressions, etc.).

The entry point to these tools is the *Track view.*

New!

The Track view has been split into two specialized editors in VIZ 2005 called the Curve Editor and the Dope Sheet.

NOTE   The term Dope Sheet comes from classical animation and was a vertical chart that displayed instructions to the cameraperson.

The Curve Editor is for function curve editing and can be used to fine-tune the trajectory of an object in all three spatial dimensions. The Dope Sheet is for editing time ranges and key management. In the following exercise, you'll be introduced to both aspects of the Track View of the camera you've been working with.

1. With the Camera.View.3DFRONT camera selected, choose Graph Editors ➤ Track View - Dope Sheet... to open the dialog box.

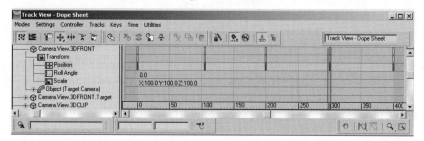

2. The list automatically expands to show the animation hierarchy of the selected object.

TIP   Right-click in the tree view on the left side of the Track View - Dope Sheet dialog box to open a kind of quad menu that is specific to the dialog box. You can choose Auto Expand the Selected Object, Transforms, XYZ Components, Base Objects, and Children. Then you won't have to click plus (+) symbols to manually expand these levels in the hierarchy. The plus symbols disappear when you choose to auto expand their types.

3. Click the Zoom Horizontal Extents tool in the View toolbar, found in the lower right corner of the Track View - Dope Sheet dialog box. You can also zoom and pan within this dialog box using the built in navigation controls.

The Zoom Horizontal Extents tool expands the Track view to display the entire timeline of your animation.

TIP *If at any time, your Track View dialog boxes do not show the timeline as described in this book, click the Zoom Horizontal Extents tool shown in step 3 to display the entire timeline.*

Take a moment to study the Track View - Dope Sheet dialog box. In the left panel, you see a hierarchical listing of the camera's tracks. The camera name is at the top, followed by the Transform track. Under Transform are three options labeled Position, Roll Angle, and Scale. These are the three types of transforms—move, rotate, and scale—that you can apply to any object, as you've learned from earlier chapters. In this case, they represent the transforms applied to an object over time, such as the Move transform you applied to the camera.

In the panel to the right, you see a graph representing the camera's motion. The frame numbers are shown on the scale at the bottom of the panel. You see the familiar keyframe bars that correspond to the Position track in the left panel. These bars represent the same bars that you see below the time slider and are referred to as *keys*. You'll also see a light blue double vertical line in the graph. That line indicates the current frame in the animation.

You can think of the Track View - Dope Sheet dialog box layout as a mini version of the VIZ main window. Across the top of the dialog box, you see a set of tools that let you work on various aspects of the animation. You'll get a chance to work with some of these tools in the following exercises. At bottom right, a set of navigation tools allows you to control the view of the graph. You can zoom in or out, or pan using these tools. Two input boxes toward the bottom middle of the dialog box display the current position and value (if applicable) of a selected key. To the left of the input boxes is a message box that provides messages for the current operation.

Finally, in the preceding exercise, you opened a Track View dialog box that expanded and panned to show the tracks for the selected object. You can also pan through all the nodes for the entire scene. Pan the tree view on the left side of the dialog box to the upper left. Observe that all the scene nodes are children of the World. Other scene nodes include tracks for Sound, Environment, Renderer, Objects, and many others.

Notice that some of the Object nodes have two plus symbols, both a square and a round one. The plus symbols display as minus (−) symbols after they have been expanded. Figure 12.14 shows the node for the WALL.13 object expanded.

The round plus symbol is used to get at the *keyable* tracks for the objects. Keyable tracks are those that can be animated. The WALL.13 object has a category inside the round plus symbol called Transform which holds the three keyable tracks for Position, Rotation, and Scale.

FIGURE 12.14

Two plus symbols in the Dope Sheet's tree

Click the square plus to expand a group, assembly, or linked hierarchy.

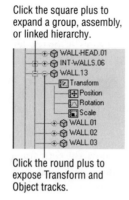

Click the round plus to expose Transform and Object tracks.

Some objects may also have an Object category that can be expanded using the round plus symbol in Track views. In VIZ, only the nodes appropriate to animating architectural visualizations have keyable object tracks. For example, Camera.View.3DFRONT has an expandable Object category that can be expanded to expose a number of keyable tracks like the Field of View (FOV), Target Distance, and many others.

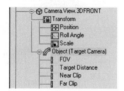

NOTE   *In discreet 3ds max, all objects have keyable object tracks, which makes it much more powerful for animation.*

These parameters can be animated in the object itself, like those you can manually edit on the Modify tab of the Command Panel. If you do create keys on object tracks, the corresponding parameters on the Modify tab of the Command Panel receive red outlines around their spinners. Here the Lens and FOV parameters feature red spinner outlines showing a visual reminder that they are animated.

So far you have been in Edit Keys mode within the Track View - Dope Sheet. This mode is perfect for editing individual keys and their tangents.

There is another mode of the Dope Sheet that is better suited for editing the timing of entire series of keys called *ranges*.

1. Click the Edit Ranges button next to Edit Keys at the top left of the Track View - Dope Sheet dialog box.

2. You can drag range bars in the middle to move the entire range to another time, or you can drag the starting or ending handle to change the overall duration of the range (Figure 12.15). Experiment with these features and undo your actions after you're satisfied that you understand them.

FIGURE 12.15
Edit Ranges mode of
Dope Sheet

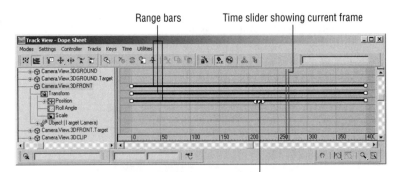

NOTE   *Editing ranges becomes important when you want to adjust the timing of multiple animated objects and sequences relative to each other. It is much like video editing in this respect.*

Compressing and Expanding Time

Now let's see how the Curve Editor portion of the Track View can be used to adjust the camera's transition through keyframe 4.

1. Inside the Track View - Dope Sheet dialog box, Choose Modes ➤ Curve Editor. You can switch back and forth between the Dope Sheet and Curve Editor in this way.

   You can also use the main menu bar and choose Graph Editors ➤ Track View - Curve Editor to open both dialog boxes simultaneously.

TIP   *Get two or more monitors and graphics cards to maximize screen real estate. It is much better to place floating dialog boxes like the Track views on a secondary monitor while you are working within the main VIZ window.*

2. Move the Track View - Curve Editor dialog box down if necessary so that you can get a clear view of the Top viewport.

3. Adjust the Top viewport so it looks similar to Figure 12.16.

FIGURE 12.16

The Top viewport

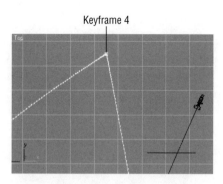

Keyframe 4

4. In the Motion tab of the Command Panel, make sure that the Key Info (Basic) rollout shows key number 4. You should see the camera in the Top viewport at keyframe 4.

5. In the Track View - Curve Editor dialog box, click the Position track in the left panel. Notice that there are three tracks below Position—one for each spatial direction.

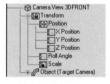

New!

There are three tracks for position because objects now use the Position XYZ controller by default in VIZ 2005. In earlier versions of VIZ, objects used the Bézier Position controller as the default that combined all three directions in one track.

These two controllers store the animation data in different ways mathematically, but they function similarly.

You will change the Camera.View.3DFRONT's controller to the older one so that you can control all three directions with a single Ease curve.

6. Click the Motion tab of the Command Panel and click the Parameters button if it is not already active. Open the Assign Controller rollout. Select the Position controller in the list box.

7. Click the Assign Controller button at the top of the rollout. The Assign Position Controller dialog box appears. You can also choose Controller ➢ Assign from the Track View - Curve Editor dialog box.

8. The right angle bracket indicates which animation controller is currently assigned to position. Select the Bézier Position controller from the list and click OK.

NOTE *You can reassign a default controller by clicking the Make Default button in the Assign Position Controller dialog box. There is a message at the bottom of the dialog box showing that Position XYZ is currently the default controller.*

WARNING *All tangent assignments are lost when you change controllers.*

9. Select the Position track in the Curve Editor. Notice that it no longer has any subtracks.

10. Within the Track View - Curve Editor dialog box, choose Curves ➢ Apply - Ease Curve or type Ctrl+E on the keyboard.

You now see an Ease Curve track indented below the Position track.

11. Click the Ease Curve track in the left panel. The Ease Curve function curve appears in the panel to the right.

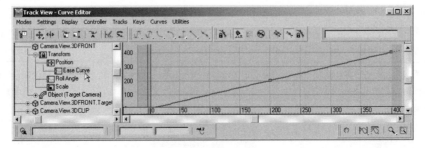

When you changed controllers, all the tangents were overwritten with the Auto type, which is now the default in VIZ 2005. To remedy this situation, you will reassign two tangents.

1. Using the arrows in the Key Info rollout on the Motion tab of the Command Panel, go to key 1 at time 0. Change the Out tangent type to Slow.

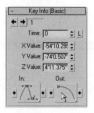

2. Go to key 4 at frame 300 and change its In tangent to Slow. Now the camera is slow to start moving and it decelerates at key 4 as it did earlier in the chapter.

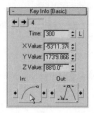

The Ease Curve graph displays a time scale in a straight line from 0 to 400. This is the current time you are using for the camera. You can adjust this curve to compress or expand time at various points along the camera trajectory. This may seem like a peculiar concept at first, but to help you understand the Ease Curve graph more clearly, consider how you used the In and Out keyframe parameters to select a tangent option. Selecting the Slow option for the first key had the effect of *compressing* or slow-ing time around that first keyframe. You see this graphically by the way the frame dots on the camera trajectory bunch up as they get closer to the key.

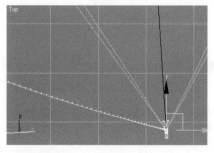

The result is a smooth transition from a stop. Likewise, you added the Slow tangent option to the In parameter of the last key to make the camera slow to a stop, instead of abruptly stopping. This is similar to compressing time before the last key.

The Ease Curve graph lets you compress or expand time in a way similar to the Slow or Fast tangent options for the In and Out key parameters. Let's try adjusting the In and Out speed around key 4 to make the transition around key 4 a bit smoother. First, add a key to the position on the Ease Curve graph that corresponds to keyframe 4. You'll then adjust the key to compress the time around the key.

1. Click the Add Keys tool on the Track View - Curve Editor toolbar.

2. Click the graph at the point that corresponds to frame 300, as shown in Figure 12.17.

   Notice that the two input boxes at the bottom of the Track View dialog box show the time coordinates of the key you just created.

NOTE   *The numbers you see may be different from the ones shown here depending on how accurately you clicked in step 2.*

3. You can fine-tune the location of the key by entering the exact coordinate values in these boxes. Click the box to the left and enter **300**; then press the Tab key and enter **300** again if necessary.

4. Right-click the key that you just added. You'll see the Camera.View.3DFRONT Ease Curve dialog box.

5. In the In parameters flyout, click the Select the Slow Tangent option.

6. Do the same for the Out parameter, and then close the dialog box.

Now notice how the Ease Curve looks. It levels off just before and after the new key. This leveling off indicates a compression in time around the key. A straight diagonal line as seen in the rest of the graph indicates a smooth, continuous flow of time.

Also notice that dots in the camera trajectory seen in the Top viewport are compressed a bit more than before as they approach keyframe 4. This tells you that the camera now slows down as it transitions into keyframe 4.

FIGURE 12.17
Click here to add a
key at frame 300.

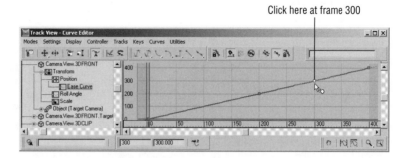

If you want even more control over the Ease Curve graph, you can use the Custom Tangent option.

1. Click the Custom Tangent button on the main toolbar of the Track View - Curve Editor dialog box.

Notice that now you have a Bézier handle appearing at the key. You can adjust this handle vertically to control the shape of the curve through the key.

2. Click the Move Keys tool in the Track View - Curve Editor toolbar.

3. Click and drag the Bézier handle on the key upward. The curve follows the handle. Notice how the dots arrange themselves in the trajectory in the Top viewport. They start to compress, and then expand again as they approach the keyframe.

WARNING   If you hold down the Shift key while dragging tangent handles, it breaks them so that they no longer function in parallel. After they are broken, you can move the handles independently of each other. This creates a velocity discontinuity and can look jerky if the curve has a sharp point.

4. You don't really want this configuration for the key, so click the Undo button on the VIZ standard toolbar to undo the change in the curve.

5. Now let's get rid of the key that's in the middle of the graph. Click that key to select it as shown in Figure 12.18. It turns white to show that it has been selected.

FIGURE 12.18

Making the Ease
Curve more gradual

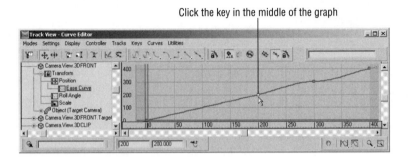

6. Press the Delete key.

The key disappears. Notice how the curve changes. The transition into keyframe 4 is now more gradual.

Go ahead and make similar changes to the Ease Curve settings for the first and last keys.

1. Click the first key to the far left of the curve. You may need to use the scrollbar at the bottom of the window to gain access to the first key. Then, click and hold the Slow tangent flyout and select the option for the Out parameter (Figure 12.19).

FIGURE 12.19

Three options for
tangent buttons

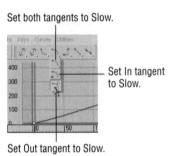

2. Click the last key to the far right of the curve and select the Slow tangent flyout option for the In parameter. The curve now looks like a gentle slope with gradual transitions between keys.

It is important to keep in mind that the Ease Curve tangent settings are really independent of the Position keys. You can compress and expand time anywhere along the timeline. For example, if you wanted to have the camera slow down between keyframes 1 and 2, you could create a key in the Track view at frame 62 of the Ease Curve and adjust the key in a way similar to the way you adjusted the key in the previous exercises.

If you decide that you don't want to use the Ease Curve settings you've created, you can delete an Ease Curve by selecting the Ease Curve track in the left panel and press the delete key.

WARNING *The camera will move backward along its own trajectory if the ease curve ever slopes downward.*

Next, let's see how to adjust the camera motion to avoid going through the roof of the villa as the camera approaches the courtyard. To do this, you'll need to use the Position track of the Track View - Curve Editor dialog box.

Adjusting the Camera Trajectory Using the Track View

Now let's take a look at another way that the Curve Editor can help you fine-tune the camera motion.

1. Move the Track View - Curve Editor dialog box up so that you can get a clear view of the Left viewport.

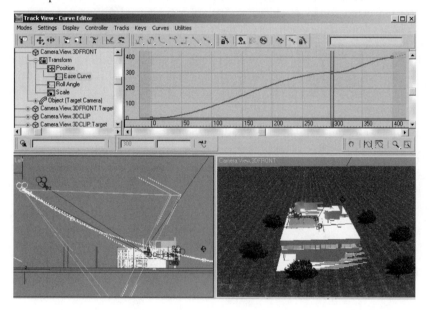

2. Click the Position track in the left panel. You see the graph in the left panel change to show three curves. (See Figure 12.20.)

FIGURE 12.20

The Track View - Curve Editor dialog box showing the (Bézier) Position track

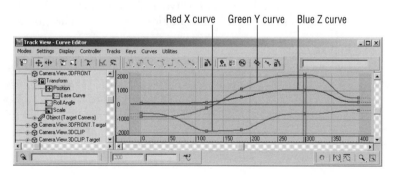

NOTE *The Position XYZ controller has one function curve each on three separate tracks. The Bézier Position controller puts all three curves on one track. Each controller has its strengths and weaknesses depending on what you are doing. You have more control over each axis with Position XYZ, but you saw how the Ease Curve could be simultaneously applied to all three curves with the Bézier Position controller.*

The Position Function curves are a graphic representation of the camera motion through three-dimensional space. Unlike the camera trajectory, the Position Function curves display the changes in the X, Y, and Z coordinates as separate lines. Each line represents a different axis in the coordinate system: The Red is X, the Green is Y, and the Blue is Z. One way to remember this relationship is that the red, green, and blue colors are usually abbreviated as RGB, so you can correlate RGB with XYZ. Don't worry if the graph doesn't make any sense to you right now. You'll see in the next exercise how you can make practical use of it.

If you created a preview of the animation so far, you'd see that the camera passes through the roof of the villa before landing in the courtyard. To avoid this, you can use the Position Function curve to adjust the shape of the camera trajectory so that it avoids the roof. Try the following exercise to see how this works.

1. Use the Zoom and Pan tools to adjust the Left viewport to look like Figure 12.21.

FIGURE 12.21
The Left viewport adjusted to show the camera trajectory approaching the courtyard

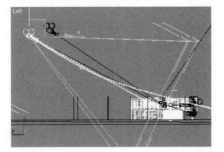

2. Back in the Curve Editor, on the right end of the Position Function curve, click the key at the far right end of the blue curve, as shown in Figure 12.22. Remember that the blue curve represents the Z axis for the position transform applied to the camera.

FIGURE 12.22
Click the key at the far right end of the blue curve, as shown here.

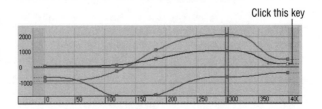

3. Change the In tangent of this key to Custom. You'll see a Bézier handle appear at the selected key on the curve.

4. With the Move Keys tool from the Track View - Curve Editor toolbar selected, move the Bézier handle upward so it looks similar to Figure 12.23.

FIGURE 12.23

The Function curve with the Bézier handle pointing upward and a view of the resulting camera trajectory

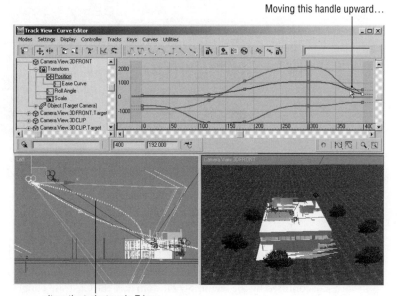

Moving this handle upward…

…alters the trajectory in Z here.

Notice what happens to the camera trajectory in the Left viewport in Figure 12.23. It now curves upward. This helps move the trajectory away from the roof.

By altering the Z curve of the Position Function curve, you altered the trajectory of the camera in the Z axis. If you take time to study the blue curve, you see that it is really a graph that represents the Z coordinates of the camera over the 400 frames. The same is true for the X and Y red and green curves. You can manipulate the keys using a combination of the Custom In and Out tangents.

As you can see from this and the previous section, you have a great deal of control over the motion of an object through time and space. Next, you'll look at ways of adjusting the time so that you can add motion to the beginning of your animation.

The Custom tangent and the resulting curve in the Position track and its resulting trajectory are affected by the prior tangent setting that the Custom tangent replaces. Had the prior In tangent setting for keyframe 5 been the Smooth tangent instead of the Slow tangent, the resulting curve in the trajectory and the Z-axis curve of the Track View - Curve Editor would be different. Instead of the curved trajectory shown in Figure 12.23, you would see a curve that resembles the one in Figure 12.24.

FIGURE 12.24

The Track View curve and trajectory after changing the In tangent option from Smooth to Custom

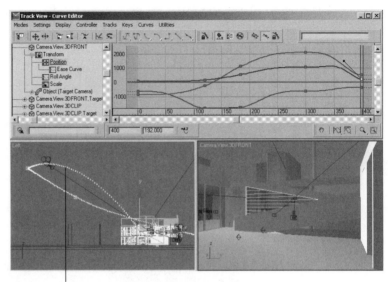

The trajectory is biased toward keyframe 4

The curve in Figure 12.24 is biased toward keyframe 4 at the upper left corner of the Left viewport. This is quite different from the Left viewport view in Figure 12.23, where the trajectory curve is biased toward keyframe 5. This is a subtle feature and one that often goes unnoticed until you become confused by the seemingly random way the Custom Tangent option affects a curve. The Custom tangent does not change the shape of the existing curve when it is applied. That's why the previously used tangent makes a difference when you apply the Custom tangent.

TIP   *You can adjust the camera trajectory while watching a playback of the animation in the Camera viewport. Make the Camera viewport active; then click the Play button in the Time controls. As you watch the playback of the animation in the Camera viewport, adjust the curve in the Track View dialog box.*

USING THE TCB METHOD FOR ADJUSTING KEYFRAME TRANSITIONS

If you find that the Track view is too complex, you can also use the Tension Continuity Bias (TCB) controller for your keyframe transitions. Instead of offering a set of tangent options for the In and Out keyframe parameters, you use three settings—Tension, Continuity, and Bias—to control a keyframe transition.

The default Position controller is called a Position XYZ controller. You can change to a TCB controller by doing the following.

1. With an animated camera selected, select a keyframe key. Then, in the Motion tab of the Command Panel, open the Assign Controller rollout.

Continued on next page

USING THE TCB METHOD FOR ADJUSTING KEYFRAME TRANSITIONS *(continued)*

2. In the list box of the Assign Controller rollout, open the Transform track and click the Position track to select it.

3. Next, click the Assign Controller tool in the upper left corner of the rollout.

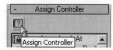

The Assign Position Controller dialog box displays.

1. Select TCB Position and click OK. The Key Info rollout of the Motion tab will change to show parameters for a TCB controller.

Continued on next page

USING THE TCB METHOD FOR ADJUSTING KEYFRAME TRANSITIONS *(continued)*

You see the familiar Time and X, Y, and Z Value spinners, but you also see a graphic and five new settings named Ease To, Ease From, Tension, Continuity, and Bias. The graphic shows you an example of how the frames approach and recede from the current keyframe. The default setting shows the keys as black crosses transitioning through a bell-shaped arc. At the top of the arc is a red cross representing the actual keyframe.

You can adjust the Ease To and Ease From settings to compress the frames around the keyframe in a manner similar to the Slow tangent option you used in an earlier exercise. Using negative numbers expands the frames around the keyframe.

The Tension option alters the duration of the frames around the keyframe. A value greater than the default 25 increases the density of the frames around the keyframe, while a 0 value spreads the frames out.

The Continuity setting affects the curvature of the trajectory through the keyframe. A value greater than 25 pushes the trajectory outward, while a value of 0 causes the trajectory to form a straight line to and from the keyframe.

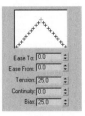

Finally, Bias pushes the trajectory curve to one side of the keyframe or the other, literally biasing the curve. A number less than 25 adds bias to the left side of the graphic, and a number greater than 25 biases the curve to the right side.

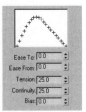

You can use the TCB controller to perform the same tasks as the Bézier Position controllers. For example, in place of the Slow tangent option in the In or Out key parameter, you can use the Ease To or Ease From settings to slow the camera as it approaches the keyframe. The TCB controller offers finer control from a single rollout than does the default Position XYZ controller. Also, you still have access to many of the same Track view functions you've used in previous exercises. You cannot, however, make changes to the individual X, Y, and Z Position Function curves as you can with the Bézier and Position XYZ controllers.

Increasing the Number of Frames between Selected Keys

You saw earlier how you could increase the number of frames to increase the overall time and slow down the animation. You can also increase the number of frames within a specific range of frames through the combined use of the Time Configuration dialog box and the Dope Sheet. To see how this works, try increasing the number of frames between keyframe 4 and the end of the segment. Right now there are 100 frames between these two keyframes, and they are numbered from 300 to 400.

The first step is to create some additional frames to work with.

1. Click the Time Configuration tool to open the Time Configuration dialog box.

2. In the Animation group, change the Length input box to read **500**; then click OK to close the dialog box.

You've just added 100 frames to the animation, though you haven't actually changed the camera motion in any way. If you look at the time slider, you can see that the keyframes are still in the same location relative to the frame numbers. The next step is to expand the time between keyframes 4 and 5. You do this through the Track View - Dope Sheet.

1. With the Camera.View.3DFRONT object selected, choose Graph Editors ➢ Track View - Dope Sheet.

2. Select the Position track under the Camera.View.3DFRONT Transform track. Expand the Position track by clicking the round plus symbol and note that the Ease Curve track is also selected.

3. Hold down the Ctrl key and click the key in the Ease Curve track at frame 400. The key bar will turn white when it is selected.

4. On the Track View - Dope Sheet toolbar, click the Scale Keys tool.

5. Now click and drag the cursor from the Position key at frame 400 to frame 500. You'll see the position and ease curve keys move in the Dope Sheet graph to frame 500 as shown in Figure 12.25.

You have just scaled the keys from frame 400 to 500, without altering anything else about the animation. The camera remains hovered above the building at frame 300 (keyframe 4) and there are now 100 additional frames between keyframe 4 and the end of the animated segment. The camera's trajectory remains the same as it was before you increased the number of frames between the selected keys.

TIP   If you find that, after scaling a key or range of time, an object's motion does not complete its full range of motion, check the Ease Curve settings in the Track view. Frequently, if the Ease Curve data are not adjusted correctly, portions of an animated object's trajectory will appear to be missing or misplaced. It is important that any Ease Curves you have maintain their one-to-one correspondences with the tracks they are affecting.

FIGURE 12.25

Scaling selected keys

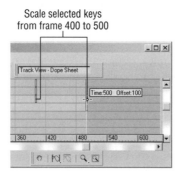

Speeding Up the Preview Rendering Time

Let's take another look at a preview of the animation. Since you've increased the number of frames, you may want to adjust the preview so it doesn't take quite so long to process.

1. Choose Animation ➢ Make Preview.

2. In the Make Preview dialog box, change the Every Nth Frame value in the Frame Rate group to **2**. This causes the preview to render every other frame, reducing by half the overall time it takes to create the preview.

3. Change the Playback FPS setting to **15**. Since you've got half the number of frames being created, you will also want to cut the frame rate in half to maintain the correct speed for the animation.

4. Click the Active Time Segment radio button in the Preview Range group to make sure that the entire animation is rendered. This is important, because you added some frames to the end of the animation.

5. Make sure that the Camera viewport is selected in the Render viewport drop-down list at the bottom of the dialog box; then click Create.

The preview animation won't be as smooth as before, but you'll get a fairly good idea of the camera motion.

If you really want to have VIZ render all of the frames in the preview but you also want to speed up the rendering time, you can reduce the detail of the preview in a number of ways. For example, you can select a rendering level in the Rendering Level drop-down list that is less demanding on the system. The default is Smooth + Highlights, which takes the most time to process. You might choose Wireframe or Facets from the list to help shorten the rendering time. Another option is to change the image size to something smaller than 320¥240. The Image Size group offers an input box that lets you control the image size as a percentage of the finished output.

TIP   If your rendering is destined for video and you plan to render to fields, it is a good idea to create a preview rendering at twice the number of frames of the final output. (Fields are the interlaced scans that make up a single frame in NTSC video.) This will help you detect any object collisions that might occur between fields. For example, a camera may momentarily collide with an object in the design, temporarily causing a blank field. This collision may occur only in a single field of your animation, and would go undetected when turning off field rendering. Such a collision would cause an annoying flash in the final animation when you use field rendering but would not be detected if you created a standard preview of each frame.

Adding Frames to the Beginning of a Segment

You've seen how to add time to the end of a time segment. Now let's look at how you add time to the beginning. You've already been exposed to some of the tools to do this. As before, you'll use the Time Configuration dialog box to add more time to the overall animation. Then you'll use the Track View dialog box to shift the animation sequence forward in the time track.

1. Click the Time Configuration tool to open the Time Configuration dialog box.

2. In the Animation group, change the Length setting to **550**, and then click OK.

3. Open the Track View - Dope Sheet dialog box if it isn't already open.

4. Click the Position track of the Camera.View.3DFRONT object in the left panel. The Ease Curve track is automatically selected.

5. Click the Edit Ranges tool on the Track View - Dope Sheet toolbar.

The right panel will change to show a set of range bars instead of the keys.

6. Click and drag the topmost Camera.View.3DFRONT bar to the right. As you do, watch the Key Time box at the bottom of the Track View dialog box and adjust the range bars so that the Key Time shows 550. Notice that all of the bars move in unison.

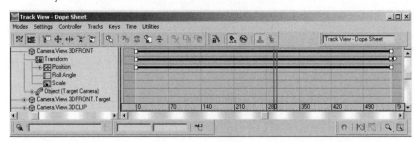

7. Play the entire animation in the Camera.View.3DFRONT viewport.

Notice that the last 50 frames are cut off; the camera seems to hang above the building and never reaches the courtyard. The camera motion that you had before is still stored in the scene, but some of the keys extend beyond the Active Time Segment. You will fix this next.

1. Switch to the Curve Editor by choosing Modes ➢ Curve Editor from the Track View - Dope Sheet dialog box.

2. Select the Position track for the animated camera. Note how the function curves extend into the dark gray area past frame 550, which is now the end of the Active Time Segment.

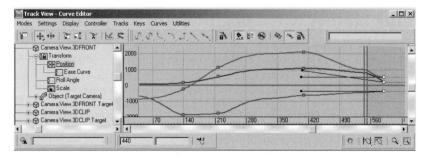

3. Click the Slide Keys tool in the main toolbar of the Track View - Curve Editor dialog box.

The slide keys tool allows only horizontal motion in the Curve Editor graph.

4. Drag a selection window around the three keys at the ends of the function curves at frame 600.

5. Zoom into the area near the end of the Active Time Segment in the Curve Editor. You should be able to see frame 550 listed on the track bar within the dialog box.

6. Drag the selected keys to the left and place them at frame 550.

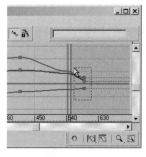

7. Play the animation again and observe that the camera motion is complete and the entire segment has been increased now to 550 frames.

You now have a fairly smooth animation that shows off the building from several vantage points. At this point, you may want to explore some different ways to study the results of your work.

Throughout this chapter, you've created preview animations or used the time slider to check your camera motion. The next section will show you some additional ways to preview the motion in your model.

Other Options for Previewing Your Motion

Earlier in this chapter, you learned how to create a preview animation that gives you a pretty good sense of the speed and overall time of your animation. You can also use the time slider to get an idea of the camera motion by manually sliding the bar at a slow rate and watching the result in the Perspective view.

A third way to study the motion in your animation is to use the time controls located at the bottom of the Command Panel (see Figure 12.26).

FIGURE 12.26
The time controls

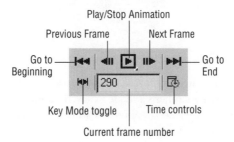

These tools work in a way similar to buttons on a VCR or DVD player, with some additions. The Go to Start button moves you to the first frame of the active segment. The Go to End button moves you to the last frame. The Next Frame and Previous Frame buttons move you one frame at a time either forward or backward. If you make the Key Mode toggle active by clicking on it, the Next Frame and Previous Frame buttons will advance the time slider to the next keyframe. The Play Animation button plays the active segment in a continuous loop. The Play Animation button is also a flyout, offering you the option of playing the animation of a single selected object.

The playback is useful for getting a quick idea of how your animation is working. Try it out on what you've got so far.

1. Click the Perspective view to make it active.

2. Click the Playback button below the icon panel and watch the playback for a few seconds.

3. While the playback is still running, choose Views ➤ Adaptive Degradation Toggle, or type letter **O**.

   The playback changes to a wireframe view and displays a smoother motion only if your graphics card cannot keep up with the speed of the animation. Toggling adaptive degradation off can be helpful in very large scenes that challenge the limits of your graphics card.

4. Click the Stop button to stop the playback. The Playback button turns into a Stop button when the animation is playing.

When the Adaptive Degradation toggle is unchecked in the Views menu, it forces the camera view to maintain a Smooth + Highlights shaded view even while playing back the camera motion. VIZ attempts to play back the animation at the full 30 FPS. When this option is checked, VIZ uses what is adaptive degradation to achieve a full-frame rate. You can alter the way your view is displayed to help improve the playback speed. For example, by default, VIZ degrades the image to a wireframe for the playback. You can force VIZ to limit the degradation to a shaded view with facets.

1. Choose Customize ➤ Viewport Configuration. The Viewport Configuration dialog box appears.

2. Click the Adaptive Degradation tab, then click Facets in the Active Degradation group.

3. Click Z-buffered Wires to turn off this setting.

4. Click OK; then make sure the Degradation Override is turned off and click the Playback button. Now the playback maintains a shaded view. The animation is a bit rough, skipping frames to maintain the desired frame rate, but it is a bit smoother than it would be with the Degradation Override turned on.

NOTE   *You may have noticed that the Viewport Configuration dialog box shows two groups with the same settings. The General Degradation group affects inactive viewports while the Active Degradation group affects active viewports.*

If you want smoother playback at the expense of detail, you can use the Bounding Box setting as the degradation setting. Bounding Box is the fastest display mode and you should only need it in very complex scenes with millions of polygons where other display modes lag behind.

WARNING   *Due to advances in Direct3D driver (DirectX 9) technology, you may not be able to get your viewport to adaptively degrade except in very complex scenes. Graphics cards have made amazing progress in the last few years and can usually keep up with real-time playback except in the most complex scenes.*

As you've just seen, these different options offer a variety of ways of previewing your animation. These tools will give you a sense of the motion in the animation at each change you make. They will help you refine your animation, so make liberal use of them.

Moving the Camera Target through Time

So far in this chapter, you've touched on all the major editing activities you might run into while creating a keyframed camera path. You can also make changes to the camera target. The target can be manipulated independently of the camera it is attached to. A camera target's trajectory can be completely independent of the camera itself, though you'll want to carefully choreograph the motion of both the camera and the target.

Try the following exercise to see the effects of camera target motion.

1. In the Top viewport, adjust the view so that you can see the villa courtyard as shown in Figure 12.27.

2. Move the time slider to the last frame so that you can see the camera in the Top viewport.

3. Click Select by Name to open the Select Objects dialog box.

4. Locate and select Camera.View.3DFRONT.Target from the list, and click Select.

5. Turn the Auto Key button on if it is not already active; then use the Select and Move tool to move the camera target to the location shown in Figure 12.28.

FIGURE 12.27
Adjust the Top viewport to show this view.

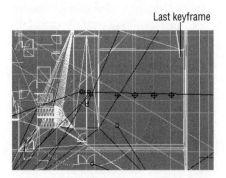

Last keyframe

FIGURE 12.28
Move the camera target to this location.

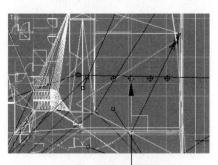

Move the camera target here.

Now you've created a motion for your target. The target has just two keyframes. Just as with the camera path, you can adjust the keyframe's In and Out settings, as well as function curve settings in the Track View window.

1. In the Motion tab of the Command Panel, change the In parameter flyout of the Key Info (Basic) rollout to Slow Tangent.

2. Use the keyframe selector arrows at the top of the Key Info (Basic) rollout to go to keyframe 1, and then select the Slow tangent flyout in the Out parameter.

3. Click the Playback button to see how the changes in the target affect the animation.

The target trajectory is often forgotten as the cause of erratic camera motion. Remember that when you start to add camera target motion, you will need to pay attention to its effect on the overall animation. If part of the animation seems too jerky and you know that you've adjusted everything for the camera path to create a smooth animation, check the target path for abrupt changes.

Controlling Lights over Time

This chapter has been devoted to showing you ways of controlling the motion of objects. In this section, you'll learn how properties of a light, such as intensity, can be made to change over time.

Now let's suppose you want to fade the sunlight while simultaneously brightening the interior lights. In addition, let's suppose you want this done at the end of the animation, viewing the courtyard while the camera is no longer moving. To accomplish this in the following example, you'll use several of the tools you've already learned in this chapter.

1. First, add some time to the end of the animation. Click the Time Configuration tool to open the Time Configuration dialog box.

2. Enter **600** in the Length input box, and click OK to close the Time Configuration dialog box.

3. In the VIZ main toolbar, click the Select by Name tool to open the Select Object dialog box.

4. Select SUN from the Select Object list and click Select.

5. Choose Graph Editors ➤ Track View - Dope Sheet.

6. Expand the round plus symbol under the Object (Target Directional Light) track.

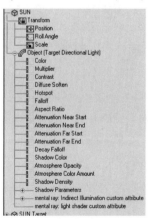

The SUN directional light is not currently animated. In the following exercise, you'll add keyframes to the SUN through the Track View – Dope Sheet dialog box.

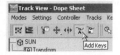

1. Click the Edit Keys tool in the Track View – Dope Sheet dialog box.

2. Using the Dope Sheet's navigation tools, zoom in to the area near the end of the Active Time Sequence until you can see 550 appear on the scale.

3. Select the Add Keys tool on the Track View - Dope Sheet toolbar.

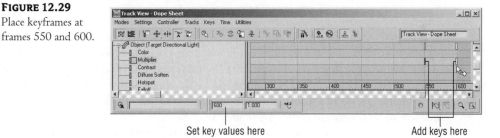

4. Click the Multiplier track in the left panel.

5. In the right panel, click the Multiplier track at a location that is close to frame 550, as shown in Figure 12.29.

FIGURE 12.29

Place keyframes at frames 550 and 600.

6. Click the Key Time box at the bottom of the Time Track window and enter **550**↵ to set the new key to frame 550.

7. Click the Multiplier track at a location that is close to frame 600, as shown in Figure 12.29.

8. Click the Key Time box again, and this time enter **600**↵ to set the new key to frame 600.

The Multiplier track of the SUN directional light now has two keys that control its value over time. These keys don't change anything yet. Remember that the Multiplier setting gives you control over a light's intensity. The final step is to adjust the Multiplier value at frame 600.

1. Right-click the key at frame 600. The Sun\Multiplier dialog box displays.

2. Make sure Auto Key is still on, then change the Value input box to **0**, and close the dialog box.

You've just set up the SUN directional light to dim from full intensity to zero intensity between frames 550 and 600.

3. Switch to the Curve Editor and then click the Multiplier listing in the left panel. In the right panel, you see the curve for the Multiplier value over time.

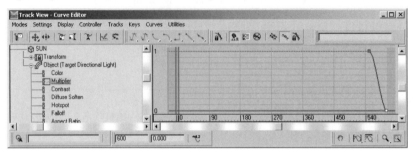

In this last exercise, you added two keys to the Multiplier track. You could have added just the last key at frame 600 and set the Multiplier value to 0 at that key. This would have caused the SUN directional light to dim gradually over the entire length of the animation. The key at frame 550 ensures that the Multiplier value stays constant at 1.0 until frame 550. The Multiplier function curve gives you a graphic representation of how this works by showing you a straight line from frame 0 to frame 550. The line then drops from frame 550 to frame 600, showing you the change in the Multiplier value from 1 to 0 between those two frames.

To see whether the modification you made really affects the model, you can create a preview animation of the Camera viewport.

1. Choose Animation ➢ Make Preview.

2. In the Make Preview dialog box, click the Custom Range radio button in the Preview Range group.

3. Change the range values to read **550** and **600** in the two input boxes just below the Custom Range radio button.

4. In the Render Viewport drop-down list at the bottom of the dialog box, select Camera.View.3DFRONT, and then click Create. After building the preview, you'll see a short animation showing you roughly how the lights dim over time.

Notice that in the last frame of the sample animation, the design is still lit. To really darken the design, you'll need to change the ambient lighting over time in the same way that you changed the SUN directional light object.

1. Open another Track View - Dope Sheet dialog box.

2. Scroll up the left panel to the Environment listing, under the World node.

3. Click the plus sign next to the Environment track, and then click the Ambient Light track that appears below Environment.

4. Click Edit Keys mode. Then click the Add Keys tool and add two keys at frame 550 and at frame 600 in the Ambient Light track, just as you did for the Multiplier track of the SUN directional light.

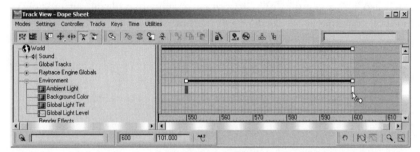

5. Turn on Auto Key mode and right-click the key at frame 600. The Ambient Light dialog box displays.

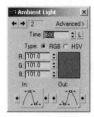

6. Right-click the spinners for the R, G, and B input boxes to set their values to 0. You can also click the color swatch to open the Color Selector, and then adjust the Value setting to 0.

7. Turn off Auto Key mode.

8. Close the Track View - Dope Sheet dialog box, and then rerender a preview animation. This time the design darkens to a greater extent.

9. Save the file as **Myfirstanimation.max**.

You still have the Omni court lights illuminating the courtyard and the Omni interior lights lighting the interior of the villa. You can perform the same steps you used with the SUN directional light to change the Omni lights' multiplier over time.

Summary

You've had an opportunity to try out most of the tools you'll need to create keyframed walk-through or flyby animations. As you've seen, there are many ways that you can control the motion of a camera, or of any object, for that matter. You've focused your efforts on a camera, but you can apply the same methods to any object in VIZ.

In the next chapter, you'll continue your exploration of VIZ's animation tools. You'll learn how objects in the environment affect the look of your animation and how you can work with objects to produce study and final animations.

You'll also learn about the different options for animation file output and how you can use the animation tools to automate the rendering of multiple still images.

Chapter 13

Creating Animations

IN THE LAST CHAPTER, you got a fairly detailed look at how you can animate camera motion. In this chapter, you'll continue your exploration of animation by looking at methods for saving your animations as files. You'll explore how using rendering presets can save you time.

You'll also look at how animations differ from still images in the way you put a VIZ design file together. The arrangement of objects and methods you use to create a still image has different requirements from those of an animation. You'll examine some of those differences and their effect on your work.

- ◆ Rendering File Output Options

- ◆ Automating Output of Multiple Still Images

- ◆ Rendering a Sun Shadow Study

- ◆ Creating a Walkthrough

- ◆ The Animation File Output Options

Rendering File Output Options

Now let's take a look at the options you have for animation output. This is really a big subject, so you'll start with the basics of study animations versus finished animations.

Before you've gotten to a point where you think you're ready for a final animation, you'll want to generate a study animation to make sure all of the elements are working together. You'll want to do this because of the time it takes to generate a full, finished animation. For a very elaborate design, a 20-second animation can take days to render, so before you commit your computer to 48 hours of nonstop rendering, you'll want to be completely sure that everything is perfect.

You can create a study animation by turning off some key features that may not be crucial for studying the motion of objects in your animation. You can also reduce the resolution of the animation to help speed things up.

Creating a Study Animation

In the following exercise, you'll create an animation file to be viewed in VIZ. It won't be a finished product by any means. The advantage of using the Renderer output, as opposed to making a Preview animation (see Chapter 12), is that you will be better able to see the lighting change over time, and you'll also see how the shadows affect the animation.

The first animation you'll do will focus on the last few frames of the animation, to ascertain that the spotlight is indeed dimming at the end.

1. Open the file you saved in the last chapter. You may also use `Myfirstanimation.max` from the companion CD.

2. Right-Click the Camera.View.3DFRONT viewport to make it active if it is not already.

3. Click the Render Scene tool on the main toolbar.

4. At the bottom of the Render Scene dialog box, click the Preset drop-down list.

VIZ lets you maintain multiple sets of rendering presets, as you can see from the Preset list.

5. Select Load Preset from the drop-down list. In the Render Presets dialog box, select viz.scanline.no advanced lighting.draft.rps then click Open.

6. The Select Preset Category dialog box appears. Here you can select which categories you would like to load. Leave all three categories selected and click the Load button.

Now the appropriate settings are loaded from the `viz.scanline.no advanced lighting.draft` settings file.

NOTE   *Render Presets are stored by default in* `C:\Program Files\Autodesk VIZ 2005\RenderPresets` *on your hard drive.*

In this case, the Default Scanline Renderer was chosen, and settings were altered in the Advanced Lighting and Raytracer tabs of the Render Scene dialog box. Of course, these are settings that you could have changed manually in the Render Scene dialog box, but it saves time to load them all from a file.

1. In the Render Scene dialog box, make sure the Common tab is selected. In the Time Output group of the Common Parameters rollout, click the Range radio button and enter a range from **550** to **600** in the range input boxes.

2. Click the 320×240 button in the Output Size group to reduce the size of the output if it is not already set at that output size. Fewer pixels take less time to render.

TIP   *Right-click the Output size buttons to change their preset pixel sizes.*

3. Click the Renderer tab of the Render Scene dialog box and note that the Antialiasing check box in the Antialiasing group isn't selected. This was unchecked when you loaded the preset earlier. This will greatly improve the speed of the rendering, but it will create a rendering that shows jagged edges on objects.

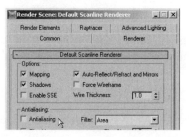

4. Switch back to the Common tab. Click the Files button in the Render Output group of the Common Parameters rollout; then in the Render Output File dialog box, select the AVI File (*.avi) option from the Save as Type drop-down list and enter **Myfirstanimation** as the filename. Use the Save In drop-down list to browse to the folder where you've been saving your project files.

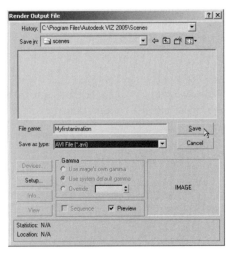

5. Click Save. You'll see the Video Compression dialog box for AVI files.

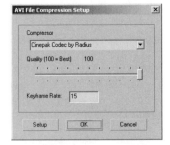

This dialog box lets you control the quality of your AVI animation file. You can also select the method of compression used on your animation. You'll get a closer look at these issues in "The AVI Codecs" later in this chapter.

6. Click OK to select the default values.

7. Click Render in the Render Design dialog box. VIZ begins the rendering process.

At this point, you may want to take a break and do something else. Even with the timesaving measures, the animation will take about 5 minutes to fully render on a newer computer.

Once the animation is created, you can view the rendered animation from within VIZ using the Display Image command or by locating the AVI file using the Windows Explorer and double-clicking it.

1. Choose File ➤ View Image File. The View File dialog box displays.

2. Locate, select, and save `Myfirstanimation.avi`, then click Open. The Windows Media Player opens and plays back the animation. If you have another application set to play back AVI files, then that application will open and play the AVI file.

As you can see, the animation is still pretty crude, but at least we can tell whether the lights are doing what we want them to.

Creating a Quick Overall Study Animation

Now suppose you want to get a quick view of the overall animation to make sure everything is working as planned. In the next exercise, you'll adjust some of the frame output settings to limit the number of frames that are animated. This will help reduce the total animation time so that you'll see the results more quickly. You'll use a different file format that offers a bit more control at file creation.

1. Make sure the Common tab is selected in the Render Scene dialog box, and then click the Active Time Segment radio button in the Time Output group.

2. In the Every Nth Frame input box, enter **3**. This will cause the renderer to create an animation that renders only every third frame. Consequently, the animation will take approximately $1/3$ of the time to render all the frames.

3. Click the Files button in the Render Output group; then, in the Render Output Files dialog box, enter **Mysecondanimation** for the file name.

4. Select MOV Quick Time File (*.mov) in the Save as Type drop-down list and click Save. As you'll see in a moment, the QuickTime file format lets you set the playback frame rate.

5. In the Compression Settings dialog box, change the Frames per second setting to **10**. Note that you can set the Quality slider and also select the color depth for the MOV file. Click OK after setting the frame rate. The lower the Quality setting, the smaller the file size will be. Decreasing color depth can also reduce file size. Click OK to close the Compression Settings dialog and return to the Render Scene dialog.

NOTE *Rendering at 10 frames per second (FPS) is near the limit of flicker fusion, where you start to perceive individual frames, rather than the illusion of continuous motion. The animation will be a bit jerky, but is still a valuable sample that allows you to get a sense of timing in the segment.*

6. Click the Render button in the Render Scene dialog box. This time the rendering will take a bit more time because you will be rendering about 200 frames overall ($^1/_3$ of 600 frames).

7. Use the View Image Filedialog box (File ➢ View Image File) to play back the animation when it finishes rendering.

This animation is still crude, and you may detect that it is not quite as smooth in the playback as the prior animation, but it gives you a far better idea of how the final rendering will look than did the preview animations you used in the last chapter, because it includes rendered light and shadow. The test animations that you render may also show you problems that need fixing. This is exactly the kind of feedback you want from tests before you commit all the time required to render the entire animation.

Adding a Moving Car

Your animation work so far has involved moving a camera around the villa. Of course, you can animate other objects in your model. Let's add a car to the villa animation to see how to control the behavior of objects other than cameras. By animating a car, you'll explore how you can rotate an object through time. You'll use a simple box to represent a car to see how you can make an object move smoothly in an animation.

NOTE *You can substitute a real car model for the box at a later time (see Chapter 15 to model a car using photographs).*

First create the box that will represent the car.

1. Right-click the Top viewport; then click the Min/Max Toggle tool to enlarge the view.

2. Click the skydome object; then, in the Display tab, click Hide Selected.

3. Click the Create tab in the Command Panel; then click the Geometry button. Select Standard Primitives from the Create tab drop-down list and click Box.

4. Click and drag the box shown in Figure 13.1; then click again to fix the height of the box.

FIGURE 13.1

Adding the box representing the car

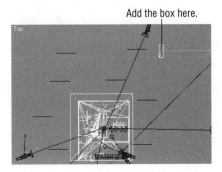

5. In the Parameters rollout, set the Length to be **15′**, the Width to be **5′ 6″**, and the height to be **40″**.

6. Change the name of the box to **Car01** in the Name and Color rollout on the Command Panel.

Now that you have a box representing a car, it's time to animate it. Just as with the camera, you'll need to enter the Auto Key mode, select a time in the time slider, and then move the car.

1. Click the Auto Key button at the bottom of the interface.

2. Move the time slider to frame 200.

3. Click the Select and Move tool; then move the car to the position shown in Figure 13.2.

FIGURE 13.2
Move the car to the new location at frame 200.

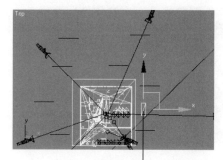

At frame 200, keyframe the box here.

To help you visualize the path of the car, turn on its trajectory.

1. Right-click the car and select Properties.

2. In the Display Properties of the Object Properties dialog box, click By Layer to change the display property of the car to By Object.

3. Click the Trajectory check box and click OK.

Now you've got a visible trajectory. Let's adjust the beginning and ending keyframes so the car starts and stops smoothly on its path.

1. Click the Motion tab in the Command Panel.

2. In the Key Info (Basic) rollout, click and drag the In flyout and select Slow.

3. Click the Key number arrow in the upper left corner of the Key Info (Basic) flyout to go to keyframe 1.

4. Select the Slow tangent option for the Out parameter.

5. Move the time slider from frame 0 to frame 200 and watch what the car does.

You can see that the car moves in a straight line between the two keyframes. The orientation of the car has not changed, so the car looks like it is moving slightly sideways. Finally, the car is driving through a tree.

Next, you'll modify the trajectory of the car so that it avoids the tree. You'll also add some rotation to the car so that it looks like it's turning into the building.

1. Move the time slider to frame 120. This is where you'll add another keyframe in order to move the trajectory away from the tree.

2. With the Select and Move tool still active, move the car to the location shown in Figure 13.3.

FIGURE 13.3

Moving the car

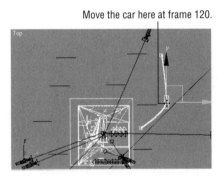

Move the car here at frame 120.

3. Click the Select and Rotate tool, and rotate the car clockwise so that it is aligned with the trajectory at this keyframe (see Figure 13.3). By rotating the car at this point you are adding a rotation key.

4. Now click and drag the time slider between frames 0 and 200 to see the motion of the car.

The car moves around the tree and turns, though the turning is not well coordinated with the trajectory. The car also does not complete its turn at frame 200 where it comes to rest. You need to add a few more rotation keys to make the car's motion fit its trajectory.

1. Go to frame 200, which is now keyframe 3 of the trajectory.

2. With the Select and Rotate tool still selected, rotate the car so that it is oriented with the trajectory as shown in Figure 13.4.

3. Go to keyframe 1 and orient the car with the trajectory.

4. Now check the animation again by moving the time slider between frames 0 and 200.

The car now turns, but it is still somehow out of sync with the trajectory. To fine-tune the car's motion, you'll need to add some additional key locations for the rotation.

1. Set the time slider to frame 93; then use the Select and Rotate tool to orient the car to the trajectory. This location was chosen because it is about where the car begins to increase its turning rate.

FIGURE 13.4

Orient the car with the trajectory at key-frame 3.

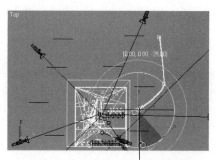

Orient the box with the trajectory.

2. Now test the animation again by sliding the time slider from 0 to 200 and back.

3. Add additional keyframes if necessary to make the car rotate along its trajectory.

The car now follows the trajectory in a more natural, car-like fashion.

You've added several rotation keys in this exercise. Unlike the position keyframes, rotation keys do not appear on the trajectory. They do, however, appear below the Time slider as additional key bars while the car box is selected. The rotation keys also have parameters that can be adjusted in the Motion panel and in the Track Views.

1. With the time slider set to 200, click the Rotation button at the bottom of the PRS Parameters rollout (not the Rotation button in the Create Key group). The Rotation key parameters appear in the Key Info rollout.

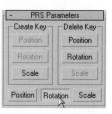

2. Scroll down the Command Panel to the Key Info rollout. You now see the Key Info panel for the rotation parameters.

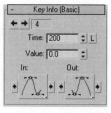

Notice that it is a Euler XYZ controller instead of the Position XYZ controller you worked with in the camera animation. You can change the Rotation controller to Tension Continuity Bias (TCB) if you prefer (see Chapter 12 for more on the TCB controller.) You can fine-tune the rotation of the car using the TCB parameters at each key, though the current settings may be just fine for this project. You've seen how you can use the Rotate transform tool over time to make the car move through its trajectory as a car normally would. You have the same types of control over the rotation of the car as you do with the position. You can also use both Track views to fine-tune the car's motion, just as you did with the camera in Chapter 12.

Automating Output of Multiple Still Images

Animations are great tools for presenting designs, and they can really help you to understand what a design will ultimately feel like to inhabit. However, animations can take a great deal of time to key-frame, preview, study, and finally, render. The tools you use for animation can also be used to help you automate the creation of still images. In particular, they can be great timesaving tools for creating the more traditional elevation views of a building or the top, front, and side views of objects for technical illustrations. When you automate the rendering of stills, you can leave the computer unattended while each one of the stills you specify is rendered.

In this section, you'll see how you can automate the creation of elevation views of the villa by animating another camera in the design.

Setting Up a Camera for Elevations

The first step in this automation project is to set up a camera to display an orthographic projection instead of a perspective view.

1. Click the Auto Key button to turn off Auto Key mode. Go to the Top viewport and, if it isn't already enlarged, enlarge it using the Min/Max Toggle tool.

2. Adjust the viewport so it looks similar to Figure 13.5.

3. Click the Create tab in the Command Panel; then click the Camera tool.

4. Click Target in the Object Type rollout; then click and drag the point indicated in Figure 13.5 directly to the left of the villa.

FIGURE 13.5

The Top viewport and new camera

Place the new camera here

5. Drag the cursor to the center of the villa plan and release the mouse.

6. Rename this new camera **Elevation01**.

The camera parameters need to be altered so that it will display a typical elevation view, which is a type of orthographic projection view.

1. First, click the Min/Max Toggle tool to view all of the viewports.

2. Right-click the Camera.View.3DFRONT viewport label in the upper left corner of the Camera viewport, and then select Views ➤ Elevation01. This will allow you to see the changes you make to the Elevation01 camera settings.

3. With the Elevation01 camera selected, click the Modify tab of the Command Panel; then, in the Parameters rollout, click the Orthographic Projection check box.

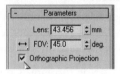

Notice that the Elevation01 viewport changes to show a side view of the building.

4. Adjust the FOV spinner (FOV stands for field of view) so that you can see the entire building in the Elevation01 viewport.

You'll need to make one more adjustment to the camera—lower the view in the Elevation01 viewport; it is a bit too high. You will also want to hide the background image behind the building by using Truck Camera.

5. Use the Truck Camera tool in the Elevation01 viewport to drag the building to the center of the viewport, over the background image as shown in Figure 13.6. This has the effect of moving the Elevation01 camera and its target up above the ground to the center of the building.

FIGURE 13.6
The Elevation01 viewport, showing the orthographic projection of the villa

Setting Up the Four Elevations

With the Elevation01 camera created and its parameters set, the final step is to set up the four views using the animation features of VIZ. You'll turn on the Auto Key mode, and then, at three different frames, you'll set up three camera positions, one for each of the other three elevations.

1. Turn on the Auto Key button on the Time Controls toolbar.

2. Move the time slider to frame 1 because it is the next frame after frame 0.

3. In the Top viewport, move the Elevation01 camera to the location shown in Figure 13.7. Make sure that you move only the camera and *not* the camera *and* the target. You can use the Elevation01 camera viewport to help align the camera.

FIGURE 13.7
Move the camera to this location for the second elevation.

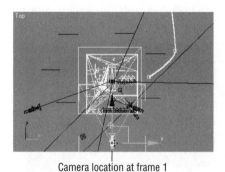

Camera location at frame 1

4. Move the time slider to frame 2; then move the camera to the position shown in Figure 13.8. Again, make sure that the camera is perpendicular to the surface of the building. You may also use the Elevation01 viewport to make sure that the camera includes the entire building in its view.

5. Move the time slider to frame 3, and then move the camera to the last elevation position shown in Figure 13.9.

FIGURE 13.8
Move the camera to
this location for the
third elevation.

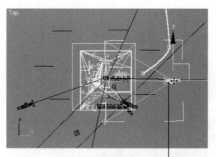

Camera location at frame 2

FIGURE 13.9
Move the camera to
this location for the
last elevation.

Camera location at frame 3

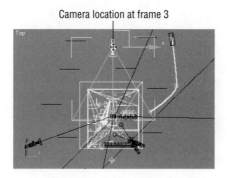

You now have four frames (frames 0 through 3) that show the villa's four elevations. As a final step, you'll need to create a copy of the SUN directional light that follows the camera. Typically, rendered elevation views use a light source from the upper corner of the view behind the camera, so you'll need to create a copy of the sun to simulate that orientation.

1. Move the time slider to frame 0.

2. Shift+click and drag the SUN directional light to the location shown in Figure 13.10.

3. In the Clone dialog box, give the new directional light the name **SUNelevation01**.

4. Click the Copy radio button to make the clone unique and click OK.

5. Move the time slider to frame 1; then move the new Sunelevation01 direct light to the location shown in Figure 13.11.

6. Repeat step 5 for frames 2 and 3. Use Figure 13.11 to guide you in the location of the Sunelevation01 directional light.

FIGURE 13.10
Copying the SUN

Make a copy here.

FIGURE 13.11
Positioning the sun
for each elevation

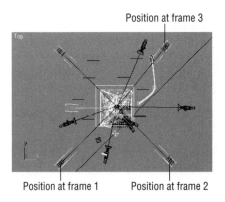

Position at frame 3

Position at frame 1   Position at frame 2

7. Select the original SUN directional light; then, in the Modify tab of the Command Panel, click the On check box in the General Parameters to turn off this light. You don't want the original SUN directional light to over-illuminate the scene, now that the elevations have their own animated SUN light source.

Now that you've got the design set up with a camera for the elevations, the rendering part is simple. VIZ gives you the option to render selected frames of an animation instead of the entire sequence of frames. You'll use this feature to create your elevations.

1. Click the Render Scene tool on the main toolbar to open the Render Scene dialog box.

2. In the Render Scene dialog box, click the Frames radio button in the Time Output group.

3. In the Frames input box, enter 0–3. This tells VIZ to render only frames 0, 1, 2, and 3.

4. Click the Files button in the Render Output group; then, in the Render Output File dialog box, enter **Myelevations** for the name, and select TIF in the Save as Type drop-down list.

5. Click Save. In the TIF Image Control dialog box, click 8-bit Color and then OK.

6. Make sure Elevation01 is selected in the Viewport drop-down list at the bottom of the dialog box, then click Render. VIZ proceeds to render the four elevation views.

VIZ will create four files, each with `Myelevations` as the first part of the name. A four-digit number is appended to the name to indicate which frame of the animation the rendering represents (for example, the first frame will be called `Myelevations0000.tif`).

Of course, you can use VIZ's animation tools to automate the rendering of a set of perspective or isometric views. You can now walk away and take care of other things while VIZ renders your views unattended. If your views take a long time to render, you may want to set things up to render overnight.

The elevations you render will look a bit stark. You can add 3D trees and opacity-mapped people to add some life to the images (see Chapter 7). The addition of landscaping, people, and cars to liven up a rendering is referred to as *entourage*. You can add entourage to your still images later in an image-editing program, or you can include trees and people in the model to be rendered with the building. Trees such as the flat magnolia trees already in the model can be used in front of the building by making them slightly transparent. You can also use trees that show no foliage, such as the trees from the Foliage palette of the AEC Extended objects set to canopy mode.

Rendering a Sun Shadow Study

Another great nontraditional way to use of VIZ's animation tools is to create sun shadow studies. In some situations, a project may require a shadow study of a building to make sure its shadows do not adversely impact a landscape feature or another building nearby. You may also be called upon to create a sun shadow study to help analyze a building's heat gain and energy usage. The Daylight system tool in conjunction with the Animation tools can make quick work of such a task.

In the following section on Adjusting for True North, you'll learn how you can use the Animation features to create both stills and animations of the building's shadows over time.

Adjusting for True North

Chapter 10 shows you how to place a Daylight system into your scenes. Instead of repeating those instructions here, you'll use a file that has the Daylight system already placed for you. The file named `Shadowstudy.max` from the companion CD has a Daylight system placed in the scene with the sun position set for 2 o'clock on April 21, 2004, and for the location of Paris, France. No adjustment has been made for true north yet, so you need to orient the sun correctly in relation to the building. For the villa, north is actually in the lower left corner of the Top viewport. You can change the orientation of the compass rose and thereby change the true north direction for the project site.

1. Open the file `Shadowstudy.max` from the companion CD.

2. Click the Select by Name tool in the main toolbar and select [Daylight01] from the list.

3. Click the Motion tab in the Command Panel and turn off the Manual Override setting at the top of the Control Parameters rollout. This option locks and unlocks the control parameter settings.

4. Scroll down to the Site group of the Control Parameters rollout.

5. Change the North Direction setting to **225**. You'll see the compass rose and Sunlight directional light change position to reflect the new north direction.

6. Turn the Manual Override option back on.

The North Direction setting interprets values as degrees in a clockwise direction, so to point north directly to the right in a positive X axis direction, you would enter **90**. The North Direction input box does not accept negative values, so to point true north to the lower left corner of the top viewport, you need to enter **225**.

Now let's set up some times for the shadow study. Suppose you want to see the shadows at 3-hour intervals, starting at 6 o'clock. You'll want to set the first hour a bit before the 6 o'clock time in case you want to create an animated study of the sunlight.

1. Use the Select by Name tool to select the Daylight01 Daylight system if it is not still selected; then click the Motion tab of the Command Panel.

2. Uncheck Manual Override in the Control Parameters rollout.

3. Set the Hours parameter in the Time group of the Control Parameters rollout to **3**.

4. Click the Auto Key button to turn on the Animate mode.

5. Move the time slider to frame 70 and change the Hours setting to **21**. Note that the Hours spinner turns red to show it has been keyframed.

6. Turn off Auto Key mode.

You now have a range of time that you can use to generate single images or a 2-second animation showing the movement of shadows across the ground on April 21, 2004. There is one more detail you'll need to adjust before you create your study renderings.

Changing from IES Sun to a Standard Light

You may recall from Chapter 10 that the Daylight system uses an IES Sun, which is a photometric light. Such a light produces a coarse-looking shadow when not used with the radiosity renderer.

You'll want to change the Daylight system from IES Sun to a standard directed light to get a smooth, even shadow when you're using the default scanline renderer.

1. Click the Modify tab.

2. In the Daylight Parameters rollout, change the IES Sun selection in the Sunlight drop-down list to Standard.

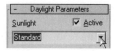

3. You don't need the Skylight option, so turn off the Active option for Skylight at the bottom of the Daylight Parameters rollout.

Now you are ready to create the shadow study renderings.

1. In the Top viewport, adjust the view to look like Figure 13.12.

FIGURE 13.12
Adjust the Top viewport so that it looks like this figure.

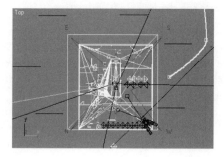

2. Open the Render Scene dialog box and select Load Preset from the presets drop-down list. In the Render Presets dialog box select viz.scanline.no advanced lighting.high.rps then click Open.

3. Click Load in the Select Preset Categories dialog box.

4. Click the Frames radio button in the Time Output group on the Common tab of the Render Scene dialog box.

5. Enter the frame numbers that correlate with the times of day that you want to render, separated by commas. For four single views at three-hour increments, enter **20,30,40,50** without spaces.

6. Use the File button to enter the name **Shadowstudy** for your file output and then click Save. Use the Save In drop-down list to browse to the folder where you've been saving your project files.

7. Make sure Top is selected in the Viewport drop-down list at the bottom of the dialog box and click Render.

VIZ will render four views of the Top viewport, each showing the shadows of the building on the ground at the times indicated for each frame.

To create a short, animated shadow study, do the following:

1. Set up the Top viewport as described in the last set of steps.

2. Open the Render Scene dialog box, click the Range radio button, and enter a range from frame 0 to frame 60.

3. Click File and enter **Shadowstudy** for the filename and **.AVI** for the Save as Type drop-down list.

4. Click Render to create the shadow study animation.

Both the still images and the animation can be helpful tools in your work, and as you've seen from these exercises, they don't really take that much time to generate.

As you've seen from the exercises in this chapter, you can have several animations in a single design. You just have to select a camera to animate, depending on which animation you want to use, then select the time range or set of frames for your final output.

You've seen how you can create a wide variety of animations from flybys to shadow studies. There's one more method for animations that you'll want to know about. You can generate a more intimate look at a design, called a *walkthrough*, by simulating the view of a building as you walk along a path. Let's see how it is done.

Creating a Walkthrough

Walkthroughs can give you a sense of what an interior space is really like. They can play a major role in selling a project to a client. They can also show you what is good or bad about a design in ways that still images cannot. Before you can start a walkthrough, you'll need a spline that indicates the walkthrough path.

Start by creating a path for your walkthrough, using a line shape.

1. Use the Min/Max Toggle tool to enlarge the Top viewport.

2. Click the Create tab in the Command Panel, click the Shapes button, and then click Line.

3. You'll want a curved path, so click and drag the start of the line at the point indicated in Figure 13.13.

4. Click and drag two more points to form the curved spline shown in Figure 13.13. Right-click to complete the path.

FIGURE 13.13

Draw this spline for the camera path.

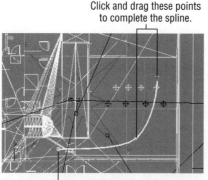

Click and drag these points to complete the spline.

Click and drag the start of the spline from here.

5. Give your new line the name **Walkthroughpath** in the Name and Color rollout on the Command Panel.

6. Click the Select and Move tool. Move this path up to 16′ in the Z direction, so that it is at eye level on the second floor.

You've just created the path for the walkthrough. Remember that you can edit the curve using the Vertex option at the sub-object level in the Modify tab. You also don't have to worry if your path isn't perfect. You can edit the spline to fine-tune the walkthrough animation path even after you've created the animation.

Now you're ready to create a camera for the walkthrough:

1. Click the Create tab of the Command Panel. Click the Cameras category and click the Free button in the Object Type rollout.

2. Use the Min/Max Toggle tool to show all of the viewports. Click a point above the building in the Left viewport to create the new camera. The camera is automatically oriented to look out at the horizon by creating it in the Left viewport.

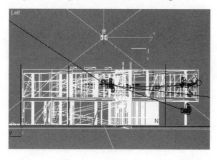

3. Rename this new camera **WalkthroughCamera** in the Name and Color rollout on the Command Panel.

4. Right-click the Top viewport and pan if necessary so that you can see both the new camera and the walkthroughpath spline simultaneously (Figure 13.14).

FIGURE 13.14
Walkthrough cam-
era and path

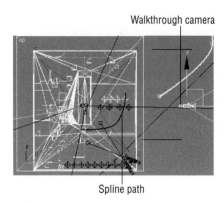

Walkthrough camera

Spline path

5. Select the Walkthrough camera and choose Animation ➤ Constraints ➤ Path Constraint. A rubber band is attached to your cursor.

6. Click the Walkthrough path to constrain the motion of the selected camera to this path.

7. Right-click the perspective viewport label and select Views ➤ WalkthroughCamera from the pop up menu to change the Perspective viewport to the Walkthrough camera.

When the Path constraint was applied, the camera moved to the beginning of the path but maintained its orientation. The path constraint only controls the position of the object by default. You have the option of keyframing its orientation as seen before, or using the built-in follow option as you'll see next.

1. Drag the time slider from frame 0 to frame 600. Observe that the WalkthroughCamera follows along the path it is constrained to, and arrives at the end vertex of the line at frame 600.

2. Click the Motion tab of the Command Panel and scroll down to the Path Parameters rollout.

3. Check Follow in the Path Parameters rollout to control the camera's rotation with the same path.

NOTE *The Bank option in the Path constraint allows a camera to roll along a path that curves in three dimensions, like a roller coaster.*

4. Drag the time slider back and forth and observe that the camera now rotates to follow the path.

NOTE The camera will maintain the same orientation relative to the path as it had in the first frame of the animation. Since the camera was initially facing forward, it will always face forward as it traverses the constrained path. If your camera is facing the wrong way, simply rotate it and it will maintain the same relative orientation thereafter.

Notice that the WalkthroughCamera is animated across the entire active time segment. If you'd like the walkthrough to take less time, you can keyframe the percentage the camera has progressed along its path to end at an earlier frame.

5. Drag the time slider to frame 150.

6. Toggle Auto Key mode on and make sure the WalkthroughCamera is still selected.

7. Change the % Along Path parameter to 100.

8. Toggle Auto Key off.

9. Play the animation and observe as the Walkthrough camera now completes the walkthrough by frame 150, while following the path.

10. Click the Go to Start tool.

One of the best things about using the Path constraint is that you can easily change the camera's trajectory by editing the path.

1. Right-click in the Top viewport. Select the Walkthroughpath spline object.

2. Switch to the Modify tab of the Command Panel.

3. Enter Vertex sub-object level by clicking on that level in the stack.

4. Select the last vertex and move it upward.

5. Drag the vertex handle as shown in Figure 13.15.

6. Exit Vertex sub-object level.

7. Right-click the Walkthrough Camera viewport and Play the animation.

FIGURE 13.15
Editing the Walk-
throughpath to con-
trol the camera
trajectory

Drag this handle to the right and downward.

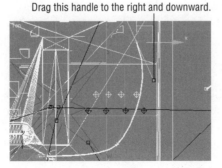

Observe the camera following the new trajectory. You may keep editing the spline path as needed to complete an entire walkthrough animation.

TIP   *You can get a camera to go up or down stairs by constraining it to a path that has its vertices moved in the Z direction to accommodate the changing elevation. It is best to use Bézier or Smooth vertices in a walkthrough path to ensure gradual and continuous motion.*

The Animation File Output Options

Before we end this chapter, you'll want to know about the animation file formats. Most of these formats are the same as those for single still images, with a few twists.

You have several format options for animation file output, each with its advantages and disadvantages.

Autodesk Flic image file (*.flc, *.fli, *.cel)   This is Autodesk's own animation file format. It is limited to 256 colors. You need the Autodesk animation player to view files in this format; however, it has become such a commonly used format that many desktop video player applications, such as the Windows Media Player, will play it.

The playback rate will vary depending on the power of the computer and the speed of your hard drive. The smaller image size of 320×200 will play back faster, and for test animation, this can be more than adequate.

AVI file (*.avi)   AVI stands for Audio Video Interleaved, and it is perhaps the most common type of animation file on the Windows platform. You can use AVI files for both animated materials and animated backgrounds.

These AVI files can use any number of compression schemes, known as codecs (*codec* is short for compressor/decompressor). When you use this file format, a dialog box appears, allowing you to select a codec. The usual choices are Cinepak, Intel Indeo 3.2, Microsoft Video 1, and Autodesk RLE. You may also install other codecs onto your system such as MPEG-1, or Motion JPEG codecs for specialized video output devices. (A complete discussion on codecs is beyond the scope of this section.) You may want to experiment with the codecs you have available to see which one gives you the best results.

Other AVI file settings include compression quality and Keyframe Every N Frames. The compression quality slider offers a tradeoff between image quality and file size: the better the image quality, the larger the AVI file will be. The Keyframe Every N Frames lets you control AVI keyframes that are not the same as the keyframes you've encountered in VIZ animations; AVI keyframes have more to do with the way animation files are compressed.

Targa (*.tga)   This is perhaps the most universally accepted format for high-quality video animation. Like the GIF file format, it produces a single file for each frame. Since a typical Targa file is close to 1 megabyte in size, you will use up disk space in a hurry using this format. Still, it is the format of choice when you want the best quality video output. It offers a wide variety of resolutions, and color depth up to 32-bit color (24-bit plus alpha channels). You can use Targa files for still images, and it is a good format for transferring to Apple Macintosh systems, because it usually requires little if any translation for the Mac platform.

Color and Mono Tiff (*.tif)   These file formats offer high-quality color or monochrome output. They are similar to the Targa format for quality, though Tiff files are used primarily for still images and prepress. This format also produces one file per frame of animation. If your images are destined for print, this file format is the best choice, but be aware that both PC and Mac versions of this file format exist. If you're sending your file to a Mac, make sure you've translated it into a Mac Tiff file. This can be done easily with Photoshop or with another high-end image-editing program.

BMP RGB and 256 (*.bmp)   The BMP format is the native Windows image format. It is not as universally used as the Targa format for video animation; still, most Windows graphics programs can read BMP files. RGB refers to 24-bit color, or color depth of 16 million.

JPEG (*.jpg, *.jpeg)   This format is a highly compressed, true color file format. JPEG is frequently used for color images on the Internet. The advantage of JPEG is that it is a true color format that offers very good quality images at a reduced file size. One drawback of JPEG is that it does introduce distortions into the image. The greater the compression used, the more distortion is introduced.

GIF (*.gif)   Although GIF files are not supported by VIZ as an output file format, it is an important file format that should be mentioned here. This is a highly compressed image file format that is limited to 256 colors. This file format is popular because it is easily sent over the Internet and is frequently used for graphics on web pages. GIF files can also contain very small animations. You can convert a series of animated GIF frames into an animation by using a number of software tools, including Adobe Image Ready, which is a product that ships with Adobe Photoshop. Also, free and shareware products can turn a series of animation frames into animated GIF files.

PNG (*.png)   The PNG file format is similar to GIF and JPEG in that it is primarily used for web graphics. It has a variety of settings, mostly for controlling color depth.

EPS (*.eps, *.ps)   EPS, or Encapsulated PostScript, is a file format devised by Adobe for describing page layouts in the graphic arts industry. If you intend to send your renderings to a prepress house, EPS and TIFF are both popular formats.

Kodak Cineon (*.cin)   The Kodak Cineon file format is intended for the film industry. It is a standard format for converting motion picture negative film into a digital format. Many special effects houses use this format and other software to help create the special effects you see in movies. Frames rendered to this format are recorded as individual files.

MOV (*.mov)   QuickTime is Apple's standard format for animation and video files. Its use is not limited to the Mac OS, however. It is somewhat equivalent to the AVI file format native to the PC, but MOV animations are of generally better quality.

While not directly related to animations, MOV files can also be QuickTime VR files. QuickTime VR is a kind of virtual reality that uses images stitched together to simulate a sense of actually being in a location and being able to look around. QuickTime VR is frequently used on the Internet on real estate sites to show the interiors and exteriors of homes. It is also popular at auto sales sites that show a 360-degree view of the interiors of new cars. Photostitching applications are available to construct QuickTime VR files from a set of images.

SGI's image file format (*.rgb) and the RLA format   The Silicon Graphics Image (SGI) has a following in the film and video industries, and they have developed a format designed to work with their own animation software and hardware. The RGB (red, green, blue) format offers 16-bit color and alpha channels. The RLA format offers a greater set of options, including additional channels for special effects.

RPF image files (*.rpf)   The RPF file format is an Autodesk VIZ file format that supports arbitrary image channels for special effects and other types of post-processing of images. It is similar to the SGI RLA format.

New!   **Radiance image files (*.pic, *.hdi)**   Also known as High Dynamic Range Images (HDRI), radiance image files are used for high-contrast datasets that capture a greater dynamic range than can be generally photographed in one shot. HDRI are usually composited from multiple shots taken from the same point of view at different exposure settings into one dataset. Generally, you shouldn't use these in animation output due to increased memory requirements. HDRI files can be used as backgrounds and reflection maps within animated scenes. See Chapter 11 for more information.

Several of these file formats create a single animation file, like the AVI and FLC file formats. Other file formats are intended as single files per frame such as the TGA and CIN formats. The single-frame formats require an application, such as Adobe Premiere or Discreet combustion, to turn them into viewable animations. Their chief advantage is that you can maintain a high level of quality in your animation files and then use the files as a source to produce other formats for different applications. Targa files, for example, can be rendered for the highest level of resolution and picture quality. The Targa files can then be processed through Adobe Premiere to generate AVI or MPEG-1 files for the Internet, or Motion JPEG for video output.

TIP   If you are using 3ds max, you can use the Video Post feature to do nonlinear video editing of your animated sequences including advanced transitions. Unfortunately, Video Post is not part of VIZ.

True Color versus 256 Colors

Three of the formats we have discussed—Flic, GIF, and BMP—offer 256-color output. You can get some very impressive still images from 256 colors, but when you start to use animation, the color limitation starts to create problems. One major problem is called *color banding*. This occurs when an image has a gradient color. Instead of a smooth transition of colors over a surface, you see bands as shown in Figure 13.16. The effect is similar to that of the Posterize option in many paint programs.

This color banding may be fine for limited applications such as previewing animations, but you will want to use true color output for your finished product. True color images, such as those offered by Targa, Tiff, and JPEG files, do not suffer from banding. They also offer smoother edges on models with lots of straight edges. If you don't need the absolute best quality, you might consider the JPEG output option. It provides high resolution and true color in a small file size. You can render a 10-second animation with JPEG files and, in some cases, use less than 40 megabytes of disk space. Most of today's desktop graphics and video editing software can read JPEG files.

FIGURE 13.16

Two images rendered in VIZ. The one on the left shows what the image should look like under good conditions. The one on the right shows color banding caused by a limited color palette.

File Naming in Animations

When you choose any of the file formats other than Flic, AVI, or MOV, VIZ generates a separate file for each frame of your animation. The name of each frame is given a number so that their sequence can be easily determined by video editing programs such as Adobe Premiere or Discreet combustion.

VIZ will use the name you provide in the Animation File Name dialog box. For the rest of the name, VIZ will add a number. For example, if you enter the name **Savoye** for the animation file output using the Targa file format, VIZ will create a set of files with the names Savoye0000.TGA, Savoye0001.TGA, Savoye0002.TGA, and so on.

Choosing an Image Size

Still image sizes will vary depending on the medium of presentation. A minimum resolution for 8×10-inch prints, for example, is 1024×768. Larger poster-size prints will require much higher resolutions. Video animations, however, will not usually exceed 752×480. The resolution will be determined by the type of device you are using to record to videotape. For example, if you were using the obsolete step-frame recording method that recorded a single frame at a time directly to videotape, you would typically render to an image size of 512×486. Other real-time video playback devices can use seemingly odd sizes such as 320×486 or 352×240. The horizontal resolution is stretched to fit the size of the screen, so the higher the horizontal resolution you use, the more detail appears in the final output. The aspect ratio of the animation does not change. You should check the documentation that comes with your video recording board for the specific sizes you can use for videotape.

The AVI Codecs

Earlier in this chapter, you had to choose a video compression method for your animation files. There are many video compression methods available, all of which degrade the video quality to some degree. Some of the methods are intended for presenting video only on a computer, while others are intended for TV monitors.

If your animation is destined for computer presentation, chances are you'll use the AVI file format. AVI allows you to select from a variety of compression/decompression methods, commonly known as *codecs*. You've already been introduced to a few of these codecs, but as a reminder, here's a rundown of the most common codecs and their uses.

Cinepak   Designed for high-quality video playback from a computer. This codec is considered to produce the best quality.

Intel Indeo   Designed for high-compression ratios, it is best suited for multimedia.

Intel Indeo RAW   Applies no compression to video. Use this to maintain the highest level of image quality while transporting your file to other digital video programs like Adobe Premiere.

Microsoft RLE   Designed to keep file size down by reducing the color depth. It is primarily designed for 8-bit animations.

Microsoft Video   Similar to RLE in that it reduces the color depth of the file. It is designed for 8- and 16-bit animations and videos.

None   Applies no compression at all to your file. Like the Intel Indeo RAW format, this option is for storing image files at their best level of quality, sacrificing disk storage space.

TIP   You can render sizable animations and burn them onto an inexpensive DVD-ROM that holds 4.7GB of data. You can buy a DVD writer for around $200, and most new computers have them now. Many DVD burners come with the software needed to produce DVDs that are viewable on consumer DVD players connected to television sets.

Summary

This concludes our animation tutorials for VIZ. There are many animation issues I didn't touch on in these chapters, including network rendering to help speed up processing, character animation, and the use of video editing programs such as Adobe Premiere, to aid in the editing of animations. But you've learned the basic tools you'll need to get up and running with animation. There are also some good resources in the VIZ user reference.

In the final four chapters, you'll learn how you can use other programs to enhance your work with VIZ. Both Adobe Photoshop and Autodesk AutoCAD are great partners to VIZ, and chances are, if you're involved in design, you are already using these or similar programs. The next chapter gets you started using Photoshop with VIZ.

Chapter 14

Using Photoshop with VIZ

YOU PROBABLY HAVE A number of other programs that you use on a daily basis. Most people have a word processor and a spreadsheet program, along with utilities for virus protection and Internet security. Business users typically have a personal information manager and database. Frequently, computer users use one program to create data that ends up in a different program. For example, you might create a spreadsheet, then move the spreadsheet data to a word processing document, or you might insert text from a word processing document into an AutoCAD drawing.

As a VIZ user, you'll have the same needs as others to create data in one program and move it to another. As in most of this book's examples, your designs will most likely begin in a CAD program before they are brought to VIZ. At the other end of the process, VIZ images may also be destined for a page on the Internet, which may require the use of a web page–design program.

On the other hand, your rendered image from VIZ may be part of a printed presentation that is being produced in Adobe Photoshop or in another image-editing program.

There are also VIZ features and operations that involve working with an image-editing program like Photoshop. For example, you will want to create and edit custom material maps, which requires an image editor. In this chapter, you'll explore ways that you might use an image-editing program with VIZ. You'll explore Photoshop as a tool to help create a texture map, specifically the tree image and opacity map you used in Chapter 7. You'll also learn how you can use Photoshop to embellish an existing rendering or even to edit geometry in VIZ.

To start your exploration of Photoshop, you'll begin by looking at how the tree bitmaps in Chapter 7 were created.

- ◆ Creating a Tree Map in Photoshop
- ◆ Creating the Opacity Map
- ◆ Using Photoshop to Create a Montage
- ◆ Creating Bump Maps for Elaborate Textures
- ◆ Modeling with Displacement Maps
- ◆ Using the Material Editor to Create Displaced Geometry

The Photoshop Interface and VIZ

An image-editing program is a must if you're working with VIZ. Many very good image-editing programs are available, but the most widely used is Adobe Photoshop, the current version of which is Photoshop CS. Photoshop is almost the *lingua franca* today for most kinds of digital imaging, and this chapter assumes you have some familiarity with it (as well as access to it along with VIZ). As a quick refresher, Figure 14.1 shows a typical view of the Photoshop CS interface.

NOTE   *All the features covered in this chapter will work equally well in Adobe Photoshop 7 or Photoshop Elements.*

FIGURE 14.1

The Photoshop CS interface

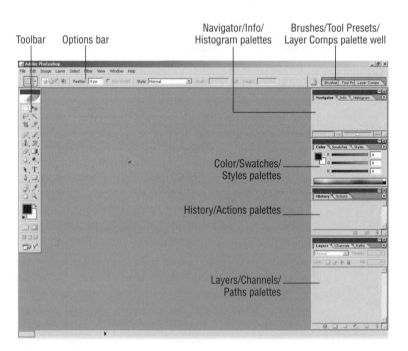

To the left, you see the main toolbar; to the right, are several tool palettes arranged vertically. The toolbar contains tools for specific tasks such as painting, line drawing, masking, and color selection, to name a few. Figure 14.2 shows the name of each function on the toolbar.

The palettes on the right give you control over tool and image settings and display functions. Each palette serves multiple functions that can be accessed through the tabs at the top of the palette. For example, the palette at the top offers Navigator and Info tabs: The Navigator tab gives you control over the view of your image, and the Info tab displays color information as you drag the cursor over your image. You'll get a chance to use a few of these palettes and tabs as you work through the Photoshop exercises.

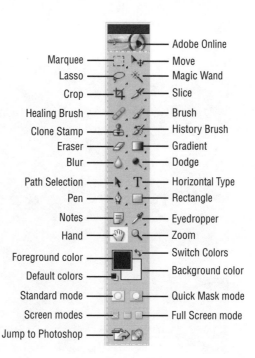

FIGURE 14.2
The Photoshop toolbar

Creating a Tree Map in Photoshop

In Chapter 7, you saw how to hide unwanted surfaces with opacity mapped materials. You used two separate image files of a magnolia tree in the tutorial. One of the images acted as the diffuse color map, and the other image acted as the opacity map. Working together in the material, the result was the image of the tree mapped onto a surface so that only the tree itself appeared in VIZ. The tree was cut out from its original background in the photograph.

You will now learn techniques for extracting the opacity image from the original color photo using the tools in Photoshop.

Selecting Areas in an Image

Now that you've gotten a brief orientation to Photoshop, let's jump in and use it to create a tree map for VIZ. The first thing you'll do is remove the extraneous parts of the image around the photograph of the magnolia tree.

1. Start Photoshop, then use File ➢ Open to open the Magnolia.tif file (Figure 14.3) in the maps folder from the companion CD.

FIGURE 14.3
The magnolia
tree that will be con-
verted to a map

2. Select the Magic Wand tool from the toolbar.

The Magic Wand selects areas of similar colors when you click a color in the image.

3. In the Options bar at the top of the Photoshop window, make sure that the Tolerance is set to 50 and that Anti-Aliased is not checked. The Tolerance setting determines how much variance from the selected color Photoshop will accept into the selection. A high number means a higher acceptance of different colors.

4. Click the image in the area shown in Figure 14.4.

5. Hold down the Shift key and continue to click in the areas around the outside of the tree to select them, as shown in Figure 14.5.

FIGURE 14.4
Click here to start selecting areas to be deleted.

Click in this area.

FIGURE 14.5
Selecting additional areas around the tree

Select additional areas.

The Shift key in conjunction with any selection tool will allow you to add additional areas to the selection. If you happen to select a portion of the tree by accident, choose Edit ➤ Undo Magic Wand or press Ctrl+Z to undo the last Magic Wand selection.

Don't worry if you haven't selected all the areas of the image outside the tree. You'll need to use some additional tools to outline some of the areas that cannot be selected with the Magic Wand tool. The Magic Wand is really good at selecting areas of similar color, like the sky in the magnolia image. However, you'll have to use a different technique to select areas of the image below the tree.

You've got a lot of the areas selected for deletion. Before you actually delete those areas, change the default background color to something closer to the tree leaf color.

1. Click the Eyedropper tool on the toolbar.

2. Click an area of the tree as shown in Figure 14.6.

FIGURE 14.6

Click an area of the tree with the Eyedropper.

The Eyedropper copies the color you click into the Foreground color swatch on the toolbar.

3. If the color swatch appears too yellow, try clicking another part of the tree until the color swatch is light green. You can click and drag the Eyedropper over the image to see the color swatch change in real time as you move the dropper.

4. Click the Switch Colors icon just above and to the right of the toolbar color swatches, or type **X**. The Foreground and Background color swatches switch places.

5. Press the Delete key. The background color displays in the selected area.

The steps you've just taken ensure that the background color matches a neutral color from the tree. This is done in case the opacity map that you create later doesn't completely align with the image.

Selecting Areas with the Lasso

Many more areas in the image need to be removed. You've accomplished just about as much as you can by using the Magic Wand tool. Now you'll have to use the Lasso tool to manually outline other areas. First, enlarge an area to work on.

1. Click the Zoom tool on the toolbar.

2. Click the lower left corner of the image so that your view looks similar to Figure 14.7.

3. Click the Lasso tool.

4. Make sure the Anti-Aliased option isn't checked on the Lasso Options bar at the top of the Photoshop window; then click and drag the Lasso tool around the edge of the tree to trace its outline as shown in Figure 14.6. Be as accurate as you can around the trunk of the tree, but you needn't be too fussy about the leaves.

FIGURE 14.7

Select the area outlined in this figure.

5. When you're done outlining, release the mouse button. If you're not happy with the outline, just start over again.

6. Press the Delete key when you're satisfied with your outline.

This exercise shows the limitations of the mouse. If you plan to use Photoshop a lot, it's a good idea to get a small tablet with a stylus.

Now continue with the other areas around the tree.

1. Use the Hand tool or the scroll bars in the image window to pan the view over to the right, as shown in Figure 14.7.

2. Use the Lasso tool again to outline the area to the right and the areas where the tree trunk begins to branch out, as shown in Figure 14.8.

3. As you finish outlining one area, hold down the Shift key and outline the next. The Shift key lets you create multiple selections.

4. When you're done, press the Delete key.

5. Continue to pan to the next area of the image and use the Lasso tool to delete the unwanted areas around the tree.

6. When you're done, select the Zoom tool; then right-click the image and select Fit on Screen from the shortcut menu. Your image should look similar to Figure 14.9.

FIGURE 14.8
Select the areas outlined in this figure.

FIGURE 14.9
The image after removing most of the area around the tree

Selecting Specific Colors

Some areas within the tree still need to be removed. You could use the Lasso tool to remove them, but that would be a bit tedious and time consuming. The Color Range command can help expedite the selection of areas that are of a particular color.

1. Choose Select ➤ Color Range. The Color Range dialog box displays.

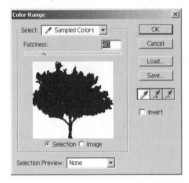

2. Click and drag a location in the image that shows some of the blue sky background through the top of the tree, as shown in Figure 14.10.

3. As you drag the mouse, watch the color swatch on the toolbar. When the swatch becomes a light-blue color, release the mouse. The Color Range dialog box shows a graphic depicting the areas that match the color swatch.

4. In the Color Range dialog box, move the Fuzziness slider to the right until the Fuzziness input box shows 100. As you do this, notice that the white areas in the sample image increase in size.

5. Click OK. You see the selections appear in the image.

6. Press the Delete key to delete the selected area.

7. You've finished editing the image. Save it as `MagnoliaIM.tif`.

The *IM* in the filename tells you that it is the image, as opposed to the opacity map. You'll create the opacity map next.

FIGURE 14.10
Click this area.

Click here.

Creating the Opacity Map

You may recall that the opacity map is the map that tells VIZ which part of the image is to be transparent and which is to be opaque. The next set of exercises will guide you through the process of creating an opacity map directly from an image map of the tree.

The first step is to select the area defining the transparent part of the bitmap.

1. Click the Magic Wand tool on the toolbar.

2. On the Magic Wand Options bar, make sure that both the Anti-Aliased option and Contiguous option are turned off.

3. Click the green background outside the tree.

Notice that this time the Magic Wand selected all the areas that match the color of the background. This is the result of turning off the Contiguous option on the Options bar. Although the Magic Wand with the Contiguous option turned off seems to offer the same functionality as the Color Range dialog box, remember that the Color Range dialog box additionally offers the Fuzziness slider to control the acceptable range of colors for the selection.

Using Quick Mask to Fine-Tune Your Selection

If you look carefully at the Magic Wand selection, you'll see that there are a few spots in the tree that really shouldn't be part of the background. You can use the Quick Mask mode to fine-tune your selection. Here's how the Quick Mask works:

1. Click the Quick Mask tool on the toolbar.

The image changes to show a red mask around the tree. The red indicates the areas that are *not* selected.

2. Zoom in to an area that needs some additional editing. In our example, an area near the top of the tree needs some work, as shown in Figure 14.11.

3. Click the Brush tool; then paint in the areas where the Magic Wand selected parts of the tree. The areas you paint are covered with the red mask color (see Figure 14.11).

FIGURE 14.11
The top of the tree, showing some spots selected by the Magic Wand tool that you don't want selected

Spots that should not be selected

4. You can adjust the size of the Brush tool by clicking the Brush preset picker on the Brush Options bar at the top of the Photoshop window.

When you do this, the Brush preset picker opens. You can then select from a list of brush types.

5. Pan around the image and paint over any areas that you want to exclude from the selection. As you work, you can temporarily switch back to a normal view of the image to check the selection; that way, it's easier to see the outline of the marching ants selection.

6. Click the Zoom tool; then right-click the image and select Fit on Screen to view the entire image.

7. Click the Standard Mode button.

The image returns to normal without the red mask.

NOTE *Photoshop uses red as a mask color because that is the color of a material called rubylith, which graphic artists use to mask unwanted portions of an image when they're preparing art for printing. When you enter the Quick Mask mode, you see the image just as a graphic artist using rubylith would see it.*

Although you can use the Brush tool to paint in masked areas that were missed by the Magic Wand tool, you can also use the Eraser tool to erase portions of a mask to create additions to the selection.

Transferring a Selection to a New File

Now that you've got the selection you need for the opacity map, the next step is to transfer the selection to a new file.

1. Choose Edit ➢ Copy or press Ctrl+C to copy the selection to the Windows Clipboard.

2. Click File ➢ New. The New dialog box displays, and the parameters for the new file appear.

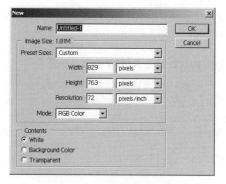

Note that the Image Size Width and Height values are based on the contents of the Windows Clipboard to which you just copied the selection from the `MagnoliaIM.tif` image.

3. Click OK. A blank window displays and becomes the active window.

4. Choose Edit ➤ Paste or press Ctrl+V to insert the contents of the clipboard.

Changing a Color to Black

You've just about got the opacity map created. Remember that black is supposed to represent the transparent area of a map, so you'll need to change the green to black. Here's how it's done:

1. Choose Image ➤ Adjustments ➤ Replace Color. The Replace Color dialog box displays.

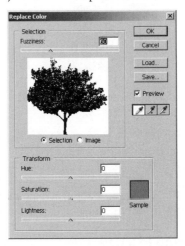

2. Use the Eyedropper tool to select the green background.

3. In the Replace Color dialog box, move the Lightness and Saturation sliders all the way to the left. This will change the selected color to black.

4. Click OK to close the Replace Color dialog box.

At this point, if you detect any stray areas you want to remove from the image, you can use the Brush tool to paint them out.

Softening the Edges with the Airbrush Tool

In addition, if some of the edges of the tree seem too regular or smooth, the tree may take on an unnatural look in VIZ. You can *roughen* the edges of the opacity map to introduce some irregularity to the edges and create a more natural appearance.

Let's try using the Airbrush tool to do this.

1. Click the Brush tool on the toolbar; then click the Airbrush tool at the right end of the Brush Options bar.

2. Select Dissolve from the Mode drop-down list of the Brush Options bar. This will give the airbrush a spattered texture. The default Normal option gives the airbrush a smooth-gradient appearance, which isn't what you want in this situation.

3. Set the Flow value to 10%. This keeps the airbrush flow to a manageable level, allowing you to gradually build up coverage.

4. Open the Brush preset picker and select brush number 19 because it has a good size and hardness for airbrushing this image.

5. In the Layers palette, click the Background layer.

6. Click and drag the airbrush near the left side of the tree at the location shown in Figure 14.11. Starting in the black area, carefully and gradually move the airbrush into the white area to introduce some irregularity to the edge, as shown in Figure 14.12.

7. If you get carried away, you can use Edit ➢ Undo Brush Tool. You can also use the trash can on the History palette. In fact, you can undo several steps back by selecting the step from the History panel and then clicking the trash can.

The opacity map is ready to be saved. This final step is not as obvious as it may seem.

1. Choose File ➢ Save As.

FIGURE 14.12
Airbrushing the edge
of the tree to intro-
duce some irregulari-
ty to the tree edge

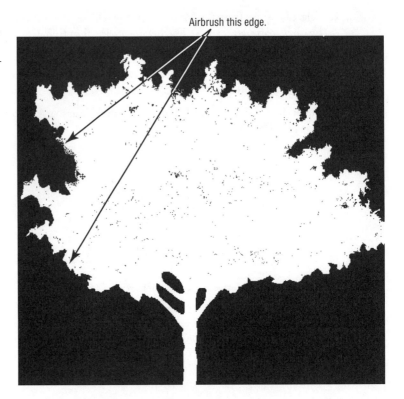

Airbrush this edge.

2. In the Save As dialog box, locate the directory where you've stored the sample files from the companion CD.

3. In the Save As drop-down list, select TIFF. Actually, you can select any file format that VIZ will recognize, including JPEG or GIF. Using one of these formats can save some file space.

4. In the File Name input box, enter the name **MagnoliaOP** to distinguish this file as the opacity map for the magnolia tree.

5. Click Discard Layers and Save a Copy in the Layer Compression Group of the Tiff Options dialog box and then click Save. If you're using Photoshop 7, check As a Copy in the Save Options group of the Save As dialog box and then click Save. You've got your tree maps ready to go.

You may wonder why you didn't use the standard File ➢ Save As option to save your opacity map image. When you pasted the image into the new window, Photoshop automatically created a new layer. Layers in Photoshop are similar to layers in VIZ and AutoCAD. They act as tools to help you organize parts of an image. You can see the layer on the Layers palette in the bottom right corner of the Photoshop window.

If you think you'll be editing an image file further, it's a good idea to use the PSD file format because it does store types of data that other formats do not. In fact, it would, in any case, be a good idea to save your opacity map as a PSD file in case you find that it isn't quite right when you view it in VIZ.

Now that you've got your image and opacity maps, you could use the Material Editor in VIZ to combine the two image files into a material, as you did in Chapter 7. A more efficient technique is presented next, where you will learn how to use an alpha channel to store the opacity data alongside the color data in a single image file.

Saving Images with Alpha Channels

In the previous sections you saved two separate image files for use in an opacity-mapped material. The procedure in Chapter 7 where you applied these bitmaps involved managing two image files: one color image file (stored with the suffix IM), and one opacity file (stored with the suffix OP).

Another approach to making an opacity-mapped material is to store both the diffuse map and the grayscale opacity map in the same image file. The advantage is fewer files to manage, which therefore, reduces the potential of misplacing a dependent file.

Channels are used to store color information in images. An image in the Rendered Frame Window has three channels: red, green, and blue. Each channel is an 8-bit grayscale image (256 shades of gray per pixel) that, when composited together, form the overall color picture, which is 24 bit (8×3).

An image's *alpha channel* is traditionally used to store grayscale opacity data. The alpha, meaning the first, is an extra channel in addition to the three color channels, making the overall image 32 bit (8×4). It is technically possible to store as many channels as desired, although, in practice, the alpha channel is usually the only extra needed.

WARNING   *Not all image formats support alpha channels. The* .psd, .tga, *and* .tif *formats are good choices for storing opacity data in an alpha channel.*

1. Open both magnoliaIM.jpg and magnoliaOP.jpg from the CD if they are not already open.

2. Make sure magnoliaIM.jpg is the active file and Choose File ➢ Save As... and save this file as Magnolia.tga (Targa format) on your hard drive. You will be using the .tga format because it can store an alpha channel that is readable by VIZ. Make sure Alpha Channels is checked in the Save As dialog box prior to saving the file.

3. Select 32 bits/pixel in the Targa Options dialog box to store all 4 channels.

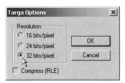

4. Click the window of `magnoliaOP.jpg` to make it active. Type Ctrl+A to select all and then Ctrl+C to copy the entire opacity map to the clipboard.

5. Click the window of `Magnolia.tga` to make it active. Click the Channels palette to bring it to the top. There are three channels—one for each of the colors in RGB color mode.

6. Click the Create New Channel button at the bottom of the Channels palette as shown in Figure 14.13. The Alpha 1 channel appears.

FIGURE 14.13
Create a new channel

7. Press Ctrl+V to paste the data from the clipboard you copied in step 4 to the Alpha 1 channel.

8. Click the RGB channel at the top of the Channels palette to view the color data.

9. Finally, press Ctrl+S to save the color image with a grayscale alpha channel, as shown in Figure 14.14.

FIGURE 14.14
Image with alpha channel

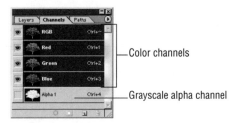

Using Alpha Channel Images in VIZ

Now that you've learned how to create alpha channel images in Photoshop, your next task is to learn how they can be used in VIZ. See Chapter 7 for a review if any of the basic material procedures in the following exercise aren't familiar.

1. Launch VIZ if it is not already running.

2. Open Villa14.max from the CD.

3. Right-click in the Camera viewport. Press Shift+Q to do a Quick Render. There is a plane that has been rotated to face the camera in the rendering (Figure 14.15) onto which you will map the magnolia tree.

FIGURE 14.15

Plane for mapping material

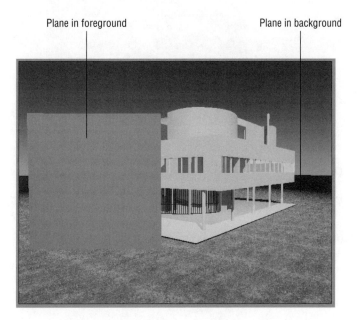

Plane in foreground

Plane in background

4. Type **H** to open the Select Objects dialog box. Select Tree1 and click Select.

5. Type **M** to open the Material Editor. Scroll down through the samples and click the green sample slot in the lower left of the material slot area to select it.

6. In the Physical Qualities rollout, click the Diffuse Map button (currently labeled None).

7. Double-click Bitmap in the Material/Map Browser.

8. Select the Magnolia.tga file from where you stored it on your hard drive in the last section. This file is also available on the CD for your convenience.

9. Click the Go to Parent tool in the Material Editor to return to the top level of this Architectural material.

10. Click the Show Map in Viewport button. Figure 14.16 shows the result in the Perspective viewport.

TIP   Clicking Show Map in Viewport displays different information in the viewports depending on what level of the material hierarchy you use it. If you toggle it on at the top level, you will see the maps in all channels simultaneously in the viewports.

FIGURE 14.16
Plane with Diffuse Map only

11. Open the Special Effects rollout in the Material Editor.

12. Drag the map in the Diffuse Map slot in the Physical Qualities rollout into the Cutout slot in the Special Effects rollout and release the mouse button (Figure 14.17).

FIGURE 14.17
Dragging maps between material slots

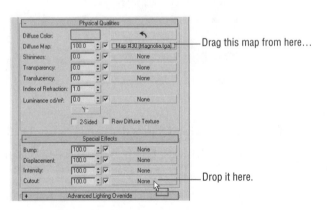

13. Choose the Copy radio button from the Instance (Copy) Map dialog box. You want a Copy so that the map can have different parameters from the diffuse map.

14. Click the map in the Cutout slot to go to the child map's rollouts in the Material Editor.

15. Click the Alpha radio button in the Mono Channel Output group in the Bitmap Parameters rollout. By selecting Alpha here, you are instructing VIZ to cut the diffuse map according to the grayscale data from this one channel.

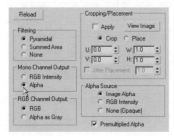

16. Do a Quick Render to see the results (Figure 14.18). You can see two tree trunks because there are two intersecting planes to which the material is mapped.

FIGURE 14.18
Alpha channel
cutout

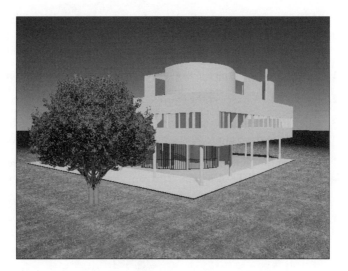

Although you've seen how you can create an image-based tree in these exercises, you can apply the same process for creating people and other entourage in your VIZ scene (see Chapter 7). As long as you're not creating an animated walkthrough, entourage such as the flat tree in the Villa Savoye model can be great time-savers; and if carefully done, they can add a high degree of realism to your renderings.

Using Photoshop to Create a Montage

You've seen one example of using Photoshop as a tool to create a material to be used with VIZ's Material Editor. You can also use Photoshop to enhance finished, rendered images from VIZ. For example, you can insert different backgrounds into a VIZ rendering, or you can add people and trees to an elevation created in VIZ.

In this section, you'll learn how to combine graphics into a rendering in a montage. You'll use the northeast elevation of the villa, which was rendered during an exercise in Chapter 13. This particular rendering has the background turned off so that you can more easily add a sky.

Start by adding a sky to the background. The main trick in performing this task is to limit the area in which the sky will appear.

1. In Photoshop, open the file `Sample_elevation.tif` in the maps folder from the companion CD.

2. Click the Magic Wand tool on the toolbar; then click the Contiguous option on the Magic Wand Options bar to make it active.

3. Click in the blank area where you want to place the sky, as shown in Figure 14.19.

4. Shift+click in the isolated area below the second floor that should also show sky (see Figure 14.19).

In other situations, you may find that there are additional areas that need to be selected for the sky. You can continue to Shift+click those areas using the Magic Wand tool.

The next step is to open the file you'll use as the sky background and paste it into the elevation.

1. Locate and open the file `Ksc-sky1a.jpg` from the companion CD. It is in the maps folder.

2. Press Ctrl+A to select the entire image; then press Ctrl+C to copy the image to the clipboard.

3. Click the Sample_elevation window to make it active; then choose Edit ➢ Paste Into. The sky displays in the Sample_elevation window, only in the selected area.

The sizes of the Sample_elevation file and the sky file are different, so when the sky is inserted, it doesn't quite fit in the elevation. You can adjust the size and location of the sky using the Move tool and the Transform options.

1. Click the Move tool on the toolbar.

2. Click and drag the sky background to the left so that it looks similar to Figure 14.20.

3. To adjust the size of the background, choose Edit ➤ Free Transform. You see a transform border, and handles appear on the background image, as shown in Figure 14.21.

FIGURE 14.19
Click the areas that are shown as selected in this figure.

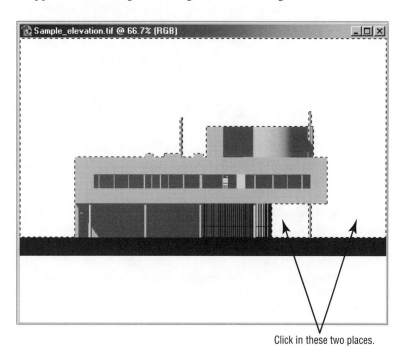

Click in these two places.

FIGURE 14.20
Move the sky background to the left, as shown here.

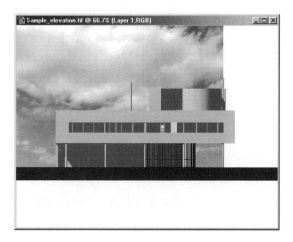

FIGURE 14.21
Background with
border and handles

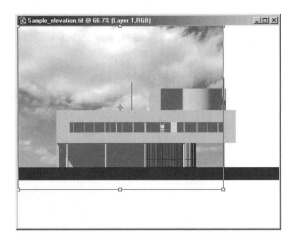

4. Click and drag the handle in the lower right corner of the background to the right so that the background fills the entire image.

5. When you've finished adjusting the size of the background, press Enter.

The background is now in place. Notice that you now have a new layer called Layer 1. If you need to use the Free Transform option again later to change the background, you can select Layer 1 and then choose Edit ➢ Free Transform with Layer 1 active.

Adding a Tree in the Foreground

Adding a background to the VIZ image is tricky, only because you need to know how to paste an image into selected areas. For pasting images into the foreground, the trick is making sure that you select only the portion of the pasted image that you want.

Next, try adding a tree to the image in front of the villa elevation. In this exercise, you'll select a tree in a way that will make the tree somewhat transparent. This is done so that the tree doesn't hide too much of the building.

1. Open the file `camphorAM.tif` from the `maps` folder on companion CD (Figure 14.22).

   This is an image used for a tree map that you saw in the aquatic center rendering in Chapter 6.

2. Choose Select ➢ Color Range.

3. Use the Eyedropper tool to click the green area outside the tree.

4. Set the Fuzziness setting to **60**; then click OK. The green area around the tree is selected.

5. Choose Select ➢ Inverse. This inverts the selection so that the tree—but not the background—is selected.

6. Press Ctrl+C to copy the tree to the Clipboard.

FIGURE 14.22
The camphor tree that you'll add to the foreground

7. Go to the Sample_elevation window and press Ctrl+V to paste the tree into the image. The tree is a bit too big for the image.

Once again, you'll want to employ the Free Transform option to adjust the size of the addition to the elevation.

1. Choose Edit ➤ Free Transform.

2. While holding down the Shift key, click and drag the Transform handle in the upper left corner downward and to the right. By holding the Shift key, you maintain the width and height proportion of the tree (this proportion is called the *aspect ratio*).

3. Adjust the tree using the Transform handle so that it is roughly the size shown in Figure 14.23.

4. Move the tree so that its base is on the ground. Press Enter when you're done.

FIGURE 14.23
Adjust the tree size as shown here.

The tree has a somewhat transparent look. This is because you were directed to set the Fuzziness value to 60 in the Color Range dialog box. With the Fuzziness value at 60, Photoshop selected a range of colors a bit beyond the green background, including parts of the tree. By making the tree slightly transparent, you can place it in front of the building without obscuring the building too much. As long as you don't get carried away, the transparency of the tree lets you add landscaping to the image without obscuring the view of the building. You may also want to apply a blur filter to the tree layer to subordinate the tree image.

TIP   You can also reduce the Opacity setting on the Layer palette to give the tree some transparency.

You may want to add other entourage to the elevation, such as people and cars (see Figure 14.24). Just follow the same steps you used to add the tree.

FIGURE 14.24
The elevation with
the addition of
people

Creating Bump Maps for Elaborate Textures

You've seen how you can mix a diffuse map and an opacity map to create the illusion of a tree, or by using the alpha channel to cut out the diffuse map like an opacity map. But diffuse, cutout, and opacity maps aren't the only combination of maps that are useful in VIZ. For example, you can combine bump maps with diffuse maps to very quickly create complex forms. For example, suppose you want to create a wall made of stone or splitface block. You would drive yourself crazy creating such a detailed item by trying to model the object block by block or stone by stone. By combining diffuse and bump maps, you can make quick work of such a project.

Try the following tutorial, which combines Photoshop, AutoCAD, and VIZ to help create an elaborate block wall.

Using AutoCAD for the Outline

Start by using AutoCAD to create the basic outline of the block wall. If you're using a different program, try to follow along to create the 96-inch by 48-inch block wall described here.

1. Open AutoCAD; then click the Rectangle tool on the Draw toolbar on the left side of the AutoCAD window.

2. Type **0,0↵** to start the rectangle at the origin of the drawing.

3. Type **96,48**↵ to place the other corner of the rectangle. This creates a rectangle that is 96 inches wide by 48 inches high. These dimensions will accommodate 6 vertical courses of block.

4. Click the Zoom Realtime tool.

5. Right-click and select Zoom Extents to view the entire rectangle. Click and drag downward with the Zoom Realtime tool to get a better view.

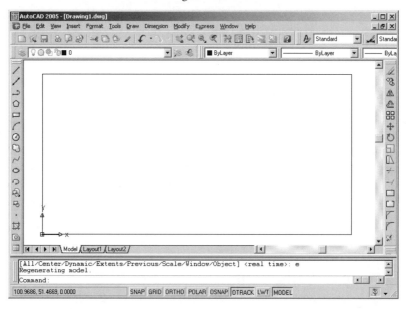

You've got the basic outline now. The next step is to add the block pattern.

1. Click the Hatch tool on the Draw toolbar.

2. In the Boundary Hatch and Fill dialog box, click the sample swatch.

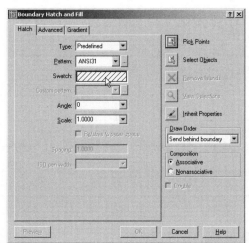

3. On the Hatch Pattern palette, click the Other Predefined tab.

4. Click the AR-B816C pattern shown in the dialog box; then click OK.

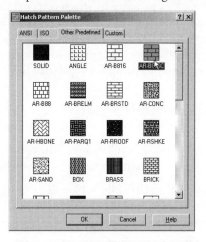

5. Back in the Boundary Hatch and Fill dialog box, click Select Objects. The dialog box temporarily disappears to allow you to select an object.

6. Use the Square cursor to select the rectangle; then press Enter. You return to the Boundary Hatch and Fill dialog box.

7. Click OK. The hatch pattern appears in the drawing.

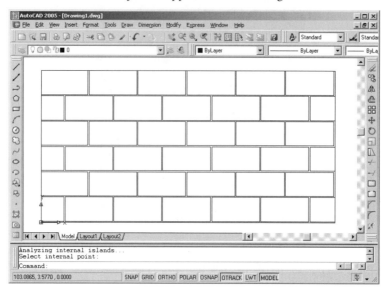

You now have the basic block pattern over which you can build an image map for a splitface block wall. AutoCAD is perfect for this particular task. It would take quite a bit longer to create this pattern accurately in a non-CAD graphics program.

Next, you need to transfer the AutoCAD image to Photoshop. There are several ways to do this. AutoCAD can be set up to print a bitmap file capable of being read by Photoshop; however, you'll use a simpler method for the block wall.

1. If you see the UCS icon in the lower left corner of the screen, type **ucsicon**↵ **Off**↵ to turn it off. You don't want the UCS icon to appear in the image that is copied to the clipboard.

2. With the AutoCAD window in full view and the cursor out of the block area, press the Print Screen key. This copies the entire content of your screen to the clipboard.

3. Return to Photoshop; then click File ➢ New. Remember that a new file in Photoshop will be sized according to the content of the clipboard, so you'll see the New dialog box, showing the size of your display for the new file size.

4. Click OK. When the Untitled window displays, choose Edit ➢ Paste or press Ctrl+V. The image of your screen displays in the window.

5. Once you've successfully copied the AutoCAD screen to Photoshop, close AutoCAD. You don't need to save the block drawing.

Transferring the AutoCAD image through the clipboard is adequate for what you're doing here. You don't need a super-accurate AutoCAD image to create the block pattern because you will be enhancing the drawing by using it in a material in VIZ.

WARNING *The clipboard is only capable of transferring images between applications at screen resolution, which isn't sufficient for direct high-resolution printing.*

Building Textures in Photoshop

The next step is to start to build a pattern that VIZ can use to create a texture. Remember that VIZ uses shades of gray to create a sense of bumpiness when using a bitmap image as a bump map. The splitface block has a rough surface that can be simulated with a pattern of random gray dots. Photoshop offers a filter called Noise, which is similar to the Noise material map you used in Chapter 7 to give the ground in the villa design a rolling effect. In the next exercise, you'll use Noise as a background.

Before you get to the Noise tool, you'll need to crop the image down. This will be a bit easier than cropping the tree image.

1. Click the Zoom tool and then zoom in to the upper left corner of the image so that your view is similar to Figure 14.25.

FIGURE 14.25
Enlarged view
of the image

Click and drag the Marquee tool starting here.

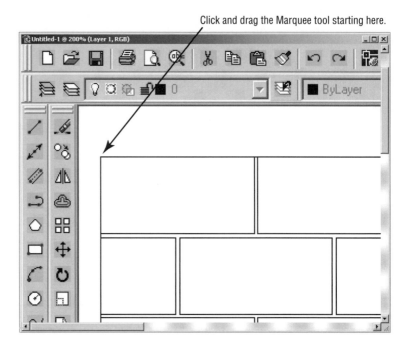

2. Click the Marquee tool.

3. Click and drag the mouse at the location shown in Figure 14.25, but don't release the mouse quite yet.

4. Drag the mouse downward and to the right. The display will automatically pan to the lower right corner of the image.

5. When your image looks similar to Figure 14.26, release the mouse button. You should see the marching ant marquee, indicating your selection.

You could have placed the Marquee selection while viewing the entire image, but it would have been difficult to select a point close to the corners of the block wall outline. By using the Zoom tool, you can get close enough to make an accurate selection, and when using the Marquee tool, you can automatically pan to other parts of the image by moving the cursor to the edge of the image.

FIGURE 14.26

The completion of the Marquee selection

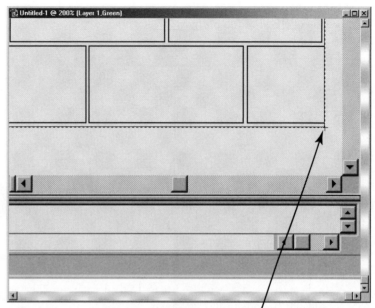

Drag the Marquee to this corner and release the mouse button.

Now that you've made the selection, you need to crop it.

1. To get an overall view of the image, click the Zoom tool; then right-click within the image and select Fit on Screen.

2. Choose Image ➤ Crop. The image is reduced to the block pattern. If your AutoCAD display was set to a black background the image will be inverted at this point. To reverse it, press Ctrl+A to select all and then press Ctrl+I to invert the image so that black lines appear on a white background.

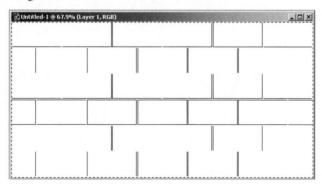

Now you're ready to add some noise. First, take a look at the Layers palette in the bottom right portion of the Photoshop window.

You'll see two layers listed in two slots: the background and Layer 1. The background is the content of the image before you pasted the AutoCAD screen into the image. Layer 1 contains the pasted image. Photoshop automatically creates a new layer when something is pasted into a new RGB file. The Layer 1 label isn't visible in the Layers palette, although the name *Layer 1* is shown in the image viewport.

In the next exercise, you'll add noise to the background; the noise will be used by VIZ to create the rough texture of a splitface block.

1. In the Layers palette, click the Background label to make it the current active layer. The label appears highlighted in blue to show that it's active. Also note that you can now see the Layer 1 label above the Background layer slot.

2. Turn off Layer 1 temporarily by clicking the Eye icon to the far left of the Layer 1 listing on the Layers palette. This is the Layer Visibility button.

The eye disappears and the block pattern also disappears in the Untitled image window.

3. Choose Filter ➢ Noise ➢ Add Noise. The Add Noise dialog box displays.

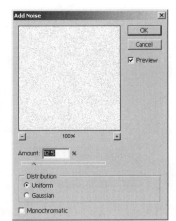

4. Click the Monochromatic check box; then adjust the Amount slider to around 400%. Notice that both the sample image in the dialog box and the Untitled image window change as you do this.

5. Click OK to accept the Add Noise setting.

6. On the Layers palette, click the Layer Visibility box for Layer 1 to turn it back on. The noise disappears in the image window because Layer 1 completely covers it.

You've added the noise to the background, but you need to make some adjustments to Layer 1 to allow the noise to appear in the image. You also need to fill in the mortar joint in the Layer 1 image. Start with the mortar joints.

1. Click the Zoom tool; then zoom in to the block pattern so that you can see the mortar joint clearly, as in Figure 14.27.

FIGURE 14.27

Enlarged view of the block pattern

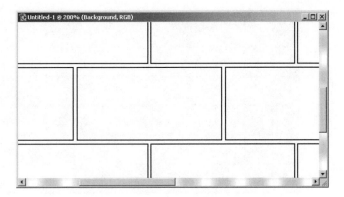

2. Make sure the Foreground color swatch shows black. To reset the foreground to black and the background to white, you can click the Default Colors icon below and to the left of the color swatches.

3. Right-click the Gradient tool; then click the Paint Bucket tool.

4. In the Layers palette, click the Layer 1 label to make Layer 1 the active layer.

5. Click the tip of the dripping paint icon on the white area of the mortar joint in the image window. The white area is filled with black.

6. Click the Zoom tool; then right-click within the image and select Fit on Screen to get the overall view of your image.

Now you need to remove the white area so that the background can show through.

1. Click the Magic Wand tool.

2. In the Magic Wand Options bar, make sure that both the Anti-Aliased option and the Contiguous option are both turned off.

3. Click the Magic Wand tool in any white area of the image.

4. Choose Edit ➢ Clear or press the Delete key to remove the white areas from Layer 1. The background now shows through between the mortar joints.

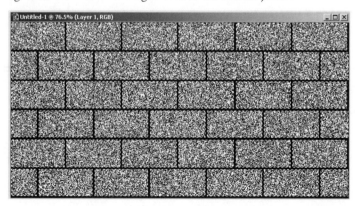

CREATING A CHAIN-LINK FENCE WITH AUTOCAD

In Chapter 6, you may have noticed a chain-link fence in the background of the aquatic center. That fence was created using the same techniques described in this chapter. Here's how the fence was created.

In AutoCAD, a simple crosshatch was created using the AutoCAD Boundary Hatch tool.

The view of the hatch pattern was adjusted so that it filled the display as much as possible. Once this was done, the Print Screen key was pressed. This copied the contents of the entire screen into the Windows Clipboard. Photoshop was then opened and File ➢ New was selected to create a new file. Remember that File ➢ New uses the contents of the Clipboard to determine the size of the new file. The Paste option was then used to paste the captured screen into the Photoshop window.

Next, the Marquee tool was used to single out the area displaying the crosshatch. Image ➢ Crop was then used to crop the image down to the selected area. The image was saved as a TIFF file, which was then used in VIZ as an opacity map.

Testing the Image in VIZ

You've got a start on a splitface block map. Let's take a look at the results so far. First, save the image in a file type that can be read by VIZ.

1. Choose File ➢ Save As.

2. In the Save As dialog box, locate the `\Autodesk VIZ 2005\Maps` folder in the Save In drop-down list.

3. In the Format drop-down list, select TIFF.

4. Enter **Splitface_bump** in the File Name input box.

5. Turn off the Layers options in the Save Options group. In Photoshop CS, click Discard Layers and Save a Copy in the Layer Compression group of the TIFF Options dialog box.

You need to use the Save As option in Photoshop because it allows you to save your work in a TIFF file format. As you've already seen, TIFF is a format that VIZ can read.

Now let's take a look at the results in VIZ.

1. Open VIZ and then open the sample file, called `Splitface.max`, from the companion CD. This is a file containing a simple box that is 192 inches wide by 48 inches high by 8 inches deep. The file also contains a light source, and the background and ambient lighting have been set to a neutral color.

2. Open the Material Editor and make sure the first sample slot in the upper left corner is selected, using the scroll bar to get to the top if necessary.

3. Scroll down to the Map rollout and open it; then click the bump map button labeled None.

4. In the Material/Map Browser, double-click Bitmap.

5. In the Select Bitmap Image File dialog box, locate and select `Splitface_bump.tif`. The sample slot now shows the bump texture on the sphere.

TIP   You can also use the noise map in VIZ to create a bumpy surface, but by using Photoshop to create a bitmap bump map, you have more control over where the bumpiness occurs.

The bump map you created in Photoshop is now part of a material definition, but you need to make a few adjustments. The color isn't quite right, and it's too shiny. Let's make these adjustments and add the material to the sample wall.

1. In the Material Editor, click the Go to Parent tool.

2. In the Maps rollout, change the bump map Amount value to **200**.

3. Scroll up the panel to the Specular Highlights group of the Phong Basic Parameters and right-click the Specular Level and Glossiness spinners to set both of these options to **0**.

4. Click the Diffuse color swatch, and in the Color Selector dialog box, set the Saturation to **0**.

5. Back in the Material Editor window, click the Ambient color swatch and set its Saturation setting to **0**; then click Close in the Color Selector dialog box.

6. The material from slot 1 has already been applied to the wall, so to get an idea of how the material looks, click the Quick Render tool in the main toolbar. You see the wall rendered with the new splitface block pattern (see Figure 14.28).

FIGURE 14.28
Rendered view of the block wall

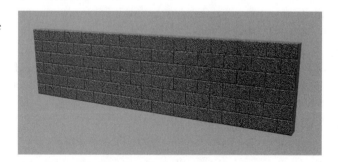

Everything that defines the wall as a block wall is there, but it looks too uniform and colorless. You'll need to add some variation to the bump map to give the wall a more natural appearance. You'll also want to start bringing in some color. In the next section, you'll learn how you can start to build your Photoshop image to include these features.

Adding Irregularity and Color to the Material

You've made a start on the bump map for the splitface block wall. In this section, you'll begin playing with the bump map image in Photoshop while keeping VIZ open, so that you can see your changes as you go along. That way, you'll get a better sense of how your Photoshop edits affect the material in VIZ.

WARNING *If you are using less than 256 megabytes of RAM, you may want to close VIZ while you're working in Photoshop. If your system is running Windows XP or 2000 and has at least 256 megabytes of RAM, having both Photoshop and VIZ open at the same time shouldn't cause any problems.*

To add some irregularity to the block surface, you'll want to include some wide patches of dark and light tones to the image while maintaining the rough appearance of the surface. You can do this by adding some dark tones with the Airbrush tool. You'll want to keep your airbrush work on a separate layer in case it doesn't come out exactly the way you want. By airbrushing on a different layer, you won't affect the other layers in an irreversible way.

1. Go back to Photoshop; then click the right-pointing arrow at the top of the Layers palette.

   This opens the Layers menu.

2. Click New Layer. The New Layer dialog box displays.

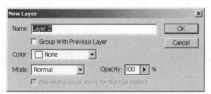

3. Enter **Airbrush** for the name; then click OK.

You now have a new, blank layer called Airbrush, and by default, the new layer is the currently active one. A new layer is transparent, so you don't see any changes to the image.

TIP *You can change the name of an existing layer by opening the Layers menu with the arrow button and selecting Layer Options. A dialog box opens, allowing you to set the layer name. You can also change the name by double-clicking the layer name label.*

Now, add some irregularity to the pattern using the Airbrush tool.

1. Click the Brush tool on the toolbar; then click the Enable Airbrush tool on the Brush Options bar.

2. In the Brush Options bar, select Dissolve from the Mode drop-down list.

3. Set the Flow value to 30%.

4. Open the Brush preset picker and select the slot labeled 45 because this is a large soft brush that's appropriate to gradually build up areas of darkness.

5. Set the color swatch on the toolbar to black.

6. Start brushing in some areas over the image. With the Flow value set to 30%, you'll be able to gradually build up areas of darkness. Brush in areas of each block in a pattern similar to that shown in Figure 14.29.

FIGURE 14.29
The splitface block image with airbrush added

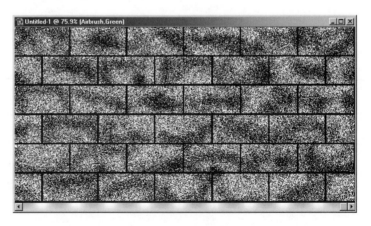

If you get carried away and blacken an area too much, use the Switch Colors icon on the toolbar to switch the foreground from black to white, and airbrush over the black areas.

After applying the airbrush, you'll begin to get a sense of depth variation, even in the flat Photoshop image. Once you're satisfied with the airbrush, take a look at its effect in VIZ.

1. In Photoshop, choose File ➤ Save As and then save the file again under the same name as before: **Splitface_bump.tif**.

2. Go to VIZ and return to the Material Editor.

3. Scroll to the Maps rollout and click the `Splitface_bump.tif` button.

4. In the Bitmap Parameters rollout, click Reload.

5. Click the Quick Render tool on the Rendering toolbar. With some variation in the surface, the block wall now begins to look a bit more realistic.

The surface of the block wall now takes on a rough appearance that was created by the random airbrush areas added to the `Splitface_bump.tif` image.

Adding Color through Photoshop

Frequently, the splitface block is used as a decorative element with color. You can add color through VIZ by adjusting the Ambient, Diffuse, and Specular color swatches in the Material Editor. Again, this results in a somewhat bland-looking surface. As you learned early on, you can apply a diffuse map to a material to add a pattern or color to a material. In this section, you'll add some color by creating another bitmap file that contains color information.

Start by creating a new layer in Photoshop that will hold the color image.

1. Go back to Photoshop. In the Layers palette, click the arrow in the upper right corner and select New Layer.

2. Enter the name **Color Pattern** for the layer name and then click OK. Remember that new layers are transparent, so the image won't change.

Now create a color for the blocks.

1. Click the Foreground color swatch.

2. Set the Hue (H), Saturation (S), and Brightness (B) settings as shown in Figure 14.30. This will create a tan color. Click OK to close the dialog box.

FIGURE 14.30
The Color Picker
dialog box with
settings

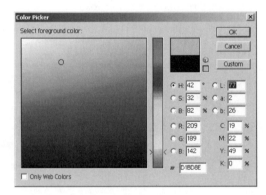

3. Click the Paint Bucket tool. Then, with the Color Pattern layer selected, click within the image. The color will fill the entire image.

Now, add some noise to the color to give it a sense of texture.

1. Click Filter ➤ Noise ➤ Add Noise.

2. In the Add Noise dialog box, set the slider to 90.

3. Click Uniform for the Distribution group and make sure Monochromatic isn't checked. Click OK to close the dialog box.

There's one more feature you need to add to the image. The mortar joint should be a darker color to set it off from the rest of the pattern.

1. Click Layer 1 in the Layers palette to make it active; then click the Layer Visibility button for the Color Pattern layer to temporarily turn it off.

2. Press Ctrl+A or choose Select ➤ All to select the entire layer.

3. Press Ctrl+C; then press Ctrl+V. This copies the layer to the Clipboard and then pastes it back into the image. You now have a new layer called Layer 2, and it's the active layer.

4. In the Layers palette, click the Color Pattern Layer Visibility button to turn it back on. You see the tan color return to the image window.

5. In the Layers palette, click and drag the Layer 2 label upward so that it's above the Color Pattern layer listing, as shown in Figure 14.31.

FIGURE 14.31
Move the Layer 2 label two layers above the Color Pattern layer.

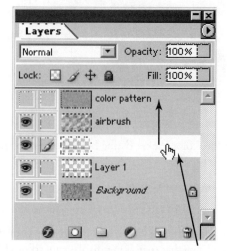

Click and drag the layer upward.

When you see the dark bar appear above the Color Pattern listing, release the mouse button. The mortar joints appear in the image.

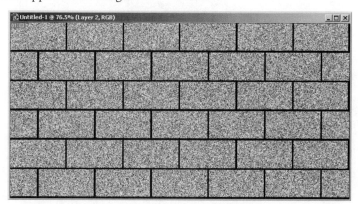

Last of all, let's give the mortar joint a dark brown color.

1. Make sure Layer 2 selected in the Layers palette.

2. Click the Foreground color swatch on the toolbar. In the Color Picker dialog box, set the H, S, and B settings as shown in Figure 14.32.

FIGURE 14.32
The Color Picker dialog box, showing the colors for the mortar joint

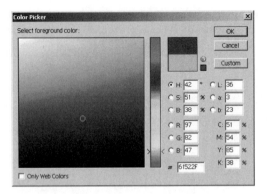

3. Click OK to close the Color Picker dialog box, zoom in to an area showing the mortar joint, select the Paint Bucket tool, and then click the mortar joint. The new color fills the joint lines.

4. Zoom back out to the overall view of the image.

5. Click the Marquee tool; then click the image to remove the selection.

You've got the mortar joints and the block color ready for your diffuse map. As an added twist, let's change one row of blocks so that they don't display any color. This will create a block wall with one course of gray block.

1. Make sure that the Color Pattern layer is selected in the Layers palette.

2. Click the Marquee tool.

3. Click and drag a rectangular selection, as shown in Figure 14.33.

4. Press the Delete key to remove the selected area.

5. The layer underneath the Color Pattern layer shows through, so you'll need to turn the lower layers off. Click the Layer Visibility buttons for the Airbrush, Layer 1, and Background layers.

FIGURE 14.33
Select one row of
blocks.

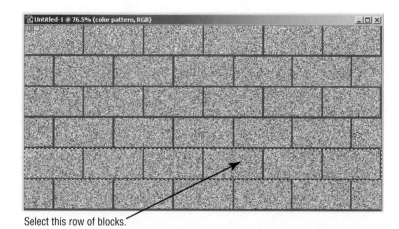

Select this row of blocks.

The final step is to save the image as a file for VIZ.

1. Choose File ➤ Save a Copy or choose File ➤ Save As.

2. Save the image as a TIFF file with the name **Splitface_Dif**.

You're now ready to add the `Splitface_dif.tif` file to the material in VIZ. Before you do that, though, take a moment to review what you've got in Photoshop.

The file in Photoshop contains several layers that make up the components for both the bump and diffuse maps. You can selectively turn layers on and off to obtain the appropriate mix of layers for each type of map. You can save the file as a Photoshop PSD file for later editing in case you decide to make further changes to the `Splitface_Bump` and `Splitface_dif` files.

Now let's see how the addition of a diffuse map will affect the block wall in VIZ.

1. Go to VIZ and click the Go to Parent button in the Material Editor to go to the Maps rollout.

2. Click the Diffuse Color Map button; then, in the Material/Map Browser, double-click Bitmap.

3. In the Select Bitmap Image File dialog box, locate and open the `Splitface_dif.tif` file.

4. Click the Quick Render tool on the Rendering toolbar. The image is rendered with some additional color.

Now you can clearly see the mortar joints. In addition, you can see the band of gray block in the second row from the bottom. The color of the gray band can be controlled by adjusting the Ambient, Diffuse, and Specular color settings for the material, without affecting the rest of the block wall.

If you want, you can make other changes to the `Splitface_dif.tif` image in Photoshop. You can add another color to the block course you deleted earlier, or you can modify the colors of all the blocks. By keeping and editing bitmap information in Photoshop, you can keep parts of materials, such as the blocks and mortar in the splitface block example, aligned. You needn't limit the materials to bump and diffuse maps. Some fairly elaborate decorative architectural elements can be generated using specular and reflection maps that are carefully aligned.

While you've learned how to use Photoshop to create textures and colors for VIZ materials, you've also seen that the Windows environment lets you use the two programs simultaneously in an almost seamless way. By switching from Photoshop to VIZ and back again, you can fine-tune a material's appearance in a VIZ rendering.

Modeling with Displacement Maps

You've seen how you can use a bump map to simulate a rough surface like the splitface block in the previous exercises or a rolling surface like the ground in the villa design. Another map option, called a displacement map, performs a function similar to that of bump maps, but instead of applying a texture, it actually deforms geometry into new shapes. The effect is akin to a vacuum mold in which a flat surface is stretched over a form to create an object. In this case, the form is a bitmap where dark areas represent lower levels of a surface and light areas represent higher levels, in a way similar to bump maps. Figure 14.34 shows how a displacement map alters the geometry to which it is applied.

FIGURE 14.34

A sample displacement mesh

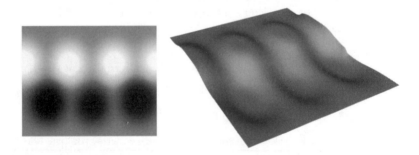

The image, named `disp_dots.jpg`, was created in Photoshop by using the Airbrush tool to create the dots. The background was first filled in with a gray tone; then the black and white dots were sprayed in, using the Airbrush tool. As you compare the image with the mesh, you can see that the black dots correspond to the dips in the mesh, and the white dots correspond to the bumps. Since the dots are airbrushed with soft edges, they create a smooth transition from high to low in the resulting mesh.

There are two ways that you can create mesh forms with displacement maps. You can go through the Material Editor and create a material containing a displacement map, or you can use the Displace modifier to apply a bitmap directly to an object to deform it into a new shape.

Using the Displace Modifier

Using the Displace modifier is probably the easiest way to convert a bitmap into a deformed surface. In the following exercise, you'll use the modifier to get a feel for how the process works. You'll create the object in Figure 14.32 by using the sample `disp_dot.jpg` image file from the companion CD.

1. In VIZ, choose File ➢ Reset. At the warning message, click No. You don't really need to keep the changes to the wall. Then, at the second warning, click Yes to continue with the reset.

2. In the Create tab of the Command Panel, click Plane; then click and drag a plane that is roughly 125 by 100. Then use the Arc Rotate and Pan tools to get a Perspective view from the Front viewport, as shown in Figure 14.35.

FIGURE 14.35
Draw the plane shown here.

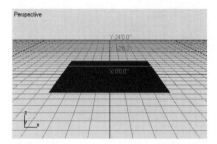

3. Adjust the Length parameter to 125 and the Width parameter to 100. For now, leave the Length Segs and Width Segs at the default 4 value. You'll adjust these settings later.

4. Open the Material Editor and assign the default material in the upper middle slot to the plane object. This allows you to see the surface features of the plane a bit more clearly.

The plane is perhaps the best type of geometry to use to demonstrate the effects of the Displace modifier, although you can use the Displace modifier on any NURBS surface, patch, poly, or editable mesh.

NOTE *NURBS stands for non-uniform rational B-Splines. It is a type of object that is especially suited to creating smooth curves. You can find out more about NURBS in Appendix C.*

Now let's go ahead and apply the bitmap from Photoshop.

1. Click the Modify tab; then select Displace from the Modifier List drop-down list. You'll find it under the Object-Space Modifiers heading.

2. In the Image group of the Parameters rollout, click the Bitmap button labeled None.

3. Locate and open the file named `disp_dot.jpg` from the installed samples of the companion CD.

4. Go to the Displacement group and change the Strength setting to **12**. You'll notice that the plane starts to distort, although it doesn't look anything like the one in Figure 14.32.

You've applied the `disp_dot.jpg` bitmap but haven't gotten the results you might have expected. The reason is that the mesh contains only a 4 by 4 array of segments. You'll need to increase the number of segments in the plane before you begin to see the form of the bitmap.

1. To get a better idea of what's going on with the mesh, right-click the Perspective label in the upper left corner of the viewport and select Wireframe.

2. Select Plane from the modifier stack list.

3. In the Parameters rollout, change the Length and Width Segs values to **40**. Now you can see the form more clearly.

4. Click the Quick Render tool to see the mesh as a rendered surface. (You may need to change the background color to gray to see the shape clearly in the render window.)

Now you can see that you can use a bitmap image to deform a surface. You don't have a lot of control over the details of the form, but you can create some interesting geometry using this method. For example, you can use a bitmap to create a free-form terrain.

NOTE *You may have noticed that the Image group of the Displace Modifier parameters offered two sets of options: Bitmap and Map. Although you used the Bitmap option, you could also have used the Map option to apply a bitmap. The Map option lets you use other types of maps such as the procedural maps offered in the Material/Map Browser. You can use both Bitmap and Map options to combine maps to displace a mesh.*

Now let's go back to the Displace Modifier parameters and see what some of the other options do.

1. In the modifier stack list, select Displace.

2. In the Displacement group of the parameters, click and drag the Strength spinner upward to 2′6″, or 30″. The Strength value indicates the distance from the black portions of the bitmap to the white portions.

3. Click the Luminance Center check box and make sure the Center value is set to **0.5** if not already set. The mesh drops down. The Luminance Center lets you control which shade of gray in the bitmap determines the center of the displacement.

4. Scroll down to the Map group and change the length value to **95** and the Width value to **75**. Now the surface really looks like a vacuum-formed plastic object with a flange.

5. Use the U Tile spinner to increase the U Tile value, and then do the same for the V Tile value. As you increase these values, the number of bumps across the width of the plane increases.

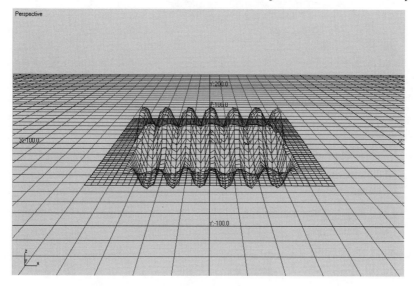

Notice that in the Map group, the Planar radio button is selected. This is the default Map gizmo setting. In fact, since the Displace modifier works with maps, the Map group mimics the map settings for the UVW Map modifier.

You used the Displace modifier on a plane geometry object, but you can also use it on any NURBS surface, patch, or editable mesh. Once you've finished working with the object, you can collapse its stack using the Edit Stack button in the modifier stack. By doing so, you will help conserve memory and help improve VIZ's performance. You can then start to edit the mesh by going to the sub-object level.

Using the Material Editor to Create Displaced Geometry

If you want to apply a displacement map to an object other than a NURBS surface, patch, poly, or editable mesh, you can use the Displace Map option in the Material Editor. This option works in conjunction with the Displacement Approximation modifier to perform the same function as the Displace modifier, but on a wider range of objects. For example, you can form a decorative feature on a building or create signage using the combination of displace, opacity, and diffuse maps in the Material Editor and then apply the resulting material to a cylinder or other geometry.

In this section, you'll create a fictitious concrete landscaping bench using an image file to create the details of the geometry (see Figure 14.36).

FIGURE 14.36

A concrete bench

/ The image file was created entirely in Photoshop using the Pen tool for the top and bottom bars and the Horizontal Type tool for the word *Brilliant.* This could really be anything from a scanned photograph to an imported AutoCAD line drawing. The point is that it's a bitmap image in which the dark areas represent low surfaces and the light areas represent high surfaces.

Let's get started with the bench by creating the basic geometry.

1. Choose File ➢ Reset to reset VIZ.

2. Make sure the Geometry button is selected in the Create tab of the Command Panel; then click Cylinder.

3. Click and drag from the origin of the perspective view and give the cylinder a radius of 30 inches. Make the height 24 inches.

4. Click the Modify Tab in the Command Panel and then select the UVW Map modifier from the Modifier List drop-down list.

5. Scroll down the Parameters rollout and click the Cylindrical Mapping radio button.

6. If the Map gizmo doesn't conform to the shape of the cylinder, click the Fit button in the Alignment group.

With the UVW Map modifier added and set to Cylindrical, any material maps applied to the cylinder will appear around the perimeter. The next step is to create a material that uses a displacement map.

1. Open the Material Editor window.

2. Select the top middle material slot and then click the material type button that says Architectural. Select and double-click Standard from the Material/Map Browser dialog box.

3. Click the Displacement Map button labeled None.

4. In the Material/Map Browser, double-click Bitmap.

5. In the Select Bitmap Image File dialog box, locate and open the file named `displace_sample.jpg` from the companion CD. The sample slot image distorts into something unrecognizable. Don't worry about it right now. You'll see the results of the displacement map more clearly a bit later.

6. Click the Assign Material to Selection button to assign the material to the cylinder.

7. Use the Arc Rotate and Pan tools to get a Perspective view of the cylinder and then change the environment background to white by choosing Rendering ➤ Environment, clicking the background color swatch, and dragging the whiteness slider to 0. Do a quick rendering to see the results.

Your rendering doesn't really look anything like the `Displace_sample.jpg` image. You need to add to the cylinder a modifier that gives you some control over the way the displacement map affects the cylinder.

1. In the Modifier List drop-down list, select Disp Approx. under the Object-Space Modifiers heading.

2. Render the image again. This time you begin to see more clearly the effects of the displacement map.

The Displacement Approx. modifier is needed to apply the displacement map correctly to the object. There are still a few changes that need to be made, however. The amount of displacement is too great, and a single version of the map wraps completely around the cylinder. You want to reduce the strength of the displacement and have the map repeat four times around the perimeter so that it's readable.

The following steps will increase the number of times the displacement map displays around the cylinder.

1. Choose UVW Mapping in the Modifier List drop-down list.

This brings up the UVW Mapping parameters.

2. Scroll down to the U Tile setting in the Mapping group of the parameters and change the U Tile setting to **4**. Remember that the U setting is similar to the X coordinate. By setting U Tile to 4, you cause the map to repeat 4 times around the perimeter of the cylinder.

3. Render the design again using the Quick Render tool. The rendering regresses to a crude form.

By increasing the number of times the map is repeated over the surface, you have increased the complexity of the displacement map in relation to the cylinder surface. You may recall that, in an earlier exercise for the Displace modifier, you needed to increase the number of segments in the mesh surface in order to have the displacement map take effect. You need to do the same in this situation. You need to increase the number of segments on the cylinder wall to give the displacement map enough segments to work with.

You can go back to the Cylinder object level to increase the number of segments for the side of the cylinder.

1. Right-click the Perspective label in the upper left corner of the viewport and select Wireframe. This will allow you to see the cylinder segments more clearly.

2. In the Modifier List drop-down list, choose Cylinder.

3. In the Parameters rollout, change the Height Segments value to **12** and the Sides value to **72**. The sides of the cylinder will show segments that are close to being square.

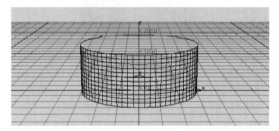

4. Click the Quick Render tool again. Now you can see the map clearly.

The depth of the displacement map shows you that it isn't just a bump map. When the cylinder is rendered, VIZ converts the flat cylinder wall into a displaced mesh that will cast shadows and stand up to close-up views, even though the cylinder remains a plain cylinder in the Design viewports.

Now let's see how to reduce the depth of the displacement to something a bit more reasonable. You'll also add some noise to the Bump Map setting to give the object a granite look.

1. Open the Material Editor; then go up one level to the Maps rollout.

2. In the Maps rollout, change the Amount setting for the displacement map to **20**.

3. Click the Bump Map button labeled None.

4. In the Material/Map Browser, select Noise; then click OK.

5. Back in the Material Editor, change the Size parameter in the Noise Parameter rollout to **0.1** and change the Blur setting in the Coordinate group to **0.01**.

6. Click the Go to Parent button on the Material Editor toolbar; then adjust the Bump Map setting to **100**.

7. Create another quick rendering of the object.

You now have a pretty convincing model of a fairly complex form, and you created it without having to do a lot of editing. The displacement map does take a toll on rendering time, but in some situations, it can save you time in building your model.

Converting a Displacement Map into an Editable Mesh

You may find yourself in a situation where you need to edit an object that you've formed using a displacement map, like the one in the preceding section. Unfortunately, displacement maps take effect only when you render the image. Meanwhile, the object to which the displacement map is applied remains in its basic form in the VIZ viewport. In the case of your exercise example, the cylinder remains a cylinder and doesn't become a displaced mesh.

You can apply two tools to gain access to the mesh that is created using a displacement map. The first is a global modifier that displays the mesh in the viewports so that you don't have to wait until the design is rendered to see the result of the displacement map.

To see the effects of the Displace Mesh World-Space modifier (WSM), make sure the cylinder is selected and then select Displace Mesh (WSM) from the Modifier List drop-down list. You'll have to wait a moment while VIZ converts the viewport display of the cylinder to show the actual mesh of the displacement map. When VIZ is done, you'll see the cylinder with the displacement map in mesh form. Figure 14.37 shows a close-up view of the cylinder with the Displace Mesh (WSM) modifier active.

You can now see why the last rendering took a bit more time. With the displacement map added, the mesh is quite dense and complex. You can reduce the complexity of the mesh by reducing the number of segments in the cylinder. You can also turn on the Custom Settings option in the Displacement Approx. rollout and select the Low settings for the Subdivision Presets group.

Using the Low setting will reduce the smoothness of the mesh and give it a rough appearance, so you may want to use the Low setting for meshes that will only be viewed from a distance.

FIGURE 14.37
A close-up view of
the cylinder mesh

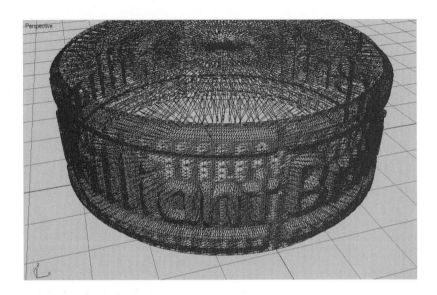

TIP *Try using the Optimize modifier to reduce the complexity of objects. Optimize reduces topology more in flat areas and leaves detail where you need it in curved surfaces.*

TEXT IN VIZ

In this example, text was used to show off the capabilities of the displacement map feature, but in most cases, you'll want to create text using the Text Shape object found in the set of Spline Shape options of the Create tab. A text shape acts just like any other shape, in that it can be extruded to form 3D objects. You can also apply modifiers to text shapes. One modifier that is especially useful with text shapes is the Bevel modifier (see Bevel in Appendix B).

You can apply any font that is available in the Windows font library to text shapes. Text can also be edited and its parameters changed, as long as it isn't collapsed into editable meshes, polys, or editable splines. For example, you can create a text shape that spells out *Brilliant*, extrude it, apply a material to it, and then later change the text to *absolutely brilliant*. Through the Text Shape object's parameters, you also have control over fonts, justification, size, kerning, leading, underlining, and italics.

Creating an Editable Mesh from a Displacement Map

The Displace Mesh (WSM) modifier allows you to see the displacement map so that you can use the transform tools to adjust the size and orientation of the object within the design. It doesn't let you edit the object's surface, however. If you need to make changes on a sub-object level, you can create a special type of clone of the object that's a full mesh representation of the object with the displacement map. You can then use the clone to make further changes and hide or delete the original object.

To create this copy, use the Snapshot dialog box as demonstrated in the following exercise.

1. Choose Tools ➢ Snapshot.

2. In the Snapshot dialog box, make sure the Single radio button is selected in the Snapshot group and that the Mesh Clone Method is selected; then click OK.

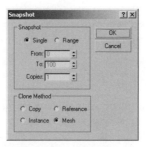

3. Use the Select and Move tool to move the cylinder to the left so that you can get a clear view of the new displacement mesh. You'll experience some lag time between the time you move the cylinder and when the cylinder actually moves on the screen.

4. Remove the Displace Mesh (WSM) modifier from the cylinder's modifier stack by selecting Displace Mesh from the Modifier Stack and then clicking the trash can button below the modifier stack list. You may have noticed that the Displace Mesh (WSM) modifier slows VIZ's reaction to your input, so deleting it will help save some time. When the Displace Mesh (WSM) modifier is removed, you see the original cylinder revert to its former shape.

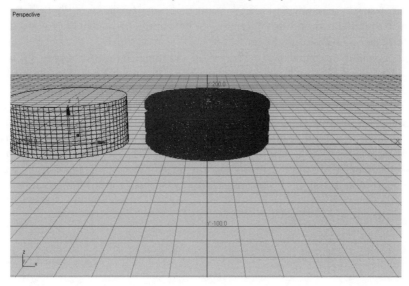

5. Render the view of the cloned cylinder. You see that it is an exact copy of the original cylinder, but that the copy is an editable mesh rather than a cylinder with several modifiers attached.

TIP *You can think of the Snapshot dialog box as a tool to collapse a displacement map object into an editable mesh.*

As you've seen in these exercises, the displacement modifiers require the surface to have at least enough segments to accommodate the form. This means that with complex forms, you'll have to create a mesh with lots of segments, which also means that you can quickly expand your file size using the Displace modifier. For this reason, you may want to restrict the use of this modifier to those types of geometry that can take the best advantage of its features.

CLONING WITH SNAPSHOT

The Snapshot dialog box is mainly intended to clone an animated object at a particular point in time. For example, suppose you have an animation of an object deforming over time and you want to create a clone of the object at a specific point in the deformation. Snapshot is designed to perform this function. As its name indicates, Snapshot takes a snapshot of an object at a particular moment in time. The clone created by Snapshot doesn't inherit the animated motion or deformation of the source object.

In architectural applications, you may rarely, if ever, use Snapshot to clone an animated object, but you may use it more often as a tool to convert a displacement map into an editable mesh, as shown in these examples.

Summary

This chapter offered a glimpse into some of the ways you can use bitmap images to enhance your VIZ designs. You started out by exploring the more traditional functions of Photoshop for editing images. Then, in the latter part of the chapter, you saw how images created in Photoshop can be used to actually form three dimensional objects.

Image-editing programs such as Photoshop add so much functionality to VIZ that, as you begin to use VIZ in earnest, you'll feel somewhat crippled if you don't have access to such a program. The importance of having an image-editing program cannot be overstressed.

You may want to take some time to explore some of the ways that you can use an image-editing program for your own work. Perhaps you can use the Displace modifier to create an otherwise difficult architectural detail, or maybe the displacement map tools can help you create a part of an object that is particularly troublesome to model. If you prefer using a program other than Photoshop, you may want to examine ways to use your favorite image-editing program to create bump and displacement maps. A judicious use of these tools can go a long way toward simplifying your design creation in VIZ.

Chapter 15

Combining Photographs with VIZ Designs

P HOTOGRAPHY PLAYS A BIG role in the design process, so it shouldn't be a big surprise that photographs are also an important part of your work with VIZ. Architects use photographs to study proposed building sites and to record the progress of a construction project. Photographs are also used to record design details that need to be reproduced or restored.

In Chapter 14, you explored the relationship between image-editing programs and VIZ. You saw how image-editing programs can be an integral part of your model creation. In this chapter, you'll continue that exploration by looking at how photographs play a role in your work with VIZ.

In the first part of this chapter, you'll learn how you can simulate detail in a model of a car by using modified photographs. You'll use a combination of mesh modeling and a series of photographs of a car to create a car that you can use as a three-dimensional entourage element in your designs and animations. This will give you a chance to try out some new mesh modeling tools and will also allow you to see how photos can help simplify the creation of certain types of objects.

In the second part of the chapter, you'll learn how to match a building to a background photograph of the building site. This process gives you a chance to see what a building will look like when it's completed in its proposed location. Matching a VIZ design to a photographic background is also an essential presentation tool that is often required as a part of a design review submission.

- ◆ Mesh Editing with a Photograph

- ◆ Adding Detail with Photographs

- ◆ Matching Your Design to a Background Image

Mesh Editing with a Photograph

In most of your work with VIZ, you'll be using the geometry and shape tools you learned about in the first four chapters of this book, but there will be the occasional odd form that will require some new and different modeling methods. In this section, you'll take a tour of mesh modeling by creating a car in VIZ.

NOTE   *Refer to Chapter 4 to review mesh modeling techniques.*

The car won't be perfect, but it will give you a chance to explore a few methods that you haven't yet learned about in VIZ. You can use the car as part of your entourage for outdoor renderings, and hopefully, with the skills you learn here, you'll be able to create other cars and design elements as well.

Establishing the Basic Form

In Chapter 4, you used a scanned image of a floor plan sketch as the basis of a 3D model. In this section, you'll create a car using a photograph as an aid. You'll start with a Left viewport side view of the car, which you'll use as a template to help mold a mesh into the shape of a car.

1. Start VIZ or select Reset VIZ if it is already open; then click the Min/Max Toggle tool to get a view of all four viewports.

2. In the Create tab of the Command Panel, click the Box tool. Then, in the Top viewport, create a box that is 160 inches long, 67 inches wide, and 28 inches high. You can roughly place the box in the Top viewport and then adjust the Length, Width, and Height parameters in the Command Panel.

3. Set the Length Segs parameter to **16**, the Width Segs to **3**, and the Height Segs to **5**.

4. Click the Zoom Extents All tool to fill the viewports with the box.

5. Right-click the Left viewport; then click the Min/Max Toggle tool to enlarge it.

Now you're ready to bring the image into the file. You'll place the image of the car in the Left viewport as an aid to help mold the car's profile. The image won't appear to be the proper size at first, so you'll have to do some adjusting once the image is brought in.

1. Click Views ➤ Viewport Background.

2. In the top of the Viewport Image dialog box, click Files.

3. In the Select Background Image dialog box, locate and open the `mazdaside.tif` file. This is a file from the `maps` folder on the companion CD.

4. In the Aspect Ratio group of the Viewport Image dialog box, click Match Bitmap; then click OK. The car appears in the viewport.

The next step is to adjust the view magnification so that the box is the same width as the image of the car.

1. Use the Zoom and Pan tools to adjust the view so that the length of the box matches the length of the car in the viewport, as shown in Figure 15.1. (You don't want to change the size of the box since it's already the appropriate size for the car; so you adjust the view to fit the background.)

2. Once you've got the length matched with the image, choose Views ➤ Viewport Background.

FIGURE 15.1
Adjust the view so that the box displays at the same length as the car.

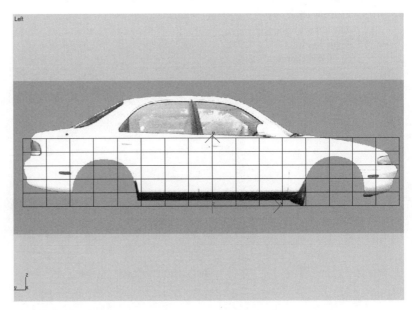

3. In the Viewport Image dialog box, click the Lock Zoom/Pan option and then click OK.

The image will shift out of view.

4. Use the Pan tool to move the image back into the center of the viewport.

5. Use the Move tool to move the box back over the car, as shown in Figure 15.1.

The Mazda has a slight taper from back to front, so you'll add a taper to the box before you start to form the box to the profile.

1. With the box selected, click the Modify tab.

2. Select Taper from the Modifier List drop-down list.

3. In the Taper Axis group, click Y for the Primary setting and click Z for the Effect setting.

4. Adjust the Amount parameter in the Taper group to .24.

5. Select Box from the modifier stack list to gain access to the Box parameters.

6. The box should look similar to Figure 15.2, with the bottom aligned with the image and the top just a bit below the side windows.

FIGURE 15.2
The box with the
Taper modifier
and the background
so far

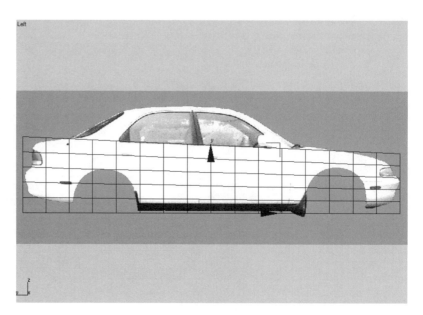

You were asked to set the vertical segments to **5** so that you would have enough vertices to work with in order to mold the form of the car. The next step is to collapse the stack to a mesh so that you can begin to edit the mesh to shape the box to the form of the car.

1. Right-click in the modifier stack list; then select Collapse All.

2. Click Yes at the warning message.

With the stack collapsed, you no longer have access to the box parameters, but you can still edit the box on the sub-object level.

WARNING *Remember that collapsing a stack is an irreversible process. If you want to experiment, you can use the Temporary Buffer (Edit ➤ Hold) to save the state of your design before applying the Collapse All option in step 1. You may also use the Undo option to un-collapse the stack as long as you haven't applied too many changes to the design since Collapse All was applied.*

Moving Vertices

You can now begin to edit the vertices of the box. As you adjust the shape of the box in the following exercise, you'll be selecting and moving vertices. You'll be selecting vertices in the Left viewport using a rectangular selection region. This selection region allows you to select several vertices at once across the width of the box, as shown in Figure 15.3.

1. Click the Vertex button in the Selection rollout of the Command Panel and make sure that the Ignore Backfacing option is not on.

2. Make sure the Rectangular Selection Region is selected on the main toolbar.

3. Click the Select and Move tool and place a selection region around the area shown in Figure 15.4.

FIGURE 15.3

Selecting a set of four vertices in the Left viewport actually selects eight vertices across the width of the box.

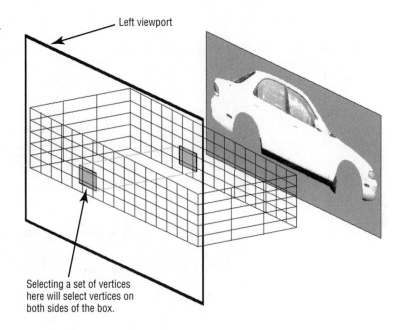

Left viewport

Selecting a set of vertices here will select vertices on both sides of the box.

FIGURE 15.4

Select this region.

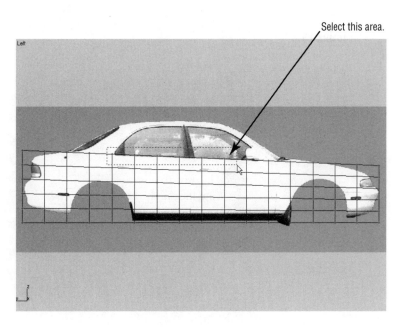

Select this area.

4. Click and drag the selected vertices upward so that your view looks similar to Figure 15.5.

5. Now, adjust the top row of vertices individually so that the top of the box follows the profile of the car, as shown in Figure 15.6. You want to hold the vertices slightly below the very edge of the profile of the car, since the car bulges outward toward its center.

FIGURE 15.5
Move the vertices upward.

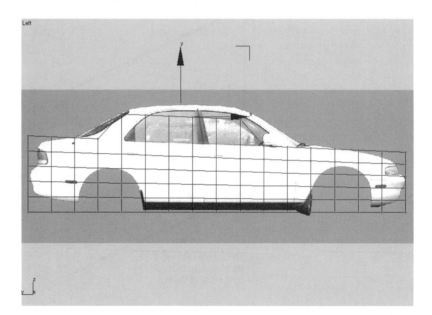

FIGURE 15.6
Adjust the top vertices as shown here.

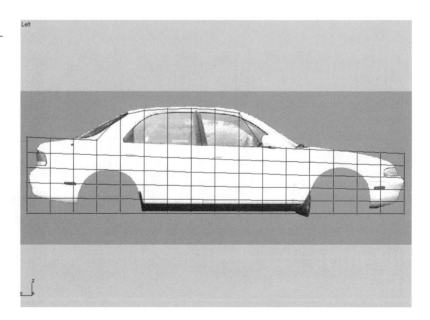

6. Continue to adjust the profile around the front, back, and bottom of the car. Also adjust the vertices on the side of the car near the front and back. Use Figure 15.7 as a guide in adjusting these areas.

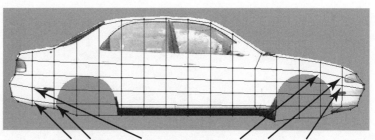

Adjust these vertices on the side of the car, as well as the profile.

TIP   In step 1, you were directed to make sure that the Ignore Backfacing option was turned off. This option, which is off by default, controls sub-object selections based on the direction of normals. When turned on, Ignore Backfacing will cause VIZ to ignore sub-objects whose surface normals point away from the view and are invisible. This is useful when you want to work on just the surface of a volume that is facing you. When the option is off, VIZ selects everything. You want it off in these exercises, to affect both sides of the box.

Adding Curvature

The next step is to adjust the vertices through the middle of the car to create a slight bulge. Although the bulge you create is really made up of flat polygons, you'll use VIZ's smoothing tools to simulate a smooth, curved surface.

1. Press the T key to switch to the Top viewport and then click Zoom Extents. By pressing T, you can bypass the Min/Max Toggle tool to jump to a different, enlarged viewport view.

2. Select the vertices in the middle of the box, avoiding the vertices at the very top and bottom of the box, as shown in Figure 15.8.

3. Press the L key to return to the Left viewport.

4. While holding down the Alt key, select a region at the bottom of the box, as shown in Figure 15.9.

Notice that while you hold down the Alt key, the cursor shows a minus (–) sign. This tells you that you are removing items from a selection. In this case, you are removing the vertices at the bottom of the box from the selection. Since you originally selected the vertices from the Top viewport, your selection included a set of vertices from both the bottom and the top of the box. You want to edit only the top vertices.

5. Move the vertices upward to match the profile of the car, as shown in Figure 15.10.

FIGURE 15.8
Select the vertices
shown here.

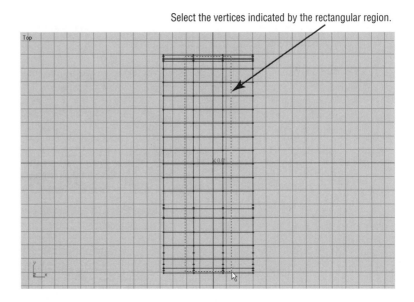

Select the vertices indicated by the rectangular region.

FIGURE 15.9
Select this region
while holding down
the Alt key.

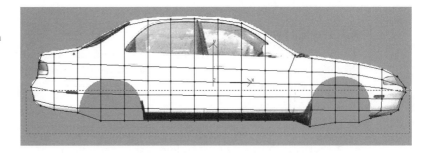

FIGURE 15.10
Move the middle
vertices upward to
match the profile
of the car.

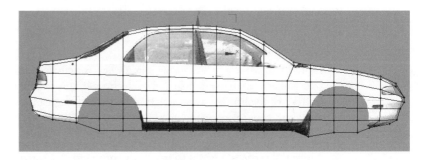

TIP   *You can also check the Ignore Backfacing option in the Selection rollout before attempting to select objects on a sub-object level. This eliminates the need to remove the vertex selection at the opposite side of the box, since, with Ignore Back-facing turned on, VIZ selects only the vertices that are visible on the side of the box that is facing you.*

You've added a bulge to the top of the car, and in the process, you saw how you could remove items from a selection using the Alt key. The front and back of the car also curve outward. Do the following to add a curve to the front.

1. Press T again to go to the Top viewport.

2. Use the Region Zoom tool to enlarge the front of the box, as shown in Figure 15.11.

3. Using a region selection, select the vertices shown in Figure 15.11; then move them downward.

4. Pan to the other end of the box and move upward the vertices shown in Figure 15.12.

FIGURE 15.11
Move these vertices
downward.

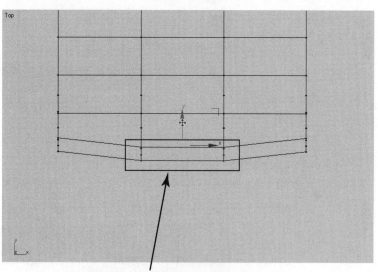

Select these vertices and move them downward.

FIGURE 15.12
Move these vertices
upward.

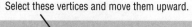

Select these vertices and move them upward.

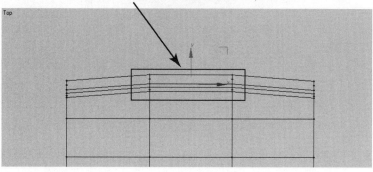

By now, the front and back of the box have been stretched beyond the profile of the car. The next step is to move the entire front and back into place.

1. Press the L key to go back to the Left viewport; then select the vertices shown in Figure 15.13.

2. Move back the vertices that are in the front of the box so that they are again roughly aligned with the car's image.

3. Do the same for the back of the car. Your view should now look similar to Figure 15.13.

4. Press the P key to view the Perspective viewport. Use the Zoom, Pan, and Arc Rotate tools on the Viewport toolbar to adjust the view so that it looks similar to Figure 15.14.

FIGURE 15.13

The car so far

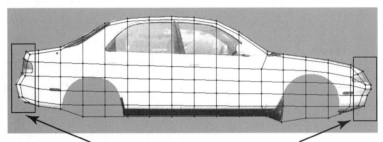

Select these regions and move them back into alignment with the background image.

FIGURE 15.14

A perspective view of the car so far

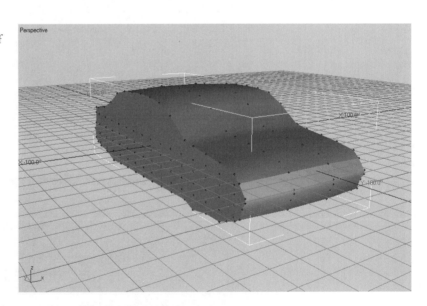

The car has really taken shape now, and you could almost use it as is. There are just a few more details that you need to take care of before the car is ready for use. Right now, the car has vertical, flat sides. You'll want to add some slope to the sides of the car and also add a slight bulge to the side to give the impression of curvature.

Start by bending the sides inward toward the top.

1. Press the F key to go to the Front viewport.

2. Click the Zoom Extents tool to enlarge the car.

3. Click the Select and Rotate tool; then use the Rectangular Selection Region tool to select the vertices shown in Figure 15.15.

FIGURE 15.15

Select these vertices in the Front viewport.

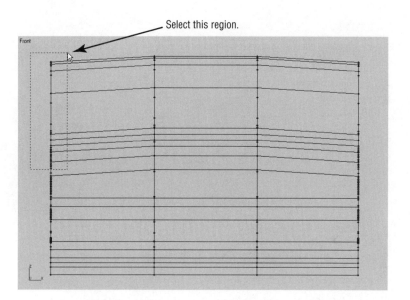

Select this region.

4. Click and drag the left side of the blue Z axis ring upward to rotate the vertices. As you do this, watch the readout on the Rotate gizmo. When the readout shows −12 degrees, release the mouse.

5. Click the Select and Move tool; then click and drag the X axis arrow to the right until the vertices at the bottom of the selected group of vertices are aligned with the rest of the side of the car, as shown in Figure 15.16.

6. Repeat the process described in steps 3 through 5 for the other side of the car, but this time, make sure you rotate the vertices in the opposite direction from that of step 4. The result should look like Figure 15.17.

FIGURE 15.16
Move the vertices so that the bottom of the selection is aligned with the rest of the side.

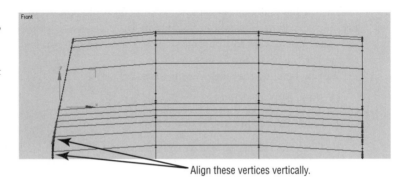

Align these vertices vertically.

FIGURE 15.17
The car after editing the vertices on the right side

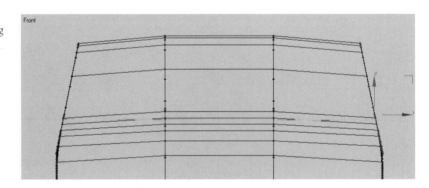

Now add the bulge in the sides.

1. Press the L key to go to the Left viewport.

2. Click and drag the Rectangular Selection Region tool on the main toolbar to open the flyout; then select the Fence Selection Region tool.

3. Click the Select and Move tool; then click and drag within the area shown in Figure 15.18 to start the fence selection.

4. Continue to select points so that the vertices shown in Figure 15.18 are selected. To close the fence selection, place the cursor over the beginning of the selection fence. When you see the cursor turn into a cross, click the mouse.

FIGURE 15.18

Selecting the fence selection area

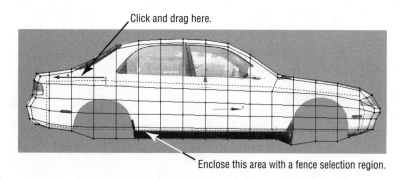

FIGURE 15.18

Selecting the fence selection area

5. Save this selection by entering **sidebulge** in the Selection Set input box in the main toolbar. You'll want to be able to return to this selection set a bit later.

Remember that because you're selecting points in an orthogonal view, you are actually selecting vertices on both sides of the car. You need to remove the vertices from one side of the car so that you'll affect only a single side when you move the vertices.

1. Press the F key to go to the Front viewport.

2. While holding down the Alt key, click and drag the location shown in Figure 15.19. Continue holding the Alt key while you select points to enclose the vertices shown in this figure.

FIGURE 15.19

Place a fence selec-
tion region around
these vertices.

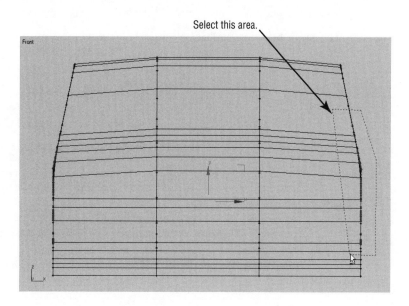

3. When you've completed the selection by closing the fence selection region, the vertices on the right side of the car will be removed from the selection set.

4. Click and drag the X axis handle of the Transform gizmo to the left, as shown in Figure 15.20, to add a slight bulge to the side of the car.

FIGURE 15.20
Move the X axis arrow to the left.

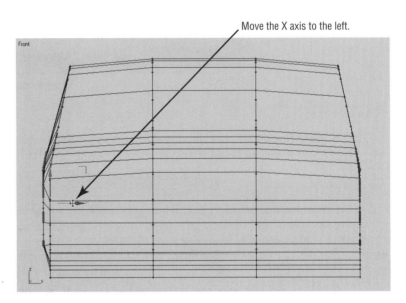

You've got one side done. Now, add the bulge to the other side.

1. On the Selection toolbar, select sidebulge from the drop-down list. This restores the vertex selection you had before you removed the vertices from the right side of the box.

2. Hold down the Alt key, and this time, select the vertices on the left side of the car.

3. Move the vertices to the right to add the bulge to that side of the car. Your view should look similar to Figure 15.21.

You've completed the vertex editing for the car. The next step is to apply smoothing to the mesh to remove some of the sharp edges.

TIP *So far, you've used a single box to represent the entire car. Since a car is symmetrical, you can also model half of the car and then mirror-clone that half and attach and weld the two halves together. If you use an instance clone, changes on one half are automatically applied to the other half. Using either a single box or two halves is acceptable, and each offers advantages over the other. The method you choose is a matter of preference.*

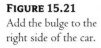

FIGURE 15.21
Add the bulge to the right side of the car.

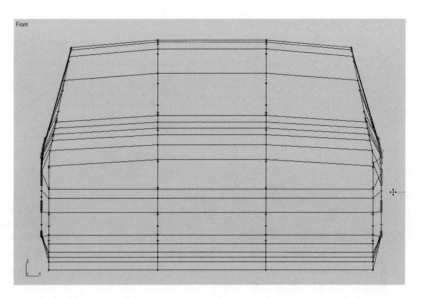

Smoothing the Surface

In the first part of this book, you saw how spheres and other types of rounded geometry appear smooth, even though the surfaces are really made up of faceted polygons. This smooth appearance is created by smoothing groups that are applied to the faces of an object.

A *smoothing group* is an integer from 1 to 32 that identifies whether two adjacent faces are to be smoothed or not. If two adjacent faces are assigned the same smoothing group—30, for example— they will appear to blend together in a smooth surface instead of showing a sharp edge between the two faces.

You can apply smoothing to geometry by using the Smooth modifier. For editable meshes, you can apply smoothing through the face, polygon, or element sub-object level. Try the following exercise to add smoothing to the car mesh.

1. Choose File ➢ Save As and save the file as **Carmesh01.max**. You'll come back later to the car that you save at this stage to look at some other mesh smoothing options.

2. Press the P key to view the car in the Perspective viewport.

3. In the Command Panel, click the Element button in the Selection rollout.

4. Click the car to select it as an element.

5. Scroll down the Command Panel to the Surface Properties rollout.

6. In the Smoothing Groups, set the Auto Smooth value to **90**; then click the Auto Smooth button and click the Element button in the Selection rollout.

The car's surface changes to a smoother appearance.

The Auto Smooth option doesn't actually smooth out the geometry of the car. It's a setting that causes VIZ to smooth over the edges of surfaces in rendered views.

Here you used the Auto Smooth option to smooth the mesh. You can be very specific about which face you want to smooth by selecting the face and applying a smoothing group to that face. Remember that adjacent faces must have similar smoothing groups before they are smoothed.

You've completed the mesh editing portion of the car. Right now, it still looks like an amorphous blob, vaguely resembling a car. The next step is to apply a map to create the illusion of the car's surface details.

REMOVING UNWANTED SMOOTHING GROUPS

If you import AutoCAD models to VIZ, you may encounter flat surfaces that show random dark patches. These dark patches are often caused by an improper application of smoothing groups during the import process. You can eliminate these dark patches by selecting the object and then selecting the Face, Polygon, or Element sub-object level in the Modify tab of the Command Panel. Select the irregular surface; then click the Clear All button in the Smoothing Groups group of the Surface Properties rollout.

Adding Detail with Photographs

The goal of the car exercise is to create a reasonably convincing car without creating a huge file. After all, the car will serve only as part of your entourage and won't be the main focus of your design. Still, you don't want the car to be too cartoon-like.

In the next set of exercises, you'll add a material to the car. The material will include a photograph of the side of the car to give the impression of the details we're used to seeing in a car. Along the way, you'll learn some tricks to preparing the bitmap for the car, as well as methods for preparing the UVW Map modifier to align the map to the car's surface.

Creating a Material for the Car Side

Start by creating the material that will be mapped to the car's side:

1. Open the Material Editor.

2. With the upper middle sample slot selected, click the Material Type button labeled Architectural on the Material Editor toolbar. In the Material/Map Browser select Standard. Scroll down and open the Maps rollout.

3. Click the Diffuse Map button.

4. In the Material/Map Browser, click Bitmap and then click OK.

5. In the Select Bitmap Image File dialog box, select and open `mazdaside dif.tif`. This file from the Maps folder on the companion CD is an edited bitmap image of the side of the car.

The `mazdaside dif.tif` image isn't exactly what the car looks like. The front and back windshield have been stretched, and so have the headlights and taillights. Also, the outline of the car has been eliminated. These changes were made to facilitate the way the image will be mapped on the car mesh. You'll see the effects of this map on the mesh a bit later.

Next, you'll want to add an opacity map for the wheel wells of the car.

1. In the Material Editor, click the Go to Parent tool on the Material Editor toolbar.

2. Click the Opacity Map button.

3. Click Bitmap in the Material/Map Browser and then click OK.

4. Select and open the `mazdaside op.tif` file. This is an image that outlines the wheel wells of the car.

5. In the Modify tab of the Command Panel, click Editable Mesh in the modifier stack list to turn off the sub-object level.

6. Back in the Material Editor, click the Assign Material to Selection button; then close the Material Editor.

Adding the UVW Map

Next, you'll need to apply a UVW Mapping modifier to the car mesh to align the material maps to the side of the car. In this situation, a planar map will work best.

1. In the Modify tab of the Command Panel, select UVW Map from the modifier list drop-down list.

2. Scroll down the Command Panel to the Alignment group and click the X radio button.

By default, VIZ assigns a planar map to the object, but the map is aligned with the Z axis of the mesh. The map needs to be aligned with the X axis in order for the map images to be aligned to the side of the car.

The map is now aligned with the appropriate axis, but it's oriented in the wrong direction. You need to rotate the map 90 degrees so that the point of the Map gizmo points upward and the green side of the gizmo points to the front of the car, as shown in Figure 15.22.

FIGURE 15.22
The UVW Map gizmo in its proper location and proportion

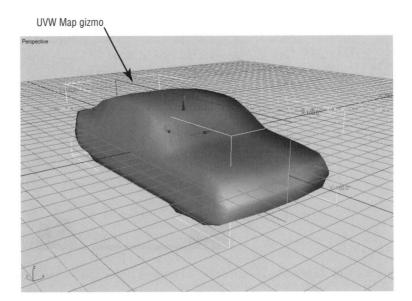

1. Expand the UVW Map listing in the modifier stack list; then select Gizmo from the list just below UVW Map.

2. Click the Select and Rotate tool on the main toolbar; then click and drag the red X axis ring of the map Rotate gizmo downward. As you do this, watch the numeric readout on the Rotate gizmo. Adjust the gizmo rotation so that it shows 90 degrees; then release the mouse button.

3. Scroll down to the bottom of the Command Panel; then click the Fit button in the Alignment group. The gizmo now fits the car mesh, as shown in Figure 15.22.

4. Click the Quick Render tool to see how the car looks with the material map (see Figure 15.23).

FIGURE 15.23

The car rendered

It's not a great-looking car, but it will be convincing when placed at a distance from the camera. There are a few adjustments you may need to make. For example, the front windshield posts may be distorted, as in Figure 15.24. This is caused by the bitmap being stretched over a broad area of the windshield. If this happens in your model, you can move the vertices of the mesh so that the windshield pillars fall on a flat portion of the mesh.

FIGURE 15.24

The windshield pillar is out of alignment.

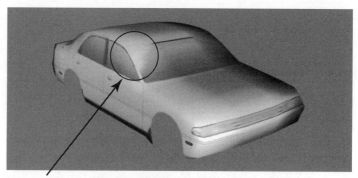

The windshield pillar loses some definition in this example.

1. Minimize the Rendered Frame Window; then press the L key to go to the Left viewport.

2. Click Vertex under the editable mesh listing in the modifier stack list.

3. Use the Select and Move tool to move the vertices around the windshield toward the right, as shown in Figure 15.25.

4. Click UVW Mapping from the modifier stack list to return to the top of the modifier stack.

5. Press the P key to return to the Perspective viewport; then click the Quick Render tool. The windshield pillar is better defined this time.

FIGURE 15.25
Adjusting the wind-
shield forward

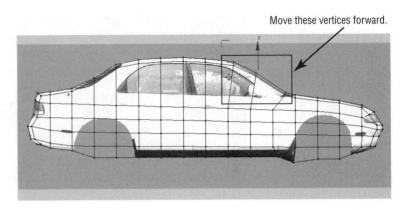

If you look at the mazdaside dif.tif bitmap image, you see that the front and back windshields were distorted to extend way beyond the boundaries of the car. This was done deliberately so that you could make the types of adjustments you made in the last exercise. You can move parts of the mesh and still maintain the appearance of the windshield. The same holds true for the headlights and taillights.

Adding the Front to the Car

Using a single bitmap for the side of the car works fine for side views and perhaps even for the rear views, but the front of the car needs a bit more detail to make it more convincing. In Chapter 14, you learned that you can add multiple bitmaps to a single object. In this section, you'll learn firsthand how to add a second map to a separate set of mesh faces to add headlights and a grille to the car.

First, create a Multi/Sub-Object material.

1. Open the Material Editor; then, if you aren't already at the Parent Material level, click the Go to Parent button on the Material Editor toolbar.

2. Click the Type button labeled Architectural on the Material Editor toolbar.

3. In the Material/Map Browser, click the Multi/Sub-Object listing and then click OK.

4. In the Replace Material dialog box, select Keep old material as sub-material? and then click OK.

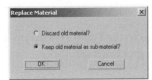

5. Back in the Material Editor, click the Set Number button in the Multi/Sub-Object Basic Parameters rollout.

6. In the Set Number of Materials dialog box, enter **2** for the number of materials; then click OK.

Next, add a material to the Multi/Sub-Object material.

1. Click the Material button in row 2 of the Multi/Sub-Object Basic Parameters rollout.

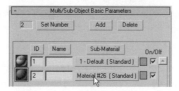

2. Scroll down to the Maps rollout and open it.

3. Click the Diffuse Color Map button.

4. In the Material/Map Browser tool, click Bitmap and then click OK.

5. Locate and open the `mazdafront.tif` file. You can see in the sample slot of the file dialog box that `mazdafront.tif` is a bitmap image of the front of the car.

6. Back in the Material Editor, change the Map Channel value in the Coordinates rollout to **2**.

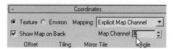

7. Click the Go to Parent tool to return to the parent level of the material.

By setting the Map Channel value to 2, you will be able to assign a UVW Map modifier to the `mazdafront.tif` bitmap.

Now let's focus on the mesh to see how to apply the `mazdafront.tif` map to the front of the mesh. Start by isolating the polygons that you'll use for the map of the front of the car.

1. Close the Material Editor window and, if the Left viewport isn't already on the screen, press the L key to display it.

2. Change the Selection region to the Fence Selection region on the main toolbar.

3. Make sure the car mesh is selected; then, in the Modify tab of the Command Panel, select Polygon from the modifier stack list.

4. Make sure Window Selection is the active selection mode.

5. Click the Select Object tool on the main toolbar and place a fence selection region around the area shown in Figure 15.26.

FIGURE 15.26
Select these polygons with the Select Object tool.

Select this region.

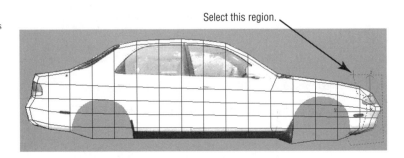

6. With the polygons selected, scroll down the Command Panel to the Surface Properties rollout. In the Material group, change the ID setting to **2** to match the polygons with the material 2 of the Multi/Sub Object material.

Next, you'll need to apply a UVW Map modifier for the polygons that you just assigned to the second material. You'll also need to adjust the orientation of the map to face the polygons.

1. While still in the sub-object level of the mesh, select UVW Map from the Modifier List drop-down list. Although it may not be obvious at first, you'll see the UVW Map gizmo appear at the front of the mesh near the selected polygons.

2. Press the P key to view the Perspective viewport; then right-click the Perspective label in the upper left corner of the viewport. Select Wireframe. This will allow you to more clearly see the UVW Map gizmo.

3. Scroll down the Command Panel and click the Y radio button from the Alignment group.

4. Click the Fit button, also in the Alignment group. As you do this, the UVW Map gizmo will become more easily visible as it is scaled to fit the object.

5. In the Channel group, change the Map Channel value to **2**.

By remaining in the Polygon sub-object level in step 1, the UVW Map modifier automatically aligns the Map gizmo with the selected polygons. This also makes it easier to use the Fit option in step 4.

You're just about ready to render your model to see the results, but first you need to do a little housecleaning.

1. Select Editable Mesh from the modifier stack list.

2. Click Editable Mesh again to exit the sub-object level.

3. Select the top UVW Mapping listing in the modifier stack list.

4. Click the Quick Render button to see the results of the UVW Mapping addition to the stack.

Now the front of the car appears as part of the model. If you look at the front corner of the car, you see that the side and front are not quite aligned. You can adjust the UVW Map gizmo to align the two maps.

1. In the modifier stack list, select the UVW Map listing that corresponds to the front of the car. This should be the middle modifier in the stack.

2. In the Mapping group of the UVW Map Parameters rollout, adjust the Width parameter to **75**, or **6′3″**. This stretches the UVW map horizontally.

3. Render the perspective view again.

This time, the headlights from the sides start to merge with the headlights from the front. You can move the gizmo vertically to get the maps to align vertically.

1. Expand the UVW Map listing; then select Gizmo. This gives you access to the Map gizmo.

2. Click the Select and Move tool; then click and drag the map downward in the Z axis to align it with the map on the side.

3. Render the perspective view again.

You may need to adjust the front Map gizmo a few times while rendering the view to get the location just right. You may also need to adjust the Length setting of the Mapping parameters to align the headlights with the side view (see Figure 15.27).

FIGURE 15.27
Adjust the UVW
Map gizmo to align
the headlights.

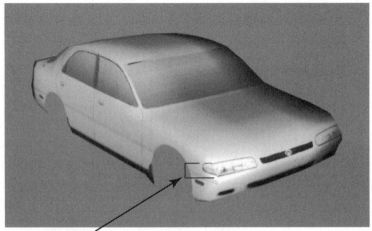

Align the headlights.

For the final touch, you'll need to add wheels. To save some time, you can import a set of wheels that were created for this model.

1. Choose File ➢ Merge.

2. In the Merge File dialog box, locate and open the `carwheels.max` file.

3. In the Merge dialog box, click All; then click OK. The wheels display in the design.

4. Use the top and side views to move the wheels into their proper locations; then render the perspective view again.

5. Save the car as **Carmesh02.max**.

The car isn't perfect. At a distance, though, it's fine, and it won't use a lot of memory. Now that you've got a basic car, you can start to make copies of it, adding different color schemes and modifying the shape a bit for each copy to create a set of cars for your entourage. You can use the methods described here to create other vehicles as well.

TIP   Once you've finished the car, you may want to use the Group command to collect the parts of the car into a single group. Alternatively, you could attach all the parts of the car into a single mesh object for tighter organization.

Smoothing the Mesh

The car you created still has some rough edges that are especially noticeable in close-up views. VIZ offers the MeshSmooth modifier. It will smooth out sharp corners of a mesh by adding additional faces or polygons. This increases the amount of memory the mesh occupies, but for some situations, the improvement may be worth the cost.

In the following exercise, you'll try out the MeshSmooth modifier on an earlier version of the car mesh. You may recall that in an earlier exercise in this chapter, you saved the car mesh as Carmesh01.max. You'll use that design file to experiment with the MeshSmooth modifier.

1. Open the Carmesh01.max file.

2. If you see only a single viewport, click the Min/Max Toggle tool to view all four viewports.

3. Select the mesh representing the car body. If the Modify tab of the Command Panel shows that the mesh is in a sub-object level, click Editable Mesh in the modifier stack.

4. Open the Modifier List drop-down list; under Object-Space Modifiers, select MeshSmooth.

5. Scroll down to the Subdivision Amount rollout in the Command Panel; then change the Iterations value to 1. The mesh becomes smoother with additional polygons.

WARNING   Be careful you don't increase the Iterations value too rapidly, because the increase in iterations greatly augments the amount of memory VIZ uses. A rapid boost in this value can cause an unstable system to crash.

The car will appear smoother after you subdivide with the MeshSmooth modifier.

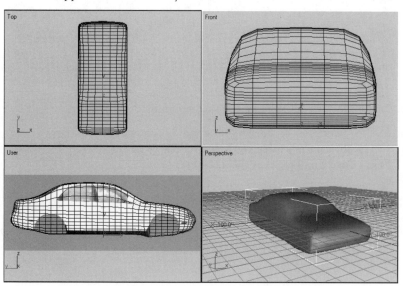

From here, you can add the materials just as you did before, but this time, the results will be a bit more realistic because of the smoother surface of the car body.

The MeshSmooth modifier actually generates a second mesh, using the original mesh's vertices as control points. The vertices of the original mesh exert a "pull" on this second MeshSmooth mesh, and you can control the amount of pull exerted by the vertices. The following exercise shows you how you can control the MeshSmooth mesh by adjusting the Local Control parameters of the MeshSmooth modifier.

1. Scroll down the Command Panel to the Local Control rollout; then click the Display Control Mesh check box.

   Now you see the edges used to control the MeshSmooth mesh. They are most easily seen in the Perspective viewport with the Smooth+Highlights option turned on.

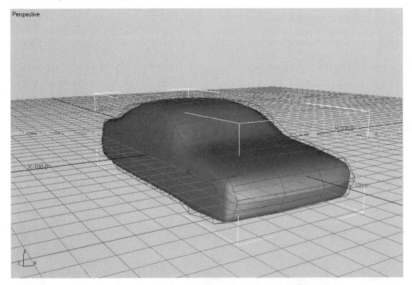

2. Right-click in the Front viewport and click the Min/Max Toggle tool to enlarge the Front viewport.

3. In the Modify tab, expand the MeshSmooth modifier; then select Vertex.

4. Use the Select Object tool with the Fence Selection Region to select the vertices shown in Figure 15.28. Remember that you can select one set of vertices and then use the Ctrl key with the Select Object tool to select the second set.

FIGURE 15.28
Select these two sets
of vertices.

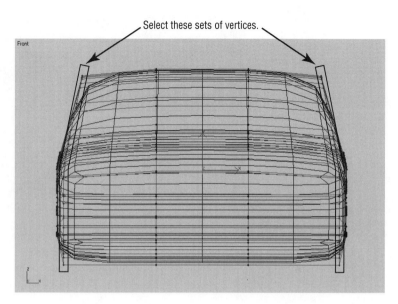

Select these sets of vertices.

5. In the Command Panel, scroll down to the Local Control rollout and change the Weight value
to **4.0**. Notice how the sides are pulled tighter toward the selected vertices.

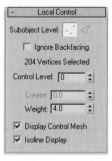

The profile of the car is now a bit more sedan-like than before.

You can continue to fine-tune the shape of the car by selecting vertices and adjusting their weight.
For example, you can round out the corners of the car by selecting the corner vertices and reducing
their weight. Once you've arrived at a shape you like, you can collapse the stack to reduce the object
to an editable mesh to conserve memory. Figure 15.29 shows the car with the MeshSmooth modifier
applied and with a few adjustments to the weight of the vertices in selected places.

FIGURE 15.29
A rendering of a car
that uses a Mesh-
Smooth modifier

One of the more common questions architects seem to ask about 3D software is whether it will allow them to do the type of free-form shaping of objects that you've seen in this chapter. Although the focus in these exercises has been on the creation of a car as a prop in your designs, you can certainly apply these methods to architectural elements, and perhaps even to the main form of your design.

Matching Your Design to a Background Image

One of the more interesting uses of VIZ is to combine a photograph with a design to create a view of a building as it will appear in its intended location. This is an excellent way to help your client understand the look and scale of your design. It can also play a crucial role in the planning phase of a project, where this type of image may be required as part of a design review submission.

In this section, you'll use VIZ's Camera Match tools to place a model of an apartment building in a background photograph of the apartment's intended site. The apartment is located in San Francisco, California, so the model has a Sunlight system light source set up for San Francisco at 1:30 A.M. on July 4, 2004. This is the same time that the background photograph was taken (see Figure 15.30).

TIP   It's a good idea to make note of all the camera settings that were used to take the background photograph. Information such as the focal length of the camera lens and the position and height of the camera can help you determine whether you are on the right track when aligning a model to the background. You will also want to keep track of the date, time of day, and the direction of true north. This information will help you accurately match the sun in your design to the location of the sun in the background.

Setting Up the Model and the Image

Before you can align a design with a background image, you need to find at least five locations in the image that you can correlate with locations in the design. In the design, you can create an object, such as a rectangular base, that can be easily located in the photograph. The photographic image for the apartment site already has an outline of the base of the apartment drawn in for you (see Figure 15.31).

FIGURE 15.30
The background image of the site for the apartment building and a sample rendering of the apartment building

This base is 5 feet, 8 inches high and matches the building's footprint. The height of 5 feet, 8 inches was used because it is a known height in the image. The sides of the base were established by locating the building's corner in the image. Although it wasn't done for this photograph, frequently poles of known heights are placed at the corner points of the building before the photograph is taken so that known points can be established more easily.

The vanishing points of the photograph were located so that the outline of the box could be established. AutoCAD was used to help locate the vanishing points. The photograph was brought into AutoCAD using the Image command. Then the vanishing points were established by drawing lines over the photograph.

The locations of the vanishing-point lines were carefully noted and then drawn in over the image in Photoshop. Photoshop could also have been used to find the vanishing points, but because AutoCAD offers some specialized tools for drawing vector graphics, it was much easier to find the vanishing points in AutoCAD.

A box was added to the VIZ design of the apartment that corresponds to the 5 foot, 8 inch–tall base that was drawn over the photograph. The box will be used to align the model to the image, as you'll see in the following exercise.

Adding the Background Image

You now know that you'll need to do a little background preparation before you can match a design to a photograph. The next step is to do the actual matching in VIZ.

FIGURE 15.31
The AutoCAD image with vanishing points drawn in

Vanishing point to the left

Vanishing point

Layout lines

Start by assigning the background to the VIZ design file.

1. Open the file called noriega.max from the companion CD. This file contains the 3D model of the apartment building.

2. Add the background image to the viewport by first choosing Views ➤ Viewport Background.

3. At the top of the Viewport Image dialog box, click Files.

4. In the Select Background Image dialog box, locate and open the noriegaview.tif image file in the maps folder from the companion CD. This is the image file that contains the additional outline of the apartment base.

5. Back in the Viewport Image dialog box, make sure that the Match Bitmap radio button is selected in the Aspect Ratio group.

6. Also make sure that the Lock Zoom/Pan check box is not checked; then click OK. After a moment, the image will appear in the viewport.

You've got the image in the viewport, but you also need to tell VIZ that you want an image to be included as the background for renderings.

1. Choose Rendering ➢ Environment.

2. In the Environment dialog box, click the Environment Map button, which is currently labeled None.

3. In the Material/Map Browser tool, click Bitmap; then click OK.

4. In the Select Bitmap Image File dialog box, locate and open the noriegaview_render.tif file from the companion CD. This is an exact duplicate of the noriegaview.tif file but without the outline of the base. You can also select noriegaview.tif, but if you do, your final rendering will contain a few stray layout lines.

5. Close the Environment dialog box to move it out of the way.

Now you're ready to start using the Camera Match tools.

Adding the Camera Match Points

The Camera Match tools are in two sets. The first set lets you place helper objects in the model. These helper objects, called *CamPoints*, will then be used with the second set of tools to match locations in the design with locations in the background image.

The model contains a box named Alignobject whose sole purpose is to facilitate the alignment of the design with the background photograph. You'll use the Alignobject box to accurately place the CamPoints in the design at their appropriate locations.

Start by setting up VIZ to select endpoint snaps and by hiding all of the geometry except the Alignobject box.

1. Right-click the Snap Toggle tool.

2. In the Grid and Snap Settings dialog box, place a check by the Endpoint option; then close the dialog box.

3. Use the Select Object tool to select the green base object named Alignobject, as shown in Figure 15.32.

4. Click the Display tab in the Command Panel; then click the Hide Unselected button in the Hide rollout.

You now have just the Alignobject box showing. This will make it easier to place the CamPoint helpers.

FIGURE 15.32
Select the Align-
object object in the
design.

The next step is to place the CamPoint helpers in the model.

1. Click the Create tab in the Command Panel; then click the Helpers button.

2. Select Camera Match from the Helpers drop-down list.

3. In the Object Type rollout, click CamPoint.

4. Make sure that the Snap mode is active; then click the bottom front corner of the Alignobject box, as shown in Figure 15.33. You've just added a CamPoint to the scene.

5. Back in the Command Panel, change the CamPoint01 name in the Name and Color rollout to **Front Bottom**. This will make it easier to identify the CamPoint you just created.

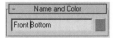

6. Next, click the top front corner of the Alignobject box, as shown in Figure 15.33.

7. Change the name in the Name and Color rollout to **Front Top**.

8. Place the rest of the CamPoints—Left Top, Left Bottom, and Right Top—shown in Figure 15.33, as you did for the Front Top CamPoint. Click the location in the design; then change the newly added CamPoint's name to reflect its location.

FIGURE 15.33
With the endpoint snap active, click the corners of the Alignobject box.

You've now got five CamPoints in place. That is the minimum number that VIZ needs to align a design with a background image. You've seen how the Alignobject box helps make quick work of placing the CamPoints in the design. You can also place the CamPoints in your design by entering their coordinates, using the Camera Match Keyboard Entry rollout. But using geometry like the Alignobject box is a bit more straightforward.

NOTE   The Alignobject box was created specifically for the Camera Match operation and isn't really part of the building, so remember to turn it off when you're rendering the model.

Aligning the Camera Match Points to the Background Image

The next set of steps will require some care. You'll locate the places in the background image that correspond to the CamPoints you've just created.

1. Click the Utilities tab in the upper right corner of the Command Panel.

2. Click the Camera Match button. You'll see the CamPoint Info rollout appear with a list of the CamPoints you just created.

3. Click Front Bottom in the CamPoint Info rollout; then click the Assign Position button.

4. Click the location (shown in the background image) that corresponds to the Front Bottom CamPoint in the design (see Figure 15.34). A small cross appears at the point you click. Try to be as precise as you can in placing the cross. If you don't like the location, you can continue to click points until you have the cross placed in a location you're satisfied with.

5. Since this is the first point you are aligning, you'll see a Camera Match warning message. Click Yes.

6. Select Front Top from the list in the CamPoint Info rollout; then click the top corner location in the background image, as shown in Figure 15.34.

7. Repeat step 6 for each of the remaining three CamPoints.

FIGURE 15.34
Click the CamPoint name in the Cam-Point Info rollout; then, with the Assign Position button active, click the points shown in the figure.

VIZ now has enough information to create a camera that matches the design geometry to the background image.

1. Scroll down the Command Panel so that you can see the Camera Match rollout clearly.

2. Click the Create Camera button.

Nothing seems to have changed, but you'll see a value appear in the Current Camera Error message in the Camera Match rollout. When you click the Create Camera button, VIZ creates a camera that matches the view of the design with the background image.

TIP   *A good value for the Camera Error is any value from 0 to 1.5.*

3. To see how the camera matching worked, right-click the Perspective viewport label in the upper left corner of the viewport and select Views ➢ Camera01. This is the camera that the Create Camera button created. The box will move into position over the image.

4. Click the Display tab in the Command Panel; then click Unhide All in the Hide rollout. The rest of the building appears in the viewport, as shown in Figure 15.35.

FIGURE 15.35

The apartment building in position

5. Select the Alignobject box and then click Hide Selected in the Hide rollout. You don't want the Alignobject box to appear in the rendered view.

6. Click the Quick Render tool on the main toolbar. The apartment is rendered with the background, as shown in Figure 15.36.

FIGURE 15.36
The rendered apartment building with the background

Once you have a rendering matched to a background, your work isn't completely finished. As you see in Figure 15.36, the building obscures some of the objects that are in the foreground. You can use Photoshop to bring those parts of the image back into the foreground, using the techniques you learned in Chapter 14.

1. Save the rendered image as a file named **Apartment.tif**.

2. In Photoshop or another image-editing program, open both the `Apartment.tif` file and the original background image, `noriegaview_render.tif`.

3. Resize the `noriegaview_render.tif` image to the size of the rendered image. To do this in Photoshop, choose Image ➢ Image Size. Then, in the Image Size dialog box, change the Width and Height settings in the Pixel Dimension group to values that match the VIZ rendering.

WARNING *Make sure that the Constrain Proportions and Resample Image check boxes are checked when you do this.*

4. Use the Lasso tool to carefully trace around the tops of the cars in the `noriegaview_render.tif` image.

5. Press Ctrl+C to copy the selection to the Clipboard. Then go to the rendered image of the apartment building.

6. Press Ctrl+V to paste the cars into the rendered view.

7. Use the Move tool to move the pasted cars into their proper locations.

8. Repeat the process for other items in the foreground, such as the mailbox and stop sign. Figure 15.37 shows the results of the changes to the image rendered in Photoshop.

FIGURE 15.37
Editing the render-ing in Photoshop

Fine-Tuning a Camera-Matched View

Not all of your camera-matching projects will go as smoothly as the previous example. Due to site restrictions or other limitations, you may be able to get only three or four points to match instead of the required five points. In these situations, you have to rely more on your knowledge of the site con-ditions, camera locations, and camera settings. Perhaps the most important item to record is the posi-tion of the camera in relation to the site, both in plan and elevation. If you can accurately place a camera in your scene, you can usually reconstruct a camera-matched view by fine-tuning your view using the Dolly, Field-of-View, and Roll Camera tools in the display toolbar. It helps to have topo-graphical information and, if possible, aerial photographs or satellite imagery, although good site plans will work as well.

Matching the Design Image Quality to the Background

You may find that the building doesn't quite match up with the background image in ways other than orientation and size. For example, the contrast in the building may be too low compared with the contrast in the background, or there may be a grain in the background that isn't present in the rendered building. These differences can cause the design to stand out from the background, making it obvious that it is a computer rendering superimposed onto a photograph.

You can make adjustments to the lighting and materials in the design to compensate for contrast and lighting differences, but noise in the background image has to be handled differently. You can deal with both noise and contrast by taking an alternate approach to final rendering of the design.

Now that you've got the design aligned with the background image, you can go ahead and render the image without the background. You can then use Photoshop or another image editing program to merge the rendered design into the background image. By doing this, you have control over the rendered image of the building apart from the background. You can add noise or adjust the contrast of the rendered design in Photoshop to match the background before the two images are merged. Figure 15.38 shows the rendering redone using this method. Compare it with the rendering in Figure 15.37 where the background and building were combined and rendered into a single image in VIZ.

TIP   To set up VIZ to render a view without the background, choose Rendering ➤ Environment and turn off the Use Map option in the Background group. You can always turn the background back on by reversing this procedure.

FIGURE 15.38
The rendered
apartment

Summary

In these last two chapters, you've seen how important an image editing program can be in your work with VIZ. In some situations, an image editing program can mean the difference between finishing a project on time and struggling for hours over some annoying detail in your design. It takes some experience working with VIZ to know when to use a bitmap image instead of creating an object. The information in these chapters should give you a head start in working with image files and photographs.

You also got a glimpse of how AutoCAD can be used in conjunction with VIZ as an image editing tool. In this chapter, you saw how a photograph can be analyzed to establish vanishing points and locations, using AutoCAD. In Chapter 14, you also learned how AutoCAD and other CAD programs can be used directly to generate bitmap images of geometric shapes. In the next chapter, you'll learn how you can use CAD files directly as a basis for geometry in VIZ.

Chapter 16

Using AutoCAD-Based Applications with VIZ

IN CHAPTER 14, YOU had some exposure to the ways that you can use Photoshop interactively with VIZ. Another set of products that are very useful with VIZ are AutoCAD-based applications including AutoCAD itself, AutoCAD LT, Mechanical Desktop (MDT), and Architectural Desktop (ADT). You can use any of these CAD programs to help create material maps and analyze photos for VIZ backgrounds. In this chapter, you'll look at ways that you can use AutoCAD-based applications more directly with VIZ in your design and visualization workflow. You'll explore the most common strategy, which is to import 2D AutoCAD line drawings as a starting point in the creation of VIZ geometry.

- ◆ Creating Topography with Splines
- ◆ Setting Up an AutoCAD Plan for VIZ
- ◆ Importing AutoCAD Plans into VIZ
- ◆ Exploring the File Link Manager
- ◆ Adding Stairs
- ◆ Importing a Truss

The tight integration between all of Autodesk's AutoCAD-based products and VIZ 2005 allows you to maximize the strengths of each program in your workflow. By using CAD and VIZ together, you can maintain a single design database that carries through your entire workflow. VIZ will never overwrite an AutoCAD DWG or DXF file that you import or link into your scene, so you can be sure of the integrity of your design database.

Depending on your particular needs and skill level with each program, you will need to consider several strategies for planning the tasks to perform in each software package.

Although it is possible to create your entire project in VIZ alone, you are not advised to do so. VIZ's real strengths are in modeling complex forms, assigning materials, lighting, scene composition, rendering, and animation. VIZ is weaker in managing the complex 2D linework that is needed in drafting—this is AutoCAD and AutoCAD LT's traditional strength. Therefore, it is more efficient to utilize CAD for what it is best at doing and use VIZ for its strengths as well.

AutoCAD and AutoCAD LT are excellent tools for creating 2D geometry. Much of your work as a designer will require accurate renditions of your designs in the traditional plan and elevation views. Frequently, designs begin as 2D plans anyway, so having the ability to import or link to a DWG or DXF drawing is a natural extension of VIZ. In the most common strategy, the 2D linework is handled by CAD, and the rest of the workflow is handled by VIZ.

Another strategy to consider is to bring a well-developed 3D model into VIZ from AutoCAD, ADT, or MDT. Some veteran AutoCAD users (or those very new to VIZ) may prefer to do basic 3D modeling in AutoCAD, and use VIZ later in their workflow.

AutoCAD's 3D modeling tools are quite primitive in comparison with VIZ's modeling tools. VIZ is much better for modeling curving forms such as those found in furniture, ornamentation, and luminaires.

ADT is designed to build a 3D model as you work, so it makes sense to link an ADT model into VIZ and use VIZ for the visualization aspects of the workflow.

There is a stripped-down version of VIZ inside ADT called VIZ Render. VIZ Render is used to assign materials, cameras, lighting, basic rendering, and simple animation to an ADT model only. VIZ 2005 is much more powerful and is preferable for modeling, rendering, and animation.

You can use VIZ Render (inside ADT) to assign materials, cameras, and lighting. Then you would open the VIZ Render file inside VIZ 2005 and optionally add furniture, ornamentation, and luminaires. VIZ can then be used to complete the workflow by creating photo-realistic renderings and complex animation.

Creating Topography with Splines

In Chapter 14, you learned to create geometry by using a displacement map. A displacement map, which is similar to a bump map, creates a deformed surface based on the light and dark areas of a bitmap image. You can create terrain in a VIZ model by painting light and dark areas in an image, and then importing that image and using it as a displacement map, as shown in Figure 16.1.

FIGURE 16.1

A bitmap image and the terrain created by using the image as a displacement map

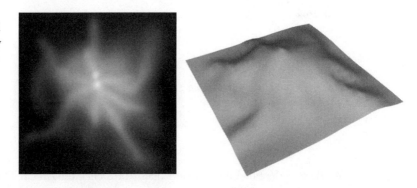

This type of terrain modeling is fine for free-form shapes, but if you want to have an accurate model of terrain based on survey data, you need to use other tools to create your terrain model. In this section, you'll learn how you can quickly create a terrain model from contour lines generated in AutoCAD. You'll also get a look at ways of linking files from AutoCAD to allow you to maintain one data source for both AutoCAD and VIZ. The importer for DWG and DXF files has been completely rewritten in VIZ 2005. Both DWG and DXF files are imported through the same dialog box, and there are new options.

New!

TIP You can still access the legacy DWG importer if you want to import files the way it worked in VIZ 4. Choose File ➤ Import. Then click the Files of Type drop-down list and select Legacy AutoCAD DWG to access the old importer.

1. Start VIZ; then choose File ➤ File Link Manager.

TIP You can also use the File Link manager as a utility. Click the Utilities tab of the Command Panel and click File Link Manager.

2. In the File Link Manager dialog box, make sure the Attach tab is selected; then click the File button.

3. In the Open dialog box, locate and open the contour.dwg file. This is an AutoCAD file that contains a series of contour lines, as shown in Figure 16.2. The contour lines are AutoCAD splines.

FIGURE 16.2
The contour.dwg file

4. Back in the File Link Manager dialog box, click the Attach This File button. The contours appear in the VIZ Perspective viewport.

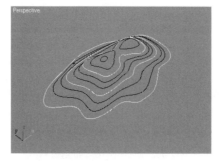

5. Click OK to accept all the default options in the File Link Setting: DWG Files dialog box.

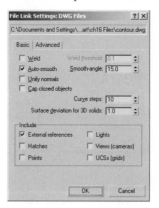

6. Click the Close button in the File Link manager.

By importing an AutoCAD file as a linked file, you keep the imported geometry linked to the original AutoCAD file. As you'll see a bit later, this link will enable you to update the VIZ scene whenever changes occur to the AutoCAD file.

Now let's see how the contours can be turned into a surface model.

1. Click Select by Name to open the Select Object dialog box. Select both objects in the list.

2. Make sure that the Geometry button is selected in the Create tab of the Command Panel; then choose Compound Objects on the Create drop-down list.

3. Click Terrain on the Object Type rollout.

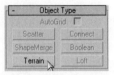

A surface appears over the contour lines.

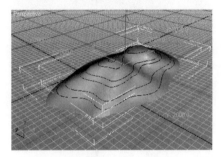

VIZ creates a terrain object based on the contour lines. You can improve the visibility of the terrain's shape by using the Color by Elevation option.

1. In the Command Panel, scroll down to the Color by Elevation rollout and open it.

2. Click the Create Defaults button in the Zones by Base Elevation group.

The Terrain object changes to show a series of colored bands.

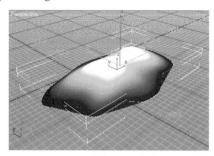

The values in the Zone by Base Elevation group list box tell you the base elevation for each of the colors. You can change the color and the base elevation.

1. Select the first elevation value in the list box of the Zones by Base Elevation group.

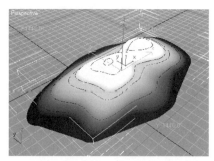

2. In the Color Zone group, click the Base Color swatch.

3. In the Color Selector dialog box, click the cyan (blue) color in the Hue/Blackness color selector.

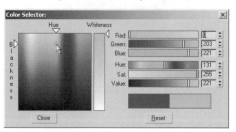

4. Click the Modify Zone button in the Color Zone group. The base of the Terrain object changes to the blue color you selected.

You can also change the vertical location for a color by changing the Base Elev value in the Color Zone group. This doesn't have any effect on the shape of the Terrain object; it only changes the location of the color.

Updating Changes from an AutoCAD File

You imported the AutoCAD contour map using the File ➤ File Link Manager option. By using this option, you link your VIZ scene to the `contour.dwg` file in a way that's similar to XRef files in both VIZ and AutoCAD. The conceptual difference between file linking and external references is that with XRefs, you are bringing in native files, whereas with file linking, you are bringing in files that were made in another application. Just as with changes made to an XRef, changes in the `contour.dwg` file will affect any VIZ file to which it's linked.

Let's suppose that you have some corrections to make to the AutoCAD contour drawing that will affect the Terrain object you've just created. You can change the AutoCAD drawing file and then update the VIZ scene to reflect those changes.

1. If you have AutoCAD 2004 or later, open the `contour.dwg` file in AutoCAD and make the changes shown in Figure 16.3.

FIGURE 16.3
Stretch these points
outward.

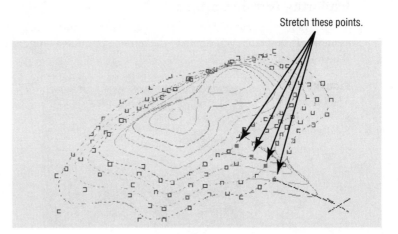

2. If you don't have AutoCAD, use Windows Explorer to delete the `contour.dwg` file; then make a copy of the `contour modified.dwg` file and rename it **`contour.dwg`** to replace the file you deleted. The `contour modified.dwg` file contains the changes shown in Figure 16.3.

3. In VIZ, choose File ➤ File Link Manager.

4. In the File Link Manager dialog box, select the Files tab; then click the `contour.dwg` listing in the Linked Files list box at the top of the dialog box.

5. Click the Reload button. The File Link Settings: DWG Files dialog box displays.

6. In the File Link Settings: DWG Files dialog box, click OK. The file will be reloaded, and the changes will be imported into the current VIZ file.

7. Close the File Link Manager dialog box. The changes are now visible in the Terrain object.

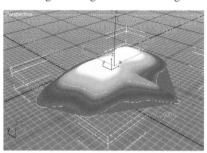

Like XRef files, VIZ scenes that are linked to AutoCAD files can be updated to reflect changes that are made to the source AutoCAD file. You'll get a chance to take a closer look at this feature later in this chapter.

Exploring Terrain Options

The Terrain object has quite a few parameters that allow you to make adjustments to the terrain. For example, if you prefer, you can have the terrain appear as a terraced form instead of a smooth one, as shown in Figure 16.4.

FIGURE 16.4
The Terrain object with the Layered Solid option

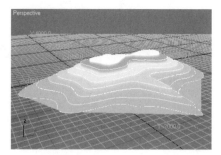

NOTE *The Layered Solid option of the Terrain object creates a surface that resembles a traditional site plan model made of foamcore.*

You've already seen how a few of the Color by Elevation rollout options work. Here's a rundown of the rest of the Terrain object parameters.

THE PICK OPERAND ROLLOUT

These options allow you to add other splines to an existing Terrain object.

The splines used for the Terrain object are referred to as the operands of the Terrain object. When a Terrain object is created, a Reference clone of the selected splines is added as part of the Terrain object. This is the default option in the Pick Operand rollout. When adding additional splines, you can choose the type of clone you wish to use instead of the Reference clone. The Override option lets you replace one operand with another.

THE PARAMETERS ROLLOUT

The Parameters rollout offers settings that control the overall form of the Terrain object. The Operands group lets you selectively delete operands from the terrain.

The Form group gives you control over the way the contour data is formed into a terrain. Graded Surface creates the type of terrain you've seen in previous exercises. Graded Solid creates a solid form that encloses the entire terrain, including the underside. Layered Solid creates a terraced form. The Stitched Border option improves the formation of terrain where open splines or polylines are used in the contour. Retriangulate helps to generate a terrain that follows the contours more closely.

The Display group allows you to view the terrain as a surface terrain, as contour lines, or as both.

The Update group lets you control the way that the Terrain object is updated when the operands are edited. The Always option updates the Terrain object as soon as a contour is modified. The When

Rendering option updates when you render the scene. You can also use the Update button with this option. The Manually option updates the terrain only when you click the Update button.

THE SIMPLIFICATION ROLLOUT

VIZ uses the vertices of the original contour polylines to generate the Terrain object. The Simplification rollout options give you control over the number of vertices used to generate the terrain.

In the Horizontal group, both the Use $^1/_2$ of Points option and the Use $^1/_4$ of Points option reduce the number of points used from the contour line. These procedures reduce the accuracy of the terrain, but they also reduce the complexity of the geometry, thereby making the terrain's memory requirements smaller. The Interpolate Points options increase the number of points used. Interpolate Points * 2, for example, doubles the number of vertices used by interpolating new points between the existing points in the contour.

The Vertical group determines whether all of the selected contour lines are used. You can reduce the terrain's complexity by using either the Use $^1/_2$ of Lines option or the Use $^1/_4$ of Lines option.

THE COLOR BY ELEVATION ROLLOUT

VIZ lets you color the Terrain object by elevation. This enables you to visualize the terrain more clearly and helps you identify elevations by color-coding them.

The Maximum Elev and Minimum Elev options display the maximum and minimum extents of the terrain, based on the contour data. The Reference Elev option lets you establish a reference elevation that is used for assigning colors to the terrain. If this value is equal to or less than the lowest contour, VIZ generates five color zones for the terrain, as you saw in an earlier exercise. If the Reference Elev is greater than the lowest contour, VIZ treats the lower elevations as water, using the Reference Elev value as the water level. Water is given a blue color by default.

The Zones by Base Elevation group gives you control over the individual colors for each color zone. As you've seen from the exercise, the Create Defaults button applies the colors to the Terrain object based on the current settings of the rollout. You can also change the color of each zone by selecting the zone elevation from the list box and using the Base Color swatch to select a color.

The Blend to Color Above and Solid to Top of Zone radio buttons let you choose to blend colors between zones or to have each zone one solid color. By default, colors are blended. You can change from blended to solid by selecting the zone elevation from the Zones by Base Elevation list, selecting Solid to Top of Zone and then clicking the Modify Zones button. The Add Zone and Delete Zone options add and delete zones.

Setting Up an AutoCAD Plan for VIZ

If you're an experienced AutoCAD, ADT, or MDT user, you may find it easier to create at least part of your 3D model in AutoCAD and then import the model into VIZ to refine it. If this is the case, simply import or link the CAD model into VIZ and then resume your design visualization workflow at the point of assigning materials, or adding lights and cameras. Then you can render and animate the scene, if desired, entirely in VIZ.

On the other hand, you can also import 2D plans and elevations and build your 3D model in VIZ. In this section, you'll explore the ways you can set up an AutoCAD or AutoCAD LT 2D drawing to take advantage of VIZ's superior modeling tools.

One of the drawbacks of importing fully developed 3D models from AutoCAD is that frequently, the surface normals of the AutoCAD model are not all oriented in the same direction. You can use VIZ to adjust the normals to point in the same direction, but that takes time. In this situation, it's usually more efficient to apply two-sided materials to the offending objects and leave it at that. Using two-sided materials increases rendering time somewhat, but this disadvantage is often offset by the enormous amount of time it would have taken to adjust misaligned normals. You can also try to use the Normal modifier, or apply the Edit Mesh modifier to selected objects and adjust individual sub-objects in order to correct problems with surface normals.

You can avoid the normals problem altogether by importing a specially prepared 2D model from AutoCAD into VIZ.

TIP   It is usually not worth doing 3D modeling in AutoCAD unless you are a veteran AutoCAD user, are unfamiliar with VIZ's superior 3D modeling tools, and are working on a deadline. It is worth learning how to model in VIZ, and importing or linking 2D linework from CAD is a way to ease into it.

In the next set of exercises, you'll use AutoCAD to prepare a plan for export to VIZ. If you don't have AutoCAD, you can skip to the section "Importing AutoCAD Plans into VIZ."

1. Open AutoCAD 2004 or later; then open the `savoye-ground.dwg` file. This is the ground floor plan of the Villa Savoye that you worked with earlier in this book.

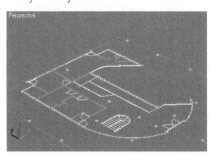

NOTE *If you have an older version of AutoCAD, a compressed archive is included on the CD called* `LegacyAutoCAD.ZIP` *that contains all the DWG files used in this chapter, saved in AutoCAD Release 14 format.*

2. Select WALL-viz-EXT from the Layer drop-down list on the main toolbar.

3. Use the Zoom Region tool to enlarge your view so that it looks similar to Figure 16.5.

4. Choose Draw ➢ Boundary. The Boundary Creation dialog box displays.

5. In the Boundary Creation dialog box, click Pick Points. The dialog box temporarily disappears to allow you to select points on the screen.

FIGURE 16.5

Selecting points
inside the exterior
walls

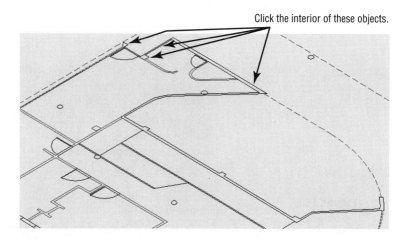

Click the interior of these objects.

6. Click the points shown in Figure 16.5. Press Enter when you're finished. A magenta outline of the wall appears, outlining the areas you selected.

The magenta outline is a continuous closed polyline, which will become a closed spline in VIZ. Closed splines are preferable entities because they extrude without any problems with surface normals in VIZ. Since Wall-viz-EXT is current, the outline is placed on this layer. The layer's color is magenta, so the wall acquires the layer's color.

TIP   *You must be able to see the entire boundary on the screen before picking a point to create a boundary object. The Boundary Creation tool will fail unless the boundary is visible because the internal hatch algorithm analyzes what is visible on the screen only. Try zooming out a bit and try selecting Draw ➤ Boundary again if you get the message "Boundary Definition Error: Valid hatch boundary not found." Boundary creation will also fail if you click outside the lines, or if the point you click is directly on an object.*

Next, continue to add the outlines of the exterior walls using the Boundary Creation dialog box.

1. Use the Pan tool to adjust your view to look similar to Figure 16.6.

2. Open the Boundary Creation dialog box again and then click the Pick Points button.

3. Select the points indicated in Figure 16.6.

4. Press Enter when you've selected all the points.

5. Adjust your view as shown in Figure 16.7.

6. Use the Boundary Creation dialog box again to select the areas indicated in Figure 16.7. Press Enter when you're done.

7. Select Wall-viz-INT from the Layer drop-down list on the main toolbar.

FIGURE 16.6
Selecting other points for the exterior wall

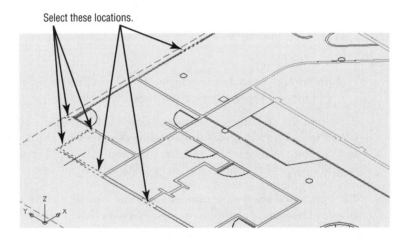

FIGURE 16.7
Select points in the walls near the curved glass.

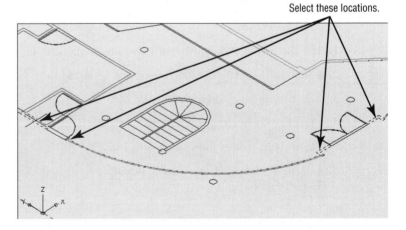

8. Use the Boundary Creation dialog box to create outlines of the interior walls. When you're done, the interior walls should all appear in the cyan color, which is the color for the Wall-viz-INT layer.

You want the interior walls to be on a different layer from the exterior walls so that when the drawing is imported into VIZ, you can apply separate materials to the interior and exterior wall objects. By default, VIZ converts AutoCAD objects into VIZ objects based on their layers, although you can have VIZ use other criteria for converting objects if you choose.

Go ahead and use the Boundary Creation dialog box to outline the other portions of the drawing.

1. Choose the Wall-viz-int-hdr layer from the Layer drop-down list; then use the Boundary Creation dialog box to outline all the door headers, as indicated in Figure 16.8.

FIGURE 16.8
Outline the door headers of the interior walls.

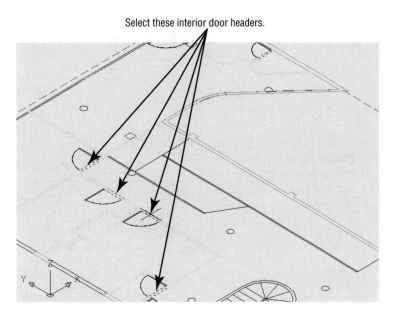

Select these interior door headers.

2. Choose the Wall-viz-ext-hdr layer; then use the Boundary Creation dialog box to outline the door headers over the exterior doors.

3. Turn off the Glass layer; then make the Wall-viz-sill layer current.

4. Use the Boundary Creation dialog box to outline the areas where the windows are indicated in the plan, as shown in Figure 16.9.

5. Finally, turn off the Mullion-vert layer, set the current layer to Mullion-horiz, and outline the areas indicated in Figure 16.10.

6. Make sure all the layers are turned back on; then choose File ➢ Save As and save the file as **MySavoye-ground-viz**.

FIGURE 16.9
Outline the
window areas.

Select the window sill areas.

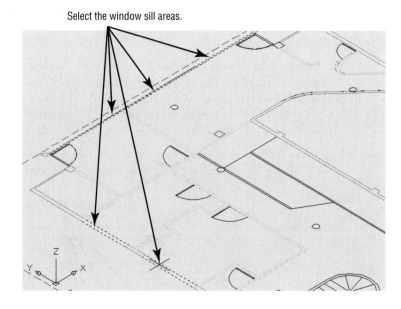

FIGURE 16.10
Outline the areas
that are the horizon-
tal mullions.

Select the outline of the curved windows.

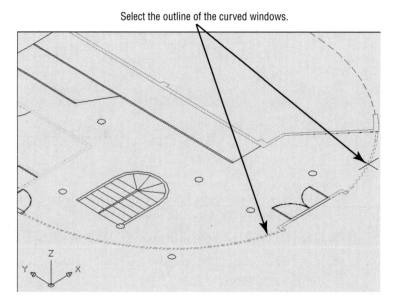

The main point of these exercises is that you want to segregate the different parts of the drawing so that later, in VIZ, you can control the extruded heights of the separate layers individually. You ensure that you can do this by using layers in AutoCAD to organize the closed polylines that are to be extruded in VIZ.

You use the Boundary Creation dialog box to ensure that the polyline outlines are continuous and closed. Alternatively, you can just use the Polyline tool on the Draw toolbar to trace over the wall outlines if you prefer. The Boundary Creation dialog box makes the work a lot easier because it relieves you from having to click every point in each boundary.

NOTE   *At times, you'll encounter an error message while selecting areas with the Boundary Creation dialog box. This is usually caused by one of two things: either the area you select isn't completely closed, or a single line intrudes into the space you're trying to outline. In these cases, you will have to manually trim away intruding lines, or join lines that do not meet.*

Importing AutoCAD Plans into VIZ

Now that you've got the plan set up, you can import it into VIZ and make fairly quick work of the conversion to 3D. You've done all of the organizing in AutoCAD, so all that is left is to extrude the building parts to their appropriate heights.

1. Open VIZ and choose File ➤ Reset. You don't need to save your changes, so click No at the "Do you want to save your changes?" warning and click Yes at the "Do you really want to reset?" warning.

2. Choose File ➤ Import. The Select File to Import dialog box displays.

3. In the Select File to Import dialog box, select AutoCAD Drawing (*.DWG, *.DXF) from the File of Type drop-down list; then locate and open the MySavoye-ground-viz.dwg file. If you haven't done the preceding AutoCAD exercises, you can open the savoye-ground-viz.dwg file from the companion CD.

4. In the AutoCAD DWG/DXF Import Options dialog box, make sure the settings are the same as those shown in Figure 16.11.

5. Be sure that the Unify Normals check box is checked. This is an important setting because it tells VIZ to align all the normals so that they are pointing outward.

6. Click OK to import the AutoCAD file. The plan appears in the viewport.

The next step is to set up a comfortable view of the model so that you can easily maneuver within it.

1. Right-click the Perspective label in the upper left corner of the viewport; then either select Views ➤ User or press U. Your view changes to an orthographic projection instead of a perspective view.

FIGURE 16.11

The Import Auto-
CAD DWG File
dialog box showing
the settings needed
for this exercise

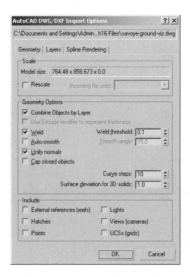

2. Arc Rotate so your point of view is above and at a 45-degree angle to the plan.

3. Click the Grid button at the bottom of the user interface for a clearer view.

4. Click the Zoom Extents tool to view the plan so that it looks similar to Figure 16.12.

FIGURE 16.12

The view so far

Extruding the Walls

The next step is to start extruding the walls. The polyline outlines that you created in AutoCAD are converted to closed splines in VIZ, so you need only to select the splines and apply the Extrude modifier.

1. Click the Select by Name tool on the main toolbar to open the Select Objects dialog box.

2. Select Layer:Wall-viz-INT, Layer:Wall-viz-EXT, and Layer:MULLION-VERT from the
list then click Select. Remember that you can select multiple, nonconsecutive items from a list
by holding down the Ctrl key while you click.

NOTE *The object naming convention has changed with the new version of the DWG/DXF importer in VIZ 2005. Objects that were combined by Layer in the translation have "Layer:" preceding their AutoCAD layer name.*

3. Select the Modify tab in the Command Panel and then select Extrude from the Modifier List drop-down list.

4. In the Parameters rollout, set the Amount input box to **9´6˝**. The walls display in the viewport.

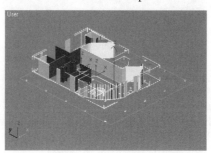

In this exercise, you applied the same modifier to three objects: Layer:Wall-viz-INT, Layer:Wall-viz-EXT, and Layer:MULLION-VERT. Whenever you change the Extrude Amount parameter for one object, it changes for the others because the Extrude modifier is instanced across the objects you selected in step 2. The two sets of walls and the vertical mullions were segregated in AutoCAD so that you could apply a different material to each of them in VIZ; but because all of these items are the same height, you applied a single modifier to all three of them.

If you decide that you need to give each set of walls its own Extrude modifier, you can do so by clicking one of the walls, selecting the italicized Extrude modifier in the stack, and then clicking the Make Unique button in the modifier stack list.

TIP *Modifiers that appear in italic in the stack are instanced.*

Extruding Headers

Now let's continue with the door headers and the walls around the windows.

1. Open the Select Objects dialog box again. Then select Layer:Wall-viz-ext-hdr, Layer:Wall-viz-int-hdr, and Layer:Wall-viz-sill.

2. Select Extrude again from the modifier list; then change the Amount value in the Parameters rollout to **1´6˝**.

3. Click the Select and Move tool; then click the Absolute/Offset Mode Transform Type-In tool next to the coordinate readout so that you are in the Offset mode. You'll see values appear in the coordinate readout.

4. In the coordinate readout, change the Z value to **96**. The door headers all move to their positions above the doors.

You may have noticed that in step 3, the coordinate readout showed values only when you selected the Offset mode from the Absolute/Offset Mode Transform Type-In tool. This is because you have more than one object selected. The Absolute mode has no significance for multiple selections because several objects can have different locations in the scene.

Also, just as with the walls, you use a single instanced Extrude modifier to effect changes to three objects.

Now, take a closer look at the windows. You have the window headers in place, but they also need a portion of wall to fill in below the windows. You'll need to copy the window headers and change their Extrude amount.

1. Select the Layer:Wall-viz-sill object. You can use the Select Objects dialog box to do this, or you can simply click one of the window headers toward the back of the building.

2. With the Select and Move tool selected, Shift+click the blue Z axis arrow of the selected header downward to make a clone of the window header object, roughly placing the copy at ground level.

3. In the Clone Options dialog box, make sure the Copy radio button is selected. You can keep the Layer:Wall-viz-sill01 name. Click OK to accept the clone settings.

4. Click the Absolute/Offset Mode Transform Type-In tool to change to the Absolute mode; then right-click the Z spinner to change the Z value in the coordinate readout to 0.

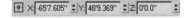

5. Change the Amount value in the Parameters rollout of the Modify tab to **32**.

Extruding the Mullions

You now have the walls in place. Because you did some prep work in AutoCAD, the work in VIZ went fairly quickly. Even so, a few items still need to be taken care of. The horizontal mullions for the curved window need to be created.

1. Use the Region Zoom tool to enlarge your view of the plan near the entrance to the right, as shown in Figure 16.13.

FIGURE 16.13
A close-up view of
the entrance and
curved window

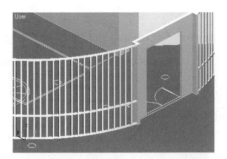

2. Select the horizontal mullion outline named Layer:MULLION-HORIZ.

3. Select the Extrude option in the modifier list; then change the Amount parameter to **2**.

4. Choose Edit ➢ Clone; then, in the Clone Options dialog box, click OK. The clone is now the selected object.

5. Click the Select and Move tool; then change the Z value in the coordinate readout to **32**.

6. Choose Edit ➢ Clone again; then click OK in the Clone Options dialog box.

7. With the Select and Move tool still selected, change the Z value in the coordinate readout to 9′4″. The horizontal mullions for the curved window are now in place, as shown in Figure 16.13.

Adding Glass

To finish off the ground floor of the villa, you need to add the glass.

1. Open the Select Objects dialog box and select Layer:GLASS.

2. Select Extrude from the modifier list; then change the Amount parameter to 9′6″.

The glass appears in only one area. This is because the Glass object is a single spline and not an outline. You may recall from Chapter 3 that the normals of a surface will render the surface visible in only one direction. To compensate for this limitation, you can turn the Layer:GLASS spline into an outline.

1. In the Command Panel, select Editable Spline from the Modifier List drop-down list.

2. Click the Spline button in the Selection rollout to enter that sub-object level for editing.

3. Click the Zoom Extents tool to view the entire scene.

4. Press Ctrl+A to select all the sub-splines within Layer:GLASS.

5. Scroll down to the Outline button in the Geometry rollout and enter **0.2**↵ for the Outline value. You won't see any changes at this viewing distance, but the glass is now an outline instead of a single line.

6. Select Extrude from the modifier stack list. The glass now appears in all of the appropriate places because it now has two surfaces that both have normals that face outward.

7. Save this file as **savoye-ground-viz.max**.

You could have left the glass as a single line. Although this makes the glass difficult to see in a shaded viewport, you can apply a two-sided material to the glass so that it will appear in a finished rendering. Although a two-sided glass material takes a bit longer to render, the single-line glass material is a less complex geometry. This makes the file a bit smaller. For this reason, if your model contains lots of curved glass, it may make sense to leave the glass as a single line. Otherwise, you may want to convert all of the glass in your model to outlines. As you've seen here, that's fairly easy to do in VIZ. It takes a bit more work to accomplish the same results in AutoCAD by using the Boundary tool.

Also, in the last exercise, you may have noticed that you gave the glass a full height of 9 feet, 6 inches, even though, in many cases, the glass only filled a height of 64 inches or less. You can do this because VIZ takes care of the small details of object intersections. In those places where the glass occurs within a wall, VIZ hides most of the glass, and it is displayed only where it appears in an opening, as shown in Figure 16.14. VIZ also takes care of the intersection of the vertical and horizontal mullions.

FIGURE 16.14
The window show-ing the glass

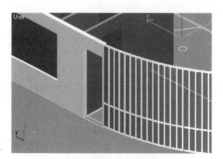

Creating a Floor with Openings

You've seen how the ground floor of the villa can be set up in AutoCAD to make quick work of the extrusions in VIZ. The second floor and rooftop can be done in the same way, but the floors between the different levels require a slightly different approach.

Both the second floor and the roof surface have openings that need some special attention when you are setting up to export to VIZ.

1. Go back to AutoCAD and open the savoye-second.dwg file.

2. Click the Layer Properties tool, and in the Layer Properties Manager dialog box, click New. Create a layer named **VIZ-floor** and click the Current button to make it the current layer.

3. Use a polyline to outline the second floor, as shown in Figure 16.15.

4. Turn off all the layers except VIZ-floor, STAIR, and RAMP; then zoom in to the stair, as shown in Figure 16.16.

5. Enlarge the view of the stair. Then outline the stair with a closed polyline, as shown in Figure 16.16. (In this operation, you're drawing the outline of the stair opening in the floor.)

TIP *You will have to toggle between Arc and Line modes while drawing with the Pline tool in AutoCAD to complete the outline shown in Figure 16.16.*

6. Pan over to the ramp. Then draw an outline of the ramp with a closed polyline (you may use the Rectangle tool), as shown in Figure 16.17.

FIGURE 16.15
Outline the second floor.

Place a rectangle or closed polyline around the perimeter of the second floor plan.

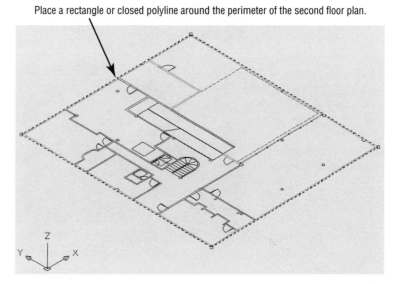

FIGURE 16.16
Outline the stair.

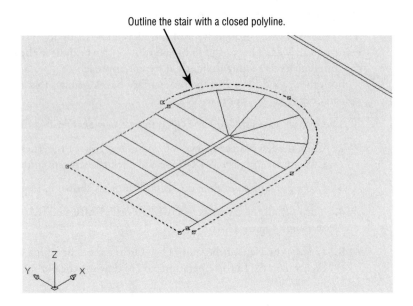

Outline the stair with a closed polyline.

FIGURE 16.17
The outline of the ramp floor opening

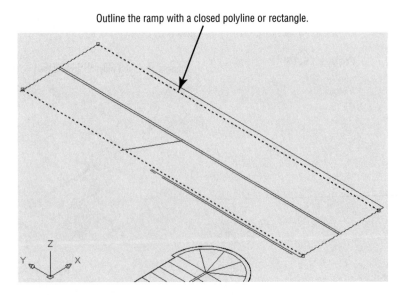

Outline the ramp with a closed polyline or rectangle.

You've got all of the additional line work you need to export the floor of the second story to VIZ, but you still need to take a few more steps to complete the setup for VIZ.

1. Freeze all the layers except the VIZ-floor layer.

WARNING   *The way layers that are off are handled has changed in the new DWG/DXF importer. You now have to freeze layers to automatically exclude them from import. However, it is possible to manually select which layers will be included upon import, regardless of their layer state in AutoCAD (but it is less efficient).*

2. Use the Zoom Extents tool to view your work so far (see Figure 16.18). You now have the outline of the second floor and the two openings through the floor.

3. Choose File ➤ Save to save your changes.

FIGURE 16.18
The outline of the
second floor

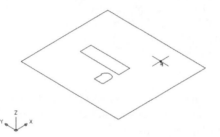

Basically, you've outlined the second floor and its openings with closed polylines. In addition, you've frozen all the layers except the floor outline and openings. This last step lets you automatically limit the objects that VIZ imports to only those items you added to the AutoCAD file.

The next step is to import your work to VIZ.

1. Go back to VIZ and choose File ➤ Reset. You can go ahead and reset the file since you've already saved your work.

2. Choose File ➤ Import. Then, in the Select File to Import dialog box, locate and open the `savoye-second.dwg` file you just saved from AutoCAD. If you don't have AutoCAD, open the `savoye-second-outline.dwg` file from the companion CD.

3. In the AutoCAD DWG/DXF Import Options dialog box, adjust the settings to match those of Figure 16.19.

FIGURE 16.19

The AutoCAD
DWG/DXF Import
Options dialog box

4. Click the Layers tab in the AutoCAD DWG/DXF Import Options dialog box. Note that the Skip All Frozen Layers radio button is selected by default. This setting lets you automatically skip importing the layers you froze in AutoCAD.

5. Click OK to close the AutoCAD DWG/DXF Options dialog box. When you click the Select from List radio button on the Layers tab of the AutoCAD DWG/DXF Import Options dialog box, you are able to manually check which layers are imported by toggling the large check mark along the left edge of the list. The layer states shown in the list (on/off, frozen/thaw, locked/unlocked) represent the current state of the DWG or DXF file, and are not functional; they are for your information only.

You now see the outline of the second floor that you created in AutoCAD.

The final step is fairly easy. You only need to extrude the spline, and the openings will appear automatically.

1. Click the Select Object tool; then click the floor outline.

2. Select the Modify tab in the Command Panel; then select Extrude from the modifier list.

3. Set the Amount parameter to **18**. You now have the second-story floor, complete with openings.

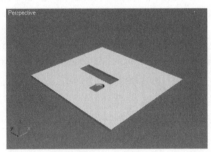

4. If you'd like, save this file as `savoye-secondfloor.max` for future reference.

VIZ automatically subtracts closed splines that are enclosed by other splines. On the second floor, ramp and stair openings are automatically subtracted from the second floor perimeter.

USING BUILDING ELEVATIONS AND WALL PROFILES FROM AUTOCAD

In the last section, you learned how to convert outlines of a building plan into a floor with openings. You can employ the same procedures for converting building elevations from AutoCAD to VIZ scenes. For example, in AutoCAD, you can outline an elevation of the villa using concentric rectangles for the second floor outline and the windows. You would then import the outlines to VIZ and extrude them, just as you did with the floor. That would give you the exterior walls of the building that you could rotate into a vertical position. This VIZ technique is similar to real-world tilt-up wall framing construction.

Using this method, you can even include other detail such as the window mullions. Once you've done this for all four exterior walls, you can join the walls to form the second floor exterior walls, complete with window openings and even window detail.

Another great tool for forming building exteriors and interiors is the Loft tool. Sometimes a simple vertical extrusion won't be enough for walls. You may be working with a design that makes use of strong horizontal elements, such as a wide cornice or exaggerated rustication. You can make quick work of such detail by using VIZ's Loft tool. Draw the profile of the wall and the building footprint in AutoCAD. Make sure each of these items is on a separate layer and is made of polylines. You can then import the AutoCAD file into VIZ and use the Loft Compound object tool to loft the wall profile along the building footprint in a way similar to the Ronchamp roof exercise in Chapter 5. This is especially helpful if the building footprint contains lots of curves and corners that would otherwise be difficult to model.

TIP As an alternative, in AutoCAD, you can convert the closed splines of the stair, ramp, and floor into regions, and then subtract the stair and ramp regions from the floor outline. AutoCAD regions are converted into VIZ mesh surfaces. You then have to extrude the floor with the tools within the polygon level of the editable mesh, rather than with the Extrude modifier.

You were asked to freeze all the layers in AutoCAD except the Viz-floor layer. This allowed you to automatically limit the objects that were imported from AutoCAD into VIZ. You can go back to the AutoCAD file, thaw the wall, header, and other layers, and then freeze the VIZ-floor layer. Once you've done that, you can import the other second-story elements into a VIZ file and then merge the floor and the walls. On the other hand, you can choose exactly which layers will be imported on the Layers tab of the new AutoCAD DWG/DXF Import Options dialog box. Of course, you can also thaw all the layers and import all the AutoCAD drawing at once. But importing parts of an AutoCAD file can help simplify your work and keep it manageable.

Exploring the File Link Manager

Earlier in this chapter, you were introduced to the File Link manager when you imported topographic contour lines from AutoCAD. In that example, the File Link manager allowed you to update the VIZ terrain model when a change was made to the AutoCAD DWG file. You can also use the File Link manager with floor plans to help maintain design continuity between AutoCAD and VIZ.

Try using the File Link manager with the second floor of the villa in the following exercises.

1. Choose File ➢ Reset to reset the file.

2. Choose File ➢ File Link Manager.

3. In the File Link Manager dialog box, select the Attach tab and then click the File button.

4. Locate and open savoye-second-viz.dwg from the companion CD.

Now let's take a closer look at some of the options in the File Link manager.

1. In the File Link Manager dialog box, click the Presets tab.

2. Click the New button; then, in the New Settings Preset dialog box, click OK to accept the default name of New Presets.

3. Back in the File Link Manager dialog box, select New Preset from the list; then click Modify. The File Link Settings: DWG Files dialog box displays.

4. In the File Link Settings dialog box, select the Advanced tab.

5. In the Derive AutoCAD Primitives By drop-down list, make sure Layer, Blocks as Node Hierarchy is selected.

6. Click the Basic tab and check Weld and Unify Normals.

7. Click Save. Then, in the File Link Manager dialog box, select the Attach tab and select the New Preset from the Preset drop-down menu.

8. Click the Attach This File button. The plan displays in the viewport.

9. Click the Close button in the File Link Manager dialog box.

10. Click the Layer Manager tool in the main toolbar. The AutoCAD layers are re-created in VIZ in the Layer dialog box.

With the file link settings, you can control layers as you would in AutoCAD, using the AutoCAD layer names preserved in VIZ. You can also create your own settings for special conditions by using the File Link Manager Presets tab and selecting your custom presets as you need them.

To confirm that you have full control over the linked drawing, try the following steps.

1. Open the Select Objects dialog box; then select the Layer:Wall-viz-INT and Layer:Wall-viz-EXT objects.

2. Click the Modify tab in the Command Panel; then click the Extrude button.

3. Set the Amount parameter to **114**. The interior and exterior walls display in the model.

As you can see, the method for extruding the walls is exactly the same for the imported AutoCAD file. You can now select and extrude objects as you did for the `savoye-ground.dwg` file that you imported earlier. The difference with the linked file is that changes made in the AutoCAD file can be updated in VIZ, much like the way XRefs work in both AutoCAD and VIZ.

Editing Linked AutoCAD Files

Now let's take a look at one of the key advantages of using the File Link manager instead of the simpler DWG file import.

1. Go back to AutoCAD and open the `savoye-second.dwg` file.

2. Turn on and thaw all the layers and use the Stretch command to stretch the walls as shown in Figure 16.20.

3. Choose File ➢ Save to save the changes.

FIGURE 16.20
Stretch these walls as shown here.

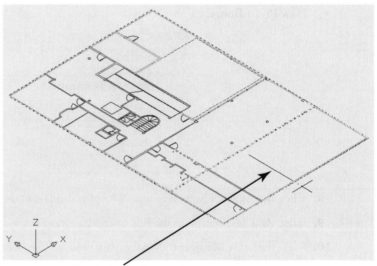

Stretch these walls outward.

NOTE   *If you don't have AutoCAD, use Windows Explorer to make a copy of the* `savoye-second-viz-mod.dwg` *file from the companion CD as* **`savoye-second.dwg`**. `Savoye-second-viz-mod.dwg` *contains the modifications described in the preceding exercise.*

4. Go back to VIZ; then click File ➤ File Link Manager.

5. In the File Link Manager dialog box, select the Files tab; then select `savoye-second.dwg` in the Linked Files list box.

6. Click the Reload button. The File Link Settings dialog box displays.

7. In the File Link Settings dialog box, click OK. Then close the File Link Manager dialog box.

The VIZ scene is updated according to the changes made in the AutoCAD file.

You've seen how you can update VIZ scenes when changes occur in a linked AutoCAD object. If you add objects in AutoCAD, those objects are also added to the VIZ scene. If the new object is added to a layer that already exists, and the objects associated with that layer are attached to a modifier, then the new object is also controlled by the modifier. For example, if you add a rectangle to the AutoCAD drawing on the Wall-viz-EXT layer, the new rectangle will be extruded to the 9′6″ height, just like all the other objects on the Wall-viz-EXT layer. New objects on that layer that have a thickness or that are extruded within AutoCAD will be ignored by VIZ unless they are placed on a newly created layer.

Understanding the Block Node Hierarchy

New!

The way AutoCAD blocks are handled in VIZ has changed in the new File Link manager. In VIZ 4, AutoCAD blocks translated into VIZblocks, which were collections of entities treated as a single object (which worked like a compound object).

NOTE   *You can still encounter VIZblocks in VIZ 2005 if you choose to derive AutoCAD primitives by Layer, Entity, Color, or One Object only.*

In VIZ 2005, blocks are linked in a *node hierarchy* when you choose to derive AutoCAD primitives by Layer, Blocks as Node Hierarchy, or Entity, Blocks as Node Hierarchy. To understand how this works, let's do a short tutorial.

1. Choose File ➤ Reset and do not save the changes you made to the scene earlier.

2. Choose File ➤ File Link Manager and click the Attach tab.

3. Click the File button and select the `Blocks.dwg` file from the CD; then click Open.

4. Click the Presets tab and click New. Give the new preset the name **Entity Blocks** and click OK.

5. Select Entity Blocks in the Named Presets list and click Modify.

6. Click the Advanced tab in the File Link Settings: DWG Files dialog box. Click the Derive AutoCAD Primitive By drop-down list and select Entity, Blocks as Node Hierarchy. In this example, it makes sense to also combine by Entity (rather than Layer) because there are only a few simple objects.

7. Click Save to close the File Link Settings: DWG Files dialog box.

8. Click the Attach tab of the File Link Manager dialog box and select Entity Blocks from the Preset drop-down list if it is not already selected. Finally, click Attach this file and close the dialog box. The drawing appears in the viewport as shown in Figure 16.21.

FIGURE 16.21
Block node hierarchy

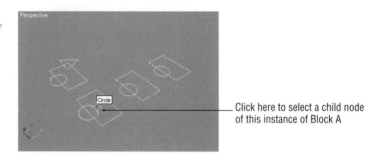

Click here to select a child node
of this instance of Block A

The `Blocks.dwg` contains two simple blocks called BlockA and BlockB. BlockA contains a circle and a rectangular polyline. There are three instances of BlockA in the scene. BlockB has only one instance and contains a triangular polyline and BlockA nested inside.

9. Choose Tools ➤ Selection Floater to open the Select Objects dialog box. The advantage to opening the floating version of this dialog box is that it persists after selection so that you can examine the relationship between what is selected in the viewport and the selection list. Click the circle of BlockA as shown in Figure 16.21.

You can visually see the node hierarchy illustrated in the Select Objects dialog box. As long as Display Subtree is checked (it is by default), you will see the child nodes indented in the list.

10. Click the Select and Move tool and move the Circle you selected a short distance in the XY plane.

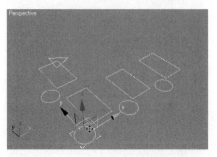

Notice that all the child circle nodes move relative to their block headers (like the insertion point of AutoCAD blocks). In AutoCAD lingo, entities in the block definition are moving relative to the insertion points in their block instances.

11. Press Ctrl+Z to undo the transform you did in step 10.

12. Hit the PageUp key to traverse the node hierarchy upward to the block header. Notice which node is selected in the Selection floater—the third instance of Block:BlockA—this is the block header node. The block header node contains all the nested objects but doesn't represent an object itself.

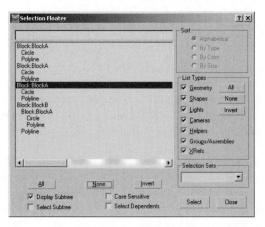

13. Using the Select and Move tool, drag the selected block header a short distance in the XY plane. Notice that this time, the entire block moves, and only the third instance of BlockA moves.

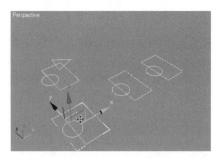

14. Click the Modify tab of the Command Panel. Notice that the block header shows up as Block/ Style Parent in the stack. Click the Reset Position button in the Linked Geometry rollout to return the block instance to the original position it had in the linked DWG file.

15. Save your work as MyBlocks.max.

As you can see from this tutorial, selecting a block node on the screen selects a child in the block hierarchy. Transforming a child node actually transforms all instances of that child relative to their block headers.

On the other hand, you only have to hit the PageUp key to select the top node in the hierarchy, called the block header; moving the block header allows you to transform a unique block instance independently of all other block instances. When you transform a parent node, the relative positions of its children do not change, just as you learned in forward kinematics in Chapter 10. AutoCAD blocks are now handled essentially as kinematic chains in VIZ.

NOTE *The block node hierarchy works much like it does in AutoCAD, with the exception that you do not have to explicitly redefine a block each time you make a change to the constituent geometry of the block definition. In VIZ it is very easy to change the relationship between what is inside a block definition (by moving the child nodes), and the block instance (by moving the block header). No block redefinition is required in VIZ because it all happens automatically, depending on which node you select in the block hierarchy. The entire block node hierarchy brings block behavior much more in line with how AutoCAD handles blocks as compared with the more limited functionality of VIZblocks.*

Understanding the File Link Manager Options

In the preceding exercises, you were able to try out a few of the File Link manager options. The File Link manager, like so many other VIZ features, offers numerous options to tailor your work to the particular needs of your project. Given the limited space of this book, I won't show an example of every option available, but you can get started with this feature after reviewing the exercises. Here's a summary of the File Link manager's options, organized by tabs.

THE ATTACH TAB

As you've already seen, this tab lets you locate a file using the File button. The File drop-down list shows a history of previously attached files that you can select from. The Preset drop-down list lets you select from a collection of presets that you've saved previously. There will also be a (Last Used Settings) option in this drop-down list after your first link is complete. You can select Last Used Settings if you don't want to bother saving a preset by name and just want to link the DWG or DXF file same way you did last time.

The Select Layers to Include button opens a Select Layers dialog box that allows you to select or deselect specific layers that you may want to include or exclude from the link. Note that this feature was geared toward excluding only in VIZ 4.

The Attach this file button lets you attach an AutoCAD DWG or DXF file to the current VIZ scene. Files can be attached from versions 12 through 2004 of AutoCAD. If you're using a CAD program other than AutoCAD, you can use the DXF file format instead of the DWG format, although many CAD programs today support the DWG file format directly.

THE FILES TAB

The Files tab allows you to control how a file is linked to the current VIZ file.

As you've seen in previous exercises, the Reload option lets you manually reload a linked AutoCAD file. An abbreviated form of the File Link Settings dialog box displays when you click this button if you have the Show Reload Options check box checked.

Detach removes a linked file from the current VIZ scene. Use this option with caution, as it deletes all of the linked objects in the scene.

The Bind option detaches any links to the source AutoCAD file while maintaining the objects in the current VIZ scene. The VIZ scene then becomes an independent scene file and can no longer be affected by the source AutoCAD file.

WARNING *Binding a former link will increase your file size as the data is migrated from CAD into VIZ and the link between them is broken. Do this with caution as changes made in CAD will no longer affect VIZ.*

Finally, the Files tab displays a list of AutoCAD DWG and DXF files that are currently linked to the VIZ scene file. An icon next to the filename indicates the status of the linked file:

◆ A paper clip indicates that the source file has not changed and that there are no errors in the link.

◆ A question mark indicates that the file cannot be found.

◆ A red flag indicates that the file has changed since import and that it must be reloaded using the Reload button.

◆ A grayed-out page indicates that a different file has been selected through another path.

◆ A curved arrow indicates that the Dynamic Reload option has been turned on for the file.

THE PRESETS TAB

You saw in an earlier exercise how you can create a preset, which determines how files are linked. The Presets tab also lets you modify an existing preset through the Modify button or rename or delete an existing preset. When you create a preset, it appears as an option in the Attach tab's Preset drop-down list. You'll learn more about the actual preset settings in the next section.

THE RENDERING TAB

You may recall from Chapter 3 that you can cause a spline shape to be rendered as a tube through parameters in the Rendering rollout of the Command Panel. The Rendering tab offers the same function but applies its settings to all imported shape objects.

New! There is a new modifier in VIZ 2005 called Renderable Spline that offers the same functionality given on the Rendering tab of the File Link manager. The difference is that by using the modifier version, you have greater control over which splines are renderable.

For example, if you linked a large number of spline layers from a DWG into VIZ using the File Link manager, you may not want all of those spline layers to be renderable. The Renderable Spline modifier gives you a chance to apply it only to the linked spline nodes that you want to be renderable, and it lets you have different settings for each node. Use the Rendering tab when you want all the linked spline nodes to be renderable with exactly the same settings.

Understanding File Link Settings

When you import a linked AutoCAD file, you have the option of controlling the way that file is imported through the File Link Settings dialog box. This dialog box appears by default when you've selected a file for linking, but you can set up VIZ to avoid this dialog box by turning off the Show Reload Options check box in the File tab of the File Link Manager dialog box.

As you saw in previous exercises, the options selected in the File Link Settings dialog box can make a huge difference in the way the resulting VIZ file is organized. Since AutoCAD and VIZ use entirely different ways of organizing data, this dialog box is necessary to make some sense of the way AutoCAD DWG files are converted to VIZ files. To help in the translation process, VIZ uses a type of node called Linked Geometry. All linked AutoCAD objects are converted to Linked Geometry or VIZblocks, which occurs only when you choose to derive AutoCAD primitives by Layer, Entity, Color, or One Object.

For example, objects in an AutoCAD file that reside on layer 0 are collected into a single VIZblock. The name of the VIZblock will depend on the settings you choose in the File Link Settings dialog box. In an earlier exercise, you chose the Layer option in the File Link Settings dialog box's Attach Options group. You can further refine the way VIZ combines objects through a combination of layer, thickness, and color, or you can have VIZ import each AutoCAD object as a single object in VIZ.

Most of the time, you will probably choose to derive your AutoCAD primitives using one of the Blocks as Node Hierarchy options in the File Link Manager dialog box, due to the improved way that you can work with blocks using these options. Therefore, the objects that appear in VIZ will most often be Linked Geometry nodes.

Linked Geometry nodes have only one parameter on the Modify tab of the Command Panel: the Reset Position button. Click Reset Position when you want to restore the node to the location it has in the linked DWG or DXF file. Any transforms you apply to Linked Geometry nodes are stored in VIZ alone and there is no chance that VIZ will ever overwrite your AutoCAD files at any time.

WARNING *You'll want to avoid several things when working with Linked Geometry due to its connection to a foreign file format. System instability may occur (meaning VIZ may crash) if you include Linked Geometry in groups or assemblies, attach to a mesh or poly, change animation controllers, create hierarchical links in Schematic View, or make instance clones of Linked Geometry. However, you can confidently make copy clones, and apply transforms, modifiers, and materials to Linked Geometry without any problems.*

THE BASIC TAB

The options in the Basic tab give you control over the way imported objects are converted into VIZ objects. These options are similar to those found in the Geometry Options group of the AutoCAD DWG/DXF Import Options dialog box. This is the dialog box that you see when you import a DWG or DXF file using the File ➤ Import option.

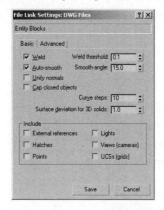

Weld   Determines whether coincident vertices of imported objects are joined, or *welded*, together to form a contiguous object. When Weld is turned on, the Weld Threshold setting is used to determine how close together objects need to be before they are welded.

Auto-smooth   Determines whether to apply smoothing to contiguous surfaces in imported objects. When Auto-Smooth is turned on, the Smooth-angle setting is used to determine the minimum angle to which smoothing should be applied.

Unify normals   Attempts to align all the normals of an object so that they point outward from the center of the object.

Cap closed objects   Causes VIZ to apply an Extrude modifier to closed objects such as closed polylines or rectangles.

Curve steps   Gives you control over the way curves are converted. A low Curve Steps value causes curves to appear as straight segments, while higher values generate a more accurate curve.

Surface deviation for 3D solids   Controls tessellation in VIZ on objects that are converted from AutoCAD 3DSOLID entities. Small numbers produce accurate surfaces with greater number of faces whereas larger numbers use less memory but produce less accurate surfaces with fewer faces.

Include group   This group has a number of check boxes that can be toggled to indicate which categories of objects you want to link into VIZ. The choices include External references (these are XRefs from AutoCAD, not VIZ), Hatches, Points, Lights (from AutoCAD Render formerly known as AutoVision), Views (cameras), and UCSs (grids) (USC stands for User Coordinate System).

WARNING   *It is generally not a good idea to include Hatch patterns in a file link. VIZ cannot store the entities making up the pattern in as efficient a way as AutoCAD, and the result usually consumes far too much memory, file size, and translation time into VIZ.*

THE ADVANCED TAB

The options in the Advanced tab give you control over the way AutoCAD primitives are derived, as well as several important settings and the possibility of selectively reloading only a portion of the linked file.

Derive AutoCAD primitives by   Lets you determine how entities from AutoCAD are treated in VIZ. Perhaps the simplest choice from this drop-down list is Layer, Blocks as Node Hierarchy which converts AutoCAD layers to Linked Geometry and blocks into a node hierarchy. The next option is Entity, Blocks as Node Hierarchy, which converts AutoCAD entities to Linked Geometry and blocks into a node hierarchy.

You may also choose Layer, Entity, or Color, which groups AutoCAD objects by their layer, entities, or color and then converts them to VIZblocks. The Entity option creates an object for each entity in the AutoCAD file. The One Object option turns the entire AutoCAD drawing into a single VIZblock.

Select Layers to include   Click this button to open the Select Layers dialog box where you can choose to Skip all frozen layers (default), or Select the layers to include from the list. This button is grayed out unless you choose to derive AutoCAD primitives by Layer. Layers that are checked are linked, regardless of their layer state in AutoCAD. Note that the layer state data shown in the dialog box is for your information only, is not functional, and does not update in AutoCAD.

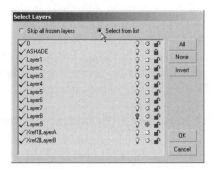

Create helper at drawing origin   Will include an Origin Point helper object with the linked file. This helper is placed at the origin of the linked file to help identify its origin and to facilitate alignment of other files.

Use Extrude modifier to represent thickness   When checked, this setting will apply an Extrude modifier, matching the height of any entities that have a thickness value. Note that thickness is a very old concept (pre–release 12) from the early days of 3D modeling in AutoCAD and is not in wide use today. Most contemporary 3D modeling is done with surfaces or solids in AutoCAD.

Use scene material definitions   Matches material names coming from an AutoCAD file with material names in VIZ. When there is a match, the material names in VIZ are used when checked. When unchecked, the material names are always taken from the DWG file. Note that DXF files do not support materials.

Use scene material assignments on Reload   This important option allows you to maintain the materials you have assigned in VIZ after you reload a DWG file. When unchecked, the materials from AutoCAD will overwrite materials made in VIZ when the linked file is reloaded.

Selective Reload   Check Selective Reload when you want to reload only a subset of all the objects in the linked file. You may want to do this if you do not want subsequent changes made in the CAD file to be linked into VIZ. Selective Reload can also be used in very complex scenes to minimize the time spent loading the entire linked database.

When Selective Reload is on, either you can select the objects to reload in the scene manually, or you can select them from the Select Linked Objects dialog box by clicking the Linked Objects button.

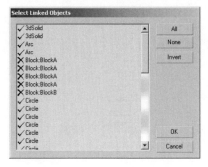

Linking files into VIZ allows you to maintain a single design database that begins in AutoCAD and continues seamlessly into VIZ. File Linking makes it a good alternative to simply importing an AutoCAD file directly using the File ➤ Import option because of the connection that carries into the future between the AutoCAD and VIZ databases. You can always use the Bind option to sever the link and make the imported data a stand-alone VIZ file, but beware that you lose the benefits that accrue to those who use both AutoCAD and VIZ together in a continuing relationship throughout the design workflow.

Using the Substitute Modifier with Linked Geometry

You can substitute a complex piece of furniture modeled in VIZ for a simple outline drawn in AutoCAD. Designers often do space planning in AutoCAD with simple 2D blocks that are drawn to scale. You can link a space planning drawing into VIZ and then proceed to substitute a complex 3D version of a piece of furniture for a simple 2D block. After seeing the more realistic depiction of the scene in VIZ, a designer may wish to revise the space plan in AutoCAD. The AutoCAD DWG file can then be reloaded in VIZ and the changes automatically affect the complex 3D models in the scene. Let's try this idea out here:

1. Open the `MyBlocks.max` file you saved earlier, or open `Blocks.max` from the CD.

2. Select the rectangular polyline in the foreground. Note that it appears as Linked Geometry in stack view on the Modify tab of the Command Panel.

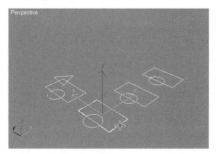

3. Apply the Substitute modifier to the Polyline.

4. Click the Select XRef Object button in the Parameters rollout. Note that you also have the option to pick an object that is already in the scene for the substitution.

5. Select the `Worktop.max` file from the CD and click Open. This is a free 3D model of a desk worktop from `ScottOnstott.com`.

6. The XRef Merge dialog box appears listing the objects that are in `Worktop.max`. Select Worktop01 and click OK.

7. Answer Yes to the Substitution Question dialog box that says "Do you want to assign the substitute object's material to this object?" The 3D model appears in the viewport, now substituting for the rectangular polylines that were there before.

8. Click the Circle in the foreground and apply the Substitute modifier to this Linked Geometry.

9. Click the Select XRef Object button again and select the `Chair.max` file from the CD (this also is part of the collection of free designer furniture models at the same website). Click Open.

10. Select the object Chair01 from the XRef Merge dialog box and click OK.

11. Answer Yes again to the Substitution Question dialog box that appears.

12. Rotate the chair and observe that it behaves exactly as the circle did within the linked block node hierarchy. All the block instances of the chair rotate accordingly.

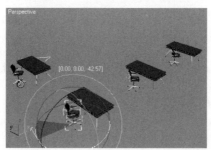

13. Type **H** to open the Select Objects dialog box. Notice that each of the nodes in the block hierarchy (except the triangular polyline in BlockB) show curly braces around their names. This indicates that these nodes have XRefs that are substituting for them in the scene. The triangular polyline nested inside BlockB was not substituted for, and thus it still appears in the viewport as a non-rendering spline.

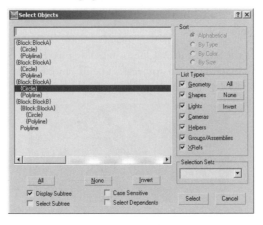

NOTE *You can make linked splines render by applying the Renderable Spline modifier.*

You have now seen how easy it is to link a space plan drawn in AutoCAD into VIZ, and then substitute more complex geometry in VIZ for the simple blocks from CAD. The benefits of such an approach are that you are using each application for what it does best: AutoCAD is used for drafting and VIZ is used for the visualization of 3D models. Not only are you focusing on the strengths of the applications you use in your workflow, but there is a dynamic link between the programs so that there can be a design dialog back and forth and changes can be incorporated using the best tools for the job.

Adding Stairs

VIZ offers a number of architecture, engineering, and construction (AEC) tools that can make quick work of the more common building-design functions. You've already seen how walls, doors, foliage, and terrain work. In this section, you'll use a few of the stair tools to build one flight of stairs in the villa design. In general, the stair tools are pretty straightforward.

Tracing over Imported Lines

To practice adding stairs, you'll use the ground-floor file that you created earlier in this chapter. The imported stair plan in the `savoye-ground-viz.max` file will provide the framework for your stairs.

1. Open the `savoye-ground-viz.max` file that you created earlier in this chapter.

2. Open the Select Objects dialog box and then click All.

3. Ctrl+click the Layer:STAIR item in the list to remove it from the selection; then click Select.

4. Click the Display tab in the Command Panel and then click Hide Selected.

5. Click the Zoom Extents tool to view the stair.

6. Right-click the Snap button at the top of the VIZ window and make sure Endpoint is selected in the Grid and Snap Settings dialog box. Then close the dialog box.

7. Click the Snap button or type **S** to turn on the Snap mode.

You'll create the stair in three sections: the two straight runs and the circular portion. Since the straight runs are identical, you'll create one and then copy it to the other side.

To create the first stair run, do the following:

1. Click the Create tab in the Command Panel.

2. With the Geometry button selected, select Stairs from the drop-down list.

3. Click Straight Stair from the Object Type rollout.

4. With the Snap mode turned on, click and drag from the corner indicated in Figure 16.22.

5. Drag the cursor to the second location shown in Figure 16.22; then release the mouse button.

6. Click the third location shown in Figure 16.22.

7. Move the mouse upward to set the height; then click OK. You'll set the exact height in the next exercise, so you don't have to worry about the look of the stair for now.

FIGURE 16.22
Click and drag from the corner, as shown here.

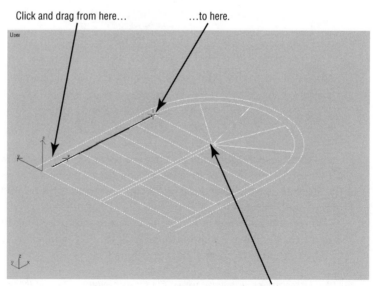

Click and drag from here...   ...to here.

Then click this endpoint to set the stair width.

You've established the stair in the design. Now you can make some adjustments to its parameters so that the stair dimensions are appropriate to the villa dimensions.

Adjusting Stair Parameters

The total distance from the ground floor to the second floor is 11 feet, or 114 inches. This makes each of the 18 steps 7.333 inches high. There is a bit of a trick to setting stair heights with the stair tools. You want to first tell VIZ the number of steps, and then work on the overall height and the height of the risers.

1. In the Create tab of the Command Panel, scroll down to the Rise group of the Parameters rollout.

2. Click the Pin Riser Ht button. Set the Riser Ct setting to **7**; then click the Pin Riser Count button to the left of the setting. This locks the riser setting to 7.

Notice that now the Overall and Riser Ht settings are both available, while the Riser Ct setting is grayed out. Also note that one pin is always down.

3. Set the Riser Ht value to **7.333**. The Overall setting automatically adjusts to the height of 51.331 inches.

4. Scroll up to the Layout group and change the length to **76.0**.

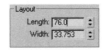

5. Scroll up to the Type group and click the Closed radio button.

VIZ will draw a set of stairs with one less riser than indicated in the Riser Ct parameter. VIZ leaves off the top riser of the stair because the stair length parameter measures the stair from the nosing of the first stair tread to the nosing of the top stair tread. This means that the top stair tread is left out of the length calculation.

When setting up the stair height, it's easiest to start by setting the number of stair risers. The trick is to use the Pin Riser Count button to lock the riser number. You can then easily adjust the height by adjusting either the overall or riser height.

TIP   *Here's another method that works: Pin the riser count and then set the overall height. Next, pin the overall height and then set either the riser count or the riser height.*

Creating a Circular Stair

You now have the first part of the stair ready. The circular portion is next.

1. Click the Min/Max Toggle tool to view all four viewports.

2. Click the Zoom Extents All tool to enlarge the view of the stairs in all the viewports.

3. In the Top viewport, move the straight stair to the left to give yourself some room to create the circular portion of the stair, as shown in Figure 16.23.

Now you are ready to use the Spiral Stair tool.

1. Turn off the Snap mode.

2. Scroll to the top of the Command Panel and click the Spiral Stair option.

3. In the Top viewport, click and drag the center of the circular portion of the stair plan, as shown in Figure 16.23.

4. Drag the mouse to set the radius of the spiral to the width of the stair and release the mouse, as shown in Figure 16.23.

5. Move the mouse upward and click to set the height of the stair. Once again, you can click any height, since you'll adjust the height accurately in the Command Panel.

FIGURE 16.23

Selecting points to place the circular portion of the stair

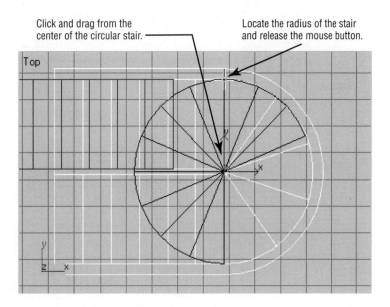

Click and drag from the center of the circular stair.

Locate the radius of the stair and release the mouse button.

There are a few problems with the circular portion. It's turning the wrong way, and it extends beyond the 180-degree arc of the stair in the plan. The following steps will quickly take care of these problems.

1. Click Closed in the Type group to match the straight portion of the stairs.

2. Scroll down to the Layout group and click the CW (clockwise) radio button.

3. In the Rise group, change the Riser Ct value to **6**; then click the Pin Riser Count button.

4. Set the Riser Ht value to **7.333**.

5. In the Layout group, set the Revs value to **0.602**.

6. Use the Select and Rotate tool to rotate the circular stair in the Top viewport so that it is oriented correctly in the plan.

7. Use the Select and Move tool to move the circular stair vertically in the Left viewport so that it is aligned with the top of the straight stairs.

At this point, you only need to align the circular stair in the vertical axis. You'll move the stair components into position once you have them all constructed and in the proper orientation.

Finishing the Stair

Now, make the clone of the straight stair and move the clone into position.

1. Click the Zoom Extents All tool to get a clear view of your work so far.

2. Click the straight stair in the Left viewport; then Shift+click and drag the Y axis upward so that the bottom of the straight stair aligns with the top of the circular stair, as shown in Figure 16.24.

FIGURE 16.24
Copy the straight stair run vertically.

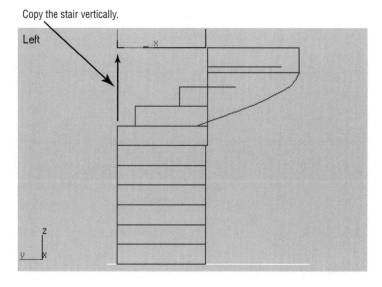

Copy the stair vertically.

3. In the Clone Options dialog box, click OK.

4. Right-click the Top viewport; then click the Select and Rotate tool.

5. Select the Center pivot option from the Pivot flyout on the main toolbar.

6. Click and drag the Z axis of the cloned stair upward in the Top viewport to rotate the stair 180 degrees.

7. Move the cloned stair downward to align with the circular stair, as shown in Figure 16.25.

FIGURE 16.25
Move the clone into position.

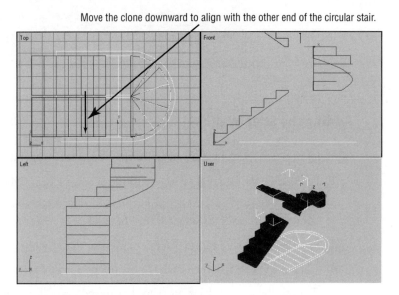

Move the clone downward to align with the other end of the circular stair.

8. Move the two straight stairs to the left so that they're connected to the circular stair, as shown in Figure 16.26.

You don't have to worry about being absolutely accurate when placing the stair components together. When you consider construction methods, an eighth-inch tolerance for locating building components is about as accurate as you can expect; and for most rendering and modeling purposes, positioning objects visually is usually good enough. Remember, you are making a visualization in VIZ, not in construction documents.

FIGURE 16.26

The straight stairs
moved into position
next to the circular
stair

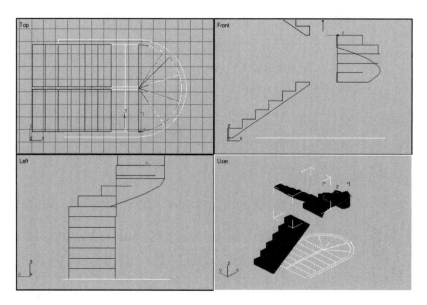

Adding the Stair Walls

You've now got some stairs from the ground floor to the second floor. You still need the walls that surround the stairs. Start by drawing a line that forms the inside edge of the wall.

1. Right-click the Perspective viewport; then click the Min/Max Toggle tool to enlarge it.

2. Right-click the User label in the upper left corner of the viewport and select Wireframe. This allows you to easily select points on the stair.

3. Use the Arc Rotate tool to rotate the view so that it looks similar to Figure 16.27.

4. Click the Create tab; then click the Shapes button and select Line.

5. Turn the Snap mode back on; then click the points indicated in Figure 16.27. Remember that you can press the Backspace key if you select a point by accident.

You've got a path set up, but the curved portion of the path needs to be smoothed out to form a curve. You'll employ a method you learned in Chapters 4 and 5 to change the vertices at the curved portion of the path.

1. Click the Modify tab; then click the Vertex option in the Selection rollout.

2. Turn off the Snap mode, because it may interfere with the following steps.

3. Use the Select Object tool to right-click one of the vertices in the curved portion of the stairs, as shown in Figure 16.28.

FIGURE 16.27
Drawing the inside
edge of the wall

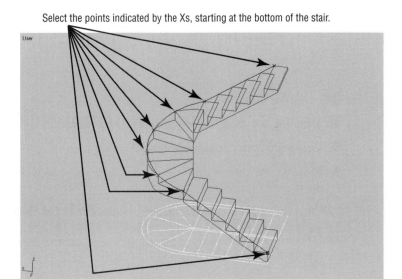

Select the points indicated by the Xs, starting at the bottom of the stair.

4. Select Smooth from the right-click menu.

5. Repeat steps 2 and 3 for each of the vertices in the curved part of the stair, as indicated in Figure 16.28.

FIGURE 16.28
Change these vertices
into smooth vertices.

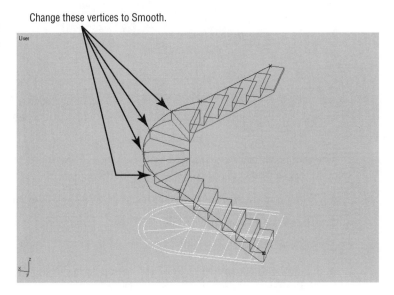

Change these vertices to Smooth.

The final step for the stair walls is to turn the lines into outlines and then extrude the outline.

1. Click the Spline button in the Selection rollout.

2. Click the spline you just created.

3. Scroll down to the Outline parameter and set the Outline value to 6. You see the line turn into an outline.

4. Select Extrude from the Modifier List drop-down list.

5. Change the Amount parameter to **50**.

6. Move the wall downward in the Z axis about 7 inches so that the bottom of the wall aligns with the bottom of the stair.

7. Click the Zoom Extents tool to get a complete view of the stair, as shown in Figure 16.29.

FIGURE 16.29
The stair so far

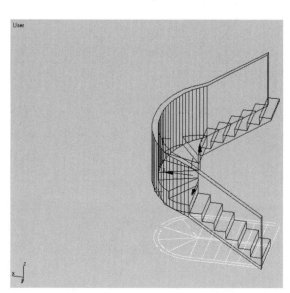

The wall needs to be extended by one stair step at the top of the stairs. You can go back to the spline vertex sub-object level to make this modification.

1. Zoom into the top stair step so that your view looks similar to that of Figure 16.30.

2. Choose Line from the modifier stack list.

3. Select the Vertex sub-level.

4. Click the Select and Move tool and then place a rectangular selection region around the two end vertices indicated in Figure 16.30.

FIGURE 16.30
Select these two
vertices.

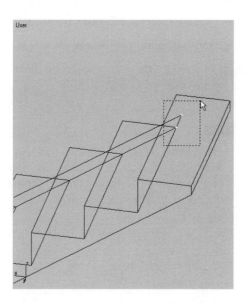

5. Click and drag the blue axis corner mark of the Transform gizmo to move the vertices into the position shown in Figure 16.31. By using the corner marks of the Transform gizmo, you can restrict the motion to the two axes indicated by the corner mark while in a Perspective viewport.

FIGURE 16.31
Move the vertices
into this position.

Click and drag this corner mark to adjust the location of the end vertices.

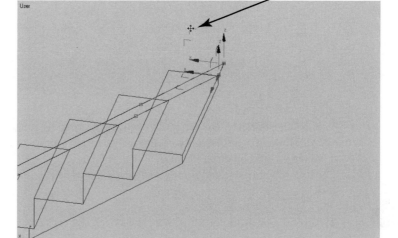

6. Select Extrude from the modifier stack list to return to the extruded version of the wall.

7. Click the Zoom Extents button to get a view of the stairs.

You've made one flight of stairs for the villa. The second flight is the same as the first, so for the second floor, you can clone the stairs you just created.

Importing a Truss

Frequently, you may be called upon to include a truss in your design. If it's a flat truss, you can draw a side view of the truss in AutoCAD using closed polylines, and then import the drawing to VIZ and extrude it in a way similar to the floor of the earlier `savoye-second.dwg` example. If you import the truss line drawing as a single object, VIZ will automatically subtract the truss web from the outline of the truss, as shown in Figure 16.32.

FIGURE 16.32
An AutoCAD drawing of a truss at the top, and the resulting VIZ scene below

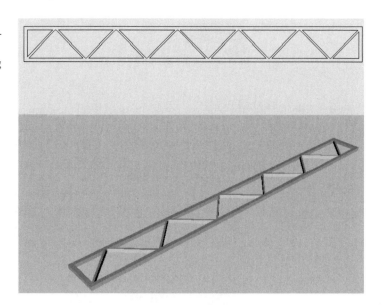

Tubular trusses can be created easily from engineering 3D line diagrams. Figure 16.33 shows an AutoCAD diagram of a truss whose components are to be made of tubular steel. The different diameters are represented by different layers in this model.

The following exercise will show you how the model can be turned into a renderable truss in VIZ.

1. Choose File ➢ Reset to reset VIZ.

2. Choose File ➢ Import; then select and open the `truss.dwg` file from the companion CD.

FIGURE 16.33
A 3D line diagram of
a truss in AutoCAD

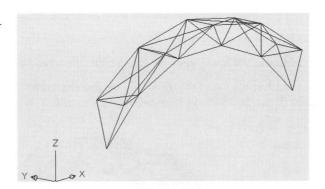

3. In the DWG Import dialog box, click OK. The AutoCAD DWG/DXF Import Options dialog box displays.

4. Make sure that the settings in the AutoCAD DWG/DXF Import Options dialog box are the same as those shown in Figure 16.34. Click OK.

FIGURE 16.34

The AutoCAD
DWG/DXF Import
Options settings

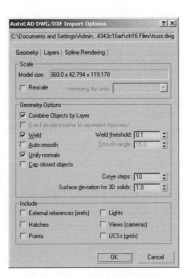

The truss displays in the VIZ viewport.

With the truss imported into VIZ, you only need to change a parameter to alter the way VIZ renders the lines.

1. Select one of the blue struts of the truss.

2. Click the Modify tab of the Command Panel.

3. Open the Rendering rollout, turn on the Renderable option, and change the Thickness to **4**.

4. Select one of the magenta lines in the Perspective viewport.

5. In the Command Panel, click the Renderable option and change the Thickness value to **6**.

6. Do a quick rendering of the truss. You see that the rendered view converts the line work into tubes. Figure 16.35 shows a rendering of the truss from a different angle.

FIGURE 16.35
The rendered truss

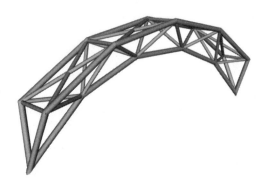

TIP *You can use the File Link manager to import linked AutoCAD drawings and still use the Spline Rendering tab parameters to create the truss shown in the preceding exercise. You can also use the Renderable Spline modifier if you prefer.*

You saw this earlier in Chapter 4, where I introduced you quickly to the Rendering rollout. Here you see a practical use for this set of options. Without much work in VIZ, you can create a reasonable-looking truss. You just need to remember to place the different-diameter truss members on different layers in AutoCAD before you import the file to VIZ.

You can also make quick work of window mullions using this method. Typically, mullions are square, but if they are to be viewed from a distance, you can use single lines for mullions and set up the Rendering rollout to have them render as 4-sided tubes (you can't easily get rid of smoothing that makes them appear rounded). From a distance, you won't really be able to tell that they are tubes. Another obvious use of this method is creating guardrails.

Summary

CAD programs are the workhorses of the design industry. They offer a way to accurately represent designs and to communicate design ideas to others. By allowing you to use your existing CAD data, VIZ enables you to quickly provide the all-important third dimension to your design visualizations. You have seen the particular advantages to linking to, rather than directly importing CAD data into VIZ. By maintaining a connection between any of the AutoCAD-based applications and VIZ, you can essentially maintain a single linked design database throughout your project design workflow, increasing productivity efficiencies in the process.

Chapter 17

Exporting to the Web

VIZ OUTPUT MOST COMMONLY takes the form of rendered images. You are probably aware that you need to render large images in order to have enough resolution for quality color printing (at least 300 pixels/inch), and it takes a long time to render such images for large format printing. It is not uncommon for a single detailed photo-realistic scene to require many hours or even overnight to render.

Perhaps the second most common form of VIZ output is animation output to videotape or DVD. If you thought printable images took a long time to render, wait until you try to render a one-minute animation! One consolation is that the rendered frame size in most animations is relatively small, so each frame can be rendered much more quickly as compared with images destined for print. However, you'll have to render many, many frames to complete the animation. Do the math (30 frames/second × total frames × time/frame), and you can see that you'll likely have to wait days for a single processor to render your animation.

TIP *You can use VIZ's backburner technology to render images over a network. Each processor in the network, and each processor in multiprocessor machines, can be harnessed to render your still image or animated sequence. Rendering networks are sometimes called* render farms. *You should contact a knowledgeable network administrator before attempting to install backburner. Please refer to Help ➤ User Reference for more information.*

Fortunately, getting your project done before the deadline is not as bleak as it sounds. Other forms of VIZ output that require far less processing time can be just as compelling (if not more so) than large printed images and animations. You should carefully consider several options for exporting to the Web.

The first and most simple option is to render relatively small images and put them on a website. You'll be able to render many still images in the time you have left by keeping your required image size small. You should use Adobe Photoshop's Save for Web tool to optimize JPEG images for small file size and a reasonable level of quality. The other side of this equation is building a website for your project, which clearly goes beyond the scope of this book. A project website can have tangential marketing benefits worth considering as well.

NOTE *Sybex publishes many books where you can learn how to build compelling project websites; most of them are written for specific authoring tools, such as* Microsoft FrontPage 2003 Savvy, *by Christian Crumlish and Kate J. Chase (2003). See the catalog listing at* www.sybex.com *for titles on other web design tools.*

If you feel that your client needs more than just a still image to visualize your design, create a QuickTimeVR panorama, explore an interactive virtual reality world, build a custom presentation with Shockwave 3D content in Macromedia Director, or use a third-party real-time graphics engine to build a simulation with advanced lighting data stored in baked textures from VIZ. In this chapter, you will learn how to use VIZ to export to the Web.

◆ Creating Panoramas

◆ Making Virtual Reality Worlds

◆ Exporting Shockwave 3D Content

◆ Using Render to Texture for Real-Time Models

Creating Panoramas

If you've ever shopped for a car or looked at real estate online , you've probably come across a type of "virtual tour" or "wraparound panorama" that offers a 360-degree view of a space. Spawned by Apple's QuickTimeVR, many software packages are available that make panoramas from a series of images. Panoramas can be made from photographs of real places or from your virtual architecture in VIZ.

TIP   *REALVIZ's Stitcher software is an excellent tool for stitching together a series of digital stills into a high quality seamless panorama. You can also use this software to build higher resolution in a background image (that exceeds any camera's ability to capture megapixels) by stitching together many smaller images. See them on the Web at* **www.realviz.com**.

All panorama software uses an image distortion technique to create the seamless wraparound illusion. Because the panorama effect is image based, it is essentially a pixel phenomenon and can be efficiently transmitted on the Web. VIZ can export 360-degree cylindrical and spherically distorted images that you can use in a wide array of panorama-creating software. In addition, VIZ can also export panoramas directly to Apple's popular QuickTime format. Let's use the Villa Savoye model one last time to export an interior panorama.

1. Open Savoye17a.max from the CD.

2. Right-click the Left viewport to activate it.

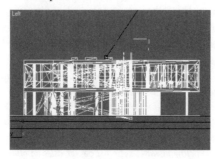

VIZ's Panorama utility requires a camera to be placed at eye level, looking straight ahead in an interior space.

3. Click the Create tab of the Command Panel. Select the Cameras button and click the Free button in the Object Type rollout.

4. Click a point in the middle of the second floor to place a free camera looking straight ahead as shown in Figure 17.1.

5. Right-click the Top viewport and zoom out until you can see the new camera.

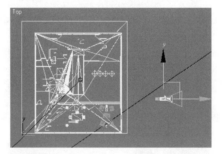

It does not matter which way the camera is oriented for a panorama, as long as it is facing straight ahead at eye level. The Panorama utility will automatically rotate the camera as needed to generate the panoramic image, as you will see shortly.

6. Using the Select and Move tool, move the camera to the center of the room containing furniture near the bottom of the floor plan (Figure 17.2). Zoom in to get a better look at the room.

FIGURE 17.1
Place the free camera
for a panorama

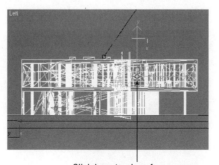

Click here to place free camera.

FIGURE 17.2
Move the camera
to the center of
the room

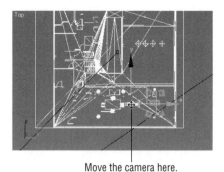

Move the camera here.

7. Using the Select and Move tool, move the camera to a height of 15′ in the Z direction to approximate eye level on the second floor.

8. Right-click the Perspective viewport and press **C** to look through the free camera in this viewport.

Do not worry that the composition through this camera leaves something to be desired. The Panorama utility will make use of this camera and automatically adjust it to generate the panorama.

9. Click the Utilities tab of the Command Panel. Click the Panorama Exporter button on the Utilities rollout.

10. Click the Render button in the Panorama Exporter rollout.

11. In the Render Setup dialog box that appears, click the 2048×1024 button in the Interactive Panorama Exporter Common Parameters rollout. This sets a much larger pixel size for the entire panorama and yields higher quality output.

12. Make sure that Camera01 is selected in the Viewport drop-down list at the bottom of the Render Setup dialog box and click the Render button.

A series of six still images corresponding to the six sides of a cube are rendered and appear sequentially in the Rendered Frame window. At the end of the automatically scripted sequence, the Panorama Exporter Viewer appears.

The image that appears in the Panorama Exporter Viewer window looks blurry because of the distortion filter that was applied to create the wraparound illusion.

You can make the image look crisper by dragging the Panorama Exporter Viewer to make it smaller. On the other hand, you could have rendered more pixels in step 11 to make the panorama less blurry, but this takes additional render time. Generally, panoramas will be rather small when posted on a website, so the additional resolution may not be needed.

13. Drag the edge of the Panorama Exporter Viewer window to a smaller size for better apparent quality.

TIP *Try rendering the panorama at a much higher resolution to decrease the inherent blurriness. The tradeoff for a sharper image is a larger image size and consequently a longer download time when the panorama is posted on a website.*

14. Place your mouse directly in the center of the Panorama Exporter Viewer window as shown in Figure 17.3. Carefully drag the mouse about 1/8″ in any direction and watch as the image dynamically wraps around as if you are turning your virtual head in the interior space.

You can look from side to side, up and down, and all around. Be careful not to drag too far or the rate at which the panorama spins increases and you might get dizzy. Stop dragging to stop moving. For increased control, or to turn small amounts, try right-clicking and dragging in the viewer window.

15. Place the mouse in the center again and hold down the middle button or wheel button on your mouse and drag down. You will "zoom out" of the panorama as shown in Figure 17.3. Drag up to "zoom in."

FIGURE 17.3
Place your mouse in the center and drag

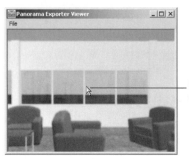

Place your mouse here before dragging a short distance.

WARNING *Be careful not to "zoom in" or "zoom out" too much in a panorama. Since it is a 2D image, you are actually changing the field of view of the effect, and the extremes exhibit wild distortion.*

16. In the Panorama Exporter Viewer window, choose File ➤ Export ➤ Export QuickTimeVR.

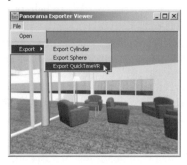

NOTE   *You can also export your panorama with cylindrical or spherical distortion for use in third-party panorama-generating software.*

17. Save a file called **Panorama.mov** in the QuickTimeVR File Output dialog box.

18. Close the Panorama Exporter Viewer window and the Render Setup dialog box.

19. To view your new QuickTime VR file, double-click the file where you saved it in the file system. QuickTime will launch and display the panorama in a similar fashion to VIZ's built-in Panorama Exporter Viewer. Drag in the center to spin the panorama.

The advantage of having your panorama in QuickTime format is that you can post it on a website and anyone who has the free QuickTime plug-in will be able to enjoy your interactive artwork; no other software is required.

TIP   *QuickTime 6.1 is on the VIZ 2005 installation CD. You can also download it for free from* www.apple.com.

Making Virtual Reality Worlds

Virtual Reality (VR) is the name given to any computer-generated environment in which you can place your *avatar* (representing your point of view like a mobile camera) and freely move around a three-dimensional space in real time. This approach differs from the image-based panoramas you've just created in that in panoramas, your point of view is in a fixed location. In contrast, VR allows your avatar to actually move through space like walking into another room. Some of the first applications of VR were in flight simulators designed to help train pilots. Today there is a huge market in real-time simulation for military training and in the game market. As interest in VR grew, it was viewed as a potential tool for the design industry—to help architects interactively visualize and experience spaces in time.

In its early days, VR was a high-tech tool accessible to only a few big companies that could afford it. But as personal computers became more powerful, its use caught on in the home computer game world. Now, a technology that was once considered exotic seems fairly commonplace, especially to computer game users. In the mid '90s, VR became a prominent part of the Internet and the World Wide Web. Through the Virtual Reality Modeling Language (VRML, pronounced "vermal"), VR became cheap and easily accessible to the general public.

VRML was created through the efforts of a handful of people closely involved with the development of virtual reality and the World Wide Web. They sought a means of conveying 3D worlds through the Internet and found what they were looking for in a system developed by Silicon Graphics, Inc. (SGI). That system, called Open Inventor, was a programming library used to help create 3D applications. A subset of Open Inventor was developed and placed in the public domain through the good graces of SGI. That subset was at the root of a software specification called VRML 1.0. VRML 1.0 has evolved into later releases such as VRML 2.0 and VRML97. Autodesk created its own flavor of VRML, called virtual reality behavioral language (VRBL), which is based on VRML 1.0.

Although VRML created a stir when it first became available, architects have been slow to embrace it. It remains more a curiosity than a well-used tool.

When SGI, a major proponent of VRML, dropped its highly regarded VRML viewer named Cosmo in 1998, most VR users feared that VRML was all but dead. But VR is far from dead on the Internet. VR is now experiencing a rebirth in a form called Web3D. Since there are no big companies like SGI promoting Web3D, many competing companies have their own ideas about what VR can be. Many of the Web3D software offerings are better than VRML97, but they remain proprietary systems. See the following links for more information as of this writing:

www.web3d.org

www.cult3d.com

www.viewpoint.com

www.parallelgraphics.com

www.kaon.com

Despite the decline of VRML, the VRML file format remains a viable medium for VR today. There are many programs that can import and export VRML files. If you're the least bit interested in VR, you may want to become familiar with VIZ's VRML options. You can export VRML worlds from VIZ without having to purchase any other software.

Installing a VRML Client

You will need to download a plug-in to view VRML content in your browser. For best results, I recommend using the free Cortona VRML Client. Cortona offers the best performance and support for VRML97 format (among free clients) as of this writing. Let's get started.

1. Open your browser and type the following URL in the address bar:

   www.parallelgraphics.com

2. Navigate to the Products section on their website and choose to download the free Cortona VRML Client plug-in. The actual steps may vary as their website evolves.

3. When the installation is complete, close your browser.

   Now you are ready to view VRML content on the Web. You will not have to install the plug-in again to view VRML content with your browser in the future.

Virtual Helpers

VRML97 is the de facto standard for VRML worlds today; it is amazing that this vintage format still persists (think of it like Latin).

WARNING *VIZ no longer can export to the VRML 1.0 or VRBL formats. Most Web3D clients no longer support these early VR formats due to their limited feature sets. However, VIZ can still import these early formats, so legacy worlds are not lost.*

The way you build a virtual reality world is to model your design as usual in VIZ, and then add helper objects to enhance the behavior of the virtual world you will be exporting. You will be adding many of these helpers to a VIZ scene in a tutorial in the next section. VIZ offers the following set of helpers that can aid you in taking advantage of the features of VRML97:

The Anchor helper   Lets you assign a trigger action to an object. The action can be a hyperlink or a camera jump.

The AudioClip helper   Lets you include sound files in your VRML file. It's used in conjunction with the Sound helper. The sound files must be posted at a URL (not locally), so you'll need access to a web server for testing.

The Background button   Gives you control over the background of your VRML file. You can select colors or images, or a gradient of colors.

The Billboard helper   With the Billboard helper, you can set up an object so that it always points in the direction of the viewer. Place the Billboard helper in the design and use the Select and Link tool (in Schematic view) to link an object to the Billboard helper. Place the Billboard helper at the axis of rotation (usually centered on the object to which it is linked).

The Fog button   Opens a rollout that lets you add fog to your VRML environment. Fog can help create a sense of atmosphere and space by obscuring objects in the distance. This can also help the performance of the interactive real-time display in very complex scenes, because objects that are hidden by the fog are not rendered.

The Inline helper   You can include other VRML97 files in the current design. Such files are like XRefs for VRML files at the browser level. The Inline helper acts as a proxy object to which you can assign a URL pointing to the inline VRML file.

The Level of Detail (LOD) helper   With this helper, you can set up your VRML file to adjust the level of detail of an object depending on the distance between the object and the viewer. This helper requires you to create two copies of the object that you want to control with LOD. Each copy must have a different level of detail. (See the VIZ Online Reference for a detailed description of how to use this helper.)

The NavInfo button   Lets you determine the characteristics of the viewer within your VRML97 world. It places a NavigationInfo node in your design that tells the browser how to move about in your world. You can specify the type of movement, such as walk, examine, or fly. You can also specify the height of the viewer's eye level (Avatar Size). You can even include headlights and set visibility limits.

The ProxSensor button   You can have sounds or animations play whenever the viewer of your VRML world enters a region of your world. The ProxSensor button lets you place a Proximity-Sensor node in your design that's associated with an action object. Whenever the viewer crosses into the node, the associated action object will be activated.

The Sound helper   Lets you add spatial or ambient sounds to your design. You can control the direction and intensity of the sound. To use Sound, you must use the AudioClip option to specify a sound file for your design. Once you've done that, you can use the Pick Audio Clip option in the Sound rollout to assign a sound to the Sound helper.

The TimeSensor options   An animation in your VRML world can be split into different time segments using the TimeSensor options. You can set a trigger object to play different segments of an animation.

The TouchSensor options   With the TouchSensor options, you can have an object act as a trigger for playing animations.

Building a Virtual World

Now that you have seen what helpers are available, let's add them to a 3D scene in preparation for exporting a VRML world. The 3D scene that has been prepared contains many features that will expose the power of VRML97.

1. Open `World01.max` from the CD. Familiarize yourself with its objects as shown in Figure 17.4.

FIGURE 17.4
World before help-ers are added

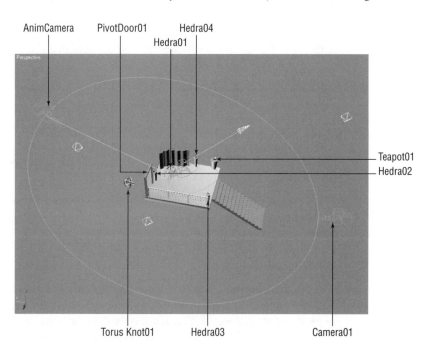

Several hedra objects will be used as triggers that your avatar can activate to perform various actions in the browser. These hedra are like buttons on top of the three small podiums in the sample scene.

The first helper to add, and perhaps the most important, is the NavInfo VRML97 helper. It determines what kind of VRML world you are exporting.

2. Click the Create tab of the Command Panel and then click the Helpers button. Choose VRML97 from the drop-down list and click NavInfo in the Object Type rollout.

VRML helpers do not appear in the exported world. As the name suggests, they help you to control the world's behavior. Each VRML helper has a graphical icon representation that can be placed anywhere in the scene.

3. Drag to place and size the NavInfo helper icon. Although it does not matter where you put it in the scene, it's a good idea to place all your helpers in the same area just so you can stay organized and easily find them later on.

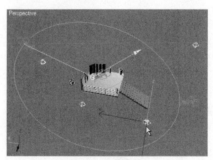

4. In the NavigationInfo rollout, leave Type as Walk, change Speed to **3´**, Terrain to **5´**, Step Height to **8˝**, and the Icon Size to **4´**.

By leaving the NavInfo Type as Walk, you are indicating that you want your avatar to walk on the ground. There are also options for Fly, and Examine, which let you make flythrough and spinning object worlds. Setting the Speed to 3′ means your avatar will be able to walk a maximum speed of 3 feet/second. Setting the Terrain to 5′ indicates you want your avatar's eye level to float 5′ above the ground. Setting Step Height to 8″ means your avatar will be capable of going up steps that are 8″ or smaller. The icon size can be anything, but a setting of 4′ ensures you'll be able to see it in the viewport.

5. Click the Background tool in the Object Type rollout. Drag a Background helper to place and size the icon adjacent to the NavInfo helper. Zoom in and Arc Rotate about 180 degrees to get a better view as shown in Figure 17.5.

FIGURE 17.5
Two VRML helper icons

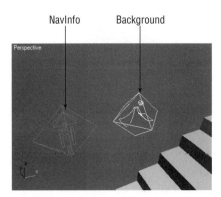

6. Click the Modify tab of the Command Panel. In the Sky Colors rollout, change the Number of Colors radio button to Three. Click the color swatch next to Color One to open the Color Selector. Change Color One to a pale blue, click the Color Two swatch and change it to a bright blue, then click the Color Three swatch and change it to a deep blue. Finally, change the Icon Size to **4′**.

By making a three-color sky, you are creating a gradient of color that changes depending upon your avatar's viewing angle with respect to the horizon. It will be pale blue near the zenith, bright blue at a 45-degree angle overhead, and a deep blue at the horizon.

7. Open the Ground Colors rollout. Similar to step 6, choose the Three radio button for the Number of Colors. Then select brown, orange, and medium green for colors one, two, and three. You are creating a similar color gradient for the ground.

TIP In the Images rollout in the Background VRML helper, you can specify six bitmap URLs to be used for the background.

8. Click the Create tab of the Command Panel and click the Fog tool in the Object Type rollout. Drag to place and size the Fog helper adjacent to the other helpers. Change the Visibility Range to **200′** and the Icon Size to **4′**.

The Fog helper creates a white fog that completely obscures the objects at a distance of 200′ from the avatar. The fog increases exponentially, so it happens suddenly as you approach the end of the visibility range. Fog can be helpful in complex scenes to hide far away objects, and it gives a sense of atmosphere and mystery to a world.

In the next stages of this exercise, you'll use three of the hedra objects that were included in the scene to trigger various actions that are often included in VRML animations—opening a door in the scene, changing cameras, and jumping to a hyperlink, for example.

NOTE Hedra01 is the latticed object that animates when the avatar triggers the proximity sensor. Unlike the other hedra in the scene, Hedra01 does not act as a trigger, but as an action object instead.

9. Press **T** to switch to a Top view and navigate to the area near Hedra01 as shown in Figure 17.6.

10. Toggle Autogrid mode on in the Extras toolbar. You will use autogrid to create an object on top of the platform. Click the ProxSensor tool in the Object Type rollout.

11. Drag out a proximity sensor that surrounds the area where Hedra01 is located as shown in Figure 17.6. Do not enclose the camera that is on the platform within the sensor volume. Turn Autogrid mode off.

FIGURE 17.6
Adding a ProxSensor volume

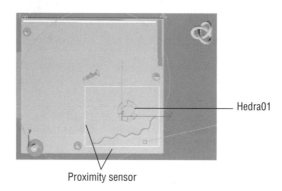

Hedra01

Proximity sensor

12. Click the Modify tab of the Command Panel. Change the Height parameter to **6′** to ensure that the avatar (which is 5′ high as set by the Terrain parameter in the NavInfo helper) can trigger the sensor when it enters into the volume of the proximity sensor.

13. Click the Pick Action Objects button and then press **H** to open the Pick Object dialog box. Select Hedra01 from the list and click Pick. Hedra01 appears in the list box. Toggle the Pick Action Objects button off.

NOTE   *Many of the objects in this scene are animated. When you pick an action object, you are setting up the VRML Client to play that object's animation tracks when the action is triggered in the browser. For example, when you click the hedra object on top of the podium by the doors, the doors will open in the browser.*

When the avatar triggers the proximity sensor by walking next to the object, the VRML Client in the browser will play the animation of Hedra01. This hedra will move and spin on a looping trajectory when its action is triggered.

14. Click the Create tab of the Command Panel. Click the TouchSensor tool in the Object Type rollout. Navigate so that you can see the other VRML helpers on the ground. Drag to place and size the icon adjacent to the other helpers.

15. Click the Pick Trigger Object button and then press **H** to open the Pick Objects dialog box. Select Hedra02 from the list and click Pick.

16. Click the Pick Action Objects button and then press **H**. Select PivotDoor01 from the list and click Pick. Click again on the Pick Action Objects button to turn it off. Change the Icon Size to **4´**.

Now when the scene is exported, the avatar will be able to click Hedra02 (which is placed like a button on a pedestal in the scene) to trigger the animation of the doors opening.

17. Click the Anchor tool in the Object Type rollout. Drag out a new icon adjacent to the others on the ground.

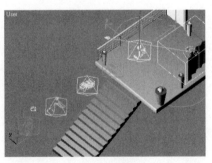

18. Click the Pick Trigger Object button and then press H to open the Pick Objects dialog box. Select Hedra03 from the list and click Pick.

19. Click the Set Camera radio button in the Camera group. Then open the drop-down list and select AnimCamera from the list. Change the Icon Size to **4′** as usual.

This anchor will serve to switch cameras in the browser when the avatar picks Hedra03.

Besides triggering a jump between cameras, an anchor can trigger a jump to a hyperlink. If you were building a virtual world for a retail store, for example, you could anchor hyperlink jumps from virtual objects to web pages that have product details and e-commerce links to buy the real objects. For this demonstration, you'll simply link to an existing web page.

20. Click the Anchor tool in the Object Type rollout again. Drag out a new icon adjacent to the others on the ground.

21. Click the Pick Trigger Object button and then press **H** to open the Pick Objects dialog box. Select Hedra04 from the list and click Pick.

22. Type in the URL of a website in the Hyperlink Jump group you'd like to visit when the avatar triggers this anchor. You can type in **http://ScottOnstott.com** if you would like to trigger a jump to the author's site from this virtual world. Otherwise you can type in the URL of your choice.

The last type of VRML helper we will cover is the Billboard. The Billboard is designed to automatically rotate the object it is linked to in the browser as the avatar moves to keep the linked object oriented towards the viewer.

23. Click the Billboard tool in the Object Type rollout. Drag out a new icon anywhere on the ground.

24. Press Alt+A to invoke the Align tool and then press **H**. Select Teapot01 from the Select Objects list and click Pick to use it as the align target.

25. The Align Selection dialog box appears. Check the X, Y, and Z Position check boxes and make sure that the Center radio buttons are selected for both the Current and Target objects and then click OK. The Billboard icon is now centered on the teapot.

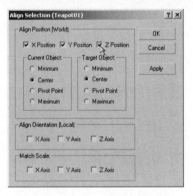

26. Use the Zoom Extents Selected tool to get a closer view of the teapot and the Billboard helper. Press **A** to activate angle snap and then use the Select and Rotate tool to rotate the billboard 90 degrees clockwise in the Z direction so that the billboard icon's sign faces forward in the direction of the teapot spout as shown in Figure 17.7.

Now that you've created, aligned, and oriented the billboard, the last step is to link the teapot to it.

FIGURE 17.7
Rotate the billboard.

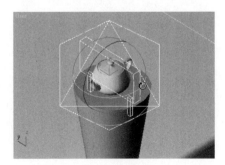

27. Press **H** to open the Select Objects dialog box. Select Billboard01 and Teapot01 (by holding down the Ctrl key) and click Select. Choose Graph Editors ➢ New Schematic View.

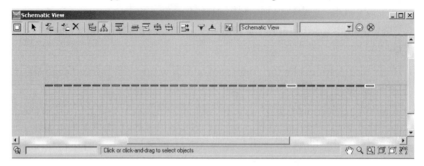

The two selected nodes are far apart in the node graph.

28. Visually keeping track of where Teapot01 is in Schematic view (it is the selected node on the left), click inside the Schematic View window to deselect the objects. Next, drag the Teapot01 node below the last nodes on the far right as shown in Figure 17.8.

29. Click the Region Zoom tool at the bottom of the Schematic View window. Drag a window around the last two nodes on the right to enlarge them.

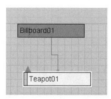

30. Click the Connect tool at the top of the Schematic View window. Drag a link from the Teapot01 to Billboard01 nodes in Schematic View. Close the Schematic View window.

A green link appears to indicate the nodes are linked with the billboard as the parent to the teapot. When the world is exported, the spout of the teapot will always face the avatar.

FIGURE 17.8
Arranging nodes in
Schematic view

Drag Teapot01 from here...   ...to here.

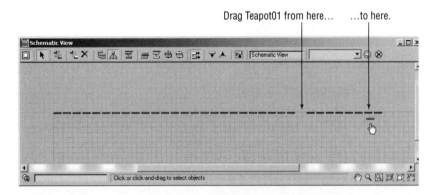

Exporting the VRML File

At this point, you have added many VRML helpers to the scene. Many of the helpers trigger animated actions when certain events occur in the browser. Other helpers were used to set up the behavior of the virtual world, making it a walkable experience for the avatar that will represent you in virtual space. To experience the world you have built, the next step is to export the WRL file from VIZ.

1. Open `World02.max` from the CD or continue from where you left off in the previous section.

2. Choose File ➢ Export. Change the Save as Type drop-down list to **VRML97 (*.WRL)**. Navigate to a folder on your hard drive where you want to export this file and type **MyWorld** in the File name box and click Save.

3. The VRML97 Exporter dialog box (Figure 17.9) appears. In the Generate group, make sure Normals, Indentation, Primitives, and Coordinate Interpolators are checked.

FIGURE 17.9
VRML97 Exporter
settings

Normals allow smoothing data to be exported, Indentation makes for a human readable WRL file, Primitives make for more efficient data structures, and Coordinate Interpolators are necessary for exporting animation. Make sure all the settings are as shown in Figure 17.9 and then click OK.

Exploring the World

Now that you've done all the work, it is time to have the pleasure of exploring the world you have built. You cannot experience the world in VIZ; you must load it in your Internet browser using the VRML Client you installed earlier in this chapter.

1. Launch your Internet browser.

2. Open the MyWorld.WRL file you exported earlier, or open the one from the CD. The way you open it depends on which browser you are using. One sure way to load the world is to drag the MyWorld.WRL file from Windows Explorer into an open browser window. The Cortona VRML client displays the world as shown in Figure 17.10. The toolbars at the edges of the world are part of the Cortona client.

3. To make your avatar walk, position your mouse in the center of the VRML Client and drag forward (up). The farther you drag, the faster your avatar walks, up to the maximum speed you set in the NavInfo helper in an earlier section. If you drag to the left, you turn left. Drag right to move right, drag backward to back up. It is very intuitive navigation. Try walking up the stairs. When you get to the top, your avatar will be on a platform with a Hedra lattice, some closed doors, and other hedra on pedestals.

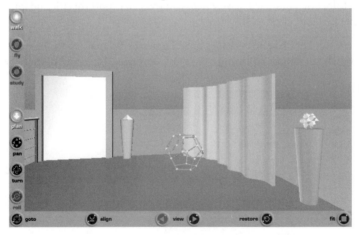

FIGURE 17.10
Exploring the virtual world in a browser

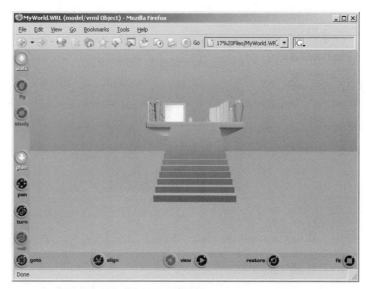

4. Walk toward the Hedra lattice (Hedra01 in VIZ). When you get close enough, you should trigger the proximity sensor and the hedra will start to move.

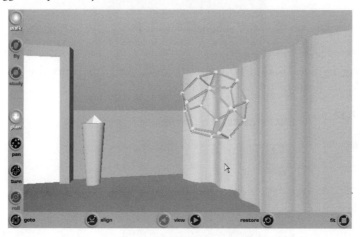

NOTE *The Hedra lattice is on an animation loop, so it returns to its original position after the animation is done. You can trigger it again and restart the animation loop by walking out of and back into the (invisible) proximity sensor.*

5. Walk over near the doors and click the yellow hedra on the pedestal near the door as shown in Figure 17.11.

FIGURE 17.11
Triggering the
TouchSensor

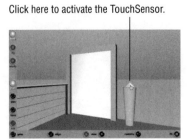

Click here to activate the TouchSensor.

When you click the Hedra "button," the doors open. A rotating Torus Knot is revealed behind the doors, and it rotates continuously. The doors remain open once triggered because their animation track does not loop.

6. Drag the mouse to the left to turn left. Walk over to the pedestal at the end of the railing and click the hedra on top as shown in Figure 17.12.

FIGURE 17.12
Triggering a
camera jump

Click here to activate the camera jump.

The avatar will switch into the point of view of the AnimCamera, which has been animated to follow a spline path that encircles the model. The jump to a new viewpoint was made with the Anchor helper in VIZ.

TIP *You can include animated cameras that follow a predetermined path in a virtual reality world. This is helpful during a live demo and lets you discuss aspects of the model while the motion captivates the audience.*

7. Click the Previous Viewpoint button on the lower Cortona toolbar. This switches you out of the animated camera loop.

Go ahead and explore the other features of the Cortona VRML Client on your own. Hopefully your imagination has been stimulated by this exploration and you can now consider publishing interactive worlds of your own design.

TIP *You can make WRL files much smaller (for faster downloading) by applying gzip compression to them. Many programs on the Web offer such a compression algorithm. There is a convention of using the file extension* .WRZ *to indicate the world is gzipped and all major VRML Clients can un-gzip the compressed worlds on the fly. Note that this trick does not work for other compression types, only gzip.*

Exporting Shockwave 3D Content

New!

Now in VIZ 2005, if you want to build a custom presentation with Shockwave 3D content in Macromedia Director, you can export a W3D file from VIZ. Then you can use the features of Director to craft a custom presentation interface that showcases the 3D content that you made in VIZ.

1. Open Shockwave.max from the CD. This is the same scene you were using when you were making virtual reality worlds.

2. Choose File ➤ Export. Select Shockwave 3D Scene Export (*.W3D) from the Save as Type drop-down list. Type in **MyShockwave** in the File Name box and navigate to a folder where you would like to export this file on your hard disk and then click Save.

3. The Shockwave 3D Scene Export Options dialog box appears. Select AnimCamera from the Camera drop-down list as shown in Figure 17.13.

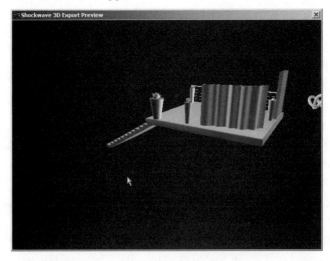

Select the animated camera here.

4. Click the Preview button. After a while, the objects are processed and the Shockwave 3D Export Preview window appears.

The view in the window is moving as the camera is following its animation path. Close the window after you have seen what your exported file will look like in Director.

5. Click the Author Check button in the Shockwave 3D Scene Export Options dialog box. A dialog box appears showing possible problems converting a scene to Shockwave 3D.

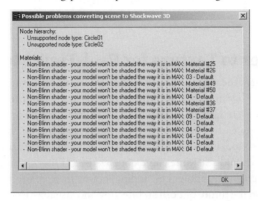

The possible problems with this scene are listed under node hierarchy and materials.

The node hierarchy issues are raised to warn you that the circle splines won't be exported from the scene. That's really not a problem because those circles were only used to animate the camera but aren't needed in the Shockwave 3D file.

The material issues are all related to the fact that many of the materials aren't using the Blinn shader, which is the only shader that is supported in Shockwave 3D. All your materials will automatically be assigned the Blinn shader upon export, which is perfectly acceptable for a web presentation.

TIP   *Read the User Reference for more information on the Shockwave 3D format.*

6. Click the Analyze button. A Shockwave 3D File Analysis dialog box appears showing a breakdown of the different categories of nodes. Director users can interpret this data to help them plan a successful file conversion.

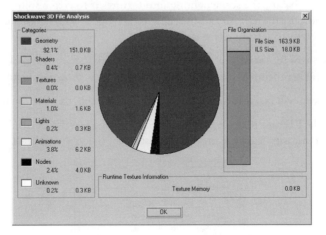

7. Click the Export button when satisfied with the options chosen to save the file to your hard drive.

Macromedia Director users can open the exported W3D files and now use the 3D assets from VIZ in their projects.

Using Render to Texture for Real-Time Models

New!

VIZ 2005 now offers the ability to *render to texture*, or *bake* rendering information into the model by storing the advanced lighting data as bitmaps that are mapped onto objects' surfaces. Baked objects look like they are lit even though the original light sources may be removed from the model. Basically, graphics cards have an easier time displaying baked textures than they do calculating lighting information in real-time. Models whose lighting data is rendered to texture can be displayed efficiently in graphics display cards and real-time game engines using DirectX and OpenGL technologies.

Real-time game engine technology is finding its way into architectural visualization through those who have insight into the future of both architecture and visualization. Game engine technology is much more advanced than VRML (format frozen in 1997) thanks to active development for the multi-billion dollar worldwide game market, which is also partly driven by graphics card manufacturers.

Real-time interactivity isn't just about presenting designs to clients, although that can be quite impressive. The "killer app" of real-time technology is allowing designers to be "in" their architecture during the design process, which shortens development time considerably (a lesson learned in the game industry).

Real-time models can also be used for design, client approval, planning authorities, and construction site management, even marketing and sales. If you've played a modern console game, you will know how compelling moving around architectural spaces in real time can be. You still develop a model in VIZ and then export it to a proprietary real-time editor where you prepare a simulation. Most of the work still happens in VIZ. Render to Texture is the bridge to getting your advanced lighting data into a form that can be displayed in real time. Let's see how it works.

Calculating Advanced Lighting Data

The first step to baking the scene lighting into textures is to create some lighting that is worth capturing. Let's now use the radiosity advanced lighting renderer to generate some appealing lighting that we can later render to texture in the next section.

1. Open `Interior.max` from the CD. This is a model of a single room that is set up with photometric luminaires and a few pieces of furniture as shown in Figure 17.14.

Next, you will be creating advanced lighting data that can later be rendered to texture.

2. Press the **F10** key to open the Render Scene dialog box. Click the Advanced Lighting tab and select Radiosity from the drop-down list in the Select Advanced Lighting rollout.

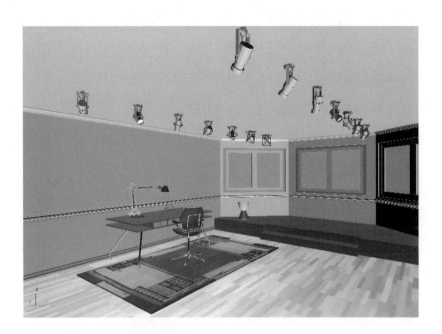

3. In the Radiosity Processing Parameters rollout, set the Initial Quality to 50% in the Process group. Set Filtering to **2** in the Interactive Tools group.

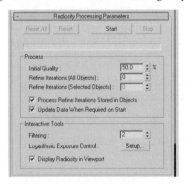

4. Open the Radiosity Meshing Parameters rollout, check Enabled, and change the Meshing size to **2′**.

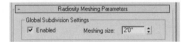

5. Click the Start button at the top of the Radiosity Processing Parameters rollout. You will have to wait a few minutes for the lighting solution to reach a 50% level of quality. You will see a progress bar move across from left to right for each refine iteration that is processed. It will stop processing automatically when it reaches 50%.

6. Click the Setup button in the Interactive Tools group of the Radiosity Processing Parameters rollout. This opens the Environment and Effects dialog box where you'll find the Logarithmic Exposure Control Parameters rollout. Change the Brightness to **72**.

Figure 17.15 shows the Radiosity data in the viewport. You see the vertex color data, which is stored in the mesh that results from radiosity processing, appear automatically in the viewport. Notice there are display artifacts showing on two pieces of furniture.

7. Select both the stool and the chair by Ctrl+clicking both of them in the viewport. Click the Render Scene dialog box to bring it to the front. Change Refine Iterations (Selected Objects) to **4** and click the Continue button.

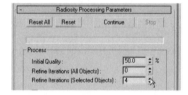

The selected objects are given additional processing to remove the display artifacts.

8. Click the Render button at the bottom of the Render Scene dialog box. Close both the Render Scene and Environment and Effects dialog boxes. Deselect all by pressing Ctrl+D. Figure 17.16 shows the rendered scene with advanced lighting data shown in the Rendered Frame Window.

9. Close the Rendered Frame Window and save the model as `InteriorRadiosity.max` on your hard drive.

TIP *You can use the mental ray renderer instead to provide advanced lighting data that could be rendered to texture.*

There are display artifacts on these pieces of furniture.

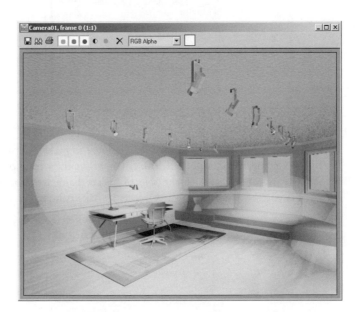

Baking Lighting into Textures

In order to use this nice looking scene in a real-time game engine, you will have to bake the lighting into textures. It wouldn't be possible for a real-time engine to go through the lengthy radiosity calculations and still maintain real-time interactivity. However, the real-time engine will be able to display any number of textures that look like they are illuminated. Texture Baking can also save processing time by reducing the required calculations for static objects in animation. The Texture Baking process is highly automated in VIZ 2005 as you will see now.

1. Choose Rendering ➢ Render To Texture, or press **0** (zero). Open the Objects to Bake rollout if it is not already open.

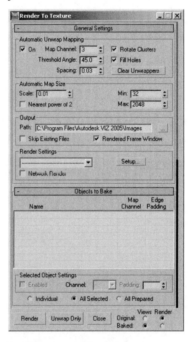

2. Using the Select tool, hold down the Ctrl key to make multiple selections and click on the Floor, Ceiling, Wall, and Platform. If you select the wrong object, deselect it and try again. Alternatively, you could use the Select Objects dialog box if you prefer to select by name. The objects you select appear in the Objects to Bake rollout.

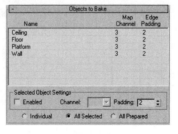

3. Change the Path in the Output group of the General Settings rollout to the same folder where you have saved the scene file on your hard drive by clicking the ellipsis button to the right of the path text box (your path will differ from the illustration). By default, Render To Texture saves the textures it bakes to `C:\Program Files\Autodesk VIZ 2005\Images`.

4. Click the Add button in the Output rollout in the Render To Texture dialog box.

5. The Add Texture Elements dialog box appears. Select CompleteMap and click Add Elements. There are many different elements to choose from that correspond to different aspects of illumination.

6. Open the Target Map Slot drop-down list in the Selected Element Common Settings group in the Output rollout. You see a list of the different map slots that the CompleteMap can correspond to within each object's material. Select Diffuse Map if it is not already selected.

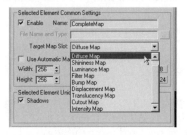

In this exercise, you are baking all of the mapping information for the material and outputting it to the Diffuse Map group, which is the most direct way of Texture Baking. In some cases, it may be useful to isolate particular elements. For example, the Lighting Map element could be output only to the self-illumination Map group.

7. The size at which the baked texture will be output depends on what your real-time engine can display. In this example, you will choose a large size that captures greater detail. Click the 1024×1024 button.

8. Open the Baked Material rollout. Here you can select how the baked output will interact with the materials in the scene. You have the option of Output into Source or Save Source (Create Shell). The Output into Source option replaces the original source material with the new baked material and is generally useful for final output in a completed scene. The Save Source (Create Shell) creates a Shell material that contains both the original source material and the baked material and is useful when you anticipate making further modification or tweaking. Choose Save Source (Create Shell) and Duplicate Source to Baked if these choices are not already selected.

9. At the bottom of the Render To Texture dialog box, there are radio buttons on the right side that correspond to the way you would like to view and render your new Shell materials. By default the Baked Material is shown in the viewport and the Original Material is shown in the renderings. Select both radio buttons in the Baked row so that you will see the new Baked materials both in the viewports and in renderings.

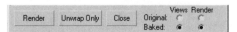

10. Finally, click the Render button at the bottom of the Render To Texture dialog box and the automated process begins. After a while, you'll see a Rendered Frame Window appear and the baked textures will get rendered using the advanced lighting data in the scene. Close the Rendered Frame Window and the Render To Texture dialog box when the process is complete. You see the illumination data baked into the textures in Figure 17.17.

Now that you have successfully rendered the advanced lighting to textures that are mapped onto the largest surfaces in the model, you can dispose of the advanced lighting data.

FIGURE 17.17
Baked textures displayed in viewport

11. Press the **F10** key to open the Render Scene dialog box and click the Advanced Lighting tab. Open the drop-down list in the Select Advanced Lighting rollout and select <no lighting plug-in> from the list.

12. A small dialog box appears that states, "Changing the advanced lighting plug-in will discard its solution. Are you sure?" Click the Yes button and the radiosity data is gone. Close the Render Scene dialog box. Note that the baked textures showing the lighting are still visible in the viewport as shown in Figure 17.17, even though the lighting data itself is no longer in the model.

13. Save the scene as InteriorBaked.max.

Examining the Baked Materials and Mapping

The scene is essentially ready for export into a proprietary real-time authoring environment at this point. The advanced lighting data has been baked into textures and the radiosity data has been discarded. However, you may still be interested to know how the scene's materials were automatically altered and what kind of mapping was used. Let's take a quick look.

1. Press **M** to open the Material Editor. Click a blank sample slot on the bottom row to select it.

2. Click the eyedropper tool to pick a material from an object in the scene. Click the Wall and its material fills the selected sample slot in the Material Editor.

New!   The Shell material is new to VIZ 2005 and is very simple as you can see. It holds two child materials. Each material can be set to display in the viewports and/or renderings with the corresponding radio buttons. Render To Texture automatically set this up in the last section.

The Original material goes in the first slot and has the `orig_` prefix added before the material name, so it reads `orig_Wall Paint`. The Baked material likewise had `baked_` added as a prefix before the name, so it reads `baked_Wall Paint` now.

3. Click the `baked_Wall Paint` material to go deeper into the material hierarchy in the editor.

4. Click the `WallCompleteMap.tga` bitmap in the Diffuse Map slot.

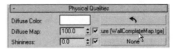

5. Click the View Image button in the Bitmap Parameters rollout. You can see that the different surfaces that are part of the Wall object are all arranged neatly in the bitmap, each having the lighting data baked into the textures. Close the Image window and the Material Editor.

At this point you should be asking yourself how this complex image was mapped onto all the various surfaces in the Wall object.

6. To discover the truth about the mapping that was applied by Render To Texture, select the Wall object and then click the Modify tab of the Command Panel.

The stack view shows an Automatic Flatten UVs modifier at the top, which was added by Render To Texture.

TIP   *The Automatic Flatten UVs modifier has the same functionality as the Unwrap UVW modifier that you can apply manually, but it has a different name to differentiate it from other Unwrap UVWs that may be applied in a scene. Choose Help ➢ User Reference for more information.*

7. Click the Edit button in the Parameters rollout. The Edit UVWs window appears.

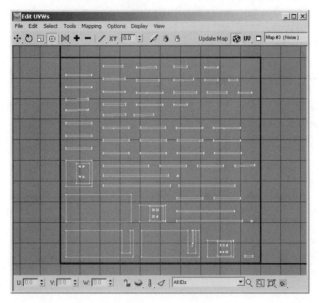

You can see that all the surfaces in the Wall object were automatically unwrapped, flattened, and arranged neatly in this window. The mapping coordinates (in UVW space) are controlled here and correspond exactly with the baked bitmap you saw in step 5. As you can see an amazing amount of automation takes place when you use Render To Texture.

Hopefully your curiosity about how Render To Texture automates the baking process has been partially satisfied. Remember that the baked model is ready for export to a real-time engine, but such engines are not part of VIZ. Here are a few websites for you to investigate for more information about real-time visualization engines that interface with VIZ:

www.cubicspace.com

www.vr4max.com

www.wildtangent.com

Summary

In this chapter you have been exposed to alternatives to the traditional rendered still images and animations that VIZ is known for. You can now consider exporting interactive media from your own projects including panoramas, virtual reality worlds, Shockwave 3D content, and baked textures used in real-time visualization engines.

This brings you to the end of *Mastering Autodesk VIZ 2005*. You weren't shown every conceivable feature in VIZ, but you were introduced to the main tools you'll need to produce professional-level work.

We hope you've enjoyed your exploration of VIZ and that you'll find this book a useful tool in your ongoing work in VIZ.

If you'd like to offer comments regarding this book, or if you have any questions about the program, feel free to contact the authors. Thanks for choosing *Mastering Autodesk VIZ 2005*.

George Omura
Gomura@yahoo.com

Scott Onstott
Scott@ScottOnstott.com
http://ScottOnstott.com

Appendix A

Installation Notes

To USE THE TUTORIALS in this book, you'll want to be sure you've installed most of the components that are available on the VIZ installation CD. This means that you'll need at least 464 megabytes of free disk space for the VIZ files alone. You may also want to install the tutorials, samples, and partner files from the *Partners CD*. This will require another 360 megabytes of space. In addition, you'll want to install the sample files from the companion CD for this book, which will require another 500 megabytes of space. All together, you will need between 464 megabytes and 1.3 gigabytes of space on your hard drive, depending on the options you choose.

Installing VIZ

Installing VIZ is fairly straightforward. When you insert the VIZ disk into your CD-ROM drive, the Windows Autorun feature will automatically start the installation program on the VIZ CD. If Autorun is disabled, open Windows Explorer and double-click the startup application (`setup.exe`) on the VIZ CD. You will be given the options for installing VIZ and a number of other related applications, including Microsoft DirectX, Apple QuickTime, and the Autodesk 2005 Software Development Kit (SDK) as shown in Figure A.1.

TIP   *Click the Network Deployment button in the Setup dialog box if you have purchased a network license.*

Click the Install button in Step 2 in the Install area of the Setup dialog box. After selecting the Install option, a smaller Autodesk VIZ 2005 Setup dialog box appears and you will be asked to make sure that no other applications are running; then you'll be presented with the licensing agreement. After clicking the I Accept button and clicking Next, you'll see a dialog box asking for your name, company name, and the serial number. You can find this number on the product box. Next, you'll see the Select Features page of the dialog box where you can select the components you want to install and the installation path.

You'll want to do a full installation so that you can take advantage of all the files available on the VIZ CD. Thus, when you get to the Select Features page of the Autodesk VIZ 2005 Setup dialog box, choose the Complete option; leave the installation path at the default setting of `C:\Program Files\Autodesk VIZ 2005`.

FIGURE A.1
VIZ Setup
dialog box

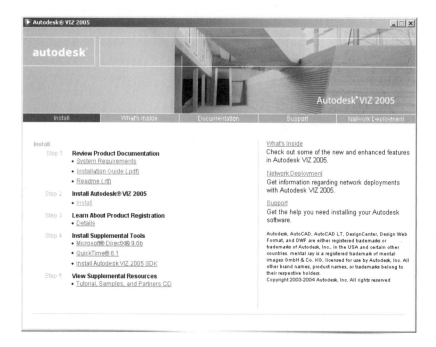

It's a good idea to make sure you have enough disk space for VIZ by clicking the Disk Cost button at the bottom of the Select Features dialog box. You'll then see a dialog box that shows you the drives on your computer and the amount of total and free disk space for each drive. If you find that your currently selected installation drive is too low on space, click OK. Then use the Back button to return to the Destination Folder dialog box and select a different drive location for VIZ.

Once you've selected the appropriate options, you can proceed with the rest of the installation.

If this is the first time you've installed VIZ, you'll then be asked to supply an authorization code when you start VIZ. You can choose to postpone the entry of your authorization code to a later date, but if you do so, you'll have a 30-day grace period until VIZ refuses to start without the code. You can obtain the code by phone, fax, or e-mail, or through your Internet connection as instructed by the VIZ opening screen.

After the installation of the main program is done, go back to the original Setup dialog box and complete Steps 3 through 5 as shown in Figure A.1. You will want to install the latest versions of DirectX and QuickTime if you haven't done so independently before. Unless you are a C++ programmer writing plug-ins, Autodesk does not recommend most users install the Autodesk VIZ 2005 SDK. Finally, you can insert the second CD and install extra tutorials, sample files, and sample partner plug-ins.

Moving VIZ to Another Computer

VIZ incorporates a licensing software lock system. To allow users to use VIZ at different locations, VIZ offers a utility called the *Portable License Utility*. This utility allows you to maintain a pool of computers to which you can transfer your license. That way, you can use a single license on several computers, but you may run VIZ on only one computer at a time. For example, you can install VIZ on both your home and office computers and then use the Portable License Utility to enable VIZ on one computer or the other as needed.

The idea is simple, but the process of transferring your VIZ license may seem a bit complicated at first. The following steps describe the process. To begin, you need to do some preparation.

1. Start by installing VIZ on your main computer and authorizing it.

2. Go to the other computer, which I'll call computer 2. Install VIZ on it but don't attempt to authorize it.

3. While still on computer 2, choose Start ➢ Programs ➢ Autodesk ➢ Autodesk VIZ 2005 ➢ Portable License Utility. The Portable License Utility dialog box displays.

4. Select the Import tab. You'll see a number in the Machine Identification Code text box. Write this number down, since you'll need it later.

5. Go back to the main computer that has the authorized version of VIZ; then choose Start ➢ Programs ➢ Autodesk ➢ Autodesk VIZ 2005 ➢ Portable License Utility.

6. Make sure the Pool tab is selected; then click the Add button. The Add Machine Details dialog box displays.

7. Enter a name for computer 2 in the Machine Name input box; then enter the code you obtained in step 4 in the Machine Identification Code input box. Click OK.

You now have a pool consisting of one other computer. You can add other computers to the pool as you need them.

To use VIZ on computer 2, you need to export your license from the main computer.

1. On the main computer, start the Portable License Utility; then select the Export tab.

2. Select the name of the computer to which you'll export your license; then click Export. If you see more than one computer listed, select the computer name under the Status–Active listing. The Exporting dialog box displays.

3. Verify that the information is correct and then click OK. The Export Type Selection dialog box displays.

Here you have two options: you can export your license using a transfer code, or you can use a file. If this is the first time you have transferred a license to computer 2, you'll have only the Transfer File option.

1. Select the Transfer File option and make note of the filename and location in the Transfer File input box. By default, the filename and location is \Program Files\Autodesk VIZ 2005\License.ctl.

   2. Click Transfer. You may see a message telling you that you must enter a name for this (the current) machine. The Add This Machine dialog box displays.

   3. Enter a name for the current computer and then click OK. You see a message saying that the license was successfully exported.

The final step is to import your license to computer 2. As you might guess, you need to take a copy of the `License.ctl` file from your main computer to computer 2 to complete the transfer of the license.

   1. Copy the `License.ctl` file from the main computer to a floppy disk. If the computers are connected over a network, you may alternatively move the `License.ctl` file to a shared directory on the main computer or server.

   2. Start the Portable License Utility on computer 2.

   3. Select the Import tab; then select the Read Transfer File radio button.

   4. Click the Browse button; then locate and select the `License.ctl` file you exported from the main computer.

   5. Click the Import button. After a moment, you'll see a message indicating that the transfer was successful.

   6. Exit the Portable License Utility and start VIZ.

To transfer the license back to the main computer, start by retrieving the machine identification code from the main computer. You need to add the main computer to the list in the Pool tab of the Portable License Utility in computer 2. Once this is done, you can export the license from computer 2 and import it back to the main computer. By the way, once you record and enter the machine identification code, you won't have to record or enter it again during subsequent license transfers. You just need to remember the name you gave to each computer in the pool.

Although the process may seem lengthy in these instructions, once you've gone through it a few times, it becomes a simple and quick operation.

UNDERSTANDING THE VIZ SOFTWARE LOCK

VIZ's software lock uses three components of your computer to verify the VIZ license. VIZ places licensing data on the primary boot disk and in a license folder. In addition, VIZ correlates your installation with your system date and time so that your software license is sensitive to your computer's date and time settings. For this reason, you'll want to pay close attention to your date and time settings when you install VIZ. Make sure they are correct before you begin the installation.

Once you've installed and authorized your software, you can make changes to your date or time within two days. You are also limited to two backward time changes. Since VIZ is sensitive to changes in your system, you need to take some extra steps when you want to make changes to your computer or if you want to move VIZ to another computer.

If you intend to make other changes to your system, use the Portable License Utility to export your license before the changes; then import the license when you've completed your changes. For more information on VIZ licensing, consult the Autodesk VIZ 2005 installation guide that comes with VIZ.

Visit the Autodesk Website Often

Once you're up and running with VIZ 2005, you'll want to check the Autodesk website often for news, links, discussion groups, and other helpful information on VIZ 2005. You'll also want be on the lookout for any service pack that may be available for download.

To find the latest service packs and updates, go to the Support page of www.autodesk.com. You can choose Help ➤ Autodesk VIZ on the Web ➤ Online Support to go directly to the Autodesk website, then select your country or region to enter the site. Click Support to get to the Support page. On the Support page, select Autodesk VIZ from the Technical Support drop-down list. At the Autodesk VIZ page, click Data & Downloads. Links to the most current Updates & Service Packs, Utilities & Drivers, Viewers, and Tools will appear.

Installing the Companion CD

Before you start the tutorials in this book, you'll want to install the sample files from the book's companion CD. The CD contains many other programs and sample files that you may find useful in your work with VIZ.

To install the software from the companion CD, place the CD in your computer's CD-ROM drive and then follow these steps:

1. You'll see a message telling you that you need QuickTime to play sample movies included on the CD. Click the type of operating system you have or click Continue to skip the QuickTime installation.

2. Next, you'll see the software license agreement. Click Accept.

3. The next screen is a menu that lists the different programs and files on the CD. To install the sample files, click Book Files.

4. In the WinZip Self-Extractor dialog box, click Unzip. If you want to install the files in a location other than the one shown in the Unzip to Folder input box, enter a different directory before you click Unzip. You may also click Browse to find the location for the sample files.

5. Once the Unzip operation is complete, you can exit all the dialog boxes.

After step 4, you can continue to install other options or exit the installation. You can always return to the installation menu later.

TIP   If for some reason the installation process doesn't occur automatically when you insert the CD in step 1, use Windows Explorer to view the contents of the CD. Locate the clickme.exe *file and double-click it.*

Appendix B

Modifiers and Materials

VIZ OFFERS A MULTITUDE of modifier and material options—so many, in fact, that to do a tutorial on all of them would require a multivolume book. After reading the first few chapters of this book, however, you'll have a good understanding of how VIZ works, and you'll be able to use most, if not all, of the modifiers and materials with a little experimentation and some help from this appendix.

This appendix is intended to give you general information about the modifiers and materials and to show you what types of features are available. If you need more detailed information about the modifiers and materials, the VIZ User Reference offers full descriptions of the options and parameters for all the items discussed in this appendix. Choose Help ➢ User Reference. Click the Search tab in the panel to the left, enter the name of the item in the Type In The Word(s) To Search For input box, and then click List Topics. If you see only a single panel in the User Reference, click the Show button in the User Reference toolbar.

Modifiers

The tutorials in this book cover the more commonly used modifiers in VIZ. Every now and then, you'll find a need to use one of the other modifiers that are not discussed at any length in the User Reference. For those situations, you can find a description of the modifier in this section, and hopefully, this description will be enough to get you started. Even if you don't need all these modifiers now, you may want to review their functions so that you'll know what's available.

The modifiers are all on a single drop-down list named Modifier List. The list is broken down into three categories. This appendix presents the modifiers in the same order as they appear in the Modifier List drop-down list, starting with the Selection modifiers. Not all of the modifiers appear in the Modifier List simultaneously, because the list changes, depending on the type of object currently being edited. Only the modifiers that work with the selected object are displayed in the list.

Selection Modifiers

The Selection modifiers allow you to gain access to the sub-object levels of objects. Once sub-objects are selected with a selection modifier, other modifiers can be placed above them in the stack to affect only the sub-object selection. This process is also called *passing a sub-object selection up the stack.*

MESH SELECT

The Mesh Select modifier allows you to gain access to the sub-object level of an object to select part of the object. You can then apply another modifier to affect only what you selected with Mesh Select. For example, you could use Mesh Select to select part of an object, and then you could apply Bend to only the selected part. You can use Mesh Select to pass selections up the stack to other modifiers or to gain access to mesh sub-object selection for Patch and NURBS surfaces.

PATCH SELECT

The Patch Select modifier allows you to gain access to the sub-object level of an object to select part of the object. It works in a similar manner to the Mesh Select modifier, but Patch Select treats objects as if they were editable patches rather than meshes.

SPLINE SELECT

The Spline Select modifier lets you affect sub-object selections of splines. This is useful for making sub-object selections for modifiers that are removed from the source object in the modifier stack.

POLY SELECT

The Poly Select modifier lets you select sub-objects of Editable Poly objects. This is useful for making sub-object selections for modifiers that are removed from the source object in the modifier stack.

VOL. SELECT

The Vol. Select modifier lets you make sub-object selections based on a volume. You have the choice of three volume types: Box, Sphere, and Cylinder. A Selection gizmo in the shape of the volume type you select appears in the design. You can then select the sub-object level of the Vol. Select modifier to move the Volume gizmo into place to make the selection.

NSURF SEL

NSurf Sel allows you to place sub-object selections anywhere in the stack of a NURBS objects. This is similar to the Mesh Select modifier but is used only for NURBS.

World-Space Modifiers

World-Space modifiers (WSMs) are modifiers that use the world space as their point of reference, as opposed to the object space of the object to which they are attached. The Map Scalar modifier is a good example of a WSM, since it associates the map of an object with the world space and isn't affected by the object space of the object to which it's attached. An object using the Map Scalar can be scaled to any size or shape, and any maps attached to the object won't be scaled.

TIP   The World-Space modifiers can be recognized by their (WSM) postfix.

CAMERA MAP (WSM)

At times, you may want an object to be invisible while it maintains a presence in a design. For example, suppose you have a fairly detailed background image that shows a garage, and you want to create the illusion of a car entering the garage. You can create a simple box with an opening similar in shape to the background garage opening, and then use the Camera Map modifier to blend the box into the background. Once you do that, you can animate the car to drive into the box. The net effect is that the car appears to drive into the garage in the background image in your final animation. This allows you to keep the geometry simple, yet still have an animation that shows a fair amount of detail.

The Camera Map modifier applies a planar UVW map to an object, and it aligns that map so that it's perpendicular to a specified camera. The map is typically the same as the background, giving the illusion of an invisible object. Since the object can cast and receive shadows, you can create different effects. For example, if you're using the Camera Match tool to match a building design to a photo of a building site, you can use the Camera Map modifier to include shadows on buildings in the background.

This modifier can be used when a camera is in motion, as it updates the map at each frame. There is also an Object-Space modifier (OSM) version.

DISPLACE MESH (WSM)

Displace Mesh lets you form a surface using a bitmap image. It's similar to applying a bump map material to an object, but instead of simply creating the illusion of a bumpy surface by changing the surface normals, Displace Mesh actually changes the geometry to a bumpy surface. See Chapter 14 for a detailed description of the Displace Mesh modifier.

If you assign a displacement map to an object, you usually won't be able to see the effects of the map until it's rendered. The Displace Mesh modifier allows you to see the effects of a displacement map while you're editing. Displace Mesh can also let you convert a displacement map into an editable mesh, as described in Chapter 14.

DISPLACE NURBS (WSM)

The Displace NURBS modifier performs the same function as the Displace Mesh modifier, but it is applied to NURBS objects.

LS COLORS (WSM)

The LS Colors modifier converts Lightscape radiosity mesh colors to Autodesk VIZ vertex colors. This is useful when you import a lighting solution (*.ls file) from Lightscape into VIZ.

TIP   You can also use the Lightscape Materials utility to aid in the conversion of lighting solution data into VIZ.

MAP SCALAR (WSM)

Apply this version of the modifier when you want the material map to maintain its original scale, regardless of the scale of the object to which it is applied. This modifier allows you to "lock" a map's scale so that changes to the object don't affect the associated map. Use the OSM version to lock the associated map's scale to object space instead.

PATCH DEFORM (WSM)

This modifier allows you to deform an object based on the form of a Patch object. A Patch object is an object that can be formed into a smooth, curved surface by editing its vertices. You can, for example, create a plane and then convert the plane into an editable patch. The vertices of the editable patch can then be edited to shape the plane into a smooth, curved surface of any shape you want. Such a surface can be used to deform other objects, using the Patch Deform modifier. The object moves to the location of the patch with the WSM version. See also the OSM version of this modifier.

PATH DEFORM (WSM)

The Path Deform modifier works in a way similar to the Patch Deform modifier but uses a spline or NURBS curve instead of a Patch object. For example, you can use this modifier to deform an object along the path of the spline. An example of this would be the curving of text to conform to the shape of a round column or sphere. The object moves to the path used for the deformation in this version of the modifier. See the OSM version also.

SUBDIVIDE (WSM)

The Subdivide modifier allows you to manually apply a radiosity mesh to an object. Subdivide works in a similar way to the Radiosity Meshing parameters discussed in Chapter 10, but instead of applying a mesh globally, Subdivide lets you apply a mesh to single objects or even sub-object levels. Since it's a modifier, it can be edited directly from the modifier stack. The size of the subdivided mesh is locked to world space with this modifier; if you scale the object, the mesh stays the same size.

SURFACE MAPPER (WSM)

The UVW Map modifier has a fixed set of seven mapping options that allow you to apply a map to most forms. But what happens when none of those options will work for your design? If you have an organic form that requires custom mapping, you can use the Surface Mapper modifier.

The Surface Mapper requires that you create a NURBS surface that you edit to the form of the required map. You form the NURBS surface around the object to which you are applying the map and assign the same material to both the NURBS surface and the object. Once this is done, you apply the Surface Mapper modifier to the object or objects. The map is projected onto the modified object(s), based on the direction of the normals on the NURBS surface. In this version of the modifier, the scale of UVW space is tied to world space; if you scale the object, the UVW coordinates remain in their original size.

SURF DEFORM (WSM)

The Surf Deform modifier works in a way similar to the PathDeform modifier but uses a NURBS surface instead of a curve. You can use this modifier to deform an object, based on the shape of a NURBS surface. This version stays locked to world space.

Object-Space Modifiers

These modifiers directly affect the object that they are applied to in the local coordinate system of the object itself. Object space is generally described in UVW coordinates when dealing with texture maps.

AFFECT REGION

The Affect Region modifier lets you apply a bump to a surface. Two points control the bump. One point sets the base of the bump, while the other locates the tip of the bump. Each point can be adjusted independently of the other. You can control the bump's shape through Falloff, Pinch, and Bubble parameters.

Automatic Flatten UVs

This is the same as the Unwrap UVW modifier, automatically applied by Render to Texture (see Chapter 17).

Bend

You can bend an object on any axis by using the Bend modifier. You can control the degree of the bend, the place where it occurs, and the axis about which it occurs. This modifier is demonstrated in Chapter 2.

Bevel

Bevel allows you to extrude a 2D shape and add a beveled edge. The Bevel Values rollout for this modifier allows you to set the height of the extrusion. You can use three levels of beveling. Each level has its own height and outline settings, so you can control beveling by adjusting the height and changing the outline value, and then expanding or contracting the shape of the outline at the selected level. The Surface parameters let you control the segments of the extrusion and whether the sides are curved or straight. Typically, Bevel is used to bevel text, but it can also be used for other 2D shapes (see Figure B.1).

Bevel Profile

Bevel Profile is like a simplified Loft tool. You can use it to extrude a shape along a path. This modifier is an excellent tool for creating extruded forms such as elaborate picture frames or curved stairs. To use it, you draw an outline of the object, using a spline. Draw another open spline indicating the profile of the object. Select the outline and then apply the Bevel Profile modifier. In the Parameters rollout of the Bevel Profile modifier, click the Pick Profile button and select the spline you want to use as the profile. The outline is extruded to the shape of the profile (see Figure B.2).

Figure B.1

A sample of the Bevel modifier used on text

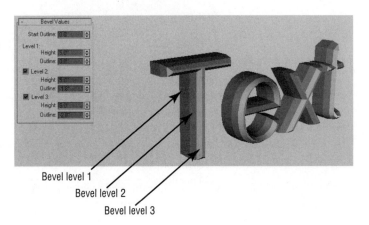

FIGURE B.2
An example of
the Bevel Profile
modifier

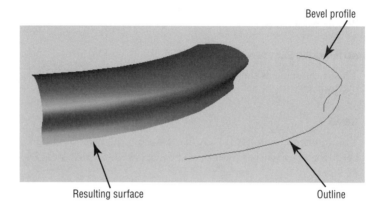

Bevel profile

Resulting surface

Outline

Once you've extruded a shape using the Bevel Profile modifier, you can modify the shape by adjusting either the profile spline or the original extruded shape.

CAMERA CORRECTION MODIFIER

Wide-angle camera views tend to exaggerate the three-point perspective view of tall objects. The tops of buildings, for example, appear to taper to a sharp point too quickly. The Camera Correction modifier enables you to reduce this distortion.

The Camera Correction modifier is unusual in that it isn't found in the Modifier List drop-down list. To use it, you must first select the camera you want to work on, right-click the camera, and then select Apply Camera Correction Modifier from the shortcut Quad menu.

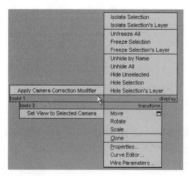

TIP   You can also apply the Camera Correction modifier by first selecting the camera and then choosing Modifiers ➢ Cameras ➢ Camera Correction.

Once you've done that, you can adjust the camera view using the options in the 2-Point Perspective Correction rollout that appears in the Modify tab of the Command Panel.

CAMERA MAP

At times, you may want an object to be invisible while it maintains a presence in a design. For example, suppose you have a fairly detailed background image that shows a garage, and you want to create the illusion of a car entering the garage. You can create a simple box with an opening similar in shape to the background garage opening, and then use the Camera Map modifier to blend the box into the background. Once you do that, you can animate the car to drive into the box. The net effect is that the car appears to drive into the garage in the background image in your final animation. This allows you to keep the geometry simple, yet still have an animation that shows a fair amount of detail.

The Camera Map modifier applies a planar UVW map to an object, and it aligns that map so that it's perpendicular to a specified camera. The map is typically the same as the background, giving the illusion of an invisible object. Since the object can cast and receive shadows, you can create different effects. For example, if you're using the Camera Match tool to match a building design to a photo of a building site, you can use the Camera Map modifier to include shadows on buildings in the background.

The Object-Space version of this modifier is a better choice when there is no camera motion. (See also "Matte/Shadow" later in this appendix.)

CAP HOLES

Some editing procedures will leave openings in a mesh. You may, for example, use the Slice modifier to slice a cylinder into two halves. Each half will have an opening at the Slice plane. The Cap Holes modifier can be used to close the openings.

In VIZ, a hole is a closed loop of edges with a single face. Cap Holes works best on planar holes, but it also works on non-planar holes.

CROSSSECTION

The CrossSection modifier is a powerful tool that lets you connect splines to form surfaces. (If you're an AutoCAD user, you can think of CrossSection as a super Rulesurf or Edgesurf command.) This modifier is called CrossSection because with it you can draw cross sections of an object and then join the cross sections together to form a surface.

When used in conjunction with the Surface modifier, CrossSection lets you form elaborate patch surfaces by defining the surface edge with two or more 3D splines. First you draw the splines; then you attach them to form a single object, using the Attach option in the Modify tab. You then apply the CrossSection modifier, which connects the vertices of the separate splines. Finally, you can "skin" over the splines with the Surface modifier (see Figure B.3).

The order in which the splines are created is as important as the location of the starting vertex of the splines. You want to be sure that the splines *point* in the same direction, with the beginning vertex of each spline placed in the same orientation relative to the rest of the spline. Figure B.4 shows how all the splines are oriented with their starting points to the left of the figure.

If you collapse the stack of a surface created using the CrossSection and Surface modifiers, you have a patch surface that can be edited in the same way as any other patch surface.

FIGURE B.3

Creating a surface using the CrossSection modifier and the Surface modifier

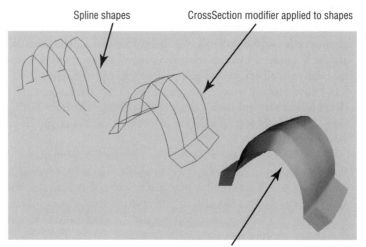

Spline shapes

CrossSection modifier applied to shapes

Surface modifier applied to cross-sectioned shapes

FIGURE B.4

Aligning the spine vertices

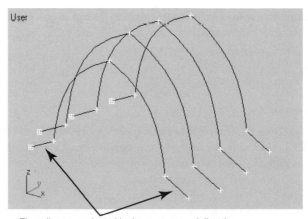

The splines are oriented in the same general direction.

DELETEMESH

You can think of the DeleteMesh modifier as a tool that lets you try out deletions in a mesh. Since it's a modifier, it can be placed anywhere in the modifier stack. Here's how it works: go to the sub-object level of an object and make a selection of the item you want to remove. If it's a surface patch or NURBS surface, you can isolate mesh surfaces for deletion by using the Mesh Select modifier. Once you've made your selection, apply the DeleteMesh modifier. The selection will be deleted. Since DeleteMesh is a modifier, you can restore the deleted items by removing DeleteMesh from the stack.

DELETEPATCH

You can think of the DeletePatch modifier as a tool that lets you try out deletions in a Patch object. Since it's a modifier, it can be placed anywhere in the modifier stack. It works in a similar way to the DeleteMesh modifier (described in the next section). Since DeletePatch is a modifier, you can restore the deleted items by removing DeleteMesh from the stack.

DELETESPLINE

Delete Spline is similar to DeleteMesh except that it works on splines rather than on meshes. Sub-object selections are limited to vertices, segments, and splines.

DISP APPROX

The Disp Approx modifier allows you to apply a displacement map to an object through a material channel. A tutorial for this modifier can be found in Chapter 14.

DISPLACE

The Displace modifier allows you to apply a displacement map directly to an object without having to do it through a material. This is similar to the Disp Approx modifier but no materials are required.

EDIT MESH

Like the Edit Spline modifier, Edit Mesh seems a bit redundant, as it duplicates the parameters for editable meshes. However, Edit Mesh offers great flexibility in editing meshes by allowing you to position edits in the modifier stack. You can experiment with changes in a mesh, maintain other modifiers and parameters that would otherwise be altered by mesh edits, or edit multiple mesh objects.

The Edit Mesh modifier uses much more memory than does a simple Editable Mesh object. For this reason, try to avoid using this modifier unless you really need the flexibility it offers.

EDIT PATCH

The Edit Patch modifier lets you edit an object as if it were an Editable Patch object (see Appendix C for more on Editable Patch objects). The Edit Patch modifier uses a good deal of RAM, as it must make a copy of the selected geometry in RAM in order to perform its functions. Nevertheless, Edit Patch is offered for those occasions when you want to try out options, or when prior modifiers or parametric options must be left in place.

EDIT SPLINE

The Edit Spline modifier may seem redundant, because it duplicates the parameters for Spline objects, with a few limitations. Edit Spline offers flexibility in editing splines by allowing you to position edits in the modifier stack. For example, you can use Edit Spline to test out spline edits. Since it's a modifier, you can easily discard changes made using Edit Spline by deleting it from the modifier stack—something you cannot do using the basic parameters for a spline. Edit Spline is also useful for applying changes to several shapes at once by applying a single Edit Spline modifier to a set of objects. You may also want to maintain other modifiers that would otherwise be affected by changes to the basic parameters of the shape.

WARNING *The Edit Spline modifier uses much more memory than does a simple Editable Spline object. For this reason, try to avoid using this modifier unless you really need the flexibility it offers.*

EXTRUDE

Extrude is used to extend 2D shapes into the third dimension in a linear fashion. Both VIZ shapes and shapes imported from other CAD programs can be extruded. The Extrude modifier offers the option to cap ends, which closes the openings formed by the top and bottom of an extruded, closed shape. You can also select the type of mesh that is created with Extrude.

FACE EXTRUDE

The Face Extrude modifier allows you to extrude selected faces of a mesh. You must first make a selection of faces on the sub-object level of an object. You can then apply the Face Extrude modifier to affect the selected faces. Although you can use the Extrude option at the sub-object level of a mesh, the Face Extrude modifier offers a few additional options, such as Scale and Extrude from Center. You can achieve a beveled effect with these options.

FFD ($2 \times 2 \times 2$, $3 \times 3 \times 3$, $4 \times 4 \times 4$)

The Free Form Deformation modifier lets you deform objects in a general way by offering lattice control points to pull and stretch objects. When you apply the FFD modifier, a lattice box appears around the selected object. You can use the control points on the box to push or pull the object's form (see Figure B.5). The lattice box is a type of gizmo and doesn't represent actual geometry.

The FFD modifier is offered in three types: $2 \times 2 \times 2$, $3 \times 3 \times 3$, and 4 4×4. Each type places a different box around the object. The FFD $2 \times 2 \times 2$ modifier, for example, places a box with control points at each corner.

FIGURE B.5

A chair with the FFD $4 \times 4 \times 4$ modifier

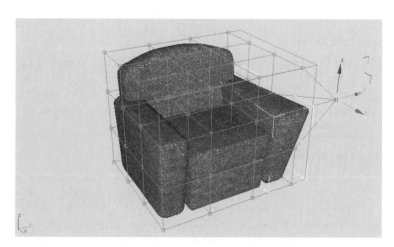

FFD (Box)

The FFD (Box) modifier is similar in function to the FFD modifier but adds the capability to control the number of control points. With FFD (Box), you aren't limited to the 2 × 2 × 2 through 4 × 4 × 4 lattice of the FFD modifier, as shown in Figure B.6.

FIGURE B.6

An FFD (Box) modifier applied to a chair using a 5 × 6 × 7 lattice

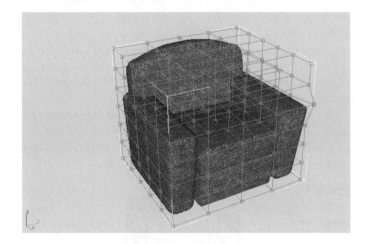

FFD (Cyl)

Like the FFD (Box) modifier, FFD (Cyl) allows you to set the number of control points in the control lattice, but instead of a box, FFD (Cyl) places a cylindrical lattice around the object.

Fillet/Chamfer

The Fillet/Chamfer modifier lets you convert a spline vertex into a filleted (rounded) corner or a chamfered corner. It works only on vertices that connect straight segments, and it won't join two disconnected segments. To use it, select a shape and then apply the Fillet/Chamfer modifier. The Vertex sub-object level is automatically opened, allowing you to select a vertex for editing. You can either select a vertex and enter a fillet or chamfer value in the Edit Vertex rollout, or set a fillet or chamfer value first and then select a vertex and click the Apply button.

HSDS

HSDS stands for Hierarchical Subdivision Surfaces. The HSDS modifier subdivides the surface of an object. You can use it to help smooth out a curved surface of an object without reducing the object to a mesh.

NOTE   *The HSDS modifier was developed by mental images, the makers of mental ray.*

LATHE

Lathe is used to revolve 2D shapes into the third dimension in a circular fashion. Both VIZ shapes and shapes imported from other CAD programs can be extruded. The Lathe modifier offers the option to cap ends, which closes the openings formed by the beginning and end of an extruded shape. You can also select the type of mesh that is created with Lathe.

LATTICE

The Lattice modifier lets you convert the segments of a shape or the edges of an object into joints and struts. The effect is similar to that of converting a mesh object into a wireframe, but expressing the wireframe as renderable geometry (see Figure B.7). A geodesic dome is a good architectural example of using a latticed geosphere.

You can change the selected object so that only its vertices appear, as shown in Figure B.8.

In addition, Lattice allows you to display both vertices and struts to form some unusual objects. You have control over the number of sides of the struts or the type of geometry used at the vertices. You can also change the scale of the joints and struts.

FIGURE B.7
A tapered cylinder converted into a lattice

FIGURE B.8
A tapered cylinder with its vertices converted into octahedrons

LS MESH

This modifier refines a Lightscape mesh object (imported from Lightscape). This modifier is designed to be used in conjunction with the Lightscape material, and the LS Colors modifier.

MAP SCALAR

Apply this version of the modifier when you want the material map to maintain its scale relative to the scale of the object. Changes to the object's scale will affect the associated map's scale also. Use the WSM version to lock the associated map's scale to world space instead.

MATERIAL

When you apply a Multi/Sub-Object material to an object, you need to assign a material ID to selected faces of the object in order to correlate the sub-material with the selected faces (see Chapter 7 for a look at Multi/Sub-Object materials). The Material modifier lets you do just that.

The Material modifier isn't needed for editable meshes. It's intended for other types of objects that don't offer access to mesh-level editing. For those objects, you need to apply the Mesh Select modifier first in order to select mesh faces. You can then apply the Material modifier to assign a material ID.

MATERIALBYELEMENT

The MaterialByElement modifier applies the different materials of a Multi/Sub-Object material to the different elements of an object. This is done randomly.

MESHSMOOTH

MeshSmooth does just what the name implies: it smoothes a mesh so that sharp corners are rounded. It does this by increasing the complexity of the mesh. The smoothed form can be edited by using control vertices (CVs) in a way similar to NURBS CVs (see Appendix C for more on NURBS CVs). See Chapter 15 for a detailed description of this modifier.

MIRROR

Mirror performs the same function as the Mirror tool on the VIZ main toolbar to the left of the VIZ window. Since it's a modifier, you can control the mirror effect as part of the object's modifier stack.

MULTIRES

The MultiRes modifier is similar to the Optimize modifier, with the added option to specify the level of simplification as a percentage.

NOISE

The Noise modifier randomly repositions the vertices of an object to simulate an uneven surface. You can adjust the strength of the noise to create a relatively smooth surface or a mountainous terrain. The effectiveness of Noise is dependent on the amount of segmentation of the object.

NORMAL

When you create geometry in VIZ, the normals of the geometry are pointing outward and you don't have control over their orientation. You can gain control of the normals of VIZ geometry by collapsing the stack and reducing the geometry to an editable mesh. Unfortunately, once you do that, the geometry loses its parametric functions. The Normal modifier lets you control the normals of VIZ geometry without forcing you to give up parametric functions.

NORMALIZE SPLINE

The Normalize Spline modifier places additional control points along a spline. The control points are spaced at regular intervals. This can be useful when using splines for motion paths where a constant speed is required.

OPTIMIZE

The Optimize modifier simplifies the geometry of an object while maintaining an acceptable level of detail. This offers the benefits of faster rendering time and less RAM usage.

PATCH DEFORM

This modifier allows you to deform an object based on the form of a Patch object. A Patch object is an object that can be formed into a smooth, curved surface by editing its vertices. You can, for example, create a plane and then convert the plane into an editable patch. The vertices of the editable patch can then be edited to shape the plane into a smooth, curved surface of any shape you want. Such a surface can be used to deform other objects, using the Patch Deform modifier.

The object remains in its current location while being deformed. See also the WSM version of this modifier.

PATH DEFORM

The Path Deform modifier works in a way similar to the Patch Deform modifier but uses a spline or NURBS curve instead of a Patch object. For example, you can use this modifier to deform an object along the path of the spline. An example of this would be the curving of text to conform to the shape of a round column or sphere. The object does not move to the path with this modifier. See the WSM version also.

PRESERVE

The Preserve modifier lets you "clean up" a mesh that has been edited on a vertex sub-object level. Often when a mesh is edited by moving vertices, the resulting form takes on a rough appearance. The Preserve modifier will help smooth out that rough appearance.

To use the Preserve modifier, you must first make a copy of the object you wish to modify. Make your changes to the copy's vertices, and then, with the vertex sub-object level still active, apply the Preserve modifier. Use the Pick Original button of the Preserve modifier to select the original object from which you made the copy. You can then use the other Preserve modifier controls to adjust the mesh.

PUSH

If you need to create a bulging or shrunken appearance, you can use Push. The Push modifier has a single parameter that pushes or pulls the vertices of an object from its center.

RELAX

Relax is similar to Push, but instead of pushing vertices out from the object's center, Relax softens the corner edges of an object or generally relaxes an object's shape to something smoother, with less-pronounced surface change.

RENDERABLE SPLINE

New!

This new modifier lets you set the renderable parameters of spline objects including those that are brought into VIZ through importing or file linking (see Chapter 16) from an AutoCAD-based application without collapsing the splines to editable splines.

TIP   Splines made in VIZ do not require the use of the Renderable Spline modifier because they already have the same controls available in their Rendering rollout.

RIPPLE

Ripple modifies an object's surface to produce a concentric rippled effect. You can control the amplitude, wavelength, phase, and decay of the ripple.

SHELL

New!

This new modifier extrudes a flat or curved two-dimensional or three-dimensional surface, giving it volume and solidity. See Chapter 5 for a tutorial.

SKEW

The Skew modifier skews an object, as shown in Figure B.9. You can control the direction and strength of the skew. You can also limit the skew to a section of the object.

FIGURE B.9
A cylinder skewed using the Skew modifier

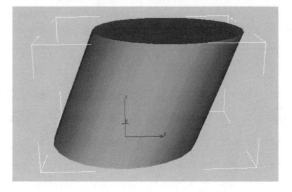

SLICE

Slice allows you to define a plane through which objects can be cut. There are two ways that Slice can affect an object. The most obvious is to split an object into two objects. Slice gives you the option to keep both parts of the split object, or you may hide one part. Slice also lets you refine an object along the intersection of the slice plane with the object.

SMOOTH

The Smooth modifier applies auto-smoothing to the surface of an object. Although you can usually apply smoothing to an editable mesh at the sub-object level, Smooth allows you to control the smoothing as an item in the mesh's modifier stack.

SPHERIFY

The Spherify modifier lets you distort an object into a spherical shape. It offers a single parameter that lets you control the amount of distortion you can apply to the object.

SQUEEZE

Squeeze lets you move the vertices of an object along the Z axis. The vertices closest to the object's pivot point are moved the farthest. If you apply Squeeze to a box, for example, the vertices at the center of the top surface are pushed or pulled farther than the ones toward the edge, creating a bulging effect or a cupping effect, as shown in Figure B.10.

Squeeze can also be made to affect the vertices along the Y and Z axes to create a flare or a crimping effect, as shown in Figure B.11.

STL CHECK

If you plan to export your VIZ model for use with stereolithography (STL) equipment, you can use the STL Check modifier to check your design for correct export.

STRETCH

If you just want to squash or stretch an object along a single axis, you can do so using the Stretch modifier. If you apply a positive Stretch value to this modifier, the object elongates along the selected axis while contracting along the other two axes, as shown on the left in Figure B.12. Applying a negative Stretch value causes the object to shrink along the selected axis while bulging out in the plane of the other two axes, as shown on the right in Figure B.12.

FIGURE B.10
Using the Squeeze modifier on a box

 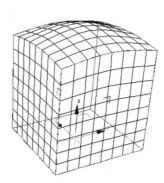

FIGURE B.11
Flaring and
crimping a box

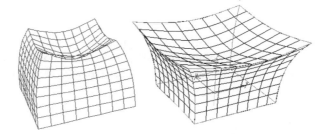

FIGURE B.12
Sample boxes that
are stretched and
squashed using the
Stretch modifier

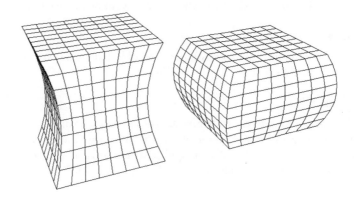

SUBDIVIDE

The Subdivide modifier allows you to manually apply a radiosity mesh to an object. Subdivide works . in a similar way to the Radiosity Meshing parameters discussed in Chapter 10, but instead of applying a mesh globally, Subdivide lets you apply a mesh to single objects or even sub-object levels. Since it's a modifier, it can be edited directly from the modifier stack.

SUBSTITUTE

The Substitute modifier lets you substitute one object for another. This feature is useful if you have a very complex design and want to simplify part of it to help speed up editing or rendering. You can substitute a simple object for a complex one while editing. Then, at render time, you can have VIZ restore the original complex object. You may also do the reverse for quicker rendering of sample views. The Substitute object can come from the current design or from an external file. Substitute objects are removed by deleting the Substitute modifier from the stack.

The Substitute modifier is view-dependent, so when you apply it, you must choose the object you want to substitute and the viewport that is to be affected. You can select an object from an external file using the Select XRef Object option in the Substitute parameters.

SURFACE

The Surface modifier applies a patch surface over a set of interconnected spline segments. The segments must all be of one object and must be joined at their vertices. The Surface modifier applies patch surfaces to three- and four-sided polygon formations of the interconnected segments. See "CrossSection" earlier in this section and "Understanding Patches" in Appendix C. Also see the tutorial in Chapter 5 that uses this modifier.

SURF DEFORM

The Surf Deform modifier works in a way similar to the Patch Deform modifier but uses a NURBS surface instead of a Patch object. You can use this modifier to deform an object, based on the shape of a NURBS surface, similar to the way you would use a patch surface.

TAPER

The Taper modifier allows you to taper an object along a specified axis. See Chapters 2 and 4 for a more detailed look at the Taper modifier.

TESSELLATE

The Tessellate modifier divides the faces of a surface into multiple, smaller faces. It can have the effect of smoothing a surface. You can also use it to increase the number of faces in a region of a surface for further editing. If Tessellate is applied to an object, all the faces of the object are tessellated. You may also enter the Face sub-object level to select a specific set of faces for tessellation (See Figure B.13).

FIGURE B.13
A surface before and
after tessellation

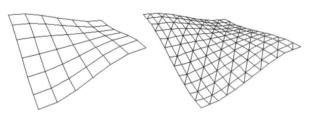

Tessellate is also an option in the Face, Polygon, and Element sub-object levels of editable meshes.

TRIM/EXTEND

The Trim/Extend modifier works just like the Trim/Extend options in the sub-object level of Shape objects. You can trim open spline segments to other existing, overlapping segments within a single object, or you can extend open segments to other segments within the same object that lie in the direction of the segment end. The Trim/Extend modifier is offered for those situations where it's preferable to include Trim/Extend operations within the modifier stack.

Turn To Modifiers

Turn To modifiers let you convert objects from one type to another with the modifier stack. You can then apply other modifiers to control the converted object.

Turn to Poly   Converts a triangular face edge to a polygon.

Turn to Patch   Converts objects to patches.

Turn to Mesh   Converts objects to meshes.

Twist

The Twist modifier deforms an object by twisting it along a selected axis. Figure B.14 shows a box that has a Twist modifier.

Figure B.14
A twisted box

Unwrap UVW

This modifier is used to assign planar texture maps to sub-object selections. Unwrap UVW can also assign UVW coordinates to a model. The Automatic Unwrap UVW modifier is applied during the Render to Texture process where each object is UV mapped so that the resulting textures can be applied to the object surfaces.

UVW Map

This modifier, also called UVW Mapping, lets you control the orientation of maps on the surface of an object. It also lets you control the size and aspect ratio of a map in relation to the object to which it is mapped. UVW Map offers a set of mapping types that allow you to tailor the map to the shape of an object. For example, if you are applying a material to a cylindrical shape, you can use the Cylindrical Mapping parameter that projects the map in a cylindrical form. A UVW Map gizmo gives you a visual reference for the location and orientation of the mapping parameters. You can use the transform tools to adjust the Map gizmo.

UVW XFORM

You can use the UVW XForm modifier to control the way a material map is applied to an object. Many VIZ objects offer built-in mapping, such as the general coordinates for standard primitives and lofted objects. Unfortunately, those built-in mapping coordinates don't offer the tiling and offset options found in the UVW Map modifier. The UVW XForm modifier is offered to allow tiling and offset control over mapping in objects that have built-in mapping.

WAVE

The Wave modifier produces a wave effect on the selected geometry. The number of segments in the object determines the smoothness of the wave. More segments produce a smoother wave.

XFORM

The XForm modifier is intended to allow transforms within specific locations in the modifier stack. This makes it useful for trial purposes, since you can easily delete the XForm modifier from the stack—something you cannot do with the standard XForm tools on the main toolbar.

Materials and Maps

The main part of *Mastering Autodesk VIZ 2005* focuses on a few of the materials available in VIZ, and for 80% of your projects, your needs won't go beyond the material types shown in the tutorials of this book. For the remaining 20%, you'll find the range of materials offered by VIZ indispensable.

NOTE *The specialized mental ray material and map shaders are covered in Chapter 11. You can refer to the User Reference for detailed notes on the many mental ray shaders that are available.*

This section provides a description of all the materials available in the VIZ Material/Map Browser for use with the default scanline renderer. Just as with the preceding Modifiers section, you may want to read about these material options for future reference.

Materials (Blue Sphere)

When you select both the Materials and Maps options in the Show group of the Material/Map Browser, you'll see a list of options that show either a blue sphere or a green parallelogram. The items at the top of the list with the blue spheres are materials; the green parallelograms indicate the maps. The main difference between the two is that the materials in the list represent types of materials available, whereas the maps are components of materials.

NONE

This option allows you to remove a material or map specification.

ADVANCED LIGHTING OVERRIDE

This material is used to fine-tune legacy radiosity materials. This material gives you direct control over the radiosity properties of a material. This material is an adjunct to the base material and has no effect in non-radiosity renderings. You can control properties like reflectance, color bleed, and transmittance. It used to be called Radiosity Override in VIZ 4.

TIP   The Architectural material has an Advanced Lighting Override rollout with the same controls available in this material.

ARCHITECTURAL

New!

This is the new default material in VIZ 2005. It is physically accurate and designed to be used with the radiosity renderer. See Chapter 7 for more information and a tutorial on its use.

BLEND

You can mix two materials into a single material by using the Blend material. Blend offers the ability to control the strength of each material.

COMPOSITE

Composite materials allow you to superimpose up to 10 materials. You can apply additive or subtractive opacity to each material or control the strength of the individual materials.

DOUBLE SIDED

You can assign a different material to the front and back of an object with a single surface by using the Double Sided material. When you select this material type, you can use the Double Sided basic parameters to select a material for the Facing material and another material for the Back material.

LIGHTSCAPE MTL

If you work with Lightscape and you want to import or export your Lightscape models to VIZ, VIZ needs a way to handle the translation of Lightscape materials. This is where the Lightscape Mtl material comes in. Lightscape Mtl allows VIZ to manage the transport of material properties between the two programs.

MATTE/SHADOW

A Matte/Shadow object has the effect of making itself and anything behind it invisible. It's most frequently used in conjunction with environment maps where a design is to be blended into a photograph. For example, suppose you have a fairly detailed background image of a photograph that shows a garage, and you want to create the illusion of a car entering the garage. You can create a simple box with an opening that's similar in shape to the background garage opening, and then apply the Matte/Shadow material to the box. Once this is done, you can animate the car to drive into the box. The net effect is that the car appears to drive into the garage in the background.

You can also use Matte/Shadow objects to add shadows to objects in a background image. For example, suppose you are using the camera match tools to match a car design to a background image of the building's site. In the real world, your design would cast shadows on the ground, but in your VIZ design, you would leave out the ground so that the ground in the background image could come through in the rendering. Unfortunately, when you do this, the design doesn't cast a shadow on the ground. This unnatural absence of a shadow creates an odd, floating appearance. You can add a ground plane to your design and assign the Matte/Shadow material to this ground plane. The ground plane will be invisible when it's rendered; yet it will receive a shadow, creating the illusion that the car is casting a shadow on the ground of the background image.

Figure B.15 shows a rendering of the car from Chapter 15, using the background from the camera match exercise of Chapter 15. Notice the shadow of the car in the image. To obtain that shadow, a surface was placed under the car, and a Matte/Shadow material was applied to the surface. The Receive Shadow option was also turned on for the Matte/Shadow material.

FIGURE B.15
A 3D car model is rendered onto a background image.

Matte/Shadow materials behave in a way similar to the effect of the Camera Map modifier. The main difference here is that the Camera Map modifier is view dependent, while the Matte/Shadow material affects all views.

MULTI/SUB-OBJECT

The Multi/Sub-Object material is like a collection of separate materials under a single material name. Multi/Sub-Object materials are useful in situations where you want to assign multiple materials to a single object. See Chapters 7 and 15 for more on the use of Multi/Sub-Object materials.

RAYTRACE

Ray Traced materials reflect and refract light in a way that simulates one of the ways that light actually works. The term *raytrace* comes from the way the program traces the path of light from a pixel in the rendered image back to the light source. Ray Traced materials are best used for transparent or shiny materials, such as glass or water that reflect or refract light. Figure B.16 shows a rendering of a sample file from VIZ. The goblet in the figure uses a Ray Traced material.

SHELL

This material is used for storing and rendering baked textures created by the Render to Texture feature when the Baked Materials setting is Save Source (Create Shell), which is the default setting (see Chapter 17). The Save Source (Create Shell) option allows for the creation of a shell material while saving the original one with options for displaying either in the viewport and/or rendering.

FIGURE B.16

A goblet using a Ray
Traced material

SHELLAC

A Shellac material lets you create a shellac effect by combining two materials. One, called the Base material, is used for the underlying base. The second, the Shellac material, is applied over the base with some transparency. You can control the transparency and blending of the Shellac material.

STANDARD

The Standard material was formerly the default material in the Material Editor. It's covered in some depth through the tutorials in this book. It offers a wide variety of shaders, and you can include several different types of maps (described in the next section). With the available combination of shaders and maps, you can create nearly any effect you need for materials.

TOP/BOTTOM

The Top/Bottom material lets you assign a different material to the top and bottom of an object. An example of this might be a two-tone car body. You can control the position and blending of the two materials.

Maps (Green Parallelogram)

The standard materials discussed in this book allow you to apply maps in several different ways. Maps can be used to control reflection, opacity, bumpiness, and transparency, and so on. This book focuses on the use of bitmaps for most of the material map applications, but there are several other map types that you'll want to know about. Here is a listing describing the different map types and how they might be used.

NONE

This option is used to remove a map assignment from a material.

BITMAP

The Bitmap option is described thoroughly in this book. It allows you to use any bitmap image as a material map. It's perhaps the most flexible option, since thousands of bitmaps can be acquired from a wide variety of sources. You can create fairly credible materials through the use of bitmaps.

CELLULAR

The Cellular map is a procedural map that creates a variety of cellular, or granular, material effects. With this map, you can create materials ranging from terrazzo to polystyrene foam. The VIZ Online Reference also mentions using the Cellular material for the ocean surface. The Cellular map is fairly complex, so you may want to experiment with it on your own to see what types of results it produces.

CHECKER

The Checker map is a procedural map that creates a checkerboard pattern. You can assign a color or another map to the squares of the checkerboard. You can also add noise to create a more natural appearance.

COMBUSTION

Works in conjunction with Discreet combustion compositing software.

COMPOSITE

A Composite map is a map formed from the combination of other maps. Alpha channels are used to control blending of the composite maps.

DENT

Dent is a procedural 3D map that produces a random, dented surface. You can control the depth and size of dents through the map's parameters. You can also apply other maps to the Dent map to create a multicolored surface.

FALLOFF

The Falloff map is primarily used as an opacity map. When applied to a sphere as an opacity map in its default mode, the sphere appears most transparent at its center and least transparent around its edges, like a clear balloon or glass ball. This is the same effect as the Falloff setting in the Extended Parameters rollout of the Standard material, with some added control.

FLAT MIRROR

The Flat Mirror map is used primarily as a reflection map. It produces a mirror-like finish on a flat surface, reflecting the environment and objects nearby. To use this material, you must apply it directly to coplanar faces of an object on a sub-object level. This can be done by including Flat Mirror in the reflection channel in a sub-material of a Multi/Sub-Object material.

GRADIENT

The Gradient map lets you create a color gradient using two or three colors. You can perturb the gradient by applying a noise parameter.

GRADIENT RAMP

The Gradient Ramp map is similar to the Gradient map, but it allows for a greater range of colors.

MARBLE

The Marble map simulates the appearance of marble. You can control the color of the marble veins and the background. You can also adjust the size of the veins.

MASK

The Mask map uses two maps. One map is used as a base map, while the second map is a mask. The mask controls the visibility of the base map.

MIX

The Mix map allows you to combine two colors, two maps, or a color and a map.

NOISE

The Noise map creates random noise in the form of a grayscale pattern. It looks a bit like the static from an older TV set. Noise can be used to create a bump pattern or a granite surface. Parameters let you adjust the scale and intensity of the noise.

OUTPUT

Bitmap maps offer control over the bitmap image through the Output rollout. Such controls aren't available for many of the other procedural maps. The Output map is like a modifier for procedural maps that gives you the same Output rollout options as Bitmap maps. See Chapter 7 for a detailed look at the Output rollout for Bitmap maps.

PERLIN MARBLE

Perlin Marble creates a marble pattern using what is called the Perlin Turbulence algorithm. The Perlin pattern has a more swirled appearance.

PLANET

The Planet map is designed to simulate the surface of a planet, complete with oceans and continents. It's designed to be used primarily as a diffuse map.

RAYTRACE

Like the Raytrace material, the Raytrace map provides Ray Traced reflection and refraction for objects to which it is assigned. It's most suitable for highly reflective surfaces or transparent materials. See "Raytrace" in the earlier Materials section for more information.

REFLECT/REFRACT

The Reflect/Refract map simulates reflection and refraction of backgrounds in the environment of the design. It does this by mapping the environment onto a cube surrounding the mapped object, and then using that cube as a reflection map.

RGB MULTIPLY

The RGB Multiply map combines the effects of two maps. This map is commonly used for bump maps.

RGB TINT

The RGB Tint map lets you apply a color tint to another map. You first insert the RGB Tint map; then, through its parameters, you attach a second map. You can then use the R, G, or B color swatch in the RGB Tint parameters to tint the second map.

SMOKE

The Smoke map creates a smoke-like pattern. It's more commonly used as an opacity map for simulating smoke.

SPECKLE

The Speckle map creates a speckled appearance using two colors, two maps, or a color and a map. You can use it for diffuse or bump maps to create a speckled-egg look.

SPLAT

Splat produces a splattered-paint look. Its controls are similar to those for Speckle. You can use two colors, two maps, or a color and a map to produce the splat effect.

STUCCO

The Stucco map is designed to create a stucco surface and is commonly used as a bump map.

SWIRL

Swirl creates a swirl pattern from two colors or maps.

THIN WALL REFRACTION

The Thin Wall Refraction map creates the illusion of refracting glass. When applied to a thin box representing a glass panel, it offsets the view behind the glass panel, simulating a refracted appearance. This map requires less time to render than the Reflect/Refract map or the Raytrace map. Therefore, in well-lit, close-up views, it offers a good alternative to those maps.

TILES

The Tiles map is a procedural map that allows you to parametrically control the map's appearance. You can control the type of tile joint as well as the color and texture of the tile pattern through this map.

NOTE   The Tiles map was called the Bricks map in previous versions of VIZ.

VERTEX COLOR

You can apply regions of color to an editable mesh by assigning color to vertices in the mesh. These vertex color assignments become visible when you apply the Vertex Color map to the mesh. To apply a color to a vertex, select the mesh and then click the Modify tab. Click the Vertex option in the Modify Tabs Selection rollout, select a vertex or set of vertices, scroll down to the Vertex Color group, and edit the colors. After assigning a color to a vertex, create a material that uses the Vertex Color map as a diffuse map; then apply the material to the object.

WATER

The Water map simulates the surface of water. It can be used as a diffuse and bump map at the same time to create a rippling, water-like surface. You can control the amplitude and size of ripples.

WOOD

The Wood map simulates the qualities of wood grain. It is a 3D procedural map, which means that the wood-grain effect is carried through the volume of the object to which it is applied. If you cut a notch out of the object, for example, you'll see the grain accurately reproduced in the notch, as in a real piece of wood. You have the option of controlling two colors for the wood grain, the grain thickness, and the amount of noise or straightness in the grain.

Appendix C

Patches and NURBS Surfaces

THERE ARE TWO VIZ objects that haven't been covered in the main body of this book, although they certainly play a major role in VIZ designs. Patches and NURBS surfaces are objects that allow you to form curved surfaces quickly by deforming their geometry. If you want to be able to sculpt a shape, you'll want to know about these objects. Patches and NURBS are often used in character animation and other design disciplines in which forming curved shapes are a major part of the design tool set.

Understanding Patches

A patch object is a collection of Bézier patches that consist of vertices, edges, and surfaces similar to mesh objects. The main difference between mesh objects and patches is that the patch vertices can be controlled using Bézier handles. These handles can be moved to apply a curve to the edges of the patch. The segments connecting patch vertices are splines that can be curved. Meshes always have straight-line segments connecting their vertices. In a sense, patches are like splines that have surfaces.

Perhaps the best way to understand patches is to see how one can be created and edited. Most of the standard primitives can be converted into editable patches. Let's take a look at how a plane standard primitive can be converted into an editable patch and then edited.

Converting a Plane into an Editable Patch

First, create a plane using the Standard Primitives option of the Geometry tool in the Create tab of the Command Panel. The Length Segs and Width Segs parameters will influence the number of vertices of the patch. Once you've created the plane, use the Edit Stack tool in the Modify tab to convert the surface to an editable patch. The plane will appear to be subdivided into smaller segments.

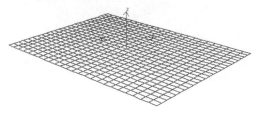

These subdivisions are a visual aid. The resulting editable patch contains vertices at the locations of the segment corners of the original plane. You can see the vertices clearly if you select the Vertex sub-object level from the Selection rollout of the editable patch.

Notice that the rows and columns of vertices are in the same location as the segments of the original plane standard primitive. If you increase the number of segments in the plane, the resulting editable patch will contain more vertices.

At the Vertex sub-object level of the editable patch, you can move the vertices to sculpt the surface. The subdivisions on the plane, called *view steps,* let you see the deformation of the surface as you move the vertices, as shown in Figure C.1.

The Surface group of the editable patch's Geometry rollout lets you control the number of view steps within each patch.

You may also use the Edge or Patch sub-object level to sculpt the surface of an editable patch.

Converting Other Standard Primitives to Editable Patches

You can convert any standard primitive into an editable patch object. The resulting patch depends on the type of object you use for the conversion. A sphere, for example, becomes an editable patch whose surface facets are arranged like those of a geosphere.

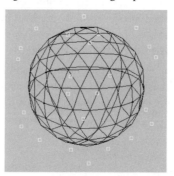

The density of vertices is dependent on the number of segments of the original sphere from which the editable patch is derived.

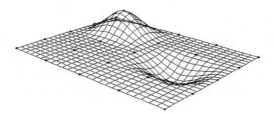

When a box is converted to an editable patch, the corners of the box become the vertices of the editable patch. There are no intermediate vertices on the surface of the box.

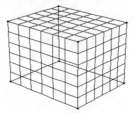

At the sub-object level, the corner vertices display Bézier handles that can be moved to deform the box.

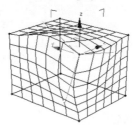

You can deform the surface of any box by using the Patch Deform modifier. This modifier allows you to deform the surface of an object, based on the deformation of an editable patch. For example, you can apply the deformation of the patch shown in Figure C.1 to the top of a box to achieve the shape shown in Figure C.2.

FIGURE C.2
An editable mesh
box with its top de-
formed by using the
Patch Deform modi-
fier and the editable
patch shown in Fig-
ure C.1

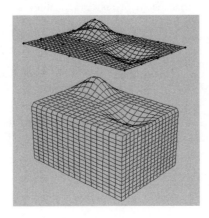

You first select the object or sub-object level you want to deform and then add the Patch Deform modifier. The modifier then offers a button that lets you select the patch surface that you want to use to describe the deformation. You can then sculpt the object by editing the patch surface.

Cylinders, cones, tubes, and pyramids will all convert to editable patches, with their vertices limited to the edges of the planar surfaces. For example, a cylinder will convert to an editable patch with vertices at the top and bottom surfaces in the four quadrants of the cylinder, as shown in Figure C.3.

FIGURE C.3

A cylinder showing the vertices of the editable patch

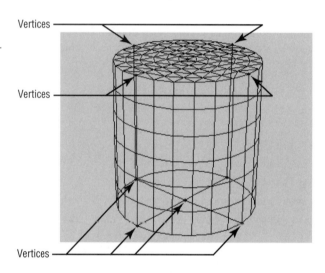

Understanding NURBS

NURBS stands for non-uniform rational basis-splines. I won't try to explain what all of that means. Just be aware that NURBS have their basis in a mathematical structure that plays an invisible role in their formation. Don't let this scare you away from using them. You can use NURBS surfaces and curves in a very practical way without delving too deeply into their structural underpinnings. However, it will help to understand their behavior on a practical level.

Looking at NURBS Curves

Let's start by looking at a NURBS curve and how it behaves. If you click the Shape tool in the Create tab and then select NURBS Curves from the Shapes drop-down list, you are presented with two options: Point Curve and CV Curve. The Point Curve option lets you draw a curve by indicating points through which the curve passes, as shown in Figure C.4.

The CV Curve option lets you draw a curve by indicating the location of *control vertices*. A single control vertex is referred to as a CV. Instead of passing through a CV, the curve is "pulled" in the direction of the CV, as shown in Figure C.5.

FIGURE C.4
A NURBS curve
using the Point
Curve option

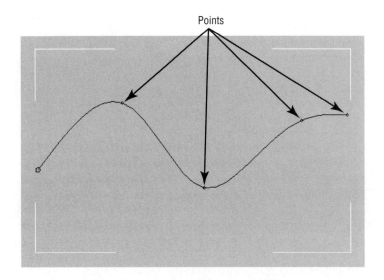

FIGURE C.5
A NURBS curve
using CVs

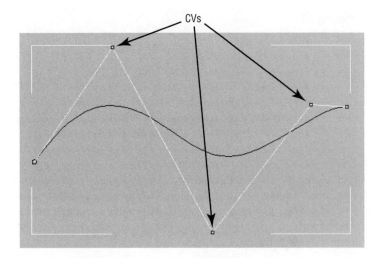

VIZ offers parameters that allow you to control the weight, or pull, of a CV to sharpen or soften the curve at the CV location. Multiple CVs can be combined to increase the pull at a given location. For example, you can combine three CVs at one point to form a corner, as shown in Figure C.6. You can also increase the weight of a single CV. CVs can be added using the options in the Refine group of the CV parameters.

FIGURE C.6
A curve shown with three CVs combined in one location

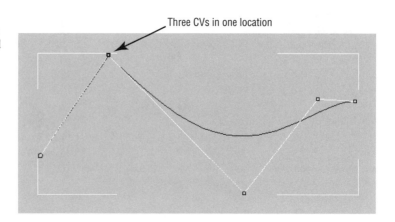

Three CVs in one location

A NURBS surface works in a way similar to a NURBS curve. Vertices of a NURBS surface can be either points on the curve or CVs. Figure C.7 shows a NURBS surface with point curves. The surface makes contact with the vertex. Note that the segments of the surface aren't related to the number of vertices in the surface.

FIGURE C.7
A NURBS surface using point curves

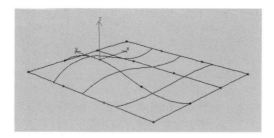

CVs in a NURBS surface exert a pull on the surface but aren't necessarily on the surface itself, just as CVs on a curve aren't on the curve itself (see Figure C.8).

FIGURE C.8
A NURBS surface using CVs

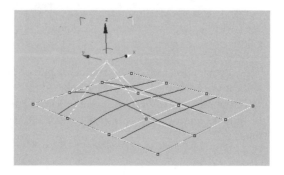

Just as with NURBS splines, you can increase or decrease the pull of a CV by adjusting its weight parameter. You gain access to the weight parameter of a CV by entering the Surface CV sub-object level of the NURBS object. You can then select a vertex and adjust its weight parameter in the CV rollout.

Creating NURBS Surfaces from Standard Primitives

You can create a single NURBS surface by selecting the Geometry tool in the Create tab and then selecting the NURBS Surfaces option from the Geometry drop-down list. You are presented with the Point Surf and CV Surf options. Each of these options lets you create a flat NURBS surface that you can edit by adjusting its vertices.

Just as with the editable patch, you can convert standard primitives into NURBS surfaces by selecting the NURBS option from the Edit Stack button in the modifier stack. Such converted surfaces use CVs by default. Unlike editable patches, the vertices are distributed over the surface of boxes, cylinders, cones, and pyramids, giving you a bit more flexibility in shaping these objects. However, the number of vertices of a converted NURBS mesh doesn't correlate with the number of segments of the original object, as shown in Figure C.9.

You can increase the number of vertices on a surface or change CVs to points on the surface by using the Convert Surface dialog box. To access this dialog box, first select the NURBS surface and then select the Surface sub-object level. Select the surfaces you want to edit; then click the Convert Surface button in the Surface Common rollout. The Convert Surface dialog box appears.

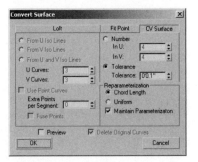

The Fit Point will change the vertices defining the surface from CVs to points on the surface. Click the Number radio button and adjust the In U and In V options to change the number of vertices on the surface.

FIGURE C.9

The box to the left is the original box, and the one to the right is the converted NURBS box

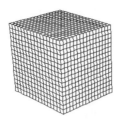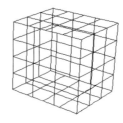

Applying a NURBS Deformation to an Object

You can use the Surf Deform modifier to apply the deformation of a NURBS surface to the surface of another object. This works in a way similar to the Patch Deform modifier described in the earlier section, "Converting Other Standard Primitives to Editable Patches." You first select the object you want to deform; then you add the Surf Deform modifier. This modifier then offers a button that lets you select the NURBS surface that you want to use to describe the deformation. If you need to, you can then turn the NURBS surface off to hide it from view.

You can use the Surf Deform modifier in conjunction with a NURBS surface to add the trough in the roof of the Ronchamp tutorial in Chapter 5. Instead of using the Soft Selection parameters to move the vertices of the roof, you can create the trough shape using a NURBS surface and then apply the NURBS surface deformation to the roof. You would do this after the Boolean operation to remove the smaller towers from the roof.

Helpers and Effects

MASTERING AUTODESK VIZ 2005 focuses on the tools you'll need to create presentations of your designs. There are a few tools that you'll want to know about that weren't discussed in the main part of the book.

Helpers are nonrendering objects that can assist you in creating your model. Some helpers are designed specifically for animation, while others help you take measurements in your design. Another set of helpers gives you control over the effects tools.

Effects are tools you can use to add a dramatic touch to your final renderings. For example, you can add film grain if your rendering is to be matched to a grainy background, or you can add a lens flare. You can also add atmospheric effects such as fog or smoke and light from a fire or explosion.

This appendix is intended to give you general information about the helpers and effects and to show you what types of features are available. If you need more detailed information about the helpers and effects, the VIZ Online Reference offers full descriptions of the options and parameters for all the items discussed in this appendix. Choose Help ➤ User Reference, click the Search tab in the panel to the left, enter the name of the item in the Type In The Word(s) To Search For input box, and then click List Topics. If you see only a single panel in the Online Reference, click the Show button on the Online Reference toolbar.

Helpers

Chapter 15 shows you how to use the Camera Match helpers to align a design to a background image. There are also a number of other types of helpers. The Standard helpers are general-purpose helpers that aid in measuring and linking objects. The Atmospheric Apparatus helpers are gizmos that help you control atmospheric effects. The Virtual Reality Modeling Language (VRML) helpers assist you in creating VRML worlds and are covered in Chapter 17.

Standard Helpers

Standard helpers can assist you as you build your design models. You can use them to mark location, measure distances, and create a local grid system.

DUMMY

A Dummy helper is simply a box with a center location. It's used primarily as a linkage point for hierarchical linkages. At first glance, dummy objects seem fairly useless, but they can be powerful aids when you are editing your models and are especially useful for animations.

Here's an example of a dummy used for editing. You may find that when using the transform tools, you need a pivot point that's not available from the standard set of pivot centers on the main toolbar. You can link an object to a dummy and then use the dummy's center point for transformations. The dummy can be located anywhere in the design. Depending on how the link is set up, you can apply transforms to the dummy instead of to the linked object, and the object will use the dummy's center for the transforms. The following steps describe how you can set this up.

First, create the dummy:

1. Click the Helpers button in the Create tab and then select Standard from the Helpers drop-down list.

2. Click Dummy; then click and drag within a viewport to place and size the dummy object. Remember that the dummy does not render, so you can make it a size that is convenient for editing.

3. Move the dummy to the desired pivot point.

Next, link the dummy to an object.

1. Click the Select and Link tool on the IK toolbar on the left side of the main toolbar.

2. Click and drag the object that you want to link to the dummy. A dashed line appears from the selected object.

3. Continue to drag the mouse to the dummy. When you see the link cursor appear, release the mouse. This makes the dummy the parent in the linkage.

Next, use the Rotate tool to test the link. By rotating the dummy, you also rotate the object that is linked to it.

1. Click the Select and Rotate tool.

2. Select the dummy object and rotate it. Notice that the linked object rotates with the dummy about the dummy's center.

Links are hierarchical, which means that one object in the link has dominance over the other. This is usually described as a parent-to-child relationship. In the example described here, the dummy is the parent of the object. Wherever the dummy goes, the child object goes. On the other hand, the child can go anywhere. You can move the object to change the relationship between the dummy and the object, but if you move the dummy, the child object must follow.

Multiple objects can be linked to a single dummy. You can also have objects linked to other objects in a chain. Remember that when linking an object using the Select and Link tool, the first object you select becomes the child object.

You can also link objects to a dummy and then animate the dummy. For example, you can link a camera and camera target to a dummy to move both the camera and the target in unison. In fact, the target is the camera's child.

GRID

Most of the time, you'll use the world-space coordinates while creating and editing objects. You can also create a user or custom grid as a local coordinate system in which to work. For example, you may have a need to create a set of objects that are oriented at a 45-degree angle from the plane of the world-space grid. You can create a user grid and rotate it on any axis. Once this user grid is created, you can add objects whose orientation is based on the user grid instead of on the world-space grid. The following steps demonstrate how user grids work.

1. Click the Helpers button in the Create tab and make sure that the Standard option is selected in the Helpers drop-down list.

2. Click and drag within the Perspective viewport to place the user grid.

3. Click the Select and Rotate tool on the main toolbar; then click and drag the red X axis of the Rotate gizmo to rotate the grid approximately 45 degrees about the X axis. You've just created a user grid and rotated it.

4. Click the Geometry button in the Create tab; then create a box. Notice how the box is aligned with the grid. When you create a user grid, it automatically becomes the active grid on which objects are built.

5. Try creating other objects. Try moving objects to see how they react.

The objects are aligned to the user grid and use the user grid for transformations.
To return to the world-space grid, do the following:

1. Click the Select Object tool and select the Helper grid.

2. Right-click within the viewport.

3. Select Activate HomeGrid from the Tools1 group of the quad menu. The viewport displays the home grid, which is the grid for the world-space coordinates.

You can use the Active Grid option in the viewport's shortcut menu to gain access to other user grids that you may have created. User grids have parameters to set grid size and spacing, and you can name them for easy reference.

NOTE *Along with the user grid, you'll want to know about the Autogrid feature. Autogrid creates a temporary user grid that is aligned to the surface of an object. To use Autogrid, click the Autogrid button at the bottom of the VIZ window. Select an object to create from the Create tab of the Command Panel; then place the cursor on the desired surface of an object. A Center gizmo will appear and align itself to the surface on which the cursor rests. You can then click and drag to create the new object on the surface. Click the Autogrid button again to turn it off.*

POINT

If you need to mark a location in your model for future reference, you can use the Point helper. A Point helper is just a point to which you can snap using the Pivot snap option. Points can be named for easy reference. They appear as small Xs along with coordinate arrows.

TAPE

You can find the distance between two objects using the Tape helper.

1. Click the Tape button in the Standard Helpers Object Type rollout.

2. Click and drag the first point you want to measure.

3. Drag the cursor to the second point and release the mouse. The Tape helper appears as a box at the first point you click and as a vector at the second point. The distance measured by the Tape helper is displayed as the grayed-out Length parameter in the Tape helper's parameters rollout.

Once placed, the Tape helper (or its target) can be moved to measure other distances—or you can just delete it.

PROTRACTOR

You can find the angle between two objects by using the Protractor helper.

1. Choose the Protractor button in the Standard Helpers Object Type rollout.

2. Click and drag the protractor to the location for the pivot point of the angle between the objects.

3. Click the Pick Object 1 button in the Protractor's parameters rollout; then select the first object.

4. Click the Pick Object 2 button and click the second object. The angle between the two objects is displayed in the parameters rollout just below the two Pick Object buttons.

Once placed, the Object 1 and Object 2 target locations can be changed by repeating either step 3 or step 4.

COMPASS

The Compass helper displays a compass rose in your design. It is typically inserted as part of the Sunlight System tool for placing the sun accurately in your model, but you can also insert the Compass helper independently of the Sunlight System tool.

Atmospheric Apparatus

VIZ offers atmospheric effects to simulate fog, glowing lights (volume light), and flames from fires. The fog and fire effects can be confined to a specific volume through the use of Atmospheric Apparatus helpers.

The Atmospheric Apparatus helpers are three gizmos that define the space to which the atmospheric effects are confined. These gizmos have the effect of giving form and location to the fog and fire effects. (Volume light doesn't need an atmospheric apparatus because it's given a location by association with a light source.)

The three Atmospheric Apparatus gizmos offered are BoxGizmo, CylGizmo, and SphereGizmo. Their names tell you the shape that they apply to the effect you assign them to. (See the "Effects" section later in this appendix to learn how to assign an apparatus to an effect.) You can place an atmospheric apparatus in a design by selecting the apparatus from the Atmospheric Apparatus Helpers Object Type rollout and clicking and dragging on a location in the design. You can then adjust the dimension of the Apparatus gizmo through its parameters.

Camera Match

The Camera Match CamPoints are used to locate points in your design that are matched to points on a background image. You place at least five CamPoints in your design that you can associate with the background image by using the Camera Match option in the Utilities tab of the Command Panel. Chapter 15 provides a detailed tutorial on how to use these helpers.

Assembly Heads

Assembly heads are the part of an assembly that houses a light fixture. Assemblies are collections of VIZ objects; these collections are similar to groups, but with the addition of a custom user interface. The assembly helper option offers the Luminaire helper, a nonrendering object that lets you control the light associated with the assembly. See Chapter 10 provides for a tutorial on using assembly heads in building a luminaire.

VRML97

VRML97 helpers allow you to customize virtual reality worlds before you export them from VIZ. The helpers in this category are covered in Chapter 17.

Effects

There may be times when you need to apply an effect to your design to simulate certain conditions. For example, you can create a foggy environment by using the Fog atmospheric effect, or you can simulate a shallow depth of field by using the Depth of Field rendering effect. You can gain access to these effects and others like them in the Environment and Render Effects dialog box.

Atmospheric Effects

You can open the Environment dialog box by choosing Rendering ➤ Environment. Once it's open, you can scroll down to the Atmosphere rollout.

This is where you'll find the Atmospheric Effects. If you click the Add button in the Atmosphere rollout, you'll see the Add Atmospheric Effect dialog box.

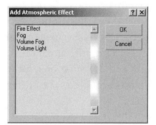

When you select one of the listed options, the option is placed in the Effects list box of the Atmosphere rollout. You can then click the listed item to open its parameters rollout and begin to use the effect. The following subsections describe the atmospheric effects and how to use them.

FIRE EFFECT

The Fire Effect creates the appearance of smoke and light from a fire or explosion. You can choose either a Fireball effect or a Tendril effect to simulate the fire from a fireplace. Flame characteristics and motion can also be set.

NOTE   *This effect used to be called Combustion in earlier versions of VIZ. It was renamed Fire Effect in VIZ 2005 to avoid possible confusion with Discreet's software product called combustion.*

To place a Fire Effect in your model, you must first place an Atmospheric Apparatus gizmo in the design (see "Atmospheric Apparatus" in the "Helpers" section of this appendix). Once you've placed the gizmo and given it the appropriate size, click Add in the Atmosphere rollout of the Environment dialog box and select Fire Effect. In the Environment dialog box, select Fire Effect in the Effects list of the Atmosphere rollout. Scroll down the dialog box to the Fire Effect parameters rollout and click the Pick Gizmo button.

Select the Atmospheric Apparatus gizmo you placed in your design. Once you've done that, you can render your perspective or camera view to see the Fire Effect. You can experiment with the settings in the Environment dialog box to achieve the effect you want. You can use other Atmospheric Apparatus gizmos to add more complexity to the effect.

You can also add multiple Atmospheric Apparatus gizmos to adjust the shape of the Fire Effect. Figure D.1 shows a candle flame that uses three SphereGizmos and a CylGizmo to shape the flame.

FIGURE D.1

Several Atmospheric Apparatus gizmos are used to create the flame on the candle.

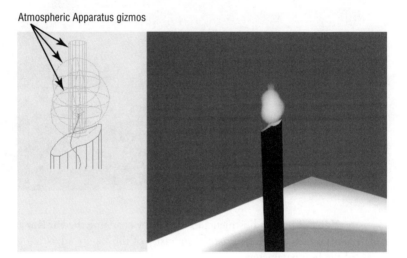

Atmospheric Apparatus gizmos

FOG

You can create fog in your design by using the Fog Atmosphere effect. There are two types of Fog effects, Standard and Layered. To use the Standard type, take the following steps:

1. If you don't already have a camera for your rendered view, create one before you add fog.

2. Select the camera you are using for your rendered view; then go to the Environment Ranges group of the camera's parameters.

3. Turn on the Show option; then set the Far Range value to a distance just beyond the objects in your design.

4. Adjust the Near Range value to a location just in front of the objects nearest the camera. These Environment Range settings affect the range in which the fog will take effect.

5. Open the Environment dialog box.

6. Select Fog from the Effects list box of the Atmosphere rollout; then scroll down the Environment dialog box to the Fog parameters and select the Standard radio button.

7. Set the Far% value in the Standard group to 50 as a starting point for the fog.

Once you've taken these steps, you can render the camera view and see the results. See Figure D.2.

FIGURE D.2
A rendered view of fog

You can make adjustments to the fog by changing the Far Range and Near Range settings for the camera. You can also adjust the intensity of the fog by adjusting the settings in the Standard group of the Fog parameters.

The Layered fog option creates the effect of a blanket of fog or a mist rising from a water surface. For example, you can simulate ground fog by doing the following:

1. After adding Fog to the Effects list in the Environment dialog box, choose the Layered radio button in the Fog group of the Fog parameters.

2. In the Layered group of the Fog parameters, set the Top value to the height of the fog—10 inches for example—and set the Bottom value to 0 (assuming that the ground level is a 0 in world-space coordinates). Set the fog Density to 30- or 40%.

3. Turn on the Horizon Noise and click the Top Falloff radio button.

4. Render the view to see the results. (See Figure D.3.)

FIGURE D.3

A sample rendering of ground fog

VOLUME FOG

Volume fog creates a more cloudlike fog effect with varying densities. It can be used to create a puffy cloud effect. You can apply volume fog to an entire design by adding it to the Effects list in the Atmosphere rollout of the Environment dialog box. If you want to confine the volume fog to an area, you can add an Atmospheric Apparatus helper to the design and assign the helper to the volume fog. You can do this by clicking the Pick Gizmo button from the Gizmo group of the Volume Fog Parameters rollout and selecting the Atmospheric Apparatus helper. The shape and size of the Atmospheric Apparatus determines the area in which the volume fog appears.

VOLUME LIGHT

One of the more popular effects for night scenes is the glowing light fixture. Unfortunately, you can't just add a light source in a VIZ design and expect it to look like it's glowing. To create a glowing effect around an Omni light, for example, you need to use the Volume Light effect. Here are the steps to set it up:

1. Choose Rendering ➤ Environment; then use the Add button in the Atmosphere rollout to add the Volume Light effect to the Effects list.

2. With the Volume Light options selected in the Effects list, scroll down the Environment dialog box to the Volume Light Parameters rollout, click the Pick Light button, and select the Omni light that you want to appear to glow.

You can render your design at this point and see the effects of the Volume Light. You may find that the glow is too large. To adjust the size of the glow, you need to make some changes to the lights parameters.

1. Use the Select Object tool to select the Omni light you selected in step 2 of the preceding procedure.

2. Click the Modify tab of the Command Panel; then scroll down and open the Attenuation Parameters rollout.

3. Turn on the Show option in the Far Attenuation group. This turns on the gizmo that shows you the limits of the far attenuation for the selected light.

4. Adjust the Far Attenuation end value so that the Far Attenuation gizmo is the size of the desired glow.

5. Render your view again to see the results.

You can use the Volume Light effect on spotlights and directed lights to create a glow around their light paths. A spotlight's or directed light's cone will glow when it's added to the list of lights under the Volume Light effect.

Rendering Effects

In addition to the Environment effects, you can apply other visual effects to the final rendering of your design by using the Environment and Effects dialog box. You can open the Environment and Effects dialog box by choosing Rendering ➢ Environment and then clicking on the Effects tab.

Just as with the Atmosphere rollout in the Environment dialog box, you add effects by clicking the Add button in the dialog box and selecting an effect from the Add Effects list. Once you've added an effect, it appears in the Effects list box of the Environment and Effects dialog box. You can then render your design to see how the effect changes the rendering.

Once you've rendered the design with an effect, you can experiment with the effect settings and then click the Update Effect button in the Preview group of the Environment and Effects dialog box to see the results of your changes. You don't have to rerender the design. This saves time when you need to fine-tune the rendering effects settings.

To adjust the parameters of an effect, select it from the Effects list box. Then scroll down the dialog box to set the parameters for the selected effect.

The following subsections describe the standard rendering effects that are available in VIZ. Note that to gain access to all the effects listed here, you must install all of the extra features from the VIZ installation CD. See Appendix A for information on installing VIZ.

LENS

The Lens effects are a set of effects that simulate the way camera lenses refract light. To use these effects, you need a light source somewhere in front of the camera. When you add the Lens effects to the Effects list in the Environment and Effects dialog box, you gain access to the Lens Effects Parameters rollout, which appears below the Effects rollout in the Environment and Effects dialog box.

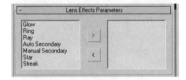

In the Lens Effects Parameters rollout, you can select an effect to add to the design. You select the desired effect from the list on the left and then click the right-pointing arrow to add that effect to the right-hand list.

Once you've added an effect to the right-hand column, you can assign it to a light source. To do this, scroll down the Environment and Effects dialog box to the Lens Effects Globals rollout.

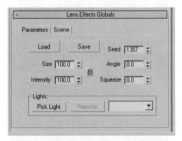

Select the Parameters tab and then click the Pick Light button in the Lights group. Select the light source in any viewport. You can then render your design to see the results. VIZ first renders the view without the effect; then it applies the effect to the finished rendering. It may take a second or two before the effect is applied. Once you've viewed the rendering, you can adjust settings for the effect in the Lens Effects Globals parameters. You can use multiple lens effects as your needs require them.

Following are descriptions of the Lens rendering effects.

Glow   Places a glow around a light source, simulating atmospheric diffraction.

Ring   Places a ring around a light source.

Ray   Produces an array of single pixel lines radiating from a light source, emulating scratches on a lens.

Auto Secondary   Produces multiple lens flares, simulating refraction from lens elements.

Manual Secondary   Produces a single lens flare, simulating lens refraction.

Star   Creates a star-like pattern of highlights with up to 30 points.

Streak   Creates a light streak similar to a pair of rays from a star pattern.

BLUR

The Blur effect blurs the final rendered image. You can blur the whole image or blur selectively based on non-background or luminance settings. Figure D.4 shows an image that uses the Blur effect with the Luminance option in the Pixel Selection tab turned on. Notice that the candle and the tabletop show sharp edges, while areas around bright areas are blurred.

The Map Mask option lets you mask specific areas for blurring.

BRIGHTNESS AND CONTRAST

The Brightness and Contrast effect is useful for matching the brightness and contrast of a design to a background. You can set this effect to act only on the objects in the design and not affect the background. The Update Effect option is especially useful with this effect.

FIGURE D.4
A Blur effect with the
Luminance option

COLOR BALANCE

The Color Balance effect lets you adjust the red, green, and blue color balance of your rendering. The Update Effect option is especially useful with this effect, since you can alternately adjust color balance and then click Update Effect to see the results.

FILE OUTPUT

The File Output effect lets you save the results of a rendering before certain other effects are applied. For example, you can add the File Output effect after a Lens effect, but before a Blur effect, to save a snapshot of the rendering before the Blur effect takes place. You control where the snapshot takes place by the location of the File Output effect in the Effects list. You can also select a channel to save rather than a whole image.

To place the File Output effect in a particular location in the Effects list, first add it to the list using the Add button. Then use the Move Up or Move Down button to move the File Output effect up and down in the list.

FILM GRAIN

You can add a film grain to a design by using the Film Grain effect. This is useful if you are matching your design to a grainy background image. You have the choice to add grain to the background or to leave the background untouched. The Update Effect button is useful with this effect, as it lets you fine-tune the graininess of your rendering to match a background.

DEPTH OF FIELD

The Depth of Field effect creates the effect of a shallow depth of field by blurring objects that are a certain distance from the camera. This is useful for blending a design into a blurred background.

To use this effect, choose Rendering ➢ Environment, then click the Effects tab and click the Add button. Select Depth of Field from the Add Effects dialog box and click OK. Once this is done, click the Pick Cam button in the Cameras group to select the camera that will use the effect. You also need to select an object on which to focus, by selecting the Focal Node radio button.

TIP   You may also set the depth of field by using the Depth of Field Parameters rollout in the Modify tab for any selected camera. The Depth of Field Parameters rollout does not allow you to select an object for the focal point of the depth of field, however. mental ray also can simulate depth of field (see Chapter 11).

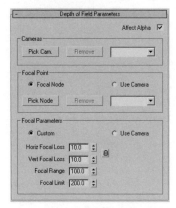

Other options let you set the degree of blurring.

Index

Page numbers in *italics* refer to illustrations; page numbers in bold refer to significant discussions of the topic

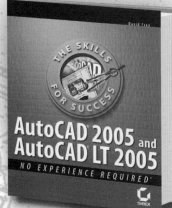
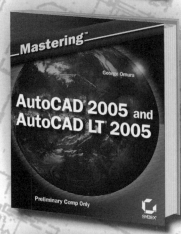

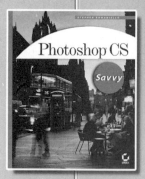
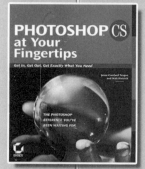